CISTERCIAN STUDIES SERIES: NUMBER ONE HUNDRED NINETY

PRAYING WITH BENEDICT

D1082488

CISTERCIAN STUDIES SERIES: NUMBER ONE HUNDRED NINETY

PRAYING WITH BENEDICT

Prayer in the Rule of St Benedict

KORNEEL VERMEIREN OCSO

Translated by
RICHARD YEO OSB

CISTERCIAN PUBLICATIONS
Kalamazoo, Michigan — Spencer, Massachusetts

First published in the English language in 1999 by
Darton, Longman and Todd Ltd
1 Spencer Court
140–142 Wandsworth High Street
London SW18 4JJ

and by

Cistercian Publications
WMU Station
Kalamazoo, Michigan 49008

First published as *Bidden mit Benedictus* in 1980
by Abdij Bethlehem, 2820 Bonheiden, Belgium.

ISBN 0 87907 790 5

A catalogue record for this book is available
from the British Library

Designed by Sandie Boccacci
Phototypeset in 11/14.5pt Joanna by Intype London Ltd
Printed and bound in Great Britain by
Redwood Books, Trowbridge, Wiltshire

Contents

Abbreviations

Apophthegmata: *Apophthegmata Patrum*
Conferences: Cassian, *Conlationes*
Institutes: Cassian, *De institutis coenobiorum*
RB: Rule of Benedict
RM: Rule of the Master

Translator's Note

Unless otherwise stated, The New Jerusalem Bible, copyright 1985 by Darton, Longman & Todd Ltd and Doubleday & Co. Inc., is normally used for Scripture quotations; *RB 1980* for quotations from the Rule of St Benedict and Eberle's translation for quotations from the Rule of the Master.

Translator's Introduction

This book was first published in 1980, during the year marking the fifteenth centenary of the traditional date (480) of the birth of Saint Benedict.

It grew out of some lectures given by Korneel Vermeiren, a Cistercian monk from the Netherlands, to religious communities of men and women in the Netherlands and Belgium following the Rule of Benedict. The lectures were about prayer in the Rule, looking at both common and individual prayer, and giving an idea of the spiritual tradition which forms the background to Benedict's ideas.

Prominent among Benedict's forebears were the ordinary folk from the villages of Egypt who went out into the desert, from the middle of the third century onwards, to live the monastic life. We find their wisdom and experience in the Sayings of the Fathers, in the Lives of Anthony and Pachomius, and in the writings of Evagrius and Cassian. Benedict knew these writings and was influenced by them, both consciously and unconsciously. He supplemented and corrected them out of his own experience and the experiences of others.

I picked up a copy of the book in the early 1980s, and was greatly impressed by the clear presentation of monastic spirituality. It shows how St Benedict's teaching is strongly rooted in the earlier monastic spiritual tradition, and how the different elements of monastic life complement each other. Common prayer, individual prayer, reading and Eucharist are not isolated from each other and from the rest of our lives, but all are interdependent and essential elements in a life lived according to the spirit of Saint Benedict.

Even then I thought that it would be good to translate it, and I am grateful to the author for giving me permission to present his book to English-speaking readers. I am sorry it has been fifteen years before I got round to doing the translation!

Korneel Vermeiren has in the meantime become Abbot of the monastery of Koningshoeven. Back in 1980, he expressed the hope that his book might help those who pursue the monastic life, and that it might also offer some guidance in the life of prayer for those who live in the world and are conscious of God's call, addressed to all Christians, to a life of trustful intimacy with him. This is my hope too.

RICHARD YEO OSB

I

PRAYER IN THE RULE
AND CONTINUOUS PRAYER

The biblical call to uninterrupted prayer stands at the heart of monastic spirituality and, indeed, of any spirituality. In the whole of the Rule, there is no chapter where Benedict formulates his teaching on prayer, so it is not immediately apparent whether he stands in the great tradition of prayer of the early centuries of Christianity.

We are told that Abba Isidore said, 'When I was young, and was sitting in my cell, I did not measure out my time for prayer. Night and day were my time for prayer.'[1] So Abba Isidore had no 'metron', that is, no set limits for his prayer.

This reference to his way of life as a young man prompts us to ask what happened to him with the passing of the years. Did he slacken off later on? Did he have to accept, in the end, a well-defined timetable? We do not know.

What we do know is that St Benedict, after a long experience as a hermit, and with an eye to the weakness of his monks, dealt with the matter in a very different way. In one sense he is diametrically opposed to Abba Isidore. In any case he has a very different accent. Benedict is famous precisely because he does have 'measure'. His moderation and measure shine out everywhere in his Rule.

Benedict has 'measure'. It is not only a matter of the measure of wine the monk may drink[2] or the amount of bread he receives each day,[3] nor just a matter of the measure of sleep[4] and work,[5] but he also has measure in relation to prayer and time for prayer. He measures everything with a true sense of rhythm. He is more measured than the zealous young monk Isidore: 'In community prayer should always be brief, and when the superior gives the signal, all should rise together.'[6] To the fervent young Isidore, it would have seemed an excessively human measure that Benedict is here setting out for prayer!

Has he given up all his zeal and abandoned his idealism? It looks as though he has fallen into a rather cautious and unspiritual compromise. At most, enough to pacify our guilty conscience, but hardly enough to whip up enthusiasm.

This is a vital question. Prayer, like life itself, by definition has no limits and no boundaries.

Is the rhythm of prayer, as organised by Benedict, something devised by monks who were rather too hard headed and disillusioned, men of little faith and a bit too much realism? In one sense, this is true: the pages of Scripture clearly put Isidore in the right; there is nothing that we could call Prime, Terce, Sext, None, etc. We also know that we are not to take literally the words of Psalm 119, where we read, 'At midnight I rise to praise you'[7] and 'Seven times a day I praise you . . .'.[8] These are symbolic numbers to express the whole of the day; just as in Psalm 55, 'evening, morning and noon'[9] is a way of saying 'the whole day long'. It means a lot more than three disconnected moments in the day.

In Scripture we read that we should pray without ceasing. This is stated by Jesus himself and also by Paul with a great deal of emphasis. The most important texts, which also played a big role in the tradition, are the following ones:

'Pray constantly', from the first letter to the Thessalonians.[10] Paul repeats this call in the letter to the Ephesians: 'In all your prayer and entreaty keep praying to the Spirit on every possible occasion.'[11] Also in the letter to the Colossians and to the Romans, 'persevere in prayer'.[12]

In the Gospels it is Luke, above all others, who passes on the call to constant prayer. He is the only evangelist who gives the parable of the importunate prayer of the widow: 'He told them a parable about the need to pray continually and never lose heart.'[13]

This New Testament call has a central place in ancient monasticism. This is why, in the eyes of the earliest monks, the prayer of the hours never has the character of a specific obligation, in our modern understanding of the term. The real obligation was, and remains: 'Pray without ceasing'. The ancient monks trod paths of every kind and made all sorts of effort to live out that injunction of the Lord. It was not so simple for them, just as it is not easy for us.

It is striking that the words of Jesus about praying together, 'where two or three meet in my name . . .',[14] are never used in the monastic literature to justify the prayer of the hours. This is noteworthy as we should have expected it. Jesus himself did not leave behind for us any set order of prayer. There is not even any trace of a prescription about the Jewish prayer called the Eighteen Benedictions, to be said three times a day, which the Lord and his disciples, as pious Jews, would undoubtedly have prayed. This prayer, performed in the direction of Jerusalem in union with the sacrifice in the temple, was the mark of the true Israelite in late Judaism, especially among the Jews in the dispersion.

We read in the Book of Daniel,

[3]

When Daniel heard that the document had been signed, he retired to his house. The windows of his upstairs room faced towards Jerusalem. Three times each day, he went down on his knees, praying and giving praise to God as he had always done . . . Then they said to the king, '. . . this man Daniel, one of the exiles from Judah, disregards both you and the edict which you have signed: he is at his prayers three times each day.'[15]

And in 1 Kings, the faithful Jews pray '. . . turning towards the country which God gave to their ancestors, towards the city which God has chosen and towards the Temple which has been built for his name'.[16] After she is insulted by her maidservant, Sarah, the future wife of Tobias, prays by the open window, 'You are blessed, O God of mercy . . .'[17]

In the life of Jesus and in the Gospels, there is no trace of this. Later, in the Acts of the Apostles, we find that the disciples are at prayer at the sixth hour[18] and at the ninth hour.[19]

But all this is far outweighed by the evangelical call to continuous prayer. God has a right to the totality of our life, the whole of the day and the whole of the night, and not just certain moments. God is our all. And the only fitting way of giving him honour is by giving him everything, which includes giving him all our time.

This affects the whole of our life, and also governs our attitude towards the celebration of the hours. Praying at particular hours is ambiguous. It has value only as a means of arriving at continuous prayer, and must therefore be directed at all the other hours of the day and night. This was how the early fathers of the monastic life combined the ideal of 'prayer without ceasing' with the prayer of the hours. They spent the whole day, including time for work and part of the night, in prayer. They did not feel the need for the ecclesiastical hours as they were celebrated, following the Jewish pattern, in the churches and basilicas of the young Church after the peace of Constantine in 313.

They were well acquainted with the practice of formal prayer in the morning at sunrise and in the evening at sunset. It is one of our natural, deep-rooted religious instincts to mark these moments and hallow them with prayer. According to Cassian, who died in Southern Gaul around 430, the only set times of prayer known to the most zealous of the early monks were the services in the morning and in the evening.

We have to make a distinction between the most zealous, or rather the most mature monks who, after a lengthy period of 'ascesis' and the practice of virtue, have been purified and come to continuous contemplation, and the beginners, who are taking their first footsteps in the monastic way of life. And a modest 'rule for beginners' is exactly what Benedict is writing.[20]

The beginners and the disciples in the Egyptian desert had more prayer services. The more mature the monk, the fewer offices he needed. Today it seems to be exactly the opposite. By reducing the classical schema of prayer services a few years ago down to three, four or five hours, perhaps we have not taken this tradition sufficiently into consideration. It may be that we did not pay sufficient attention to the connection between continual prayer and the prayer of the hours.

In the Egypt of the Fathers, in any case, the rule was 'more hours for the beginners, less offices for the proficient'.

Cassian tells us that in Egypt there was a prayer service only in the morning and in the evening. This, however, is perfection, and an austere discipline which cannot be imitated. The custom of praying at the third, sixth and ninth hour in Palestine and Mesopotamia was a mitigation and a relaxation of the perfection of the Egyptian monks, and of the austerity of their lives, which others were not able to attain. We need to be encouraged to pray now and then, but the monks in Egypt prayed spontaneously, the whole day long, while they were doing their work. 'For that which is offered continually is better than that which is offered intermittently; and an offering freely given is more acceptable than duties which are performed because they are prescribed by a rule.'[21]

We are conscious of a tension between continuous prayer which Cassian sets forth as the ideal and goal of the monastic life, and prayer as exercise or training, undertaken in order to reach that state of prayer. We see how in his heart Cassian always remained a hermit.

Maybe he is such a true monastic father that, while as a monk he yearns to reach perfection in prayer, he can still indicate a practical method of attaining that ideal. This is what makes Cassian so attractive: he combines the zeal of Abba Isidore with the realism which does not disdain the assistance provided by the prayer of the hours.

Now the perfection of continuous prayer is characteristic of the hermit. The monk who lives in a community has not yet attained the heights of prayer. The cenobite is a learner, a beginner. That leads to the question whether the cenobite can come to the same perfection of prayer as the hermit. We shall come back to this later, when we look at the characteristics of the prayer of the Benedictine monk.

It is worth remembering that the exterior structure of the life in the cenobitic monastery is very different from that of the hermit in the desert, and this must have had repercussions on the prayer-life. St Benedict made a synthesis of these two lifestyles in his Rule.

The eremitical life of the Egyptian desert, as it has come down to us in the Sayings of the Fathers, has the following characteristics: there are no rules, and there is no horarium; you live and pray, day-in, day-out; there are no bells to summon you to the services, you pray spontaneously in accordance with the inspiration of the Spirit. Hospitality is practised in an outstanding way, which shows love taking precedence over ascetical rigour and moderating it. The beginner does not have to do a 'novitiate', but he attaches himself to an elder with experience. In this relationship of trust, a deeply radical form of obedience is experienced as the following of Christ. The monk remains with his 'abba' until he himself possesses sufficient wisdom and experience to continue safely on the road alone, until he, perhaps, in turn becomes an 'abba' who attracts disciples. The only law or rule in the desert is the spoken word of the 'abba'.

There are innumerable sayings of the Fathers which illustrate this. On the other hand, cenobitic monasticism, as it was lived especially in Southern Egypt by Pachomius (died 346) and his followers, offers the picture of a highly organised and structured group of monks and nuns. They laid great emphasis on the community life. There was a strongly hierarchical organisation to this community, with superiors and subordinates. It bears a certain resemblance to our

modern congregations, with motherhouses and depen-
dencies.

According to this pattern, the monks live a well-balanced
daily life, as they work together, eat together, sleep together
and pray together. Bells mark changes of occupation. There
is an 'enclosure', and even an 'enclosure wall', which means
a division between the sacred and the profane, between the
world and the monastery. The cenobium of Pachomius is a
foreshadowing and a picture of the heavenly Jerusalem,
where the praise of God is continuously sung and where
everything becomes sacred, down to the everyday utensils.
We find an echo of this last element in the Rule of Benedict.[22]
One who is admitted is bound to carry out certain specified
obligations, and abandoning the monastery is considered to
be 'going back to the world'. The Pachomian monks and
nuns have a Rule. That Rule is holy, as it was given by God
himself by means of an angel who dictated it to him.

This structure naturally has consequences in the prayer-
life, and in the organisation of the prayer-life. We can now
get a clear picture of the two different lifestyles. The hermit
prays alone, in his cell, in his own way, in freedom, always
following the inspiration of the Spirit. The cenobite prays
together with others, in the oratory, at specified times, in an
agreed way, following an arrangement which has the
character of an obligation.

Something of this we all experience even in modern times
in our communities: the tension between the individual and
the community. In Benedict we find traces of these two
elements, the unfolding of the personal call within the life
in community. We too, in a sense, are the heirs of both the
eremitical life of Northern Egypt and the cenobitical life of

Southern Egypt. Every individual and each community as a whole has to find an equilibrium between these two fundamental elements.

As regards prayer, we could put it like this: what the hermits used to do privately during the whole day and night, the cenobites do together, publicly, and at agreed times.

We find more traces of this in the fact that, in the Rule, St Benedict maintained in principle the numerical order of the psalms. The monks knew the psalms in their numerical order by heart. Is Benedict having recourse to legislation in an area where the older monks had greater liberty? Is the call of Christ being reduced to rules and regulations? Is freedom being turned into duty and uniformity?

Those were important questions then, and they are also important for us today. However we can only give an answer if we keep on seeing Benedict's prayer of the hours in the light of the Lord's command: 'Pray continually'.

The prayer of the hours, then, is not an end in itself, but a means. It is a device: a humble method devised by human beings, in order to give a better response to the call of Christ and to afford some protection against human weakness and sloth. It is a little way, a way for small people who undertake it in order to arrive at continuous prayer. In this sense, the choral office can be compared with the Jesus prayer.

The Jesus prayer and the prayer of the hours are like the supports of a bridge, or like the human skeleton. The skeleton is not an end in itself: it exists as a framework for the body. The supports exist for the benefit of the road which runs over the bridge. The most important function of the prayer of the hours is to be the foundation of continuous prayer.

This is why John Cassian, and all the monastic fathers with him, express a clear preference for spontaneous ardour, for the continuous private prayer of the hermit, rather than the interrupted prayer of the hours which is the duty of the cenobites. 'If a monk only prays when he is kneeling down,' says Cassian, 'then he is praying very little'.[23]

In the tradition of the monks of Gaza who lived in Palestine in the sixth century, we see how continuous prayer was characteristic of the proficient. Barsanufius writes, 'the hours of prayer and the chants belong to the Church's tradition, and they contribute in an outstanding way to the unity of the Church's people and to the solidarity of our communities; but the inhabitants of Scetis do not have any hours of prayer, and they do not sing any chants': the souls of those who pray without ceasing are occupied with prayer all the day long.[24]

The first monks felt their way hesitantly towards the realisation of the Lord's instruction to pray continually. They sought all sorts of ways of achieving this goal; some had good results, others ended in failure.

Before looking at some of these attempts, we need to bear in mind that the monks were most reluctant to speak about prayer. Evagrius (died 399) was the first to write a proper theory of prayer. The monks of the Apophthegms usually refused to speak when someone came to interrogate them about their experience of prayer.

Abba Poimen at a certain moment received a visit from another monk who had come from a very long way away. He asked him questions about spiritual things. But to his annoyance Abba Poimen persisted in stubborn silence. The visitor went and complained to one of Poimen's disciples. This man knew his spiritual father, and advised the monk to speak about the battle that he had been obliged to fight against temptation. Then he went back to Poimen and got a reply to his questions.[25] We too need guile to get the old monks to reveal their experiences of prayer.

In order to understand Benedict's prayer of the hours as a means of coming to continual prayer, we need to investigate some of the early monastic experiences. How did the first monks try to pray continually?

1. MESSALIANISM

This was a religious movement which is found all over the Middle East and Asia Minor from about 350 onward. The mentality it fostered had a deep imprint on the Christian life. The most characteristic effect was a confusion between grace and the experience of grace. The objective mediation of grace in the sacraments is seen as secondary or even superfluous. It was opposed to the Church as an institution. This movement can be compared with the so-called 'sect of the Holy Spirit' of the time of Ruysbroeck, or with some of the religious movements of our own time. It has a strongly experiential flavour.

We find traces of Messalianism in monastic literature. The adherents are known in monastic circles as the followers of the sect of the Euchites, 'those who pray'. They intended to arrive at continual prayer through saying as many prayers as possible, piling them up and repeating them, and excluding all other activities. Even manual labour was viewed by them as incompatible with a life of prayer.

At the Council of Constantinople in 426, the Messalians were condemned. This condemnation was repeated at Ephesus in 431. At Shahapivan in Armenia in 447, the Messalians were once again harshly dealt with.

John Damascene has handed down to us a number of their ideas. One of these theories dealt, among other things, with the manual labour of the monks: 'they say that manual labour is to be shunned as something disgusting, and on this account they reckon themselves to be spiritual. They think it is impossible and wrong for such people to be still involved in physical work, and thus they break the apostolic tradition.'

We find Messalianism, or at least a Messalian tendency, in the following Apophthegm:

A certain brother came to Abba Silvanus on Mount Sinai. Seeing the brothers at work, he said to the old man, 'Labour not for the bread which perishes; for Mary has chosen the better part.' The old man said to his assistant, 'Zachary, give this brother a book, and take him into a cell without anything else.' At the ninth hour, the brother started looking at the door, to see if they would send someone to call him to the meal. When nobody came, he got up and went to the old man. 'Abba,' he asked him, 'have the brothers not eaten today?' 'Yes,' he was told. 'Then why did you not call me?' The old man replied, 'Because you are a spiritual man, and you have no need of food of this type; we, however, who are made of flesh, need to eat, and that is why we work. But you have chosen the better part, and you read the whole day long, and have no desire to eat human food.' When he heard this, the brother prostrated himself in penance, and said, 'Forgive me, Abba.' And the old man told him, 'Mary also needs Martha, and it is thanks to Martha that Mary is praised.'[26]

All human beings, including monks, have to face the daily reality of working for their living, and will not go unpunished if they try to escape it. The following Apophthegm of Abbot John the Dwarf gives a humorous account of the cure of a monk from his Messalian leanings:

It was said of Abba John the Dwarf that one day he said to his old elder brother, 'I should like to be free of all cares, like the angels, who do not work but serve God continuously.' He took off his cloak, and went out into the desert. A week later he came back to his brother. When he knocked on the door, his brother asked, 'Who are you?' 'I am John, your brother,' he replied, but his brother said to him, 'John has gone to become an angel, and no longer lives among men.' He insisted, 'It is I!' But his brother wouldn't open up, but left him there in distress until the next day. Then he opened the door, and said to him, 'You are a man, and you need to work again if you want to eat.' John made a prostration before him, and said, 'Forgive me.'[27]

The efforts of the Messalians are here held up to ridicule as a deviation. You cannot escape from the human condition. Maybe the cap fits us better than we might at first sight have thought. The great temptation for people who wish to live a spiritual life is the desire to stay above the ordinary human condition, wanting not to get their hands dirty. This expresses itself in a false piety with no firm theological foundation.

In the first saying of Abba Anthony, the old man in a moment of temptation asks an angel, 'How can I be saved?' The saying goes on,

> Shortly afterwards he got up and went outside, and he saw someone like himself who was sitting and working; he then got up from his work to pray; then he sat down again to weave a rope, then again he got up to pray. This was an angel of the Lord, who had been sent to correct Anthony and to reassure him. Then he heard the angel saying, 'Do this, and you will be saved.' At this, Anthony was filled with joy and confidence. He did just that, and he was saved.[28]

That was the problem for the Messalians: continual prayer doesn't allow you to do anything else. The angel shows Anthony the way out of the dilemma.

2. BASIL THE GREAT

In his youth, Basil the Great (died 370) visited the monastic settlements of Egypt. However, he returned to Asia Minor, where he gave the monastic life a distinctive character. He is also cited by St Benedict, in chapter 73 of his Rule, as an important monastic authority.

Basil certainly felt the attraction of Messalianism. In his so-called 'longer Rules' he dealt in question 37 with the relationship between prayer and work. He asks himself the question, 'Is work to be neglected for the sake of prayer and psalmody?' He replies,

Our Lord Jesus Christ does not say that everybody deserves his food, but 'the labourer is worthy of his hire.' The Apostle Paul also orders us to work and to do good with our own hands, so that we may have something to give to those in need. It therefore follows clearly that we ought to work diligently. Piety will not serve as an excuse for laziness or as a way of escaping hard work; rather it incites us to strive and exert ourselves more earnestly, and to practise patience in tribulation, so as to be able to say, 'in labour and in much watching, in hunger and thirst' (2 Cor. 11,27). And therefore, not only in order to chastise the body, but also for the sake of charity to our neighbour, this rule of life is to be observed, so that God may supply through us what is necessary to our infirm brothers . . .

While our hands are occupied, we can with our tongue praise God with psalms and hymns and spiritual songs, when this is possible or useful for the edification of believers; but if not, we can at least in our heart thank God who has endowed our hands with the capacity to work, bestowed on our minds the ability to acquire skills, and given us the matter from which our tools are shaped. Finally we shall ask God that the work of our hands may be guided towards their object, in order that they may be acceptable to God.[29]

This text offers an important perspective on the integration of prayer and work, on the unity of prayer and life.

The world around us is not just a source of dissipation, but also a privileged place for our encounter with God. Basil has a high appreciation for everything human, and so he reacts quite sharply against the Messalians.

Faith and piety are only authentic to the extent that they can be brought into harmony with the reality of our lives. Otherwise, they will be fruitless and illusory.

St Benedict, in chapter 48 of his Rule, is fully in accord with the thought of St Basil when he writes, ' . . . then they are truly monks, when they live by the work of their hands, like our fathers and the apostles.'[30]

3. ABBA LUCIUS

Before coming to prayer in the Rule, we shall look at a few more examples from the pre-Benedictine tradition.

The Messalians multiplied their acts of prayer to such an extent that they had no time left for other activities. We saw that this was a dead-end spirituality in practice. Others tried to steer clear of this danger by having recourse to the help of other people when they themselves had to give their attention to other matters. One who took this approach was Abba Lucius, who came a little closer than the Messalians to solving the problem of continuous prayer.

In the one saying of his which has been preserved, we hear the following:

> Once there came to Abba Lucius at Enaton a number of those monks who are called Euchites, 'those who pray'; and the old man questioned them, 'What manual work do you do?' They replied, 'We do no manual work, but we pray without ceasing, in accordance with the Apostle's precept.' The old man asked them, 'Do you eat?' 'Of

course,' they answered. Then the old man asked, 'Then when you are eating, who prays for you?' He also asked them, 'Do you sleep?' 'Yes,' they answered. 'Then when you sleep, who prays for you?' They did not know how to reply.

So the old man said, 'Forgive me, but your practice does not correspond to what you claim. I will show you how I pray without ceasing while I am doing my manual work. I sit in the presence of God, and as I moisten my supply of palm branches and plait them together I say, "have mercy on me, God, according to your great goodness, and according to the multitude of your great mercies blot out my iniquity". Is this prayer?' 'It is,' they said. He went on, 'When I spend the whole day like this, working and praying, I earn about sixteen sesterces. Two of these I give away at the gate, and the rest I spend on my food. The person who receives the two sesterces prays for me while I am eating and sleeping; and thus, by the grace of God, I am able to fulfil the command to pray without ceasing.'[31]

Messalianism is seen as offering no solution. At first, it looks as though Lucius has found the answer. It is well thought out; he has worked out how to unite prayer and work. He continues to pray while he works: he has progressed beyond the Messalians. However, the time he has to spend in eating and sleeping remains a problem. He thinks he has solved it by having others pray in his stead. But this is only half a solution, and in fact he is only tinkering with the problem. At the deepest level the question remains: what is his mind filled with during his meal-times and during his night rest?

Substitution as a means of achieving continuous prayer was attempted not only by individuals but also by communities. In the sixth century, the 'akoimetoi', 'those who do not sleep', made their appearance on the monastic scene, an offshoot of Messalianism. The entire community was divided into three groups, each of which took turns to spend eight hours in prayer. Thus the entire community, but not the individual, prayed continuously. Sigismund of Burgundy in 515 founded the monastery of St Maurice so that the monks might sing the continuous praises of God. In the foundation document, he said, 'I, Sigismund, found this monastery for the salvation of my soul and I endow the monks who will pray on my behalf.'

This idea of continuous praise or 'laus perennis' took on a number of different forms in the Middle Ages. Commendable and impressive though it is, this form of laus perennis does not really fulfil the command to pray continuously. Anthony has a saying which is relevant here: 'A brother said to Abba Anthony, "Pray for me". The old man replied to him, "I am not going to have mercy on you, and nor will God, unless you also make an effort, and pray to God." '[32] However valuable the prayer of another may be, it does not mean that I do not have to pray too.

4. MELANIA THE YOUNGER

In fifth-century Jerusalem, Melania the Younger was an experienced spiritual director. Many monks, nuns and lay people came to ask for her advice. Thus it was that Evagrius of Pontus came to Melania in Jerusalem after his adventures in Constantinople, and it was under her influence that he became a monk in the Egyptian desert. She had set up a sort of reception centre, or a house for pilgrims. Because of the great number of guests, she said that she was no longer able to lead the life of a nun.

Her biographer tells us:

> wounded as she was by the love of God, . . . she conceived the project of shutting herself in a cell, of having no more contact with anyone, but of devoting herself to continuous prayer and fasting. But that was impossible, because many benefitted from her teaching which was full of God; this meant that everybody came to her. So she did not cut herself off completely, but fixed certain times when she would help her visitors with her good advice. The rest of the time she spent with God and accomplished her spiritual work through her prayer.[33]

Here we have a very different solution from that of Basil, who saw work as the breeding ground for prayer. Melania is aware of the competition between the time spent in helping others and the time which is devoted to God.

Melania divides her time: so much for Martha and so much for Mary. Prayer is often portrayed in the early tradition as the soul's opportunity to breathe: if this is true, then Melania's solution is no answer to the problem. You either pray all the time, or you aren't praying.

Often we get stuck with Melania's solution. What is missing is a unity at a deeper level which enables our work and occupations to be taken up into prayer, and our prayer to penetrate into the bustle of our lives. We have to look elsewhere for a more deep-rooted integration of prayer and life.

5. ORIGEN, EVAGRIUS AND CASSIAN

Origen (died 253/254), Evagrius (died 399) and John Cassian (died 435) point out to us new ways towards a deeper unity between prayer and life, a greater interdependence between attention to God and attention to the people round about us. Many later monks and spiritual writers have built on their insights and experiences.

Origen has rightly been called the founder of Christian spirituality. His personality was so strong and his work so important that even centuries later all spiritual writers were obliged to follow Origen's lead, acknowledge his influence or to be conscious of rejecting it.

In his treatise on prayer, Origen speaks about the links between prayer and work. He does this with a moderation and wisdom which are a surprise coming from a man who was always prone to extreme and radical solutions.

> Deeds of virtue or fulfilling the commandments are included as part of prayer, so we pray 'constantly' if we unite our prayer with the deeds required, and the right deeds with prayer. For the only way we can understand the command to 'pray without ceasing' as referring to a real possibility is by saying that the entire life of the Christian, taken as a whole, is a single great prayer, and what we normally call prayer is only a part of this.[34]

Later on in the same treatise, he goes on to say, 'Let us not suppose that the Scriptures teach us to say "Our Father" only at the appointed time of prayer. Rather, if we really understand the earlier discussion of "prayer without ceasing", then our whole life is to be a constant prayer.'[35]

Origen's approach to continuous prayer was to seek for unity in the interior life. The human heart is where this profound level of unity is to be discovered. In this way, he offered a way forward – and ultimately the only way forward – to a form of continuous prayer which does not alienate the individual from human nature, but allows human nature to develop.

Evagrius was a disciple of Origen, and after his death his writings were condemned on account of his Origenistic sympathies. He was the first monk to leave a literary legacy behind him. Starting with the ascetical experiences of the Desert Fathers, he tried to create a coherent teaching on the monastic life, based on Origen's great theological synthesis.

In his 153 *Chapters on Prayer*, he speaks in several places about the state of prayer: in numbers 2,3,27,47,51 and 52. In n. 52 he says, 'the state of prayer can aptly be described as a state of habitual calm ("apatheia"). It snatches to the heights of intelligible reality the spirit which loves wisdom and which is truly spiritualised by the most intense love.'[36]

By 'state' of prayer, Evagrius here means a lasting condition, a persistent attitude of the soul which is no longer disturbed by passionate thoughts. For Evagrius, acts of prayer result in an attitude of prayer.

Cassian has with justice been described as the 'novice-master of western monks'. He continues the line which runs from Origen and Evagrius and on towards the Rule of Benedict, which in chapter 73 expressly mentions the two famous works of Cassian, 'then there are the Conferences of the Fathers and their Institutes . . .'.

In the third, ninth and tenth Conferences he speaks, or

rather lets the Egyptian monks speak, about the state of prayer. In the third Conference, Cassian allows the three renunciations to develop into an attitude of continuous reflection on the things of God. In this state, human beings walk with God, as Enoch did (Gen. 5:24).[37]

When Cassian describes the goal of the monastic life in Conference IX, it is clear he is dealing with an attitude of the heart.

> The whole aim of the monk and the perfection of his heart consists in a continual and uninterrupted perseverance in prayer, and as far as is possible for human frailty, it is a striving for immovable tranquillity of mind and lasting purity . . .
>
> Just as the building up of all the virtues is directed towards the perfection of prayer, the virtues, in their turn, will not be secure or strong unless they are bound together and united by this high goal.
>
> And just as the continuity and tranquillity we have been talking about cannot be acquired or perfected without the virtues, neither can those virtues which build up such prayer be perfected without assiduity at prayer.[38]

In Conference X, he indicates a simple, practical way of arriving at this state of prayer. The cry for assistance from Psalm 70, 'O God, make speed to save me; O Lord, make haste to help me' (v. 2), should be repeated as often as possible, no matter what the monk is busy with, until it becomes a habitual attitude of the heart.

> In order to be perpetually mindful of God, this holy formula should be always in your mind.

This verse should be our constant prayer: in time of adversity, that we may be delivered; in time of prosperity, that we may be preserved, and not puffed up.

Always, I say, you should be turning this verse over in your heart. Whatever work you are engaged in, whatever journey you have embarked on, do not cease to repeat it. Meditate on it when you are going to bed, while eating and when engaged in any kind of occupation our nature requires.

Be meditating on this verse when sleep overtakes you until, by unremitting repetition of this exercise, you find yourself repeating it even in your sleep. As you wake up, let it be the first thing that comes into your mind. Let it anticipate all your waking thoughts. Let it accompany you as you rise from your bed and fall to your knees, and then let it lead you on to every action you perform and every deed you do. Let it accompany you all the day long.

When you kneel down to pray, it will be your refrain, and when you rise to go about the necessary occupations of your life it will be your constant prayer.[39]

We shall come back to this text later on.[40] Cassian defines the link between this short prayer formula and the habitual state of recollection which the praying person brings to everything. The problem of prayer is no longer seen in terms of quantity but quality, not in terms of what a person does but of what a person is.

The question then is not how I ought to pray while I have a lot of work, or when other people need me, but what the attitude of my heart must be if I am to pray continuously.

To put it in a negative way: how do I come to the point that my conscious relationship with God is not disturbed by my occupations or by the people round about me?

In theory, there is no rivalry between action and contemplation. The story of Jesus with Martha and Mary in Luke 10:38–42 is often misinterpreted, and the contemplative life is often constructed on a faulty interpretation of the 'better part', to the disadvantage of all those in the Church who give their best in an 'active' way. The real problem, though, is the deep tension between God and the world, between the sacred and the profane, between the vertical and the horizontal. And this tension does not lie outside us, but in the heart of every human being.

This tension is felt by the monk and nun, even after they have made their fundamental choice. The world is in our heart; we cannot just escape from it, as the Messalians tried to do. Here lies the challenge to the monk at the deepest level: to turn into reality what is signified by his name, *monachos*, to become 'one'. The root of the word *monachos* is *monos*, which can mean 'alone' just as much as it can mean 'one'.

Living with other people and earning one's living is an important part of being human. This has to be integrated with our 'seeking God'. The monastic patriarch Benedict is rightly concerned to integrate the monk's humanity into the great commitment to which the monk is called.

The Messalians, Basil the Great, Abba Lucius, Melania the Younger, Origen, Evagrius and Cassian: all of them tried to give a shape to the basic human commitment. What they achieved is not simply a matter of history. They are not just episodes from the past. They are rather our own attempts, today, on our own pilgrimage towards unifying and integrating all our human energies and abilities.

We now need to go back to the question we started off with: whether St Benedict's teaching about prayer and times of prayer is in line with the commitment to continuous prayer which was seen by his predecessors as the primary monastic value, and the centre of the monastic vocation. Is prayer 'seven times a day' and 'at midnight'[41] a mitigation of the continuous prayer of the Desert Fathers, or is it a practical, human and realistic version of it, a method or technique of arriving at the state of continuous prayer? Is this work of God, consisting of hours of prayer, dynamically directed towards the great work of God which encompasses and embraces the whole of life? Or should Benedict feel the force of the reproach which Epiphanius, Bishop of Cyprus, in his third saying, directed towards the abbot of a monastery in Palestine:

> The blessed Epiphanius, Bishop of Cyprus, received a report from the abbot of a monastery in Palestine: 'thanks to your prayers we do not neglect our canon [that is, the list of psalms to be recited daily], but we carefully celebrate prime, terce, sext, none and vespers.'
>
> But Epiphanius in reply showed his disapproval, saying, 'Evidently you are neglecting the other hours of the day when you are not praying. The true monk should be ceaselessly praying and saying psalms in his heart.'[42]

ADDENDUM

Maybe this is a good place to ask whether it is a somewhat one-sided approach to say that the prayer of the hours described in the Rule is a means of arriving at continuous prayer. Surely it is also the praise of God, offered in the name of the whole human race? And is not this one of the defining characteristics of the monastic life?

This raises the question of the place of praise in choral prayer. Time and time again in chapters 8 to 20, Benedict refers to this. The psalms of praise, 148, 149 and 150, are repeated daily at morning prayer.[43] And in chapter 16, when dealing with the so-called little hours, he says: 'at these times we should ring out our songs of praise to our creator . . .', and later on: 'at night we should rise to praise him'.[44]

The introduction of the 'Glory be to the Father and to the Son and to the Holy Spirit' at the end of the psalms[45] and at the end of the responsories at the night office[46] points in the same direction. He goes on, 'as soon as the singer begins this, all rise up from their seats out of honour and reverence towards the Holy Trinity'.[47]

Here and there in these chapters, a clear prominence is given to the element of praise in the prayer of the hours. In chapter 19, the monk's praise of God is even seen as a work of service[48] which he shares with the angels.[49] Nevertheless, we should take care not to read into the text a contrast when Benedict never intended to make one. The distinction between praise and continuous prayer is completely alien to ancient monastic spirituality, and also to the Rule of Benedict. Praise and contemplation are essentially complementary.

There is the exterior liturgy, with its prescribed forms,

celebrated together with others, and there is the personal liturgy of the spirit, in the inner chamber of the heart. The exterior liturgy springs from the need to give a communitarian aspect to the interior liturgy. The exterior liturgy flows into the continuous liturgy of the heart, and uninterrupted prayer is the prolongation of the exterior liturgy. Uninterrupted prayer, in turn, needs to be nourished by the Word of God, which comes to us in the psalms and in the readings from Scripture.

Prayer and the liturgy of the hours, as we meet it in the Rule, can best be described as 'contemplative praise'. This title is, indeed, given to n. 13 of the *Directory for the Celebration of the Work of God*, published in 1977 by the Benedictine Confederation.

> The first and fundamental attitude of the praying community which celebrates the memorial of the mystery of Christ, which is the content of the Opus Dei, should be one of contemplative praise.
>
> The first prayer which goes up from the heart of the monks, as they gather together each morning, is the supplication addressed to the Lord, 'Lord, open my lips and my mouth shall proclaim your praise' (RB 9, 1). The Opus Dei, just like the sacrifice of the altar, is intended to be an 'eucharist', a thanksgiving and an act of praise for the wonderful things that God in his goodness has done for us, and which we contemplate in his mystery. In the Opus Dei we enter into that privileged time of common praise to which the Father has called us in Christ: 'In Christ we too are called and predestined . . . to be a song of praise to his glory' (Ephes. 1, 11-12).

In the Rule of St Benedict the element of praise in the Opus Dei is clearly in the forefront when it cites the words of Holy Scripture (Ps. 118,164) and goes on to say, 'at these times we should offer our praise to our Creator for his just judgments' (RB 16, 5).

Furthermore, in the Rule it is ordered that the psalms of praise, that is, the three last ones of the Psalter, are to be said at the solemnity of lauds on Sundays and weekdays, that is to say, daily. It reminds us that the angels, who are the singers 'par excellence' of the praise of God,[50] and whose nature it is to adore God,[51] are present at the choral prayer of the monks; 'with them we are joined as we adore in joy, and together with them cry out in praise'.[52] All this clearly shows that the laudative character of the Opus Dei is of supreme importance for monks. They are not alone in praising God, but are conscious that through their voice 'every creature under heaven'[53] praises the name of the Lord, and that they follow the example of the angels, whose role it is not only to praise the Lord but also to 'fulfil his commands, attentive to the sound of his words',[54] and so they strive to bring their mind into harmony with the words they proclaim. Indeed, our praise will only be authentic when 'our hearts are in harmony with our voices' (RB 19,7).[55]

II

'NOTHING IS TO BE PREFERRED TO THE WORK OF GOD'

W hy does St Benedict attach so much importance to the prayer of the hours?

'Indeed, nothing is to be preferred to the work of God.' This verse from chapter 43 of the Rule is of particular significance and is often quoted to underline the importance of the Divine Office. In this verse, and also in many other places, Benedict emphasises that the prayer which is consti- tuted by the Church's canonical hours fills an essential role in the monastic day. In this chapter we shall take stock of these instructions.

The first surprise for the reader of Benedict's Rule is the way he suddenly and unexpectedly starts to talk about the prayer of the hours. The Prologue and chapters 1 to 7 contain important spiritual teaching, and these are immedi- ately followed by an arid list of liturgical prescriptions, in chapters 8 to 18, inclusive.

Together with chapter 52, the most important source of Benedict's teaching on prayer is to be found in chapters 19 and 20. These two chapters follow on very naturally after chapter 7, on humility: it could be said that in chapters 19 and 20 he applies his teaching on humility to the monk's prayer. But the placing of chapters 8 to 18, before the other chapters about the organisation of the monastery, says something about the importance of the prayer of the hours. The length of this section, in relation to the rest of the Rule, is also striking. Here we find many more detailed regulations than elsewhere in the Rule. In general, Benedict manages with many fewer rubrics than the Master,[1] but in this section he has more. In addition, the Master has placed the chapters dealing with the organis-ation of the prayer of the hours among the other regulations about the monk's occupations. Benedict has lifted them out of their place and put them at the beginning.

Exceptions and flexibility are no less significant than posi-tive injunctions as indications of the importance of some provision. 'The exception proves the rule', and the exception ensures that the positive prescriptions will be safeguarded. So the making of adequate and sensible exceptions is a sign that we are dealing with a truly wise lawgiver. Benedict's Rule bears witness to this wisdom.

Thus the brothers who have work far from the place of prayer, and those who are on a journey, are excused by Benedict: not excused from the prayer, but excused from coming to the community's oratory. But this only holds good when there is a big distance involved, when the abbot is in agreement, and when the reason for the absence is that the monk has been sent on a journey.

Brothers who are so far away at work that they cannot return to the oratory at the proper time – and the abbot determines that this is indeed the case – accomplish the work of God there at the place where they are working, and let them kneel out of reverence for God. So too, those who have been sent on a journey should not omit the prescribed hours . . .[2]

Benedict thus indicates here the conditions which need to be fulfilled if monks are to be allowed to perform on the spot the service to which they are pledged. The monk cannot arbitrarily drop this special moment of prayer, because he must indeed pray at all times. He must recognise that this moment of prayer is a means of arriving at continuous prayer and of being faithful to it.

This special attitude of Benedict comes to the fore most strongly when we compare this chapter with the parallel text in the Rule of the Master. The Master writes:

> As soon as the signal struck by the abbot has sounded, let the brother who is working, whether alone or with others, let go of his iron tool and by a quick visual calculation determine whether or not he should hasten to the oratory. At a distance of fifty paces from the entrance of the monastery, his decision must be to hasten with gravity to the oratory. But if the place is at a greater distance than this, then they do not go; but having dropped the iron tool from their hands and bending their neck, just as they would bend the knees in the oratory, they too recite the work of God quietly by themselves there where they are.[3]

Benedict underlines what is important by dropping the things of lesser significance, and by reserving the matter to the decision of the abbot. The importance of presence in the oratory is safeguarded, but at the same time Benedict leaves open the possibility of a monk not being present and making his prayer while on a journey or at work. The road and the field are a meeting-place with God, no less than the oratory.

These brothers who are absent are always prayed for in

the last prayer of the work of God: 'and in the closing prayer of the work of God all the absent brothers should always be remembered.'[4]

The one who is on a journey or is far away at work is not forgotten. By this commemoration of the brothers who are legitimately absent in the concluding prayer, Benedict seems to be making the point that no one is truly absent. Here and in chapter 50 it is apparent that presence at the community prayer is a source of grace in itself. In this way, the support of the brotherhood is experienced. The brother who cannot be present has a greater need of the support of the praying community.

Giving the signal for the work of God – dealt with in chapter 47 – is a particularly important task in the monastery. Indeed, Benedict gives the responsibility to the abbot himself, 'or he may entrust this responsibility to a brother who is so conscientious that everything may be done at the proper time.'[5]

In entrusting this task to the abbot, Benedict again points to its importance. There are other chapters where the Rule shows the same concern for the smooth running, peace and good order of the monastery.[6]

It is clear that we are not just dealing with precautionary measures in an age when they only had things like hour-glasses to tell the time. Giving the signal for the work of God is not like any other announcement. It is God himself who calls us to accomplish this work: that is why it has to be punctual. That is also why tasks must be performed with care and why it is not everybody who can read or sing without further ado. 'Only those who are authorised are to lead the psalms and antiphons after the abbot, according to their rank. No one should presume to read or sing unless he is able to benefit the hearers; let this be done with humility, seriousness and reverence, and at the abbot's bidding.'[7]

Humility, seriousness and reverence are the attitudes which Benedict always looks for when the monk speaks. 'The eleventh degree of humility consists in this: that the monk, when he speaks, does so gently and without laughter, humbly and seriously . . .'[8]

Later on we shall again see that Benedict expects the monk to behave in the same way when he is at prayer as when he is in the company of his brethren.

At first sight it may seem odd that the chapter on 'how the monks are to sleep' (chapter 22) should contain such important directions about the value of the common prayer. Nevertheless, this is one of the chapters of the Rule where Benedict says a great deal more than one might think after a superficial reading.

> [In the dormitory] a lamp must be left burning until morning. They sleep clothed, and girded with a belt or cord, but they should not have their knives on them when they sleep, lest they should accidentally cut themselves in their sleep. Thus the monks will always be ready, and as soon as the signal is given, they will rise without delay and each will hasten to the work of God before the others, yet always with dignity and decorum. . . On arising for the work of God, the brothers are to encourage each other, in an unobtrusive way, to overcome the excuses of those who are sleepy.[9]

Here too, it is much more than merely practical details. We

can deduce that Benedict sees the office as an important work of God when he writes, 'a lamp must be left burning until morning'. The monk has to sleep with the attitude of the wise virgins who had their lamps ready when the arrival of the bridegroom was announced.[10] It is the lamp of prayer and of worship that should never go out. It is also the symbol of God's protecting presence.

> The Lord would not destroy the House of David, because of the covenant which he had made with David, promising to provide him and his sons with a lamp for ever.[11]

> Aaron and his sons will tend it in the Tent of Meeting, outside the curtain hanging in front of the Testimony, from dusk to dawn, before the Lord. This is a perpetual decree for all generations of Israelites.[12]

This lamp in the Jewish sanctuary is to be filled with pure olive oil, and must be kept burning continuously from evening to morning before the Lord.[13]

Even while he is asleep, the monk must be ready and vigilant, always prepared to come to the work of God, so Benedict asks his monks to sleep 'clothed and girded'. They are to be ready at all times, and always prepared for the coming of the Son of Man.

> 'See that you have your belts done up and your lamps lit. Be like people waiting for their master to return from the wedding feast, ready to open the door as soon as he comes and knocks. Blessed those servants whom his master finds awake when he comes. In truth I tell you,

he will do up his belt, sit them down at table and wait on them. It may be in the second watch that he comes, or in the third, but blessed are those servants if he finds them ready. You may be quite sure of this, that if the householder had known at what time the burglar would come, he would not have let anyone break through the wall of his house. You too must stand ready, because the Son of man is coming at an hour you do not expect.'[14]

The monks are to let the urgent call from the Apocalypse resound continuously in their ears: 'Look! I shall come like a thief. Blessed is anyone who has kept watch and has kept his clothes on, so that he does not go out naked and expose his shame.'[15] The monk's habit is the wedding garment of the Bible. It may never be put off.

The following saying of Abba Dioscorus may have been an influence on Benedict when he wrote chapter 22.

Abba Dioscorus once said, 'If we wear the heavenly garment, we shall not be found naked. If we are found not wearing this garment, what shall we do, brothers? We shall then hear the voice, saying, "Throw him into the darkness outside, where there will be weeping and grinding of teeth."[16] If we have been wearing the monastic habit for so many years, great will be our shame then, brothers, if we are found lacking a wedding garment in our hour of need! What sorrow will overcome us! What darkness will overcome us, before the eyes of our fathers and brothers, when they see us being punished by the angels of wrath!'[17]

Benedict writes in chapter 22, 'Each will hasten to the work of God before the others, . . . they are to encourage each other.'[18] We are reminded of Paul's image of the runner in a race.

Everywhere, Benedict calls for this sense of urgency on the part of his monks, particularly in the Prologue and in chapter 72: 'Run while you have the light of life';[19] 'If we wish to dwell in the tent of this kingdom, we will never arrive unless we run there by doing good deeds';[20] 'They should each try to be the first to show respect for each other'.[21]

Encouraging each other reveals something of the significance of living in community. The cenobite is to be trained in the ranks of the brothers and with the support of the community.[22] The emulation and the mutual support that they should always practise is to be shown above all in connection with the work of God.

In chapter 43, 'On those who come late to the work of God or to table', Benedict is strict when it comes to those who are careless and arrive late.[23] He goes into detail about the treatment to be meted out to them. Instead of making haste, the monk can become slack, and for want of zeal he can fall into spiritual lethargy.

For Benedict, this is not just a matter of good order being disturbed or damage to the smooth running of things. It indicates a certain sloth, and a monk being attached to his own work and his own will. His own work is put before the work of God, or else it is only with difficulty that he can disengage himself from what he himself has in hand. This is why coming late to the work of God is a serious matter. The work of God is the principal expression of everything the monk seeks to be and do, the main way in which his charism is manifested. As in chapter 22, we are not just dealing with a disciplinary measure. 'On hearing the signal for the hour of the divine office, the monk will immediately set aside what he has at hand, and go with utmost speed, yet with gravity and without giving occasion for frivolity. Indeed, nothing is to be preferred to the work of God.'[24] To understand the full significance of these verses we have to go back to chapter 5, on obedience.

Chapter 5 deals with the monk's readiness for the work of God in the wider sense of the term. This is what the whole of his life embraces and what his life stands for. In the first verses of chapter 43 we find the concrete application of this readiness in his immediate response to the signal for the specifically liturgical work of God.

The first step of humility is obedience without delay, which comes naturally to those who cherish Christ above all . . . They admit of no delay . . .[25]

Such people as these immediately put aside their own concerns, abandon their own will, lay down whatever they have in hand, leaving it unfinished. With the ready step of obedience they follow the voice of the one who commands. Almost at the same moment as the master gives the instruction the disciple quickly puts it into practice in the fear of God; both actions together are swiftly completed as one.[26]

What is given is not just an external response; more importantly, it is a swift response of the heart: 'but this obedience will be acceptable to God and agreeable to men only if compliance with what is commanded is not cringing or sluggish or careless, but free from any grumbling or any reaction of unwillingness . . . the disciple's obedience must be given cheerfully . . .'[27]

In chapter 43, just like chapter 22, haste, zeal and emulation are qualities which Benedict calls for in the monk, but especially in connection with the work of God: 'Indeed, nothing is to be preferred to the work of God.'[28] The work of God, then, takes precedence over all the monks' other activities.

This sentence stands out even more sharply when we read it in the light of two other orders: the monk is 'to place nothing before the love of Christ',[29] and 'let them prefer nothing whatever to Christ.'[30]

In each of these three phrases, the word *præponere* is used. Both in connection with the instruments of good works in chapter 4, and also when talking in chapter 72 about the good zeal which should animate the monk, the love of Christ is placed above everything. The work of God is thus given a particularly high value, and this is underlined by the use of the same word, *præponere*.

It must be added, both as a supplement to what has just been said about the importance of the work of God, and in a certain sense also as a corrective, that Benedict always remains very flexible in regards his regulations for the prayer of the hours. This can be seen most clearly when comparing the parallel texts from the Rule of the Master.

Benedict's liturgical prescriptions are not absolute. This is because he always sees the common prayer both as an expression of continuous prayer and also as a means of achieving it. This continuous prayer is the complete work of God for the monk, and that is why the prayer of the hours can easily be moved to another time, unlike the regulations given by the Master, who wants the hours to be celebrated at exactly the prescribed time. It is instructive to read chapter 48, 1–14, of the Rule of Benedict side by side with chapter 50 of the Rule of the Master.

Benedict moves the time for the office when this is necessary. For example, in relation to the night hours, he wants them to be sung, but he also wants the brothers to get a good night's rest. For this reason, in chapter 8, 1–4, he moves the hour for rising a bit, so as to cater for the human need for sleep.

He allows a certain flexibility about the beginning of each hour: there may still be brothers coming in after the first psalm has been intoned.[31] They are to come to the reading for Compline when they have finished the work they have been assigned.[32] Here he seems to correct what he has said elsewhere: in chapter 43 the monk must act immediately when the signal calls him to the work of God, but in chapters 13 and 42 Benedict allows him some leeway. You could say he has had second thoughts, and softened his demands a bit.

For some celebrations, only a part of the community will be present. In chapter 48, Terce is not mentioned. This raises the question: is this hour to be prayed out in the fields or the place where the monks are working? Verses 10–12 present us with other questions: in winter, is None in fact celebrated in common? And why is Sext not mentioned at all? Benedict doesn't push anything to extremes.

'Nothing is to be preferred to the work of God.'[33] The various texts we have quoted here show that presence at the liturgy of the hours is of the greatest importance for St Benedict. This is the method of prayer which is characteristic of the monk of the Benedictine tradition, and which constitutes his special patrimony. Benedict knows from experience that if we wish to arrive at continuous prayer and to achieve a radical redirecting towards God of all our thoughts and emotions, we need to reserve specified times during the day when we do nothing else but pray.

The whole of our conscious and unconscious life can only be totally directed towards God when there are specific times during which we allow God to be the sole object of our consciousness. This is also the reason why the times of prayer are spread out very evenly throughout the day. At specified times the monk returns to the source from which wells up the stream of his continuous prayer. He neglects it at his peril.

III

THE WORK OF GOD

On more than one occasion in the last chapter, we came across the expression 'work of God'. This term does not always have the same meaning. Sometimes it is identical with the prayer of the hours, as in the phrase 'when the work of God has been completed,'[1] which occurs twice in chapter 52. Here the meaning is practical, concrete and obvious. In other places a whole range of possible meanings lies in the background, as for example in chapter 43, which we have already looked at: 'indeed, nothing is to be preferred to the work of God.'[2]

We need to find out what lies at the back of Benedict's mind when he uses the expression 'work of God' in his Rule. All the expressions used in the Rule have a history behind them, and this term is no exception. All the words we use have a background of their own, and the history of language reflects the history of a people and of the whole human race.

'Work of God' is one of those expressions which is heavily laden with meaning. It had a number of different meanings before Benedict used it in his Rule. He comes at the end of a period of evolution, which he brought to a conclusion with his Rule. In order to understand what he means by this expression, we have to trace its history. First we go to the

Bible, which speaks of the works of God. Then we take a look at early Christian literature. Finally we try to discover why Benedict uses this stock phrase, with a very general meaning, when he wants to refer to a small element of the great work of God: the prayer of the hours.

A. THE 'WORK OF GOD' IN HOLY SCRIPTURE

The creation was God's first great work. 'On the seventh day God had completed the work he had been doing. He rested on the seventh day after all the work he had been doing.'[3]

No passage in the whole of the Bible speaks so clearly about the works of God. It is the most important and most fundamental text, because God himself is the subject, God himself is the one who works. All human works and activities find their origin in God and his works. When human activity is detached from God, selfishness comes in and the activity will come to nothing. The men and women of the Bible are acutely conscious of this. They know it is not their own works that justify them, but only the grace of God, working in them and in history. It is good to keep this in mind when speaking about the work of God in the Rule for monks.

The whole of the Old Testament is full of praise for God's work for the human race and for the people of Israel. 'Great are the deeds of the Lord':[4] this is the message which resounds throughout the temple liturgy, referring to the work of creation and redemption. There are also places where human beings are the agents: in such cases, the work of God is the commission which God has given them and which God calls them to accomplish. 'Accursed be he who does the Lord's work negligently!' warns Jeremiah.[5]

Human beings participate in God's activity, and they are responsible for doing the work of God. They do this especially through fulfilling the Law of Yahweh. This is their most essential duty and includes both the unwritten law of conscience and the written law of Sinai.

In the New Testament, Jesus accomplishes the work of God, his Father. 'My Father still goes on working, and I am at work, too.'[6] The work of Jesus and that of his Father is one. In everything the Son does, the works of the Father are revealed.

The synoptic Gospels rarely speak explicitly of the 'works of Jesus', although reports of his works reach the prison where John the Baptist is confined. 'Now John had heard in prison what Christ was doing . . .'[7]

The miracles wrought on behalf of the downtrodden and the handicapped are in fact Jesus' works. In the Fourth Gospel, John sees this activity of Jesus as proceeding from the Father. The works of Jesus are 'the deeds my Father has given me to perform',[8] and they show that he is the Son of God. The Son and the Father are together in their work. The unity of action stems from the love of the Father for the Son, and of the Son for the Father. 'By himself, the Son can do nothing; he can do only what he sees the Father doing: and whatever the Father does, the Son does too.'[9] 'It is the Father, living in me, who is doing his works.'[10] So Jesus glorifies the Father 'by finishing the work that you gave me to do.'[11]

In Jesus, the work of God and human work come together. The work of Jesus reaches its high point and its completion on the cross. Then he can say in truth, 'It is fulfilled.'[12] Then he can enter the rest of the great Sabbath, the rest of God who on the seventh day ceased from all the work he had done.[13]

Another theme emerges in the sixth chapter of St John's Gospel. The Jews ask Jesus, 'What must we do if we are to carry out God's work?'[14] Jesus replies, 'This is carrying out God's work: you must believe in the one he has sent.'[15] Believing is the work which human beings have to do, but we cannot do it by ourselves: 'No one can come to me unless drawn by the Father'.[16] Even believing is a gift of the Father, and so it is at the same time the work of God and human work. The one who receives the gift of believing, therefore, is doing the work which the Son does. 'Whoever believes in me will perform the same works as I do myself'.[17] In this way, the work of God, the work of Christ and the work of the believer come together.

It is part of our human and Christian vocation that all we do has a relationship with the work of God and with God's creative activity. It is good to keep before our eyes the wider biblical background to the work of God and of Christ when we consider the expression 'work of God' in the Rule of Benedict.

B. THE 'WORK OF GOD' IN ANCIENT MONASTIC LITERATURE

Once again we go to the Sayings of the Fathers, in our search for the true meaning of the term 'work of God' in the Rule.

In the Greek texts of all the most ancient monastic writings, including the Sayings of the Fathers, the 'work of God', '*ergon tou Theou*', never means the liturgy or the prayer of the hours, but always the monastic programme or way of life, taken as a whole.

Thus, for example, in the thirteenth saying of Abba Anthony,

> There was a man who used to hunt the wild animals in the desert, and when he saw Abba Anthony at recreation with the brothers, he was scandalized. The old man wished to show him that we have to meet the needs of our brothers every so often, so he said to him, 'Put a bow in your arrow and bend it!' He did what he was asked, and the old man said, 'Bend it further!' He did so, and again the old man said, 'Bend it still further!' The huntsman replied, 'If I bend the bow too far, it will break.' Then the old man said, 'it is the same with the work of God. If we test the brothers beyond endurance, they could well break. Now and then, we have to meet the needs of the brothers.' When the huntsman heard this, he felt ashamed. He had learnt a lot from the old man, and went away. The brothers were also encouraged, and went back to their own cells.[18]

The whole of the monastic way of life, solitude, ascesis and prayer, is here included in the expression 'work of God'. Everything the monk has to do in order to become and remain a monk is the 'work of God'.

The text that follows is important for the two meanings of the term 'work of God'. In the Greek, the speaker uses two different expressions, namely '*ergon tou Theou*', 'work of God', and '*synaxis*', the prayer of the hours. In the Latin version, both are translated by the single phrase '*opus Dei*', 'work of God'. The speaker in the original Greek would not have used two different expressions if he had not wanted to say two different things.

> One of the fathers said, 'There was a certain monk who did not shirk difficulties and was watchful over himself, but it once happened that he committed an act of negligence. He was in despair about this, and said to himself, "My soul, how much longer will you neglect your salvation? Do you have no fear of God's judgment? nor of being snatched away in the midst of your negligence and delivered to everlasting punishment?"

> 'Spurred on by this thought, he once again settled down to the work of God. One day, while he was fulfilling his prayer service, the demons came and made an uproar. He said to them, "how much longer are you going to torment me? Wasn't my act of negligence in the past enough for you?" Then the demons answered him, "when you were negligent, we neglected you. But when you started to stand up against us, then we started to stand up against you." When the monk heard this, he set himself to do the work of God, and through the grace of Christ he made progress.'[19]

The devil tempts the ardent warrior more than the negligent one, not less. Because he is filled with zeal, he perceives the onslaughts of the devil for what they are.

For our purposes, the point of interest in this saying is that the work of prayer is shown to be a high point of the work of God performed by the monk, and it is because this is the case that the devil makes his attack: on a certain day, 'while he was fulfilling his prayer service, the demons came and made an uproar.' It is when the monk directs his heart to God in the work of prayer that the temptation and the evil thoughts come to him all the stronger.

Here we have the two meanings of the 'work of God' side by side, expressed by two different terms: '*ergon tou Theou*' and '*synaxis*'.

There is another very short saying which expresses this point particularly well: 'an old man said, "when the bee flies away, she collects honey everywhere. It is the same with the monk: wherever he goes, everywhere he does the work of God." '[20]

Most of the Greek texts of the Sayings of the Fathers were translated into Latin by Pope Pelagius I (died 560). A curious feature of this translation, however, is that everywhere the prayer service (*synaxis*) is translated as 'the work of God' ('*opus Dei*'). Thus, for example, in the thirty-second saying of Abba Poimen, 'It was said of Abba Poimen that whenever he was to go to the prayer service, he would first sit apart, examining his thoughts, for about an hour; only then would he set off.'[21] In the Greek the word is *ergon tou Theou*; in Pope Pelagius's Latin it is *opus Dei*.

We are aware of the difference; a shift of meaning has taken place. It is not just a matter of terminology, but something of an alteration in the very way of life. We could summarise this change of meaning like this: we start with the biblical concept of God working in and for the human race; in his Son, this is transformed and we see a man working for God. In the monastic literature, the expression 'work of God' acquires a new meaning: the monastic programme, which is a practical way of living out the Christian life. In the Western, Latin-speaking monastic literature, the name 'work of God' is given to one of the occupations of the monk, namely the prayer of the hours.

The meaning becomes ever more specific. When we hear Benedict speaking about the work of God, it is important to bear in mind the whole range of meanings if we are to understand the true significance of the phrase.

C. HOW DID THE SHIFT OF MEANING OCCUR?

Two attempts to answer this question will once again bring us close to the essential nature of the monastic life. In the first place, the Latin tradition, including Benedict, uses the expression 'work of God' to mean the prayer of the hours, in order to stress its outstanding significance. The great importance attached to the prayer of the hours does not require us to downgrade the other observances of the monastic life. All the areas where the monk has to exercise his zeal are summed up by Benedict in his fourth chapter, 'the tools for good works'. Here are all the things that go to make up the whole of the monk's 'work of God', presented with a wealth of detail. This is where we see that the monk is a 'worker' in everything he does. He is a workman and the monastery is his work-place. He accomplishes his work with the tools of good works, a long list that includes, 'listen readily to holy reading', 'devote yourselves often to prayer', 'every day with tears and sighs confess your past sins to God in prayer'.[22]

At the end of this fourth chapter, Benedict clearly has in mind the work of God in the broad sense when he writes,

These, then, are the tools of the spiritual craft. When we have used them without ceasing day and night and have returned them on judgment day, our wages will be the reward the Lord has promised: 'What the eye has not seen nor the ear heard, God has prepared for those who love him' (1 Cor. 2, 9). The workshop where we are to toil faithfully at all these tasks is the enclosure of the monastery and stability in the community.[23]

Among the different works that the monk has to accomplish every day – day and night – first and foremost comes prayer. The whole of his work is focused on prayer. This is why the expression 'work of God' is Benedict's preferred term when speaking about prayer.

A second reason for using the term 'work of God' for the prayer of the hours is the fact that, according to the ancient fathers, it calls for a great deal of effort to apply oneself to prayer. In the earliest monastic literature, to be a monk is an 'effort' and an 'exertion'. So Abba Macarius asks Abba Zacharias,

'Tell me what is the work of the monk.' He replied, 'How is it that you are asking me, my Father?' Abba Macarius then said, 'I am well satisfied with you, Zacharias, my son. There is someone who asks me to put this question to you.' Then Zacharias replied, 'In my opinion, Father, to make a real effort in everything, that is to be a monk.'[24]

When one of the Fathers asked Abba John the Dwarf, 'What is a monk?' he got the answer, 'It is hard work! For the monk is hard-working in whatever he does. That is to be a monk!'[25]

This determined effort is asked of the monk at all times, but especially during prayer. The monk is asked to make an interior effort to be attentive and vigilant, so that his prayer may flourish. Flowing out from this, his whole life is slowly transformed and sanctified and raised up to become life in God.

Prayer, then, is pre-eminently the tool which the monk has to use. It involves a great deal of time and effort, until we reach the point of allowing the Spirit within us to pray with groans that cannot be put into words.

Some brothers put a question to Abba Agatho,

'Which virtue, Father, is the most difficult?' He said to them, 'Forgive me, but I think that there is nothing so difficult as praying to God. Whenever we wish to pray, our enemies the demons set to work to prevent us. They know that the only thing that really stops them is prayer to God. If we engage in any good work and persevere in it, we shall without doubt receive rest, but praying involves effort right until our final breath.'[26]

Prayer sums up the monk's work, but also his struggle. This saying gives us a realistic glimpse into the life of prayer and the spiritual life. Sometimes we almost have guilt feelings when we find prayer difficult. But if we follow Abba Agatho's advice, it is obvious that this is wrong!

Prayer sums up the whole of our monastic commitment. That is why Benedict can justifiably call the work of prayer 'the work of God'. Although Benedict always uses the term 'opus Dei' to mean the prayer of the hours, the older, wider meaning is certainly still present at the back of his mind, and he sees the prayer of the hours as one of the defining moments of the monastic way of life. We need to keep in mind the wider background, as Benedict was conscious of this when he used the expression. It was for him, and remains for us, an expression full of significance, a term with many layers of meaning.

CONCLUSION

Prayer, including liturgical prayer, takes first place in the 'opus Dei' – meaning the 'work of God' in the wider, all-embracing sense of the word. It is the work of God in the monk as well as the monk's work for God. Benedict says that the senior who is assigned to look after newcomers is to be concerned about 'whether the novice truly seeks God and whether he shows eagerness for the work of God . . .'.[27] Seeking God is thus linked up to the work of God.

To seek God truly must of necessity find its expression in eagerness for the work of God, meaning the prayer of the hours. The two are linked together. Sometimes the two are experienced as being equally significant in the life of the monk. 'They said of Abba Sisoes of the desert of the Thebaid, that when the service in the church was concluded, he used to flee to his cell. They said that he was possessed by a devil, but he was doing the work of God.'[28] Here the work of God is not the prayer of the hours, but the whole of the monastic life, spent unceasingly in the presence of God. What is more, the prayer of the hours comes across as something of a danger and an imposition in place of the real work of the monk. To go back to the beginning, all work is ultimately God's saving, creative activity, operating in us. It is good for monks to remain very conscious of this. Being a monk, after all, is 'effort' and 'difficulty'.

We labour, striving with God's energy which works in us mightily.[29] Benedict several times in the Rule urges the monk, 'first of all, every time you begin a good work, you must pray to him most earnestly to bring it to perfection.'[30] Who will enter the tent of God's temple and dwell on his holy mountain? Only those who

> fear the Lord and do not become elated over their great deeds; they judge it is the Lord's power, not their own, that brings about the good in them. They praise the Lord working in them, and say with the Prophet, 'not to us, Lord, not to us give the glory, but to your name alone'.[31] In just this way the Apostle Paul refused to take credit for the power of his preaching. He declared 'By God's grace I am what I am'.[32] And again he said, 'he who boasts should make his boast in the Lord.'[33]

All the good that the monk accomplishes, and all the evil which he is able to avoid, is the grace of God at work in him. 'If you notice something good in yourself, give credit to God, not to yourself, but be certain that the evil you commit is always your own and yours to acknowledge', says Benedict in his list of the tools for good works.[34]

As we said before, Benedict wants this attitude towards God to be experienced in the everyday reality of community living, rubbing shoulders with the other monks. The monk is not to ascribe to himself achievements great or small, or take pride in them. 'If perhaps one of these deans is found to be puffed up with any pride, and so deserving of censure, he is to be reproved . . .'.[35] The cellarer, too, above all, is to be humble.[36] Readers at table and those who lead the singing have it impressed on them that, above all else, they must fulfil their task with humility.[37] As for the artisans of the monastery,

> they are to practise their craft with all humility, but only with the Abbot's permission. If one of them becomes puffed up by his skill in his craft, and feels that he is conferring something on the monastery, he is to be removed from practising his craft and not allowed to resume it until, after manifesting his humility, he is so ordered by the Abbot.[38]

The same holds true for the priests of the monastery: 'the monk who is ordained must be on guard against conceit or pride'.[39]

The whole of the monk's life is the work of God, the service to which he has committed himself. This work finds its fullest and most clear expression in the prayer of the hours, given pride of place by St Benedict as pre-eminently 'the work of God'.

$\overline{}$

HOW, WHEN AND WHERE IS THE MONK TO PRAY?

In the first chapter we asked whether St Benedict is really faithful in his Rule to the ancient monastic tradition of prayer. Is the monk in Benedict's cenobitic monastery really engaged in continuous prayer? Does the life 'under a Rule and an abbot'[1] lead to the continuous prayer of the heart? It is now time to give an answer to these queries by asking three practical questions, which will give us an insight into the prayer-life of the cenobitic monk:

> How does the monk pray?
> When does he pray?
> Where does he pray?

The best answer, and, indeed, the answer given by the Rule, is short and simple:

> How does the monk pray? In the way he lives!
> When does he pray? Always!
> Where does he pray? Everywhere!

This is the reply given by St Benedict in the twelfth degree of humility. Here we see the mature monk, praying at all times and in all places, throughout the whole of his life.

The twelfth degree of humility is that a monk always

manifests humility in his bearing no less than in his heart, so that is evident at the work of God, in the oratory, the monastery or the garden, on a journey or in the field, or anywhere else. Whether he sits, walks or stands, his head must be bowed and his eyes cast down. Judging himself always guilty on account of his sins, he should consider that he is already at the fearful judgment, and constantly say in his heart what the publican in the Gospel said with downcast eyes: 'Lord, I am a sinner, not worthy to look up to heaven'.[2] And with the prophet: 'I am bowed down and humbled in every way.'[3]

This continuous repetition of the Jesus Prayer, the prayer of the publican, brings the monk to 'that perfect love of God which casts out fear. Through this love, all that he once performed with dread, he will now begin to observe without effort, as though naturally, from habit, no longer out of fear of hell, but out of love for Christ . . .'.[4] The goal of prayer is perfect love, which is not regulated by times and places. It penetrates all the consciousness of the monk and all his activities.

We now go back to those three questions. To respond to the first question, 'How does the monk pray', we shall be looking at the way our heart is to be formed and the characteristics of our prayer. Then we examine the role played by the body in prayer. Finally we shall look at the different forms of prayer in the Rule.

The question 'When does the monk pray' brings us to the symbolism of the prayer of the hours. And the question 'Where does he pray' leads us into the oratory, the space in the monastery which is set aside for prayer.

HOW?

a. The dispositions of the heart

St Benedict frequently speaks about the heart which is engaged in prayer. When we compare this with what the Rule of the Master says in parallel texts, it is striking how Benedict leaves out nearly all the external regulations. This heightens the emphasis on the interior nature of the monk's prayer. The Master says in chapter 47, 'Furthermore, care must be taken while singing that there is not a lot of frequent coughing or prolonged gasping or constant spitting out of saliva.'[5] Again, in the following chapter, 'There should not be a great deal of frequent coughing or constant spitting or gasping, because the devil uses all these as a hindrance to prayers and psalms.'[6]

Benedict consciously omits these external details. He goes back to the older teaching on prayer, earlier than the Rule of the Master, that we find in Cassian and Evagrius. It is obvious where St Benedict is drawing his teaching on prayer from, especially in chapters 20 and 52.

> Whenever we want to ask some favour of a powerful man, we do it humbly and respectfully, for fear of presumption. How much more important, then, to lay our petitions before the Lord God of all things with the utmost humility and sincere devotion. We must know that God regards our purity of heart and tears of compunction, not our many words. Prayer should therefore be short and pure, unless perhaps it is prolonged under the inspiration of divine grace. In community, however, prayer should always be brief; and

when the superior gives the signal, all should rise together.[7]

Moreover, if at other times someone chooses to pray privately, he may simply go in and pray, not in a loud voice, but with tears and heartfelt devotion. Accordingly, anyone who does not pray in this manner is not to remain in the oratory after the work of God, as we have said; then he will not interfere with anyone else.[8]

There is a link with chapter 7 when Benedict speaks about the monk manifesting humility in his bearing. Indeed, this chapter provides a key to understanding what humble prayer consists of and what humility means for the monk when he prays.

As well as humility, Benedict indicates some of the characteristics of prayer which have become a classic part of the spiritual tradition since Evagrius. This leads us to the conclusion that the monk who lives in Benedict's cenobitical monastery is called to the same heights of prayer as the hermit in the Egyptian desert. In the *Dialogues*, St Gregory shows that sanctity was not just a thing of the past, reserved for the great heroes of the Egyptian desert or Syria, but that it was something achievable, reached by many ordinary saints in his own times, and by one great saint, namely Benedict. In the Rule too, Benedict offers his own monks the same attainable ideal.

Life according to the Rule of Benedict is a truly contemplative life. In the chapters quoted above, Benedict says that prayer must be pure, brief and with few words, full of compunction and ardent. Three times in chapter 20, he emphasises purity of prayer and purity of heart: we are to pray with 'pure devotion', we shall be heard for our 'purity of heart', and prayer should be 'pure'.[9]

Purity of heart is a precondition of genuine prayer and also a consequence of it. Evagrius writes in his *Chapters on Prayer*, 'First of all, pray to be purified from your passions. Secondly, pray to be delivered from ignorance. Thirdly, pray to be freed from all temptation and abandonment.'[10] As we come to God, we are called to go through three degrees of purity of heart, of increasing intensity. Through prayer we are purified and emptied of all that makes us attached to ourselves and to the world.

Prayer which is pure can only come from a heart which is purified. 'Blessed are the pure in heart: they shall see God.'[11] The monastic fathers could not find enough words to describe this purity of heart, the indispensable stripping away of everything that is not God. It is the culmination of monastic asceticism, as it is described in chapters 5 to 7 of the Rule. 'After ascending all these steps of humility, the monk will quickly arrive at that perfect love of God which casts out fear.'[12] 'All this the Lord will by the Holy Spirit graciously manifest in his workman, now cleansed of vices and sins.'[13]

Purity of heart and perfect love correspond to each other. Purity of heart is the precondition, the disposition needed if God is to instil perfect love into the heart. Purity of heart is the point when we can put the active life completely behind us and be content to wait for the total fulfilment of God's will. Then, using Cassian's words, we will be able to speak of the 'great fire of love' burning within us.

The attainment of purity of heart is the reason why the

monk has embarked on his journey. 'The whole aim of the monk and the perfection of his heart consists in a continual and uninterrupted perseverance in prayer and, as far as is possible for human frailty, it is a striving for immovable tranquillity of mind and lasting purity.'[14]

Through the working of the Spirit, the heart of the one who prays changes from chaos to cosmos, from uninhabitable wilderness to a fertile dwelling-place where the tree of love can bring forth fruit in abundance, the fruits of the Spirit.

As well as talking about a 'pure' heart, we can also talk about a 'cheerful' heart, or a 'clean' heart: 'cleansed' from all sins and vices,[15] and also cleansed of all thoughts and sentiments that obstruct the coming of the Lord and prevent purity of prayer.

Because Cassian, in his ninth conference, gives such a clear exposition of this concept of purity and the process of purification, it is helpful to give the relevant passage in full.

In order to be able to offer up prayer with the earnestness and purity which is appropriate, we must at all costs observe the following rules. First anxiety about earthly things must be got rid of completely. Next, it is not enough just to banish worries about business matters: we must even put aside the thought of them. We must also put aside all backbiting, vain and unnecessary chattering, and frivolity. Above all, the disturbance caused by anger and melancholy must be thoroughly cut out, and the deadly taint of carnal lust and covetousness be torn up by the roots.

These faults, and other similar ones, which are visible

even to human eyes, have to be entirely removed and cut out. The purification and cleansing we spoke about needs to take place: this is accomplished through purity, simplicity and innocence. Then the secure foundations of a deep humility needs to be laid. This will have to support a tower reaching up as far as the sky, which will carry a spiritual building consisting of the virtues. Finally, the soul needs to be restrained from all distractions and roving thoughts so that it may gradually rise to the contemplation of God and fix its gaze on that which is spiritual.

For whatever has been on our mind before the hour of prayer is sure to come back to us while we are praying, through the activity of the memory. Before the time of prayer, therefore, we need to transform ourselves into what we want to be like while we are praying. The attitude of the mind in prayer is conditioned by its previous state. When we apply ourselves to prayer, the images of our previous actions, words and thoughts will dance before our eyes and, depending on our previous attitude, they will make us angry or sad, they will make us dwell on our desires or on business matters, maybe we begin to shake with foolish laughter (I am ashamed even to mention this) at some silly joke, or smile at some action, or we go back to our previous conversation.

Before our time of prayer, therefore, let us do our utmost to chase away from the entrance of our heart everything that we do not wish to be distracted by when we are praying. In this way we fulfil the Apostle's injunction: 'pray constantly',[16] and 'in every place lift hands up reverently in prayer with no anger or argument'.[17]

For we shall not be able to carry out that command unless our mind is purified from all stain of sin, and dedicated to virtue as though this were natural to it, so that it may be nourished by the continual contemplation of Almighty God.[18]

Of course, the fruit of this cleansing or purification of the heart is deep joy and cheerfulness. From this point on, we can have a clear conscience as we pray to God and live in communion with each other.

The heart of the monk, when it is thus purified, will be like the oratory of the monastery. This, according to chapter 52, must be what its name implies: a place where nothing is to be done or kept which would obstruct prayer. This purity of heart spills over from the monk's prayer into the rest of daily life. The monk's manner of life should be kept most pure during Lent,[19] but not only in this time: 'the life of a monk ought to be a continuous Lent.'[20] In chapter 20, Benedict says that prayer is to be 'short' and to consist of 'few words': 'we must know that God regards our purity of heart and tears of compunction, not our many words. Prayer should therefore be short . . . In community, prayer should always be very brief. . . .'[21]

It should be pointed out that, in chapter 20, Benedict is speaking about personal private prayer, while in the last verse he is referring to the silent prayer which followed each psalm during the prayer of the hours.

At first sight it seems contradictory: a monk is supposed to pray long and hard! Surely a person who only prays for a short time is lacking in fervour? For Benedict, the brevity of prayer is directly linked to its purity. For prayer to remain as pure as possible, it is especially important that it should not be unduly protracted. You can quickly switch back from this short and pure prayer to listening to the psalms and readings in the divine office, or to meditating on them while working. Brevity of prayer is very much part of the traditional monastic spiritual teaching.

When some people asked Abbot Macarius how they ought to pray, he replied, 'There is no need to make long discourses; it is enough to stretch out one's hands and say, "Lord, as you will, and as you know, have mercy." '[22]

Benedict did not need to give a long explanation of this characteristic of prayer, as his monks knew the texts from the monastic tradition as well as their abbot did.

In his Institutes, Cassian anticipates the ninth and tenth Conferences, where he will speak at length about prayer. In the Institutes, he says, 'The fathers think it is best if prayers are short but offered up frequently. They should be frequent, so that by praying often we may be able to cleave to God without ceasing. They should be short so that we may avoid the assaults of the devil, who threatens us particularly when we are at prayer.'[23]

Cassian comes back to this in the ninth Conference, where he speaks about short repeated prayer as the way that leads to the pure heights of prayer where love is made perfect.

We ought, then, to pray often but briefly. For if we draw it out, the enemy may succeed in planting something in our heart. This is what true sacrifice is: 'sacrifice to God is a broken spirit.'[24] This is the saving offering, the pure oblation; this is the 'sacrifice of righteousness', the 'sacrifice of thanksgiving', these are true and fat victims, 'holocausts full of marrow',[25] which are offered with a contrite and humble heart. When we offer these sacrifices, in the proper way and with the attitude of heart which we have explained, then we can truly sing with power, 'may my prayer be like incense in your presence, my uplifted hands like the evening sacrifice'.[26]

We have already seen[27] how, in the tenth Conference, Cassian completes his teaching on brief prayer by offering Psalm 70:2 as the finest example of a text which puts into words all that we can express to God.

You have rightly compared teaching someone to pray with educating children. They are not able to take in the whole of the alphabet, and they cannot recognise the letters, or write with a steady hand, until they have spent a lot of time studying the forms and patterns, copied them out many times and become accustomed to them. Now I am going to give you a pattern of spiritual contemplation, to which you should apply yourself steadfastly, with great persistence. In that way, you will learn to pray without ceasing and so come to be saved, and through practice and through meditation you will be able to climb to a still higher level of contemplation. What will be proposed to you is the model which you must learn, the prayer formula which you are seeking. Every monk who is striving to be continually mindful of God has to grow into the habit of reflecting on it incessantly in his heart, while he chases out all the distractions from his thoughts. For he cannot possibly keep hold of this unless he is free from earthly worries and concerns. This formula was handed on to us by a few of the fathers of the older generation who were still alive, and we only entrust it to those very few who truly yearn for it.

In order to be continually mindful of God, you should keep this holy formula in your mind without ceasing: 'O God, make speed to save me: O Lord, make haste to help me.'[28]

With the whole arsenal of Scripture to choose from, it is not unreasonable that this is the verse that should have been chosen. It expresses all the feelings that can be found in human nature and it can be easily adapted to every condition and used in any type of temptation. It contains an appeal to God against all dangers, it includes a humble and pious confession; the watchfulness of anxiety and continual fear; recognition of one's own weakness, a clear expectation that we shall be heard, confidence in receiving help always and everywhere, for if we constantly call on our protector, we can be sure that he is constantly present. This verse expresses the charity of an ardent and loving soul, which is conscious of the ambushes that threaten it. It expresses the soul's fear of its enemies, seeing itself hemmed in by them day and night, and acknowledging that without the aid of its defender it cannot be set free.[29]

St Benedict recommends that when praying we should not indulge in many words, and this fits in with what has just been said. He harks back to the Sermon on the Mount: 'In your prayers, do not babble as the gentiles do, for they think that by using many words they will make themselves heard.'[30] Augustine also makes an allusion to the Egyptian monks' custom of using frequent but short prayers in his letter to Proba.

> We are told that in Egypt there are brothers who offer up frequent prayers, but that these are very short, like arrows loosed off in rapid succession, for fear that the vigilant, alert attention, so necessary for one who prays, should be weakened or blunted if too long an interval is left between them. Thus they show quite clearly that our attention is not to be forced if it cannot be prolonged, while on the other hand it should not be quickly broken off if it is capable of being prolonged.

> So a multiplicity of words should be absent from prayer, but as long as an ardent attention remains, let there be frequent supplications ... Praying intensely means repeatedly and fervently stirring the heart, knocking at the door of him to whom we are praying. Indeed, this is more a matter of sighs than of words, and consists of weeping rather than eloquence. So our tears come into his sight and our sighs do not pass unnoticed by the One who created all things by his Word and who has no need of our words.[31]

When Benedict discourages prayer made with many words, he is referring to the Sermon on the Mount.[32] It is striking that he alludes to these words of Jesus not only when talking about prayer, but also when he talks about the relationships between the brothers. In this context too, he warns that they should not become lost in a multiplicity of words. 'The monk controls his tongue and remains silent, not speaking unless asked a question.'[33] 'The eleventh step of humility is that a monk speaks gently and without laughter, seriously and with becoming modesty, briefly and reasonably . . ., as it is written: "a wise man is known by his few words".'[34]

One of the tools of good works runs as follows: 'not to love much speaking.'[35] The whole of the sixth chapter, on taciturnity, reflects the same attitude towards speech.

Once again, the Rule links up prayer with life. Our living with one another is a training for our relationship with God, and our life with God should make our mutual love for each other more sensitive. Benedict seems to be saying, 'Relate to God in the same way that you relate to each other, and relate to each other in the same way that you relate to God.'

Returning to the silent prayer dealt with in chapter 20, we see how Benedict takes the opportunity to describe the qualities that should characterise the heart of the monk who prays, and to give a description of the prayer of the heart. The pure and short prayer of chapter 20 is, in fact, the prayer of the heart that is called 'one-word prayer' in the tradition, or '*monologistos*' in Greek. It is the individual calling to God from the bottom of the heart that has been wounded by sin and at the same time wounded by the love of God. This form of prayer goes hand in hand with the gift of tears.

Thus we come to the third disposition which should be found in the heart: compunction. 'Every day with tears and sighs confess your past sins to God in prayer.'[36] 'We know that we shall be heard . . . for our tears of compunction.'[37] During Lent we are 'to devote ourselves to prayer with tears.'[38] When a person wishes to pray alone in the oratory, he is to do this 'not in a loud voice, but with tears . . .'[39]

It is only in the context of prayer that Benedict speaks about tears as a sign of compunction. He considers them to be a feature of prayer. They are not a sign of sentimentality, as we hard-headed Northerners too easily assume. They show that the heart has been touched by grace. According to the Fathers, the water from tears purifies the heart and washes it clean. Tears wash away sins, which are like a hard crust on the soul and make it unfeeling.

Evagrius writes, 'pray that you may be able to weep tears, so that through compunction they may soften the hardness of your soul; and then you will obtain forgiveness from the Lord whenever you confess your offences to him.'[40]

The soul, the human heart, is obdurate. You could say it has been frozen, and needs to be defrosted in order to be capable of loving once again. The gift of tears will be able to break through this hardness and make it possible to reach through to the heart once more.

Obduracy affects our relationship with God, and also our relationships with each other. Sometimes it is in our relationships with our neighbour that we first notice our lack of sensitivity. Something can happen, a hard word can be uttered, and slowly there grows a hard shell which obstructs our relations with each other and with God. This is why, according to Evagrius, we first need to pray for the tears that will once again soften the soul. Benedict was inspired by Evagrius's teaching about prayer with tears: he learned about it through Cassian, who speaks of it in his ninth Conference. Cassian says in chapter 28 that it does not depend on us whether we have the gift of tears or not; it is a grace from God. In the following chapter he explains that a great variety of feelings can be expressed in tears:

Sometimes tears flow because our sins prick us like

thorns ... at other times they may be caused by the thought of everlasting joy and by desire of the glory which is to come .... Again, even without having a single deadly sin on our conscience, tears may flow for fear of hell and remembrance of the dread day of judgment. ... There is another kind of tears, too, which are shed, not because of our own conscience, but because of the rebelliousness and the sins of others.[41]

In chapter 30, Cassian warns that we should not try to force tears when they do not come spontaneously. It is a useful warning given by many spiritual writers when dealing with religious emotions.

The heart is purified by the gift of tears and by the soul-searching process, so now there is room in it for the presence of God. From now on there will also be room for our neighbour. Compunction helps me to see the beam in my own eye and to concentrate less on the splinter in the eyes of others. Abba Moses says, ' "Unless we have in our heart the conviction that we are sinners, God does not hear us." One of the brothers asked, "What does it mean, to have in our heart the conviction that we are sinners?" The old man replied, "When we are concerned about our own sins, we do not see those of our neighbour." '[42]

The tears are an outward expression of our inner feelings. Through them, body and soul are joined together. The thoughts of the soul become bound up with the sensations we experience in our bodies.

When Benedict says that we should pray with tears, he is harking back to the traditional teaching of the early monks about compunction or *penthos*.

The final characteristic of the heart mentioned by the Rule in connection with prayer is fervour. This characterises short and pure prayer with tears. The monk is to pray 'intentione cordis', 'with heartfelt devotion':[43] that is to say, his heart is to be filled with fervour, tenderness and earnestness.[44] 'The heartfelt devotion' of chapter 52 of the Rule is a fervent, affectionate, dynamic and tender devotion, which directs the loving heart towards God.

Behind this concept of heartfelt devotion, we once again find texts of Cassian. Those who practise the fourth and highest degree of prayer

> attain with fervent and ecstatic heart that ardent prayer which cannot be understood or expressed in human terms. . . . Sometimes, however, the soul which has arrived at that state of true purity, and is already acquiring a certain stability in it, will use all these forms of prayer at the same time. Like some incomprehensible but all-comprehending flame, it darts from one to the other, and pours out to God inexpressible prayers of the purest force, prayers which the Holy Spirit, with ineffable sighs, offers up to God on our behalf, in a way that is beyond our understanding . . .[45]

Fervour and tenderness are two of the qualities of prayer that are closely related to each other. Fervour of heart is also a characteristic of the whole of the monk's life, according to the Rule of Benedict. In the Prologue, he urges the monk to listen with enthusiasm to the call of the Lord. 'If we wish to dwell in the tent of his kingdom, we shall never arrive unless we run there by doing good works.'[46]

The life of the monk is filled with spiritual zeal. Ardent enthusiasm is not only a mark of his personal life; it also characterises his love for his brethren. 'This, then, is the good zeal which monks must foster with fervent love: they should try to be the first to show respect to each other.'[47] Ardent love knows no boundaries. The visitor is also received with ardent love. 'As soon as anyone knocks . . . the porter provides a prompt answer with the warmth of love.'[48] Ardent love is nourished by fervour in prayer.

Benedict describes the prayer of the monk who lives according to his Rule as pure, short, full of compunction and fervent. The whole of the primitive monastic tradition lies behind these highly significant expressions. It also shows the extent to which Benedict in his Rule lays stress on the interior aspect of monasticism. All his emphasis is on the monk's interior disposition.

b.   Bodily posture

To answer the question 'How does the monk pray?' we also have to look at his external bearing: how his prayer is reflected in his bodily posture. The body has its proper role to play in our dialogue with God. Through contact with Asian traditions of prayer, we have become much more conscious of this. Benedict gives no systematic reply to our question about the role of the body. He and his contemporaries were certainly much more aware than we are of the unity of body and soul.

During the community prayer services, the monks were seated when they were listening to readings. The same was true during the so-called responsories, when they sang and

[70]

meditated on the passages of Scripture that they had read and listened to. 'When all are seated on the benches, the brothers in turn read three selections from the book on the lectern. After each reading a responsory is sung.'[49] After the six psalms of the Sunday office, 'while they are seated on the benches and arranged in their proper order, there are read from the book . . . four readings with their responsories.'[50] At night too, 'all the monks will sit together . . . and someone should read from the "Conferences" or the "Lives of the Fathers" . . .'.[51]

The sitting position is one of rest and relaxation, receptivity and readiness to listen. It is a suitable position for listening to the Word of God.

This sitting posture has something to do with Jesus' sitting down beside Jacob's well. 'Jesus, tired by the journey, sat down by the well.'[52] Listening to the Word of God is like going to sit by the well from which we can draw comfort, where we can take a rest from the fatigue of our journey through life. To go and sit down implies that somehow we take the time to put aside rush and agitation.

Standing up always implies for Benedict an inner attitude of reverence and awe. 'All stand in reverence when the cantor begins the "Glory be to the Father".'[53] 'The Abbot reads from the Gospels while all the monks stand with respect and awe.'[54] He explains why the monks rise when the 'Glory be to the Father' is commenced: 'in honour and reverence for the Holy Trinity.'[55] While the psalmody is being sung, the monks also remain standing.[56]

Standing in the presence of God is the service to which the monks have dedicated themselves, the duty to which they are committed.[57] Standing expresses readiness and vigilance, reverence and respect towards the person we serve. It is an attitude owed to God, but also an appropriate attitude towards our fellow human beings, especially when these have an additional right to honour and respect because of their age or the authority vested in them. 'Wherever brothers meet, the junior asks his senior for a blessing. When an older monk comes by, the younger rises and offers him a seat, and does not presume to sit down unless the older bids him.'[58] This standing is never a haughty attitude, but that seen in the tax collector in the Gospel: 'the tax collector stood some distance away, not daring even to raise his eyes to heaven . . .'.[59]

Kneeling certainly points to an attitude of intense prayer. It is not clear whether the silent prayer was done kneeling or lying prostrate on the ground. It was certainly not done sitting, as the silent prayer required a more intense posture than singing psalms or listening to the readings. According to chapter 20, the monks rise after the silent prayer when the abbot gives the signal.[60] When they are not in the oratory, the brothers say the psalms standing, and make their silent prayer kneeling: '. . . they kneel out of reverence for God.'[61] Kneeling is also appropriate when asking other people for their prayers: the kitchen servers kneel to ask their brothers to intercede for them.[62]

The most striking way of expressing repentance and sorrow is by prostrating oneself on the ground. This is appropriate for the monk who has been excommunicated on account of his disobedience. Making a prostration expresses humbling ourselves before God and before each other.

The monk prostrates himself in a gesture of humble adoration when Christ is received in the guest. 'By a bow of the head or by a complete prostration of the body, Christ is to be adored because he is indeed welcomed in them.'[63] A prostration is the gesture of humility made towards the brothers when a serious fault has been committed. 'Anyone excommunicated for serious faults from the oratory and from the table is to prostrate himself in silence at the oratory entrance, at the end of the celebration of the work of God. He should lie face down at the feet of all as they leave the oratory.'[64] The monk should also adopt this attitude of humble submission when he perceives that one who is his senior, or even the abbot himself, is angry with him or secretly vexed. 'He must, then and there, without delay, cast himself on the ground at the other's feet'.[65] When the novice asks to be received into the community, he 'prostrates himself at the feet of each monk to ask his prayers'.[66]

Each of these four postures – sitting, standing, kneeling and prostrating – expresses the monk's attitude towards God and towards his brothers. It is the fundamental attitude of humility towards God which is lived out in our relationships with each other. Bodily posture is linked up with the disposition of the heart, and reinforces it.

Benedict repeatedly comes back to the connection between body and soul and the unity between them. Both body and soul are to be transformed through the conversion process implicit in the monastic way of life, and so become bearers of the presence of God. 'We must, therefore, prepare our hearts and bodies for the battle of holy obedience to God's instructions.'[67]

The ladder by which we climb through humility is formed by two sides. 'We may call our body and our soul the sides of this ladder, into which our divine vocation has fitted the various steps of humility and discipline as we ascend.'[68]

We are body and soul, and the two cannot be separated. This fact has many far-reaching consequences. The monastic life cannot be reduced to the external accomplishment of ascetical observances or the adoption of a structured lifestyle, nor can it be a purely interior matter. These two roads lead to nothing but aridity and barren sentimentality, no matter how beautiful and exalted the sentiments may be. Fervour, purity and a loving heart: these are the indispensable companions of correct external observance. '. . . A monk always manifests humility in his bearing no less than in his heart . . . whether he sits, walks or stands . . .'.[69]

Both the inner person and the outer body need to be purified by grace. 'He guards himself at every moment from sins and vices of thought or tongue, of hand or foot, of self-will or bodily desire.'[70] Some manuscripts, such as the Oxford one, add 'eyes' after 'tongue'.

The whole person needs to be transformed. When Benedict presents his programme for achieving this complete transformation, he foresees the danger that the monk may only get as far as being humble in words, and fail to take the necessary further step. 'The seventh step of humility is that a man not only admits with his tongue but is also convinced in his heart that he is inferior to all and of less value.'[71] We have to speak the truth not only with our tongue, but also with our heart.[72] On the level of obedience too, it is worse to grumble in the heart than with the tongue.[73]

Harmony between body and soul is especially important when the monk is at prayer. 'Let us stand to sing the psalms in such a way that our minds are in harmony with our voices.'[74] The prayer of the hours is very definitely a form of prayer in which the whole person is engaged, body and soul. A proper, disciplined posture keeps the soul vigilant and attentive in the presence of the Word of God which is pronounced and hearkened to. The danger is always present that the monk will sing with his voice but that his mind will be in a different world. The ability of his imagination to wander is boundless. Abba Elias said, 'If the spirit does not pray the psalms together with the body, its labour is pointless.'[75]

When Benedict speaks about the harmony between mind and voice,[76] he is giving a very brief summary of the following text from the Rule of the Master.

So the singer of psalms must always be careful not to let his attention wander elsewhere, lest God say to us when our mind has strayed to some other thought: 'this people honours me only with lip-service, while their hearts are far from me',[77] and lest it likewise be said of us: 'with their mouth they blessed and in their heart they cursed',[78] and lest when we praise God with the tongue alone, we admit God only to the doorway of our mouth while we bring in and lodge the devil in the dwelling of our heart. For he who goes inside is held in higher esteem by the one who brought him in than is he who is left waiting outside. Therefore for a duty so great and so important the heart should be in consonance with the tongue, in order to render with fear what is due to the Lord every day. And in his heart let the singer of psalms pay attention to each and every verse he says, because if each verse is noted the soul derives profit for salvation and therein finds all it seeks, for 'the psalm says everything for edification';[79] as the prophet declares: 'I shall sing and understand in the way of integrity, when you come to me'.[80] Let him who resounds in the voice also be in the mind of the singer. Let us therefore sing with voice and mind in unison; as the apostle says, 'I will sing with the spirit, but I will sing with the understanding also'.[81] We must cry out to God not only with our voices, but with our heart as well.[82]

In the method of prayer which we find in the Rule of Benedict, heart and body are in harmony with each other, and both of them are agents in bringing about God's presence. The monk desires to make the whole of his life a prayer, and to make the whole of his being into a man of prayer.

c. Types of prayer

In practice, the monk's spiritual experience will be determined by the different forms which prayer takes in his everyday life.

We can identify four different types of prayer in the Rule: the prayer of the hours, the silent prayer which is closely related to the prayer of the hours and takes place during it as well as at other times, *lectio divina* or spiritual reading, and finally *meditatio*.

1. Prayer of the hours and silent prayer

Although Benedict expressly mentions the monk's personal prayer outside the prayer of the hours,[83] it is also clear that he considers the prayer of the hours to be an important time for personal prayer. According to the Rule, the prayer of the hours consists of two elements: one part is sung or read, the other part is silent. Thus in chapters 19 and 20 these two essential elements of the prayer of the hours are treated one after the other. It has often been assumed that chapter 19 deals with the divine office and chapter 20 with private prayer, but this involves introducing an anachronistic Western distinction that is not to be found in the Rule.

Since the rise of the apostolic Orders and Congregations in the sixteenth and seventeenth centuries, a strong emphasis has been laid on a separate time for silent prayer. The silent prayer in the Rule is certainly no mere afterthought: it is the heart of the prayer of the hours. It is not a moment of relaxation or a pause for rest after the psalm or reading. This time is intended so that the Word of God which has been listened to can become personal prayer. This is the time when the Word of God can resonate in my heart, so that it can become my response: from being God's Word to me, it becomes my word to God.

It is of secondary importance how long the prayer of the hours lasts or what it contains; it is the silent prayer which gives the real value to the psalm or the reading. You could even say that the silent prayer is more truly prayer than the psalm that goes before it. The psalms, like the readings and *lectio divina*, are the first step: they are an invitation to prayer, which comes from the heart. This also explains why Benedict generally prefers consecutive reading from the psalter, taking the psalms in their numerical order. We find traces of this in chapter 18. Benedict's monks, like their forebears, knew by heart long passages of the Bible, including the psalms, which they would have known in numerical order.

In the most ancient monastic tradition, then, and also in the Rule, the psalms are in the first place God's word to us. The monk first sits and listens to the Word, letting it penetrate into the heart as deeply as possible, so that it may achieve what it was sent to accomplish.[84] Caesarius of Arles speaks of this in one of his homilies: 'Singing psalms, my brothers, is like scattering seed on a field; praying is like ploughing over the land and burying the seed.'[85] There is a play on the Latin words '*orare*' (to pray) and '*arare*' (to plough), which does not come across in translation.

The silent prayer is like ploughing: by ploughing over the ground of our heart, we enable the Word we have heard to penetrate it deeply. Earlier in the homily, Caesarius asks,

> What good does it do you to sing psalms faithfully, if you refuse to make your supplication to God when the psalms are over? Each of us, therefore, when finishing the psalm, should pray and put his petition before the Lord in all humility, so that, with God's help, he may be able to accomplish in his deeds what he has spoken with his lips.

The whole of the prayer of the hours consists of a twofold action: the psalmody and the reading sow the Word of God in our heart, while the silent, personal prayer ploughs it in, so that it may germinate and bear fruit in our lives.

Reading and psalmody both come before the prayer. This is the case with the liturgy in the oratory, and also the liturgy outside the oratory: during work, at the table, and everywhere else. 'God has the first word'; 'It was he who loved us first.' Our prayer and our love cannot be anything more than a response or an answer. Listening, then, is the indispensable preparation for pure, silent prayer.

Maybe what really needs to be kept together has, in practice, been drawn a bit too far apart. After all, the psalter is full of prayers, and in the psalter God himself teaches how we should pray. You could say that he puts the words for our prayer into our mouth.

There is a difference, though, between the value of the psalms and that of the silent prayer after the psalm. In the monastic tradition, and also for Benedict, pride of place is given to the silent prayer which the monk prays in his heart. In the course of history, however, this silent prayer was rapidly downgraded into a useless appendage. Silence is a difficult thing to cope with in the liturgy; there is a horror of an empty space. Nature abhors a vacuum, and it seems that the liturgy does too. Hence the tendency to fill up the silence and the empty spaces in the liturgy with the spoken word. The psalmody – the very thing which was supposed to nourish the silent prayer – quickly came to swallow it up instead. The 'Glory be to the Father', which was added to the psalm early on, started to fill up the period of silence after the psalm and to take its place.

As early as Cassian, we see the beginning of a trend which will result in the silent prayer being replaced by the 'Glory be to the Father'.

We have noticed the following practice in this country: when the soloist has reached the end of the psalm, all those present join together and sing in a loud voice the 'Glory be to the Father'. In the East, we never saw anything like this. There, perfect quiet is observed when the singer has finished the psalm, and the silent prayer follows.[86]

This diversity is an indication of a change in practice. We can follow this development, step by step, from Cassian, via the Master, and on to Benedict. In Cassian, the whole emphasis is still on the silent prayer. The psalms are less numerous, and they are divided into two or three groups. They are done slowly and carefully by soloists taking turns, one after the other. These singers

are not concerned about the number of verses they sing, but about the spiritual understanding of them. They do all they can to follow the advice of the apostle, who says, 'I shall pray with the spirit, but I shall pray with the mind as well.'[87] So they consider it better to sing ten verses with understanding than to reel off a whole psalm with a bewildered mind.[88]

For Cassian, the goal is to foster prayer in the heart of the listening monk, by means of the reading done by a soloist. 'For sometimes a verse of some psalm which we have sung provides us with an occasion for ardent prayer. Sometimes a brother's tuneful voice stirs the hearts of those who hear it to intense prayer. We know also that the dignity and reverence of the chanter contribute greatly to the fervour of those who are present.'[89]

The psalmody here is still principally the Word of God addressed to us, which is listened to attentively. For the Master, the psalmody is increasingly seen as homage rendered to God. He reckons that the silent prayer is less important than the psalm that goes before it, less important also than the 'Glory be to the Father' which follows.[90] The spoken word becomes more important than silence, emphasis is laid on texts in preference to personal prayer, and prescribed formulae are enhanced at the expense of the spontaneous prayer of the heart.

When the office has to be cut down for lack of time, the Master lets the silent prayer be dropped. Sometimes even the psalmody is cut down, but the 'Glory be to the Father' has to be sung at all costs. 'If a very urgent necessity of some kind puts constraint on those in choir, let them recite one section of each of the psalms to be said, with one doxology, and then leave the oratory. Thus, whatever the necessity may be, the Word of God will in any case not be openly skipped.'[91]

In Benedict, we see traces of both Cassian and the Master. The structure is still that of Cassian, with the silent prayer after the psalm, but the 'Glory be to the Father' has the same emphasis as it had for the Master. Thus the element of worship becomes ever more dominant. This is a development that will be taken still further after Benedict.

The silent prayer during the office vanishes, and with it goes the vital link between word and silence: each of these elements is necessary in order to nurture the other. The times of silence introduced into the prayer of the hours and the Eucharist in recent years can be an important way of helping us to integrate the prayer of the hours and personal silent prayer, and to rediscover the relationship between them.

2. *Lectio divina*

In the Rule of Benedict, and in all the texts about organised monastic life, reading holds a very important place in the daily life of the monk. This becomes apparent when we read chapter 48 of the Rule. The traditional title of this chapter reads 'Concerning the daily manual labour'. It would be quite appropriate to rename it 'Concerning spiritual reading'. The day is divided between three principal occupations or duties: work, *lectio* and prayer. 'Prayer' for Benedict includes common and personal prayer, and also *lectio* as a first step towards prayer.

This chapter of the Rule aims at pointing the monk towards the unity between prayer and work; reading binds these two elements together. This is why reading is so prominent, and Benedict sets aside the best part of the day for it, not just a few snatched moments when the monk is too tired to do anything worth while. Reading is so important because, in all teaching about prayer, it is the first step towards the pure, continuous prayer of the heart. It leads to the state or condition of prayer about which Cassian speaks. Reading is itself the first type of prayer. This does not mean that it is the form that has to be completely mastered first; rather it is the first element in a sort of cycle: time and time again, we move from reading on to prayer.

Reading means a listening and watchful openness to the Word of God. First we have to listen, and go on listening long and hard. 'Listening' is a dominant theme running throughout the Rule. It lies at the root of obedience, humility and taciturnity. They are concrete ways of leading a life of listening. Listening is one of the principal characteristics which mark out the monk.

There is a masterly exposition of the importance of reading, and its place in a life of prayer, in the *Ladder of Monks* of Guigo II the Carthusian. When he was a young monk he wrote one day a long letter to his friend Gervasius about an important discovery he had made.

> One day when I was busy working with my hands I began to think about our spiritual work, and all at once four stages in spiritual exercise came into my mind: reading, meditation, prayer and contemplation. These make a ladder for monks by which they are lifted up from earth to heaven. It has few rungs, yet its length is immense and wonderful, for its lower end rests upon the earth, but its top pierces the clouds and touches heavenly secrets.
>
> Reading is the careful study of the Scriptures, concentrating all one's powers on it . . . . Reading seeks for the sweetness of a blessed life, meditation perceives it, prayer asks for it and contemplation tastes it. . . .

Further on, Guigo compares reading with tasting a grape. 'Wishing to have a fuller understanding of it, the soul begins to chew upon the grape, as though putting it through a wine press. . . .'

When he has given a description of each of the stages, he summarises them as follows:

> You can see . . . how these degrees are joined to each other. One precedes another, not only in the order of time but of causality. Reading comes first, and is, as it were, the foundation: it provides the subject matter we must use for meditation. Meditation considers more

carefully what is to be sought after; it digs, as it were, for treasure which it finds and reveals, but since it is not in meditation's power to seize upon the treasure, it directs us to prayer. Prayer lifts itself up to God with all its strength, and begs for the treasure it longs for, which is the sweetness of contemplation. Contemplation when it comes rewards the labours of the other three; it inebriates the soul with the dew of heavenly sweetness.

Reading is an exercise of the outward senses; meditation is concerned with the inward understanding; prayer is concerned with desire; contemplation outstrips every faculty.

The first degree is proper to beginners, the second to proficients, the third to devotees, the fourth to the blessed. . . . At the same time, these degrees are so linked together, each one working also for the others, that the first degrees are of little or no use without the last, while the last can never, or hardly ever, be won without the first. For what is the use of spending one's time in continuous reading, turning the pages of the lives and sayings of holy men, unless we can extract nourishment from them by chewing and digesting this food so that its strength can pass into our inmost heart.

Blessed is the man whose heart is not possessed by any other concern and whose desire is always to keep his feet upon this ladder.[92]

We say, rather too easily, that prayer is about being

emptied, becoming silent, eliminating our thoughts. Sometimes we launch into prayer, and then become discouraged
because we find it so hard. Maybe this is because we have
missed out one of the stages, the first rung described by
Guigo. We are building without foundations. The first stage
towards achieving that deep silence and becoming emptied
is that of letting our thoughts be fashioned and transformed,
and directed towards the Good and the Beautiful, towards
God himself. This is the function of reading.

This is the background which enables us to understand
why Benedict, faithful to the whole of the monastic tradition
that went before him, attached such importance to regular
spiritual reading, or *lectio divina*. The discovery of Guigo the
Carthusian can help us understand the importance and spiritual significance of *lectio* in the Rule. Whenever Benedict
speaks about *lectio divina* or spiritual reading, the first thing
he is referring to is the common reading when one monk
reads aloud and the others listen, in other words public
reading. Readiness to listen should characterise the whole
life of the monk, and this applies in particular when he is
at the community's common reading.

There are a number of places where St Benedict speaks
about *lectio* in the Rule.

(1) In the list of the tools for good works, he mentions
reading in the context of prayer: 'listen readily to holy
reading'; this is followed immediately by: 'and devote yourself often to prayer' and 'every day with tears and sighs
confess your past sins to God in prayer'.[93] Reading is clearly
the foundation on which prayer is built, just as it is for
Guigo the Carthusian.

(2) In chapters 8–18 there are repeated references to the

reading that takes place during liturgical prayer. At the night office, Benedict lays down that 'besides the inspired books of the Old and New Testaments, the works read at Vigils should include the explanations of Scripture by reputable and orthodox catholic Fathers.'[94] At the morning liturgy 'a reading from the Apostle is read by heart'[95] on weekdays, while, on Sundays, it is worth noting that the reading is to be from the Apocalypse of St John.[96] At the other hours there is always mention of a reading, although we are not given details about the book of the Scriptures which is to be read.

(3) Chapter 38, on 'the reader for the week', stresses the importance of reading during meal-times. This chapter begins with the rather stately declaration that 'Reading should always accompany the meals of the brothers.' Benedict determines how the reading should be done: 'The reader should not be the one who just happens to pick up the book, but someone will read for a whole week',[97] and only those whose reading will benefit the hearers.[98] Because it is such an important matter, the reader is to ask for the prayers of the whole community at the beginning of his week of service.[99] 'Because of Holy Communion and because the fast may be too hard for him to bear,' he is to be given 'some diluted wine before he begins to read'[100] so that he may discharge his duty with care. 'Complete silence' is to be observed, so that everybody can hear the reading.[101]

By devoting the whole of the chapter to reading and the reader, Benedict brings out very clearly the importance of this reading in the refectory, all the more so because, as usual, he does not really give any reasons: he obviously takes it for granted that these will be well known. His monks would certainly have known what the Rule of Saint Augustine says: 'From the time of your coming to table until you rise from it, listen without noise and wrangling to whatever may be read to you; let not your mouths alone be exercised in receiving food, let your ears also be occupied in receiving the Word of God.'[102] They will also have been acquainted with what the Master wrote: 'In this way divine food will never be wanting at a carnal meal; as Scripture says, "Man does not live by bread alone, but by every word of God",[103] and the brothers' meal will be double when they eat through the mouth and are nourished by the ears.'[104] From these two quotations we can assume that, in Benedict's monastery too, all the refectory reading will have been from Holy Scripture.

A particular sort of spiritual reading took place in the evening, just before Compline. The monks came together specifically in order to listen together to this reading. Benedict indicates the texts to be read for preference: Cassian's Conferences or the *Lausiac History*, 'or at any rate something else that will benefit the hearers.'[105] Some of the books of the Old Testament, nevertheless, are expressly excluded, with an eye for those who are weak, whose imaginations could cause them problems during the night.[106]

(4) In chapter 53, on the reception of guests, 'the divine law is read to the guest for his instruction' when he is newly arrived.[107] The Word of God and prayer are to determine the spirit in which the guest is received.

(5) Reference has already been made to chapter 48, and we saw how the Word of God constitutes the leaven of the whole of the monk's day. The liturgical readings at the hours of prayer, the reading at meal-times, the evening reading and the two or three hours spent in private reading mean that the whole of the monk's life is shot through and transformed

by the Word. In this chapter, Benedict uses the expression 'vacare lectioni/lectionibus' no less than six times: reading presupposes inner freedom, spiritual receptivity, readiness to make ourselves available for God and for his Word to us.

(6) During Lent Benedict calls for special attention to reading, although reading really ought to have at all times the importance that is given to it during the forty days of Lent.[108] Here, as in the list of the tools for good works in chapter 4, reading is closely linked to prayer: we are called to devote ourselves 'to prayer with tears, to reading, to compunction of heart and self-denial.'[109] Prayer, reading and compunction go together. There comes a moment when listening to the Word and reading it confronts us with ourselves. The Word will penetrate through to the depths of our consciousness where we are completely dependent on God and his mercy. This confrontation leads to the compunction which makes the monk capable of prayer in his heart. Then God will be able to dwell in him, together with his Word, as in the Ark of the Covenant.

At the beginning of the forty days of Lent, the codices containing the Scriptures were distributed. As these were to be kept until the following year, the monks would spend a lot of time with this text of Holy Scripture, committing it to memory through meditatio, and making it a part of their inmost selves.

As we have already said, the preferred choice for reading was the Bible, which is the Word of God and the wellspring of life. One indication of this is the fact that forty per cent of the Rule consists in quotations from the Bible. You could say that Benedict's monks lived immersed in Scripture. Their whole life was lived under the guidance of the Gospel, '*per ducatum Evangelii*'.[110] The Bible is a guiding light, the rule which governs the life of each of the monks. 'What page, what passage of the inspired books of the Old and New Testament is not the truest of guides for human life?'[111]

The Rule does not take the place of Scripture for the monk. It shows him the way to the Scriptures and to a way of life that is in conformity with them: it is Scripture that is normative. It is also medicine for the weak brother, and that means everybody at some time or another. The abbot is to employ 'the medicine of divine Scripture'[112] for those who have been frequently punished and will not amend.

Towards such brothers, the abbot needs to act like that great visionary, Abba Silvanus. A brother was suffering from heavy despondency because he had sinned grievously and had not been able to confess the sin. He came to Abba Silvanus and asked him,

> 'If thoughts of such a kind should come to someone, can he be saved?' The father opened his mouth and, beginning with the Scriptures, said to him that in no way was there condemnation for those who have thoughts such as these. The brother listened to this and took hope, and explained his situation to him. The father listened, and like a good physician made a plaster for his soul out of the Holy Scriptures, saying that repentance is possible for those who sincerely turn to God.[113]

The monk's meeting with the Word of God in *lectio divina* will give him an ever-increasing hunger and thirst for the Word. Cassian speaks of this in one of his Conferences.

No matter how often we listen to the Holy Scripture, it

will never satisfy our hunger or leave us feeling disgust for it. . . . Every day we receive it as something new, something longed for, and the more often we approach it, the more eagerly we will listen to it and speak of it. Repetition will not lead to boredom, but will rather reinforce our understanding.[114]

As we become totally engrossed by the Word of God, God is glorified by the whole of our life.

3. *Meditatio*

What is absorbed during *lectio* is assimilated and received into the heart through *meditatio*. *Meditatio*, then, follows on from *lectio*. After listening to the Word of God in the community reading, or after reading it on his own, the monk repeats the Word to himself, chewing it over. He whispers or murmurs it quietly to himself, probably audibly, but not noisily, especially when others are trying to sleep.[115] This *meditatio* is clearly something different from what we mean nowadays by 'meditation'.

For the original meaning of *meditatio* we can look to texts in Cassian's Institutes. He writes, 'All do the work assigned to them, all the while repeating by heart some psalm or passage of Scripture. Thus they have no opportunity or time for dangerous schemes or evil designs, or even for idle talk, as mind and heart are ceaselessly occupied with spiritual meditation.'[116]

This gives us a picture of the practice of *meditatio*. The whole day was spent engaged in it. Cassian writes, 'Each of them is continually engaged in manual labour in their cells

in such a way that meditation on the psalms and the rest of
the Scriptures is never entirely omitted.'[117]

Cassian talks in the Institutes about eavesdropping on a
monk who was engaged in this type of *meditatio*.

> I remember an old man, when I was staying in the desert
> of Scete, who went to the cell of a certain brother to pay
> him a visit. When he reached the door, he heard him
> murmuring inside, so he waited outside for a little while,
> wanting to know what passage of Scripture he was
> reading or repeating from memory while he was at work,
> as is their custom.[118]

The fruits yielded by this sort of meditation are well
described by Cassian himself.

> This continuous reflection ('*iugitas meditatio*') yields fruit
> in two ways. In the first place, while our attention is
> fixed on reading and studying, it cannot become snared
> in the nets of evil thoughts. Secondly, it may happen that
> some passages, which we have repeatedly reflected on
> and striven to commit to memory, still remain obscure
> to us because at the time our mind does not enjoy the
> freedom it needs. But later, when we have been freed
> from distracting occupations and images, and as we con-
> tinue to repeat these passages to ourselves in silence,
> especially during the night ('*nocturna meditatio*'), then the
> text which has been committed to memory emerges in
> a clear light. When we were fully awake we had not the
> slightest idea of these hidden things. But when we are
> sunk in deep sleep, its meaning is revealed to us.[119]

Through *meditatio* we grasp the significance of what our

intellect had taken in through *lectio*. You could say that *meditatio* brings it from the head to the heart. This process is prolonged during sleep in an unconscious nocturnal *meditatio*. For the monks of old, the day was not complete without meditation of this sort. *Meditatio* was the prolongation of reading, and turned what had been read into *oratio*, prayer.

Benedict talks about this sort of *meditatio* three times in the Rule. 'In the time remaining after Vigils, those who need to learn some of the psalter or readings should study them ("*meditationi inserviatur*")'.[120] On Sundays, the biggest part of the day is spent in reading and *meditatio*. 'If anyone is so remiss and indolent that he is unwilling or unable to study ("*meditare*") or read, he is to be given some work in order that he may not be idle.'[121] The novitiate is the place where the newcomers 'study ("*meditent*"), eat and sleep.'[122]

If we compare these passages of the Rule with the texts from Cassian quoted above, we notice that by St Benedict's time *meditatio* has acquired an additional and slightly different meaning: 'study' or 'learning by heart'. It certainly still includes repeating what has been learnt by heart, murmuring it during work, but the emphasis has shifted towards the exercise of learning by heart. For Cassian, *meditatio* was to occupy the whole of the monk's day. For Benedict, it has become a distinct occupation, to be engaged in at certain times. Cassian's *meditatio* was much more obviously a form of prayer.

Benedict is still close to the primitive tradition, and his *meditatio* is always closely linked with prayer and *lectio*. We need to discover afresh the meaning and purpose of *meditatio*. It may be that this is one of the practices of ancient monasticism which we find it most difficult to rediscover. The shift towards discursive thought, the sense of rush that pervades our mentality, together with the surfeit of ideas and written material, make it extremely difficult for us to pause in silence with what we have absorbed in our reading.

Meditatio, or ruminating over the Word of God, is indispensable if this Word is to become an integral element of our daily life. In modern conditions, it will need a strictly organised work schedule (such as we find in many places in the Rule), together with a careful and responsible use of the mass media, to ensure that there is room for *meditatio*, which is essential for a genuine monastic life.

WHEN, ACCORDING TO THE RULE OF SAINT BENEDICT, IS THE MONK TO PRAY?

After considering at some length the question, 'How does the monk pray?', we next need to ask which moments of the day should be dedicated in a particular way to prayer.

Following the Lord's example, Benedict asks his monks to pray unceasingly, and make one single great prayer out of the whole of their lives: all their thoughts and actions are concerned with their relationship with God. Nevertheless, this unceasing prayer is focused on certain important moments of the day. In chapter 16, he lays a great deal of emphasis on describing the times of day when this is to happen.

> The Prophet says, 'Seven times a day have I praised you.'[123] We shall fulfil this sacred number of seven if we satisfy our obligations of service at Lauds, Prime, Terce, Sext, None, Vespers and Compline, for it was of

these hours during the day that he said: 'Seven times a day have I praised you.' Concerning Vigils, the same prophet says: 'At midnight I arose to give you praise.'[124] Therefore we should praise our Creator for his just judgments at these times: Lauds, Prime, Terce, Sext, None, Vespers and Compline; and let us arise at night to give him praise.[125]

Benedict is making use here of the ancient world's fourfold division of the day, with the breaks at the first, third, sixth and ninth hours. The night was divided into four watches, starting at sunset, midnight, cock-crow and dawn. From the very beginnings of Christianity, following Jewish usage, these moments were special times for prayer.

When Benedict refers with such emphasis in chapter 16 to the 'seven times a day' and 'at midnight', he is fully in accord with the tradition found in the Bible and in primitive Christianity. Moreover, the two biblical citations (Psalm 119:62 and 164) are quoted twice over: these verses constitute a sort of refrain to the chapter. 'Seven' is the number of completeness. The seven sacraments impart to us the whole of God's salvation, and in the seven days of creation the whole of God's work is brought to perfection. Praising God seven times a day, then, is the expression of the dedication of the whole day to God. These moments of prayer take on a strong symbolic meaning in the Christian tradition. Benedict, however, nowhere refers to this. He presumes that his monks know about it. It was common knowledge in the Church in his time, so it was unnecessary to explain it.

In the early Church, various meanings are given to the different times of prayer. Generally speaking, the hours of prayer were linked with the events in the story of Christ's passion or in the history of salvation. Tertullian was the first to connect the successive moments in the story of our redemption to the times of prayer. In his *De Ieiunio*, he writes that it was at the third hour[126] that the Holy Spirit was sent down upon the Apostles, at the sixth hour[127] that Peter was at prayer on the housetop at Joppa and received the vision about Cornelius, and at the ninth hour[128] that Peter and John cured the lame man at the entrance to the temple.[129]

In the same treatise, Tertullian gives a more Christological interpretation to the hours of prayer, one which is taken over by Cassian in his Institutes: the sixth hour, when the monks sing Sext, is the time when Christ was nailed to the cross, and at the hour of None they reflect on the death of the Lord.[130]

Cyprian sees praise being offered to the Father, Son and Holy Spirit in the three hours of Terce, Sext and None respectively. He also mentions the symbolism given by Tertullian.

In a treatise *On Virginity* attributed to Athanasius, the morning prayer is linked with the moment of Christ's resurrection from the dead. The writer then goes on,

> At the third hour come to prayer, for at that hour the wood of the cross was put together. At the sixth hour too, make your prayers together with psalms, tears and supplications, for at that hour the Son of God was crucified; and at the ninth hour pray to God with hymns and praise, and confess your sins, for at that hour the crucified Lord gave up his spirit. . . . Remember the twelfth hour, when our Lord descended into hell. . . .[131]

For the celebration of the morning hour of Lauds, Cassian looks to Psalm 63: 'God, you are my God, I pine for you; my heart thirsts for you, my body longs for you, as a land parched, dry and waterless',[132] and 'On my bed when I think of you, I muse on you in the watches of the night'.[133] The allusion to morning prayer is more obvious in the Latin: '*Deus meus, ad te de luce vigilo*' and '*in matutinis meditabor de te*'. Later he draws on two verses from Psalm 119: 'I am awake before dawn to cry for help'[134] and 'My eyes are awake before each watch of the night to ponder your promise'[135] (in Cassian's Latin, '*Praeveni in maturitate, et clamavi*' and '*Praevenerunt oculi mei ad te diluculum: ut meditarer eloquia tua*').

For evening prayer, he quotes Psalm 141: 'May my prayer be like incense in your presence, my uplifted hands like the evening sacrifice.'[136] The remembrance of the Jewish evening sacrifice in the temple and of Jesus' Last Supper sanctifies this hour of prayer in a special way.

Cassian sums up the symbolic significance of the hours of prayer as follows:

> These were also the times when the householder in the Gospel hired labourers to go into his vineyard. For he is said to have hired them in the early morning, which is the time for our morning office, then at the third hour, the sixth, and also at the ninth hour; and last of all at the eleventh hour, meaning the time of the evening office.[137]

God comes to us in a very special way at these hours of prayer to recruit us for the work – the work of God – which he wants to assign to us in his vineyard.

In chapters 8 to 11 St Benedict gives his prescriptions

concerning the night office, and here too he follows the tradition of the early Church and ancient monasticism. In the early Church, the Easter Vigil took pride of place, and there were also nocturnal vigils at the tombs of the martyrs on the anniversaries of their death. In monastic circles, the prevailing custom was to spend an entire night in prayer once or twice a week. This took place either from Friday to Saturday, or from Saturday to Sunday, or both. This night of prayer was concluded with morning prayer.

Both the Master and Cassian were acquainted with what was called 'agrypnia', literally a sleepless night. The monks of the Orthodox Churches have preserved this tradition until the present day. According to the Master, 'Every Saturday, in the monastery, Vigils are to be celebrated from evening until the second cockcrow is heard, with Matins then following. The very name Vigils means that the brethren refrain from sleep, singing psalms and listening to those reading the lessons. Then after Matins they take repose in their beds.'[138]

On Sunday, however, the Master let his monks sleep: 'They also have complete freedom to go back to bed. Thus they should rejoice in having Sunday assigned them for resting.'[139]

Cassian had been much stricter on this point, and warned his monks that after an agrypnia they were not to spend the whole day sleeping. That would be no more than moving the night to a different time.[140]

St Benedict has replaced the complete vigil from Saturday to Sunday with a night office, centred on twelve psalms. It is appreciably longer than the service on other days, having twelve lessons, but it does not start until the monks have had a good night's rest. That meant that Benedict could let the whole of Sunday be devoted to *lectio* (there was no need to make up lost sleep).

A very important difference between the Rules of the Master and Benedict is that Benedict does not let his monks go back to bed for a second sleep after the night office: they have had enough sleep before the office. He has the time between vigils and morning prayer devoted to *lectio divina*. The monks keep watch, engaged in dialogue with the Word of God, waiting to meet the dawn, symbol of the coming of the Lord. This waiting in expectation for the Lord's coming takes place every night: not just on Sunday, as in the Rule of the Master.

WHERE, ACCORDING TO THE RULE, DOES THE MONK PRAY?

As we have already said, the monk who has climbed the twelfth step on the ladder of humility prays everywhere, wherever he is. Henceforward, his prayer and his life are intertwined. He no longer needs words to pray with; he prays secretly in his heart, 'at the work of God, in the oratory, the monastery or the garden, on a journey or in the field, or anywhere else; whether he sits, walks or stands . . .'[141]

This, however, is for the mature monk. As for the others, the beginners and cenobites, Benedict asks them to pray for preference in that part of the monastery which is reserved for this purpose. This applies both to common and to private prayer. Hence we find in the Rule chapter 52, dealing with 'The Oratory of the Monastery'.

As far as the layout of the monastery is concerned, St Benedict certainly wrote in a time of transition. In chapter

22, and also in chapter 48, 5, we see hints of the shift from the individual cell to the communal dormitory. We see something of this development in chapter 52 as well. The individual cell, where the monk can pray freely without being disturbed during his work, was a thing of the past. We can understand the precautions which Benedict takes to ensure that no one should be distracted by others in the place of prayer:

> The oratory ought to be what it is called, and nothing else is to be done or stored there. After the work of God, all should leave in complete silence and with reverence for God, so that a brother who may wish to pray alone will not be disturbed by the insensitivity of another. Moreover, if at other times someone chooses to pray privately, he may simply go in and pray, not in a loud voice, but with tears and heartfelt devotion. Accordingly, anyone who does not pray in this manner is not to remain in the oratory after the work of God, as we have said; then he will not interfere with anyone else.[142]

The fact that the monk no longer has a room where he can pray to God alone – pray behind locked doors, hidden from the eyes of the brothers, to God who dwells in that secret place and sees all that is done in secret[143] – emphasises all the more that it is his own heart which is pre-eminently his place of prayer. In his practical instructions too, St Benedict is concerned with the prayer of the heart. The opening sentence of this chapter is applicable above all to the heart, which is the most important place for prayer. Nothing is to be done or kept in it which is in contradiction to prayer. It is to be cleansed so as to be a space fit to receive the Lord as its guest. This place of prayer then becomes God's place: God and the individual can encounter each other in the human heart.

The oratory occupies a central place among the buildings in Benedict's monastery. Just as prayer is the monk's most important occupation, and everything is geared towards it, so too the oratory has its place in the centre of the monastery. This space is the material symbol of the ceaseless prayer to which the monk is called. The visible sign is of immense value: but it is also a danger. There is a risk of a deepening gulf between prayer and work. The sacred and the secular threaten to move further and further apart from each other. Benedict stands at a crucial point in the development of ancient monasticism: something charismatic is slowly being institutionalised. The work of God ought to be related to the remainder of the day and night, and in the same way the door of the oratory should really always be left open. Maybe disturbing sounds from outside will get inside and interfere with our singing. Maybe there will be a draught. But there is a danger that otherwise prayer will become fossilised, cut off from real life and from the world.

In the Rule of the Master there is a striking reminder that in ancient monasticism the whole monastery was a place of prayer. At the end of chapter 53, dealing with food and drink during Lent, the Master writes, 'In general, the monastery should always be so well-appointed and clean that when viewed from all the entrances, themselves neatly kept and adorned with hangings, it may everywhere have the appearance of a church, and thus no matter where any gathering occurs it will be in a place suitable and pleasant where prayer gives delight.'[144]

Benedict is indebted to chapter 68 of the Rule of the Master for his injunction to keep silence when leaving the oratory. He uses this as a peg on which to hang borrowings from Cassian and Augustine. He takes over chapter 2 of the Rule of Saint Augustine almost to the letter:

> Be regular at prayers at the appointed hours and times. In the oratory let no one do anything else than the duty for which the place was made, and from which it has received its name; so that if any of you, having leisure, wish to pray at other hours than those appointed, they may not be hindered by others using the place for any other purpose.[145]

Benedict is also influenced by Cassian in what he says about the place of prayer. The full significance of this chapter of the Rule becomes more obvious in the light of the following text from Cassian's ninth Conference:

> We should be very careful to put into practice the Gospel precept, which bids us enter into our private room and shut the door and pray to our Father. This is how we are to do it. We pray inside our private room when we shut out of our hearts the din of our thoughts and anxieties, and make our prayer to the Lord in an intimate and private manner. We pray with the door shut when we pray with our lips sealed and in complete silence to him who does not listen to words but who searches the heart. We pray in secret when we make our petitions to God alone, speaking only in our heart and with our minds fixed on him, in such a way that not even the demons are able to discover what our petitions are about. This is

why we should pray in complete silence: not only to avoid distracting the brothers who are nearby through our whispers or cries, and disturbing those who are praying, but also to conceal the purpose of our petition from our enemies, who watch us most intently while we are at prayer. Thus we shall fulfil the injunction: 'Do not open your mouth to the wife who shares your bed.'[146]

The oratory was so important for St Benedict's monks that Gregory the Great, in his second book of the Dialogues, tells us how the father of the monastery is brought to the oratory where six days later he was to die; and 'with his disciples supporting his feeble members, and his hands held up heavenwards, he stood and prayed, and while still saying his prayer he gave up his spirit.'[147]

THE EUCHARIST IN THE RULE

Twentieth-century monks would naturally expect to find a chapter in the Rule of Benedict with a title such as 'On the daily celebration of the Eucharist'. This is completely absent. All we find in the Rule is a few indirect and casual allusions to eucharistic practice.

To our minds, it is particularly astonishing that Benedict says nothing about the Eucharist in the liturgical section of the Rule. We should have expected something on the subject in the section directly concerned with the prayer of his monks. The same gap is to be found in the other monastic rules of the period.

The Master speaks just as casually as Benedict in his forty-fifth chapter:

> On every Sunday, from the saying of the blessings to the end of the Mass in the church, let this verse always be said at the work of God: 'The saints will exult in their glory, they will rejoice upon their couches'.[1] In other words, wherever any saints have their chambers, that is, churches, Mass is celebrated with exultation. . . . Moreover, if it is the feastday of the saint in whose oratory the psalmody is being sung, there is no kneeling from the saying of the blessings until the procession

for the Mass to be celebrated there that day by a priest.[2]

Cassian makes one passing reference to the Eucharist in his Institutes: 'Wherefore, except Vespers and Nocturns, there are no public daily services among them, except on Saturday and Sunday, when they meet together at the third hour for the purpose of Holy Communion.'[3]

1. WHERE DOES BENEDICT SPEAK ABOUT THE EUCHARIST?

In chapter 38, on the reader for the week, he writes, 'After Mass and Communion, let the incoming reader ask all to pray for him so that God may shield him from the spirit of vanity.'[4] 'Because of Holy Communion and because the fast may be too hard for him to bear, the brother who is reader for the week is to receive some diluted wine before he begins to read.'[5]

In chapter 59, on the children of nobles or of the poor who are offered, we read that 'at the presentation of the gifts' the nobles are to 'wrap the document itself and the boy's hand in the altar cloth, and this is how they offer him.'[6] Poor people do the same, but 'those who have nothing at all simply write the document and, in the presence of witnesses, offer their son with the gifts.'[7]

In chapter 62, Benedict says that a priest in the monastery is to take his place in the community according to the time of his entry, just like the rest of the monks, 'except in his duties at the altar'.[8] Furthermore, 'When the monks come for the kiss of peace and for Communion . . . they do so in the order determined by the abbot or already existing among them.'⁹

There are two other references to '*missae*',¹⁰ but it is not clear whether these refer to the concluding prayer of the office or the dismissal at the end of the Mass.

This is a very meagre harvest. Bearing in mind the importance of the Mass in the Christian life, it is extremely sparse. Nevertheless, there are important texts from the early monastic sources which show that the celebration of the Eucharist occupies a central place in their spiritual lives.

2. EUCHARISTIC PRACTICE IN PRE-BENEDICTINE MONASTICISM

Cassian puts the following words into the mouth of Abba Theonas:

> We should not abstain from the Lord's Communion because we know we are sinners, but should hasten to it all the more eagerly, so that our soul may be healed and purified; but with great humility and considering ourselves unworthy to receive so great a grace, let us beg for a cure for our wounds. Otherwise we should not receive Holy Communion even once a year, as is the practice of some monks, who interpret the dignity, holiness and value of the heavenly sacraments in such a way as to think that only saints and perfect people should dare to receive them, forgetting that receiving the sacraments make us saints and pure. In truth, they do not avoid presumption and arrogance, but they fall into these vices all the more, because when they do receive the

sacraments, they think they are worthy to do so. Instead of getting the silly idea that at the end of the year we are going to be worthy to receive the sacraments, it is much better to receive them every Sunday as a cure for our infirmities, believing and confessing with humility that we can never approach these holy mysteries in view of our own merits.[11]

Cassian, then, recommends a weekly Mass. He does not approve of monks who only communicate once a year. This text of his reveals to us the reasons often put forward by monks for infrequent communion: scruples, a sense of sin and a feeling of unworthiness. However, Cassian and others insist on the importance of communion, as the Body and Blood of Christ heals our sinfulness.

An element which comes into play here is a rather low valuation of the sacramental life in the Church and in Christian life. These external symbols which mediate salvation were viewed by spiritual people with Messalian tendencies as being suitable for 'ordinary' believers. John Damascene in his *Compendium of Heresies* states the Messalian position as being that 'Baptism in no way makes a person perfect, nor does participation in the divine mysteries purify the soul, but only earnest prayer.'[12]

Palladius, in his *Lives of the Fathers*, writes about the proud monk Valens who abstained from communicating. 'Another time he became very conceited, so much so that he felt he was too good to participate in the mysteries . . ., saying, "I have no need of Holy Communion, for I saw Christ this very day".'[13]

In circles close to the great monastic founder St Basil, daily Communion was not uncommon. He writes, 'All the monks who live in the desert, where there are no priests, keep the Holy Eucharist, and administer it to themselves with their own hand.'[14] The hermits would come together for the celebration of the Eucharist, and then take the sacred elements back to their hermitages with them.

In contrast to the text quoted above from Book III of the Institutes, Cassian also appears to be acquainted with daily Communion: 'With what purity should we keep our body and soul, we who every day need the holy Flesh of the Lamb, which even the old Law declares[15] may not come into contact with anything unclean.'[16] Maybe he knew the same practice as Basil.

We can assume that daily Communion was normal in St Augustine's monasteries, although there was also a rigorist element that wished to limit the reception of Holy Communion to those days when greater abstinence and purity was observed, rather than allowing daily Communion. Augustine recognises that both practices have good reasons behind them and both wish 'to honour the holy Sacrament'. He points to the tax-collector Zacchaeus, who welcomed the Lord into his house full of joy,[17] and to the centurion who acknowledged his unworthiness.[18]

> Both honour the Saviour, though in different and almost contradictory ways; both are wretched as a result of sin, and both obtain the mercy they need. . . . For the one who dares not take it every day, and the one who does not omit it any day, are both alike moved by a desire to do it honour. That sacred food will not submit to be despised, just as the manna could not be loathed with impunity.[19]

In his own church at Hippo, Augustine sticks to the practice of daily Communion, and strongly recommends it. Thus he explains the fourth petition of the Lord's Prayer as referring to daily Communion: 'The Eucharist, then, is our daily bread.'[20] These texts allow us to deduce that daily Communion was fairly widespread among monks, but that they only came together for the celebration of the Eucharist on Saturday and Sunday.

One of the sayings of the great Abba Poimen gives us a striking idea of the nature of the experience of Holy Communion and the celebration of the Eucharist.

> He also said, 'It is written: "As the hart longs for flowing streams, so longs my soul for Thee, O God."[21] For truly harts in the desert devour many reptiles and when their venom burns them, they try to come to the springs, to drink so as to assuage the venom's burning. It is the same for the monks: sitting in the desert they are burned by the venom of evil demons, and they long for Saturday and Sunday to come to be able to go to the springs of water, that is to say, the body and blood of the Lord, so as to be purified from the bitterness of the evil one.'[22]

Saturday and Sunday are like an oasis for the monk who has spent the whole week alone in solitude. The interior combat, which he must of necessity conduct, will have left behind in him feelings that lie heavy like poison on his soul. He needs the Body and Blood of the Lord as an antidote to take away the sour taste of the Evil One.

The weekly Mass was also a *synaxis*, that is to say, a reunion with the other hermits. The encouragement brought about by meeting with the others was part of the refreshment associated with Saturday and Sunday. The Eucharistic celebration is the expression of their fellowship: they also experience this fellowship while apart from each other, but every time the Eucharist is celebrated it builds the community up once more into the Body of Christ. In this community, it is good 'to live as brothers together'.[23]

The practical expression of this community comes with the meal, the *agape* which concludes the celebration of the Eucharist. In Abba Poimen's saying, it is striking how the Eucharist and Holy Communion stand in such a clear relationship with the spiritual combat which is the monk's daily occupation.

Taken as a whole, mention of the Eucharist and of the *agape* feature prominently in the sayings of the Fathers. A particularly touching story is that recounted by Abba Phocas, about the monk who had been severely tempted by the demon of unchastity. He isolated himself for forty days and asked the Abba to bring him Holy Communion.

> . . . Having heard this, when the forty days were fulfilled, I took Holy Communion and a whole loaf with a little wine and went to find him. As I was drawing near to the cave I smelt a very bad smell which came from its mouth. I said to myself, 'The blessed one is at rest.' When I got close to him, I found him half dead. When he saw me he moved his right hand a little, as much as he could, asking me for the Holy Communion with his hand. I said to him, 'I have it.' He wanted to open his mouth but it was fast shut. Not knowing what to do, I went out into the desert and found a piece of wood and with much difficulty, I opened his mouth a little. I poured in

a little of the Body and the precious Blood, as much as he could take of them. Through this participation in the Holy Communion he drew strength. A little while after, soaking some crumbs of ordinary bread, I offered them to him and after a time, some more, as much as he could take. So, by the grace of God, he came back with me a day later and walked as far as his own cell, delivered, by the help of God, from the harmful passion of forni-cation.[24]

3. EUCHARISTIC PRACTICE IN THE RULE OF THE MASTER AND THE RULE OF BENEDICT

It is generally the case that the Rule of the Master is much more detailed than that of Benedict, and this is also the case in relation to the Eucharist. Indeed, the Master gives detailed instructions about the Communion service. A reading of chapters 21, 22 and 45 indicates that the Eucharist was probably not celebrated within the monastery, and that there was only a Communion service. Holy Communion was received daily under both kinds just before the meal, which means immediately after None.

Holy Communion, then, concludes the day's fasting, and is prepared for by fasting. The meal follows immediately as the daily *agape*. The Master says that the monks should wash their hands before the Communion service. They received Holy Communion in the hand, according to the practice of the primitive Church. This is evident also from the saying of Abba Phocas. The abbot is not a priest in the Rule of the Master, but he distributes Holy Communion.[25] This has led to the suggestion that on Sunday a local priest had to come in to celebrate the Eucharist, or alternatively that the community went to a nearby church.

Benedict is certainly accustomed to having priests in the community. This is clear from chapters 60 and 62. On Sunday there was certainly a celebration of the Eucharist. This can be deduced from chapter 38. The refectory reader begins his weekly duty by asking for the prayers of all the brothers on Sunday 'after Mass and Communion'.[26] From verse 10 of the same chapter we can conclude that during the week only a Communion service would have been held. Benedict speaks about 'the Communion' in the daily course of things. We also find the Communion service once again, in the context of viaticum, when Benedict is about to die: 'On the sixth day he had his disciples take him into the oratory, and there he fortified himself for his departure by partaking in the Body and Blood of the Lord.'[27]

This eucharistic practice is clear evidence of the lay character of Benedictine monasticism. This was to change rapidly after Benedict. In the Carolingian era (700–800), the practice of having a large number of monks ordained to the priesthood became general. These celebrated Mass daily at the numerous side altars that are to be found in abbey churches.

That St Benedict gave extensive prescriptions about the liturgy of the hours and nothing about the celebration of the Mass indicates that he wanted to adhere unreservedly to the eucharistic practice of the local church. This practice required no special explanation or adaptation to the monastic life.

4. ESTEEM FOR THE EUCHARIST

Simply because the early monks and Benedict celebrated the Eucharist less frequently, it does not necessarily follow that they had a lower opinion of its value. They expressed their appreciation by reserving the celebration of the Eucharist for Sunday and/or Saturday. This meant that the Mass and Sunday acquired a special quality. The characteristic of the day of the Lord's resurrection is more strongly underlined if that is the only day when the Eucharist is celebrated. On weekdays, they were content with a simple Communion service.

Nowadays, we express our appreciation of the Mass by celebrating it daily. The appreciation is the same, although it is expressed in another way. Our practice certainly entails a greater risk of it becoming a matter of routine. In the majority of Orthodox monasteries, the eucharistic practice of the early Church and of primitive monasticism has been adhered to, right up to the present time.

Conclusion

The Rule of Saint Benedict is not a compendium of spirituality. It was not Benedict's intention to give a developed theology of the spiritual life and prayer. Instead, he gives a practical description of a particular form of life, and one which will bring those who commit themselves to it with faith to an experience of God. He does this above all in the spiritual section of the Rule, namely the Prologue and chapters 1 to 7.

For a more developed teaching about prayer he explicitly refers to other sources which were generally known to his monks. These were, in the first place, the Holy Scriptures, and 'the teachings of the holy Fathers, the observance of which will lead to the very heights of perfection.'[1] 'What book of the holy catholic Fathers does not resoundingly summon us along the true way to reach the Creator?'[2]

We always have to read the Rule against the background of the spiritual climate in which, consciously and unconsciously, Benedict and his monks lived. This study has attempted to capture something of the background to what the Rule says about prayer.

E. Manning writes in his *Règle de Saint Benoît*, in a note on chapter 52 of the Rule, 'It would be dangerous, then, to try and talk about "Saint Benedict's ideas on prayer" on the basis of the small number of texts to be found in the Rule.'[3]

In spite of this warning, this is what we have ventured to do. The Rule still contains, even today, a rich treasure; it is a storehouse which will yield what is old and new for the monastic life of our times.

Looking back at what Benedict said about prayer, this is what we would conclude:

1. St Benedict is faithful to the ancient monastic call to continuous prayer. Everywhere we find traces of the traditional teaching on prayer given by his great predecessors, especially Evagrius and Cassian.

2. The prayer of the hours in the Rule is a sort of bridgehead in the monastic day; it underpins the monk's continuous prayer. Observance of the regular daily rhythm of the prayer of the hours leads to the heights of contemplative prayer.

3. In the Rule, prayer and life are closely interwoven so as to constitute a single whole. This is shown most clearly in the convergence between the attitudes of the heart and the position of the body, both during prayer and at other times (during work and when the brothers meet together). Prayer reaches out beyond itself and brings us to the love of Christ, love of the brothers and love of our neighbour.

4. Because of this, life 'under a rule and an abbot' is a training-ground for prayer, a method of prayer which embraces the whole of our life. It is a healthy and balanced method of prayer which brings unity to the life of the monk, who thus becomes truly a *monachos* and is led

into the realm of God's love. It is there, at the deepest level, that we discover ourselves, we find other people and encounter the world in which we live.

Notes

I: Prayer in the Rule and Continuous Prayer

1. Apophthegmata: Isidore the Priest 4.
2. RB 40, 3.
3. RB 39, 4.
4. RB 8, 1.2.4.
5. RB 48.
6. RB 20, 5.
7. Ps. 119:62.
8. Ps. 119:164.
9. Ps. 55:17.
10. 1 Thess. 5:17.
11. Eph. 6:18.
12. Col. 4:2; Rom. 12:12.
13. Luke 18:1–18.
14. Matt. 18:20.
15. Dan. 6:11–14.
16. 1 Kings 8:48 (my adaptation).
17. Tob. 3:11.
18. Acts 10:9.
19. Acts 3:1.
20. RB 73, 8.
21. Institutes, III, 1. 2.
22. RB 31, 10.
23. Conferences, X, 14.
24. Barsanuphe et Jean de Gaza, *Correspondances* (Solesmes, 1971), pp. 127–8.
25. Apophthegmata: Poimen 8.
26. Apophthegmata: Silvanus 5.
27. Apophthegmata: John the Dwarf 2.

28. Apophthegmata: Anthony 1.
29. St Basil, *Regulae fusius tractatae*, 37.
30. RB 48, 8.
31. Apophthegmata: Lucius.
32. Apophthegmata: Anthony 16.
33. D. Gorce (ed.), *Life of St Melania*, Sources Chrétiennes 90 (Paris, 1962), p. 33.
34. Origen, *De oratione* 12, 1, tr. R.A. Greer, Classics of Western Spirituality (New York, 1979), p. 104.
35. ibid., 22, 5, cited in Greer, p. 125.
36. Evagrius, *153 Chapters on Prayer*, ed. J.E. Bamberger, Cistercian Studies 4 (Spencer, 1970), n. 52.
37. Conferences, III, 7.
38. Conferences, IX, 2.
39. Conferences, X, 10.
40. See pp. 63f.
41. RB 16, 3–4.
42. Apophthegmata: Epiphanius 3.
43. RB 12,4; 13,11.
44. RB 16, 5.
45. RB 9, 2.
46. RB 9, 6.
47. RB 9, 7.
48. RB 19, 2.
49. RB 19, 5.
50. RB 19,6; cf. Ps. 102:20 in the Vulgate.
51. Ps. 97:7; cf. Heb. 1:6; Rev. 4:6–11; Jer. 6:2.
52. *Roman Missal*, Preface of the Angels.
53. ibid., Eucharistic Prayer IV.
54. Ps. 102:20.
55. *Directorium de Opere Dei persolvendo*, in *Thesaurus Liturgiae Horarum Monasticae*, Rome 1977, n. 13.

II: 'Nothing Is to Be Preferred to the Work of God'

1. 'The Master' is the name given to the anonymous writer of a rule which is generally thought to have been written before the Rule of Benedict and to have been Benedict's most important source.
2. RB 50, 1–4.
3. RM 55, 1–4.
4. RB 67, 2.

5. RB 47, 1.
6. RB 31, 19; 35, 13; 41, 5.
7. RB 47, 2–4.
8. RB 7, 60.
9. RB 22, 4–6.8.
10. Matt. 25:1–13.
11. 2 Chr. 21:7.
12. Exod. 27:21.
13. Lev. 24:1–4.
14. Luke 12:35–40.
15. Rev. 16:15.
16. Matt. 22:13.
17. Apophthegmata: Dioscorus 3.
18. RB 22, 6.8.
19. RB Prol. 13.
20. RB Prol. 22.
21. RB 72, 4.
22. cf. RB 1, 4–5.
23. RB 43, 4–12.
24. RB 43, 1–3.
25. RB 5, 1–2.4.
26. RB 5, 7–9.
27. RB 5, 14.16.
28. RB 43, 3.
29. RB 4, 21.
30. RB 72, 11.
31. RB 13, 2.
32. RB 42, 7.
33. RB 43, 3.

III. The Work of God

1. RB 52, 2, 5.
2. RB 43, 3.
3. Gen. 2:2.
4. Ps. 111:2.
5. Jer. 48:10.
6. John 5:17.
7. Matt. 11:2.
8. John 5:36.
9. John 5:19.

10. John 14:10.
11. John 17:4.
12. John 19:30.
13. Gen. 2:3.
14. John 6:28.
15. John 6:29.
16. John 6:44.
17. John 14:12.
18. Apophthegmata: Anthony 13.
19. Apophthegmata: Nau 401, in *Les Sentences des pères du désert, nouveau recueil*, ed. L. Regnault (Solesmes, 1977), p. 51.
20. Apophthegmata: Nau 399, in *Sentences des pères*, p. 50.
21. Apophthegmata: Poimen 32.
22. RB 4, 55–7.
23. RB 4, 75–8.
24. Apophthegmata: Zacharias 1.
25. Apophthegmata: John the Dwarf 37.
26. Apophthegmata: Agathon 9.
27. RB 58, 7.
28. Apophthegmata: Sisoes 37.
29. Col. 1:29.
30. RB Prol. 4.
31. Ps. 115:1.
32. 1 Cor. 15:10.
33. 2 Cor. 10:17; RB Prol. 29–32.
34. RB 4, 42–3.
35. RB 21, 5.
36. RB 31, 13.
37. RB 47, 3–4.
38. RB 57, 1–3.
39. RB 62, 2.

IV: How, When and Where Is the Monk to Pray?

1. RB 1, 2.
2. Luke 18:13.
3. RB 7, 62–6.
4. RB 7, 67–9.
5. RM 47, 21.
6. RM 48, 6.
7. RB 20, 1–5.

8. RB 52, 4–5.
9. RB 20, 2–4.
10. Evagrius, 153 *Chapters on Prayer*, ed. J.E. Bamberger, Cistercian Studies 4 (Spencer, 1970), n. 37.
11. Matt. 5:8.
12. RB 7, 67.
13. RB 7, 70.
14. Conferences, IX, 2.
15. cf. RB 7, 70.
16. 1 Thess. 5:17.
17. 1 Tim. 2:8.
18. Conferences, IX, 3.
19. RB 49, 2.
20. RB 49, 1.
21. RB 20, 3.4.5.
22. Apophthegmata: Macarius 19.
23. Institutes, II, 10.
24. Ps. 51:17.
25. Ps. 51:19; 50:23; 66:15.
26. Ps. 141:2; Conferences, IX, 36.
27. See pp. 22f.
28. Ps. 70:2.
29. Conferences, X, 10.
30. Matt. 6:7.
31. St Augustine, *Letter to Proba* (= *Letter* 130), 19–20.
32. Matt. 6:7.
33. RB 7, 56.
34. RB 7, 60–1.
35. RB 4, 52.
36. RB 4, 57.
37. RB 20, 3.
38. RB 49, 4.
39. RB 52, 4.
40. Evagrius, *Chapters on Prayer*, n. 5.
41. Conferences, IX, 29.
42. Apophthegmata: Moses 16 (= Instructions sent to Abba Poimen, 3).
43. RB 52, 4.
44. See Basilius Steidle's translation of 'intentione cordis' as 'mit Inbrust des Herzens': see B. Steidle, *Die Regel St. Benedikts* (Beuron, 1952), p. 256.
45. Conferences, IX, 15.

46. RB Prol., 22.
47. RB 72, 3–4.
48. RB 66, 3–4.
49. RB 9, 5.
50. RB 11, 2.
51. RB 42, 3.
52. John 4:6.
53. RB 11, 3.
54. RB 11, 9.
55. RB 9, 7.
56. RB 19, 7.
57. RB 18, 24; 50, 4.
58. RB 63, 15–16.
59. Luke 18:13.
60. RB 20, 5.
61. RB 50, 3.
62. RB 35, 15.
63. RB 53, 7.
64. RB 44, 1–2.
65. RB 71, 8.
66. RB 58, 23.
67. RB Prol., 40.
68. RB 7, 9.
69. RB 7, 62–3.
70. RB 7, 12.
71. RB 7, 51.
72. RB 4, 28.
73. cf. RB 5, 17.
74. RB 19, 7.
75. Apophthegmata: Elias 6.
76. RB 19, 7.
77. Matt. 15:8.
78. Ps. 62:4.
79. 1 Cor. 14:3, 26.
80. Ps. 101:2.
81. 1 Cor. 14:15.
82. RM 47, 9–20.
83. RB 20, 5 and 52, 4–5.
84. Isa. 55:10–11.

85. Caesarius of Arles, *Sermon 76*, 1: *Sermons au Peuple III*, ed. M.-J. Delage, Sources Chrétiennes 330 (Paris, 1986).
86. Institutes, II, 8.
87. 1 Cor. 14:15.
88. Institutes, II, 11.
89. Conferences, IX, 26.
90. RM 33; 55.
91. RM 33, 52–4.
92. Guigo II, *The Ladder of Monks and Twelve Meditations*, tr. E. Colledge and T. Walsh (London, 1976), II, nn. 2–14, pp. 81–96.
93. RB 4, 55–7.
94. RB 9, 8.
95. RB 13, 11.
96. RB 12, 4.
97. RB 38, 1.
98. RB 38, 12.
99. RB 38, 2–4.
100. RB 38, 10.
101. RB 38, 5.
102. St Augustine, *Rule*, 4.
103. Luke 4:4.
104. RM 24, 4–5.
105. RB 42, 3.
106. RB 42, 4.
107. RB 53, 9.
108. RB 49, 1.
109. RB 49, 4.
110. RB Prol., 21.
111. RB 73, 3.
112. RB 28, 3.
113. Apophthegmata: Nau 217, in *Revue d'Orient Chrétien* 14 (1909), 357–8.
114. Conferences, XIV, 13.
115. RB 48, 5.
116. Institutes, II, 15.
117. Institutes, III, 2.
118. Institutes, XI, 16.
119. Conferences, XIV, 13.
120. RB 8, 3.
121. RB 48, 23.
122. RB 58, 5.

123. Ps. 119:164.
124. Ps. 119:62.
125. RB 16, 1–5.
126. Acts 2:15.
127. Acts 10:9.
128. Acts 3:1.
129. Tertullian, *De Ieiunio*, 10.
130. Institutes, III, 3.
131. Ps-Athanasius, *De Virginitate*, 12. 16.
132. Ps 63:1.
133. Ps. 63:6.
134. Ps. 119:147.
135. Ps. 119:148.
136. Ps. 141:1.
137. Institutes, III, 3.
138. RM 49, 1–3.
139. RM 75, 6–7.
140. Institutes, III, 8.
141. RB 7, 63.
142. RB 52, 1–5.
143. Matt. 6:6.
144. RM 53, 64–5.
145. St Augustine, *Rule*, 2.
146. Micah 7:5; Conferences, IX, 35.
147. St Gregory the Great, *Dialogues* II, 37.

V. The Eucharist in the Rule

1. Ps. 149:5.
2. RM 45, 14–15. 17.
3. Institutes, III, 2.
4. RB 38, 2.
5. RB 38, 10.
6. RB 59, 2.
7. RB 59, 8.
8. RB 62, 6.
9. RB 63, 4.
10. RB 35, 14 and 60, 4.
11. Conferences, XXIII, 21.
12. St John Damascene, *De haeresibus*, 80 (4).

13. Palladius, *Lausiac History*, tr. R. Meyer, Ancient Christian Writers 34 (Westminster, 1965), 25, 2.5.
14. St Basil, *Letter* 93.
15. Lev. 7:19–20.
16. Institutes, VI, 8.
17. Luke 19:5ff.
18. Luke 7:6.
19. St Augustine, *Letter* 54.
20. St Augustine, *Sermon* 57.
21. Ps. 42:1.
22. Apophthegmata: Poimen 30.
23. Ps. 133:1.
24. Apophthegmata: Phocas 2.
25. RM 21, 1.
26. RB 38, 2.
27. St Gregory the Great, *Dialogues* II, 37.

Conclusion

1. RB 73, 2.
2. RB 73, 4.
3. H. Rochais and E. Manning, *Règle de Saint Benoît* (Rochefort, 1980), 125.
4. RB 1, 2.

Select Bibliography:

PRINCIPAL MONASTIC AND PATRISTIC SOURCES CITED

Apophthegmata Patrum, in Migne, *Patrologia Graeca* 65, 71–440. See also *Histoires des Solitaires Egyptiens*, ed. F. Nau, in *Revue d'Orient Chrétien; Sayings of the Desert Fathers, The Alphabetical Collection*, tr. Benedicta Ward (London, 1975); and *Les Sentences des pères du désert, nouveau recueil*, ed. L. Regnault (Solesmes, 1977)

Augustine, Rule of Saint, = letter 211, in Migne, *Patrologia Latina* 33, 958. See also *The Confessions and Letters of St Augustine*, tr. P. Schaff, The Nicene and Post-Nicene Fathers, First Series I (Edinburgh/Grand Rapids, 1988)

Basil, *Regulae fusius tractatae*, in Migne, *Patrologia Graeca* 31, 901–1305. See also W. Clarke, *The Ascetical Works of St Basil* (London, 1925)

Cassian, John: see Jean Cassien, *Conférences*, ed. E. Pichery, Sources Chrétiennes 42.54.64 (Paris, 1955–9); *Institutions*, ed. J.-C. Guy, Sources Chrétiennes 109 (Paris, 1965), English translation in John Cassian, *Works*, tr. E. Gibson, The Nicene and Post-Nicene Fathers XI (Edinburgh/Grand Rapids, 1991)

Evagrius, *153 Chapters on Prayer*, ed. J.E. Bamberger, Cistercian Studies 4 (Spencer, 1970)

Palladius, *Lausiac History*, tr. R. Meyer, Ancient Christian Writers 34 (Westminster, 1965)

The Rule of Benedict: *Sancti Benedicti Regula Monachorum*, ed. R. Hanslik, Corpus Scriptorum Ecclesiasticorum Latinorum 75, second edition (Vienna, 1977). See also *RB 1980. The Rule of St Benedict*, ed. T. Fry (Collegeville, 1981)

The Rule of the Master: *La Règle du Maître*, ed. A. de Vogüé, Sources Chrétiennes 105–107 (Paris, 1964–5). See also English translation, *The Rule of the Master*, tr. L. Eberle, Cistercian Studies 6 (Kalamazoo, 1977)

Index of References to the Rule of Benedict

Through a Glass, Darkly

I have resumed my love affair with Martha Morgan, with the full approval of my wife. It is twelve months since I had any contact with Martha, and I had assumed that our mysterious and beautiful relationship was over and done with, to be remembered wistfully on walks to the bluestone summit of Angel Mountain or on visits to the ruined house which is inhabited by her free spirit.

The regeneration of this particular passion came about under the most peculiar of circumstances, which I will try to explain. First, the story of my original infatuation. Three years ago a handwritten diary came into my hands, with very few clues as to its origins. After a good deal of sleuthing, it turned out to have been written in 1796–97 by a young lady called Martha Morgan. She was mistress of the small estate of Plas Ingli, on the flanks of Carningli near Newport in Pembrokeshire. The diary was written in an archaic dialect of Welsh, and it was only with the translation of the manuscript by my friend Abraham Jenkins that Martha's dark and disturbing tale was finally revealed. It was published and received kind reviews, and that was that.

Or so I thought. I assumed that I would have no

further contact with young Martha, but about seven months ago, early in the month of February, I received a surprising telephone call. 'Hello,' said an elderly female voice in a strong South Pembrokeshire accent. 'Is it you that did the book about Martha?'

'Yes, that's correct.'

'Jenny Evans from Paddington speaking. Me and my husband liked the story. Very exciting. We think we might have something that will be of interest to you.'

'Indeed? And what might that be?'

'A little watercolour painting of an old house, with a mountain in the background,' said Jenny. 'No date or anything, but the painting is signed with the initials "MM" in the bottom right-hand corner.'

My left ear immediately pricked up, insofar as such a thing was possible with a telephone handset clamped to it. I knew from her diary that Martha had enjoyed painting with watercolours, and that she had once given a little painting to her husband David. So I asked whether there were any other indications on either the back or the front of the painting which might assist in deducing its provenance.

'Oh yes,' replied Jenny. 'On the back there is some handwriting, a bit faint but quite tidy, that says *To my beloved David, with much affection, on the occasion of his twentieth birthday*. It occurred to Robert and me after reading your book that the "MM" might be Martha Morgan and that David might be her husband.'

'You may well be right!' I exclaimed. 'Would it be possible for me to see the painting? I am coming to London soon, and could call on you.'

'By all means, you just come and see us. You can't have the painting, mind you. Too fond of it, we are. Not that it's worth anything – it was valued once and the man said it was worthless apart from sentimental value.'

Following this conversation, as the days passed, I found that my thoughts returned over and again to the strange story revealed in Martha Morgan's original diary, most of it written when she was only nineteen years old. I recalled her descriptions of coast and country and her songs of praise about her beloved Carningli and its changing moods in sunshine and snow, in driving rain and drifting cloud. Her narrative told of the appalling events that had turned her from a naive teenage girl into a tough defender of the Plas Ingli estate – miscarriage, flood, cholera epidemic, and finally vindictive and public humiliation. I remembered the final words of her diary: *I trust that the good Lord will bless my life, and the lives of all whom I love, to the extent that nothing else will happen that will be worth writing about.* Could it be that something else did happen, and that Martha, later in life, found solace in writing about it? I hardly dared to hope.

My obsession with Martha, having lain dormant for six months, had gripped me again. On one crisp, bright morning, as the first faint signs of spring appeared in the woods, I was drawn once more to the mountain and to the ruins of Plas Ingli. I walked through springy heather and broken bracken stalks and smelt the sweet fragrance of winter-flowering gorse, just as Martha might have done two centuries before. I watched a pair of ravens hovering on an eddy above the bluestone summit. I splashed across Ffynnon Brynach, the sacred spring from which the inhabitants of Plas Ingli had once obtained their water supply. I traversed the boulder-strewn slopes to the cave which had been, for Martha, a place both of sanctuary and of terror. Then I scrambled across the frosty summit and down to the ruins of the old house, where I sat on the massive oak beam which had once been part of the kitchen's open fireplace. I could still make out, among the rubble, the outlines of the main rooms, the doorways and windows, the scullery and the dairy. I closed my eyes and heard clanking pots and pans, laughter and snatches of conversation, a crying baby, an excited dog outside. I opened my eyes again. I did not see Martha, but I knew that she was still there.

A fortnight later I found myself in the front parlour of the Evanses' terrace house not far from Paddington Station, enjoying cup-cakes and Typhoo tea under the stony gaze of assorted stuffed creatures in a glass case. The room was almost identical, down to the rosewood piano and the smell of camphor balls, to my grandmother's parlour as I remember it from childhood days in Haverfordwest. Jenny and Robert were both sprightly despite being well into their eighties, and had moved to London from Pembroke Dock after the Second World War.

They showed me the painting. It was smaller than I had anticipated, but colourful and charming. It was set in a nondescript modern frame. The mountain in the background could only have been Carningli. The house could only have been Plas Ingli. I had never before seen an image of it as it appeared at the end of the eighteenth century, but it was much as I had imagined – whitewashed and with a purple slate roof, prominent against the uncurling green bracken and the tumbled blue stones of the mountainside. It was painted from the south. There were eleven windows on the front facade, and three stumpy Pembrokeshire chimneys. Smoke was coming from the one on the western gable end. I knew from Martha's diary that this was where the kitchen had been, and that the fire in the *simnai fawr* was never allowed to go out. The painting was obviously done in May, for in the foreground there was a sheet of bluebells and a may tree splattered with little white blossoms. Everything fitted perfectly. I was now absolutely certain that Martha had painted the picture in Spring 1797 and had given it to David on 10 June, the date of his twentieth birthday, as described in her diary. When I turned the painting over the dedication was just as Jenny had described it – in Martha's unmistakable handwriting.

We started to speculate on the route followed by the painting from Plas Ingli to Paddington. As far as they knew, neither Jenny nor Robert had any family connections with North Pembrokeshire, and they had always assumed that the little mountain in the painting was one of those close to the coast of the St David's peninsula – either Carnllidi or Penbiri. Robert said that the painting had been given to him by his grandfather Levi Evans around 1935 because he had liked it as a child; but he could not remember how the old gentleman had obtained it. He knew, however, that his grandpa had worked in the Royal Naval Dockyard at Pembroke Dock, and all three of us now thought it reasonable to speculate that he or his parents might have moved from Newport to the growing dockyard town in search of work some time in the late nineteenth century. Hundreds of other poor Pembrokeshire families had done just that. Maybe Levi had bought it or been given it by one of the Morgan family before he left his community. Maybe – even more intriguingly – Levi and his grandson were themselves descendants of the Morgan family of Plas Ingli.

Excited as I was by this turn of events, and by the reappearance of Martha Morgan in my life, there was no reason to read any great significance into the discovery of the painting, or into my conversation with Robert and Jenny. I offered to send the old couple a photograph of the ruined house as it appears today, and in return they would arrange for a photographic copy of the painting to be made for me. They also promised to delve deeper into Robert's family history with a view to uncovering any links with the Newport area generally or with Plas Ingli in particular. Robert said that his brother Gareth had once drawn up a family tree and sent it to him; he would hunt it out.

Having thanked them for their time and for my delightful tea, I was about to take my leave when Jenny said: 'Oh dear, oh dear! I almost forgot to show you this.' She pulled out from behind the mantelpiece clock a tightly folded piece of paper which was frayed at the edges, and presented it to me. It was clearly very old. As I opened it gingerly she continued: 'A few months ago the picture cord behind the painting snapped, and the glass smashed when it fell on the floor. When we had it reframed, the young man in the shop found this piece of paper folded up and stuffed between the painting and the backing board. He almost threw it away, but then he noticed the writing on it and saved it for us.'

'The writing is the same as that in the dedication,' volunteered Robert, 'and it seems to be some sort of riddle. God knows what it means. It's no good to us. Take it, and if you ever manage to sort out the answer, mind you let us know!'

So it was that I spent much of my journey from London to Pembrokeshire poring over an old piece of paper with the following words on it, written by my old friend Martha Morgan: *If you would know the secrets of my heart, search at the stone bridge between Venice and Verona.* It was a riddle, to be sure, but why was it written in English when I knew perfectly well that Martha preferred to use either everyday Welsh or her own peculiar and long-defunct Dimetian dialect? Had she placed the note behind the painting at the time of the original framing in 1797, or much later on when she was old and grey? And what on earth can have been Martha's involvement with Italy? Had she gone off, as the mistress of a wealthy estate, on a Grand Tour to the great cities of Mediterranean Europe? My imagination was running away with me.

Two weeks passed, and I was so obsessed with the riddle that I became furious with Martha. She was playing games with me, and she had the better of me. Did she really want me to go off to Italy and examine every old stone bridge between Venice and Verona? The two cities were more than 150 kilometres apart, and there must surely have been a hundred stone bridges between the one and the other. I went to the trouble of getting a large-scale map of the area but gave up when I counted more than sixty route crossings of rivers and streams.

At last I could contain myself no longer, and I called in to see my friend Abraham Jenkins at Waun Isaf. As I walked up the Cilgwyn road a thin March drizzle was drifting about in the wind, and the top of Carningli was hidden behind a veil of muddy cloud. The roadside gullies were full, transporting murky water from mountain slope to river valley. It was one of those raw days in which chilblains thrive. When I arrived, Abraham was in the yard, having just finished his task of feeding two molly lambs. 'Good afternoon, young man!' he said, instantly lifting the spirits of a bona fide holder of a Senior Railcard. We went inside and he made a pot of tea. As he rummaged in his pantry for some bread and butter and blackberry jam I told him all about my latest encounter with Martha. He looked at her handwritten note for a few minutes, with a furrow or two upon his earth-brown brow, and then his eyes sparkled and he roared with laughter.

'You have been too literal by far, my friend,' he chortled. 'Our dear Martha had a strong sense of

21

humour – we knew that already. Of course she was playing a little game when she wrote the note, but I doubt that she ever went to Italy. Have you not translated "stone bridge" into Welsh?'

'Maybe "*pont*" or "*bont*" somewhere, with "*maen*" or "*faen*" either in front or behind?' I hazarded.

'Would "Pontfaen" fit the bill?'

'Abraham, you are a genius!' I exclaimed, banging my fist on his kitchen table. 'Of course! How stupid of me!'

After that breakthrough the deductive process moved along at a much happier pace. Over our jam sandwiches and cups of tea we agreed that Martha was pointing us towards Plas Pontfaen, the home of her good friend Mary Jane and a place where she had enjoyed laughter and stimulating company on many occasions. Was there something in or near the house that we now needed to find? Not a treasure, surely, for that would not have been described by Martha as containing 'the secrets of my heart'. A bundle of letters or other documents, perhaps? Another volume of her diary? On balance, we both doubted that, since it was clear at the end of 1797 that she intended never to write another word, and to devote herself from that point on to her beloved David and to her children as yet unborn. But women have been known to change their minds.

And what of the Italian connection? An Italian garden, perhaps? Marble figures or columns, or even oil paintings imported from Venice and Verona? We were greatly attracted by the idea of one painting by Canaletto and another by Veronese fixed on an ancient wood-panelled wall, with a secret chamber located halfway between the two. And then, exhausted by our intense mental activity, we called it a day. I told Abraham that I would ring the present-day owners of Plas Pontfaen and ask them if we could pay them an investigative visit.

22

So it was that next morning I picked Abraham up and we set off in hot pursuit of Martha Morgan. An early March sun was occasionally visible above the valley side, feebly illuminating the south-facing slopes as we followed the Cwm Gwaun road. The daffodils were at their cheerful best, and there were lambs at play in the warm dry fields at Llannerch, overlooked by woodlands of oak and ash. I recalled from Martha's diary that this place of calm beauty had once been owned by one of her blackest and most implacable enemies. We continued westwards through sunshine and shadow on the single-track valley road, with occasional glimpses of the high moorlands to north and south across which Martha had wandered two hundred years ago. Now and then, where the road was overhung by catkin hedges, we drove though sprinklings of gold dust. Four buzzards wheeled overhead, scanning the countryside for edible remnants from the lambing season.

Then we drove across the old stone bridge at Pontfaen, and into the gravel driveway of Plas Pontfaen. I had forgotten what a rural paradise the place was; even in early spring it was quite charming, down in the valley away from the wind, with house, stables, gardens and the little church clustered together under the protection of a score of tall beech trees. Somewhere behind the house a male peacock was making that strange and ugly noise which presumably passes, in polite peacock circles, as a serenade. We knocked on the front door and were welcomed by Julia Laugharne, who had lived in the house for only ten years but explained that it had never passed out of the family over fifteen generations. She was intrigued by our mission, and as we talked she became more and more involved in the hunt for the secrets of Martha's heart. In fact Julia knew all about her, for it turned out that she had read the diary, *On*

Angel Mountain, while snuggled up in front of her open fire between Christmas and New Year.

We drank coffee in the flagstoned kitchen, basking in the warmth of the Aga. Then we set off on a guided tour of the house, with the intention of examining everything remotely connected with Italy. We focused on the paintings hanging on the walls, but were unsurprised to find that few of them were old and that none of them was an original Canaletto or Veronese, or even a reproduction. We had exhausted almost all possibilities and were looking at the last paintings in the house, alongside a steep staircase, when I noticed a door which opened off a landing halfway between top and bottom.

'May I ask where that heavy door leads to?'

'Oh, that's just the old library. Full of dry old tomes from floor to ceiling. My father-in-law, before he died, tried to give the whole collection away to the National Library in Aberystwyth, but they weren't interested, so the books are still there. There are no pictures in there, if that's what you are wondering about.'

Abraham and I exchanged glances, and we both sensed that the trail, which had been getting colder by the minute, might suddenly become red hot. So Abraham said: 'Do you mind if we have a look inside? You never know – there might be something there.'

Julia opened the door and switched on the light. The room was quite small, with finely crafted oak bookshelves covering three walls. At the far end was a high leaded window, with a table and chair placed beneath it for the benefit of readers. I was disappointed to see that the place was spotless: not a cobweb, or a ghost, or a dead bat in sight. None the less I asked Julia how old this part of the house might be.

'My husband says it is probably Elizabethan,' she replied. 'But none of the books are older than about 1750;

the older ones were taken out years ago and sold to an antiquarian dealer in Cardiff.'

'So Martha Morgan could have visited this library when she was alive, and it would have been much as we see it today?'

'Well yes, I suppose so.'

Before Julia could blink Abraham and I were scanning the rows of books for anything out of the ordinary. We picked out many volumes with faded or illegible lettering on their spines, looked at them briefly, and put them back again. We were both certain that we were now very close to the solution of the riddle. As we worked, Julia gave us a running commentary. 'I looked through all this before the book dealer called,' she said. 'Over there are some translations of Greek tragedies; this shelf has got old medical texts on it; over here are the collected plays of William Shakespeare—'

'William Shakespeare!' shouted Abraham and I in magnificent harmony, and we dived across to the relevant section of the shelving adjacent to the window. All thirty-five of the plays were there, arranged more or less in alphabetical order. 'You look for *The Merchant of Venice*,' said Abraham, 'and I will look for *Two Gentlemen of Verona*.'

There they were, at the end of one shelf, side by side – or rather, almost side by side, for sandwiched between them was a bound volume of the same size and colour but with no marking on the spine. With perspiring fingers I eased it away from the loving embrace of the merchant and the other good gentlemen, hardly daring to believe that we were about to enjoy another encounter with the Mistress of Plas Ingli. But indeed we were. I carried the book to the table. It was well bound in soft pigskin. Inside the front cover, written in English, were the words *For Owain, who kept faith when I did not*. On the

25

pages which followed there was another diary, written in Martha's inimitable hand and once again using her strange and almost incomprehensible Dimetian dialect. I looked at it but understood virtually nothing. Julia, who had studied Welsh Literature at university, could decipher only a little more. All eyes turned to Abraham, who said: 'Well, my friends, I see that I have more to do.'

After a quick scan, he declared the entries to be intermittent, all having been written between 13 January 1805 and 23 December 1806. There were some long gaps; in other places the entries were scrappy and even staccato. There was no title page, but there was a signature at the end. Many people must have scanned these shelves in the past, but here the volume was, still in its appointed place. Maybe those who had looked at it had thought of it as some boring old diary of a daughter of the house, written in an illegible hand, just like some of the other old handwritten volumes scattered about elsewhere on the shelves. It might as well have been written in Arabic, and there was nothing about it to attest to any significance.

With the permission of Julia and her husband Jack, Abraham took the volume away and that evening I rang Jenny and Robert to tell them about developments in Pembrokeshire. The couple were thrilled by the news. They then told me that they had found their old family tree and discovered that Grandpa Levi's family had once lived near Newport but had moved to Pembroke Dock in 1875. His parents Rose and Henry had been Baptists, and had married in a chapel called Caersalem in 1849. Was that not the chapel, asked Robert, which was mentioned occasionally in Martha's diary? Indeed it was, I replied, delighted that a firm link was now established between painting, places and persons. I knew that Martha Morgan had not died until 1855, and

I now formed in my mind a theory that Rose and Henry might have been servants or friends of Martha or (more likely) of one of her children.

Abraham worked intermittently on the translation for six months. He and the Laugharnes and I met up socially on a number of occasions while the work was in progress, and he was amused by our speculations on the meaning of the inscription inside the front cover and the reasons for Martha's renewal of literary activity. Who might Owain have been? Why had Martha written nothing between 1797 and 1805? When – and why – had she placed the diary in the library at Pontfaen? We got nowhere with these questionings, and Abraham refused to give us any clues, let alone any answers, until he had completed his task.

Summer has come and gone, and now it is done. Recently Abraham stopped me as I was walking past his house on the way up to the mountain on a bracing autumnal day. 'I've got something for you at last!' he yelled from his back door. 'Sorry it has taken so long. My eyesight has got worse, and so has Martha's handwriting. Wretched woman! Never mind – I refused to let her get the better of me, and eventually I found my way back into her head and her soul. What an extraordinary creature. I do believe that I am more than a little in love with her. Take the secrets of her heart away with you, young man, and treat her with the care and sensitivity which she so richly deserves.'

So here, is Martha's second diary, a strange tale from another age – written in a house inhabited by angels.

MARTHA MORGAN'S STORY

EXTRACTS FROM THE PAGES OF HER
DIARY FOR 1805–1806, TRANSLATED FROM
THE DIMETIAN WELSH DIALECT BY
ABRAHAM JENKINS

Black Clouds

13 January 1805

I have seen a battle in the sky, and from experience I know that before many days have passed some poor innocent soul will be subjected to unimaginable terror. I have seen slaughter in the sky once before, some seven years since, and the consequences of that sighting are still with me in the form of deep scars upon my back and upon the very fabric of my being. The scars will never heal. I trust that on this occasion cruel fate will spare me and the little mite who has been growing in the warm darkness of my womb for seven months. I trust that she will also spare my beloved husband David, Grandpa Isaac and Grandma Jane, and my three beautiful children whose innocence has thus far been unsullied by a wicked world.

It happened thus. Last evening was the occasion of *Hen Galan*, the Old New Year, when according to tradition the Morgans of Plas Ingli pay a social visit to the Laugharnes of Pontfaen. We were all invited. Discretion and good manners dictated that I should not flaunt in public the fact that I am all too clearly seven months gone, and in truth I thought that the excesses of a bumpy drive, a loaded table and a jovial meeting of old

31

friends until well past the midnight hour might be a little too much for me. But I prevailed upon David and his grandparents to attend, for I knew that they would enjoy the conviviality and felt that they should not deny themselves on my account.

'Off you go,' I said as they climbed into the light coach. 'Be sure to give my warmest regards to Squire and Mistress Laugharne and to their family. David, will you tell Mary Jane that I hope to see her soon and that I shall appreciate a visit?'

'Of course,' said David, settling into the driver's seat. 'Now, are you sure you will be comfortable without us?'

'My dear husband, let me assure you that you are by no means indispensable!' I laughed. 'Even in my expanded state I can manage perfectly well on my own. I will tell a story to the children when Sian has finished bathing them. I will settle them down for the night, and then I will take a short walk on the mountain. I can assure you that I will be tucked up in bed, fast asleep, by nine of the clock.'

And off they went, chatting happily together, along the drive down to the Dolrannog Road. I stood at the gate and watched them go into the enveloping darkness, faintly illuminated by their candle lanterns. How I loved them, all three! At last the sounds of their voices, and the crunching of the wheels upon the gravel, and the clatter of the horses' hooves were swallowed up by the night.

An hour later, when Sian had delivered three shining and sweet-smelling children into my care, I told them a fantastical tale about a fairy and a mermaid and a terrible sea monster, and tucked them up cosily in their warm cots. I kissed each of them in turn on their foreheads, as I love to do every night. Little Dewi was already fast asleep. I blew out the candle on their window sill, closed the shutters and wished the girls sweet dreams.

The night was calm and clear, and I decided that my short walk should take me up the track towards Ffynnon Brynach. I wrapped my warmest winter cloak about me, and left the servants to enjoy the warmth of the kitchen. Mrs Owen had seized the opportunity offered by Grandma Jane's absence to sit in her settle by the open fire, and her head was nodding onto her ample bosom; Shemi and Billy were playing chess on the kitchen table; and Bessie and Sian were knitting socks and passing on to each other the latest news from town. Now that I look back, I realize that my senses were heightened in some mysterious way in the moment before I went out into the yard. I recall that Billy had three pieces of straw sticking to the back of his jacket, and that Bessie's nose was dripping, and that there were four flies on the big ham hanging from the ceiling. There was a green flame in the fire, and one of the burning logs looked like the head of a dragon. Sian was wearing a shawl that I had not seen before, and I observed that Shemi would lose a bishop on the move after next.

'Be careful, Mistress,' said Bessie, as solicitous as ever. 'There is frost in the air, and no moonlight to speak of. Where are you going?'

'Just up to the spring,' I said. 'I will take a candle lantern, but there is enough starlight to fill a cathedral. I shall celebrate *Hen Galan* briefly, and almost by myself this year, with only the tawny owls and red foxes for company. I will be back very soon.'

So I walked up the track onto the mountain, with frozen grasses crackling underfoot and a sparkling sky over my head. There was a thin new moon. Three tawny owls were calling from different parts of the *cwm*. The rocky summit of the mountain stood in silhouette

33

against the northern sky, and to the south I could see a multitude of faint lights flickering from the sooty windows of the cottages and hovels of Cilgwyn. Now and then a whiff of woodsmoke reached my nostrils. A dog barked at Dolrannog Isaf, and then its barking turned into a howl. I did not think this particularly strange, but then other distant sounds reached my ears, and I became aware that the hairs on the back of my neck were rising and that my pulse was quickening. I sat down on a rock near the icy spring and placed my lantern on the ground, not sure what to expect.

Then, as I let my gaze wander along the far horizon, I saw a bright haze of light in the sky towards the south. At the same time I heard hoofbeats and marching feet and bugles and drums and war chants, far away but getting closer. Then I realized that similar sounds were coming from the north, and when I turned I saw that the sky behind Carningli was also growing lighter, with streaks of blue and green and orange like those which we see occasionally in the gleaming of the Northern Lights. But I knew, with rising apprehension, that these lights were coming not from some cold northern ocean but from a world in which time and place were confused and tangled together into some horrid knot which would bind itself round my heart. And so it proved. I could not take my eyes off the sky and I could not cover my ears as the sky became brighter by the second and the sounds of marching armies drew closer. Soon all the stars had been overwhelmed by the glow in the sky, and the landscape around me was bathed in light. Then I saw the men, the horses, the battle standards, the shields and the weapons – two armies marching towards each other, intent upon slaughter and upon overturning my own calm and loving little world.

The northern army marched overhead, as if supported

on some invisible bridge across the firmament, and the southern army halted in its tracks. Then a great shout went up, and the drumbeats quickened and reached a climax. Bugles blared, riders spurred their steeds to the gallop, and the sound of marching feet was transformed into a thunderous cacophony of running soldiers and clashing weapons, falling horses and mortally injured men, war cries and screams of agony. Armour, helmets and shields glinted as sheets of lightning flared from horizon to horizon. There were no clouds, but thunder crashed and rolled above me, disobeying all the rules of nature. Dark sweeps of arrows flashed overhead, lances and spears were cast into the mêlée, and I could hear the sounds of heavy swords clashing, metal on metal, cutting through the thin cold air and into limbs, heads and torsos. Flails and battleaxes were used to terrible effect. I saw cleaved heads and severed limbs, horses with wild eyes struggling in their death throes on the blood-covered grass, and men insane with blood-lust, killing in order to save themselves. I watched, transfixed, until I could stand it no longer, and then I fell to the ground and buried my head beneath my cloak, shaking with terror. For minutes or hours (in truth, I know not which) the battle continued, and then I heard a shout of triumph as the ragged remnants of one army put the other to flight. I raised my head and opened my eyes, and saw horsemen and foot soldiers rush down towards some far western horizon, leaving behind them a scene of utter carnage on the battlefield. The sounds of drums and bugles faded away, until the only things audible were the faint cries for help of men who still had breath for crying, and the sighs and moans of those who were sinking into the sweet oblivion of death.

The bright light began to fade, and I stood up and sought to compose myself. I realized that the battle had occurred in the sky above Mynydd Morfil, in exactly the same place as I had observed it some seven years ago. I also knew that I had witnessed again, some seven hundred years after its occurrence, the conflict known in Pembrokeshire as the Battle of Mynydd Carn, in which the forces of Trehaearn and Caradog of Gwynedd had fought the armies of Gruffydd ap Cynon and Rhys ap Tewdwr. Old Morris Higgon of Trepant, who has the misfortune to live close to the scene of the battle, had told me that those who witness it are either blessed or cursed by what happens immediately afterwards. Seven years ago, after the battle, I watched as the sky was bathed in a white light which enabled me to find my way to Mr Higgon's humble abode. All he had asked me then was to tell him what colour light I had seen, and I perceived from his response that I had given him the desired answer: white. It must have been a sign that I was well blessed, and destined to emerge triumphant from the trials which were later to afflict me. And emerge I did, on that occasion, with my faculties more or less intact, though literally battered and bleeding after having been dragged through hell.

Now I waited to see what would happen next, and as I watched the landscape was bathed in an ethereal light which surrounded me and even seemed to pass through me. With a cold horror which I felt in the pit of my stomach I had to accept that the light was not white, but red. Then in a few seconds it faded away, leaving me shaking and shivering with emotion and gasping for breath beneath the gleaming stars of the January night.

This all happened twenty-four hours ago. This morning, having slept hardly at all, I determined that tonight I would resume my diary after a break of some years, for better or for worse. In writing, I may derive some comfort and find order in the midst of the chaos which will now surely overtake me. David is fast asleep, as innocent as little Dewi and the girls in the nursery next door, blissfully unaware of the turmoil which exists in my heart and my head. I will not tell him what I have seen and heard in the wide sky over Mynydd Morfil and Carningli; he would probably not believe me anyway, and what is there to be gained by feeding my own fears into the hearts and minds of others?

In resolving to keep this matter to myself, I am trying to hold in my mind the wise words of my old friend Joseph Harries the wizard, who told me some years ago that premonitions are never to be shared. They are, he said, signs from some other world intended to prepare and strengthen the resolve of the recipient; and he added that the sharing of them always, without fail, does more harm than good. So I will take my responsibility in this matter seriously, and will be silent. And in writing these words I am reminded of the many secrets which I have already gathered in my heart here at Plas Ingli.

Suddenly I feel crushed by the weights, old and new, which I have to bear on my scarred shoulders, and my hand is shaking as I write. Now I must weep, silently so that I do not wake David. I cannot continue in this state.

17 January 1805

Four days have passed, and my black mood has lightened. No disaster has overtaken us, and I am coming to think that my viewing of the battle in the sky was after all a premonition of some fearsome event which may affect others and yet leave my own dear family unscarred. In any case, how could I possibly go about the place with a furrow upon my brow when Dewi and his big sisters spend every minute of the day filling the house with sunbeams? Betsi, who is almost seven, and Daisy (near four) are making a house for their dolls in an old chest, and they require my constant assistance; and little Dewi, who will be two in a fortnight's time, is the most cheerful and contented of children even when left entirely to his own devices. David and I spend as much time with them as we can, for our different reasons – he because he knows that spring ploughing and sowing will soon be upon us, and I because there will soon be another small baby who will demand almost all of my attention.

I must continue my narrative from the eve of *Hen Galan*. After my terrifying experience on the mountain I picked up my candle lantern and made my way cautiously back down to the house. Frosted grass crackled beneath my feet and crisp starlight illuminated the heavens. The tawny owls were still talking to each other in the woods, and an invisible curlew called as it flew overhead. I have to admit that I was still shaking with fear when I entered the kitchen. Without looking up Sian said, 'Mistress! Very glad I am that you've returned. That saves us from sending out a search party on this cold and frosty night.'

Bessie helped me off with my heavy cloak and noticed immediately that all was not well. 'Mistress, what have you been doing?' she asked in a voice which she normally reserves for scolding the children. 'Your face is the colour of a shroud, and you are shivering so much that you might have been dragged straight out of a snow drift. Are you all right?'

'Yes, thank you Bessie,' I lied. 'The air is very cold, and perhaps I should have changed into my woollen dress before going outside. Let me sit by the fire, and I will soon be myself again. But I must say that a tot of brandy would not go amiss in the process of thawing out.'

By now Mrs Owen had woken up, and she looked at me momentarily as she had done years ago when I suffered the loss of my first baby. Then she and the others clucked about me like five brown hens claiming ownership of a single chick. The brandy, and the noise, and the warmth of the fire soon restored me to some sort of equilibrium, although in truth my mind was still full of the most appalling images. I was released from my self-obsession by the realization that I was not the only one in the room with pallid cheeks, wild eyes and shaking hands. I knew immediately on catching his eye that young Shemi Jenkins, twenty-three years old and as strong as a prize bull, had also seen the battle in the sky. I surmised that he had been outside checking the animals, as he did every evening, and I also knew that the ability to 'speak' to animals was but one of the special talents handed down to him by his strange father.

Next morning David and his grandparents all had sore heads, having drunk too much at Plas Pontfaen and slept too little on arriving home. After breakfast I left them to the tender mercies of the children and found Shemi cutting turnips behind the cowshed. 'Good morning, Mistress Martha,' said he. 'Not often I sees you out here.'

'Good morning, Shemi. I felt like some fresh air, and the children are too boisterous for a sensitive soul who is approaching her time. May I ask you something?'

'Anything, Mistress.'

'When you checked the animals last night, did you observe anything strange?' Shemi lowered his eyes and looked embarrassed. 'I see that you did. Would you like to tell me about it?'

'Well, Mistress,' he replied, losing his diffidence, 'since I feels in my bones that you saw it too, I can tell you. The battle in the sky. Terrible, terrible it was. I was frightened almost out of my wits. I have heard say that my uncle Caleb saw it once, but he never talked about it. What am I to make of it, Mistress?'

'I am afraid I do not know myself, Shemi. It may be some portent of fearsome things to come, but it is best that we tell nobody else lest they think us mad. Shall we preserve this knowledge as a secret between ourselves?'

'Yes, Mistress, if you say so. I promise I will not say a word to any other soul.'

'There is a duty placed upon us to protect those who do not see such things from needless worries. Life is hard enough as it is, and the others who live beneath our roof are better off without wild imaginings of the end of the world.'

'I agree, Mistress,' replied our young labourer. 'I dare say that in this delicate matter silence is kindness.'

I then appealed to Shemi to let me know if he saw or heard of any other strange omens in the community over the forthcoming days, and he agreed to keep a careful watch. And so he returned to his frozen turnips and I returned to the warm kitchen, feeling that an unexpected bond had been created between us.

25 January 1805

Five days ago the weather turned. A bitter east wind sprang up, and within a few hours a slate-grey blanket of cloud had extinguished the sun and obliterated the heavens. The snow started almost immediately, and we only just had time to get the animals down to the bottom fields before we were all enveloped in a wild banshee of a blizzard. It lasted for three full days, and the men had to battle unremittingly against the elements to keep the animals alive. In places the snow drifts were twelve feet deep. At times the wind was so strong that we had to shout to make ourselves heard, even within the house. All shutters were kept closed, which made the rooms very dark, and even so flurries of snowflakes insinuated themselves through cracks and crannies, making curtains and furnishings cold and damp. Six sheep were rescued by Billy and David out of a veritable mountain of snow in Parc-bach, and since the water in the pipe from Ffynnon Brynach was solidly frozen the women's task was to maintain a supply of ice blocks to three great 'melting cauldrons' over the kitchen fire just to provide drinking water for the cattle, horses and pigs. All the feed – hay, turnips, chaff and oats – was hauled by sledge from the barn to the feeding points in the fields; our best cob, Champion, sank to her belly in a snowdrift behind the orchard and had to be dug out. From past experience, David had placed all the animals in the fields and paddocks to the west of the house, where there was some shelter from the evil easterly wind; but on their journeys back to the house, into the teeth of the storm and with snowflakes as hard as sand grains assaulting their eyes and cutting into their faces, the men had a hard time of it. Yesterday David was worried that Shemi may have suffered frostbite on the fingers of his right hand.

Mealtimes were thrown into chaos, with the four men coming and going at all hours, and the smell of cawl and fresh bread filling the house through day and night. Grandma Jane and Mrs Owen tried to run the kitchen like a military headquarters, but their best efforts were disrupted by piles of thawing smocks, coats, cloaks and mittens thrown into corners and across benches, by men stamping their boots and leaving puddles of melting dirty snow everywhere, and by the constant demands for dry clothes and hot soapy water. Mrs Owen was not

41

at all amused by the presence of four horse harnesses hanging from the hooks in the kitchen ceiling which are normally reserved for salted hams; but they had to come in, for it was so cold in the stable, even close to the horses, that they were frozen solid within two hours of being used. Bessie kept the rest of the house in order, and Sian took on responsibility for the children. Her constant good humour in the face of adversity is a source of wonderment to me.

In my present condition I was worse than useless as the blizzard raged on, but the children loved every minute of the crisis. Betsi was the only one allowed outside, and she took care of feeding the chickens and geese and collecting the eggs. With remarkable discipline, at three-hourly intervals during her waking hours, she took it upon herself to place out bowls of breadcrumbs and warm water for the little birds that have congregated in the barn; there is nowhere else for them to go, poor fluffy things, and she said that she counted more than thirty sparrows, twenty tom-tits, six chaffinches, fifty starlings and even some blackbirds and thrushes beneath the roof. I did not have the heart to tell her that the main beneficiaries of this feathered invasion were the farm cats. Daisy and Dewi 'helped' with carrying logs and washing dishes and hanging soggy clothes out to dry. All the fires in the house were kept going, and we were blessed in this regard by a well-stocked wood-shed. In truth, we managed remarkably well in difficult circumstances. There has not been such a prolonged blizzard since I arrived at the Plas in the year before the French Invasion, but the old folks have seen it all before, and Grandpa says that when he was a boy some of the blizzards were so long, and living conditions were so primitive, that you were lucky to get through them with all of your family, let alone all of your animals, still alive.

This morning I awoke with a start. I saw that David had already slid out of bed, and heard him singing a tuneless song downstairs. In his place, by my side, there was a small boy, warm and fast asleep, with his favourite stuffed toy sheep held tightly in his arms. For some minutes I lay there, loving the child and the moment. Then I realized that the wind had stopped, and that the only sounds I could hear were coming from the kitchen – snatches of conversation, clanking utensils and the music of metal cutlery on stoneware plates. A strange brightness was filtering through a crack in the shutters. I slipped out of bed with a distinct lack of grace, put on my dressing gown, and folded back the shutters. The world was transformed, and my eyes took several minutes to adjust to its glory. The sun was well up, and there was not a cloud in the sky. I thought that the snow-covered landscape looked more beautiful than anything I had ever seen. Ice crystals gleamed and glittered in the sunlight; a cascade of powder snow fell from the tall ash tree near the driveway; and a little flock of seagulls flew high overhead from some secret roosting place towards the coast. I opened the window and the coldness of the air quite took my breath away. Even in the full glare of the sun there was not enough warmth for drops of water to form or for icicles to grow beneath the gutters. And outside there was not a single sound to be heard – sheep, cattle, dogs, poultry, oxen, wild birds and domesticated humans all seemed to be holding their breath, hesitant to do anything which might disturb the virgin cleanliness of the snow-covered landscape or the sacred stillness of the air.

I was dragged out of my reverie by Betsi and Daisy, who came racing up the stairs yelling like some wild warriors from an African jungle. 'Mam! Mam! Come quickly!' shouted Daisy, wide-eyed and over-excited.

'We have had our breakfast, and the sun is shining, and the snow will all melt away in no time at all if we don't hurry, so we must put on our nice warm coats, and our thick mittens, and we must make a snowman and feed the birds and fetch more wood before it is too late!'

'Dad said we were to let you and little Dewi sleep some more,' added big sister Betsi, equally wide-eyed but somewhat more in control of her emotions. 'But you have slept for hours and hours, and if you don't get up now you will miss all the fun!'

'Now then, calm down, the pair of you,' I replied. 'Don't worry that the snow will go away – it is still far too cold for it to melt. Dewi and I will get up and get dressed, and have some breakfast, and by twelve of the clock it will be perfect for going outside. Tell Bessie, if you please, that I would like some warm water in my washing bowl and a nice dry towel.'

'Yes, Mam!' they shouted in chorus, and went racing back down the main staircase.

Now the day has gone, and the little angels, all three of them, are fast asleep, as is David. In truth I am very tired myself, and find that I need more sleep on this occasion of child-bearing than on the others. Before my quill drops from my hand I will simply record that we have had a perfect day in the snow and out of it. We have lost no animals, and the servants have gone about their duties with smiles upon their faces in spite of the hard work. Such is the miracle of sunshine. David, unexpectedly, took the day off and devoted all his attention to me and the children. We tramped about in the drifts, made a snow house and sat in it while we consumed our bowls of pea soup in the middle of the day, built a quite magnificent snowman with a frozen cow-pat for a hat, and threw snowballs at each other. Then, much to our surprise, Grandpa Isaac came out and showed us all how to make angels. We all lay flat on our backs with our legs together and our arms outstretched. Then, following instructions, we opened and closed our legs and moved our arms up and down several times, always keeping contact with the snow. Then we were all supposed to hop up and skip away, leaving behind beautiful impressions of angels with long skirts and magnificent wings. The others managed the hopping and skipping very well, but I needed more than a little assistance from David. There were screams of delight and yells of joy from the children, and tears of laughter from David and myself, and we all agreed that Grandpa, after many years of practice, made the best angels.

While we members of the Morgan clan disturbed the January silence the summit of Carningli gleamed and glistened in the sunlight, its old blue rocks completely blanketed and its perfect whiteness accentuated by the deep azure of the northern winter sky. Could anybody, I wonder, live in a place closer to the angels?

30 January 1805

The snow has gone, to be replaced by mud and slush; and the sun is once again hidden by smudgy grey cloud. No matter, for we have had our share of cold and this will be followed, according to the old saying, by a double share of harvest. Soon the first catkins, snow-drops and wood anemones will appear, and spring will not be far behind.

In writing of our family and servants I am reminded that if anyone should happen upon these written pages in years to come, they will not necessarily know who is who and what is what. My earlier little books are still safe and sound in my tin box in the attic, but for all I know they will not survive the passage of time. This evening I have a few moments of peace, with the children fast asleep and David working at his desk on the estate accounts. So I will pen a few words by way of explanation.

This beloved place belongs to David and me because his parents, three brothers and one little sister all died in 1794 in a dreadful fire which consumed the old Plas. This was the most terrible event ever to occur in the turbulent history of Plas Ingli. People think that it was the fire that killed them, but in fact they were slaughtered in cold blood by one Moses Lloyd, who was the very incarnation of evil. He too is dead and gone, and for him I shed no tears. I am the only person alive who knows how and where he died. David, the man whom I adore above all else in the world, still does not know that the fire was started by Moses Lloyd, and that his parents, brothers and little sister were all dead before the flames reached them. I am sworn to protect him from this knowledge. He still carries the scorch-marks of the inferno on his soul, but they are fading bit by bit, due in no small measure to the innocence and joy of our children. And the house and outbuildings are now rebuilt, backed against the mountain and looking out over the *cwm* towards the distant grey-green summits of Mynydd Preseli.

I cannot bear to write about the things that happened to this suffering family and beleaguered estate in the year of the French Invasion; suffice to say that we emerged from a time of terror with our honour intact. For this, no little thanks are due to David's grandparents Isaac and Jane, who are still in their sixties and who, God willing, will guide us for many years yet.

Grandpa Isaac is a man of medium height, with a mind as sharp as a silvered scythe, a bald pate and a grizzled chin. He has bright blue eyes and a weather-beaten complexion, for he is not, and never has been, the sort of country gentleman who rules his tenant farmers and his labourers from within the confines of his office or his parlour. He shares labour with the men and boys who work on the estate, and although he is a magistrate he claims to have the instincts of a pauper. Indeed, he owns no property and has no fortune under his bed; the small change which he needs for his occasional drinking sessions with his cronies in town comes, courtesy of David, from the profits made by the estate. I love him dearly, for he has a sparkling wit and his head contains a library of wisdom. He knows when and what to buy and sell, the best times to plant and harvest, and he can tell a good animal from a distance of a hundred paces. He has a network of spies without equal, and reads avidly about the latest innovations in harrows and ploughs, and the current economic and political theories. Over the past seven years David would, by his own admission, never have coped with the demands of the estate without his timely advice, his cool judgement and his occasional remonstrations. He dotes on the children, and sometimes it is as much as I can do to drag them away from his magical and interminable story-telling sessions and off to bed. If he has a fault, it is his tendency towards impetuosity; and he freely admits that he has occasionally waded into battle without thinking too deeply about the whys and the wherefores, just for the sheer pleasure of it. It has occurred to me more than once that he and I are kindred souls.

And Grandma Jane? Isaac says he would die without her, and indeed I believe he would, for she is the most felicitous and gentle of women, brought up in an old world of manners and customs very different from those of today. She is a woman of great learning, and I have discovered that when she was young she received tuition from some of the best tutors in Wales. She plays the harp like an angel, and is determined that Betsi will do the same. She is very short, and so slender that I am at a loss to understand her strength and her stamina. She has a sharp nose and piercing grey eyes, and skin as smooth as that of an eighteen-year-old. Her hair is the colour of windblown snow, and the neighbours say that it turned white in one day, after the fire. She speaks very little, except in the company of Mrs Owen, but when there are weighty matters under consideration she shows over and again that she has the mind of a true diplomat. Grandpa says that if only she had been shipped over to France some years past she would have sorted out the wild men of the Revolution without a single shot being fired, and without a single drop of the guillotine. That having been said, she has revolutionary blood in her veins, and if the King and Master Pitt had overheard some of her comments on social and political matters she would certainly have been clapped in irons long since. In her quiet way she has, I am sure, created a Plas Ingli in which love, respect, compassion and honesty have become the abiding values; and David and I have been intrigued more and more by her carefully considered view of our complicated world. She looks rather fierce to the children, and I believe they are more than a little afraid of her since she finds it hard to be frivolous and is too fond of discipline for their liking. But in a few years they will discover the treasures within her soul, and will value them a good deal more than silver and gold.

And so to my beloved David, Master of Plas Ingli and ruler of my heart. As I write I can see him through the doorway, his brow furrowed as he tries to make both head and tail of the estate finances. Mathematics is not his strongest subject, but I esteem him no less for that, since I happen to love the furrowing of his brow as I do all his other little mannerisms. We first met when I was sixteen and he was one year older, in the aftermath of the Plas Ingli fire. He was, as may be imagined, in a quite dreadful state, and at a time of heightened emotions and inadequate supervision from my parents we became besotted with each other, to the point where at last we made love beneath the old oaks of Tycanol Wood. In the late summer of 1796 I realized that I was carrying his child, and we were then swept by our families into a strange and secretive wedding. My move to Plas Ingli was a time of utter misery for me, in which I harboured thoughts of taking my own life, and then I lost the baby which was the product of our love, and plunged into several months of deep melancholia. During all this David was the pillar on whom I had to lean – with great reluctance, it has to be said, for he was already carrying more burdens than any young man should have to bear. But through the force of his will and the strength of his love we survived this time of danger and find ourselves now even happier than when we first met, our love deeper and stronger, and blessed with three (soon to be four) beautiful and beloved children.

He is, I declare, the bravest man on this earth, and would have no fear for his personal safety if his family were in danger. As soon as he heard that the French had invaded Pencaer, he rushed off in defence of the realm before the rest of us had a chance to draw breath. What is more, he came back from that strange episode a hero, carrying two captured muskets and having saved Lord Cawdor and his army from a dastardly ambush. Who knows what the course of events might have been without his involvement? On another occasion, two years since, he rushed into the path of a charging bull and swept up little Daisy, who would otherwise certainly have been killed. He is a great sportsman who knows all there is to know about the ancient game of *cnapan*; and when he and the servants come back from a day's shooting in the woods Billy always professes amazement at the speed of his reactions and the accuracy of his eye. He shares labour in the fields with the hired hands, and this has been rewarded by a very special allegiance from them. When he comes in from a day of ploughing or haymaking he is often exhausted and filthy, looking more like a common vagrant than a respected squire and magistrate.

What more can I say about him? That I love his boyish good looks and his twinkling blue eyes and his blond unruly hair? That every night in his arms is an adventure and a new discovery of love? That I care not a jot about his total disregard for fashion and his reputation as being the worst-dressed squire in Pembrokeshire? What matters is his humility, his gentleness, his humour, his fathomless love for the children, his pleasure in little gestures of romance, and his endless patience with my erratic and wilful nature. A perfect gentleman and a perfect lover, one might think. Not quite. He still requires further training in tidying his clothes up properly, putting books back on their shelves, and wiping his boots when he comes in from the yard. I have to tell him frequently that he lavishes more attention on little Dewi than is good for him, and that the two girls need far more discipline. He is so kind with others, and so trusting, that he seems on occasion to have no appreciation of the deviousness and the wickedness of mankind, and because of this he has needed rescue by his grandparents and myself on more than one occasion. He tries too hard to be a good squire, and finds it impossible to make decisions which may harm others. He refuses to hire a steward to manage the estate, although we could probably now afford it. He has no interest in cultivating contacts and forging alliances. He has little ambition, and will never be rich and famous, but who can blame him, after the traumas of his short life, for placing happiness above politics and family above fortune? He is the man I will live and die for, and he deserves every ounce of the love that is in me.

Now David is telling me that it is time for bed, and who am I to argue with my lord and master? I will snuggle down in the warmth of his embrace, although in truth embracing is just a little difficult at present, with more than seven months of love coming between us. Tomorrow, if I find the time, I may write of the faithful servants who contribute far more than we have a right to expect towards the happiness of the Plas.

31 January 1805

It is morning, and blowing a gale. David has gone into town to see Will Final Testament on some legal business, and the children are playing an elaborate game with Sian in the nursery. I am moved to write of the five good people who are referred to by others as servants but by David and myself as friends. Without them, now and in the turbulent past, the Plas would be a sorry place. As is the way with the small estates of this area, they are in truth members of our family; when they are sick, we care for them, and if any of them was to leave (as Bessie once did, to get married) we should certainly share their pleasure but mourn their loss.

Blodwen Owen, our faithful housekeeper, has been here since the beginning of time. She is to me, and to almost everybody else, 'Mrs Owen', since to refer to her by her Christian name would be to take familiarity to unseemly lengths. The only one who calls her Blodwen is Grandma Jane, but then the two of them have been working side by side in the kitchen for forty-five years. She is a big woman, just a little taller than she is wide, with a ruddy complexion, snow-white hair and a bosom so ample that it is a source of wonderment to the little ones. She was widowed many years since and has four grown-up children, Bethan, Sian, Dafydd and Will, all of whom are in service in the neighbourhood. She had six grandchildren but suffered great sadness some years back, for she lost two of them when the town and countryside of Newport were afflicted by the dysentery sickness. She knows everything there is to know about household management and the arts of the kitchen. She is quick to see the humour in things, and her belly laugh surely shakes the foundations of the universe. However, she can be exceedingly fierce when she has to be, and she suffers no nonsense from any of the other servants; under angry assaults from her tongue I have seen Bessie reduced to tears and Billy creeping out into the yard with his tail between his legs. Dewi is a little frightened of her because she can be very loud, but the two girls adore her as she adores them. I have noticed, on more than a few occasions, that candied fruits and other good things have found their way into little sticky hands when the rest of us have been debarred from some secret operation on the kitchen table. She also has the greatest affection for David, having delivered him into this world and shared in every moment of joy and tragedy to have affected the Morgan family since 1765.

Billy came to the Plas when he was only fourteen years old, and here he is still, having worked his way up from bird-scarer and stone-gatherer to handyman and gardener, then to cowman and shepherd, and most recently to carter and head man. He accepts responsibility only with the greatest reluctance, and when David asked him last year whether he might take on one of the tenancies he admitted that the very thought of it filled him with horror. He is still only a little over forty years old, of medium height and modest build, and still good-looking enough to attract considerable interest from the local girls. He does not appear to be interested in marriage, and claims that life is more educational without it. Having chanced once or twice upon his sporting activities in the hay barn in the company of young ladies, I can well believe it. He spends almost all his time in the open air, and hates this time of year because he is trapped more often than he would like within the confines of kitchen, stable and barn by sheeting rain and screaming wind. But he is a good man, utterly dependable, unpretentious and as honest as the day is long. He works well with Grandpa Isaac and greatly respects the old man's knowledge of farming matters, and he and David are as close as brothers.

Bessie, my gentle housemaid, knows me a good deal better than I know myself, having been my constant companion and guide through my first turbulent months at the Plas. She is as pretty as a picture, almost thirty years old, with wide blue eyes, a straight nose and an engaging smile. Her blond hair, for the most part rolled up beneath her cap, flows down, in her rare moments of freedom, almost to her waist. She has a petite figure which belies her strength, and she can swing a scythe at hay-making time and heave a butter churn as well as most of our labouring men. She should, if there were any justice in this world, be married to a merchant or a tenant farmer, with a brood of little children around her; but she has had more than her share of suffering. Some years ago she left our service to marry Benji Walter, the Parrog corn merchant, and was at first as happy as an April lamb. But then she lost her little boy, Tomos, when he was only three months old, and her kind husband died in an accident in his own warehouse. Bessie was left desolate and destitute, and when she was evicted from her cottage she pleaded to be taken back at the Plas. She is almost restored to her old self, as attentive and organized as ever, and although she is supposed to spread her duties across the household she spends most of her time ensuring that I look, and feel, like the Mistress of a grand estate. In truth the estate is not at all grand, but I enjoy being the object of Bessie's sweet attention in any case. She is a very special friend, and should she even now be snatched away by one of her multitude of admirers I should miss her desperately.

And then there is Shemi, twenty-three years old and the son of Daniel Jenkins of Blaenwaun. He was born and brought up only half a mile down the track, and he knows every stone on the mountain, every inch of every lane, every acre of this estate and those of our neighbours. He also knows more than he cares to admit about how to tickle a trout or snare a rabbit, and as a child he was lucky, so says his father, not to end up in Van Diemen's Land or dangling from a gibbet. But responsibility has done wonders for him, and since he came here as a slip of a lad seven years ago he has made himself quite indispensable. He is now our gardener and cowman, but as our junior manservant he has to turn his hand to everything. He is well over six feet tall, and I am mystified as to how Mrs Owen keeps him fed; but David swears that his work produces a thousand times more than he eats, and that seems good value to me. His manners are rough, but he is learning to read and write, and I suspect that he has the capacity, if only he will recognize it, to absorb information like a sponge. He

54

dotes on little Dewi and would spend all his time giving him piggybacks around the paddock if we were to let him. As one of the younger members of the Jenkins clan he has access to a vast circle of contacts; and if there is pertinent or indeed salacious news to be had he is almost always the first to deliver it. I find myself drawn to like this young fellow in a very strange way, for he has special powers which Billy is at a loss to understand. Whenever there are problems with the animals, Shemi is the one who sorts them out, and I am convinced that he sees things which others do not even dream about. His observation of the battle in the sky, some days since, was not a matter of chance; I have discreetly enquired of others who were on the mountain on the evening of *Hen Galan*, and none of them saw anything other than stars or heard anything but tawny owls.

Finally I must mention my happy friend Sian, who is nursemaid to the children. She is the daughter of our tenants Caradoc and Bethan Williams who used to farm at Dolrannog Isaf and now look after Gelli, down in the *cwm*. She is a little older than Shemi, and played in the same fields and woods as he did as a child. As soon as I met her, shortly after my arrival at the Plas, I struck up a close friendship with her, in spite of the fact that we came from two different worlds. And when, as a new mother, I started to experience difficulties in coping with little Betsi, who cried constantly and seemed to require no sleep whatsoever, I turned to Sian for assistance. She moved in, and proved to be such a blessing that she has never gone away again. Indeed, with my last seven years devoted largely to the twin tasks of producing babies and trying to turn them into civilized human beings, I could not have managed without her. She is a well-made woman in her prime, with a ruddy complexion, blue-grey eyes and a mop of golden curls which resist all her attempts at organization. I find the dimples on her cheeks quite amusing, having always assumed that such pretty features were reserved for delicate little girls. Her true calling is that of a clown or a court jester. She mimics the rest of us with cruel wit, and has the ability to elicit gales of laughter from a roomful of listeners with her 'truthful tales' of nefarious activities in Newport. But most important of all, she is a most excellent nursemaid in spite of the fact that she has no children of her own. The little ones adore her, for they are quite aware that behind her stern words and frequent admonishments there hides an overgrown child who understands their tantrums and tears and childish pranks far better than I.

Thinking about the seven strong characters who live beneath this roof with David and me and the three children, I am more than a little amazed that we all get on with one another. To be sure, there are occasional frictions and misunderstandings, but we have never yet come to blows, and that must be some sort of miracle. Perhaps we all have our jobs and our territories, and seek not to stray onto ground that belongs to somebody else. Or maybe our unusual harmony has something to do with the place where we live – for I have always felt that the Plas is a house inhabited by angels.

4 February 1805

Today Dewi was two years old, and we had a little celebration in his honour. He did not understand very much of what was going on, but he (and the rest of us) greatly enjoyed a splendid currant cake topped with marzipan and fresh cream which I had made without any help from Mrs Owen. He had lots of little presents, of which his favourite was a carved wooden horse presented, rather bashfully, by Shemi. Then David took the little fellow for a ride all round the estate on the back of Major, our calmest and biggest shire horse. By all accounts both father and son had a wonderful time.

More than two weeks have now passed since I saw the battle in the sky, and in truth I had almost forgotten about it. Domestic matters, and the need to sleep a great deal, have caused my mind to drift away from thoughts of the future, and perhaps I have been foolish and self-indulgent in writing so extravagantly about the virtues of our strange extended family. Perhaps the disaster which I fear will fall upon one of them – could it be that we are to lose dear Billy, or Grandma Jane, or my beloved Bessie? The very thought creates a knot of apprehension in my stomach.

I was forcefully reminded that all is not well with the world this very morning. It was a bright and breezy day with scudding grey cloud, and after breakfast I took a walk along the lane with Daisy. Soon we saw Shemi coming the other way, and I knew immediately that he wanted to talk to me. So I said to Daisy, 'Oh dear, I am in danger of losing this little bonnet in the wind. Daisy, *cariad*, will you run back to the house and fetch my red one with the long ribbons?'

'All right, Mam,' she replied. 'Just you wait here for me, and I will be back in five minutes.' And off she skipped, singing to herself.

'Good morning, Mistress,' said Shemi. 'May I have a word?'

'Certainly, Shemi. But be quick, as Daisy will be back soon.'

A shadow came over his face, and he said: 'I has to report, Mistress, that the *tolaeth* has been heard down on the Parrog by the harbour.'

'Down on the Parrog?' I asked, raising my eyebrows. 'Isn't that a strange place for such a thing?'

'Not at all, Mistress. In Davy Death's workshop it was, above the chandlery. With all the ships coming in and out, dying sailors are sometimes brought ashore, and there've been vagrants found dead from the poisonous fumes around the lime kilns. And after that blizzard we had last month a vessel foundered out on Pen Morfa and six corpses was washed up on the beach. Davy Death has to deal with bodies all the time.'

'Very true. What form did the *tolaeth* take, and who saw it?'

'There was nothing much to be seen, so they say. I heard about it last night in the Royal Oak. Some boys from the Parrog said that Morgan Cobb, who lives next door to Davy, was woke up at three in the morning by the sound of oak timbers being dragged across the floor of the workshop. Then I met Morgan, and he said it was true. He told me more. A lot of footsteps and so forth, there was, followed by sawing and hammering of nails and thumping and banging. He heard Davy coughing and clearing his throat. He thought to himself, "Dammo, that Davy will be the death of me, working at all hours of the night and stopping poor innocent folks from having a decent rest." So he got up and went to the window, and there was a sort of green light shining out from the workshop. Then the noises stopped, and Morgan went back to bed and back to sleep.'

'And that was that? I dare say that Davy does have to work at night sometimes if his services are in demand.'

'Well, that's the peculiar thing, Mistress,' said Shemi, looking round and lowering his voice. 'There has been no new dying in town in the last day or two, and everybody knows it. What is more, Morgan says he met up with Davy yesterday morning and told him off good and proper for all that sawing and banging and coughing in the middle of the night. Davy looked most offended, and said that he had been fast asleep all night in bed with his wife, and that he certainly does not have any cough or cold just now. Then Mistress Death said exactly the same thing.'

'So it was the *tolaeth*, and no doubting it?'

'Quite so, Mistress. Everybody on the Parrog says there will be an important coffin made in Davy's workshop sooner or later, and that the *tolaeth* was a sign from God meant to turn us all from our wicked ways.'

Then Daisy came running towards us, waving my red bonnet in the breeze, and our conversation had to end. 'Thank you very much, Shemi,' I said. 'It will be as well to keep up our vigilance.' And he nodded and went on his way while Daisy and I continued down the lane, looking for the first snowdrops.

Now that I am back at my desk I still worry that something may happen, but I gain some reassurance from the thought that a coffin made on the Parrog is most likely to be intended for the body of some old sea captain or fisherman. I heard this afternoon that three ketches are expected at Parrog on the next high tide, and while I do not wish misfortune on any man I have to admit to some slight hope that a dead mariner in need of a coffin may be brought in from the sea. To some degree this would allay my foolish fears.

7 February 1805

Today (or in truth for the last few days) we have been making soap. Mrs Owen has been grumbling about the delay, for according to her tradition the business should be completed by the end of January. This year the cold and snowy weather has got in the way. However, now she is happy, for the cakes of soap are safe and sound in the wooden box in the scullery.

As Assistant to the Chief Soap-maker, I have to say that the manufacture is a very strange process indeed. Mrs Owen has been planning for it ever since the beginning of winter. She has been storing the vital ingredients – wood ash from the fireplaces and dripping, lard, goose grease and chicken fat from the kitchen. Some days ago she brought out, from some hiding place at the far end of the barn, an old wooden barrel with holes in the bottom. She placed some straw in it, and perched it on some stones with a large pan underneath. Then she filled the barrel with wood ash and then, at precisely eight o'clock in the morning, poured onto it a bucketful of cold water straight from the spring. Four hours later she poured on another bucketful, and then repeated this every four hours until eight in the evening. She did the same on the third day and on the fifth day. Then she removed the pan, which by now was full of a strange and apparently dangerous liquid which she called 'lye'.

The children were very intrigued by all of this, but Mrs Owen would not allow them anywhere near. Although I have observed this ceremony for eight years now, I am also very intrigued, and cannot for the life of me work out the reason for the intervals between the water pouring sessions. Mrs Owen cannot enlighten me, for she does not know either.

This morning our fierce housekeeper had Bessie and Sian mix all the fat and melt it in a cauldron on the fire. I normally do this, but I was excused this year on the grounds that my extended stomach might cause an accident. When the fat was clarified Bessie had to strain it through a muslin cloth to get rid of impurities, and keep it warm in another cauldron. Then the Chief

Soap-maker came along and added some secret ingredients, including some spoonfuls of a white powder, a cupful of a yellowish liquid that looked and smelt suspiciously like urine, and cupfuls of lavender oil and rosemary oil. She warmed up the lye until it was at about the same temperature as the fatty mixture, and then poured it, very slowly and with infinite patience, into the fat. Sian, who has good strong arms, had to stir the mixture very gently, and she was scolded fiercely on two occasions for stirring too quickly. The mixture became thicker and thicker, and when it was like honey Mrs Owen smiled a beautiful smile. 'Well done, girls,' she said. 'I do declare that we have triumphed. Success cannot be taken for granted, but you have the right touch.'

She hurried out into the scullery and returned with some simple rectangular moulds made out of thin slats of wood. Sian and Bessie each took a tin jug and decanted the mixture from the cauldron into the moulds. We now have several dozen beautiful scented blocks of soap, and tomorrow, when they are firm and ripe, I shall try one of them out. However, when I go through my ablutions I shall endeavour not to think too hard about the sources of some of the ingredients.

8 February 1805

A *toili*, a phantom funeral has been seen by Jenny Gruffydd of Pen-y-bont, in the narrow lane between Tyriet and Cilgwyn church. I heard this not from Shemi but from Bessie when she returned after fetching eggs from Gelli this morning. She says that the sighting was last night, and that everybody in the *cwm* now knows about it.

Jenny, who is Bessie's cousin, works in the dairy at Cilgwyn Mawr, and yesterday she was making cheese. It

61

was past seven in the evening when she went home, with enough moonlight to see her way. According to Bessie, she was past the church and near the ford when she became aware that there was a great throng of people coming towards her. She heard low voices, both male and female, and the shuffling of many feet. At the head of the procession were two men, one of whom had a tall hat on his head. As they approached the ford the tall hat was caught by a sudden gust of wind, flew off and landed in the water. The owner bent down and retrieved it, but it was too wet to put back on his head, and so he continued with it tucked under his arm. They came closer, and Jenny recognized the shorter of the two men as the Rector of Newport, John Devonald. She did not know the other, but took him to be another reverend gentleman.

Behind the two men there was a one-horse hearse with a coffin laid upon it. The driver splashed the hearse through the ford, but all the other people in the procession had to cross the adjacent clapper bridge in single file since the water was deep and muddy. Then they all rearranged themselves and continued slowly towards the church. The throng was so great, so Bessie says, that as it passed Jenny had to press herself into the hedge. The mourners all walked past her in their dark clothes, quite oblivious of her presence. By now she was quite convinced that she was caught up in a phantom funeral, and she was very frightened.

She had to wait, squeezed up against the hedge, for about fifteen minutes, and she told Bessie that this was no ordinary funeral since there must have been two hundred people trudging past her. She recognized the chief mourners, but she has sworn that she will never divulge who they were, for fear of causing distress. She also recognized many other local people, but there was a large group of people she did not know.

Bessie says that Jenny was so frightened as a result of this encounter that she ran all the way home after the passing of the last mourners, and took several hours to recover.

The whole community is now speculating as to the identity of the person who will shortly be taken by the Grim Reaper. It is widely assumed that the unfortunate person is a member of one of the gentry families, since it is very rare for a funeral procession to consist of more than thirty people following the death of someone from a tenant farm or labourer's cottage. The consensus is that the *toili* was that of old Squire Owen of Gelli Fawr; he has been ailing for many months and some consider it a miracle that he has survived the winter thus far. Alternatively, the big houses of Brynberian, Tregynon, Frongoch, Trefach and Cilgwyn Mawr are all occupied by elderly people who suffer from rheumatism, gout, consumption and assorted other ailments, and any of them could go to their Maker at any time. All of them have pews in Cilgwyn church, and the families concerned are large and well respected.

In transcribing this news into my diary I am gripped by a tight fist of fear. I know that there is no particular logic in this, and indeed when we discussed Bessie's news at supper the story of the *toili* was greeted with some hilarity by David, and Grandpa Isaac, and Mrs Owen. The rest of us were at least prepared to give the story some credence, on the basis that there are more things involved in life and death than the men of science would have us believe. After all, is not the Bible full of true statements about the Holy Spirit, and Satan, and angels, and miracles, and have any of us seen such things? Are we to believe that the savages and elephants of Africa do not exist, simply because we have not seen them ourselves? The phantom funeral certainly seems to have been real enough as far as Jenny Gruffydd was concerned, and Bessie says she is not the sort of girl to tell lies or suffer from wild fantasies. In our discussion I challenged Grandpa on the matter of his own love of stories about ghosts and demons and such like, and when he said that they were just fantasies handed down from his grandparents and parents I got angry with him and said that maybe in the old days people were more in tune with the world of spirits than are the educated people of today.

I have now been given three signs, and admit to being both afraid and confused. I cannot make a connection between the battle in the sky, the Parrog *tolaeth* and now the *toili* near Cilgwyn church. Perhaps – and I hope to God that this is so – the three events are not connected at all, and each one points the finger at a different person and a different event. Maybe I am in receipt of these warnings owing to some heightened awareness of things beyond the reach of others, simply because I am with child? I have read that women who are close to giving birth feel things more intensely than others. And yet . . . I am very much afraid. There is a huge anguish in my heart that tells me something dreadful is about to happen within my own small world, possibly to me or one of my beloved family. And I fear that, if it is so, it may be a consequence of my own wickedness in the past. I try to be a good wife, a loving mother and a kind mistress, but I have dark secrets in my heart, and I pray to God, if retribution is to come, that it should fall on my head and not onto the heads of those whom I love.

A Storm Like No Other

26 February 1805

David is dead. I am inconsolable, desolate, utterly destroyed by the growing awareness that he is gone, never to return. He died two weeks ago, on Shrove Tuesday, one month to the day after my observance of the battle in the sky. I should have read the signs, but I did not, and this fact fills me with a sense of deep inadequacy. Should I not have realized that he was the one marked by the Grim Reaper, just as an old ewe destined for the cull is marked on the back of its neck with red dye? Should I not have protected him? In my calmer moments I know that not even Joseph Harries the wizard, using all the force of his magic, could have resisted Destiny, and nor could I. So David is dead and cold, six feet down in the sand of Cilgwyn churchyard.

At least he is at rest. As for me, my world is torn into shreds, and the pieces swept up by the four winds. I know not what to think, where to turn for comfort, what to say, or what to do. The walls of this place, which once echoed with happy laughter, now trap me with no less brute force than those of a prison; there is no key, and the doors are open, but I have neither the energy nor the will to escape. On the inside, I can live with my dark shadows, which are now, after fourteen days, so familiar to me that they give me a sort of comfort. On the outside, what will I find? Only the hard and unforgiving world which has taken him from me, peopled by those who have no understanding of the love that I have lost.

Never again will I see him across the kitchen table, or watch him at work in the hay meadow, or hear him calling the dogs across the yard. Never again will I feel the warmth of his embrace, his body against mine, his sweet lips upon my skin, his whisperings in my ear. Who now will lift me when I am laid low, calm me when I am intent upon some wild excess, give me courage when I am afraid? He promised me so much on the day we were married, and now he has betrayed me and left me alone. How could he do this to me? Colour and warmth have drained out of my life. I cannot bear even to be with the children. I will never manage them alone. They have lost me and I have lost them, and I suffer from a cold and bitter fear that I will never regain their trust and their innocent love.

Yesterday Grandma and Grandpa encouraged me to take the little ones to see the grave. I had not previously visited it myself. I know that at any moment I could go into labour, but I agreed, and went out into the fresh air for the first time since David left me. Billy prepared the small coach and took the four of us at a gentle pace down to the Cilgwyn road. As we crossed the ford at Trefelin, William Gittins and his family, who were all digging in the garden, stopped and removed their hats in a small gesture of sympathy. 'Good morning, Mistress Morgan. And good morning, children' was all that they could say. While Billy waited near the churchyard gate, we went into the Morgan family enclosure and, weeping, placed a posy of daffodils, as bright and golden as sunbeams, on the grey-green slab of slate that covered the place.

I cannot write more now. If I have the strength, I will try again tomorrow.

27 February 1805

I am calmer today. My misery has been replaced by a cold anger as I give thought to the manner of David's death. Had he died at the hand of some villain who bore him a grudge, or who needed his purse; or beneath the wheels of a heavy wagon in some muddy field; perhaps at the culmination of some long and miserable illness, I could, even in the midst of my grief, have found some logic in it. With some effort and some support, I might have come to terms with my loss.

But he died in a silly game played by grown men – the annual *cnapan* contest on Berry Sands between the men of Newport and the men of Nevern. They say that the game was played in very foggy conditions, and that he fell off his horse close to the water's edge. He was knocked unconscious, and since nobody saw what happened, or later realized he was missing, the rising tide overwhelmed him. I gain some comfort from the fact that he was insensible at the time of his death, and that when he fell he was a happy man; but what consolation can I gain from the thought that as he lay there with the waves washing over him his confederates were chasing the *cnapan* away into the distance, laughing and yelling? It does not ease my pain to know that he was one of the cleverest horsemen and one of the most admired of players on either side.

My anger at the manner of my dear man's death is doubled by the bizarre and banal circumstances which followed it. When his body was found the game was immediately abandoned. At half past three of the clock, while he was being carried across the river to the Parrog mortuary, and placed there upon a cold slate slab, I was at home in the warmth of the kitchen, playing with the children, helping Mrs Owen with the making of a golden pancake mixture, and putting out the big wash-tub which was to have been filled with hot soapy water for my returning sporting hero. Every year since we were married the Shrove Tuesday routine has been the same – the men returning from the *cnapan* contest, tired and dirty, disappointed or elated, to be flattered or consoled, then pampered, scrubbed with carbolic soap and dried with warm towels before the fire, and finally fed with syrupy pancakes and warm ale before retiring early to bed. The children loved the routine as much as I, and this year the great sporting day was to have been more wonderful than ever, with little Dewi, now two years old, so excited as he awaited the return of his father that he spent the best part of two hours skipping round the kitchen table and clapping his chubby little hands. And then Billy and Shemi came back home with the news that destroyed for ever the innocent springtime of our family life.

I have no memory of it, but I dare say the two men used up the hot soapy water and obtained some comfort from the warm towels before the fire; but since not a single person in the house felt like eating anything, the pancake mixture went to the pigs.

God, are you laughing at me? Could Satan himself have dreamt up such a cruel conspiracy of events? You, who ordain all things, rewarding those who are virtuous and condemning those who are evil, could surely have taken this gentlest of men to your bosom in a manner involving less suffering on the part of those left behind. Could you not have taken us together? Could you not have taken me instead?

Today I have raged at Bessie, poor creature, about justice and injustice. As she put up my hair she listened, for as long as she could bear it, while I sought to understand punishment and retribution and to articulate the things which have been running about in my head for the past fortnight. Why should David, of all people, be cut down at the age of only twenty-seven, in the prime of his life and so soon after finding happiness for the first time? Had he not suffered enough to satisfy the most vengeful of gods? He fought the Plas Ingli inferno with his own hands as it consumed the bodies of his dear parents and his two brothers and little sister, only to lose his only remaining brother in a fearsome storm out at sea. Neither of these occasions even provided a single body to bury as a focus for his grieving. Then after our marriage he struggled like a Greek hero to save me when we lost our first child and when I thought of taking my own life. Surely he saw enough misery and death to last a lifetime while the dysentery sickness cast its long shadow over our community? Was he not due for just a little happiness? Did he not deserve just a small reward on this earth in the company of a loving wife and a small family of beautiful children?

At last Bessie broke down and ran from the room, leaving me in a state of deepest melancholia. I could not even weep. It is now late at night, and I still hear no answers to my questions from a merciful and benign God. Since I see in the heavens nothing but fury and vengeance I declare, in the pages of this diary, that it is my wish to join my beloved David, as soon as it can be arranged, six feet down in the serene and sacred soil of Cilgwyn churchyard.

Today is the last day of the month, and I thank God for its passing. I have apologized to my dear Bessie for the cruelty to which I subjected her yesterday, and she accepted my halting words with good grace. I have also, this evening, given her the warmest of embraces, for she has – not for the first time – taken decisive action in order to save me from myself.

This morning, while Sian was doing her best to undo the damage which I must certainly have done to the children through my recent black moods and my intolerance of childish behaviour, Bessie helped me to dress and washed my hair. Then, while I rested and without any warning, she set off across the mountain in a cold and blustery wind. She returned on the back of a white horse, perched up behind my dear friend Joseph Harries from Werndew – sage, wizard, philosopher, healer and careful observer of the human condition.

When he arrived I was still fast asleep, but when at last I emerged, rubbing my eyes, I found him in the kitchen playing silly games with the children. They have had little enough of silly games in recent days, I thought, and my cold heart warmed a little.

'Martha!' he cried, on all fours with Dewi sitting on his back. 'How good it is to see you! I have to say that you look wonderful. I have always thought that there are few things in this world more beautiful than a woman who is with child, and just a few days from her time. And you, my dear friend, are more beautiful than most.'

He stood up, causing Dewi to slide gently to the floor with great glee, and neither he nor I expected my response. I rushed into his arms and cried, 'Oh, Joseph, how good it is to see you! Where have you been since the funeral? I have been so, so miserable!' and then dissolved into tears. I cried for a long time, and as he held me in the most tender of embraces somebody must have ushered the children away to the nursery, for when I recovered my composure they were nowhere to be seen. Indeed, the whole of the population of the kitchen had disappeared as silently as phantoms, and Joseph and I were alone.

'Oh dear,' said he, wiping away my tears from his collar, 'I have to say that that was an unexpected response to my small compliment. Something tells me, my dear Martha, that you have not cried enough since I saw you last.'

'I dare say you are right, Joseph. What brought you here on this rough winter morning?'

'My white horse, with Bessie sitting behind me and hanging on for dear life. I quite enjoyed the experience.'

I laughed at this, and suddenly realized that laughter had quite gone out of my life since David's death. I immediately felt uncomfortable, but Joseph said, 'That's more like it – and don't you dare feel guilty about a smile or a laugh, Mistress Morgan. Whether you like it or not, these are the things that restore the human spirit.'

'Come into the parlour, Joseph. I need to sit down, and the kitchen benches are not made for women who are more than eight months gone.' So we went into the front room and sat comfortably in the warm glow of the log fire.

'Now then,' said Joseph, just as I was about to open my heart to him. 'I need to have a serious talk with you. I understand from a number of reliable sources that you have not been very good company of late.'

'Is that surprising, Joseph?' I asked, with a flush upon my cheeks. 'You may recall that I have recently lost my husband, and that I am still in mourning.'

'I am only too aware of that. But remember, Martha,

that you are not the first nor the last young woman to have been through this particular slough of despond.'

'Knowing that is of no particular help to me, if I may say so.'

'I am aware of that. Your grief is all that matters to you, and just now you are tortured by a pain that is almost impossible to bear. If I am not very much mistaken, you are also tormented by a thousand questions running around inside your head as you try to make some sense of what has happened. I assume that on this very day, as yesterday and the day before, you have cursed the God of Love who has previously shown you much consideration.'

My eyes widened, and I said, 'You are quite correct, Joseph! How did you know that?'

'Martha, you may think that I am a crusty old bachelor who has devoted his life to the understanding of science and the pursuit of esoteric knowledge, but it is not so. I have not told this to anybody in the community before, but when I was younger than you I lost both my parents in rapid succession, and then I lost my sweet wife, who was all I had in the world, in childbirth. I was twenty-three and she was barely twenty. Our little boy, whom I called Jacob, died in my arms when he was but twelve hours old, which was a mercy since he was terribly deformed . . .' At this his voice cracked, and as he looked at me for what seemed like an age, his eyes filled with tears.

Instinctively I crossed the room, sat next to him and held his hand in mine. 'Oh, Joseph!' I said. 'I am so sorry.'

He swallowed hard and said, 'Please don't tell this to anybody else, Martha. A wizard has to preserve some mystery, as I'm sure you will agree.' He smiled a weak smile, and added, 'It would never do for ordinary folk to realize that we have parents and wives and children, and the same emotions as everybody else.'

Then, as abruptly as it had started, our interview was at an end, for the three children rushed into the room like a herd of bullocks at feeding time. 'Mam!' shouted Daisy. 'Please can we ask Master Harries if he will give us some more piggyback rides round the kitchen?'

Having been dragged back to the realization that for children, at least, yesterday is a distant memory and today is all that matters, I replied, 'Well, you may ask him, Daisy, but you should not assume that he feels like fun and games just at the moment. We have been talking about quite serious things.'

Joseph is nothing if not resilient, and before the girls could get their questions in he said: 'Oh, very well. If you are very good indeed and promise to leave your mam in peace for the rest of the day, I will give each of you three turns round the kitchen table. And just you remember that there is a new baby on the way very soon. Your mother needs a lot of rest, and she will need a very great deal of help from the three of you when the little one arrives. Understood?'

'Yes, Master Harries!' shouted the girls, and Dewi, who has not yet fully grasped this speaking business, clapped his hands and jumped up and down.

And so Joseph did as he promised, and so did the children. Now he has gone back to Werndew on his white horse, and I am left alone once again with my thoughts.

Dear Bessie and dear Joseph! I am truly blessed to have friends as honest and kind as them.

2 March 1805

St David's Day has come and gone, and I have to admit that my mood has lightened. The celebrations, which were not very sophisticated and not at all exhausting for me, occupied Sian and the children for several hours, and consisted of various activities involving leeks. They were gathered from the garden, washed, worn on hats and coats, chopped up into little pieces and finally eaten with all sorts of other good things in a wonderful *cawl* which we enjoyed for our evening meal. The girls also made some paper flags with strange red creatures on them, and told me that they were the fierce dragons of Henry Tudor which lived in a dark cave on Mynydd Preseli and would emerge in three weeks' time to drive out the wicked English with fire and brimstone.

I did not have the energy, or the inclination, to investigate the version of history which Sian might have put into their heads during their morning lessons, but I admit now to feeling more than a little pleasure at their wide-eyed innocence and their capacity for recovery from the terrible events that have overtaken all of us. I have badly neglected the poor babes while I have been overcome with my own misery and wallowed in despair. The Good Lord – whom I have so recently cursed – knows far better than I what sufferings have been carried by the children, by Grandpa Isaac and Grandma Jane, and even by the servants. I cannot doubt for a moment that they all loved David, and that my loss is shared by them. Indeed, as Bessie and Grandma have gently reminded me more than once, they have both known grief far greater than mine, and have confronted it and overcome it. I pray for strength as great as theirs, as I am coming to realize that I owe it to them to come to my senses, and to return some of the love which they have shown to me since the dark day of David's death.

The little one in my womb is being very active as I write, kicking and pushing and demanding to be let out.

I am comforted by my instinct that this little brother or sister for the children is far healthier than might be expected in the circumstances, and that there is now not long to go. Dear God, I am sorry I have been so angry with you in recent days, and I ask your forgiveness. Now I need your help, and I pray that the baby who will soon enter this world will be perfect, and healthy. If there should be anything wrong, as with the little child that Joseph lost, I believe that I would quite lose my mind.

10 March 1805

I now feel capable of writing about the funeral and the events surrounding it, and trust this will help me to confront my demons and overcome them. This already represents progress, since barely a week ago I was hardly able to confront the appalling prospect of getting up the stairs to bed.

I have no recollection of what happened when Billy and Shemi came home with the news that David was dead. Bessie and Sian were terribly shocked, and were both in tears, but according to Mrs Owen their first instinct was to take the children immediately to the nursery so as to protect them from the raw emotions of the kitchen. Apparently I collapsed onto the floor, screaming 'Oh no! Oh no! Please God, let it not be true!' over and again, and then I was carried up to my room. Bessie left the children with Sian, and took control. Because of my condition she would not allow any strong drink or medication to pass my lips. She stayed with me all night. She says that I slept not at all, and that I spent all the hours of darkness moaning and weeping, until there were no tears left in me. In my rare moments of quiet she could not communicate with me, let alone comfort me, for I appeared to be in quite another world.

Grandpa Isaac has told me everything else, as follows. Billy and Shemi had to leave David's body in the Parrog mortuary on the night of the *cnapan* game, since Havard Medical said that he would have to conduct an autopsy next day, when it was light. Billy says he had been drinking heavily, and could not in any case have done anything requiring professional skill until he was sober. Grandpa and Billy went down with the *gambo* on the morning of Ash Wednesday and met Doctor Havard just as he had finished his task. He looked as if he was suffering from the tremors. 'As I suspected, gentlemen,' he said. 'Death by drowning. Accidental, of course. A big bump on the head, and the various other scratches and bruises that all the *cnapan* players get. I conclude that Master Morgan fell off his horse at the water's edge, hit his head, lost consciousness, and was drowned by the rising tide. A very sorry business indeed. Please pass on my sympathy to Mistress Morgan and the rest of the family. I will now write my report and make ready for the inquest.'

Grandpa then asked Davy Death, who lives only three doors away from the mortuary, to take the necessary measurements and make the coffin. Davy promised that he would deliver it to the Plas that very afternoon, and started work straight away. The inquest was held at two of the clock, with the Mayor acting as Coroner. The jury looked at David's body, considered Doctor Havard's report, and recorded 'accidental death by drowning' as their verdict. Then the Mayor said: 'Gentlemen, my deepest condolences. You may take the body home.'

Grandpa and Billy wrapped David in a shroud, placed him gently on the *gambo* and drove back to the Plas.

When they arrived there were terrible scenes, and every-body wept. Bessie told me afterwards that poor Grandma Jane was distraught, and had to be looked after in her room for several hours by Grandpa and Mrs Owen. I could not bear to be present when they carried the body into the house, and I shut myself into my bed-room with the children. We all wept, although in truth I believe that of the three only Betsi really understood that her father was dead and would never return.

They put David's body into the front room on the table, and then, when Davy Death came with the coffin, the men spent a long time behind locked doors dressing him and making him look respectable enough for the vigil. Then they lifted him into the coffin, placed it on the big table, and placed a lit candle at its head and another at its foot. From then until the time of the departure of the funeral procession the flames were not allowed to go out. Neither was David left alone for a single minute. Owen Pritchard, Will Ifans, Gethin Griffiths Dolrannog, Caradoc Williams Gelli, Joseph Harries, Daniel Jenkins Blaenwaun and many other neighbours in turn sat in the room and tended the candles. As is the custom in these parts, the coffin lid was left off. For three days David lay there, and now, almost a month later, I still recall with gratitude and some comfort the sounds of lowered voices and shuffling footsteps in the yard as the watchmen came and went.

Rector Devonald came and gave a blessing to David and to all of us in the house. He insisted on seeing me, although I was very tired and very reluctant, but I am glad, upon reflection, that we spoke. He was very con-siderate and understanding. I asked him, on a sudden inspiration, if my brother Morys might help in the funeral service in spite of the fact that he was a Baptist minister. The Rector looked shocked, but admitted that there were certain parts of the ceremonial which might be given to another without the consent of the Bishop, and to his credit he agreed. He is a very sanctimonious fellow, and is puffed up with his own importance, but he does have a good heart. After seeing me he sat with Grandpa for a long time, and together they made all the arrangements.

One by one the servants, men and women, sat with David and gave him their last respects. I was very much afraid to do this myself, and indeed for much of the time before the funeral I was in such a state of despair that I knew not whether it was night or day. But Bessie and Grandma said that I must do it, and that if I did not I should regret it for the rest of my days. So I agreed. Grandpa and Grandma said that they would come into the parlour and stay with me, and after much discussion we decided to bring the children as well.

On Friday morning, the day before the burial, we faced the ordeal together. We stood beside the coffin and looked at him. His skin was pallid and had a waxy look about it, and there were some scratches on his face. There was a bump with an open wound on his forehead, but he was still beautiful. He looked as if he was asleep, and I was reassured that he was at peace. With Grandpa holding my hand, I bent over and gave him a final kiss on the forehead; his flesh was cold, cold. I told him that I loved him, and would love him for ever, and then I said farewell. We all wept, but because the children were with us we three adults kept our composure to a remarkable extent. When we returned to the kitchen I was shaking like a leaf; but Betsi, who is a most intuitive child, cuddled up to me and held me by the hand, and said, 'There now, Mam, you must be brave. And don't you worry – I am here to look after you.'

Then, inevitably, I broke down but mixed in among the anguish and grief lay gratitude and a glimpse of joy at a sudden realization that I was surrounded by love.

After this I felt so exhausted that I had to rest for the remainder of the day. The children were very understanding, as were the old folks and the servants, and as the stream of visitors built up towards the wake I was well protected. All afternoon there were horses and ponies, coaches and traps clattering into the yard. Almost all of the local families came to say farewell to David, and many of them wanted to see me, but Bessie would not allow it, reminding them that I was heavy with child. Kind and supportive messages were written down and passed on to me, and I was almost overwhelmed by the abundance of daffodils which were carried into my room.

The only people whom I agreed to see on the day before the funeral were my closest kin: my own father and mother; my unmarried sister Elen, who miraculously appeared from Bath; my sister Catrin and her husband James, from Castlebythe; my brother Morys and his dear wife Nansi from Haverfordwest; and finally Aunt Betty from Solva, who brought David and me together more than ten years ago. I was very glad that they had all made the journey to be with us. I was able to spend some minutes with each of them as they arrived at the Plas, and there were many embraces and many tears. All eight of them stayed in the house for the *gwylnos*, although goodness only knows where Mrs Owen put them all. Afterwards I came to learn that they had all been very supportive in helping with a multitude of tasks including feeding the animals and looking after the children – for even with a wake night and a funeral to organize there was still a household and an estate to run. Cows had to be milked, turnips needed chopping, cowsheds and stables had to be mucked out. Our tenants were wonderful too. They realized that there was spring ploughing to be done, and Billy had to swallow his pride about the straightness of his furrows by allowing Caradoc Williams to plough Parc Mawr and Gethin Griffiths to do Parc Glas.

Once again Mrs Owen worked wonders in the kitchen, in spite of having no less than nineteen of us in residence and more than a hundred others who came and went during the evening before the funeral and immediately after it. Grandma insisted on being thoroughly involved, and claimed that she would have gone out of her mind without something to concentrate on. On one visit to the scullery in mid-afternoon I saw something novel: my dear father surrounded by dirty dishes, up to his elbows in soap suds, assisted by three small grandchildren. And in the kitchen I saw the other members of my family at the table with Mrs Owen, chopping, mixing, shaping, stirring, pouring and pounding the contents of what was clearly intended to be a very considerable feast. On a more sombre note, at my request Morys, as a man of the cloth, said prayers over the coffin every hour. This gave me some comfort since it was he who had joined David and me in holy matrimony when we were young and very foolish.

At about five in the evening Billy asked if he might see me, and since I could not sleep or read with all the noise going on in the house, I agreed. He came into my bedroom, looking a little uncertain. 'Well, Billy?' I asked.

'Please, Mistress,' he replied, 'there is a request from the Jenkins boys. They will be here with everybody else this evening, and they wonder if you would like them to do the *hirwen-gwd* for you and poor Master David. If you says it is all right, we will need to put the parlour fire out now, so as to have the chimney cool later on.'

I was instantly appalled by this suggestion, and also amazed, since I knew that the tradition had died out decades ago in the Solva and St David's area. Here in the region of Cwm Gwaun and Cilgwyn the Bishop's instructions clearly took a little longer to reach the ears of the inhabitants. I could not for a moment countenance a bizarre ceremony in which David would be taken from his coffin, wrapped in a white sheet, and then hauled up inside the *simnai fawr* to the top of the chimney stack before being let down again. I knew that this would involve young men clambering all over the roof with ropes, at some risk to themselves; I also knew that there would be a great deal of soot about, and that those appointed for the rope-work, above and below, would need to have their courage reinforced by warm ale in great quantities.

'Thank you for the suggestion, Billy,' I said, 'and please thank Daniel and his brothers for their kind thought. However, I will not allow it. David has lain in peace thus far, and tomorrow he will be placed in his final resting place. I am sure that evil spirits have not stolen his beloved spirit. Have you and our friends not kept a constant vigil?'

'Indeed we have, Mistress. Not a minute has passed without at least one man in the room with the poor Master.'

'As I thought. Billy, I know that the *hirwen-gwd* was intended to assist the spirit in quitting the body and leaving the house. But times have changed, and we need not believe such things any longer. In any case, hauntings are for troubled spirits, and David was as good and kind a man as ever walked this earth. He will not haunt the Plas. His spirit is in my heart, and I can assure you that that is where it will stay.'

'Very good, Mistress,' said Billy, looking relieved. 'I

am sure you are right. I will tell Daniel and the other boys that this ancient tradition is best left in the past.'

There followed a long evening and night of feasting and drinking down below in the kitchen. I was too tired and distressed to go down and join the throng; but there seemed to be a multitude of revellers downstairs, talking in loud voices and, to my horror, even laughing and joking. It appeared to me that they were actually celebrating – not Christmas, or New Year, but the death of my beloved David. How could they be so cruel? Did they not realize that Mistress Martha was upstairs, holding an unbearable weight of sorrow upon her shoulders? Not only was I deeply distressed by this turn of events, but I felt abandoned by the world. Now I knew what it was to be all alone with nobody to turn to, and I became truly afraid.

Then there was a gentle knock on the door, and Grandma Jane came in. She saw the expression of weariness on my face, and the tears in my eyes, and came and sat next to me on the bed. She put her arm round me and kissed me on the cheek. Then she said, 'Martha, my dear, do you know how much we love you?'

I could not reply, but I nodded as tears rolled down my cheeks. 'Of course you know it,' she continued, 'in the moments when you can think of love. I thought you might need a little comfort just now. This is a wretched time, with the *gwylnos* in full swing and the funeral tomorrow. I know it myself, for I have seen a little more of life and death than you.'

I could contain myself no longer. 'But Grandma,' I wailed like a small child who has dropped her candied plum onto the ground, 'they are *laughing* downstairs.'

'I know,' said Grandma, smoothing my hair. 'But you must remember *why* they are laughing, Martha. They are not laughing at you, or at David, or at the tragedy which has overtaken all of us. They are laughing because they are talking about David and celebrating his life – the time he fell off the roof of the pigsty into the trough of swill, and when he jumped off his lame horse and ran half a mile with the *cnapan* in his pocket to win the game for Newport. His was a good life filled with fun and laughter, and with love, and that is something for which you, my dear, can claim most of the credit.'

'But can they not celebrate David's life quietly, and be aware that I am trying to sleep?'

'I doubt if you will sleep anyway, Martha, until they have all gone home. Just remember why they are all here rather than sitting by their own kitchen fires on this cold February evening. They are here because they are your relatives, neighbours and friends. There are squires and their wives downstairs, our tenants, local freemen and even a good many labourers. You should not be worrying about the mighty throng; you would have cause to be far more worried if the throng had failed to materialize. And you should certainly worry far more about those who have not come than those who have.'

'Grandma – what do you mean?'

'All in good time, Martha. I know exactly who is here and who is not. One other thing. Remember that all of us in this house have suffered – maybe not as deeply as you, but we all grieve. The *gwylnos* and the funeral probably go back to the days of Adam and Eve; they are occasions for recognizing the cruelty of death but also providing some relief – knowing that life will continue, people will not be defeated by misery.'

'Thank you, Grandma. You are very wise, and I must try to be more understanding. But I still feel very sad and very lonely. Will you stay with me a little longer?'

'Of course. As long as you like.'

And she sat with me, bless her, until the evening was

83

well advanced, nodding off every now and then in the armchair beside the fireplace.

I did not attend the funeral, and neither did the children, and nobody sought to press us into going. In these parts women do attend funerals, and if I had felt stronger I might have been prevailed upon to watch while David was placed in sacred ground. But I was so tired that I could not face it. Bessie and Mrs Owen stayed at home with us, but everybody else went. Breakfast was a very quiet affair, in contrast to the ebullience of the *gwylnos*. The hearse was driven up to the house at ten of the clock, by which time everybody was ready. Rector Devonald and Morys both said prayers for David, and then Grandpa and Billy fixed down the lid of the coffin. We all watched from my bedroom window as it was slid onto the hearse.

Then the procession set off, with the two men of God walking ahead of the hearse. Grandma Jane and Grandpa Isaac were the chief mourners, followed by Auntie Betty, the servants, and the members of my family. I remember thinking, very irreverently, that Billy and Shemi looked faintly comical, and very uncomfortable, in their stiff collars and heavy jackets and shiny boots. Next came Mary Jane and her husband Dafydd, Ellie and Joseph, and the neighbours and squires and their families from far and wide. I do not know how many there were when the procession left the house; there must have been a hundred at the very least. And according to Grandpa, at least another hundred joined the procession as it passed along the Cilgwyn road, over the ford at Trefelin, and thence to Cilgwyn church. The narrow lane was filled, hedge to hedge, with mourners, and I am told that many of them were dabbing handkerchiefs to their eyes. The procession moved smoothly all the way, so I hear, until it reached the little ford near the church, at which point there was a sudden gust of wind which caused Morys's tall hat to fly off and fall into the stream. Greatly embarrassed, he retrieved it, shook the water off it, and continued with it tucked under his arm. The horse-drawn hearse splashed through the ford, but it was too deep for the procession. Morys, and everybody else, made their way silently over the clapper bridge in order to keep their feet dry.

Cilgwyn church is so small that only about eighty people could get inside; the rest had to stand outside in the cold, straining their ears to hear the words of the service but joining in lustily when the hymns were sung. Then, when it was all over, the coffin was brought outside and carried to the family enclosure, where, with due reverence and suitable words from the Bible, it was lowered into the grave. Grandma and Grandpa acted on my behalf in casting handfuls of earth onto the coffin, and at my request they also cast in a small posy of daffodils which I had picked early that morning with the children.

Billy, who hides a sentimental soul beneath his rough exterior, came up to me when they had all returned home and said that the funeral was very beautiful indeed, and that he had been moved to tears by the words and the music and also by the realization of the very high esteem in which David had been held by the community. A great many people came back to the house, and I am pleased to say that on this occasion I felt a little stronger and more sociable. I was able to spend some time with them and to thank them for their affection and support.

Now I am weary, and must sleep. I have to admit to some pride in having thus described the *gwylnos* and the funeral without dissolving into tears or being gripped by

85

panic. I believe that some healing is now under way, and I thank God in his Heaven for it.

One small postscript. I received intriguing news from Shemi this afternoon. He has been down to Parrog to fetch some hemp sacks in readiness for the barley threshing. While he was there he met Morgan Cobb, the man who heard the *tolaeth* some weeks back. He told Shemi that the sounds he heard coming from Davy Death's workshop when he was making David's coffin on Ash Wednesday were exactly the same as those he had heard in the middle of that fateful night. Even the sounds of Davy coughing and clearing his throat were the same. He said that when this struck him, he started shaking with fear. I was not entirely surprised, for I had already noticed that Jenny Gruffydd's account of the *toili* which she met early in February matched in perfect detail the actual funeral procession to Cilgwyn church as described by those who were a part of it.

Sunshine and Shadow

15 March 1805

My labour has still not started, and I am beginning to hate being with child. I know that when the time is right, nature will follow its course, and I pray to God that all will be well; but I am so heavy and ungainly and uncomfortable that I long for the whole business to be over with. Betsi, Daisy and Dewi show their enthusiasm by climbing all over me, listening to the heartbeat, and watching with wide-eyed amazement the movements of little arms and legs against the stretched skin of my stomach. The children will be just as happy as I when there is a new little brother or sister to hug.

I have been trying to distract my mind by forcing myself into short walks round the farm and by some limited involvement in estate matters. The potatoes are planted. The fields ploughed in November and set aside for barley and oats are wet, but clean with a good tilth after the winter frost and snow. The winter wheat fields are already showing green. Shemi and three of the labourers from the bottom cottages have been laying the hedges along the lane; now that they are finished, their billhooks put away, the blackthorn buds can burst into leaf, and the little birds can move in to their tightly packed and thorny nesting sites, safe from predators. The first lambs have arrived.

Billy and the tenant farmers have been burning the gorse, bracken and heather on the mountain, blessed by dry weather and southerly winds. Last evening, in the pitch darkness, the children and I looked out from the nursery window in awe as a line of angry red flames curled up into the sky, illuminating the rock faces and throwing billows of black smoke over the town and out over the coast. The mountain looked for all the world like an erupting volcano, and brought to mind a description given to me as a child by my father, who once travelled in Italy and saw a fearsome outpouring of burning ashes and glowing lava from a mountain on Sicily.

Somewhat later than planned, the barley threshing is done. Last summer we rested some fields and planted less barley than usual, fearing a slump in barley prices. We should have threshed and sold the harvest last month, but in truth the household has been in such turmoil since David's death that none of us could face a barn full of busy people and a multitude of comings and goings. But over the last two weeks Grandpa Isaac has watched the market and has organized the threshing bit by bit, using just one pair of threshers and calling in some of the labour owed us by our tenants and cottagers for the hummelling, winnowing, bagging and so forth. Hettie came up from Parrog to help for a couple of days, and Bessie, Sian and the children were of course greatly involved, glad to be out of the house and sharing convivial company on the threshing floor. They came in each evening covered in dust and coughing and spluttering, but happy and tired, and in truth I could not begrudge them their times of pleasure. Caradoc Williams Gelli and Thomas Tucker Penrhiw helped with the carting. Two hundred bushels were sold to Master Probert in Fishguard, and three hundred to Master Wilson down on the Parrog. Cash on the nail, said Grandpa, and the estate is now more than five hundred pounds better off.

We still have eighty-seven bushels in bags in the barn, and according to a tradition established by my dear David some of this will be 'sold' to the poor of the parish over the next two months, which are always referred to in this district as the 'hungry months'. May is the most difficult of all for the labourers and their families, celebrated as a time of vibrant springtime energy and vivid hedgerow colours, but feared because it is also a time of empty stomachs and needless deaths. When we 'sell' half a bushel of golden grain here or a bucketful there, no money ever changes hands, but the recipients know, and we know, just how much labour they owe to us in payment over the course of the next farming year. And it is always given with good grace by men, women and children who seldom feel the weight of a single penny in their pockets.

26 March 1805

Little Sara has arrived in the world, and she is the golden sunshine in my life. As I write she is fast asleep in her cradle at my side. As I look at her I rejoice in the fact that she is her father's daughter; she has David's fair hair, his blue eyes and even his funny nose. I cannot wait for her to wake.

She arrived a week ago, later than anticipated, but around the time at which our first baby, lost only a few months after we were married, should have been born. And I also cherish knowing when Sara was conceived. It was last June, on a bed of moss and beneath a canopy of oak leaves, when David and I loved one another in our private dell in Tycanol Wood. I will never forget the time or the place, or the wonder of that moment, and every time I look at this sweet child I will be reminded of it.

My labour was hard and long and more difficult than it should have been for a fourth child. But I was weak and tired, and I dare say it was not surprising. Mrs Owen and Grandma Jane looked after me and urged me on, and when finally, at eleven in the morning, Sara first saw the light of day, I had not an ounce of energy left in me. Mrs Owen tied and cut the cord and gave my daughter to me covered in blood. And she opened her eyes and gave me a look of infinite wisdom, and took to my breast without a murmur. To this day she has not cried; she sleeps, she feeds, and she looks at me as if to say, 'There now, Mother *bach*, you have had enough of problems for the time being. I have come into this world in order to give you all the healing you need.' She is far and away the most beautiful of all the children, but of course I will never tell that to the others. And maybe my judgement in such things is a little cockeyed just now.

On the day after Sara was born, Grandma Jane said that she was worried about my milk supply in view of the difficult time I have been through, and she asked whether I might wish to have a wet nurse. 'There is no shame in it,' she said. 'Almost all of the other squires' wives have used wet nurses in recent years so as to regain their figures, and to resume their social lives, more quickly. It so happens that Mary Shinkins had a baby the day before you; she is big and strong, and could easily cope. She could do with the money, and would benefit from a diet somewhat better than that on which she has to survive at the moment.'

'Thank you, Grandma,' I replied with fire on my

cheeks. 'I do appreciate your concern, and I am aware of the fashion of the day. But I will not hear of it. I need the contact with my little child more than anything else in the world just now, and that should not be a surprise to anybody.' Grandma left with her tail between her legs, and in retrospect I did speak rather harshly to her. But her suggestion was not very diplomatic, as she has now agreed. We have made up, and laughed about it, and are now once again the best of friends.

I have just picked up my quill again. Sentimental as I am, I could not resist picking Sara *bach* up out of her cot, just to smell her, for she has that newborn baby scent that is more wonderful than the perfume of lilac or furze or bluebells in a Maytime wood. When I lifted her up she awoke, so of course I had to tell her that I love her, and then feed her. She probably did not need feeding, but she obliged in any case. Then she nodded off again, and now she is dreaming baby dreams as I rock her cradle with my foot.

Betsi, Daisy and Dewi adore their little sister. They want to hug her all the time, and perhaps that too is not surprising since they have all been short of affection lately. I tell them that she is still too small for passing about, and that they can embrace me instead. And they have obliged, in full measure. Bless them, all three; my love for them is as wide as the spring sky, and indeed I am sure that without them I would not have survived the weeks since the death of their beloved father. So now I have four little angels to amuse me, to sustain me when my spirits are low, and to give me joy.

The household has been transformed by the new arrival. More than a month has passed since the funeral, but my sense of desolation continued until a few days before the birth, when it was suddenly replaced by a sense of anticipation and hope. Father Time is indeed a wonderful healer, and I have tried to give him some assistance in his task by reading the messages which have accumulated on my desk from friends and neighbours and from scores of people whom I have never even met. I had never before realized how much respect and affection there was within the community, and far afield, for my beloved David. I was especially touched by a message from Lord Cawdor, whom David helped at the time of the French Invasion and who intervened to save me from a dreadful fate when I languished in Haverfordwest Gaol some years since.

I have had some welcome callers. A few days before my confinement Joseph arrived. He said he was just passing, and that he was on his way to Brynberian anyway, but I do not believe that for a moment. He gave me a green medicine to drink. It tasted utterly foul, but he said it would help to make me calm and relaxed. Then he gave me a bottle of a strange yellow mixture, and told me to take it as soon as I started labour, which, in due course, I did. I have no idea what was in those herbal potions concocted in his little kitchen at Werndew, but they certainly gave some assistance at the time.

Shortly after Joseph's departure I had a visit from Owain Laugharne, Mary Jane's younger brother. I had only met him once before, at *Hen Galan* last year, when he had struck me as a kind though painfully shy young gentleman. He is now installed at Plas Llannerch, the estate which was in the ownership of the Watkins family until its fall from grace, and was later purchased by his father. When he came into the parlour he blushed the colour of ripe strawberries; he must certainly have known that I was shortly due to go into labour, but I dare say he had not expected me to be quite so large. He gave me a large posy of daffodils, primroses and celandines which he had picked from the hedgerows, and said that he had heard of my very low state following David's death. He hoped that I was now feeling somewhat better, and said that I must take heart from the great surge of support and affection which was, even now, coming from all sections of the community.

'Please, Martha,' he said, 'do not hesitate to send me a message if there is anything I can do to help with either the estate or any domestic affairs. I had the greatest respect for your husband. He was a good man and an enlightened squire, to whose high standards I personally aspire now that I am learning how to manage Llannerch.' He paused for what seemed a very long time.

Then he bowed, blushed, bowed again, and took his leave. I was very touched by his demeanour, his pedantic and hesitant way with words, and by his generosity of spirit. If all our neighbours show us such kindness, perhaps something of good can be dredged out of the black pit of grief.

10 April 1805

Easter has come and gone. We tried to make the best of it, and indeed it was a blessing to see the end of Lent, which is miserable enough at the best of times and has this year been particularly difficult for all of us. Grandma Jane always dresses in black for forty days, and this year she says she will continue to wear black until six months have passed from the date of David's death. For the time being I will follow suit, but I admit to finding it distressing, day after day, to be reminded by the very clothes I wear that I am now a young widow.

On *Sul y Blodau* we all went down to Cilgwyn church and placed flowers on David's grave. We also decorated the whole of the Morgan family enclosure most beautifully. It was not exactly a private occasion, since the churchyard was thronged with other families on similar missions, tidying up graves, whitewashing headstones, and replacing turf where damage has been done by the ravages of time. There were many kind words from our neighbours, especially from those whom I had not seen since the birth of little Sara.

On Good Friday and Easter Sunday I could not bring myself to attend the early communions in the church, nor was it expected of me. But the children have had little enough cheer lately, and on Easter Eve we determined that we should maintain some old traditions for their sake. So on Sunday we arose well before dawn, and all of us, with the exception of Mrs Owen – who has long since given up climbing – and little Sara, who is of course still a tiny thing, huffed and puffed up Carningli as the eastern sky began to lighten. I wondered at first whether I should join them, but my birthing wounds have healed well and I decided that I could manage. Billy collected a small bucket of water from Ffynnon Brynach and carried it all the way to the top, spilling a good deal of it on the way. Then, as the first rays of sunshine crept over the far horizon, we all took it in turns to look at the quivering reflection of the Easter Day sun on the surface of the water in the bucket. Grandpa explained to us that Christ rose from the dead at dawn on Easter Day, and that when he was young it was part of the celebration to see the sun 'dancing on the sacred water'. Then we all anointed each other with a few drops of the water, and threw the rest of it onto the old blue rocks. Thus was the old mountain of St Brynach anointed, and its sanctity recognized by the Morgans of Plas Ingli as it has been for countless generations. Then solemnity was replaced by hilarity as all the men, including little Dewi, had to do three somersaults on the little grassy patch of ground near the summit. Dewi insisted on doing six haphazard tumbles, and much to his surprise his great-grandfather proved that over the years he has lost none of his acrobatic skill. Back at the house after our descent, we all had boiled eggs, with pretty patterns painted on their shells, for Easter breakfast – the first fresh eggs consumed in the household since the onset of Lent. Later in the day we ate our first fresh meat since David's death – a small but very tasty spring lamb cooked to perfection by the wondrous Mrs Owen.

On the seventh day of April we had another family tradition to follow – a further visit to the Morgan burial enclosure in Cilgwyn churchyard. This time there was no Flowering Sunday hustle and bustle, and we had the sacred enclosure to ourselves. We placed flowers on David's recent grave, but for Grandma and Grandpa in particular the occasion was a poignant one since this was the anniversary of the appalling fire which destroyed the old Plas and took with it five members of the Morgan family in 1794. The two old people stood in silent contemplation for some minutes, and I was forcefully reminded what an unimaginable tragedy that fire must have been for them in that they lost their only son, a beloved daughter-in-law, and three small grandchildren. As I stood behind them I was only too aware that I knew far more about that fire, its causes and its effects, than they did; but I will never tell them the truth. I also realized, in humility, how precious I and my children must be to them – and that gave me a warm glow of consolation.

Grandpa Isaac has received a newspaper from London, and has read it avidly with the aid of his magnifying glass. He informs us that Napoleon Bonaparte has declared himself Emperor of almost everywhere, and that he is causing great trouble all over Europe. The King and Master Pitt are greatly concerned. We seem to be permanently at war with the French, which is a mystery to me since all the French people I have ever met appear to me to be perfectly charming. I can understand their wanting to be rid of their corrupt and greedy royal family so as to take possession of their own country; but why Master Bonaparte should then want to invade other people's countries as well is beyond me, since such a desire is bound to lead him into trouble. Grandpa also says that there is a temporary halt in the sailings of convict ships to New South Wales and Van Diemen's Land because of the war with the French, and the reminder causes me to wonder what happened to our enemies Rice and Watkins who were, we gather, shipped off with assorted other dastardly criminals some eight years ago. Have they learned how to do a good day's work after a lifetime of indolence and corruption? Have they been transformed into good Christian gentlemen, are they healthy or sick – indeed, are they still alive?

Back to more domestic matters. On balance, I am managing to maintain my improved humour, although I have to admit to occasional days of despondence now that little Sara has discovered that she has lungs and has learned how to use them. The poor child suffers from wind more than the other babies did, and I cannot bear it when she is upset. I also find the constant feeding, night and day, more than a little wearing without David by my side to cheer me. Yesterday Bessie and Sian saw that I was only just coping with the baby, and they suggested that I might take a walk on the mountain. I thought this an excellent idea, and off I went.

It was a bright and breezy day with spring warmth in the sun. White and pink cherry blossoms were swirling about in the yard and piling up like snowdrifts behind the walls. I followed the water pipe up towards Ffynnon Brynach, and came upon Shemi and Billy in Parc Glas. They were helping a young ewe with a difficult birth, and were unaware that I was watching them from the other side of the wall. When the job was done, and the lamb was put to the teat, I clapped my hands and shouted 'Bravo! As fine a delivery as I have seen in a long time!'

They looked up, quite startled, and then broke into toothy grins. 'Mistress Martha!' shouted Billy. 'It's good to see you out and about after all this time. I hope you are well. And how is little Sara today?'

'We are both very well, thank you,' I replied. 'Bessie and Sian have thrown me out of the house for the good of the baby, and I did not object. I am rather tired, but strong enough to tackle the mountain, and it is quite wonderful to have the sun on my cheeks and the wind in my hair.'

'Just you take care, Mistress,' shouted Shemi after me. 'Remember that the rocks are wet and slippery with all the rain we have had.'

'I will be very careful, never fear,' I said, and continued on my way.

When I reached the spring I anointed myself with a handful of the sacred water, continuing a little tradition which I had invented shortly after my arrival at the Plas. Then I climbed on, pausing frequently for breath since I had less energy than I had anticipated. I stopped and sat on a big blue rock and looked back over the *cwm*. A wide and wonderful vista had now opened up before me, and the beauty of it took my breath away. I had almost forgotten how magical the slopes of Carningli are at this time of year, with the flattened foxy-red bracken stalks from last autumn now being pushed up and bypassed by the curled green shoots of the summer to come. The broken rocks on the south side of the mountain gleamed and glistened in the sunshine, and the palette of colours was more varied than I had ever noticed before: subtle greens and blues, with flashes of white crystals here and there; greys and purples, and even browns and buffs where little puddles of rainwater have been collecting in rocky hollows. I realized that the rock surfaces were populated by myriad little plants, and when I examined them closely, with my nose almost touching them, I discovered more subtle colours in them than a rainbow and more textures than a patchwork quilt.

Delicate clouds of steam swirled off the warming rocks as the sun rose higher, and patches of mist were evaporating from the soggy fields and woodlands down in the *cwm*. Moisture from here, there and everywhere was sucked up into the air far over my head, stirred and tumbled into great mountains of cloud. I was moved to lie on my back on a patch of dry bracken in order to watch the slow and mysterious transformations in the sky. As I gazed upwards five ravens drifted into my field of vision, and I wondered how our lovely world looked from their vantage point, maybe a thousand feet above the summit of the mountain.

Suddenly I felt free, with space around me and the wide sky above. I took off my bonnet and let the wind blow through my hair, and laughed when I predicted Bessie's response on my return to the house. It seemed that a lifetime had passed since I last breathed cool fresh air into my nostrils, and I was euphoric to be back on this old mountain.

I climbed on, crossing a swath of burnt bracken and gorse and getting soot all over my skirt. I made a note in my mind that I should remind Billy to do the burning somewhere else next year, and then smiled when I realized that that was exactly what he would do anyway, without any prompting from me. Then I was on the summit, with the little town of Newport beneath my feet and the wide azure acres of the bay stretching away northwards to the far horizon. Dark cloud shadows scudded across the water surface. When I turned and looked south the *cwm* was in shadow but the far summits of Mynydd Preseli were bathed in unbroken sunlight, grey and green and gold, looking like the Fields of Elysium. I sat down behind the summit rock so that I was out of the wind, and pulled my knees up to my chin. I stayed there for I know not how long, with my eyes closed, listening to the wind.

When I got back to the house little Sara was fast asleep, but my breasts were aching with the need to feed her. So, cruel thing that I am, I woke her up, settled into my most comfortable chair, and set her to it. 'My goodness, Mistress Martha,' said Bessie. 'Your hair has been blown about something terrible, and you have a wicked glow upon your cheeks. You look as if you have been up to some mischief on the mountain.'

I smiled but said nothing. Indeed I have, I thought. Indeed I have.

12 April 1805

I am still reaping the benefits of my walk upon the mountain. As might be imagined, I have been lavishing all my attention, and giving all of my time, over the week past to my new little *cariad*. I declare that never has a small baby been so greatly loved, so well fed and so dotingly cleaned and bathed. Indeed, I have nursed her with such enthusiasm that Sian has had to remind me more than once that Sara needs her sleep and I need mine. To her, it may well appear that I have become obsessed with my small child, smoothing her cheek and kissing her brow when she might well have been left alone; but surely nobody will blame me for lavishing my love on her in some small compensation for all that I have lost? What other cheek is there to smooth, I wonder in my frequent periods of introspection, and what other brow is there to kiss?

Occasionally I am dragged away from my beloved obsession with a reminder that there are indeed other cheeks to smooth, other tears to dry, other brows to kiss, other tiny hands to hold. They belong, of course, to Betsi, Daisy and Dewi. I was able to give them cause for joy two days since when the two girls had a joint birthday celebration. Betsi's seventh birthday was the 22nd day of March, but that was only three days after baby Sara first saw the light of day, and I was too weak to cope with a crowd of over-excited children rushing about the house. She agreed, sensible child that she is, to postpone her celebrations until Daisy's fourth birthday, which fell on the 10th day of April. The momentous day of the 'double party' was happy enough for the girls and their little brother, although I have to admit that I did not feel quite up to it, and remained in my room for most of the day. In the event my ill humour mattered little, since Grandma took charge of everything, preparing a fine feast of favourite titbits, organizing presents, and arranging for three or four young friends to come up to the Plas for a couple of hours in the afternoon – a proper social occasion. Sian led assorted silly games for the wild hordes, and was by all accounts the life and soul of the party.

It has also been beneficial to concede that outside our back door is a world that demands organization. Some days since, with the weather taking a turn for the better after a spell of blustery winds and heavy showers, we were gathered round the breakfast table when Billy announced: 'Mistress, the cultivating is done. The bottom two fields are ready for the barley. Edwards Trefach is sowing already, and he will have Parc Mawr finished by nightfall.'

I turned to Grandpa and asked for his advice. 'I think it is too soon,' said Grandpa, taking a sip of foaming milk from his mug. 'Billy, my eyes are not good enough to see across the valley. Go and see which horses Edwards is using with the harrow.' Billy went out into the yard and returned a couple of minutes later. 'The big grey gelding and the chestnut mare,' he said.

'Hm. In that case it is too early,' said Grandpa, and that was the end of the discussion.

This morning, at breakfast, Billy reported that Edwards was again at work, this time in the small field by the farm. He asked again whether he should start the sowing. 'Go out into the yard then,' replied Grandpa, 'and see which horses he has this time.' Billy went out and returned to report that on this occasion he could not see the horses for the clouds of dust. 'Excellent!' said Grandpa with a sly smile on his face. 'Today, Billy, you can sow the barley.'

When Billy and Shemi had gobbled down their breakfast and taken their leave I asked Grandpa about his rules for barley-sowing at the Plas. He laughed, and explained that there was an old country saying that one should sow wheat in mud and barley in dust. 'The old farmers were very wise,' he said. 'My father taught me that barley seed needs a fine dry tilth so that it will quickly spring into life. Trefach's fields are north-facing and ours are south-facing and better drained. When there is dust in the air on the other side of the valley we always put in our barley. And just you mark my words –

our harvest will be a good fortnight ahead of theirs, and twenty per cent heavier. Do you fancy a wager against my prediction?'

'No thank you, Grandpa,' said I, smiling. '*My* father taught me never to gamble at the breakfast table.'

24 April 1805

The children and I, accompanied by Bessie and Sian, have been on a Grand Tour, and we have had a wonderful time. We did not get quite as far as Rome and Athens, but we greatly enjoyed Haverfordwest, Solva and Castlebythe. We have been away for ten days, and we have all returned refreshed. I declare that even little Sara has enjoyed herself.

Unknown to me, there was a dastardly conspiracy going on, and I pronounced myself utterly bemused early one morning when my father's coach pulled into the yard. His faithful coachman George was in the driver's seat, and I was delighted to see him. I ran downstairs to greet him and to investigate who the passengers were, but there were none. When I looked at him with a quizzical look on my face he smiled and said, 'Mistress Martha, I have come to fetch you. Are you ready?'

Then Bessie and Sian and the rest of them emerged from the kitchen, and all was revealed. The entire household stood there, with broad smiles from ear to ear. Under strict instructions from my father, said Grandpa, I was to climb into the coach with the children, and with Bessie and Sian, to be whisked away on an adventure. Clothes and food and napkins for little Sara were already organized and packed into bags; and I was greatly impressed by the military operation that had been under way beneath my nose for several days without my being aware of anything out of the ordinary. The girls were privy to the secret, and they screamed with glee when they saw the disbelief upon my face. In truth, they were probably more delighted with the fact that they had succeeded in keeping quiet about our coach trip, when for days past they must have been bursting with the anticipation of the magic that was to come.

So off we went, with cheery waves from Grandpa and Grandma and the servants, rumbling down the track and thence to the Cilgwyn road. The horses stopped for a drink at the Trefelin ford, and while we were there we heard – and saw – the first cuckoo of the season. The children were entranced. Then we were away over the sunlit swelling summits of Mynydd Preseli, beneath a wide blue sky.

We spent two days with Morys and Nansi and their children in the Bethesda manse in Haverfordwest; and then five days in Brawdy at my old family home; and then a final three days with Catrin and James and their children in Castlebythe. Peaceful it was not, but the change of scene was a wonderful tonic for my troubled soul. Sian and Bessie were the best of travelling companions, and they relieved me of all responsibility. Sian attended to the children, and Bessie pampered me and flattered me, ensured I looked like a woman of substance when in the company of others; scolded me when I became over-excited; and packed me off to bed early each night.

In Haverfordwest we explored the multitude of shops in the High Street and other streets. Whilst admiring the fine houses used by the gentry during their winter season, we saw that much building was still going on in spite of the deprivations of the war. We passed quickly along an extremely rough street lined with establishments whose virtue was open to question, and down to the quays where five trading vessels were loading and unloading cargoes of all sorts. Going out were hides and wool, sheepskins and grain, and timber headed for the shipbuilding yards at Lawrenny and Milford, where a great new town is being built. Coming in were silks, fine clothes and furniture destined no doubt for some fine mansion in the neighbourhood, spices, flour and all manner of foodstuffs, pitch and canvas, salt and sugar and tobacco, limestone and coal, wine and brandy. The bustle and the rush were wonderful to behold, with merchants shouting orders and bidding for items of cargo not yet spoken for, and sailors and porters rushing up and down gangplanks with loads upon their backs. Little Dewi was fascinated by the sights, sounds and smells of the shipping basin, and created quite a scene when at last we had to drag him away.

When we were at Brawdy Sara and I stayed in the little room which I had inhabited as a child; how I loved to be back there again, this time with my treasure in her cot beside my bed! We were thoroughly pampered by my dear parents, and Father was insistent that the coach and coachman were entirely at our disposal. So we went out and about whenever we could, on one day to Solva to see the ships, then to see the great cathedral which is currently being renovated at St David's. But the best day of all was spent at a little bay called Penycwm, which David and I had explored when he was recuperating after the Plas Ingli fire. I did not reveal to the others what was in my heart as we sat on the cliffs in the sunshine, surrounded by banks of thrift and sea campion, watching the clouds of seabirds busily coming and going between their feeding grounds out at sea and their precarious nest sites. Foaming waves crashed onto cliffs and stacks and surged in and out of dark deep caves. We ate our picnic on the clifftop and then we went down to the beach. The tide was out, and the children – and Sian and Bessie – ran riot, rushing hither and thither, chasing seagulls, catching crabs in rock pools, and building canals and sand castles decorated with sea shells and pebbles. They became extremely wet and sandy, and were distraught when it was time to return to Brawdy for supper.

Then we travelled on, in the style to which we were now accustomed, to the fine old house of Castlebythe, home to my dear sister Catrin and her husband James. He is a tall and imposing young man with a somewhat severe countenance, but he is very kind, and he threw the house open to us and provided us with meals of such splendour that the memory of them will live with all of us for years to come. They have three small children of their own, and the six little cousins all had a wonderful time together. We could not tempt them away from the house and garden, so when Sara was fast asleep I took the opportunity of taking several long walks among the hills in the company of Catrin. I was able to shed some of my burden in her company, and she was – as in the days of our childhood and youth – a wise and understanding counsellor.

And so we returned to the Plas, restored and refreshed, to find that the estate had survived without us and that the grandparents and the servants had apparently enjoyed their break from the Mistress and her boisterous family. It was wonderful, in retrospect, to renew my links with my own folk, and especially important for the children to get to know their little cousins in Haverfordwest and Castlebythe. But of course we were delighted to be home; this is where we belong, on the sunny side of the old blue mountain, with the green and pleasant *cwm* stretching away beneath us. When I finally leave this place it will be in a wooden box; but even so, I will probably leave my heart and my spirit behind.

26 April 1805

Today I have had a visit from Will Final Testament. He came trotting up the drive in his trap at ten in the morning, having previously arranged the visit with Grandpa. 'Good morning, Mistress Morgan,' said he. 'I am pleased to see you looking well; and I offer my heartiest felicitations on the arrival of your new baby.'

'Thank you, Master Probert,' I replied. 'You are very kind. It is always good to see you. I assume that you have some legal business?'

'Indeed I have. May I sit somewhere quiet and comfortable with you and Master Isaac?'

So the three of us went in to the parlour, leaving instructions that we should not be disturbed. Will took out a bulky document from his bag and put it onto the table in front of us.

'Now then,' he said, speaking rapidly, as attorneys tend to do, and reminding me of a woodpecker attacking an old tree trunk. 'I am sorry to trouble you with this so soon after the death of dear Master David, but it has to be done. You knew, I presume, that David made out a will shortly before he died?'

I must admit that I had never thought of such a thing, and before I had a chance to reply he continued, 'No? Well, never mind. He came to me in January, having spoken to Master Isaac here, and asked me to help him in sorting out his affairs, for peace of mind should anything untoward happen to him.'

My heart missed a beat. 'Do you mean,' I asked, 'that

he had some sense that he might have an accident? He certainly never said anything to me, and we had no secrets from one another.'

'My dear Mistress Morgan, I have no idea. I assumed that he was simply being prudent, as any good squire should be.'

And then, continuing at breakneck speed, with digressions strictly off the agenda, he opened up the document on the table. 'Here it is. It was signed by Master David and by two witnesses, Squire Bowen of Llwyngwair and Squire Edwards of Llwyngoras, on 31 January 1805, in my presence. It is duly confirmed and legal. I suggest that I keep it in my safe in case of accident or loss, but I have with me a copy which you should keep. Much of the will consists of a listing of properties, goods and chattels, animals and crops, and there is also a list of those who owe the estate money, but may I read you the critical part of the document?'

I swallowed hard, and said, 'Yes please, Master Probert. I think I am strong enough to cope with whatever it may contain.'

So he read it out, and this is what it said:

This is the last Will and Testament of David John Morgan Esquire, of Plas Ingli in the parish of Newport and the county of Pembroke, made this thirty-first day of January in the Year of our Lord one thousand eight hundred and five.

I appoint my wife Martha Morgan as sole executrix.

Upon my death I give absolutely and with no further condition all of my worldly possessions to my lawful wife Martha Morgan, whom I love more than anything in this world . . .

At this point Will broke into his reading and said, 'Most unsuitable language that, for a legal document, and indeed I said so to Master David, but he was quite insistent upon it, so there it is.'

. . . if she shall survive me by two calendar months, and until any son of mine, Dewi or any still to be born, shall first reach the age of twenty-one.

I pass to my said wife Martha Morgan all tenanted farms of the estate, all goods, chattels, furniture and furnishings of Plas Ingli, all debtors' notes, mortgage agreements, certificates and shares and monies as may be held by other persons and in other places, as identified below.

'There is a long list here, which I have checked and which seems to be in order. You can look at this at your leisure, Martha. Shall I pass over it and continue with the essential text?'

'Please do, Master Probert.'

I authorize her without restraint upon my death to call in or realize any assets as may be identified above or in other agreements signed by me.

I further pass to my wife Martha Morgan all inventories, listings and papers relating to the estates and farms abovementioned, whether they refer to land, properties, possessions or monies owed.

In the event that no son of mine shall reach the age of twenty-one, I give to my wife Martha Morgan all of the above mentioned assets to dispose of as she will, with the only proviso that she should consider charitably the interests of my Grandfather Isaac Morgan, my Grandmother Jane Morgan, and past and present servants of Plas Ingli according to their service and loyalty.

I instruct that my daughters Betsi, Daisy and any still to be born, shall, in the event of marriage, be given such settlement as shall be helpful for their prospects without endangering the

well-being and integrity of the Plas Ingli estate.
Signed, David John Morgan Esq
in the presence of
John William Bowen Esq and Jenkin Thomas Edwards Esq
    31 January 1805

When he had finished reading all this out to Grandpa
and me, Will looked up over the top of his spectacles and
said, 'Now then, Mistress Martha, is that all perfectly
clear?'

I am untutored in legal matters, and so I said, 'I think
I grasped some of it, Master Probert, but I should
appreciate some explanation, if you will be so kind.'

'What this means,' said Will, 'is that we now have an
arrangement which is most unusual, and indeed in my
experience quite exceptional. I do not know of another
estate in west Wales which is actually owned and
managed by a woman; most wealthy heiresses go off
and get married, and their estates are then automatically
passed to their husbands. But you, Mistress Martha, are
now the owner of this estate, in effect to hold it in trust
until little Dewi reaches the age of twenty-one. Do you
fully understand the import of this?'

I nodded, and he pressed on. 'If Dewi does not survive
to that age, you may do with the estate what you will.
Indeed, it seems to me that while he is growing up you
can be as foolish or as wise as you wish in managing the
affairs of the Plas, for in the wording there are no specific
restrictions on your behaviour. I mentioned this to
Master David, but he would not have anything changed.
He said to me that he had total confidence in your
wisdom and ability to act kindly in the interests of the
family in all matters. So there we are. Do you have any
questions?'

I buried my head in my hands. 'Does this mean that I

must now pay the servants, and collect the rents, and sell our animals and our crops, and collect debts and such like things?'

'I am afraid that is exactly what you must do,' said Will. 'But don't you worry just now. You have enough on your plate at present, with a recent bereavement and a small baby to cope with. Master Isaac has helped David with all of these things over the past few years, and I am sure he will be only too happy to help you now. In due course, I would recommend the appointment of a steward to look after the estate for you. I believe you can afford it, and a good steward will bring in far more money than is needed to pay his wages.'

For the first time, Grandpa Isaac spoke. 'Thank you, Will. You have been very kind. I had a fair idea what was in the document, because David discussed it with me some months ago. I share his absolute confidence that Martha will be a wise and trustworthy guardian of the estate, and will make it prosper.' Then he turned to me and took my hands in his, and looked me in the eye. 'And as for you, my dear young lady, I will stand at your side for as long as I have the strength. I give you my word.'

At this point the emotion of the occasion got the better of me, and I dissolved in tears. Grandpa took me in his arms and comforted me while Master Probert looked away in embarrassment. I regained my composure after a few minutes, and was able to wipe away my tears and say, 'Thank you so much, Master Probert, for your generous assistance and sound advice. I hope I can justify the faith which my dear husband had in my abilities.'

'Now then, Will,' said Grandpa Isaac, becoming practical. 'In the matter of the fee and your expenses . . . ?'

'Pray do not concern yourself with that now, Isaac,' said Will, rising to his feet. 'My clerk will prepare a bill in due course.' He winked at me and said, 'The Mistress can settle up next time she comes into town on estate business!' Then he bowed deeply, and took his leave.

This afternoon, between baby feeding times, I managed to have a long talk with Grandpa, and he explained to me some of the things that are involved in the running of an estate. I fear that I have not paid enough attention to what has been going on since my arrival at the Plas, and that I have a great deal to learn. But he also told me that I must not fret about any business matters for at least six months, for there were no debts to be repaid, and no major decisions requiring careful thought. Indeed, he implied that the estate more or less runs itself. Oh, if only that were so . . .

27 April 1805

I have not time to write much this evening. Little Sara, who is fast asleep at my side in her rocking cradle, will soon wake up and demand to be fed. Today I have gone through the motions of being a good mother to Sara and the other three beloved children, and I trust I have been civil and considerate to the others who dwell beneath our roof; but throughout the day a terrible fear has been building within me, replacing the weariness which I felt yesterday after the reading of the will.

I have been quite unable to get out of my mind one small thing which Will Final Testament said. David had asked him for help in sorting out his affairs in case 'anything untoward' should happen to him. Why should David have said such a thing? Will passed it off by praising David's prudence, and yet . . . I am discomfited.

This afternoon I found Grandpa out in the garden, and asked if I might sit with him for a few minutes. I asked him directly whether David had expressed any concerns about the future. Did he have any illness that I was unaware of? Had some gypsy or witch given him a warning of impending doom? Had he heard of the *tolaeth* and the *toili* and taken them to heart, in spite of his bluff dismissals of such phenomena as the wild fantasies of non-believers?

'No no,' said Grandpa, putting his arm round my shoulder. 'To my knowledge David was not ill, and nor was he making any link between strange omens and portents and his own mortality. But we did discuss, on a number of occasions, the fact that there are still people in this area who do not necessarily wish us well, and who might even go so far as to harm one of us. We all remember only too well the appalling events which occurred shortly after your arrival at the Plas. On that occasion the Rice, Watkins and Howell families were at the root of the evil that was done to us, and we must thank God that they were all brought to justice. Moses Lloyd was another who sought to harm us until he disappeared. The Lord only knows where he is now. He may still be intent upon returning to this area, bent upon vengeance for some wickedness which he thinks we did to him.'

I knew full well that Moses Lloyd would never trouble us again, but it would not do to say that to dear Grandpa Isaac. So I said, 'Who are these people, Grandpa? Do you think that they tried to harm David?'

'I have an idea who they are, for I listen to what is going on in the taverns of Newport and Parrog. There are certain individuals who did not attend either the wake or the funeral, and these same people have tried, in one way or another while you have been preoccupied with raising your family, to cause us financial difficulty

112

and undermine our status. I will not put it any more strongly than that. I do not, in all honesty, think they ever tried to harm David. Neither will I say, for the moment, who they are. But I have my beady eye on them, never fear. And so has our old friend Joseph Harries.'

I was reassured by Grandpa's words at first, but as dusk has turned to darkness my fears have increased, and Master Probert's words have gone round and round in my head. Could it be, Heaven forbid, that what happened down on Berry Sands on Shrove Tuesday was not simply a dreadful accident?

30 April 1805

My old friend Joseph Harries has been to see me. I saw him coming up the lane on his white horse but the instant I saw his face I knew that this was not a convivial social visit, for he had a knotted brow and his eyes had pain in them. As Shemi took his horse round to the yard I met him on the kitchen doorstep.

'Good afternoon, Martha,' said he, without his usual warmth.

'Good day, Joseph. It is kind of you to call, and I am, as ever, very pleased to see you.' I tried to smile, without great success.

'I came on the off chance that you can find a small interval in your maternal duties in order that we might have a few words.'

'By all means. Sara has just had her afternoon feed, and Sian can take care of her for the next hour, I am sure. Shall we go into the parlour?'

So in we went. I told Joseph that Will Final Testament had been to read the will. Joseph nodded. He looked nervous and distracted, and finally he swallowed hard and said: 'I am not very clever in understanding the ways of women, and I know that it is still less than three months since David died. But I cannot delay any longer. I have to tell you something very serious, for if I do not, we may all be overtaken by events for which we are ill prepared.'

The blood ran cold in my veins, but in truth I knew already what my blessed friend was about to reveal. 'Continue, Joseph,' I said.

'I have to tell you, Martha, that David did not die in an accident on Shrove Tuesday. I am utterly convinced that he was murdered, and I think I know who his killers are.'

There followed a very long silence. I stared at Joseph with wide eyes, and I felt the colour draining out of my face. I did not cry. He, dear kind friend that he is, probably thought that I was about to faint, so he came and sat next to me and put his arm round my shoulder. 'You are shaking, Martha,' he said. 'I am not surprised.' He went to the sideboard, took a crystal glass, and poured a large quantity of best duty-free brandy into it. I took it in my unsteady hand, and poured some of the potent liquid straight down my throat. It gave me a jolt, but it did not make me feel any better.

Then there was another long silence. At last I whispered, 'Oh, Joseph! Is this supposed to bring me consolation? Is it better to know that the one you love has been snatched away by a tragic accident, or that he died in fear and fury at the hands of others?'

'I suspect that the former was most likely to have helped in the healing process,' he replied, looking into my wild eyes. 'But you would have found out sooner or later.'

'I know, I know. In fact my intuition had already told

114

me that some dark deed was done to David during the *cnapan* game. My mind was coming to the same conclusion as my instinct, for in recent days I have found myself wondering why an experienced horseman such as he, who knew every inch of Berry Sands and was master of every subtlety of the game, riding a calm and sturdy horse, should have fallen off and lost consciousness out of the sight of others.'

Joseph nodded. 'This was my concern right from the beginning,' he said. Then he looked at me very intently, as if trying to assess my state of mind while working out in his own head what he should do next. At last he continued. 'Are you strong enough to hear more, or shall I come back another day?'

I gave a weak smile and said, 'My dear Joseph, do you not know anything about a woman's heart? Do you think that if you go away now, I will go to bed and surrender to a few hours of sweet dreams? For better or for worse, you had better carry on until I know everything.'

'I suppose you are right. But have another drink of brandy first.' I obeyed, and at last he embarked upon his appalling narrative.

'I was at the *cnapan* game myself,' he said, 'along with almost everybody else in town. There were stalls and booths at the Parrog end of the beach, and by the sand dunes on the other side. Even before the game started the Black Lobster and the Sloop had almost run out of ale. A great deal of good money was put down on a Newport win, but I heard that some considerable sums were wagered on a Nevern victory at long odds – so significant, in fact, that most of the betting men refused to take the money on offer. I saw David, Shemi and Billy before the game – they were as cheerful as ever, and after a meeting with the footmen and the riders on the

Newport side they were confident that they had some cunning moves worked out. It was a calm day with a very low tide. There were maybe four hundred players on each side.

'As soon as the Mayor cast up the *cnapan* to start the contest a splendid game developed. I saw David several times, very prominent in the play. After about an hour the game went off into the distance towards the Nevern goal, and I saw that the fore-runners had cleared a path through the opposition forces, allowing the gamesmen to carry the *cnapan* forward in the middle of a great throng. I judged that the Newport scouts and riders were ready to take the *cnapan* on, around the flank of the throng, possibly using David on the seaward side or Billy on the landward side, and anticipated that the game would soon be won. The play was at least half a mile away from where I was standing. Then, in an instant, a thick bank of fog rolled in from the sea and all of the watchers lost sight of the action.'

'I was told of the fog,' I said. 'But I had not realized that Newport was so close to victory at the time.'

'Yes indeed. After that, we heard lots of noise away in the middle of the fog, with mighty shoutings and cheerings, but we assumed that the game would have to be abandoned since the players could probably not see each other, let alone the *cnapan*. Then after about thirty minutes I saw Matthew Lloyd from Cwmgloyn riding out of the fog and galloping towards the river, where of course the Newport goal was placed. He was holding the *cnapan* in his hand, above his head, as he spurred his horse on. He did not reach the goal, because there were several defending horsemen around the post, and they managed to ride him into the river and delay his progress. The retreating foot players caught up and defended the post, and I lost sight of the *cnapan* in the

116

chaos which ensued. Then a shout came out of the gloom: "Stop the game! Stop the game! *Heddwch!* There has been an accident!" The shout was passed on, and as they became aware of the message all the players stopped their brawling and their running and stood still and silent. A strange quiet came over the whole throng – players, spectators, gambling men, stallholders and even small children who knew not what was going on. The Mayor immediately declared the game abandoned.'

At this stage in Joseph's narrative I fear that I could contain myself no longer, for I knew what was to come. Seeing the tears rolling down my cheeks he hesitated, but I whispered, 'Go on, Joseph. Go on. I have to hear the rest of it.'

He sat next to me and held my hands in his. 'Then I saw a riderless horse emerge from the mist. I could hardly believe my eyes, for it was David's mount. With its strange colouring and its white stripe from nostril to left ear, I would have recognized it anywhere. Then, almost immediately, someone shouted: "It's Master Morgan Plas Ingli! Fetch a plank to carry him on!" There was a great commotion, with men coming and going across the river on foot, and some of the squires who had been playing in the game riding back to find the scene of the accident. Some, including myself, crossed the river in Mistress Wilson's ferry boat, and ran across the beach. We were all far too late, of course, and soon we met a group of men coming the other way. They were carrying David on a plank, and he was dead. Martha, there was a stunned silence all around me. I saw grown men in tears, and heard many of them express their deep affection for David and their disbelief at what had happened to him.'

Joseph looked at me with a look of great tenderness, and continued: 'You know, my dearest Martha, how much I loved him too. He was a precious friend to me,

117

and after everybody else had drifted away I sat by the big lime kiln on the Parrog, overcome by the stark realization that he would never again illuminate your life, or mine, or the lives of many others.'

I swallowed hard, and said: 'Thank you. But what led you to the belief that David's death was not an accident?'

'It took me a little while to realize that the simplest explanation of David's death – that it was a tragic accident – was not necessarily the correct one. Suddenly I had a multitude of questions to ask of other *cnapan* players, and I knew that if I did not ask them immediately it would be too late, as this group of men would not be gathered together again until next year's *cnapan* contest. So in spite of my own grief I spent several hours on the evening of Shrove Tuesday in the inns of Newport. I spoke to as many players as I could find, and pieced together a story that was consistent. The last time David was seen by anybody he was riding fast away from a large congregation of foot-players with four other horsemen in hot pursuit. He was galloping along at the water's edge, and some men think he had the *cnapan* in his possession. The horsemen disappeared into the fog somewhere near the Nevern goal. There was lots of noise going on, and there were several fistfights in progress, as one would expect. Many of the foot-players, and some of the gentry on their horses, were looking for the *cnapan*. Billy tells me that as part of a planned move, while David went along the water's edge with the *cnapan*, he pretended that he had it in his pocket, and led the great bulk of the players away from the sea and towards the sand dunes. That was the last time he saw David alive.

'At last somebody shouted, "Lloyd has got it, and he is headed for Parrog!" Men were milling about everywhere in the fog, but eventually they found the water's edge and ran along it, the Nevern men to support the *cnapan*'s progress and the Newport men intent upon defence. The only men who stayed behind near the Nevern goal were those detailed for defensive duties. For a moment the fog cleared, and one of them noticed a body at the water's edge. He shouted to his confederates, and they all rushed over to investigate. Of course it was David. The small waves were washing over him, and he was quite dead. They thought he might have been in the water for some minutes. They shouted for help, and you know the rest.'

'How is this significant?' I asked, just about in control of my emotions. 'There is still nothing in this tale to indicate that a crime was committed.'

'That is true, Martha, but my inquiries were leading me towards a hypothesis, and the more questions I asked, the stronger my hypothesis became. I delved into the identities of the four horsemen who pursued David. One of them, I became certain, was Matthew Lloyd of Cwmgloyn, who has always played upon the Nevern side. His brother Moses caused the Morgan family considerable trouble some years ago, as I am sure you will recall. Master Matthew, after all, was the one who emerged from the fog with the *cnapan* held aloft.'

At this point my body tensed, and Joseph felt it. But he pressed on. 'But who were the others? I talked to as many of the Nevern gentry as I could find, and ascertained that the three men who rode with Matthew throughout the game were Joseph Rice of Pentre Ifan, John Howell of Henllys, and Ifan Beynon of Berry Hill. Names to raise alarm, Martha, as I am sure you will agree. And interestingly enough, not one of the four was to be found in the inns of Newport on the evening of David's death.'

Now my mind was racing as I made connections which became more appalling by the minute. After seven years in the area I knew a modest amount about all the local gentry families, particularly those with criminal tendencies, and I possessed a very thorough knowledge of certain families which had in the past had designs upon the Plas Ingli estate. Joseph Rice was the dissolute son of John Rice, who did me great harm some years ago and was transported to the colonies for his pains. I was aware that the fellow was now struggling to make a living as a merchant following the disposal of his father's estate. John Howell's father, Squire George Howell of Henllys, took his own life following the failure of his attempt to get me convicted for a crime I did not commit. The Henllys estate also collapsed and was sold, leaving John in desperate straits and causing him eventually to seek and find a commission in the army. I was surprised to hear that he was back in the area rather than away fighting the French. Ifan Beynon is a bully and petty criminal who was once Clerk to the local justices. He was also involved in the doomed conspiracy to take over our estate, and I had heard that after his conviction he had served some years of hard labour in Portsmouth before returning to Berry Hill. Matthew Lloyd was regarded as a mean, vindictive fellow, now living in a cottage on the family estate at Cwmgloyn. It perturbed me that he might still be interested in perpetuating the ancient and silly feud between the Lloyds of Cwmgloyn and the Morgans of Plas Ingli.

While these thoughts were going through my mind Joseph squeezed my hands and continued. 'I then checked with the betting men to see who had tried to place large wagers on a Nevern victory in the *cnapan* game. The names of Rice and Howell came up again and again. This did not surprise me; they both have long histories on the gaming tables of Tenby and Haverfordwest. Rice has lately been on a winning streak, probably because he has found some new way of cheating. Matthew Lloyd and Ifan Beynon have no money to gamble with, but they make convenient accomplices. On further talking to the landlord of the Black Lion I discovered that the four of them, unlikely as it may seem, were frequent drinking companions there in the three weeks before the Shrove Tuesday *cnapan* contest.'

'But Joseph, none of this may mean anything! You are talking about speculations and conjectures, and there is nothing in what you say which could lead us to enter a complaint about the behaviour of those four men, or to ask the constables to take them in.'

'The constables!' huffed Joseph. 'Masters Wilson, Potts and Evans! They would not be quick enough to capture a dead chicken, even if they were inclined to try. All they want, like the rest of the constables in this area, is to be left in peace, so that they can pass the job over quietly to somebody else at the end of their year in office. Now I needed evidence. Are you feeling strong enough to hear more?'

I felt the warmth of his hands on mine, and this helped me to cope with my apprehension. 'Yes, I think so. Please carry on.'

'At dawn the next morning I knocked on Davy Death's front door. As the local coffin maker he has open access to the mortuary. He owes me a few favours, and he lent the key to me for half an hour. Distressing as I knew it would be, I had to examine David's body. I will spare you the details, my dear Martha, but three important facts came to light. First, his hands were covered with goose grease. The only people who get goose grease on their hands in a *cnapan* game are those who actually handle the *cnapan* ball. It is, as you may know, made of box-wood, boiled in tallow and then covered with goose grease at the start of the game to make it slippery and

121

difficult to hold. He was probably holding the *cnapan* shortly before his death. Second, there is the matter of the blow which rendered him unconscious. You have heard, I dare say, the report which Havard Medical made out for the inquest as to the cause of death?'

'Yes, Grandpa told me about it, and I believe we have a copy somewhere in the house.'

'Havard is a fool, and he drinks too much. The only thing that he got right was that the cause of death was drowning. He said that the bump on David's forehead was caused by falling off his horse and hitting his head on the sand. Quite impossible. The sand is very soft at the Nevern end of the beach, and even if David had fallen very hard he would not have had an open wound at the point of contact. If Havard Medical had looked properly under his long hair he would have seen not one but several open wounds and severe bruising on his head. He certainly bled quite profusely, although when his body was found the sea water had washed most of the blood away. But there were traces of blood on his collar, which Havard missed. Again, if the doctor had looked under David's shirt he would have found massive bruising caused, I am sure, by a welter of blows from heavy boots. These blows could not have been inflicted on a man who was astride a horse.'

Seeing that I was sitting in a sort of trance, Joseph paused and encouraged me to take another sip of brandy. 'I am sorry, my dear, but this is all very distressing, even for me,' he said very quietly, before continuing.

'Finally, several of David's fingernails were broken, and under others I found traces of debris, including human hair. I took some of the hairs away and examined them under my magnifying glass: some were black, some were blond, and others were a sort of mousy brown colour. My conclusions, Martha, from the cursory

122

examination I was able to undertake, were that David was viciously assaulted – possibly in order to wrest the *cnapan* from his grasp, or perhaps from some darker and premeditated motive – by more than one person; that he was attacked from behind and beaten about the head, probably with clubs or other heavy weapons; that he was forced off his horse and continued to fight his assailants at the water's edge until he was finally kicked senseless; and that he was then held under the water until he drowned.'

By now I was in a state of numbed disbelief. Joseph put his arm round my shoulder and prepared to complete his story.

'I returned the key of the mortuary to Davy just in time,' he said, 'for as I was riding up the hill to Newport I passed Doctor Havard riding down. But I was not quite finished with this miserable business. I decided to make a few Ash Wednesday social calls. First I visited Ifan Beynon at Berry Hill, and then I went on to Joseph Rice's lodging house, where I happened to find John Howell as well, and finally I rode out to Cwmgloyn to visit Matthew Lloyd. As luck would have it I saw all four; since they are all in reduced circumstances none of them enjoys the luxury of protection by servants. All of them had facial injuries, mostly scratches and bruises, and Ifan Beynon had his arm strapped up. I thought I might as well try the direct approach. I told each of them that I was aware of their involvement in the *cnapan* play on the previous day, and told them that I was making some investigations relating to the death of David Morgan. Had they perhaps seen or heard anything which might be of assistance to me? Now I have had some experience, Martha, in looking for guilt in people's faces, and I have to tell you that I saw it writ large in the faces of all four. Each of them flushed to a bright red, and each of them

123

became very aggressive with me. They denied any knowledge of David's "accident" and said they had been nowhere near David at any stage of the game; I already knew this to be a lie, since I had the testimony of others fixed in my head. They did not lay hands upon me, but I have to say that my interviews with them were short and unpleasant.'

'That is hardly surprising in the circumstances. But did you not ask Matthew Lloyd how he came to have possession of the *cnapan* at the end of the game?'

'Indeed I did. He claimed that he got it from another rider whom he did not know, and never saw David, and who is there to contradict his version of events? Billy has also asked him about this, and has received the same reply.'

'So we are no further forward?'

'Not on that particular matter. But later on Ash Wednesday one of my young spies informed me that Rice and Howell had left their lodgings and walked through town to the Black Lion. While the coast was clear I took the opportunity of having a few words with the lady of the house, one Mistress Billings, and found – as I had expected – that the two conspirators had returned to their lodgings directly after the *cnapan* game, soaked to the skin and in a highly agitated state. I am still making inquiries relating to Lloyd and Beynon.'

'Joseph, why are you telling me all of this now? Could it not have waited?'

'In answer to both your questions, I am now convinced that these four men suspect I have guessed the truth. That means that I may be in danger. They are not pleasant people, any of them, and I fear that you and your dear family may also be in some peril. I have written everything down, but who knows what will happen to me and my notebooks? I know that you used to record the turbulent events of your young life in your diary and that you have an almost infallible memory for conversations and small details; will you be so kind as to open that journal again and record what I have told you?'

'As good as done, Joseph,' I replied. 'I will certainly write down your findings. I have been keeping my diary quite faithfully over these last few months.'

'Well done. I am glad to hear it.'

Then he paused and breathed deeply for what seemed a very long time. He was relieved, I dare say, to have lightened his burden. Then he continued: 'You have taken this news well, Martha, and I am proud of you. You are a very brave and resilient young woman. Now I think we should all try to collect ourselves. I have shared my knowledge of this terrible affair with you, and I will also tell Grandpa Isaac. We shall support one another, and there will be three of us to keep an eye on any moves which the four gentlemen in question may choose to make. I doubt anything will happen in the very near future; Masters Lloyd, Beynon and Rice will wish to lie low, and John Howell has, I gather, recently returned to his regiment.'

That, at least, gave me some consolation. But one thing was nagging at me, and I had to ask Joseph about it. 'Dear Joseph,' I said, 'if you were convinced, right from the beginning, that David was murdered, why did you not ask the justices to make out an indictment against the conspirators and have them arrested?'

'I thought of doing that, Martha, but at first I had nothing to connect Lloyd and the others to the scene of the crime. By the time I had completed my inquiries the inquest had been held and a verdict of accidental death had been recorded. If I had then produced my evidence it would have made the Coroner, the jury and Havard

Medical all look foolish, and they would have closed ranks against me. Then Davy Death would have got into trouble, for he should not have allowed me access to the mortuary. Once David's body was back at the Plas, I felt it would have done more harm than good to make accusations against the conspirators, since that would have involved fresh examinations of the body, a delay to the funeral, and even greater distress for you personally. You had quite enough to deal with as it was. If I had raised the matter after the funeral, it would have been necessary to ask the magistrates for an exhumation order, and that would have been a terrible business for you and everybody else. No, my dear Martha – I judged that it would be better to bide my time, and I still think that was the right judgement.'

I nodded and swallowed hard, and all I could do by way of reply was to give Joseph a weak smile.

Then he took his arm away from my shoulder, and stood up. 'I have taken up too much of your time, dear Martha,' he said, bowing deeply, 'and I am aware that it is not seemly for an old man like me to be sitting here in private with a recently bereaved young lady despite our friendship. Don't get up. I will see myself out. Just you take care, and if I discover anything new, rest assured that you will be the first to know.'

Now he is gone, and a sunny April afternoon has given way to a black, black night. For a little while, in a strange and forbidden way, I have gained some solace from the touch of Joseph's hands. 'Old man' indeed! He is really not that much older than me, and at least he knows instinctively how much I need human contact at present. Most of my friends and acquaintances, confronted by my bereavement, know not what to say, or where to look, let alone how to give me the warmth which I crave.

I know that there are abundant blessings in my life, and that my four children are the most beautiful and important of them all, but what am I to do with the fearsome knowledge which is now in my possession? I am absolutely convinced of the truth of Joseph's story and the common sense of his conclusions. But oh, how I wish that I had not heard anything of what he said!

I am tonight more miserable than ever, exhausted by grief, and lack of sleep, and the huge weight of responsibility I carry as the Mistress of this estate. Could not some small part of this burden have been placed upon shoulders broader than mine? And, dear God, I now have to come to terms with the fact that my beloved David was murdered in cold blood, and that his enemies – my enemies – are still free men who may be plotting even now to do some further wickedness to me and those whom I love.

Summer at Last

29 May 1805

May has come and almost gone. It is a month since I last picked up my quill, opened my book and committed my thoughts to paper. I have missed the most beautiful month of the year, when the mountain is radiant with sunshine and fresh growth and the hedgerows are ablaze with flowers. I have been confined to my room, suffering from a period of melancholia darker, more prolonged and more intense than I could ever have imagined. It was even worse than the black despair which overtook me following the loss of my first baby soon after my arrival at the Plas. I know not what triggered it, but I dare say it was an accumulation of things, each one disturbing and burdensome in itself and becoming quite unbearable when added together. It is some small consolation to know, from Grandma Jane and Mrs Owen, that such dispiritedness sometimes afflicts women who have recently given birth, and Grandma says that she was in such despair following the birth of her daughter Betty that at one stage she almost took her own life.

I cannot begin to describe the agonies that were in my mind from the night following my last entry. As day followed day I plunged deeper and deeper into despondence. I could not cope with the noisy and – as I thought – wild and undisciplined behaviour of the children. I am sure that I was uncivil in my behaviour towards the servants and towards Grandma Jane and Grandpa Isaac, and this is a source of the greatest regret to me since they all remained through these dark weeks as gentle and solicitous as ever. Grandpa knew something of the source of my distress, but there was little he could do. On more than one occasion I reduced poor Bessie to tears, and I am sure that in the middle of the month she thought of leaving us.

Sian has found it very difficult to cope with the children; I fear that I have given them virtually no attention and no love, and I have responded to their innocent and simple attempts to bring me out of myself with scoldings and petulance. I have behaved like a spoiled brat while they, poor things, have had to put up with me as best they could. On several nights in succession Daisy, who could not sleep and could not explain why, tried to creep into my bed for consolation. All she got from me was sharp words, even when she was screaming with distress, and Sian had to rescue the poor child each night and take her into her own bed. On another occasion Dewi would not let me be. In a moment of madness I struck out at him, and although he was not hurt he wept a flood of tears. I fear that for two weeks or more I was totally unaware of the extent to which the children were feeling the loss of their father – the one who gave them fun, security and endless love. Even though I am better now, I am dreadfully concerned about Daisy; through my neglect and lack of understanding she has closed in upon herself, and has stopped playing with her big sister and little brother. She is only four years old, but the joy of childhood has gone out of her. I pray to God that I can find the mental and physical resources which I need to help her, and that there is enough love left in my battered heart to give to her and the others.

The one small mercy in all of this is that somehow I have managed to maintain my milk supply and my feeding of little Sara. She has come through her phase of wind and wakefulness, and has been a blessed light in my life when I have been surrounded by darkness.

For almost four weeks I have been through a daily routine of closing the curtains in my room every time Bessie opened them, of declining all invitations to go out, and even rebuffing the entreaties of my family to go downstairs and join them at mealtimes. Under protest dearest Bessie has been bringing my meals to me in my room, although in truth there was no physical reason why I should not have gone downstairs. My heart and my head seem to have been empty of emotion, without interest in the welfare of others, and indeed devoid even of concern for my own welfare. I do not remember it, but Bessie now tells me that for some days I refused to get out of bed or to eat; and that she had finally to accuse me of endangering the life of little Sara before I came to my senses.

My birthday came and went, and I ignored all pleas from Grandma Jane to enjoy even a little celebration. All that I remember about it is the receipt of various posies of spring flowers, and greetings cards from Owain Laugharne and my dear friend Joseph. Instead of being delighted and flattered, I became even more miserable because many others had apparently forgotten me.

Now, thank God, I am feeling much stronger again, after a week of slowly moving from darkness to light. Several things have happened which have helped to pull me back from the edge of insanity. First, on Friday of last week, Grandma Jane decided that I needed a good talking to. She chose her moment well, and sat with me in the cool shade of the garden as the sun soared over Foel Eryr. Somehow or other, without using words that might upset me, she reminded me that my self-loathing and obsession with my own grief had gone on for long enough, and that she was personally exhausted by it. She made it clear that she had had quite enough of my constant moaning and complaining, of my neglect of the children and myself, and of my lack of appreciation of the love that others were showing me.

'My dear child,' she said, holding my hands in hers and looking me straight in the eye, 'we all feel that we have lost you, and that you have lost yourself. Whatever happened to the tender, good-humoured, and sparkling Martha that we all loved so much? Whatever happened to your passion for life, to your laughter and your music? Do you really think that you are the only person in this household to have struggled with grief? Have you forgotten what I have been through, and Bessie, and Blodwen? I know you think that your pain has been greater than anyone else's, but let me assure you, Martha *bach*, that we have all explored the same landscape of despair.'

Hard, hard words. I blushed, for I knew she was right, and that this was a message from all those who love me. She smiled, and said nothing more. We stood up, and I gave her a long embrace. 'Thank you, Grandma,' I whispered into her white hair. 'Thank you so much. Of course I know what you have suffered too, not least through the loss of David. But I have never acknowledged it to you properly, and for that I am truly sorry. Please forgive me. I promise that I will abandon this self-obsession and try to give my love again to all of you who so richly deserve it.' We did not weep, but we walked back to the house holding hands like two little girls.

Subsequently, in pursuit of my promise to Grandma Jane, I have renewed my communion with the rest of the human race, and I am trying hard to make amends to those who dwell beneath this roof for the misery which I have recently heaped upon them. Monday was a day ordained by Heaven, for I went outside into the cowslip meadow and rediscovered a world of wonder in birdsong and in the colour and smell of the spring flowers. I even laughed and cried with joy when Dewi gave me a long speech, like many others he has given me in the past, and I realized that he was using real words which I could recognize. I am ashamed to say that during the last month he has learned to speak without my being at all aware of this milestone in his little life.

Then, on Tuesday, I took a walk upon my beloved mountain with Betsi. As we climbed towards the spring I pointed out to her the nesting places of skylarks and sparrows and blackbirds, and showed her that of my ancient friends the ravens. One of them was sitting on eggs while the other wheeled overhead, keeping watch for dangerous intruders but, as usual, quite unconcerned at my presence. There was no sign of the three young fledglings from last year's brood, and I explained to Betsi that they had probably been sent packing by their parents now that the latter would shortly have a new family to concentrate upon. We lay on our backs in the fresh grass. We watched swallows swooping and listened to skylarks carolling. We picked posies of red campions and buttercups and bluebells and daisies, and played a game of closing our eyes and guessing which scent was which. My little treasure chatted endlessly and breathlessly: 'Oh, Mam! Look! A pretty butterfly with blue wings and little patterns on them! Oh, look at this!

There are ants everywhere, thousands and thousands and thousands of them, scurrying in and out of this little hole in the ground. Quick, Mam! Come over here – a brown mouse with a funny tail just went and hid behind that rock!' and so on and so on. We climbed right to the summit among the tumbled boulders. Betsi was as sure-footed as a little goat, and helped me up over the most difficult sections as if I were a battered old crone suffering from rheumatism. In truth, I was appalled at my own poor condition and determined that a great deal more climbing was required if I was to get back to my old self. We sat on the summit in the warm May breeze and drank in the beauty of the world, and with Betsi beside me I saw the world again through the wide eyes of a child as a place of infinite wonder.

Then I had a visit from Mary Jane and Ellie. They had clearly co-operated with somebody in the matter (probably Grandma Jane) and had agreed a time of arrival, so that the traps from Trecwn and Llwyngwair drew up simultaneously. They stepped down onto the gravel of the yard in perfect harmony, looking as beautiful and elegant as ever, like two ladies straight out of a ball in a grand London mansion. How lovely it was to see them – Mary Jane tall, dark-haired and dark-eyed, with her sparkling wit and vivacious manner, and Ellie as calm and cultured and elegant as ever. They came, I believe, to remind me that I am a woman, and to reawaken my sense of responsibility to myself, my family and my servants. They of course also know that I am now formally Mistress of Plas Ingli, and it was certainly a part of their purpose to ensure that I do not forget what this entails in terms of etiquette and diplomacy. None of these objects was discussed openly, of course, but we took tea in my little garden beside the orchard and talked, quite literally, until the cows came home for the evening milking. I was able to talk frankly to them about my self-absorption in recent months. They listened and commented gently, but never sought to preach or advise, and somehow they lifted my spirits by telling me what else has been going on in the world since Shrove Tuesday. It was a salutary thing to discover that other families have suffered bereavement, and hardship, and joy, without my noticing, while I have been turned in upon myself. I felt ashamed that messages of condolence and congratulation which should have gone to others have not been sent, and I resolved to put matters right immediately. Goodness knows what piles of correspondence await my attention; I know that Grandpa has dealt with most things over the past months, but there is much work to do.

And finally, I walked yesterday along the mountain track to Werndew, in order to apologize to Joseph. I was mortified when Bessie reminded me that Joseph had called when I was in my blackest state and had asked to see me, and I had refused to give him even a minute of my time. I determined to make amends, and off I went, wearing the lightest dress I could get away with as a woman in mourning, and with stout boots upon my feet. It was a most beautiful morning, with a cloudless sky, and the mountain slumbering in the heat, and skylarks tumbling and singing above my head. The walk took me more than an hour, but with every passing minute I felt a calming of my soul and a revival of my spirits.

Joseph was in his little garden at the back of the cottage, pottering as he had been when I first met him as a troubled young woman shortly after my arrival at the Plas. 'Martha!' he exclaimed, breaking into a broad and welcoming smile. 'How very good to see you! How are you? Feeling better, I hope. Have you walked all this way? Was that wise, after such a long time confined to the house?'

'Calm down, Joseph.' I laughed. 'Yes, I am quite well, and I have indeed walked all this way, and am convinced of the wisdom of it.'

He embraced me warmly, and this gave me much pleasure. Then we moved to the bench beneath his big copper beech tree which was still bursting into leaf. Then he said, 'Martha, before you say anything else I must apologize profoundly. It was most insensitive of me to visit you back at the end of April in order to give you the full details of my investigation into David's death. It was too soon. This realization has tortured me ever since, and I am truly very sorry for it. Will you ever forgive me?'

'Dear Joseph!' said I. 'I agree. It was foolish of you, and in retrospect I was not ready to absorb the appalling things that came out of our discussion. But what is done is done. I had to find out about the murder sooner or later, and to come to terms with its consequences. No forgiveness is needed.'

'Thank you for your understanding,' he replied. 'If anything good has come of it, I believe that I now have a slightly better understanding of the female mind.'

'I am not at all sure, Joseph, that the average female mind is anything like as complicated as mine. But no matter. The real purpose of my visit is to apologize to you for my extreme discourtesy. Bessie reminds me that you called when I was ill, and that I refused to see you or even to send you a kind word. I am truly sorry for that. Will you forgive me?'

'My dearest Martha!' said he, bursting with laughter. 'I assure you that that little episode is entirely forgotten. What a lot of apologizing and forgiving we have here today! This is all too much for me. Let us conclude the matter by agreeing that since Shrove Tuesday we have all been acting out of character, and that this is not entirely surprising. Now then, let me make you a cup of

135

tea. You must be thirsty after that long walk.' And he sprang up, strode into the kitchen and set about his task, leaving me to enjoy the fragrances and the sounds of his magic garden.

Afterwards, as we drank our tea and consumed some little cakes which were just about edible, we discussed my period of dark melancholia, and Joseph proved to have a much greater understanding of the female mind than he may realize. We were also able to talk quite openly about David's death, the possible motives of those responsible, and what we might expect as the next moves of the conspirators. He told me that he had compared notes on several occasions with Grandpa Isaac. Much to my surprise, I was able to talk about these things with equanimity, and with the help of Joseph's wise counsel I felt that my strength and my resolve were gradually returning. Joseph understood this too, and a little later on, as I was taking my leave, he said, 'Thank you for calling by, Martha. It seems that you are ready to face the world again.'

'Oh, I do hope so, Joseph.'

He held my hands in his, and gave me a little kiss on the cheek. 'I am convinced of it. What has happened to you, terrible as it is, may in some strange way give you strength. You will, I am sure, soon be able to enjoy life again. You will bring an iron-hard resolve to all your activities at the Plas, and you will develop a passion for justice.' And he winked, and waved, and I walked home across the fresh green mountain.

2 June 1805

For the last couple of days it has been raining, and I have been forced to remain indoors. This has perhaps been no bad thing, and I have been rebuilding my damaged reputation with the children, reading them stories and playing silly games with them. I have started taking walks with them every morning, come rain or shine, now that the lanes and hedgerows of Plas Ingli are bursting with new life and ringing with birdsong. Thank God that Daisy is now joining in and responding to my affection. I have also been rediscovering some of the innocent pursuits which should occupy the time of a lady of my social standing, and I must say that my watercolours, my embroidery and my time spent in the company of my harp have all helped in the healing of my wounded soul.

However, I am increasingly frustrated by my lack of knowledge on a range of important matters that affect the prosperity of the estate and the well-being of our workers. I have come to the view that I need more education, not so much in English literature and Greek civilization as in estate management, animal husbandry, and modern farming methods. This is not a whim on my part but a matter which is inescapable now that I am formally Mistress of the estate. I tried to explain this to Grandpa and Grandma as we ate dinner at midday, and while they were initially at a loss to understand why I should be so impatient in my wish for education in men's business, they recognize that a singular set of circumstances prevails at the Plas; and at last they came to the view that some good might come of it. We agreed that I should have lessons once a week. They suggested John Bateman, the steward of Squire Laugharne's estate at Pontfaen, as a man with a great knowledge of farming economics, and old William Edwards of Trefach, now more or less retired but possessed of a sharp wit and a matchless knowledge of husbandry and the farming year. I have today sent messages to these good men to seek their agreement. Sensing that I am already much stronger, and perhaps that creative thoughts will help to drive destructive ones from my brain, Grandpa also expressed the desire to involve me in more of the decisions concerning the management of the Plas estate and the tenant farms, woodlands and commons, so that I would learn through practical experience.

'I will not be here for ever, my dear,' he said. 'You are formally in charge of this place now, and while I will continue, as ever, to do what I can in the running of the estate, what will you do if a tree falls on me tomorrow?'

'Heaven forbid, dear Grandpa!' said I, giving him a hug. 'I would be utterly lost without you. And don't you dare stand under a tree when there is even the gentlest of breezes blowing!' But in making light of this, both he and I secretly acknowledge that his health could fail at any time. He knows, as Joseph and I know, that the men who murdered my dear husband might well be planning further assaults upon the Plas and upon our family. In my own mind, Grandpa Isaac would be their prime target, for it is he who makes all the crucial judgements upon which the prosperity of the estate depends.

6 June 1805

The shearing is done. Two days since, at breakfast time, Shemi came into the kitchen and announced: 'The fly have struck five ewes in Parc-mawr, what with this hot and sultry weather we have been having. If I may be so bold as to make a suggestion, Master Isaac, I think we should start shearing tomorrow.'

'Agreed,' said Grandpa. 'The weather looks settled, so we must do it. A fortnight has passed since the dipping at Trefelin, and if we wait any longer the fleeces will get dirty. This afternoon, you and I will make a pen in the yard, in the usual place, and you, Billy, can take the dogs and get all the breeding ewes down to the paddock behind the barn. They can stay there overnight. We will start tomorrow morning.' The rest of the day was taken up with preparations: sharpening shears on the grindstone, making ready Stockholm Tar and pitch, and clearing the threshing floor in the barn in anticipation. The children were thoroughly involved in the whole process, with Betsi on the big handle of the grindstone, and Dewi and Daisy going with Billy to round up the sheep on the common and in the top fields.

Yesterday, by the time the dew had melted away under the soaring sun, the sheep were in the pen and Billy and Shemi were hard at work on the threshing floor. The children and I watched in admiration as they threw each ewe in turn and sat her up like a begging dog, clipping the thick wool first from neck and foretop, then from flanks, back, legs and rear. Grandpa was on hand at all times, dabbing Stockholm Tar onto places where the skin had been damaged by maggots and then marking each ewe with the letters PI with boiling pitch and a branding iron. There were sixty ewes to shear, and the men worked as if possessed by some fiendish energy, sweat pouring off their brows and soaking their rough shirts. Mrs Owen plied them with beer and at every second hour they took a twenty-minute break. We all sat in the yard at midday and ate freshly baked bread, salt herring, cheese and sliced mutton, followed by raspberry pie and cream. The last tasted like manna from Heaven, and I am mystified as to the manner of its creation since this year's raspberries are still far from ripe.

The children loved every minute of the day, gathering up loose pieces of wool and helping to roll up each fleece as it was flung away by the shearer. Soon they had almost as much grease on their hands and clothes as

Billy and Shemi, and the smell of lanolin lay heavy in the air. By sunset the two men had finished the task, and the shorn and snow-white ewes were back in Parc Mawr. They and their lambs made an almighty noise throughout the night, as they normally do in the hours after shearing, since the branding hurts the ewes and the lambs find it difficult to identify their mothers without their coats. We all slept well anyway; indeed, Billy and Shemi were so tired that they both nodded off at the dinner table and had to be ushered off to bed at nine of the clock.

Now the lambs have found their mothers, and they are all back on the common. We have about six hundred pounds of good clean wool in the barn. Grandpa says that he will sell it tomorrow to Shoni Shuttle, who owns the woollen mill in Newport, while the price is still high.

I have arranged the lessons with my new tutors. Both Master Edwards and Master Bateman have agreed to assist in my education, and they will give me weekly lessons. Sometimes they will come here, and sometimes I will go to Trefach and Pontfaen to meet them. I look forward most to my visits to Pontfaen, for this will give me the opportunity of visiting Squire and Mistress Laugharne when my lessons are over. It is very pleasant here at the Plas, but following David's death there is a sadness about the place, and with eight adults and four small children living cheek-by-jowl an occasional change of scene will be welcome.

Both of my tutors came to see us this morning, and I think I shall get on famously with both of them. They are as different as bread and butter, but they complement each other in a most excellent fashion. Old Master Edwards is probably over seventy years of age, rather portly, with snow-white hair so magnificent that he has no need of a wig. He is as weatherbeaten as an old rowan tree, and is clearly more comfortable helping to deliver lambs in the Easter rain than sitting in a living room making polite conversation. In teaching me he will probably prefer us to be wandering about in the mud, and this I find quite acceptable. Farming is an outside business, and cannot in any case be conducted from the office or the kitchen table. Master Bateman is a small man with a sallow complexion, sharp eyes and a beak nose, of perhaps fifty years. He speaks and moves quickly, and reminds me of a terrier about to be sent down a fox hole. He acts very formally, and when we met he bowed so deeply that I thought his nose might scrape the floor. He has a pompous way with words, as indeed do many self-made professional men. But he has a little gleam in his eye, and I fancy that he does not take himself too seriously, and once we get to know each other I am sure that we will work well together. Bookkeeping, legal matters, commodities and markets, settlements and taxes are things I know far too little about, and it will be good for me to exercise my brain in the presence of a man who is as bright as a June buttercup.

8 June 1805

I have made a number of decisions. This may not sound like a matter of great import, but for me the process has greatly improved my confidence in my own ability and has given me a warm glow of satisfaction. I have made a start.

Grandpa and Billy have clearly been talking, and they have both looked for opportunities during the day to sit down with me and discuss matters relating to the estate. First, at breakfast this morning, Billy asked if he might have a talk with me, if I could find the time between feeding little Sara and taking my walk with the older children. I readily agreed, and so we sat down later at the kitchen table. 'Now then, Mistress,' said Billy, 'we must come to a view on one or two matters. Since you are now in charge of everything on this estate, I should first like your instructions on the harvesting of the hay-fields. Then I wants to know how many labourers we should pull in from outside for doing the job. Then we must decide what to pay them. Then there is the pigs, indeed, and the matter of the . . .'

'A moment, Billy.' I laughed. 'One thing at a time! You must not overwhelm me. Remember that this is all very new. I have of course observed the working of this place for eight years or more, but I have been an interested bystander rather than an active player, and I fear that I may well need your advice. First of all, the haymaking. How many fields are concerned?'

'Five this year, Mistress, amounting to about twenty acres all told. Parc-bach, Parc Gwyn, the two small paddocks near the entrance lane, and then Parc Mrs Owen.'

'Parc Mrs Owen?' I asked, more than a little intrigued. 'I know the plans of the estate quite well, but I was not aware that we had a field with that name.'

'Unofficial, it is,' said Billy with a twinkle in his eye, looking over his shoulder in case the housekeeper should be lurking somewhere nearby. 'It's the field where she threw a large stone at a crow in 1785 and killed it dead. Never was such a thing seen before or since. Been trying to get her to take over the bird-scaring duties ever since, we have, but she prefers baking bread and cooking up *cawl*. Now if you was to *order* her to go after them old crows . . .'

'More than my life is worth! Now let us return to our discussion.'

'Yes, Mistress. We normally cuts Parc Gwyn first, since it is the driest field, and after this rain we must not cut when it is muddy. Then I would suggest the bottom paddock, then Parc Mrs Owen, then the top paddock, and last of all Parc-bach.'

'Thank you Billy,' said I. 'Of course I will take your advice. Let's do the fields in the order you suggest. Now then, when should we start?'

'That depends on the weather, Mistress. Not yet, because we need more growth, and the ground is still too wet. But some nice days of sunshine will make all the difference.'

'How many people do we need?'

'At least thirty, for at least six days. Eight scything and the rest raking and turning. If we counts six of us to be helping when we can, and one each from the Dolrannogs, Gelli, Penrhiw and Brithdir for three days, and one person for the whole of the time from each of the fifteen labourers' cottages, and then two people for a few days at a time from Trefach, Tyriet, Cilwen and Cilgwyn in exchange for time we will give them . . .'

I fear that I could not cope with the complications being placed before me. 'Stop, stop, Billy!' I said. 'Where do all of these figures come from?'

'Tradition, Mistress. Our tenant farmers each have to give us one person for three haymaking days according to the terms of their leases. The labourers have to give us people for the whole of the harvest, and that is a part of the rent they pays. The other freeholders and estates round about send us help when they can, and then we send help over to them when they are hard at it. Shemi, Bessie and Sian will probably be needed at Llannerch tomorrow, since their harvest has already started. Is that all clear?'

'I understand. But how do you keep a track of all these

comings and goings, and know who owes what in terms of time and labour?'

'That's where Master Isaac comes in. He has a little book, and every day he writes down who is here. In due course, Mistress, I suppose you will need to take over the record keeping.' My heart sank at the very thought of it, and this probably showed on my countenance. Billy grinned in response. 'But don't you worry at all, Mistress. I will certainly help you out. Very simple it is, once you gets used to it.'

'You are very kind, Billy. I know I can depend on you when the time comes. Now then, what about money, and what else must I decide?'

'There is a lot of feeding and drinking in prospect, Mistress, and you will surely have seen the supplies which Mrs Owen and Bessie have been putting aside. That all takes care of itself. Hettie will come up from the Parrog to help, in exchange for half a bushel of barley later in the year. There is very little loose money needed except to pay labourers from off the estate. If you would be so kind, I would like to know what we should pay this year, and how many to hire in.'

'And what do you suggest?'

'Well, Owain Laugharne Llannerch is paying eight-pence a day with victuals this year, and he is a good man, so if I were you I would follow suit. Since we don't know how many of our tenants and labourers will turn up each day, what with harvesting about to start all over the place, we will need up to fifteen outsiders each day. We tends to use the Rhys family from down in the *cwm*, the Tomos boys from town, the three Stubbins girls from Parrog, and maybe eight Irish.'

'Very well. Let's give them eightpence per day. I know all the ones you mention, and recall that they all work hard, so by all means tell them to be ready if needed. I also recall that David always met the Irish when they arrived from Wexford to decide which ones should have work. When do they come?'

'Any time now, Mistress. They will turn up out of the blue as soon as they hear that the Plas Ingli harvest is about to start.'

'Very well. When they come, please let me know, Billy. I want to meet them and decide which ones to use. I do not want vagrants and paupers wandering about all over the estate without our being able to put names and faces to them. Once I have met them and feel happy that they are honest in their desire for work, they can go to it, and stay in the barn.'

And that was that. We never did get round to talking about the pigs. But that will keep. Billy went on his way well satisfied, I trust, in that I have supported him and demonstrated my faith in his judgement and knowledge of harvesting matters. There is after all no point in standing against any of his recommendations until I have much greater knowledge of what happens both on and off the hayfield.

This afternoon Grandpa and I sat down on a shady bench in my garden and discussed our proposals for Ffair Gurig, the biggest event in the local farming year, which takes place in Newport over four days at the end of June. I decided (or, to be quite honest, Grandpa suggested and I agreed) that we should sell fifteen of the Welsh Black bullocks, ten porkers, thirty ewes and five rams, and a dozen geese this year. I also decided (against Grandpa's advice, which gave me great pleasure) to try to sell two of the Welsh cobs which Shemi says are not working as hard as they should. He thinks that the land here is too heavy for them, and this makes sense since they came originally from the limestone lands in the south of the county. David bought them some years ago from Mirehouse of Angle in order to improve the blood line, and in retrospect this may have been a mistake.

Then we discussed staffing matters, and considered at some length the proposal from Will Final Testament that we should employ a steward. Grandpa gave me much information about the estate finances, which appeared to me to be sound but not sound enough for wild extravagances. I decided against employing a professional man for the time being, on the basis that Grandpa does the job of a steward anyway and still appears to enjoy it; and that it may well be wiser to give Billy more responsibility in the autumn, with an increase in his wages, once I have developed a greater understanding of how everything works. Grandpa said he wished to ensure that not too many management matters were dumped upon my desk, and added that the recovery of my good health must be a priority. Indeed I agreed with him; but I said that anything to take my mind off the sadness of recent months was a good idea, and that it would become pretty obvious to everybody in the house if tiredness should get the better of me.

'Dear Grandpa,' I said, 'I want to try to become involved in all manner of things, so long as I have the strength. If you think that I am not coping, will you promise to take me aside and tell me the cruel truth?'

'My dear Martha,' said he. 'Of course I will. Just now I am very impressed with your enthusiasm and your willingness to take over at least some of the things which David did so well. Don't worry – diplomacy never was my strong point, and if there is a need to be rude to you, I will happily oblige!' Then he gave me a hug and went off to talk to Shemi and Billy about sorting out and fattening the animals for Ffair Gurig.

On other fronts, my beloved Sara has been a model of contentment today, gurgling with delight and giving me

146

little smiles as she feeds. Since the sun has been shining out of a deep blue sky the other children have spent almost the whole day out of doors, building a den with Sian's help in a shady corner of the orchard. We all know about it, but it is a top secret business, and we are all sworn to silence in the event that some stranger might come to spy on this mysterious activity.

All in all, I can report that this has been one of my better days, and late this evening I celebrated it by climbing up to Ffynnon Brynach and anointing myself with the old saint's cool clear water. It was almost ten of the clock, and still quite light. For company I had a little group of swooping bats, three rabbits, and a heron high overhead and heading west. Somewhere, far across the common, an old raven was singing his melodious song.

13 June 1805

Three days ago David would have been twenty-eight, and it was a difficult day for us all. There were not many of us in the kitchen at breakfast, since Billy, Shemi, Bessie and Sian had all gone off to Llannerch to help with the hay harvest. But the rest of us made a little ceremony while we sat round the table, remembering David as husband, father and Master of the estate; and Grandpa Isaac, who is in truth not a very religious gentleman, even said a short prayer for him which I found very moving. Of course I wept, and so did the children. But Betsi was as sweet and perceptive as ever, and held my hand and gave me a kiss, and said, 'There now, Mam, you must try to be brave. Dad was a very brave man, and now that he is in Heaven with the angels he will surely want us to be brave too.'

However, I am determined not to dwell on unhappy thoughts, and I have made a further decision. It is far more important than animals or haymaking, and even more important than anything concerning the children. I have decided to take control of my fortune and my future. This is not an easy thing for a woman, but circumstances demand it.

In thinking recently about David and how best I might honour his memory and show my continuing love for him, it has occurred to me that it is paramount to carry on his good work on the estate and develop further the reputation of the Plas. He was above all else a strong and kind squire and an honest, humane and far-seeing Master. I argued with him many times about estate matters, but I am coming to appreciate more and more the good sense of many of his beliefs: in the generous treatment of servants, labourers and tenants; in the relationship between prices and wages; and in the need to minimize debts and risks. He sought always to avoid hazardous ventures which might endanger the reputation and integrity of the family and the estate. He was prepared to explore new ways of doing things, but was always mindful of the need to manage the land for the next generation, and the one after that. He was a great believer in education for the poorer classes, and he was frequently inflamed by righteous indignation when he encountered cruelty or injustice or the oppression of the weak by the strong. He was more complacent than I would have liked on certain issues, but I dare say that allowances have to be made for the fact that he was a man.

Since my arrival at the Plas, I have been too placid, or too timid, in my dealings with the wicked world, and too reluctant to see evil when it is all too obvious. I have allowed events to overwhelm me when I should have been better prepared, and I have been swept back and forth from day to day by the surging tides of life. I was too kind to Moses Lloyd when I first arrived at the Plas, and was almost swept away by his charm before I appreciated his wickedness. By observing rather than acting, I allowed him to do untold harm to others. I suffered at the hands of Squires Rice, Watkins and Howell as they schemed and plotted against the estate, and was terrorized by Moses Lloyd in our final meeting. Finally in recent months I have almost been destroyed by the loss of my beloved David.

But now my innocence has gone, and I have to thank God for its passing. I will make my own way in life; I will take advice and heed the interests of others, but I will take steps to protect myself and those whom I love. I will not go through life haunted by the prospect that others may wish me ill, but will keep my eyes wide open and my ears pinned back in order to maintain vigilance at all times. Where I perceive a threat I will get my retaliation in first. I will build alliances and defences and will seek to discover the weaknesses of my enemies so that I may exploit them. I will try to put my misery behind me and seek happiness, for my own sake and for the children. I will endeavour to rediscover frivolity and laughter and joy. In deference to my female friends I will seek to cultivate elegance and style and that elusive thing called grace.

In thinking about these matters, I seem to have set myself a daunting task. But I have taken Bessie into my confidence, and have talked to her at some length about life and its challenges. I was greatly heartened, and gave her a warm embrace, when she said: 'Mistress Martha, you must do what you will. You have suffered the pain of loss, and for better or worse you are no longer a sub-servient and obedient wife. Indeed, I am not sure that you ever were! Make your own life, Mistress, and remember that in all your endeavours those of us who live beneath this roof will be standing at your shoulder.'

15 June 1805

I have met up with the Irish, and have given work to eight of them. They are now happily installed in the barn, and work has started in Parc Gwyn. I love the hustle and the bustle of the hayfield, with scythes swinging and voices raised in song, having been a part of it on several occasions in the past, child-bearing permitting. I wanted to participate on this occasion also, but Grandpa and Grandma absolutely refused it, saying that I am in no fit state, as a nursing mother, for heavy labour under a high sun. They are of course quite right, but the children and I have helped with the picnics and we have all enjoyed our fleeting contacts with the laughter and rude repartee of the hayfield.

I am greatly enjoying the lessons with my farming tutors. I have only had two meetings with each of them thus far, because of the intervention of the hay harvest, but we are getting along excellently.

Yesterday I had a most instructive two hours in the company of Master Bateman on financial affairs. We discussed tithes, poor relief, parish taxes and county taxes, and other inescapable burdens placed upon the shoulders of the landowning classes. I find some of these matters quite confusing, and indeed Master Bateman appeared none too sure himself as to how some of the taxes were calculated, and by whom. But he explained that many of them were worked out on the basis of some nominal annual income figure for each farm which may bear no relation at all to the actual cash handled by the farmer. He said that the assessments were the cause of great trouble every year, especially among those who sympathized with the Nonconformists and had to pay 10 per cent of their produce over to absentee vicars and rectors for services they never received. He said that the burden was normally bearable as far as the large estates were concerned, but he explained that the small freeholders and tenant farmers, with maybe no more than twenty acres to farm, lived precariously close to starvation level. According to him, many of them have less than ten shillings a week to live on by the time they have paid all their tithes and taxes, labour costs, repair costs, bills for lime and coal, and interest repayments to merciless money lenders like Daniel Mathias of Eglwyswrw. He said that some labourers who were treated well by their masters and were fed and housed were actually better off than some of the small farmers on the rough edges of the commons. And he spoke angrily about the fact that small tenant farmers with so little cash to live on had no opportunity to improve their farming techniques or their land no matter how much they might wish to do so. 'The whole system is mad!' he exploded, with lightning flashing in his eyes. 'The small farmers are still using techniques which are two hundred years out of date! They sow barley year after year on the same land, and sometimes the weight of seed harvested is only a little greater than the weight of seed sown!'

'Well sir,' said I, 'you are a steward, and you and your kind set the rents. Is it not in your power to lighten the burden of the tenant farmers and to encourage better methods?'

'My dear Mistress Morgan,' he replied, 'I wish it were so simple. Part of the problem is that there is a demand for land. I am bothered constantly, as are the other stewards in this region, by small farmers wanting tenancies and extra land. According to the ancient rhyming law of economics, where demand exceeds supply the prices will be high. Second, most of the squires and gentlemen who own the land are in desperate straits themselves, and a reduction in rent income would tip many of them over into insolvency. And third, the leases which many of the tenants hold are so short, or so insecure, that they have no incentive to breed good stock, repair buildings, or practise good husbandry.'

I was getting rather intrigued by all of this, and was about to seek enlightenment on tenancy agreements when there was a knock upon the door and Mr Bateman was summoned to deal with some stray cattle down by the river. He hastily called our lesson to a close, promised that next week he would turn me into an expert on tenancy laws and traditions, bowed deeply, and took his leave.

This afternoon, with the weather still dry, old William Edwards came over on his pony from Trefach to give me a lesson, having given me due warning, on Master Jethro Tull and his crop rotations. Apparently there had been a copy of his book in the Plas Ingli library before the fire, but it went up in flames with Shakespeare and the rest of the family collection. When the old man arrived I started to apologize for not having done my preparatory reading; but he was not at all interested in dusty books, and said, 'Now then, Mistress Martha, if little Sara is well fed and fast asleep, stout boots upon your feet and a shady bonnet upon your head if you please, and we will have a little afternoon out in the sun.'

I was delighted at the prospect, and soon we were on our way down the lane towards the Dolrannog road. We passed the haymakers who were hard at work in Parc Mrs Owen, with eight men scything in a staggered row, working clockwise around the field. The cut hay smelt as sweet and rich as clover honey.

Then Master Edwards and I found ourselves in the field called Parc-bach, wading thigh-deep through lush grasses and clovers. Clouds of pollen swirled behind us. A hare narrowly avoided being stepped upon by Mr Edwards's large buckled foot, and scampered clumsily away. Grasshoppers, bumble bees and a multitude of other small creatures whirred, hummed, clicked, buzzed, crackled and sang all around us. Butterflies of many different sorts flitted and danced, each one alighting for a few moments at a time upon its favourite food plants. It was very hot, and I felt quite sorry for the old man in his heavy jacket and breeches under the relentless sun. He would neither disrobe nor seek the shade along the hedgebanks, and I was distracted by the thought that he might collapse from heat exhaustion. But Edwards Trefach is made of stern stuff, and got on with the matter in hand. 'On the morrow, young lady, as you know, Shemi and Billy and the rest of them will cut this field,' he said, 'and it will be too late to see what it is made of. But just you look at it carefully, if you please, and tell me how many different plants you can find around you.'

I was taken aback, because I had always thought of a hayfield simply as a field of hay, but when I set to work I discovered that there were tall grasses and short grasses, some with long droopy seed-heads, some with firm straight seed-heads, and others apparently with no seed-heads at all. Some had long stalks and others short; some coarse broad leaves and others delicate wispy ones; and there were also subtle differences in colouring. Then there were the clovers, some with white flowers and others with red or purple. And the meadow flowers! Brash and brave, delicate and demure. Hidden among

153

the tall grasses there were red blossoms and white, yellow ones and blue, and to my shame I knew only a few of their names. There were orchids too, some of which I had never seen before. I took my bonnet off and laid it on the ground, and arranged my plant specimens upon it, and at last I had twenty-three different plants to show to my tutor.

'Not at all bad, Mistress Martha!' said he. 'You can be pleased with such a fine collection. But you can take it from me that there are at least fifty different plants in this field, even though it was only cleared by Isaac when he was a young man. I helped with the work myself. Hard work indeed, but good happy days . . .'

He looked dreamily into the distance for a moment, then coughed and continued: 'Some of the old meadows down in the valley have more than one hundred different plants in them, and it is said that they have never been ploughed. If you can keep a few fields like this on your estate, and get good hay crops off them, your cattle, horses and sheep will get pretty well everything they need for good sustenance – oils, juices, seeds, rough matter, herbal medicines, minerals and all manner of things given fancy names by the men of science. I have noticed myself that animals fed on hay from such pastures work harder, put on more weight, produce more milk, and stay healthier than the feeble creatures raised on the rye grass much favoured of late by some of the local squires.'

And so the old man and I looked further into the lush greenery of the hayfield, and he showed me many little grasses that I had missed, and many flowers that were different in some minute detail from those I had gathered in my bonnet, until my head was spinning with names – sorrell, bennet, crested dog's tail, vernal grass, oat grass, knapweed, burnet, meadowsweet, buttercup, yellow vetch, lucerne, trefoil, ribwort plantain and so forth. I collected a beautiful posy of grasses and flowers, some of which I have placed in a pot upon our dining-room table, and others which I shall press and mount on stiff paper with names and annotations. Like a good pupil I will try to remember at least half of the new plant names that I have learned during the day.

It is sad to think that tomorrow all this beauty will be destroyed, each blade and stalk and stem sliced with a scythe and laid out to dry, destined in due course for the stomach of a cow or a horse. But such is the cycle of the year, and hay left standing will die anyway, desiccated under the sun or flattened and rotted in the rain. The fat animals will be in this field in the autumn, grazing the stubble close, scratching up the ground surface, and preparing the land for next year's outpouring of the Lord's bounty.

18 June 1805

Some days since, old Squire Lloyd of Cwmgloyn died. The wake was held last night and the small funeral took place in Nevern church this morning, and Grandpa went along to represent the family. Indeed, he said that he attended not so much for the sake of appearances but out of a genuine respect for the old man, who has been ill for many years. Grandpa says that twelve years ago he worked hard, in conjunction with David's father William, to repair the feud which had disfigured relations between the Lloyd and Morgan families for many generations.

He says that the old Squire was a recluse in the big dark house for ten years or more, living in a fantasy world and subject to fearsome swings of mood, both

155

loved and feared by his family and faithful servants. When he was younger he was a hard taskmaster on his estate and a cruel and even brutal father to his three sons Meredith, Moses and Matthew. Moses was spoiled, pampered and abused by him before being thrown out of the house and at last disinherited; I know this from a number of sources. Moses, who brought troubles down on his own head and on the heads of many others, is rotting in Hell, but I still feel for Meredith, the oldest son who will now take over the estate. He is a sensitive and upstanding man, and I will never forget his kind message of sympathy following David's death and the greeting which came to me following the birth of little Sara. He is married to one of the Hughes girls from Moylgrove, and has two small children, and by common consent he will make an enlightened squire and a wise magistrate.

I am quite certain that Meredith does not know of his younger brother's involvement in David's death at the *cnapan* contest. He was not there at the time, and does not play the game himself; and I am gratified that I am not the only one who feels that the game is brutal and stupid, and should be banned by order of the King. There would be absolutely no point in revealing to anybody what Grandpa, Joseph and I know about David's murder; and having been in a similar position after David died, I consider it kindest to spare Meredith from further misery at a time when he is mourning the death of his father and coming to terms with his sudden acquisition of responsibility.

High Summer

25 June 1805

The hay was cut, and dried, and carted, and ricked well before Midsummer Day and the feast of St John, as was dictated by tradition. There were just a few disruptions caused by the weather, but none of the rain was heavy enough to flatten the crop, and although we had to turn the hay in the bottom paddock more than we would have liked we had adequate labour. The eight Irish labourers (five adults and three children) who were living in the barn proved to be excellent workers, although in truth one little boy and his sister spent most of their time playing with Betsi, Daisy and Dewi. I did not object; it was worth paying them a few pence a day just for the pleasure of seeing the little ones playing ball, skipping, making skittles, and generally having adventures. They needed to resume their carefree child-hoods, and the presence of other children at the Plas has helped in the healing of all of us. The head of the group, one Michael O'Connell, had his fiddle with him, and on two of the warmer evenings we all used up whatever energy we had left by dancing Irish jigs and reels on the threshing floor. As the Mistress responsible for employ-ment and discipline among the haymakers, I should strictly have watched benignly from the barn door; but I could not resist joining in for a few minutes, and this brought a great cheer from the assembled company. In retrospect, I should not have danced about as I did so soon after David's death. But dancing did give me a sort of release from the chains of grief, and I hope that none of my neighbours will have reported my actions to the fierce deacons of Caersalem.

From here the Irish moved on to Brynberian and Eglwyswrw, following the harvest eastwards. We were sorry to see them go, but I promised them all work again when the corn harvest starts in August.

With the Irish gone, Shemi's father Daniel and his uncles Abraham, George and Abel (known as 'the Jenkins boys' even though they are all in their late forties) came up to the Plas, according to tradition, to thatch the six new hayricks with wheat straw. The task was finished by St John's Eve, and we celebrated according to ancient rules which it is now my duty to uphold. First, a little birch tree was cut from the woods near Gelli and dragged back to the yard by Billy and Shemi. Dewi *bach* was a willing helper, skipping about and almost overcome with excitement. With the 'summer birch' then planted in the middle of the farmyard, Betsi and Daisy were given the privilege of dressing it with pretty wreaths of summer flowers.

As the golden sun slipped through a cloudless midsummer sky towards the western horizon, all of the residents of Plas Ingli danced round our delicate green symbol of summer providence, holding hands and singing an old carol which Grandpa says he learned from his grandparents. Bessie and Sian, helped by the girls, fixed sprigs of St John's-wort over the doors and windows of the house in order to keep evil spirits at bay, this being the second of *y tair ysbrydnos* (the three spirit nights). Then we lit a bonfire in the middle of Parc-bach and ate a wonderful picnic supper as the longest day became dusk and dusk became night. The air was so still that the smoke from the fire curled straight up to Heaven. Grandpa told some of his silly stories about ghosts and goblins, to which we all listened intently, ruddy faces illuminated by the flames of the bonfire, with bats flitting about us and stars and sparks glittering overhead. Sara lay fast asleep in her carrying cradle at my side. The children, given a dispensation to stay up late on this special night, kept awake for as long as they could; but one by one they succumbed to exhaustion, and were carried by the servants, fast asleep, back to the house and tucked up safely in bed. I watched, and said nothing, and loved them all with every ounce of my being.

At midnight Sara woke and demanded her nocturnal feed, and so she and I said our goodnights and retired to my room. At the same time Bessie and Sian left to walk down to Cilgwyn church, where they planned to pace nine and a half times round the building and then peep in through the keyhole of the church door, in the hope of discovering something about their future partners in marriage. We left the others chatting round the glowing embers of the bonfire. Grandma Jane had her favourite grey cat on her lap, and Shemi was surrounded by five warm and sleepy sheepdogs. The image stayed with me as I sat in my chair with my baby contented at my breast. I did not want the day to end, and when I drifted into sleep half an hour later I had decided that in some fashion beyond knowing this place, and these people, had a strange power to mend the most broken of hearts and cheer the most desolate of souls.

Ffair Gurig, at the end of June, was a great success for us. Cattle prices were good, and Shemi had brought the animals up to peak condition at exactly the right time for the sale on the second day. With Grandpa by my side I started to enjoy what the traders call haggling, and I obtained great pleasure when he insisted that potential buyers should haggle with me rather than him. We sold all the sheep, geese and porkers, and I managed to sell the Welsh cobs for twenty-five guineas each to my father, of all people, who turned up unexpectedly with the sole purpose of buying a couple of horses well suited to the lighter soils of the top fields at Brawdy. Most of the cattle were sold, but I withdrew two from sale just to make a point to Squire Tomos of Puncheston, who thought he would bamboozle me with science and buy them with the small change left in his pocket at the end of the Fair. I refused to budge on my price, and by now the message will have found its way round the inns of Newport that there is more to Mistress Morgan than her pretty face. Grandpa said when we got home that my bargaining technique was wonderful, and roared with laughter and gave me one of his rare embraces. Billy and Shemi were impressed too, and said that David would have been proud of me. Perhaps, in spite of my fears, I have the makings of a crusty old farmer.

Talking of Billy, Shemi and Grandpa, I have realized that my beloved Dewi has lost one father and gained three others. I hardly see him these days, for the little fellow is out and about from dawn to dusk, two and a half years old and intent upon discovering how the world works. He talks non-stop now that he has learned to use proper words. He helps Shemi to muck out the stables, he checks the bullocks with Billy, he feeds the geese with Grandpa, he helps to take the horses down to the pond to drink, he collects the chicken eggs, he helps Shemi to weed the garden, and he clears the ditches with Billy. Sometimes he does frivolous things with Grandpa, like throwing stones at long sticks stuck into the ground, or seeing who can make the biggest splashes in the puddle outside the dairy door. He literally works and plays until he drops, and when he does drop, with virtually no warning, whoever he is with picks him up fast asleep and delivers him back to the house. The tenderness and concern which the three men show to their little assistant is very touching, and Great-grandfather Isaac has, I am sure, had his flagging spirits restored by Dewi's innocence, vitality and good humour. The three of them love him dearly, and I am sure he loves them. As I write this I have a tear in my eye, and for this I make no apology.

6 August 1805

It is now almost eight years since my confrontation with Moses Lloyd in the cave on the mountain. That encounter took me to within an inch of losing my life. It also left his body rotting on the mountain which he desecrated, and his soul in Hell. Justice was done, but until today I have carried on my shoulders a heavy burden of guilt for what I did. In some ways there is a sweet poetry in acting as an avenging angel on a mountain peopled by angels, but I have discovered over the years that acts of vengeance carry a heavy price even when the weapon used is a sword of righteousness.

At irregular intervals I have been troubled by nightmares and waking recollections of the horror of that fateful day, and recently I have been unable to rid my

161

mind of the cruel idea that David's death was an act of divine retribution for my sinfulness rather than his. Why else should such a fine man be taken from me, his loving and dutiful wife, and from his beautiful children? I could not, and still cannot, accept that his death was some cruel joke played on our family by a Grim Reaper with a grin on his face and four evil men acting as his executioners.

Twice in the last month I have climbed the mountain and thought about entering the cave again. Once I climbed to within a few yards of its entrance, but then I was overwhelmed with terror and had to retreat. I still do not know why I was so afraid. Did I fear that the cave would be inhabited by a multitude of demons? Did I fear that the ghost of Moses Lloyd would be sitting just inside, waiting to grab me and drag me to my doom? Common sense told me that these fears were unfounded, and yet I could not bring myself to cast them to one side.

Three days ago, with these thoughts occupying my mind to a greater extent than I would have wished, I realized that I was in danger of sinking into despair again. But now I know myself a little better than I did, and I recalled my promise to Grandma and my recent resolution to take charge of my life. I swallowed hard, and decided that I must visit Joseph Harries in order to confront this issue and to talk about exorcism. I realized that I needed to cleanse my mind and to cleanse the cave. So early in the morning, after feeding Sara, I left the children with Sian and set off to walk the mountain path to Werndew. The grass was heavy with dew, the air was still, and the golden orb of the sun was still low enough in the eastern sky to cast long shadows beyond the mountain crags. My spirits were lifted imperceptibly with every step I took, and over the course of an hour I found myself musing on the strange relationship between weather and temperament, sunshine and spirit. By the time I arrived at Werndew I felt quite cheerful in spite of the sombre matters that were on my mind.

I was surprised to find that Joseph was out, and then thought that this was not surprising at all since he is a wizard and a healer and a solver of problems who spends a great deal of his time visiting the poor and needy. His front door was unlocked, since wizards do not need to lock their doors, and I wondered whether I should settle down in his comfortable kitchen chair to await his return; but I decided instead on the garden, and chose the wooden seat beneath the beech tree. I was awoken from my slumbers by the scent of Heaven, and opened my eyes to find Joseph wafting a posy of roses beneath my nose.

'Joseph!' said I. 'That is not a very kind way to wake a lady.'

'Oh yes it is,' came the reply. 'From many years of testing I have discovered that it is absolutely the best way to do it. In any case, it is good to see you, my dear Martha. I apologize for my absence when you arrived. I have been down in Dinas recovering a stolen cheese for Shinkins Siop Fach. I have been rewarded for my efforts with a slice of said cheese. Would you like to taste it? Yes? Just wait a minute while I go and fetch a knife from the kitchen.' And he scuttled inside.

I laughed at this and blessed the day that Joseph was born. Although he is a wizard, I thought, he spreads not shadow but light wherever he treads, and he combines in his personality eccentricity, good humour, intelligence, compassion, and not a little romance. The world would surely be a poorer place without him.

He returned and we nibbled on our slices of Dinas cheese and washed them down with a cool drink of fruit cordial. We chatted about the children, and the weather, and the harvest, and my lessons with Master Bateman and Master Edwards, and this and that. Then I said: 'Joseph, I feel strong enough today, with your inimitable assistance, to ask you about a matter that has been troubling me.'

'Well? When you call to see me there is always something to be discussed, and that is what friendship is all about. What have you to tell me?'

'I want to talk about exorcism.'

'Exorcism! Do you have a ghost in the Plas which you need to banish? The Plas has always struck me as being singularly free of unhappy spirits.'

'No, Joseph,' I replied. 'This has nothing to do with the Plas. This has more to do with my own mind, and it concerns a certain place which makes me very unhappy.'

'I am not sure, dearest Martha, that you would be talking about exorcism unless there was a great deal more to it than that. May I assume that this place does not simply make you unhappy, but that it afflicts you with something more akin to terror?'

'Yes, I confess that. I am so afraid of it that I cannot enter it or even approach it too closely.'

'Do you want to tell me where it is?'

'No. It is my secret, and I have sworn to myself and to the angels of Carningli that I will never tell another soul.'

'Very well. I respect that.'

I was relieved that he did not press me on the location or the reason for my fear, but Joseph is a man who knows all about discretion. And I suspected that he already knew a great deal more about the source of my terror than he was prepared to reveal to me. He continued: 'Why, my dear Martha, have you not gone to consult Rector Devonald? After all, you pay your tithes, and I should have thought that he could do something in

164

return in the form of a little visit equipped with bell, book and candle.'

'God forbid!' I exclaimed in horror. 'I could not possibly allow him, or any other cleric, near to this place. It is far too sacred for that.'

'So what advice do you want of me?'

'Can you perhaps call down one of your friendly spirits to drive away evil, or give me a spell which will do the trick?'

Joseph laughed and slapped his knees in that disconcerting way he has. 'Mistress Morgan!' he said with mock severity. 'I see that you still have much to learn. Yes, I could call down a whole menagerie of spirits if I wished it; and yes, I could give you a spell which would certainly alarm an unhappy ghost. But resort to the spirit world is not always appropriate, and great care is needed to ensure that things are done correctly. In addition, when I have dealings with devils, good or bad, I am so exhausted afterwards that I can hardly stand or keep my eyes open. I do not feel like subjecting myself to that sort of thing on a beautiful day such as this.'

My heart sank. Joseph noticed my dejected appearance and continued. 'I suspect that this problem is inside your own head and that there may not even be a ghost to get rid of. May I suggest that you go quite soon to this place of terror, while you have the strength and the determination to do it. Go while the weather is good and you have sunshine to cheer you on your way. Prepare yourself properly. Be calm and breathe deeply. Can you do all of this?'

'Yes, I think so.'

'Of course you can. If you wish, take something sacred. You have told me before that you have a little ritual involving sacred water from Ffynnon Brynach. Why not take some in a bottle and sprinkle it in this place of memories so that cleansing occurs? You might have some secret words which you can use. All you need, my dear Martha, is a strong will, and if I may say so you have a will so strong that I am constantly at a loss to understand its containment within such a fragile and beautiful frame.'

At this I blushed, and Joseph laughed at my embarrassment and my pleasure. I realized that I have had few enough compliments from kind gentlemen in recent months; but I put this quickly out of my mind and determined that I would do exactly as Joseph advised. 'Yes, I can do it, Joseph,' I said. 'And I already know what to say. Thank you, my dear friend.' And I threw my arms round him and gave him a grateful hug.

Then I realized that the morning was almost gone, and that it was high time for me to feed little Sara. Joseph appeared to perceive what was in my mind, and said that it would take me far too long to walk back along the mountain track. He insisted that he would take me home on the back of his white horse, and within ten minutes we were on our way. It took us less than thirty minutes to return to the Plas, but I had to hang on for dear life. As we trotted along I said to Joseph: 'This is getting to be a habit, Master Harries. First Bessie, and now me. Before we know it Mrs Owen will insist on her rights as well!' And we both roared with laughter at the thought of the precious white horse subsiding beneath the weight of our formidable housekeeper.

Today I have done it. I announced immediately after breakfast that I was taking a walk upon the mountain, and even though Betsi wanted to come with me I insisted on solitude. As I walked I prepared myself for the ordeal ahead, but I was fired with determination not to abandon the enterprise. I stopped on my climb only once, to fill my little bottle with sacred water at Ffynnon

Brynach. On I went, higher and higher, until I was among the great blue crags and boulders and their dark shadows. I found the little pathway to the cave, and saw the boulders which guarded the entrance ahead of me. The old raven watched me from his perch fifty feet above, as he had done so many times before. The rowan tree which hid the narrow slit in the rock face was larger than it had been. Its leaves brushed my face as I went down onto my hands and knees, and then I was inside. To my immense relief, nothing happened. The whole place was clean and cool and silent. My heart was beating so loudly that its pulsing echoed round the damp bluestone walls and roof. There were a few more plants than I remembered, little straggly things hanging from crevices in the rock. The bed of moss was still in the same place towards the rear of the cave. With a degree of apprehension I knelt on it and pressed on with my little ritual. I took the cork out of the bottle, poured a little into the palm of my hand, and sprinkled it around me. Then I did it again, and again, until all the water was gone. As I did my sprinkling I repeated over and again: 'And the temple was cleansed, and the angels of the mountain returned, and all was well.'

Still nothing happened. No fleeing demons, no fluttering angels, no St Brynach, no Moses Lloyd. Silence, blessed silence, disturbed only by the slightest of rustlings as the leaves of the rowan tree moved listlessly in the hot August breeze. I breathed a great sigh of relief, then lay down on the bed of moss and let the tension drain away from my body and my mind. The exorcism was complete, and I had repossessed my sacred cave.

15 August 1805

For three weeks we have had no rain, and it has been one of the hottest Augusts that anybody can remember. The landscape slumbers under a high sun which beats down without mercy day after day. There is hardly a breath of wind, and even the birds have stopped singing in order to conserve their energy. We spend as much of our time as we can in the blessed shade of the apple orchard, or indoors where it is even cooler. But I dare not complain of inclement weather, for we had a cool and damp spring and early summer, and the corn harvest is upon us. It will be a good one, so long as we do not get any disastrous thunderstorms and deluges to flatten the crop which is currently standing bright and golden in the fields. Billy says that thunderstorms are always the climax of this sort of weather, and each day he gets up and looks anxiously at the sky, seeking to interpret the signs. Shemi is much better at reading the weather, and he says he gets his information from the animals. I know not whether to believe this, but he says that if we can get harvest home by the 26th day of the month, all will be well. I am working on his advice, and have ordered that reaping should begin tomorrow in Parc-coch.

Today Joseph called round, over-dressed, hot and bothered beneath the midday sun, and asked if he might sit under a shady tree and talk to Grandpa and me. I took with me a long drink of blackcurrant cordial, and they took their mugs of ale, and we found a private place well away from servants and children.

'Now then, Joseph,' said I, 'it is good to see you, as ever. It must be at least five days since we met. I see that there is something on your mind.'

'My dear friends, I am uncertain as to the urgency of what I have to report,' he replied, 'but it is as well to be prepared. First, I have to tell you that Matthew Lloyd of Cwmgloyn is not a happy man at present. I am reliably informed that he received virtually nothing in the old squire's will, and that he has more or less broken off contact with his brother Meredith who has now moved into the old house and taken over the running of the estate. Lately Matthew has been seen frequently in the company of Ifan Beynon in the Black Lion, and my contacts tell me that they are up to something.'

'I am in agreement with that,' said Grandpa. 'Beynon is still a burgess of Newport in spite of his criminal record, and recently he has been out to cause trouble for this estate.'

I was surprised at this, and said: 'Oh indeed? I had heard nothing of this. In what ways has he been causing trouble?'

'You have had enough to cope with recently, my dear Martha, and I had no wish to trouble you with additional things which might or might not prove to be significant. But yes – in meetings of the Court Leet and other bodies he has been seeking to sow seeds in other people's minds about our placing too many animals on the common, failing to maintain our fences, turning a blind eye to encroachments on the common by Williams Gelli, and cutting more peat than our quota permits.'

'But Grandpa!' I spluttered. 'This is outrageous! Surely there is no truth in these allegations?'

'Of course not. Compared with most of the other estates round the fringes of the mountain, we operate with the utmost respect for the rules. Everybody knows that, and Beynon's assertions have thus far been given pretty short shrift by me and almost all the other burgesses. He is not well liked, and he has many enemies. We have the confidence of the Lord Marcher and the Mayor, and that is all that matters.'

169

Then Joseph pressed on. 'And the second matter of import, which may not yet have reached your ears, is that there was a duel at dawn this very morning in Coed Pengelli.'

'Oh, my God!' said I. 'Did it involve anybody we know?'

'Indeed it did. Joseph Rice on the one hand and Matthew Lloyd on the other.'

As Grandpa and I heard this our eyes widened and our jaws dropped. Joseph laughed and slapped his knees in merriment. 'I see, dear friends, that you are amazed!' he chortled. 'Two of the very people whom I suspect of the darkest of intentions as far as this estate is concerned. It is very heartening, don't you think, when members of the criminal fraternity fall out in this way?'

I did not, in truth, find this very amusing, since Joseph was talking of two of the men who were responsible for the murder of my husband only a few months ago. My body tensed and my face darkened, and Joseph immediately responded. 'I am sorry, my dear Martha,' he said. 'It was insensitive of me to speak in such a way. Please forgive me.'

'Thank you, Joseph,' I replied. Then I took a deep breath and continued: 'And what was this particular piece of male idiocy about?'

'I am not entirely sure. But last Saturday there was a furious row between Rice and Lloyd in the Black Lion, during which Lloyd insulted Rice and refused to apologize, so Rice threw down a challenge which Lloyd accepted. The same stupidity as their fathers displayed in the past. I was always taught that insanity runs in families.'

'So what happened next?' asked Grandpa, just as intrigued as I.

'Various people intervened and tried to suggest some

sort of apology which might be acceptable, but the protagonists had had far too much to drink and they would not be deterred from their course. So they turned up as planned at the northern entrance to Pengelli Woods at dawn, with Beynon as Lloyd's second and John Fenton from Glynymel with Rice. Is that not an intriguing piece of intelligence? Ellie's brother William, from Llwyngwair, was prevailed upon to turn out in order to see fair play. He came with two other witnesses, one of whom is my informant. He carried two sets of pistols; Rice chose the set to be used, and Lloyd had first choice of pistol. William tried, even at the last moment, to broker an agreement between the two which might avoid the need for a duel, but the pair simply glared at one another and would have none of it. So William measured out twelve paces, placed a marker on the ground at each end, and ordered the seconds to prepare the pistols with ball and shot. Then they stood back to back at the six-yard mark, strode to their markers, turned to face each other, and fired.'

Joseph then paused for dramatic effect, and said at last: 'You know, I never cease to be amazed at the antics of both the gentry and the criminal classes when the world is supposed to be a place of enlightenment . . .'

'Joseph!' exploded both Grandpa and I simultaneously.

'Oh yes,' said he, thoroughly enjoying himself. 'I do believe I forgot to finish my story. Rice was the quicker of the two – understandable, since Lloyd is far too emotional about everything, and calmness is needed in such circumstances. Lloyd received a ball in his thigh and his shot demolished a few leaves in an oak tree over-head. He fell to the ground with great theatricality. The seconds and the witnesses rushed to his aid and soon ascertained that his life was not threatened. They hauled

171

him off to see Havard Medical, who was just about to have his breakfast and was not at all amused at having to undertake a small operation on Lloyd's leg. Naturally enough, everybody is sworn to silence on the matter, and Doctor Havard was told that his patient had suffered an unfortunate accident.'

'And the combatants?' I asked. 'Have they now made up after the duel under the oak leaves?'

'Dear me, no. Rice offered his hand afterwards to his fallen opponent, but Lloyd simply abused him in a fashion which was most offensive to those gentlemen who were present.'

'I suppose,' said Grandpa, 'that we can gain some comfort from the fact that those two are no longer the best of friends and are likely to remain at odds for some little time to come.'

'Quite correct, Isaac,' said Joseph. 'A perfect outcome, if I may say so.' And he took a long draught of ale from his mug, smiled like an old bull in the middle of a field of buttercups, and settled back against the trunk of the tree beneath which we were sitting.

My suspicions were immediately aroused, so I said: 'Master Joseph Harries! I see all the signs before me of a man content with a job well done. Would you, by any chance, have had anything to do with this unexpected and unsavoury episode?'

'Martha! However could you suggest such a thing?'

'With the greatest of ease. Come along, Joseph. We want the truth.'

'Oh, very well,' he said, without too much reluctance. 'It is true that I had sown certain seeds of doubt in the mind of each of the duellists relating to the loyalty and discretion of the other. I will say no more. But I have found on many occasions in the past that guilty men are easily encouraged in directions which lead, eventually, to the truth.'

At this stage I had to remind Joseph and Grandpa that I should shortly have to return to the house in order to attend to Sara, and we concluded with a rapid discussion on the implications of this news. We agreed that matters might be coming to a head, and that we should keep a careful watch on Rice, Lloyd and Beynon, who were just as likely to do harm to each other as to harm the estate. Rice will have been shocked by the duel, because he is not, so far as I know, a violent man. But he is a man well used to slithering about like a viper in the long grass, and we must be careful where we step. Beynon is a bully and a petty criminal, but he is not very bright, and the methods which he is likely to use in order to make trouble will generally be straightforward and predictable. Matthew Lloyd is our biggest problem, for he is a wild and emotional man who acts before he thinks; after the duel he has injured pride and an injured thigh, and this will not have improved his humour. He is also greatly aggrieved by the manner in which he was in effect cut out of his father's will, and we assume that he is desperately close to becoming a pauper. He may well prove to be our most determined enemy.

We three are already in possession of more disturbing information than we would have liked, and we will meet again if there should be any further developments. Our Council of War is established, and Grandpa Isaac, Joseph and I trust each other absolutely. Now, as I scribble late at night by the light of my candle flame, I admit to feeling a little apprehensive. But I also have to admit to being quite excited, and I feel that an opportunity may be coming my way to demonstrate that I can control situations rather than finding myself in the role of victim.

Young Shemi was almost correct. He thought that the weather would break on 26 August, and now it has broken only two days late, and with a vengeance. The harvest was home three days since, and it was a good one. At the busiest time we had thirty-three people at work in the fields, including our tenants, labourers and some of their womenfolk, and Michael O'Connell and his extended Irish family. Billy was, as usual, Lord of the Harvest, which meant that he first decided how each field should be cut and then led the staggered line of reapers. We had two wheat fields to harvest, and these were done first, with ten men wielding hooks and four women using sickles. The men worked by hook and by crook, holding their razor-sharp hooks in their right hands, cutting the wheat straw as close to the ground as possible and moving each cut swath away with the aid of a short-handled crook. The women worked in the old-fashioned way, each reaper grabbing a handful of stalks at a time with one hand, and using the other hand to saw away with the serrated edges of her small sickle. Each reaper worked with a partner, who was responsible for making twisted bands of wheat straw and then using these to bind up enough of the cut swath to make a manageable sheaf. The other people on the field were needed to gather up the sheaves and build them into stooks, in good straight lines so as to make the carting easier. This year we left the stooks out for three nights to dry out, since the weather was so fine, and then the Jenkins boys did the carting for us and built two beautiful round ricks with conical tops in the rickyard.

Next, the small paddock of oats was cut and stooked, and left for ten days before being carted and ricked. Grandpa says oats should always be left to ripen in stooks for three Sundays, and sometimes we have done just that, but this year I followed Shemi's intuition and insisted that it should be got in as soon as the barley reaping was done. Now we have a small oats rick in the yard, for which the horses will be grateful.

I like the barley harvest best, for this is the one of greatest importance to us and the one which is attended by the most ancient of traditions. This year we cut twenty-one acres; the fields were clean and the ears were plump enough. As usual for the barley harvest the men did all the reaping, now using scythes instead of hooks or sickles. As Lord, Billy led the way round each field, setting the rhythm and the forward pace. He is reputed to be the best man with a scythe this side of Cardigan, and it is said that he can cut a barley swath a foot longer than anybody else, and leave a stubble an inch shorter. Grandpa is full of admiration for his technique, and claims that it is all down to the expert training he gave to Billy when he started at the Plas as a slip of a lad many years ago. 'Scything is not so difficult when you know how,' said Grandpa to me the other day, 'so long as you keep the heel down. But a good reaper can only become a great reaper if he has a good scythe, a good eye, a good balance, a good body and a good whetstone. Billy has all of those, and the stamina to do ten hours in a day.' In reporting all this, and in finding it interesting, I have suddenly come to the realization that I am turning, as sure as night follows day, from an elegant and refined young Mistress into a proper farmer. If this is my destiny, so be it!

Twelve men were used in the scything this year, with six women and six children raking the swaths into rows and another twelve women pitching the harvest onto wagons and carts once the carting was under way. Most of the barley was left on the stubble for two days this year, and it was so hot that it crackled and glittered in the heat haze. For much of the harvest I was preoccupied with Sara, and with poor little Daisy, who had a summer chill on her chest, but I managed to visit the harvest fields on several occasions, and I was amazed that anybody could labour in such heat. The men worked without their shirts on, their brown bodies gleaming and glistening with sweat. They all wore wide-brimmed straw hats which are used just for the harvest and are otherwise stored in the base of Grandma's settle in the kitchen. Mrs Owen and Grandma laid out wonderful picnic feasts each day for the harvesters, usually in the shade of one or another of our stunted hedgerow trees – barley bread and salt butter, cuts of veal and ham, boiled beef and new potatoes, gooseberry pie, raspberries and fresh cream. And many gallons of cider, consumed at mealtimes and also delivered in leather mugs to the men while they were at work. I am mystified as to how they all kept sober, but after three days of scything I did notice that some of the men were cutting short swaths and leaving long stubble. No matter. They did the job with great devotion and with good humour, and the younger servants – Bessie, Sian and Shemi – all declared that the harvest was just what they needed after the traumas of past months. Our days were full of jovial talk, happy singing, and mischief-making by the children. 'Mistress Martha,' said Shemi to me when it was all over, with a big grin on his face. 'You just watch that little Dewi. He has the Devil in him, just like his father. He had me in fits this morning, chasing his big sister round the field, and if Daniel Jenkins had not looked sharpish when I lost concentration I might have had his left foot off with the tip of my scythe!'

On the last evening of reaping we all celebrated the tradition of carrying the hag back to the house. The last barley field, called Cilfynydd, was scythed clockwise, like all the others, round and round until there was only a small tuft of corn left standing in the middle of the field. Billy, as Harvest Lord, then went to it reverently, and without uprooting the stalks split them into three groups and plaited them together to make a little sheaf. This sheaf is called, in this area at least, *y wrach*, the hag. Then he retired ten paces and made a little bow, and the reapers set about the task of trying to cut the old hag down by throwing their reaping hooks at her. This was the only time the reaping hooks were used during the barley harvest. The technique was to throw the hook as close to the ground as possible, spinning fast, in the hope that the blade might slice through the plaited barley stalks. Each man has only one attempt, and if nobody succeeds then the Harvest Lord has the privilege of cutting *y wrach* himself and carrying her back to the house. It is four years since any of the reapers has managed to cut this last sheaf with a thrown reaping hook, but this year Thomas Tucker Penrhiw managed it, to the accompaniment of great cheering and laughter. When this happens there is normally a great deal of horseplay in which the owner of the sheaf is chased about all over the field while he tries to get back to the Plas and into the kitchen without getting wet. The female servants normally defend their kitchen with buckets of water, and everybody gets a thorough soaking. However, this year I was very touched when Thomas, holding *y wrach* in one hand, held up the other to silence the jovial throng, and said: 'Mistress Martha, it is my privilege to hold *y wrach* this year and to be charged with delivering it to the Plas. Normally, at this point, there would be warfare between the men and women of our company of harvesters. However, may I suggest that for once, in this saddest of years, and out of

177

respect for our beloved Master David who is no longer with us, we suspend hostilities? What happened last year would not be seemly this year. Would we agree with that?'

Everybody nodded and murmured their assent. 'Then I thank you, friends,' continued Thomas, 'for your consideration and your sensitivity.' He turned to me again, and may or may not have noticed that I had a tear in my eye. 'Mistress, may I have your consent to place this last sheaf on the big beam by the fireplace in the kitchen, and may I also have your assurance that she will be protected from all intruders and left unmolested until the start of next year's harvest?'

'Thank you, Thomas,' I replied, in a choked voice, barely in control of my emotions. 'Yes, I agree.'

And so a normally riotous procession was replaced, for this year only, by a somewhat more sedate affair. Thomas took my arm and escorted me back to the house, with little Dewi given the privilege of carrying *y wrach*. The others followed behind, silent at first but soon chatting and laughing, for in truth it is well nigh impossible to suppress ebullience at the end of the harvest. I was very touched by the thoughtfulness and affection of all these good people, and it was only with the greatest of difficulty that I kept myself under control. Once we were back at the house, and *y wrach* was fixed to her beam in the ceiling, I retired to my room with Bessie in attendance. She had noticed the draining of colour from my face and the flicker of pain in my eyes, and now she helped me, as gently as ever, to compose myself. I found further consolation in giving Sara the breast, and I am pleased to say that I coped very well with this little crisis. Later the kitchen was given over to feasting, and drinking, and singing, and dancing, and the inhibitions that had manifested themselves earlier on quickly disappeared. I did not object, and indeed I take pride in the recollection that I was able to sing and dance with the best of them while retaining some decorum as far as the drinking was concerned.

By midday on Wednesday all had been paid for their labours, and the Irish had gone. The barley harvest was safe and sound, piled high and trampled down in the barn. With ugly clouds beginning to build up over the mountains, and heaviness in the air, I immediately rang the handbell from the front doorstep of the Plas. The sound echoed round the *cwm*, signalling to the wives and children of the estate labourers that they could come into the fields for the gleaning. They emerged miraculously from the hovels and cottages at Plain Dealings, Brynaeron, Brithdir Bach, Waun Isaf and elsewhere, wicker baskets and hessian bags in their hands. No men were allowed. First the gleaners tackled the wheat fields, then the barley, and then the oats, for a pound of wheat flour is worth twice the price of a pound of barley flour and six times the price of a pound of oatmeal. There must have been sixty people at work, scrabbling about in the dusty stubble, collecting every stray piece of straw and every fallen ear of corn. Later in the year the straw will be turned into chaff, for those who have animals to feed; the clean ears of corn will be milled and used for bread or gruel; and the dirty residue will be fed later to chickens, ducks and geese.

The gleanings were good this year, since I had asked Billy to move the reapers on quickly from one field to the next in the expectation of a break in the weather. David had learned from Grandpa almost as soon as he took over at the Plas that a squire who leaves nothing to be gleaned is seen as a miserable fellow indeed, and he had passed the knowledge on to me. Also, from a strictly economic point of view, if the reapers spend too long raking over the stubble they are using up much time and producing little; Grandpa maintains, and I agree, that a good gleaning helps to foster friendly relations with the labourers and their families, and helps to stave off starvation when the lean months come.

I referred above to the weather's breaking with a vengeance. Vengeance indeed. This afternoon's thunderstorm was the most ferocious I have ever witnessed, and it went on for almost four hours. After a gradual buildup of towering white clouds, the mountains in the sky turned grey and then black, and expanded until the blueness of the firmament was quite obliterated. The morning's stiff breeze quietened to a whisper and then stopped altogether. Every sound made round the *cwm* was transported and amplified like the echoes in some great cathedral; the air itself appeared to be resonating with some strange and vibrant energy. We all stood in the yard with bated breath. We knew what was coming, and the children did not know whether to be excited or frightened. Little Dewi looked at me with wide eyes, seeking reassurance.

Then there was a distant flicker of light, followed after a few seconds by a deep rumble over Foelcwmcerwyn, which Billy said reminded him of the growl of the Hound of Hell. Before I could ask him whether he had ever seen, or heard, that particular creature, the gates of Hell were flung open directly above us. Simultaneously there was a mighty flash of white light and a single gigantic crack of thunder. We were almost frightened out of our wits, in addition to being almost deafened. Instinctively we all – men, women and children – yelled and fled indoors. 'Good God!' said Shemi when he had recovered his breath, 'I think the mountain was hit!'

Little Sara, who had been fast asleep, was screaming in her cradle and needed to be consoled, but the three other children raced upstairs and looked out of their nursery window. 'Mam! Mam!' they shouted. 'Come and look! The mountain is on fire!' And sure enough, it was. The lightning strike had ignited the dry grasses and heather close to the summit, and a fiery inferno engulfed the summit crags. Still there was no wind, and the black smoke rolled up to join the even blacker thundercloud above.

'Will our house be burnt down, Mam?' asked Daisy.

'No,' I replied. 'The fire is a long way away, and before long it will be put out by torrential rain. Just you wait and see.'

That is exactly what happened, but before the rain came we were treated to a quite extraordinary display, with lightning flickering and flashing in forks and curtains at every point of the compass, and thunder rolling and crashing near and far. Several times we thought that the storm was drifting away towards the west, only to be amazed by fresh cracklings of light and roaring and booming thunderclaps above us or over the *cwm*. After about an hour, the wind started to pick up, followed shortly thereafter by the rain. What wind! And what rain! I had not seen such a deluge since the great flood which afflicted this area in 1797, and as on that occasion I formed an image in my mind of an angry God in his Heaven, assisted by a multitude of unhappy spirits, emptying a million gigantic buckets of water over our heads. The wind blew with the force of a hurricane, but I pitied the poor animals, for they could not have known which wall to shelter behind from one minute to the next. First, the hurricane slammed into the west side of the house; then suddenly it came from the north or the south. On some occasions I swear that it came from all sides at once. In brief lulls the deluge battered the roof, and then we felt that walls of water were being driven into the sides of the house with such force that we had to close all the shutters. Three windows were smashed, luckily without harming any of us who were cowering inside. We watched and listened with wide-eyed amazement, for thunder and lightning continued to batter our senses even while rain and wind were battering the house.

And then, as suddenly as it had started, the flickering lights faded away, the thunder rolled off into the distance, the wind dropped and the rain stopped. Within half an hour the evening sun was shining, and the clouds over our heads were melting away like snowballs in a tub of warm water. 'Quite right you were, Mam,' said Daisy. 'The fire on the mountain is out.'

'I pity them poor devils at Gelli Fawr,' said Billy. 'Squire Owen have been waiting for a spot of rain to fatten his barley up a bit. Always was too greedy by half, that one. Now he have had his rain, sure enough. His harvest will be flat on the ground and lost in a sea of mud. He will be lucky to rescue a few cartloads of straw, let alone a bag or two of grain.' On hearing this, I offered up a silent prayer of thanks for our own harvest, having been reminded how narrow is the line between profit and loss, bounty and famine, happiness and misery.

On the matter of our own harvest, I have one further matter to report, which may be of some significance. On the second day of the barley harvest, it was so hot at midday that I gave permission for the harvesters to take a break of one hour in the shade. I carried down a basketful of loaves and cheese to the field in which they were resting, having given up on my attempts to stop the butter from running away. I noticed that Gethin Griffiths Dolrannog was sitting apart from the others, and he immediately caught my eye and motioned for me to join him. I went over to him and sat down beside him

182

on a rough woollen blanket. 'Well, Gethin,' I said, 'you have all made the most wonderful progress in this heat. I am very impressed.'

'Thank you, Mistress Martha,' he said. 'Things are going well.' Then he looked round to ensure that there were no spies within five yards, lowered his voice, and continued. 'If I may be so bold, I have some information which I must pass on to you. You may or may not be aware that some of us hold you in great esteem and are greatly saddened by the misfortunes which you have had to bear since you came to the Plas. It is our intention, Mistress, to ensure that no further misfortune comes in your direction.'

'Why, Gethin,' said I, greatly surprised. 'You are very kind.'

'Now, to come to the matter in hand. As you may know, I have certain contacts in the free trade business, and this requires both me and them to keep our ears close to the ground in case there are any Customs officers prowling about or in case any of those accursed Excise cutters happens to come up this way from Milford Haven. Anyway, the other night one of my business acquaintances just happened to be in the Rose and Crown, minding his own business like, when who should come in but Matthew Lloyd Cwmgloyn, and Ifan Beynon Berry Hill. Nasty bastards, both of them, if you will forgive my language, Mistress. Lloyd was limping from that ball he got in the thigh in the duel with young Rice, and he was clearly in pain since by all accounts the wound went septic . . .'

'How do you know about that? I thought the duel was a secret?'

'So it is, Mistress, so it is. To continue. Beynon has still got bandages on his arm, since it was broke in the *cnapan* game on Shrove Tuesday. Did you know it was broke?

Well, it was. Normally the two of them drinks in the Black Lion, so my business acquaintance was intrigued, naturally enough, and snuggled up a bit closer to where they was sitting. Purely by chance, Mistress, he overheard that they was talking about the Plas, and also about you. Believe it or not, they was talking about a treasure! Take it from me, Mistress, they are after it. Now there's a daft thing for you, for I saw with my very eyes after the fire that destroyed the old Plas the remains of the Morgan money chest, with just hinges and bolt left, all twisted and melted by the heat. All the money was gone, turned into molten drippings and sent up in smoke. Are these boys mad, Mistress?'

I was greatly surprised by this turn of events, but tried not to show it. Choosing my words with care, I said, 'Who am I to say whether they are mad or not? I do not think that I have met either gentleman for several years, and am quite unqualified to talk about their state of mind. Neither can I say why they may think there is a Plas Ingli treasure which they might covet. I did not even know the Morgan family at the time of the fire, and like you I heard that all that was left of the money chest was a few charred scraps of metal. At least twenty people must have been witness to that.'

Gethin nodded. 'Quite so. Anyway, if they are mad and deluded, all the more reason to watch out for them. Take care, Mistress. And be assured that me and my acquaintances will be having a little eye open for those two gentlemen, and will keep you informed.'

He stood and helped me to my feet. 'Thank you very much, Gethin,' I said. 'Your quiet words, and your concern, are much appreciated.'

And that was that. I find this very intriguing, to say the least.

Some further pieces of intelligence have reached my ears, and I am even more intrigued. They have come from a new friend who occupies a part of the social scale so far away from mine as to be almost invisible, and this is a fact which I find mildly amusing.

Last weekend Hettie came up to the Plas, as usual, to fetch some eggs and vegetables for her lodging house down on the Parrog. When she had completed her business with Mrs Owen, she came up to my room and knocked gently on the door. I was feeding Sara at the time, but that presented no difficulty either for Hettie or me, or for little Sara, and I was delighted to see her. For a while we chatted about this and that. Then Hettie said: 'Mistress Martha, I have a message for you. Do you know Patty Ellis from the Parrog?'

'I know of her and of the services which she regularly provides to passing seamen,' I replied, 'but I cannot claim to know her personally, since ladies of easy virtue tend to move in other social circles.'

'Well, she met me down by the quayside the other day, very furtive, and asked me to pass you a message. She would like you to pop in and see her as soon as it might be convenient.'

'Hettie, you must realize that I could not go down to the Parrog and knock on Patty's cottage door without being seen by half the town. My reputation would be destroyed at a stroke.'

'I appreciate that, Mistress,' said Hettie. 'Is there anywhere else you can meet?'

I thought for a moment, and then said: 'I have a sudden urge to walk down to town tomorrow morning, quite early, with a view to visiting Master Price Very Nice and purchasing a new bonnet. Before I do that,

Hettie, I might take a walk along the river, from Pont Nyfer to the Parrog. I suppose that that might take me from half past eight to nine of the clock. It is such a pleasant thing to do, and one occasionally bumps into the most interesting people.'

Hettie grinned and said, 'Message understood, Mistress. Now then, I must get back to the lodgings and make up some beds. Two ships are due on the high tide, and I will have three sailors to look after by the time the sun sets.'

So it was that next morning, as I strolled along the shore of the muddy estuary, I happened to meet Patty Ellis coming the other way. I did not recognize her, but she recognized me and immediately said: 'Good morning, Mistress Martha, there's pleased I am to meet you. My name is Patty Ellis.' Then she gave a little curtsey, which I thought very charming.

'Good day to you, Patty,' said I. 'How do you do? Hettie tells me that you have something to say to me. Shall we walk together onto the mud-flats where there are no hidden ears?'

'I'll be delighted to do that,' said Patty with a smile on her face. And so we walked onto the breezy estuary, with only gulls and long-legged wading birds for company. She was a remarkably pretty girl, just a little older and taller than me, with golden ringlets, a substantial bosom and a small waist. She wore too much rouge upon her cheeks, and had too much blacking upon her eyelashes, but the cut of her cotton dress was only a little less discreet than mine, and I thought her remarkably well preserved, considering the unsocial hours that she kept and the heavy demands of her job.

'Mistress Martha, I will be as brief as I can,' she said, 'since I have an appointment to keep in one hour's time. You may not know it, but you and I share something

186

which we would prefer, I dare say, not to talk about. We have both been sorely used in the past by those two monsters Benjamin Rice and George Howell, who abused their powers as magistrates and caused untold suffering in this town. Like you, I was falsely accused of some petty larceny, refused the opportunity to defend myself, summarily convicted, and then stripped to the waist and whipped through the crowded streets.'

'Oh, you poor thing!' said I. 'I had no idea . . .'

'It happened to me a long time ago, when I was but a slip of a girl. At the time, I swore revenge, and I will have it before I go to my grave. Then I was in the crowd some years back when you were dragged behind the whipping cart – the first and the last time that such a thing was done to a lady. I was so outraged, Mistress, by what those men did to you, and so moved by your forti-tude even as they continued to beat you with blood streaming off your back, that I swore further vengeance on your behalf.'

'But Patty, revenge is not needed. You know that those men, and their accomplices, were brought to justice?'

'Of course. Thank God that Howell is dead, and Rice shipped off to the colonies in the company of other murderers and thieves. But that slimy toad Ifan Beynon, who did their dirty work for them, is still lurking about in the dark streets of this town, and as far as the Rice and Howell families are concerned, they have still not paid a proper price.'

I was greatly surprised to hear a young lady of pleasure speaking in such dark and cold-blooded terms so many years after the events which had left scars upon her back and planted malice in her heart. I said as much to her, and surmised, aloud, that she might have suffered further, and more recently, at the hands of the Rice and Howell families.

'You are quite right, Mistress Martha,' said Patty. 'Time does heal, and three years since I had all but forgotten about the miseries of the past. I was in the service of Captain Luke Morris in the big house next to the Ship Afloat. He was often away at sea, and I was frequently alone in the house. I was not well paid – in fact, very often, if the Captain was in a foul mood, I was not paid at all. One day, in a weak moment, I thought I should earn myself a few pennies by killing one of the Captain's chickens and selling it to the landlord of the Parrog Arms. The Captain was off with the *Sally Anne* to Bristol, and would not be back for a week. I was plucking the chicken in the scullery when who should come in but Joseph Rice, one of the Captain's cronies. I came over all flustered, and I dare say, Mistress, that my face turned the colour of beetroot.'

'Oh dear,' said I, quite caught up in her sorry tale.

Patty's face darkened, and I saw pain in her eyes. She continued: 'He is a hundred times more evil than his father, Mistress, you mark my words. He immediately perceived my guilt, and said that he was duty bound to take up the matter with my employer and the magistrates. He left me in no doubt that he would swear before the Sessions as to my guilt, and that I would be strung up on the gallows tree before the month was out. Who was I, a poor serving girl, to judge the truth of what he said? What was I to do, Mistress Martha – what could I do?'

The poor girl clutched my hand and looked at me with wild and tear-filled eyes. Before I could suggest an answer to her question, she continued, and my blood ran cold. 'Then he offered me a bargain. He said that he would keep quiet if I would perform certain services whenever he required them. I think, Mistress, that you understand me?' I nodded. 'I had to agree. So he used me in a most cruel way there and then, and he returned every evening until the Captain came back with his cargo from Bristol. After that it happened over and again, whenever the Captain was away at sea.'

'But what about the chicken?' I asked, and immediately felt remorse at the banality of the question in the context of her appalling tale.

'Oh, the Captain never noticed that one was missing. He left all the domestic matters to me. I would have got away with it, for sure, had it not been for that devil Joseph Rice.'

By now our walk had taken us towards Havard Nautical's shipyard, where work was in progress on a new ketch, so I urged Patty, as delicately as I could, to complete her story. 'You might as well know, Mistress, that in the matter of intimate favours, one thing led to another,' she said. 'Soon some of Rice's cronies were paying me visits in the Captain's house, and paying for the services I provided. Rice pocketed half of my takings, and I kept the other half. Tongues were beginning to wag, and Rice decided eventually that I should hand in my notice. At the same time a cottage on the sea front fell vacant, and he arranged for me to take it. I am still there, Mistress, still providing services to Rice and his cronies and to a great many other gentlemen, and still handing over half of my takings at the end of each week. Have you ever wondered, Mistress, how Joseph Rice – the landless and idle son of a disgraced and bankrupt father – survives and pays for his food, and his ale, and his lodgings? Well, now you know.'

Instinctively I put my arm round the poor girl's shoulder and gave her a little kiss on the cheek. I had, until then, without knowing her, thought of her as nothing more than a hussy, a woman beyond help, devoid of higher feelings, who spent her days and nights

189

rejoicing in fornication. But not for the first time, I was forced to accept that life is more complex than it might seem. And I felt a bitter taste in my mouth at the realization that Joseph Rice, the murderer of my husband, was living in some comfort as a pimp on the proceeds of extortion and blackmail.

We were now walking towards the bustle and the jostle of the Parrog, where herring were being unloaded from a fishing smack and the local merchants with their carts and wagons were taking advantage of the low tide to unload two vessels beached on the sand. Limestone crushings, coal, salt and other goods were coming in, and barley, timber and wool were going out. 'I must take my leave, Mistress Martha,' said Patty, having now regained her composure. 'I judge you to be a good lady, and I assume that I can count on your discretion?'

'I swear that I will not breathe a word of this to anybody.'

'Very well. You might like to know that among my clients I number Matthew Lloyd, Captain John Howell, and a certain Master John Fenton of Glynymel. I know a good deal about each of them, and I know a very great deal about Joseph Rice. They are making plans. Something of what I know may well be of interest to you. Do you know that you are in danger?'

I nodded.

'I thought as much,' she said. Then she thrust out her chin, and a fire was lit in her eyes, and she started to laugh. I was greatly taken aback. 'Mistress Martha!' she chuckled. 'You must not look so sad. We have both suffered much. You have survived cruel abuse and have lost a brave and gentle husband. I have been cruelly used by a monster of a man and have been trapped into a life of sin through a small moment of weakness. But in truth life is not so bad, either for you or for me. You have a loving family, and a roof over your head, and a fine estate to run. I have good clothes and pretty jewels, food in my belly, and a place to live. I do not need to call on Poor Relief for the essentials of life. I have freedom of a sort. I bring pleasure to others, and in truth I occasionally enjoy some pleasure myself in the course of my work. Together, Mistress, with the aid of a little female cunning, we will see off Rice and his fellows. We are quite invincible! I believe it, and so must you.'

Then she said, 'I have more to tell you. Can we meet, at the same place and the same time, on Friday of next week?'

'Yes, of course,' I said. And she winked like a courtesan, hitched up her skirts, and trotted off along the dusty Parrog track towards her cottage.

I quite forgot to visit Martin Price Very Nice, and walked home along the high summer lanes with my mind buzzing. Somehow or other I appear to have acquired another friend and another guardian, although in truth I find it difficult to see myself as a fragile female in need of constant protection. What a courageous woman! I suspect that Patty has more brains inside her skull than all of her clients put together. She is nobody's fool, and I don't think I would like to have her for an enemy. I think I will enjoy working with her, although I dare say it will be best not to broadcast our friendship too widely, given the nature of her profession and the sensibilities of my other friends.

2 September 1805

I have had a meeting with another stranger who may, I suspect, become a valued ally. The encounter followed a little note which was delivered by a horseman at breakfast time a few days since, which read as follows:

191

Glynymel, Fishguard, on the 25th day of August
in the year 1805

My dear Mistress Morgan,

We have not met, but you may know that I was present at the funeral of your beloved husband some months since, and that I sent a small message of condolence to you and your family. These were but small gestures, and will not in any way have lessened your grief; but I trust that you obtained some consolation from the spontaneous outpouring of affection which occurred at that time from all stations of society – a sign, if any were needed, that your dear David was held in the very highest esteem.

I have been reluctant, in the circumstances, to introduce myself before now, but I hear that you and your beautiful children are coping very bravely with the misfortune which has been visited upon you, ably assisted, I am sure, by my old friends Master Isaac and Mistress Jane.

You may have heard that I am undertaking a Grand Tour of Pembrokeshire with a view to recording for posterity something of the fine houses, ancient families, and remarkable antiquities of our blessed county. I have not previously called upon Plas Ingli in the course of my researches, but I am now minded to do so if you would be so gracious as to permit a brief visit. Would next Tuesday at two of the clock be convenient?

My man will wait upon a reply, and I trust that I shall soon have the great pleasure of making your acquaintance.

Yours etc., Fenton, Glynymel

I read the letter out to the assembled company around the kitchen table, and could hardly suppress a smile. 'What a charming letter!' I said. 'So measured and considerate, and so full of genteel charm! Somewhat pedantic, but the writer must be a kind sort of gentleman. This would be Richard Fenton, Grandpa?'

'Yes indeed,' he replied, still munching on a slice of bread and cheese. 'A good old fellow with whom I spent a great deal of time many years ago. He lived then at Manorowen, near Fishguard, and went away to Oxford and London to study, and made a great fortune as a barrister. He came back some years since, with a French wife whom he adores, and has built a fine house in the *cwm* near the fishing harbour. He talks a great deal, and uses two hundred words where other men might use two, but he has a good heart.'

'Shall I welcome him to the Plas?'

'Why not? I, for one, shall be delighted to meet him again after all these years.'

So I scribbled out a brief message to the effect that we would be pleased to receive him on the suggested date and at the proposed time, and asked Shemi to give it to his man, who was drinking tea in the scullery.

Squire Fenton arrived in a two-horse chaise on the appointed day. He was ten minutes late, flustered and full of apologies. Indeed, so full of apologies was he that I had to assure him over and again that I was not in the least offended. He proved to be a little older than Grandpa, with a ruddy complexion and sparkling blue eyes. I liked him immediately, and we got on famously. We drank some excellent tea newly delivered by Dai Canton, and ate some of Mrs Owen's special cocoa-flavoured sweetmeats, and I was happy to think that our refreshments, our china, and indeed the general ambience of our parlour, left nothing to be desired. He was lavish in his compliments, and said that he was delighted to encounter such style, and such pleasant company, in the new Plas Ingli. 'My goodness, Master Fenton.' I laughed. 'The house is not as new as all that. It was built straight after the fire, and has been here now for ten years. So we have had some time to settle in and to recreate a style of living of which I, as a new Mistress, can be proud.'

We talked of this and that. Master Fenton and Grandpa reminisced about old times and talked of the French Invasion. He met the children, who immediately took a liking to him, and he even got a smile out of little Sara by tickling her under her chin. Then he suddenly said: 'Mistress Martha, the rain is holding off and I have one further item of pleasure to attend to this afternoon. I have it in mind to visit the fantastical *cromlech* built by the ancient Druids at Pentre Ifan. Have you been there? No? Would you like to accompany me?'

I was instantly taken by this proposal, since I had heard much about the strange stones at Pentre Ifan. I also realized, although I did not mention it, that I had a further demon to slay by visiting the Pentre Ifan estate. The old house was once the seat of the Rice family, and it was the place where I was condemned by Squires Rice and Howell to be horsewhipped through the streets of Newport in the black year of 1797. Now the estate was owned by Richard Fenton and farmed by one Ethan Wilmot, and I judged that a visit might well help in the long-term healing of my soul.

'What a charming idea!' I replied. 'I will be delighted to come. But two requests. First, will you give me a half hour to settle the baby before we leave? And second, may we bring Betsi with us? She was talking about standing stones and such things only the other day, and she would, I am sure, love to join us.'

'By all means! By all means!' agreed the Squire. 'You go and get yourself organized, and I will talk to Isaac about sheep for a while.'

And so, shortly after four of the clock, Betsi and I set off in the company of this fine gentleman on a voyage of discovery. We left Daisy and Dewi howling in the yard, for they wanted to come too, but I gathered later on that they soon became more cheerful when Sian informed them that six little piglets had just been born, and that there were more on the way. First, we paid a brief visit to Pentre Ifan farmhouse, where we met Master Wilmot and his family, and then we travelled on a further mile to the place where the great stones stood. They were quite magnificent, and the sight of them took our breath away. Squire Fenton, who had visited them many times before, took huge pleasure in our amazement, and was in the best of humour as he pointed out the dimensions and nature of the stones, their alignment and position on the hillside, and details of the pottery fragments and so forth which he had dug up in the course of his researches.

I had seen *cromlechs* before, but nothing like this. The monument was made of a group of mighty elongated bluestone boulders, mostly standing on end like pillars seven or eight feet tall. Balanced delicately on top of three of them was a great flat slab of rock about fifteen feet long and ten feet wide, providing a roof over a sort of chamber. The slab was so high above the ground that a man on a horse could ride under it with ease. Master Fenton told us that this was a place where great Druid chieftains were buried, for he had personally found bones and skulls there. Maybe there had been treasures too, he said, but these had long since been stolen by grave robbers. For maybe half an hour we wandered around the place, and I was especially taken by the location, with the summit of Carningli visible from one side, framed by the overhead slab and two of the supporting pillars. The craggy summits of Carnedd Meibion Owen were visible away to the south-west, and far to the north we could glimpse the sea glittering in the evening sun. A magical place indeed; and I vowed, with the Squire's willing consent, to visit it again at my leisure.

Betsi also wants to go to the *cromlech* again, for she is

quite convinced that fairies live nearby and dance round the stones in the moonlight. Indeed, Master Fenton said that he had heard from an old lady who lives out at Pencaer that when she was a girl she came here often, and saw fairies dancing on many occasions. She said they were small and very pretty, dressed in green and red, and that they danced with great delicacy to the most seductive and enthralling of tunes.

Then it was time to return home. We clambered back into the chaise, and were soon clattering down the hill to Trewern and Cilgwyn. Within a few minutes Betsi was fast asleep, her blond head against my shoulder. Much to my surprise, Master Fenton then turned to me and said quietly: 'Asleep at last. What a pretty sight is a child transported to the world of dreams! Now then. I have been waiting all day to have a quiet word with you alone. My dear Mistress Martha, before she wakes up, I want to say something important. Do you know that I have three sons?'

I was very surprised by this sudden turn of events. 'Why yes,' I said softly, trying not to wake my daughter. 'I have heard of them.'

'Well, two of them are good fellows, happy and well settled. But my other son, John, who is the oldest of the three, has caused me great sadness. He has turned out to be wild and irresponsible, and spends most of his time away from the area – mostly in London, in the company of those to whom we refer as "the Prince's Set". He knows the Prince of Wales and the scoundrels and wastrels he consorts with far too well for my peace of mind, and the generous allowance I give him slips through his fingers like fine sand in coffee houses, taverns and houses of ill repute. His mother and I have remonstrated with him and have encouraged him into a profession, but all to no avail. I despair of his ever taking an interest in the estate, or indeed ever making something useful of his life.'

'But my dear Master Fenton, what has all this to do with me?'

'Mistress Martha, you are a very desirable and very beautiful young widow. You have four hundred acres of sunny south-facing land, a good home farm, five tenanted farms and rights upon the common land of the mountain. You and your family have a reputation for probity, compassion and wise land management. You may not have realized it yet, but now that some months have passed since the death of your husband, you will have a veritable procession of hopeful gentlemen coming up the mountain track to pay you visits.'

I was taken aback by this, for in truth I had not thought of myself, or the estate, in such a manner before. 'Oh dear,' I said. 'Is this all really so? And even if it is, why does your son John come into the picture?'

'Because last time he visited he was showing an uncommon interest in you and the Plas Ingli estate. He is in London just now, but when he has run out of money again he will be back in Fishguard looking for food and entertainment, just as surely as the cuckoo returns to the area every April looking for the nest of some innocent little brown bird in which to settle.'

'Do you predict that he will wish to call on me?'

'As sure as night follows day.' Then the kind gentleman took my hand and looked me straight in the eye. 'When he calls, I urge you to have nothing to do with him. Do not listen to his honeyed words. Do not trust him. It saddens me to say this about my own son, but I have already seen too much of the damage he has done to other innocent people who have fallen under his spell. I want you to know, Mistress Martha, that I and the other members of my family have absolutely no designs upon your estate, no matter how much I might welcome a gracious lady such as you into our family circle. Whatever my son John may do or say in your presence, be assured that it is all absolutely without my blessing.'

By now the chaise was well along the Dolrannog road, and the front gate to the Plas was very close. 'I thank you, sir, for your timely words,' said I. 'I will endeavour to hold them in mind, and trust that I will never have cause to act upon your advice.'

Then we were home, and Betsi was awake. We offered warm thanks to the Squire for our fascinating expedition, and he was full of praise for our hospitality. We agreed to meet socially again before the year is out, at Glynymel this time, and he said that he was sure I would get on splendidly with his beloved wife. Then, with a wave, he was gone, and I was dragged into the happy frenzy of supper time, and children's baths and bedtime stories, and busy talk about the other events of the day.

Never before have I heard a father talk to a total stranger in such a way about his own son. It appears that I now have another friend, and another enemy.

8 September 1805

I have taken the liberty of asking some more questions about Patty Ellis. When Hettie called up the other day I took her to one side and told her that Patty and I had met as planned, and thanked her for her assistance in passing messages back and forth. Since she likes to know everything about everything, she inquired as to the purpose of our meeting.

'I am afraid that I cannot tell you that, Hettie,' I replied. 'Patty was very insistent that the contents of our discussion must be confidential. Suffice to say that I found her to be a perfectly pleasant girl who has the best interests of the estate at heart.' Then I asked Hettie about the girl's background, and said that I found her well-spoken and intelligent.

'Not surprising, Mistress,' said Hettie. 'Her father Jimmy Ellis was a merchant in town, and her mother was a seamstress. There was good money in the family, and Patty had a sound education. But her father and mother both died of the consumption when she was ten or eleven, and after that she was looked after – or not looked after, as the case may be – by various relatives. She ran wild and got into all sorts of scrapes on the Parrog. She got in with some very rough people, and you probably know the rest.'

So it was that this morning I met up again with Patty on the footpath by the river. It was raining, and blowing a veritable gale, and the tide was in. So we sat together beneath my umbrella, under a wind-blasted oak tree. 'Now then, Patty,' I said. 'I fear we will get soaked to the skin sitting here, but we have to make the best of it – and be sure to talk very quickly!'

'Quite so, Mistress Martha,' said Patty, huddling up close. Then I noticed that she gasped and winced with pain as our shoulders touched.

'Patty, are you all right?' I asked in alarm.

'Yes,' she replied. Then she drew a deep breath, and said: 'Well, actually, no. I am not all right. That swine Joseph Rice . . .'

I immediately comprehended what had been happening. 'He has been beating you. Has he discovered that you and I have been talking?'

'No, nothing like that. Last week my takings were down, and he thought they should have been up. When he gets angry, he hits me. Never on the head or face, mind, since black eyes and bruised cheeks and bleeding lips tend to have a negative effect on trade.'

'The bastard!' I exclaimed, and was immediately shocked at my violent response and my intemperate language. Calming down, I asked, 'Oh, Patty, what can we do? Can I help you in some way?'

'I don't think so,' she replied, with tears, or raindrops, or both, dripping off the end of her nose. 'Anyway, you have got problems of your own. I will be all right again in a few days. I will get him one day, maybe with a knife between his ribs, if somebody else doesn't get him first.' She swallowed hard. 'You are getting wet, Mistress Martha,' she said. 'I will say what I have to say, and then you had better get up to town and find some shelter. First, on the matter of Joseph Rice. You may not realize it, but many secrets reside between the sheets in a cottage such as mine. When he uses me, Rice is often drunk. However, I never drink alcohol when I am working. He sees it as one of his privileges to stay the night, and it is one of my misfortunes to observe him when he is asleep. Take it from me, Mistress Martha, he is a very troubled man. On five or six occasions he has been racked by the most terrible nightmares. Or maybe I should say "nightmare", for I truly believe that it is the same one that tortures him over and again. He screams and groans in a most pitiful way, and writhes about in the bed, shouting in his sleep the same words over and again.'

'Oh, my God!' said I. 'What does he say?'

'He shouts, "Die, Morgan, damn you! Die now! Die now!" and then he wakes up, and sits bolt upright, with sweat pouring off his brow and his eyes wide with terror.'

There followed a long silence, during which I found it hard to control my emotions. I felt as cold as February ice, and I think I was shivering. At last I said, 'Does Rice know that you have observed his nightmares?'

'Oh no. I always pretend to be asleep, and he always turns to me afterwards, with his heart racing, like a small baby wanting the comfort of a mother's embrace. Do you have any idea what this might mean, Mistress?'

'Yes,' I replied. 'I know perfectly well. One day I will reveal everything to you.' Patty nodded and said nothing. Then she became businesslike again.

'Finally,' she said, 'I come to the matter of the other swine in whose filthy company Joseph Rice splashes about in the mud. I mentioned to you that John Howell, John Fenton, and Matthew Lloyd are also among my clients? Yes? I know too much for comfort about them too. They all drink too much, they are all rotten to the core, and they are all indiscreet when they are in my bed. Fenton has the pox and is in London just now. Thank God for that. Howell is away fighting the French, or, if I know him as well as I think I do, avoiding them like the plague. Lloyd is out of action at present, since his wound went septic after the duel with Rice. I hear that it may never heal properly, and he is very bitter. He hates Rice with an intensity that is hard to credit, which is interesting, since they were until recently the closest of friends. They all have dealings with the loathsome Ifan Beynon, who is the vilest creature ever to pollute this sweet earth. That makes five of them altogether. They do not trust each other further than a viper can spit; but do you know, Mistress, what binds them together?'

'Tell me, Patty.'

'A strange sort of hatred for you personally, although I gather that in truth they hardly know you. I am at a loss to understand it. I think that I would be right in saying that none of them has actually met you for at least seven or eight years?'

'You are correct,' I replied. 'In fact, I don't think I have ever met John Fenton or Matthew Lloyd. As for Rice and

201

Howell, I have only met them fleetingly at various social gatherings a long time ago. And I will prefer not to talk about Ifan Beynon for fear of saying something ill befitting a lady.'

Patty grinned and nodded. 'And finally,' she said, 'the other thing that binds them together is the conviction that there is untold wealth hidden somewhere at the Plas. They all dream about getting their hands on it, and in pursuit of that aim I believe they will do almost anything. I have told them that there is no Plas Ingli treasure, since my uncle Tad was one of the men who saw the twisted remains of the family money chest when the old Plas was burnt down. But they will not listen. They are convinced that there is a pile of gold and silver waiting to be dug up.'

'Oh, dear,' I said. 'Where on earth did they get that peculiar idea from?'

Patty shrugged, and our interview was at an end. She jumped up to her feet, wincing momentarily from her injuries. 'Now then, Mistress Martha,' she said. 'You are very wet. You had better take that little path by the spring and go straight up to town before you catch your death of cold. If I was you, I would call in at Siop Fach and get a nice hot cup of tea. And don't you worry. These fellows are all insane, and we will get the better of them, just you mark my words. I won't let them harm a single hair of your pretty head, and not your children either. They are too disorganized to do anything soon, and I reckon you are quite safe until Christmas at the earliest. If I find out anything at all about what they have in mind, I will pass word to you through Hettie within the day.'

And she gave a little wave, wrapped herself up in her cloak, and headed back along the path towards Parrog.

I have tried, in the past, never to succumb to hatred, for it is the most negative and destructive of emotions, with a tendency to eat away and eventually displace the virtues which mark out mankind as different from the apes. But I feel something very close to hatred when I think of Joseph Rice, who is now confirmed as one of the murderers who took my dear David away from me. I have killed one evil man, and I will kill again, with my bare hands, if I get the chance. I swear in these secret pages of my diary that Rice will not escape with his life for what he has done in the past, and for what he continues to do today to the likes of Patty Ellis. So help me God.

In stepping back from dark and depraved thoughts, and in seeking to control raw emotions, I have to try to make sense of everything I have discovered in recent weeks. My head is full of knotted threads, and I fear that I am having great difficulty in unravelling them. Today was a grey and windy day, and first thing in the morning I had a little talk with Grandpa Isaac. He agreed with me that we needed a Council of War. So I sent Shemi over to Werndew on the chestnut pony to ask Joseph if he would be kind enough to call by during the afternoon. If anybody could help me to organize my thoughts it would be Joseph Harries, part wizard and part sleuth, but for the most part wise and trusted friend.

He arrived at three of the clock, having successfully eliminated a curse which had been afflicting one of Owen Pritchard's cows. He gave me, as usual, a warm embrace, and said, 'Martha my dear, you look wonderful! Each time you have delivered a new baby into the world I am struck by the extent to which you appear to thrive on motherhood. One day, I must make a scientific study of the phenomenon!'

'Not on me, if you please, dear doctor. I have no time to be prodded and probed, and in any case I am too ticklish, as my children will attest.'

We sat down in the parlour while Bessie made some tea, and I asked Grandpa Isaac to join us, having previously put him in the picture. When the tea and butter scones had been served, I asked Bessie to ensure that we were not disturbed by the children or anybody else, and moved immediately to the matter which was on my mind. 'Dear Grandpa and dear Joseph,' I said, 'I need your help. There are two things I need to resolve in my mind, the first of which is the motive for David's murder. I feel strong today and wish to talk about it, no matter how distressing it may be. I cannot live with confusion and supposition any longer.'

'Very well, Martha,' said Joseph. 'Master Isaac, shall I start?' Grandpa nodded. 'Since we last spoke I have obtained further information about the evening following the fateful *cnapan* game. Rice and Howell you know about. I have spoken to two of my friends, one of whom is a servant in the big house at Berry Hill, and the other a cottager who lives up the lane very close to Matthew Lloyd Cwmgloyn. They both affirm that the conspirators in question came home soaking wet. Lloyd was in a filthy mood, swearing and cursing that he was about to win the game for Nevern when it was suddenly called off. Beynon, when he arrived home, was in terrible pain, holding his arm and moaning like a man standing before the gallows. He was soaking wet and shivering uncontrollably. His old mother wanted to call the doctor, but he would have none of it, so the servants had to fill him with brandy and treat his injury as best they could. You knew that he broke his arm in the struggle with David?'

Grandpa looked surprised, but I nodded. 'Thank you, Joseph. I am now utterly convinced of the truth of your version of events. I have it verified by Billy and from other directions as well. But why? Why did they wish to kill my husband? Surely they cannot have planned it in advance? They were not to know that a bank of fog would roll in from the sea. And surely they could not have anticipated an opportunity to attack David out of the sight of others? The *cnapan* game, as I understand it, may be chaotic, but from what I hear there are always people rushing hither and thither, some on foot and some on horseback, and players are protected by their confederates. David, as one of the better players, would have been constantly protected, especially if he had the *cnapan* in his hand.'

'Perfectly correct,' said Grandpa. 'But remember that Billy was acting as a decoy, and took the bulk of the players away towards the sand dunes. The poor fellow still feels guilty about that. But in any case the murder could not have been premeditated. In my view it was a spontaneous thing: and that when an opportunity presented itself the four villains followed David away from the main throng of players and tried to wrest the *cnapan* from his hands. When he refused to give it up they attacked him, and then matters got out of hand. When men have a lot of money riding on the result of a game, such as seems to have been the case on Shrove Tuesday, common sense flies out of the window and desperation takes over. I think that in their lust to win these men simply went mad with rage, and that they were appalled and terrified when they realized that David was dead. They fled from the scene, and we know the rest.'

'I agree with some of that, Isaac,' said Joseph. 'But remember that Lloyd, at least, did not flee. He remounted his horse and rode towards the Newport goal, *cnapan* held aloft, shouting wildly and intent upon winning the game. There was no panic in that. That was the action of a cold-blooded murderer devoid of remorse.'

'And emboldened by a considerable consumption of ale?' I asked.

'Quite possibly. But I think these men were planning something before the game started. Remember that Rice and Howell may well have hated David, as head of the family which was responsible, some years back, for the destruction of their families and the disposal of their estates.'

At this I flushed, and said with anger in my voice: 'But those accursed squires deserved everything that befell them. David never did anything wrong. True, he resisted them and fought against their wicked plans, but he never harmed a hair of their heads, and they were undone by their own evil and by the course of justice.'

'True, Martha,' said Grandpa, placing his old brown hand upon mine. 'But reason does not feature strongly in the minds or hearts of men who have lost everything, and are looking for somebody to blame.'

'I agree again, Isaac,' continued Joseph. 'Maybe they thought they might get the opportunity to harm David just a little, quite legally, in the course of the game. Maybe they did set their sights upon him, and maybe they followed him on their horses and waited for an opportunity. I suspect that Rice and Lloyd were the leaders, with Beynon and Howell following. I further suspect that they could not believe their luck when they had David in their sights and the fog bank rolled in. Once they had him at the water's edge, out of the sight of the main throng of players, I am sure that they decided to kill him. And kill him they did, in cold blood.'

I found it difficult to continue this analysis, for Patty's

description of Joseph Rice's recurring nightmare came flooding into my mind. But somehow I found the strength, and I said: 'But what on earth could they have had to gain from David's death? Was this just a matter of revenge, an eye for an eye and a tooth for a tooth? Surely this would not justify what they did, with all the attendant risks of being observed by a stray foot player at the game, and then accused, and found guilty of murder, and strung up on the gallows? I think that there must be more to it than that.'

'Martha, my dear, you are very perceptive,' said Joseph. 'My thoughts exactly. Lloyd may well be motivated by the ancient feud between the Lloyds and the Morgans. But would he kill just to keep the feud alive? I doubt it – he does, after all, have a wife and family to support, and this tends to be a calming influence upon the wildest of men. Beynon, with his rat eyes and small brain, may wish revenge on the family for the years he spent doing hard labour in the penal establishments of Portsmouth. But with his record, and with no handy magistrates to protect him, he would be the first to the gallows if found guilty of murder. Does one of the others, Rice or Howell, love you and hope for your hand in marriage? I doubt that, since they have hardly met you. Do they individually or corporately hope to see the estate decline, by doing damage where they can and by removing one person after another? Isaac next? And then maybe you, my dear Martha? I doubt that too, for if the estate were to be dismantled and sold off, who would buy it? Not them, for they hardly have the price of a decent cow between them.'

'So, dear Joseph, and dear Grandpa,' I said, 'we are no nearer to the truth. But I come to my second matter. John Fenton. It has come to my ears that he may have some designs upon me and the estate. He has also been observed in meetings with Rice and Howell. Have any of your contacts come up with anything to confirm my concerns?'

Grandpa nodded. 'Yes, I know all of this,' he said.

'And so do I,' said Joseph, with a wry grin on his face. 'Martha, my dear, your information sources appear to be every bit as good as ours! You are learning very well that the survival of ancient families and small estates depends upon good intelligence.'

'I cannot claim to have initiated anything in the way of intelligence gathering,' said I, feeling instantly better. 'In fact, information simply appears to find its way to me without any encouragement on my part.'

At this point there was a discreet knock on the door, and when I said 'Come in!' Sian popped her head around the doorpost and reminded me gently that Sara needed feeding.

Joseph got up to leave, and said: 'Martha, my dear, I think we are more or less agreed. Let us keep up our guard. But I am slightly more encouraged today than I was a month ago. Fenton, I hear, is in London suffering from the pox, and Howell is presumably somewhere on the continent of Europe chasing after Napoleon Bonaparte. Beynon has a broken arm, and Lloyd is suffering grievously from a septic wound in his thigh. Rice is still in residence in his lodging house, surviving on the proceeds of a number of nefarious enterprises. He is a bully and a coward, and he will do nothing against us on his own. As for the three who are still in and around Newport, I suspect that any meetings held in the Black Lion or elsewhere will have more to do with covering their tracks after the murder than with any fresh enterprise. In any case, they are all well watched.'

'Thank you, Joseph, for those encouraging words.'

And so Joseph bowed, and kissed my hand, and went

on his way. Grandpa went to the office to do some work on cattle prices. And I took myself upstairs to feed my beloved little one. I have to confess, as I now sit at my desk in the warm darkness, with my candle lantern beside me, that I feel a great deal better, and safer, than I did a short while ago. Vengeance can wait. And I am especially proud that I got through our discussion this afternoon without once mentioning the treasure.

The Turning of the Year

5 March 1806

Six months have passed since I last put pen to paper. Out in the wide world, the news is that in October Lord Nelson won a great victory against the French and Spanish fleets at a place called Trafalgar, and was killed in the action. There was a funeral in London in January, and a very grand affair it was, according to Grandpa. He also says that the threat of a French invasion has now been averted, and that the politicians in Westminster believe that Master Bonaparte will be defeated sooner rather than later. Here, my family thrives, the estate manages well enough in spite of very harsh winter weather, and I continue to be blessed by kind and faithful friends. I thank the powers that be – in Heaven and on earth – that my enemies have kept their heads down. The winter is not a good time for skulduggery, since the priority for all stations of men is to stay warm, and dry, and alive.

The children continue to be a great blessing to me. Betsi will be eight in little more than two weeks from now, and is a truly delightful character. She is lively, interested in everything under the sun, and – so I am informed by my mother – very much like me when I was a little girl. She has a wilful streak to her, and is not terribly interested in dolls and the like; and I sometimes think she should have been a boy, for she is already adept at climbing trees, exploring on the mountain, and helping with the animals. But she does not neglect her studies, and is so keen to advance in the matter of reading and writing that I have had to employ a new tutor, young Bethan Mathias from Cilwen, to instruct her on two mornings a week. This has given me great pleasure, not simply through the joy of seeing a small girl absorbed in the learning process and loving her teacher, but also because I have re-established a link with our neighbours from Cilwen. We owe an eternal debt of gratitude to the Mathias family, for Bethan's father Eli died from his burns following an ill-fated attempt to rescue David's parents and siblings from the Plas Ingli fire in 1794.

Daisy will be five next month. She is a very beautiful child, much admired by all and sundry, with long dark hair and brown eyes. She is the one with whom I have most problems, for she is very prone to tantrums when she does not get her way, and weeps interminably at the slightest provocation. And Dewi, her little brother, can be very provocative at times. I love Daisy dearly, but it is she who has suffered most from the death of her dear father, and I fear that I have been a less than perfect mother to her. Last year, in the weeks and months following my bereavement, I admit that I was more concerned with my own misery than with the welfare of the children, and on occasion I rejected their unarticulated pleas for warmth and affection. Indeed, so close to insanity was I at times that I, their own mother, did not even recognize that they were pleading with me. She has at least come out of her shell now, after a year of great difficulty for her; but I am gravely concerned about her attention-seeking ploys and disruptive behaviour. I must endeavour at all times to give her extra love and special treats.

And the little ones? Dewi is three, and thriving. As far as he is concerned, everything in the world is a miracle. He is a thoroughly pestilential small brother to his sisters occasionally, but for most of the time he plays with them well. And he is utterly adored by all the others who reside beneath our roof. I declare that the sunshine of his smile, and the sweet music of his laughter, have saved me over and again from further descents into black melancholia. He of course dotes upon his little sister Sara, who is now almost a year old, and as placid and contented as ever. I am still breast-feeding her, much to the surprise of assorted acquaintances, but I still relish the contact, and the contentment, of feeding times; and since this is something I shall never do again, I am reluctant to stop. She is highly proficient in the crawling business, and nothing is safe from her. She gurgles and burbles endlessly. Grandpa Isaac, who is quite besotted with her, says she will be climbing chestnut trees before she can walk, and singing Methodist hymns before she can talk.

Since the end of the corn harvest I have continued my delightful lessons with my tutors. Our sessions have been somewhat erratic, but I am growing quite fond of old Master Edwards Trefach, whom I now see more as a kindly uncle than as a teacher. Master Bateman is not such an easy fellow to know, and I have seen less of him because of his onerous duties as steward at Pontfaen; but I have the greatest respect for him, and I believe that he enjoys his visits to the Plas. With him I have studied book-keeping, stock records, contracts, mortgages and investments, and this has led me to a much clearer view of how our own estate is holding up in these difficult times of war overseas and rising prices at home. Master

Edwards has taught me a great amount about rotations, ditching and hedging, animal breeding, fertilizer usage and the means of controlling pests. Because of the kindness of the pair of them, I already feel much more confident in my decision-making both in my office and out in the fields. Sadly, Master Edwards is not at all well just now, which gave me cause to pay him a little visit only yesterday; but we all trust that with the warmer weather he will soon be out and about again, exploring his beloved fields and hedgerows and observing the subtle shifts of the farming year with an eye sharper than a buzzard's.

I am moved to make a brief record of Christmas at the Plas. It was of course the first one without David, and all of us, apart from the children, had to make delicate judgements as to the extent of our celebrations. Some weeks before the festive season, Grandma Jane and Mrs Owen asked if we might sit down together and decide what to do; and I greatly appreciated their sensitivity in this matter. We decided that it would be inappropriate to indulge in the wild feasting and jollification of previous years, and so we let it be known that out of respect for dear Master David, and in his beloved memory, we would be restricting our Christmas and New Year breakfasts and dinners to the immediate family and servants only. Our tenants and labourers must all have been terribly disappointed, for the festive season is the highlight of the year for them, as it is for all of us. But they were very understanding and supportive, and we were pleased to see that our tenants Gethin Griffiths, Jeb Phipps, Thomas Tucker, Caradoc Williams, and Owen Pritchard each opened their houses to various of the labouring families. Nobody, in the event, felt deprived of festive good cheer, especially since many of the products of Mrs Owen's Christmas kitchen manufactory, in addition to several barrels of ale and cider, were delivered by special courier to the two Dolrannog farms, Penrhiw, Brithdir and Gelli.

There was a constant stream of visitors throughout the Christmas and New Year season, and we had no opportunity to feel lonely or sorry for ourselves. Indeed, we were so blessed and encouraged by this multitude of brief visits, and by many messages of goodwill, that I, for one, felt greatly moved. We went to the candlelit *Plygain* service in the parish church in Newport, but otherwise made no major visits to families or friends. And in truth we had a wonderful time, with Christmas and New Year devoted very largely to the children, who were fussed over and pampered and entertained endlessly by everybody who might otherwise have been involved in seasonal activities relating to the feeding and entertainment of the five thousand. At New Year the children from the estate came and collected their *calennig*, but we celebrated *Hen Galan* at home this year, feeling that our traditional involvement in the celebrations at Plas Pontfaen on 12 January would not have been appropriate.

One thing I did allow at New Year was a visit from the *Mari Lwyd*, since the servants all felt that a refusal would lead to bad luck. And we have certainly had enough of that already. Because of the tender ages of the children I asked Billy to ensure that the creature would be somewhat less frightening than it can be, and I am glad to report that those responsible heeded our request.

On New Year morning, which was grey and drizzly, we all awaited her arrival with bated breath. The children were very excited, their noses pressed against various window panes in eager anticipation. Daisy spotted them first, and shouted 'Oh, look, Mam! Look everybody! There is a terrible monster coming up the lane!'

Then the rest of us saw – and heard – a little procession coming up the muddy path from Blaenwaun. It was led by Abel Jenkins Brynaeron, wearing a tall black hat and a grey cloak. In one hand he held a hazel staff, and in the other a set of reins jangling with little bells and connected to the head of the *Mari Lwyd*. This strange creature, part horse and part phantom, was more comical than frightening, but it had clearly been created with great care. It was quite different from the canvas beast I had seen many times before in the Brawdy district when I was a child. Its top part consisted of a shining white horse's skull, with its jaw snapping up and down. It had eyes made of red glass, and its ears were made of strips of dark-coloured cloth. There were bows and ribbons of red, green, blue and yellow tied all over it. Its lower part, presumably covering a man who carried the skull on a pole, consisted of a billowing white sheet which was also decked with ribbons and bells. Behind the horse there were four other men whom I did not recognize. The first was playing a fiddle, and another, who was playing the part of Punch, had a blackened face and a jester's hat on his head. The third, dressed in a woman's costume, I presumed to be Judy, who was followed by one dressed like a disreputable army corporal. I pointed out to Daisy that he carried a *perllan*, a wooden board with a little carved tree in the middle of it and an apple stuck to each corner and a wooden wassail bowl with two handles. As they came up the track they were singing some strange old song and doing a simple walking dance which included the occasional hop and skip.

By the time the procession approached the front door of the house we were ready for it, and Mrs Owen was in the kitchen laying out food and drink. Grandpa told me that when he was a small child the *Mari Lwyd* had arrived on one occasion when they were not expecting it, and they had all had the fright of their lives when a fearsome horse's skull had peeped in through the kitchen window with its red eyes glowing. He said that old Mary Stokes from Newport had dropped dead with shock a few years ago when the *Mari Lwyd* unexpectedly appeared at her kitchen door.

On arrival at the front door, the leader or serjeant banged on it with his staff and demanded entry. The door was opened by Betsi, her eyes wide with wonder, but Grandma refused to let them in, and there followed a strange contest between the members of the party on the one hand and Grandpa Isaac on the other. Grandma Jane had explained to me that Grandpa was an acknowledged expert at this, and I listened with fascination as the invaders demanded entry and food and drink in one witty sung verse after another, to be rebuffed each time by Grandpa with an extempore verse of his own. This went on for some time, but since Grandpa was expected to lose the contest eventually he did this with good grace, and invited the serjeant and his friends in. So at last the strangely attired group crossed the threshold into the house, singing the praises of their nimble comely mare, demanding to enjoy the wassail, and finally singing, 'Happy New Year to you all, and to everybody in the world!'

Once inside, they headed straight for the kitchen, where the grey mare proceeded to chase all of us women round the oak table, prancing and neighing, snapping her jaw, and nudging and biting us. I am afraid that my attempts to maintain decorum were of no avail. Bessie, Sian and I were flattered to discover that we received much more attention than the older women, and we screamed and giggled in the manner that was expected of us. The children thought that this was all quite wonderful, and joined in with a vengeance. Then there was more tomfoolery as the fiddler played a merry tune and Punch chased us round the kitchen, kissing all available women and children with his black lips when he caught us, and being beaten about the head with a broom by Judy whenever she caught up with him. There were more funny songs, some silly dances, some even sillier magic tricks intended for the children, and at last the corporal arrested all of them and sat them down with difficulty round the table. Shemi's father Daniel emerged from beneath the white sheet to the sweet music of laughter and applause.

Once all were seated, the *perllan* and the migratory wassail bowl were given pride of place on the kitchen table. Mrs Owen then proudly produced our own wassail bowl, a simple wooden one with three handles recently made for us by Tomos Turner as a replacement for the fine earthenware one lost in the fire. It was half filled with a special spicy apple cake made with alternating layers of baked apples, currant and wheat flour cake, and thick brown syrup. Now, as the assembled company watched with acclaim, Mrs Owen carried it to the fireplace and poured onto the apple cake a brew of warm spicy beer that had been simmering in a copper pot for some hours. The filled bowl was then passed round the table, each one drinking in turn until all the beer was gone. The extremely alcoholic cake was then cut up and distributed in slices to everybody, and when that was eaten we tucked into other cakes and scones, with fresh salty butter from the dairy and fruit marmalades, all washed down with warm beer and cider. We all chatted happily, and I asked what this strange ceremony actually meant. I am afraid I did not get very far in my quest for knowledge; all those present had learned the songs and the ceremonial from their parents and grandparents, and all Grandpa could tell us was that it was some sort of horse worshipping tradition, used in primitive times to bring good luck and fertility to the house and its inhabitants at the turn of the year.

The company having consumed as much as was polite in the presence of small children, the serjeant got to his feet and announced that *Mari Lwyd* had other calls to make. 'We must be on our way,' he said. 'We thank you, good people, for your generous hospitality and your very acceptable wassail.' Then he turned to me, shook me by the hand, and continued: 'Mistress Martha, this is the first time that *Mari Lwyd* has visited this house since the fire, and the first since the passing of dear Master David. But our purpose is to drive away sadness and to look to the future. We promise you, young Mistress of the Plas, great happiness in the years to come.' Then the little party sang, just for us, the traditional departing verse:

> Long life, long days and long beautiful years be yours;
> Live a fruitful life like pure garden plants.
> May you see many children and grandchildren.
> So now we take our leave – farewell!

The words of the verse were not entirely appropriate, I thought. But I must admit that the warmth and kindness of these good people, and the words of their song, brought a tear to my eye, and as their grotesque procession hopped and skipped its way somewhat erratically towards Dolrannog Isaf, the children and I were sorry to see them go.

I must record in my diary that more than a year has now passed since the death of my beloved David. My temperament is still inconstant, and I do have occasional days of misery, but with the help of Bessie and the children in particular, I believe that I am learning to cope with grief. Time, as everybody told me in the beginning, is a wonderful healer. Another practised healer is dear Bessie, in whose charming company I spend several hours each day. She, poor thing, knows all too much about tragedy and loss, having lost a little child and a kind husband within the space of a few weeks. She lets me talk, gives encouragement where necessary, admonishes me when I wallow in my own misery (as I have a tendency to do), and constantly reminds me that I have far more heaven than hell in my life, and a great deal more to live for than to die for. She has, over twelve months or more, dried my tears, embraced me when I have been in desperate need of human contact, and given me healing through her hands and her words.

Shrove Tuesday this year fell on 11 February, and the *cnapan* game went ahead as normal on Berry Sands. Neither Shemi nor Billy could bring themselves to participate, and to their credit none of the other players sought to press them. We ate our pancakes as usual, with as much cheer as we could muster. Next day, on the anniversary of David's death, Shemi got the two-horse chaise ready, and the children and I travelled down to the beach. We walked the last bit, to the place where David died. I felt compelled to do it, having not previously had the courage. When we were there the children and I talked about this being the place where their father had been taken into the warm embrace of the angels. Daisy and Betsi understood, and held my hands

219

while Dewi played about and went hunting for crabs. I do not know what I expected to find or experience, but there was of course no trace of anything untoward that might have happened on the spot on that fateful day. There was no wind and the sea was calm. The tide was out, and little waves murmured at the water's edge. Oystercatchers and gulls patrolled at the point where the river insinuated itself into the sea. The sand was firm and clean under our feet. Tide and time had wiped everything away, including all traces of the frantic activity that must have been going on here during yesterday's *cnapan* game.

On our return to Cilgwyn I was in a pensive mood, but there was a stillness in my breast and I felt that I had identified, and passed, another milestone in my journey of recovery and self-discovery. Instead of returning directly to the Plas I asked Shemi to take us straight through to the churchyard where David was buried. We picked some little posies of wood anemones, snowdrops, primroses and celandines, and placed them on the grave. We stood in the weak February sunshine and said a little prayer for David's soul, and asked for blessings on ourselves. Then Dewi saw a red squirrel in one of the tall yews which lined the churchyard, and lost interest in David's soul, and his own, as he ran off to observe its acrobatic skills among the lofty boughs. I had to smile. Not for the first time, the little fellow had reminded me, without saying a word, that what is past must now be left behind, and that there is a life to be lived.

My serenity gave way to a lightness of spirit, as I vowed to put negative and dark thoughts behind me and to create a warm and loving world for my blessed family. I felt, even as I stood just a few feet from David's grave, that I should soar like a white dove into a blue sky.

'Mam!' shouted Dewi from near the churchyard gate,

'Come and look! That squirrel has jumped all the way from that big tree to that other big tree, and now he is right at the very top, eating some nuts!'

25 March 1806

A great wonder has been seen down on Berry Sands. Even Grandma Jane, who is very sceptical about strange mysteries, portents and signs from Heaven, has been down to see it, and is quite amazed.

This winter has been very wet and stormy, with a succession of terrible gales blowing out of the north. This has been exceptional, since most of our storms come from the great ocean to the west. Those who live down at the coast say that millions of tons of sand have been carried away by the waves, and that the beach between Morfa and the mouth of the river has been lowered by about six feet. A week ago, at the end of yet another storm, some urchins from the Parrog were walking along the beach near the low water mark of a spring tide when they encountered something that none of them had seen before. It was very near the spot where David died, close to the low cliffs at the northern end of the bay.

There before the boys lay a wide expanse of some peaty substance, with broken branches, whole fallen trees and tree stumps littered across it. All of the trees seem to have been broken off just above the ground, and they were all lying in the same direction, as if knocked over by some fearsome tidal wave which came sweeping down from the north. Some of the tree stumps were still rooted in the peat and soil, and the branching and radiating roots could still be seen quite clearly. The branches, logs and other pieces of trees, some of them still encased in bark, were mostly stained a rich dark brown colour, and most of them were quite solid. Some other bits of wood were almost as black as coal. In little pockets in the peat, the boys discovered large quantities of acorns and hazel nuts, just as fresh as if they had fallen to the ground only a year ago. One of the boys took a pocketful of the acorns home for his pig, who by all accounts greatly enjoyed them.

This was not all. In the middle of this strange and ancient fairy forest the boys found two huge antlers, bigger by far than they or anybody else in the town had seen before. They were attached to the skull of some mighty beast. Nearby there were lots of bones, subsequently identified as the ribcage, vertebrae, pelvis and leg bones of a giant deer. None of the flesh of the animal was left, but most of the bones were more or less in the position in which the animal must have died.

Yet more was to be uncovered. Resting across the crushed ribcage of the animal was a tree trunk with a diameter of about eighteen inches, and many of us who have seen it think that the poor beast must have been killed by a falling tree during the same mighty cataclysm which obliterated the forest. And finally, embedded in the skull of the dead creature were four quite beautiful small arrow heads made of some flinty stone. I have seen them, and can vouch for their delicate workmanship.

The boys collected the arrow heads and ran home to tell their parents , who also went to observe the strange wonder; and before the day was out half of the town had been to visit it. Then the tide rose and covered everything with sea water, and the other half of the town had to wait for the next low tide before paying a visit to the site.

Luckily the weather stayed calm for a few days, and hundreds of people visited the dead beast in its woodland glade before the sand started to cover it up again with the rising and falling of each tide. On the first day somebody sent a message to Squire Fenton, who is of course the most learned antiquarian in these parts, and he was able to conduct a proper excavation of the site. We all went down from the Plas to join him on one of his excavating days and found him hard at work, with only one hour available to him before the tide came in again. He was measuring and scribbling in his notebook while his men dug away with picks and shovels. They did not find any more skeletons. He left the bones, the skull and the antlers where they were for as long as he dared, but then some of the local people started to collect the smaller bones and teeth as keepsakes. With the spring tides waning, and before the tide covered the place up for good, the Squire decided to remove everything for the sake of posterity, to be exhibited in some fine museum. He was not so interested in the timber. Many of the better logs have been collected by local people, and Davy Death the carpenter says that when they are dry they will be suitable for use in some exquisite pieces of furniture.

Joseph Harries and other learned gentlemen also visited the scene of the giant deer's untimely death, and there was even a report about it in the county newspaper. Squire Fenton now tells us that the creature was an Irish elk, the largest of all the deer to have roamed across this land in days gone by. It may have stood eight feet tall, and its huge and heavy antlers had a spread of at least ten feet. He has purchased the four arrow heads from the Parrog boys for a few pence, and says that they will also go to a museum of antiquities. He says that they are quite typical of the arrow heads made by the ancient hunters who lived in this area, but he cannot say how old they are.

In addition to the men of science, the location of this

223

strange wonder has been much visited by the men of God. Shoni Hallelujah and his fellow Baptists immediately declared that the fallen trees, and the peat beds, and the deer skeleton and antlers, were signs from God, and that they were without a doubt a direct consequence of Noah's Flood. They spent every possible moment, tides permitting, praying and singing hymns on the beach, and asking all who visited the place to repent and turn from their sinful ways. Most people were more intent upon gazing at the relics with open mouths than they were on repenting, but in truth the good Christian people did little harm apart from getting in Squire Fenton's way every now and then. Perhaps the good squire even enjoyed the musical accompaniment to his endeavours.

Other local people, recalling the local tradition that *Gwlad y Tylwyth Teg* lies out in Newport Bay, have concluded that the relics are actually a piece of that fairy land, and that similar relics might be found for miles offshore where the fairies live happily beneath the waves. Davy Daft, who is a strange fellow, has been going round town urging people not to visit the relics for fear that they might be taken away by the fairies and never seen again. So far as I am concerned, this strange and wonderful occurrence seems to be a very long way from Mount Ararat, and seems to have little to do with the fairies; but one cannot doubt, having seen it, that it provides strong evidence of a mighty inundation by the sea which overwhelmed everything that stood in its way. What was once dry land became submerged, and has stayed submerged to this day, until revealed to human gaze by some freak of winds, waves, and tides. Some of the older people on the Parrog recall a similar wonder some fifty years ago, but on that occasion all they saw were some beds of peat and stony gravels in places where there is normally soft sand.

In seeking to make sense of what we have all seen, my favoured explanation is that it is a part of *Cantre'r Gwaelod,* the Lowland Hundred, which was once a green and fertile land extending across most of Cardigan Bay. My father taught me an old lament when I was a child, reputedly written by a bard who was one of only three people to escape from the mass drowning of the population when the Lowland Hundred was flooded. Everybody in the local community still knows the story of Seithennin, the foolish prince who was supposed to guard the sluice gates in the great sea wall that protected the land belonging to King Gwyddno. One day he got drunk and forgot to close the sluices against a rising tide. In rushed the sea, and that was that – fine palaces, gardens, houses, workshops and farms all destroyed, along with all the animals belonging to the people. I discussed this with Grandpa the other day, and he said that the old story might well be true, for he can vouch for the presence of relics of ancient settlements beneath the waves. He personally recalled being far out in the bay as a young man on a fishing boat, in perfectly calm and wind-free conditions, and hearing far beneath the waves the slow and mournful tolling of a church bell.

30 March 1806

My friend Joseph is a truly amazing fellow, and in keeping with his calling as a wizard he is adept at turning natural phenomena to good account. Today he paid me a brief visit, and said: 'My dear Martha, I have to apologize for something which I have done recently, which might appear to you to be somewhat morbid and insensitive. But I have my little ways of doing things, and

225

I am afraid it had to be done.'

'Oh? I am intrigued. Please tell me about it, Joseph, and then I will decide whether to be upset or not.'

'It's just that it relates to the death of dear David, and may appear to you to be flippant or frivolous.'

'Come along then! Out with it.'

He looked slightly uncomfortable, and then said: 'What I have done is not frivolous at all, for it relates to the fact that there are four murderers out there who still have to be brought to justice. The months are slipping by. Anyway, for better or for worse, I have written a letter to each of the villains, Beynon, Rice, Howell and Lloyd, to which I do not expect a reply. But I do expect the letter to have some impact, and I do expect it to help us in our quest.'

'Have you got a copy for me, Joseph?'

'Indeed I have. Here it is.' And he handed over a folded piece of paper which had the following well-chosen words written on it, in his neat and precise hand:

Werndew, 21st day of March 1806
To Master Joseph Rice, Captain John Howell, Master Ifan Beynon
and Master Matthew Lloyd
Sirs,

You may know that I make a special study of scientific matters and that I am keenly involved in investigations of the natural world. I always seek to find out the truth of things, in the hope that my researches might in some small way contribute to the common good.

I am aware that you, gentlemen, are also careful observers of the world about you, and I hope that you may be interested and indeed stimulated by some recent discoveries that I have made. They relate to a recent wonder observed by many people on the Berry Sands near Newport; I presume that you may indeed have

226

visited the place yourselves. If not, I can explain for you that it is exactly the place where Master David Morgan met his untimely death on Shrove Tuesday of last year.

The most interesting thing about the wonderful occurrence revealed by the shifting sands was the skeleton of a graceful and regal creature, the like of which has never been seen in this country before, crushed beneath the weight of a fallen tree trunk. It has been widely assumed by the scientific gentlemen who have visited the site that the unfortunate animal was killed in an accident, and that it simply had the misfortune to be standing beneath the offending tree when it was uprooted by a cataclysmic flood of water.

You, as very learned gentlemen, might be interested to know that this theory is not correct. I have incontrovertible evidence, from examining the remains available, that the victim was in fact killed by four hunters working together. It was already dead when the tree fell on it and the rising flood condemned it to a watery grave. Deliberate slaughter, and no accident.

I have, of course, submitted the detailed evidence on which this conclusion is based to the appropriate learned institutions.
Yours etc., Harries Werndew

When I had read the letter, I shook my head and said, 'Joseph, you are quite incorrigible!'

'Are you upset with me?'

I looked at him fiercely, trying to assess the state of my own emotions. This was a matter, after all, relating to the death of my beloved husband little more than a year ago. But I could not resist a smile at the cheeky ingenuity of the man, and soon the smile turned to laughter. I trust that dear David, from his place among the angels, laughed with me.

The Wizard of Werndew looked greatly relieved, and then began to chuckle too, tentatively at first and then with some abandon, and soon I am ashamed to say that we were both in hysterics. 'Mistress Morgan, I am greatly relieved,' he said at long last, having regained some of his composure. 'I should have sought your approval before embarking on this particular course of action. But let us now hope that something will come of my little allegory. The four rotten creatures concerned will know exactly what the letter means.'

I wiped away my tears and said, 'And they will also know something of the reputation of the man who wrote it. This is not actually a curse, but I dare say it comes quite close. I hope, Joseph, that they are, all four of them, quaking in their shoes at this very moment as they contemplate the possibility that the evil eye is upon them.'

Now he is gone off on some other errand of mercy, and I am sitting here, quill in hand, still shaking my head and grinning like an idiot at the sheer effrontery of my dear friend from over the mountain.

9 April 1806

The estate has acquired a new servant, in the most bizarre of circumstances. Yesterday Mrs Owen asked me, at breakfast, whether she might have a quiet word following the washing of the dishes. She looked agitated, which is a most unusual thing for Mrs Owen, and she looked even more agitated when we met in my room some thirty minutes later.

'You look worried, Mrs Owen,' said I. 'Is there anything I can do to remove that furrow on your brow?'

'I do hope there might be, Mistress Martha,' said she. 'I am in a very bothered state just now, because of that miserable good-for-nothing boy Will.'

'Your youngest son? Why? Is he in some trouble?'

'Very serious trouble, which have just come to my notice this very morning. A message from Levi Abbs Penrhiw Fach, who got me up out of bed before five of the clock. Pitch black, it was, and blowing a gale. I am greatly afeared that Will is going to end up on the gallows this time, or else shipped off to the colonies.'

'Oh dear,' said I in response, knowing full well that Will had a propensity for getting on the wrong side of the law, and for making friends in all the wrong places. 'You had better tell me about it.'

'Well, Mistress, this has all come from his free trading activities, which I knew would get him into trouble sooner or later. You know that he works with Gethin Dolrannog Isaf and Levi and Tom Llewellyn in the handling of certain cargoes from over the water?'

'Yes, I know it,' I said, 'but I will admit it to nobody else.' Like many others in the community, I knew in broad outline that Will and his friends were part of a smuggling team that handled various goods brought ashore at Aberrhigian and other secluded coves, usually on dark and stormy nights when the Milford Customs cutter was on duty somewhere else. Little was known about the person or persons who masterminded the 'free trade' operations, for there was a long chain of command and those who brought goods ashore and carted them to caves and other hiding places were normally paid by a beachmaster who had nothing to do with distribution to the final customers. These final customers included myself and most of the other gentry families and tenant farmers of the area, who were without exception opposed to the ludicrous taxes loaded by the government in London onto the essentials of life including tea, wine, spirits, tobacco, silks and glassware. We despised Master Pitt and his cronies in Westminster, we despised the Revenue officers who

229

occasionally came prowling around Newport and the surrounding countryside, and we all took a certain innocent pleasure in helping to subvert, on behalf of the suppressed and subdued people of Wales, the taxation plans of the ruling classes of England. Grandpa Isaac was, I knew, an avid supporter of free trade activities, and his support was not always of the passive kind.

'Anyway, Mistress, from what I can gather, a cargo was due in last night, to Aberfforest. Very stormy it was, as you know. The ship came in from Waterford, on time, at midnight. The landers got the cargo onto the beach, mostly tobacco and Nantz brandy, and some tea, but there weren't enough tubmen, and so the batmen, who usually keep a lookout and deal with the Revenue men if they turn up, had to help with the carting. They got most of the goods up to the safe house, but there must have been a tip-off. Five riding officers appeared and there was a pitched battle on the turnpike road near Hendre. Duw Duw, terrible it was, according to Levi. Pouring with rain, and pitch black. Nobody killed, thank God. Most of the gang got away, together with the horse and cart carrying the last of the bundles of tobacco and half-ankers of spirits. Levi was hurt but managed to hide behind a hedge, scared to death. My Will missed the battle, having got exhausted by five journeys up and down between the beach and the safe house, and he came staggering along the road later, carrying two half-ankers of Nantz. Walked straight into the riding officers, who were licking their wounds and pretty furious to boot.'

'Do I assume that Will is now being held on a charge of assisting in a smuggling offence, avoiding customs duties, resisting arrest, and assorted other dastardly crimes?'

'Quite so, Mistress,' said Mrs Owen, close to tears.

'Something like that. Levi overheard everything when they caught Will. He says he is in the lock-up in Newport, soaking wet, exhausted and miserable, and that he will be dealt with at a Petty Sessions this afternoon. He won't rat on his friends. He refused to admit that he had anything to do with the fellows who had recently slipped through the hands of the Revenue men. Apparently all he said was that he was carrying the Nantz for a certain customer who had bought it – all legal and above board – in Dinas some days since and who now required it in Newport in time for a social occasion in the near future.'

'A likely tale indeed,' I volunteered. 'Did the Revenue men, or the Newport constables, accept without question that Will was wandering along the road in the middle of a downpour at three of the clock on a dark April morning, loaded with eight gallons of prime quality brandy, in pursuit of some lawful business?'

'No, I fear not, Mistress Martha. Apparently they did not believe a word of it.'

'I am not surprised. What happened to the brandy?'

'Confiscated, I dare say, and due to be produced as evidence when the case comes before the magistrates.'

'Did Will tell them anything else that might be incriminating?'

'Levi, being behind the hedge, found it difficult to hear everything,' said Mrs Owen, 'but he thinks Will gave them his correct name and said that he had recently set up in business under the name Newport Nocturnal Delivery Service.'

At this I immediately burst out laughing, and thought that Will deserved great credit for originality in the face of adversity, if nothing else. 'Mistress Martha!' remonstrated Mrs Owen. 'This is not a laughing matter. My Will has not got the slightest chance of getting off when he is hauled before the magistrates. There will be a duly entered complaint from the Revenue, and sworn statements, and he will be thrown into gaol pending appearance at the Quarter Sessions in Haverfordwest. Don't forget, Mistress, that hindering Revenue officers in the course of their duty carries the death penalty. Even if he escapes the gallows, and gets merciful treatment, I fear he will be transported to New South Wales or pressed into the Navy to fight the French.'

'I'm sorry. You are quite right – this is very serious. But what can I do? I am a mere woman, and I have no influence over the magistrates.'

'Please try and think of something, Mistress!' pleaded Mrs Owen, as she got up and returned to her household duties. Thus ended our interview.

So it was that at eleven of the clock I arrived at the little lock-up in Long Street and made a great scene. I obtained confirmation that Will was inside. I then confronted old John Wilson the cooper, who was doing a stint of duty as temporary constable and who was guarding the dastardly criminal. I demanded to know who had waylaid Master William Owen in the middle of the night as he went about his lawful business on behalf of the Newport Nocturnal Delivery Service. I demanded to know who had stolen my two half-ankers of Nantz brandy, which had been lawfully paid for and stored at the house of a friend in Dinas. And I demanded to know the names of the criminals involved so that I might immediately institute highway robbery proceedings against them with the help of Lewis Legal.

I went about my business outside the front door of the lock-up with such gusto that there was soon a sizeable crowd gathered round, and poor John Wilson knew not what to do. The Revenue officers were fast asleep in some lodging house down on the Parrog, having not

232

slept a wink during the hours of darkness, and there was nobody else to help the poor fellow. The crowd started to jeer and cheer, and soon there was a chant of 'Let him go! Let him go!' echoing round the street. Constable Wilson sought to do his duty by asking for proof that the tubs of brandy were indeed mine, to which I replied with as much indignation as I could muster 'My dear Constable Wilson, I have committed no crime! I refuse absolutely to show you or anybody else my bill of purchase for these articles. My commercial transactions are a matter for me, and me alone.'

Then various members of the crowd joined in the charade, and attested to my liking for Nantz brandy, and to the excellent service provided by the Newport Nocturnal Delivery Service. Also, Constable Wilson was aware that I knew that he made a few shillings now and then by hiring out his pony and cart to certain free trade operators, and I saw that his resolve was weakening. At last, when I threatened him with a Bill of Complaint for being an accessary to the crime committed by the Revenue officers, he gave in and said, 'Very well, Mistress Morgan, I see that there is not a case to answer here, and it would appear that a dreadful mistake has been made. If you will agree not to press charges against me, I will agree to release the prisoner and your two tubs of Nantz.'

So it was all settled very amicably, to the satisfaction of the crowd, William Owen, Constable Wilson and myself. I gave the constable a shilling for his trouble. Billy had the two-horse chaise waiting round the corner, and by lunch time we were back at the Plas, accompanied by William and the brandy. News reached us this evening that Squire Bowen of Llwyngwair and Squire Gittins of Tredrissi turned up at the Black Lion at two of the clock, having been summoned by the clerk to an emergency

Petty Sessions required to deal with a matter of the utmost severity. The five Revenue officers also turned up, bleary-eyed and battered, along with Constable Wilson. When the magistrates discovered that there was no prisoner and no evidence, and when they heard Constable Wilson's account of the morning's proceedings, they immediately sent the Revenue men packing and told them they were lucky to escape without being slapped into the lock-up themselves.

This evening we have enjoyed an excellent supper, and I can confirm that the Nantz is of the highest quality. Young Will, who is in truth not all that young, has received a gentle beating at the hands of his mother, but she will probably have forgiven him by tomorrow. He is now fast asleep in the hayloft of the cowshed, also suffering from a surfeit of brandy. I like Will, for he has great charm and a good deal of native wit. I have offered him a job, largely in order to keep him out of further trouble. Besides, he owes me a shilling.

I have found the day's adventure very stimulating, and I have to admit to feeling rather pleased with myself.

15 April 1806

Will is now installed as shepherd and cowman, at exactly the right time since lambing is in full swing and the amount of work on the estate has been, of late, too taxing for Shemi and Billy to manage on their own. Partly this has been due to the fact that Grandpa Isaac is beginning to feel his age, and has a stiffening of the joints which makes it difficult for him to do heavy work. There is no room for Will in the house, but he has a cosy space in the hayloft and he declares that it is far more comfortable than sleeping behind hedges, which he has done more often than he cares to admit. He has worked with animals ever since he was a lad, and has been a good friend to Shemi for some years. He has been employed, off and on, by many of the local squires, and as a consequence he knows a good deal about them. I do have some slight reservations about employing a mother and a son from the same family, but he will receive no special favours either from Mrs Owen or from me. For the moment I will pay him six shillings a week, but I have explained to him that I will hold his money for him until all of the financial repercussions of the episode with the Revenue men have been felt. The eight gallons of brandy (well, seven and half, following our celebration of the other evening) have a market value of almost eight pounds, although somebody probably bought it for about three shillings a gallon in Ireland. I half expect a knock on the door, one dark night, from some gentleman muffled up and heavily hatted, intent upon collecting his money. And there is also a possibility that Master Dickens of the Revenue will pay me a visit which might have some financial implications.

The more I come to know Will, the more of an asset he appears to be. He has been in and out of gaol, and is an expert on the treadmill, but now that I have rescued him from an unpleasant fate on the gallows he has sworn to go straight and to do nothing which might reflect badly upon the Plas Ingli estate. Whether or not he is a reformed character we shall see, but he has such a wide circle of contacts among the criminal classes, and such a detailed knowledge of the corruption by which the upper classes maintain their control in this area, that I declare myself amazed. The other evening I listened with my mouth agape as he told us about some of the escapades of his foolish youth; and his mother confirmed that there was hardly any exaggeration involved.

Afterwards I asked him to join me in the office for a few minutes, and explained to him that in return for the assistance which I had been happy to give him in Newport the other day, he might be able to provide some help in the protection of my family and of the estate. He said, 'Yes indeed, Mistress Martha. You have saved my life, and whatever I can do for you will be but a small thing by comparison. Just you say what you wants.' So I explained that certain gentlemen, namely Rice, Fenton, Howell, Lloyd and Beynon, appeared to be out to harm us in some way, and that I simply wished to keep them under observation in the hope of nipping some wickedness in the bud. 'Nasty buggers, the lot of them,' said Will. 'They have done me no favours in the past, and indeed they have done lots of innocent people a good deal of damage. Mind you, there is no way they will work together. Some of them wouldn't even trust their own right hands, if it was dark and they couldn't see them. Leave it to me, Mistress. I will have quiet words with some of my fellows, and if there is any evil afoot, you will be the first to know about it.'

This morning I got my first report from Will and his network of spies. He called me to one side after breakfast and whispered: 'News from town, Mistress Martha. Fenton and Howell are away. You knew that?'

'Yes, I was aware of it.'

'Beynon and Lloyd are around, and in a panic. My friend Benny saw them in the street yesterday, very agitated. They went into the Royal Oak and sat in a corner and talked for a long time. Benny just happened to overhear them, and they were talking about a letter. "They know everything!" said Beynon. "Impossible!" said Lloyd. "Do you think Harries has passed his notes on to the justices?" said Beynon. "Has Rice been talking?" said Lloyd. And so on, and so on. Benny says they hate Rice and reckon that a little blackmail might help to keep him under control. They also agreed to keep a low profile for the time being, in case anything nasty should happen to them. Does that make sense, Mistress? Would they have been talking about somebody called Harries? There are lots of people with that name around the town – at least six, that I can think of.'

'Yes, that all makes perfect sense, thank you, Will.'

'And one last thing. My friend Charlie lives on the Parrog, close to where Rice has his lodgings. Rice is very agitated – drinking a lot, and hiding in the house most of the time. He is in a very foul mood, and he has hired the Ifan brothers, Huw and Sion, to protect him every time he goes up to town. God only knows who or what he needs protection from.'

'Perhaps from his own conscience, Will. But he also has a lot of enemies. Thank you so much. This has been a most helpful conversation, and I appreciate the information you have given me. I must say that it helps to put my mind at rest, for the more persecuted these particular gentlemen feel, the easier will I sleep in my bed at night.'

So Will went outside into the rain to deal with the late lambing, and I got on with feeding Sara, comfortable in the knowledge that Joseph's recent letter to the conspirators was having its desired effect.

23 April 1806

I have to accept the truth of what Squire Fenton told me some months back, for I appear to have become a desirable widow. Since the anniversary of David's death

I have been greatly bothered by a succession of young men, most of them very silly indeed, and by a scattering of quite elderly gentlemen, all of whom, I suppose, wish to marry me. Of course, none of them has actually said as much, but why should they suddenly have taken such an interest in me, having previously had none at all?

There is a good deal of delicacy to be observed in courtship, and one has to go along with it. Mostly it is a nuisance, but it has its lighter side, and I have to admit that it has given me and Grandma and Grandpa some innocent pleasure. It started shortly after my visit with the children to the beach and to Cilgwyn churchyard, in February. At the supper table that evening Grandma Jane said: 'My dear Martha, you look very pensive. You were probably wise to visit Berry Sands and the family burial enclosure. But it must have taken a lot out of you. Are you all right?'

'Oh yes,' I replied. 'Perfectly all right. The day has been less of a trial than I had anticipated. I look pensive because I feel quite serene this evening. I was just thinking how the children, and all of you dear folk round this table, have helped me through the miserable events of the past year, and I have made a little resolution to myself that I shall now try to be happy.'

'God bless you in that,' said Bessie, with her lovely smile.

'Amen,' said Grandpa Isaac, 'and let us drink a toast to it, to help you in your resolve.' And they all did that, and we all laughed, and the conversation turned to other things.

After supper, as I sat in my room rocking little Sara off to sleep after giving her the breast, there was a knock on my door and Grandpa came in. 'Can I have a few words, Martha?' he asked.

'Of course. Sara *bach* is warm, and well fed, and changed, and is just nodding off.'

'It's about you and the future of the estate. Now that a year has passed since David's death, you may expect various suitors to present themselves. Delicacy has prevented earlier approaches from some quarters, but I have already had oblique enquiries, and you will appreciate that there are few things in this world more desirable than a beautiful widow with a pleasant estate and no debts.'

'Oh dear,' said I, 'don't these gentlemen realize that I have absolutely no intention of remarrying? I cannot ever see myself being in love again. By comparison with David all the other men in this world are lacking in good looks and short on virtue.'

'That may be so, and I respect your sentiments, my dear. But you cannot blame assorted gentlemen for living in hope. You are, after all, still only twenty-seven years old. And there is always a chance that somewhere out there is a well-endowed gentleman who has loved you from afar, in tortured silence, ever since you arrived at the Plas.'

I laughed at this, since endowments come in many forms and with considerable variations in size. Grandpa appreciated my line of thought, and laughed too. Then he said: 'One thing I must make clear, Martha. There will be questions relating to the estate, its finances, its assets and liabilities, and to you personally. People will want to know about the family history and wealth of your parents and ancestors, and your inheritance of the fortune – such as it is – of the Morgan family of Plas Ingli. There will be discreet enquiries as to how much of the family wealth is committed to the children under the terms of David's will, and how much of it is available as cash.'

'How dare they?' said I, no doubt with my eyes flashing. 'Nobody has any right to this information, and they will not get it from me.'

'Nor from me,' said Grandpa. 'But they will try to get it anyway. Marriages are expected to be advantageous to both families, and generally the gentleman and lady concerned are not even consulted until the negotiations have reached an advanced stage. Which brings me to my main point. I will have nothing to do with any future social arrangements, meetings between you and any admiring gentlemen, or plans for any marriage.'

'But Grandpa, you are the head of our family, and I need your help.'

'That is where you are wrong, my dear. I am not the head of this family. I am little more than a pauper. I have no property and no cash assets, and indeed I survive, and have a roof over my head, only by virtue of your beneficence. For better or for worse, you are the head of the family, and a thoroughly capable one at that.'

'Oh dear. You are right, of course. Fate has given me this responsibility, and I suppose I have to carry it as best I can. But will you at least advise me, Grandpa, should advice be needed?'

'Of course, my dear Martha. I am always here for that, if you should wish to call upon me. But the practical consequence of my position is that I will not deal with any requests for information from outside parties, nor will I accept any direct or indirect approaches from any persons if I have the slightest suspicion that dark thoughts about alliances and weddings are lurking in the back of their heads. My response will always be to advise them to approach you direct, which will immediately cause most of them to fly into a panic.'

'Am I so fearsome, Grandpa, as to strike terror into the hearts of men?'

'No, no.' Grandpa Isaac laughed. 'You are a very model of gentility and consideration. It's just that approaches of this kind are first made through fifth parties, and then fourth parties, and then eventually through an intermediary who arranges a meeting between the hopeful gentleman and the desirable lady. The system has been developing gradually, since the time when Adam and Eve were banished from that wretched garden of theirs. It will throw the whole delicate system into utter confusion if your suitors have to approach you direct, face to face.'

We agreed, in the end, that this would be no bad thing, for deviousness and double dealing would be eliminated from the process, and Grandpa admitted that he had no wish to insult my intelligence by assuming anything at all about my need for male company or about my plans for joining the Plas Ingli estate with any other. We decided that we should not take the matter too seriously, and that he would advise me of any oblique enquiries that came his way and would always be willing to make discreet investigations as to the pedigree of any young gentleman who might in the future attract my attention.

So here I was, the desirable Mistress Martha Morgan of Plas Ingli, possibly available for some grand alliance, and possibly not. Did the situation fill me with dread? Yes, and no. In truth I was not entirely averse to the idea of holding court now and then, seeing some emissaries and sending others packing, and picking and choosing which young gentlemen I might dance with at some future ball, and which ones I might graciously entertain to afternoon tea.

The process started almost immediately, with letters from five young gentlemen and another ten letters from intermediaries, all written to Grandpa and all passed straight to me. Grandpa was thoroughly entertained by this. He passed a little note back to all of those who wrote, stating that he had no status in the Plas Ingli estate and no influence whatsoever over its young Mistress. He suggested that each of them should write directly to me, and said that he was sure that a gracious reply would be forthcoming in due course, family and estate matters permitting. That immediately got rid of most of the hopefuls, but four of them persisted, and after a few days I received polite little notes from Simeon Jenkins, the son and heir of the Cilciffeth estate; Thomas Higgins, the second son of Scolton Manor; John Collyer, the heir of the Tredafydd estate, and Mostyn Gittins, the only son of the Squire of Tredrissi.

I disliked intensely the tone of Master Jenkins's letter, and Master Higgins could neither spell nor string ten words together into a proper sentence; so I sent them notes explaining that it would not be possible to arrange for any social visits in the forseeable future, so heavy were my other commitments. Master Collyer had a nice way with words, and Master Gittins sounded like a pleasant young man, and I thought that nothing could be lost by getting to know them. I invited Master Collyer to tea a couple of weeks ago, and I have to report that I was gravely disappointed. He proved to be in his mid-thirties, and was so shy that in my presence his hands shook and he blushed scarlet almost every time he opened his mouth. He had clearly led a very sheltered life. He had almost nothing to talk about apart from sheep prices and the latest developments in the breeding of the perfect turnip. On that I have to admit that he was very knowledgeable. I did my best to remain civil, but entertaining him was very hard work, and after an hour I rose to my feet and explained that I had a small baby to feed. He took his leave graciously enough, and I do not expect to see him again.

My meeting with Master Gittins was altogether more entertaining, and both he and I had a splendid time. He proved to be an attractive young man, and very self-confident, but with interests a world away from mine. As soon as he settled down to his Chinese tea and buttered scones, he opened his heart to me, which I found immediately endearing. He said that he had come to see me at the insistence of his father, who was obsessed (like most fathers, I dare say) with the idea of a 'good' marriage; but he admitted that he could not possibly seek to develop a friendship with me under false pretences, because his heart belonged elsewhere. It transpired that he was enamoured of a young lady of Eglwyswrw, who was the only daughter of a tailor of moderate means. His father had insisted that marriage to her was absolutely out of the question, given her lowly social status; and had forbidden Mostyn ever to see her again. The poor fellow was distraught, for he could not get the sweet girl out of his mind, and he explained, looking about him furtively in case anybody else might be listening, that he and Rose (for that was her name) contrived to meet about once a month in conditions of great secrecy. I was caught up immediately in this sad tale, and said I thought it outrageous, in these enlightened times, that his father should not recognize the virtues of the merchant class and should fail to appreciate that love is the greatest of all prerequisites for a successful marriage. And so we planned and we plotted, and explored the various options that he and Rose might have – and I trust that when he left, young Mostyn felt that he had found a kind ear and that his journey had not been in vain.

Subsequently there have been other visits to the Plas, and I have been prevailed upon to make three visits to other grand houses in the company of Grandma Jane as chaperon. I have met some pleasant people, and some who have been extremely foolish. As I expected, not one of them has caused the slightest flutter in my heart.

Such were my first encounters with 'suitable young gentlemen'. I have been entertained, and I trust that I have been able to do some good through my advice to Master Gittins, but my resolve never to marry again is unshaken; and I can now get back to the business of bringing up my family of young children and running the estate.

Unsettled Weather

3 May 1806

Not for the first time, I have grave concerns about the state of the poor townspeople and country folk in this area. From my conversations with my own family and with friends like Mary Jane and Ellie, I fear that either starvation or riot may be imminent. Those who have no coins in their pockets were well fed during the Christmas and New Year celebrations, but the seasonal fat has now been worn away by hard work and hard weather, and we are in the 'hungry months' when supplies of salt meat and herrings are running down and there is little fresh food to be had. It has been a cold and miserable spring, and all plantings are delayed. Mutton and beef prices have risen to levels never before seen, but wages have hardly moved up at all, so the gap between what people earn and what they have to pay for their essentials is – in the estimation of Grandpa Isaac, at any rate – too wide to be maintained.

There have been a number of very unpleasant incidents in Newport and Fishguard, and there is much public anger directed at merchants like Master Luke Morris and Master Hubert Harry and landowners including Price Llanychaer and Owen Gelli Fawr. They are accused, as they are almost every spring, of exporting grain from the Parrog and holding back supplies so that the price is forced up. Their greed is beyond question, and the operation of their 'ring' is common knowledge although they suppose it to be a closely-guarded secret. They are also accused of stupidity, in that some of them have been growing barley continuously on their best fields for four years, against the advice of their own farm servants. Eggs and rotten vegetables have been thrown at Master Harry, and he hardly dares to show his face out in the streets of the town, and last time Squire Owen went to town his carriage was almost tipped over by an angry crowd. The squires and gentlemen are now looking for scapegoats, and if they can catch one or two poor labourers and portray them as agitators or ringleaders they will put on their justices' wigs and sentence them to whipping or transportation. They seem to think that brutality and the weight of the law will press the people into submission, but in my view they will in all probability get insurrection instead.

In these difficult circumstances I have done my best to avoid conflict with my own tenants and labourers. Because our last harvest was a good one, for both hay and corn, the estate has done well while others have not. On the advice of Grandpa I bought in thirty good Castlemartin Black cattle in the winter, when prices were low, and sold them in April to Walter Morris Drover at an average price of £15 per head. They went off with the first drove of the season, with a thousand animals headed for London. I insisted on cash on the nail; I will have nothing to do with credit and commission when there is even the slightest risk of fraud. I have also heard, too often for comfort, of drovers heading home from Smithfield Market who have been waylaid by highwaymen or footpads and relieved of large sums of other people's money. I have sold half of the wheat harvest and half of the barley harvest, again at good prices, having correctly surmised that there would be a substantial demand for grain to feed the army and the Navy in the war with the French. I also reckoned – correctly – that with a quarter of a million men under arms there would be a shortage of labour on many farms, and that this would drive up the costs of growing and harvesting grain and, in turn, the market prices paid by the merchants. The upshot of all this financial business was that I decided, at Easter, to increase the daily rate for labourers to tenpence and to bring the senior servants' wages up to £9 per year and the junior ones up to £6, all found.

Before doing this I consulted widely with those whom I respect. My tutor Master William Edwards thought my increases were too steep, and said that in his day a carter or a housekeeper would have been delighted with £4 a year. 'My dear Mistress Martha,' he said, 'I fear that the world is going mad. These high costs cannot be sustained, and I consider that the only one to benefit from our problems is Master Bonaparte, who will be delighted to see a collapse in the finances of the nation.' Master John Bateman, on the other hand, was very pragmatic, and said that the price of labour on the land would probably double before peace with France was finally achieved, and that at times of a labour shortage it was worth paying over the odds for servants who were experienced and skilful. I canvassed the views of some of the other squires, and found that while some were paying less than I, the larger estates were paying more. I found an unexpected ally in Meredith Lloyd, who is proving to be a great deal wiser than his old father in the running of the Cwmgloyn estate. He came to visit me and we had a pleasant conversation, in which family matters figured prominently. A very likeable fellow indeed, devoted to his wife and little children, embarrassed by the antics of his brother Matthew, and in my estimation entirely open and trustworthy. He does his hiring of servants at Ffair Gurig in June, and as from that date will pay the same as I.

The other person whose views I am coming to respect is Owain Laugharne of Llannerch. I wrote him a little note requesting his advice on wages in the light of the recent great increases in the cost of living for labourers, and he replied with a perfectly charming note in which he said that he was thinking of seeking my advice on exactly the same thing! I was very flattered, since I dare say that no squire has ever consulted a woman on the matter of farm wages before. Indeed, Owain is no more experienced in estate management than I am, although I am sure that plenty of advice is available to him from his father at Pontfaen and from my tutor John Bateman, who looks after the Pontfaen estate. At any rate, Master Laugharne and I met at Newport market last Friday, and I invited him back to the Plas for a cup of tea. He was, as I anticipated, very shy and stiff in his manner at first, but after a little while we discovered that we had much in common, including a love of harp music and Welsh poetry, and I was amazed to find that he too was familiar with the old Dimetian dialect which I had assumed to be almost my own private language. He said that he had made a study of it at Oxford, and that it was his mission in life to keep it alive. We were soon chatting away like lifelong friends, but I had to break off our interview because Sara was demanding to be fed. We hurriedly consulted on the cost of farm labour, having completely forgotten that this was the very purpose of our meeting. He agreed to pay the same rates as I, and this gives me great confidence.

Bessie told me, when he had gone, that we had laughed a great deal. I had not noticed that myself, but I have to admit to greatly enjoying his company.

Having informed the staff of their new rates of payment, I have to say that they were all very delighted, and insisted on a little celebration. This was a few days since. It has subsequently reached my ears that certain other squires from the neighbourhood, including Owen Gelli Fawr and Huws Bayvil, are not amused. But it is not my task to amuse them. In truth, there is not a lot that they can do to disrupt my plans, and they will soon discover that my ideas about reasonable wages are shared by other progressive squires.

7 July 1806

I have stopped breast-feeding little Sara. She is now fifteen months old, and she was so intent upon chewing me that I thought she might as well chew something else instead, now that soft fruits and vegetables are available in abundance in our garden. Also, the sweet contentment and physical pleasure which I have obtained from breast-feeding since her birth are no longer such necessities for me, with life now restored to some sort of normality. She is still the happiest of children, toddling about the place with unbounded energy and exploring every nook and cranny in the house. I dare say she will soon be talking. She is adored by Dewi and Daisy; and Betsi would spend all her time dressing and undressing her and playing with her if given the opportunity. Who needs dolls, she thinks, when she can have a little sister instead? Now and then I have to shoo big sister out of the house and tell her that she needs to be a child while she has the chance, and that motherhood will likely come along in due course.

Birthdays have come and gone. I celebrated mine very modestly on 12 May, just with the family and servants, and a few guests including Joseph, Owain, Mary Jane and Ellie. The weather was less than perfect, but we had a jolly time dodging showers and rushing into and out of the garden. On David's birthday, 10 June, we said a little prayer for him at breakfast, and I went later on to his grave and placed a posy of early summer flowers on it. There were some fresh ferns growing over the slate slab, and I thought that it was looking less fresh and raw than it had on my last visit. Thus does nature restore and refresh, and heal old wounds.

The hay harvest has come and gone, but it was not a good one, since some of the grass was flattened by heavy rain and scything was made difficult by mud and pools of standing water. Some of the hay was dried by a weak sun, and our haystacks are built; but Billy is worried that there is too much moisture in them and that we will have problems later on with mildew or even with combustion. He says he will have to monitor their condition very carefully. I pray that we will have some decent weather soon, so that the wheat and barley fields can ripen; if this miserable weather continues we may have a disaster on our hands, with starvation and disease added to discontent among the poorer classes.

Last night I had a powerful premonition that something will happen soon which will test my resolve to the limit. It was in the middle of the night. I was wide awake, with a blustering west wind and heavy rain assaulting the house. Suddenly the face of Alban Watkins came into my mind and would not go away. I did not enjoy looking at it, since it is a face which is at once devious, arrogant and mean-spirited, with eyes set too close together and a tight mouth with thin lips. I had not seen the face of this particular monster since 1797, but it figured strongly in the family dramas of that appalling year. Squire Watkins was one of the three local squires who had designs upon our estate, and it was he who instigated a criminal conspiracy in which he claimed that the estate was rightly his. He caused David and Grandpa Isaac and their allies to travel all the way to London to fight things out in the Court of Chancery. Their conspiracy was exposed through the skills of Lewis Legal and Squire Bowen of Llwyngwair, and Watkins was subsequently convicted and transported to the penal colonies of new South Wales some eight years ago. Squire Benjamin Rice of Pentre Ifan went the same way after a spell in the prison hulks of Portsmouth, and we understood that he had gone on a vessel headed for Van Diemen's Land. We assumed that we would never see either of them again, for both were transported for fourteen years.

I am learning to trust my premonitions, no matter how unpleasant most of them appear to be. What am I to make of this one? Will we shortly receive news of Watkins from the other side of the world? How would I react if he were suddenly to appear again in our midst? Strangely, in thinking about this, I was not at all afraid; and indeed I felt the same sort of stirring within me as in the year of the French Invasion when I uncovered, bit by bit, the trail of evil left by the late and unlamented Moses Lloyd.

10 July 1806

Today, while Sara was having her afternoon nap and while the other children were picking berries in the garden with Grandma Jane, I asked Bessie to help me with my hair, which was in need of some loving attention. While she was putting it up she asked, in that sweet and innocent way of hers, what I thought of the latest batch of suitors who had beaten their way to my door.

'Very little,' said I. 'Of the gentlemen who have come on social visits over the past month or two I declare that I cannot remember the name of a single one, nor have I any wish to do so.'

'That sounds a bit regal, Mistress, if I may say so.'

'Yes, I am sorry, Bessie. You are right. I must try not to act above my station, and to remember that neither I, nor the Plas Ingli estate, are so desirable as to attract the attention of the really important families of this county. Maybe I should recognize that nobody will ever replace David in my heart, and that rather than accept some fresh-faced son of a minor squire I might as well remain a merry widow for the rest of my life.'

'That would be a waste, Mistress Martha,' said Bessie, comb in hand. 'You have too much love in you for that.'

'Do you really think so?'

'Of course. You will never replace David, nor should you try to, for he was a fine gentleman, a good husband to you, and a loving father to the children. But you have a big heart. You need a man in your life just as the golden sun needs a blue sky and as a perfect rose needs a gardener.'

I was somewhat taken aback by the poetic images opened up before me by my beloved friend and confessor, and was trying to work out their meaning when she said, as casually as you like: 'I see that young Master Laugharne from Llannerch has a gleam in his eye whenever your name is mentioned.'

'Owain Laugharne? Do not mock, Bessie. He is more

than two years younger than I, and must surely be intended for one of the rich heiresses of the neighbourhood.'

At this Bessie burst into a fit of giggles and said: 'I notice, Mistress, that the mention of his name brought a very pretty touch of colour to your cheeks, and possibly even a light to your eye.'

I had to laugh too, and confessed to Bessie that indeed I did enjoy his company when he visited me a while back. 'But there was nothing in his behaviour,' said I, 'which might lead me to believe that I have any special place in his affections.'

'Mistress, you appear to have become a little rusty in the feminine art of reading the signs. Did he not visit you and bring you flowers, and show great concern towards you following Master David's death?'

'Yes, he did. But so did many others.'

'Did he not visit you again when you were suffering most grievously from the melancholia, and did he not bring you a posy in the hope that it might give you some comfort?'

'Quite correct, Bessie.'

'Do you think, Mistress, that Master Laugharne runs around delivering posies to everybody who might have suffered from bereavement or some other misfortune?'

'Well, maybe not,' I replied. 'It was a kind gesture from a considerate gentleman, but I have no reason to believe that there was anything more to it than that. Indeed, his demeanour towards me has always been somewhat stiff and formal.'

'He is very shy, and if I judge him correctly, not very used to talking to ladies. But just look at his eyes, Mistress. They are blue and beautiful, and very romantic. The eyes of a poet. I have looked at them during each of his visits to the Plas, and in my estimation they are the eyes of a man in love.'

'Bessie! How dare you presume such a thing?' I asked, feeling once again a blush upon my cheeks.

'Forgive me, Mistress,' said Bessie cheekily. 'In future I will stick to washing your hair and ironing your dresses.'

I had to laugh, and as we laughed together, I gave her a long embrace. 'No, dearest Bessie,' I said to her at last. 'If I cannot read the signs you had better do it for me. I appreciate your loving concern, and cannot imagine what I would do without you. There may well be something in what you say. But what should I do now?'

'Bide your time, Mistress, and possibly do a little research. If Master Laugharne feels a flutter in his heart every time he thinks of you, he will soon reappear on the front doorstep of the Plas. You can count on it.'

Now it is late at night. The children are fast asleep, having had a good supper and a long story from me about the dragon who guards a pile of gold and jewels on top of Mynydd Preseli. As I transcribe the details of my enlightening conversation with dear Bessie, I have to admit that I too feel a slight flutter in my heart.

15 July 1806

I have been to visit my dear friend Mary Jane, who just happens to be the sister of Master Owain Laugharne. She now lives in the splendid mansion of Trecwn, having married Dafydd Stokes, the young master of that estate, some years back. I had given her advance warning of my visit, and she was waiting for me as Shemi helped me down from the light chaise. Dafydd was by her side, and her little boy William, who is now two years old, was rushing about hither and thither.

It was wonderful to see them again, and since it was a bright and breezy afternoon we all enjoyed tea and sweetmeats in the garden. We looked round the mansion and the farm buildings, admired the Trecwn peacocks, and Mary Jane showed me the new furniture and fabrics which she has recently acquired in order to brighten up and modernize the old house. Then Dafydd took little William off on some urgent errand, understanding (as a good husband should) that it was time for two old friends to talk, beneath an apple tree full of plumping fruit, about female things.

So we talked of clothes and the latest hairstyles and the new fabrics just in from London, and purely by chance I asked her how Owain was settling in at Llannerch. Mary Jane laughed and said: 'Settling in? You may not have noticed, Martha, that he has been there now for some years. He is not greatly fond of the business of running an estate, for he would prefer to be making music and writing poems, but he has applied himself well to the task that life has set him, and Dafydd says that he is proving to be a good squire. Have you not heard the same thing from others?'

'Indeed I have. Grandpa Isaac says that the servants are very fond of him, and that Llannerch is now a place of happiness and music, following the years of misery and fear under that tyrant Alban Watkins.'

'Why do you ask about my little brother?' asked Mary Jane, with mischief in her eye and the slightest of smiles upon her lips. 'Do you not also wonder about the welfare of my older brother James and my sister Liza?'

'Oh, of course I do,' I lied. 'I wonder about them frequently.' This caused Mary Jane to chortle with delight as she noticed the colour on my cheeks; and it caused me to wonder why I, at the ripe old age of twenty-eight, was blushing like a fourteen-year-old rather too frequently for comfort.

So I came clean and told my dear friend that I had been delighted by Owain's brief visits to the Plas even though they had been under the most difficult of circumstances. I said that I enjoyed his company a good deal better than the company of the other young men of my recent acquaintance, and wondered why he was not already settled with a new wife and a young family at Llannerch.

Mary Jane laughed again and said: 'My dear friend, I have noticed – and I perceive that you have too – that my little brother has eyes only for a certain lady who happens to be a dear friend of mine.'

'Do you really think so?'

'I am sure of it. He may or may not have discussed things with Father, but on each of our recent meetings he has shown an uncommon interest in your health and in the etiquette surrounding bereavement. He has also sought my advice on approaches to beautiful ladies in general who might have families of small children to look after. My brother is a great one for doing things correctly, and I have told him frequently that to be pre-occupied with good manners is to remove all excitement from life.'

'Oh dear,' I sighed. 'I am not sure that I am ready to deal with excitement just yet. It is, after all, less than eighteen months since David's death.'

'Don't be concerned, Martha,' said Mary Jane. 'Owain will not rush things, and most of all his priority will be not to embarrass you or otherwise hurt you. Let events take their course. If it is intended by happy fate that you two should move closer together, I will be the first to rejoice and to wish you all the love in the world. But I hardly dare hope for it.'

And before we could talk further on matters of the heart William came running into the garden to show his mother and me a beautiful slow-worm which he had found under a slab of slate.

17 July 1806

Shemi has whispered in my ear, and I have bad news to report. As I feared from my recent premonition, Alban Watkins has returned from the colonies. Apparently he is a free man and in possession of a piece of paper signed by the Governor of New South Wales granting him an absolute pardon for the crimes he committed against our family in 1797. What he did in order to obtain the pardon is as yet unknown. Well, he has obtained no pardon from me, nor will he get one, unless he is man enough to meet me face to face and to swear that he will spend the rest of his days repenting his sins and working to right past wrongs. If he is still as I remember him, he will not even set foot within a mile of Plas Ingli.

It is also something of a mystery to me why he should have come back to Newport, for he has no property and no family here any longer. After his imprisonment the Llannerch estate was sold to pay off his biggest creditors, and at that time he owed more than a thousand pounds to various local merchants and landowners. As sure as winter follows summer, they will be after his blood as soon as they realize that he is back in circulation. When he was convicted his wife Myfanwy and daughters Rose and Daisy could not cope with the humiliation heaped upon them, and indeed Mistress Watkins was so heavily involved in the wickedness perpetrated by her husband and his cronies Rice and Howell that she must have feared retribution herself. So off they went to Scotland,

and nobody has heard of them since. So far as I know, Watkins has only one cousin left in the Newport area, and he is an elderly gentleman who may or may not be pleased to see him. I await further news from my spies.

18 July 1806

I am pleased to report that my newly established spy network is operating excellently. From no fewer than five sources did I hear of Watkins's return, beginning this morning, bright and early, when Hettie came up to bring us some fresh herrings and fetch some butter and cheese, and joined us for breakfast. As she tucked into her bread and butter and salted ham she said: 'There's news from the Parrog. A stranger arrived two nights since on Captain Morris's schooner *Charlotte*, in on the high tide from Bristol. Alban Watkins, no less.'

Grandpa, Grandma and the female servants looked amazed, and there were various expressions of disbelief, but I was not at all surprised. Hettie continued: 'I recognized him at once, even though he is now heavily bearded and has a scar across the bridge of his nose. He had a thick cloak about him, and came off the ship carrying very little. Nobody met him. Looked around furtively, he did, and then went off into the Queen's Head with a couple of the sailors, no doubt desperate for a drink since Captain Morris keeps a dry ship.'

'This is quite incredible!' said Grandpa. 'It is virtually unheard of for a convicted man to return from the penal colonies, especially if he has served only half his time. Do you think he has escaped, and is a fugitive from the law?'

'Oh, no,' said Hettie. 'One of my lodgers was in the Queen's Head, and Watkins was apparently in high spirits. He was quiet at first, but after he had had a few ales he bought drinks all round, announced who he was, said he was a reformed man, and showed everybody a piece of paper signed by the Governor of the penal colony. It seems to be all above board.'

There followed a good deal of speculation as to the reasons for Watkins's return, but we were unanimous in the view that he will not have come back in order to help the poor or to repair the roof of the church, and we agreed that we would need to keep a very careful eye on the wretched fellow.

No sooner had Hettie left than one of Will's cronies from town turned up and spent a long time chatting to him as he mucked out the cowshed. I was in the garden picking peas at the time, and as the lad went off back to town he doffed his cap and said cheerily, 'Good morning, Mistress Morgan!' I smiled and gave him a wave, and minutes later, as expected, Will appeared and asked if he might have a word. I sat with him on the garden bench, although he did not exactly smell of roses. 'Further developments from town, Mistress Martha,' he said in a conspiratorial tone of voice, presumably assuming that the runner beans had ears. 'My fellows have been talking to – or rather, listening to – some of Captain Morris's sailors. They tells me that Watkins was on the quayside at Bristol, looking for a passage back to Newport. He did not want to work his passage, Mistress. Good money was in his bag, and plenty of it. Gold sovereigns. He was not a nice fellow to have on board. Arrogant and bitter, so they says, and very troublesome since the Captain would not allow any drinking. He got in with one or two nasty fellows, but even they did not take to him overmuch.'

'How did he get to Bristol?'

'On another ship from Portsmouth. Paid for with

sovereigns again. The news is that he came back from Botany Bay or wherever on one of the convict ships, empty at first but then picking up goods in Canton and Calcutta. He says he was ten months at sea, hated every minute of it and suffered greatly with the scurvy. Twice the ship almost foundered, and he says he is lucky to be alive.'

'Well, I am sure we are all greatly blessed by his survival. He must indeed be a driven man to have undertaken such a voyage.'

'My thoughts exactly, Mistress. Either a driven man, or else just mad as a March hare.'

And that was that. Will said that he would pass on any further news as it reached him, and I thanked him very sincerely for his efforts. Then he got on with his day, and I with mine. No sooner had I returned to the kitchen with my basketful of peas than a very small boy arrived from the Parrog bearing a sealed envelope which smelt of lavender water. His clothes were ragged, and he wore no shoes. He insisted on handing the envelope to me personally, which he did with a shaking hand and a feeble smile. I gave him a kiss on the cheek, thanked him very much, and asked Mrs Owen to feed him up on fresh bread and cheese and a good mugful of creamy milk, which I thought would do him more good than a ha'penny. The letter was from my friend Patty Ellis, and this is what it said:

Parrog, 17th day of July 1806

My dear Mistress Martha,

I have fresh news for you. I have a new customer, name of Alban Watkins. You will no doubt share my dismay at his reappearance in town, for he is almost as vile as Joseph Rice, and has done neither me nor you any great favours in the past. I was mightily surprised when I saw him, and hardly recognized him at first, but he did not seek to hide his identity. He had good money in his purse, and showed it to me when he came knocking at the door, so I thought I might as well relieve him of some of it since times are hard. I thought that I might also be able to collect some useful intelligence between the sheets, and so it proved.

I will spare you the details of our bedroom encounter, which I did not greatly enjoy, since he is a crude fellow lacking in finesse and had drunk far too much besides. But I can report that he is as mean-spirited and arrogant as ever, and as far from being a gentleman as it is possible for any fellow to be. He showed me his free pardon papers and boasted of his special friendship with the Governor of New South Wales. Full of his own importance, he was, and talking of the manner in which he had saved the new settlement on that distant shore from disaster through his bravery and determination. He would not say more.

He asked about you and about the Plas, and I was very measured in my replies. He had already heard about David's death from one of the sailormen on the Charlotte, and could not resist gloating about it. He was very insistent on asking about the estate finances, and I had to tell him in all honesty that I knew nothing about such things.

He also told me a few things about his ancient friends. Very bitter, he is, about the manner in which old Squire Howell took his own life, and about the death of old Squire Benjamin Rice on one of the convict ships heading for the penal colonies. This was news to me, and I dare say, Mistress Martha, it is news to you too? Watkins says he heard it from one of the officials at Port Jackson who had the lists of prisoners carried, prisoners died, and prisoners sent to the different settlements. Joseph Rice does not know this either, for only the other day he was pondering, in my company, on the whereabouts of his father, and his state of health.

Watkins knows that Joseph Rice is in lodgings on the Parrog, and he also knows that John Howell is in the army fighting the French. He will no doubt make contact with both of them, Rice sooner and Howell later, next time he comes home on leave.

As to Rice, he is as nasty a fellow as ever, but he leaves me more to my own devices these days, and trusts me more, especially since I am very faithful in paying over his quota of my takings. I still wish to see him rot in hell, and will do whatever it takes to send him there. I am biding my time, and the opportunity will no doubt arise. If I was you, Mistress Martha, I would not worry too much about him just now since he is very busy with contraband and other little schemes for earning a dishonest penny. He has not mentioned you or the Plas lately, but he still has that nightmare occasionally, and I am sure he is still greatly troubled by some dark secret.

That is all I have to report for now. Send me a message by Hettie if you want to know more, and we can meet.

Otherwise I am well, and am enjoying the sunshine when I can. From your loving friend, Patty.

Dear sweet, suffering girl! How kind of her, I thought, to go to such trouble to keep me up to date, and indeed to commit things to writing that would immediately cause Rice to slit her throat if her letter should fall into his hands. I felt this morning – and indeed I still feel – a very warm regard for her, coupled with huge admiration for her fortitude.

This afternoon, as I went out for a walk along the summer lanes with the children, I thought that that was quite enough news for one day, and I was trying to work out the implications of all that I had heard and read. But no, there was more to come. As we went past Dolrannog Isaf Gethin Griffiths was at work in the farmyard, and called us over. He gave us a hearty greeting, and shouted to his wife: 'Liza! Mistress Martha and the children are here!'

She popped her head round the kitchen door, and we chatted for a couple of minutes, and then she said, 'Children! Come and see! I have got a new little calf just two days old, and it is as white as snow, and it has pink eyes. You never saw such a thing! Would you like to come and see it?'

'Oh yes please, Mistress Griffiths,' shouted the three bigger ones in unison, and off they rushed, leaving me to guard little Sara who was fast asleep in her pushing-chair.

'Tidings from town, Mistress Martha,' said Gethin, and proceeded to give me the same intelligence, now somewhat lukewarm, as the others about the arrival of Alban Watkins. I professed surprise and appreciation, for to have done otherwise would have left the dear man very disappointed and even deflated. But he did have one or two pieces of fresh news. 'Master Lloyd and Master Beynon are still keeping very quiet,' he said, 'and I hear say that they think the evil eye is on them. They have been down to Mary Higgins Witch at Allt Clydach and asked her to see if there was a curse on them, and she confirmed that there was. They asked her to remove it, and she tried some old incantations and what have you, and then said it was too strong for her. Then she charged them five shillings. They were not amused, so I hear, and refused to pay, and so she has placed a curse on them as well!' And Gethin slapped his knees with delight, and roared with laughter.

I could not resist joining in, and said at last: 'That means that they will now feel even more threatened than they did before. And how are relations between Lloyd and Rice? Have you heard anything of late?'

'Only that Lloyd hates him more with every week that passes. His injury from the duel has still not healed properly, and he will be left with a permanent limp. He blames Rice for his misfortune, although it was he who precipitated the duel in the first place. He and Beynon are trying to blackmail Master Rice at the moment; but I

263

know not what the details are. My friend Harry Half-mast is on the case, and as soon as I hear further details, Mistress, be sure that I will let you know.'

Then our conversation was ended by the arrival of three small children bearing brown eggs newly collected from Gethin's chicken house and wildly excited with news of the white calf. We said our farewells, and walked home at about four of the clock, only to find Joseph Harries waiting for us. This caused even more excitement among the children, for they love him dearly, and he had to devote some little time to entertaining them before he and I could find a moment to talk. Then Sian took all four of them off our hands, and Joseph and I sat in the garden surrounded by nasturtiums and hollyhocks, and fragrance, and busy bees. 'Hot news from town,' said Joseph, and looked very disconcerted when I burst into a fit of giggles. At last, having regained my self-control, I explained that I had received hot news from town from at least four other people during the course of the day, and that I had a fair idea what that news might be. 'Alban Watkins?' asked Joseph.

'Yes, of course. I know all about his arrival, and much else besides.'

Then he laughed too, and expressed his admiration for the network of spies that I appeared to have under my control, and the effectiveness of their intelligence-gathering operations. 'Dear Joseph!' said I. 'I can assure you again, as I have before, that I control nothing and request nothing. Information simply finds its way to me, from good people who wish me well and who may have some reason for mistrusting or fearing the very same people whom I consider to be enemies.' So we compared notes, and I was very proud to discover that my information was more comprehensive than Joseph's.

'Mistress Martha Morgan!' he gurgled with obvious

delight. 'I am impressed! I see that you need no help from me, and that you are fully in charge of the situation. One further thing. You knew that Watkins met up with Joseph Rice in the Rose and Crown at dinnertime today?'

'No, that is fresh news. Please tell me more.'

'One of my friends tells me that Watkins told him of the death of his father. It appears that he was not surprised, but that his face became set with hatred. He then said, "Those damned Morgans! The fault is all theirs. I swear that I will avenge his death and the misfortune that has overtaken my family. Estate gone to greedy predators, mother insane, father dead. Master Watkins, I may need your help, for it appears that there is work to do." And that was that. Martha, we must keep up our guard, for it seems to me that a new alliance has been forged, renewing the old and evil co-operation of the Rice and Watkins families. In truth, there is nothing much left of either family, and we are confronted by two hungry wolves, snarling in a corner, with nothing to lose from whatever hunting expedition they may embark upon.'

'I agree, Joseph,' I said. 'What we have to do is try to work out what they may have to gain from attacking the estate, what their next moves might be, and how we may best protect ourselves.'

I promised that I would bring Grandpa Isaac up to date on these latest developments, and indeed I did just that after supper this evening. We must be very watchful over the coming weeks and months.

15 August 1806

Another month has passed. The barley harvest is under way, and thank God we have had a slight improvement in the weather, with a week or two of good sunshine and southerly breezes. Since receiving the news about Watkins, Rice and the other evil fellows who lurk in the bushes hereabouts, I have been mulling over at great length the reasons for their continuing interest in the Plas. The only thing that makes sense to me is that they must all be driven, to some degree, by the conviction that there is a Plas Ingli treasure in the ground, and that they deserve to get their hands on some of it at least, and preferably all of it.

I have been trying to work out who knows what. Gethin Dolrannog told me almost a year ago that Matthew Lloyd and Ifan Beynon have some information about the presence of a treasure at the Plas, and are driven by the desire to possess it. Patty Pleasurable told me that Joseph Rice, John Howell, and John Fenton are also driven by the conviction that untold wealth lies somewhere beneath the green acres of the Plas estate. I am utterly convinced that I am the only person who knows the whereabouts of the treasure. The man who buried it in the first place was Moses Lloyd, long since dead and decomposed. He put it into the ground in April 1794 as the Plas Ingli fire was raging about him, having already murdered David's parents and emptied the money chest in the master bedroom. He was certainly the only person to know, within five yards or so, where the bags of coins were buried, but he never had the opportunity to dig them up again, and was somewhat disoriented when the new Plas Ingli was built in a position slightly different from that of the old house. Having killed at least eight people during his evil life, he was driven in his last years by the insane desire to destroy the remnants of the Morgan family and to recover the money which he seemed to think was his by right. I am sure that I was the only person he ever told about the fateful events on the night of the fire, and he only told me because it was his intention to use me and then kill me. I still shudder with terror to recall what happened in St Brynach's cave on the day when I survived and Moses Lloyd did not.

I have sworn to St Brynach that I will not touch the treasure unless the estate falls upon such hard times that its very survival is at stake. But Moses Lloyd, as he made his bloody and erratic course towards the Gates of Hell, was both insane and clever, and he had allies in Squires Benjamin Rice, Alban Watkins and George Howell. He knew that they had designs upon the estate, and I am sure that he told them about the presence of the Plas Ingli treasure without revealing its location. Thus did he encourage them in their endeavours to destroy the estate. He probably promised them shares in the treasure when it was finally recovered, while not having the slightest intention in reality to share it with anyone. So the three squires knew about the treasure. It is also possible that they admitted their families into the secret so as to ensure their co-operation in one criminal conspiracy after another. Rice and Howell are dead, and Alban Watkins, against all the odds, and at considerable risk to himself, has returned to Newport. The lust for gold can be the only possible motive.

I confess that I am confused by the involvement of Matthew Lloyd and Ifan Beynon in the treasure hunt. Moses Lloyd would never have breathed a word about the treasure either to his father at Cwmgloyn, or to his brothers Meredith and Matthew, for he was an outcast from the family and appeared to hate all its members in equal measure. As far as Matthew is concerned, Moses was the brother who went the way of the Prodigal Son but never repented and never returned. He cannot possibly know that Moses is dead; like most people in the neighbourhood, he probably assumes that with the forces of law and order (such as they were and are) in Newport in hot pursuit, and with a price on his head, he simply 'went away' to pursue his criminal career in London or some such place where richer pickings were to be had. Beynon, on the other hand, was heavily involved in the conspiracies perpetrated by the three squires, and when they were all convicted his prison sentence reflected that. All three squires were on the verge of bankruptcy, and how could they have paid Beynon for his dirty work? The answer must be that he was paid with a promise of a share in the wealth of Plas Ingli when the treasure was dug up. When he was let out of prison some years ago, and with the three squires out of the way, Beynon might have assumed he was the only one left in the neighbourhood to know about the treasure. He probably needed a partner if he was to recover it, and I surmise that his drinking friend Matthew Lloyd was the man chosen to share his secret.

In the last couple of years, Lloyd and Beynon must have discovered, in the darkest corners of the inns of Newport and Parrog, that Joseph Rice and John Howell also knew about the treasure. So was formed the alliance of four evil men who killed my dear man David on Shrove Tuesday of last year. Those are the very men with whom I have vowed not to exchange a single word until they are condemned to dangle on the gallows.

So where does this leave me in my deliberations? How many people know about the treasure? Beynon, Lloyd, Rice, Howell and Watkins, for sure, and – if Patty is to be believed – John Fenton as well. All that I have ever heard about that particular man is bad, and I can only assume that he has come upon the scene because he is a drinking and gambling partner of Rice and Howell and is probably involved with them in assorted criminal enterprises. I will take his father's advice and assume that he has a character little better than that of Moses Lloyd and that it is best to give him a very wide berth.

The months are flying by, and none of these murderous villains is making any moves. I find this perplexing. What are they waiting for? The schism between Lloyd and Rice has turned one gang into two. I do not fear Lloyd and Beynon all that much, but Rice is a much more dangerous individual, especially when he is in the company of Howell and Fenton. Thank God that both of them are conspicuous by their absence at the moment. The four who murdered David fear that Joseph has all the evidence he needs to prove their guilt; and they also fear that they are cursed both by Joseph and by old Mary Higgins. That will be preying on their minds in an appalling fashion. But the arrival of Alban Watkins, and his meeting with Rice, puts a different complexion on things. He is an evil man who is now on dangerous territory, with creditors knocking on his door and assorted bullies with past scores to settle. He has gold sovereigns in his pocket at present, but they will not last long, and he will, I am sure, soon wish to precipitate some action against the estate.

A further question runs in my mind continually. How do all of these despicable characters know that the treasure is still in the ground? They all know that Moses Lloyd buried it, and they must believe that he was the only person to know its precise location. Moses is gone. They do not know that he is dead. Would it not be logical, then, for them to assume that he betrayed his fellow conspirators in 1797 when their wicked plans were thwarted, that he dug up the treasure one dark night, and that he then disappeared off to some other part of the world to make a new life for himself as a man of substance? If I had been in their shoes, that is certainly what I might have concluded. But they have probably been through all of this business and have come to the view that if the treasure had been dug up an open hole would have been left behind,which would certainly have become public knowledge in a small place like Newport. They might also have concluded that if the treasure was close to the house, Moses may never have had the opportunity to get at it, for there are always people about the place, and dogs and geese to react to strangers and unusual goings-on. They must therefore feel, on balance, that the treasure is still there for the taking.

And could they possibly think that I, or Grandpa, or some other resident of the Plas, might know the whereabouts of the treasure? Surely not, for if any of us had known about it would we not have dug it up long since? Maybe yes and maybe no. A smart fellow might assume, quite correctly, that anybody knowing the whereabouts of the treasure might just leave it there until golden sovereigns were necessary for the good of the estate or the welfare of the family. And an even smarter fellow might assume that if the estate could be forced to the verge of bankruptcy, I or somebody else in possession of that sacred knowledge might just need the treasure, and lead the way to its location.

Suddenly I am weary of all this speculation, and my head is spinning. I know not what to think about the intentions of others, and I feel that I should be able to predict the actions of Rice and Lloyd and the rest of them, but cannot. I have the germ of an idea in my head as to how I might precipitate a conclusion to this convoluted affair, but I am too tired and too confused to develop it. I feel lonely and isolated, especially since I cannot reveal the existence of the treasure, let alone its location, to anybody else. To do so would be to invite questions about the past and about the disappearance of Moses Lloyd, and I am not inclined to discuss that particular matter with anybody.

I know that I have fine and faithful friends and a multitude of good people who seek to protect me from harm, but tonight more than on any previous night I feel a mighty weight of responsibility upon my shoulders. I have an estate to run, servants and labourers and tenants to look after, and a family of beautiful and vulnerable young children to bring up in a dangerous world. Suddenly I sense the loss of David in quite another way. He is gone as a father and guide for the children. I have already, to some degree, come to terms with the loss of him as a lover and a friend, and adjusted to the fact that I no longer feel his body against mine and his sweet lips touching my flesh. He cannot be replaced, but I still feel a great longing for a good man at my side as someone to talk to, to clarify things when confusion reigns, to advise when I know not whether to turn right or left, and to provide resolve when my instinct is to give in or retreat into comfortable security.

I go to my bed tonight tired and miserable. However, I trust that I will sleep, and that the children will wake me in the morning with some rays of golden sunshine.

16 August 1806

I have had a day dominated by panic and terror, precipitated by the thing that all parents dread – a lost child. My darling Daisy.

The morning started well enough. The children came bouncing into my room at six of the clock, full of energy and laughter, immediately lifting my spirits out of the confusion and exhaustion of last night. We played some

271

little games, and Sian helped to get them dressed and fed. At breakfast we talked happily of this and that, with most of the conversation directed at the harvesting plans for the day. The barley needed to be cut in the field called Parc y Ffynnon, and Billy and Grandpa and I discussed our labour requirements and the arrangements for carting the last of the wheat harvest. Mrs Owen, Grandma Jane and Bessie discussed the feeding and watering of the harvesting hordes. All was well with the world, for the weather was calm and the sun was gold and hot in a clear sky. By nine of the clock the dew had lifted sufficiently for work to get under way.

The children were intent upon helping with the harvest, and I said that they could go into the field at eleven of the clock, following the completion of Betsi's morning lesson with Bethan Mathias. Sian said she would look after the three little ones in the garden and would pick in some vegetables for supper. I had some bills to pay, and settled into my room, leaving them all to their appointed pursuits.

At ten minutes to eleven (the time is inscribed on my heart) Sian knocked on my door and entered without being invited. 'Mistress Martha!' she said, gasping for breath. 'Daisy is missing!'

I swear that my heart stopped beating for several seconds, and I felt the colour drain from my face. If I had not been sitting at the time I would probably have collapsed. 'Oh, my God!' I said when I could speak. 'Where and when did you see her last?'

'About half an hour ago, in the garden. She and Dewi and little Sara were picking runner beans, perfectly happily, and I popped back to the kitchen with a basketful of potatoes for Mrs Owen. I was away for maybe five minutes. When I got back to the garden she was gone – not a sign of her anywhere. I immediately asked Dewi where she was, and all he would say was, "Gone for a walk." I hunted all over the yard, in the barn and the cowshed and the stable, then back to the garden again in case she was hiding somewhere, then back to the house to look in the nursery and all the other rooms. There's no trace of her, Mistress Martha. Betsi and Bethan were reading a book, and had not seen or heard anything of her. So I tried to get some more sense out of Dewi, and still all he would say was, "Gone for a walk." So then, Mistress, I thought I had better come and tell you, quick as I could.' Then the poor girl started to cry. 'It's all my fault, Mistress,' she wailed. 'I should not have left them for a single moment . . .'

'Let's not get into cause and effect yet, Sian,' I said, recovering some of my composure. 'Let us just find her if we can.'

We rushed downstairs and instituted a full search, first of all involving all the womenfolk of the house. We searched in cupboards and wardrobes and chests and boxes; we scoured the scullery and the dairy and the pantry; we ransacked every room, upstairs and downstairs, and then we hunted through all the other farm buildings, shouting 'Daisy! Daisy!' at the tops of our voices and digging into piles of hay and turnips and threshed barley in case she had had some terrible accident. Betsi and Bethan abandoned their lesson and joined in the search. But there was still no sign of her anywhere.

By now my state of relative calm had given way to something more akin to panic, and I had to struggle to behave rationally. I realized that Dewi might hold the key to her disappearance; but the poor little fellow, and little sister Sara, had by now responded to the highly charged atmosphere around them and were both wailing, with Sian doing her best to console them. I took

Dewi in my arms and at last managed to calm him down. Wiping away his tears with my kerchief, I said to him as quietly and calmly as I could: 'Now then, Dewi, do you know where Daisy might have gone?'

'No, Mam.'

'Did you see her going out of the garden?'

'No, Mam. I was picking beans.'

'Did she go out of the garden all by herself, or did somebody go along with her?'

'I don't know. I never saw anybody else . . .' And then the little fellow's bottom lip began to quiver, and he burst into tears again. He held on to me desperately, and in the midst of his weeping he managed to ask, 'Mam, Mam! Is Daisy dead, and has she gone to join the angels just like our dad?'

This was not what I wanted to hear, and I found it almost impossible to control my own emotions. Somehow I did, and handed Dewi over to Grandma Jane, whose lined face was the colour of wood ash. I knew that there were four possibilities: Daisy had run away, having got upset about something or other; she had simply decided to wander off, lost in some fantasy world, oblivious of time and the concerns of others; she had gone off somewhere and had had an accident; or she had been abducted by someone motivated by the desire to harm our family. The thought flashed into my mind that if Rice, or Watkins, or any of the other villains on whose motives I dwelt last evening wished to turn me into a snivelling wretch, prepared to do anything they asked, the easiest way to do it would be to abduct one of the children. Even the threat of harm to them, I thought, would be enough to persuade me to hand over the treasure, the estate, anything, in order to prevent it. And with the harvest in full swing and thirty people hard at work, trotting between Parc y Ffynnon and the farm and the Cilgwyn road, it would be easy for a stranger to slip in unnoticed and reach the farmyard and the garden.

'Mistress Martha!' said a loud voice in my ear. 'Are you still with us? I am sorry to interrupt your deep thoughts, but I just came down from the barley field and discovered what has happened here. Do I have your permission to abandon the harvest and to get everybody searching for Miss Daisy?' It was Billy, blessed fellow that he is, taking control. I nodded weakly, and then all the energy drained out of me and I think I might have fainted. My next recollection is that I opened my eyes on the chaise longue in the parlour and consumed a large brandy which was fed to me by Bessie.

'Don't worry, Mistress Martha,' she said, trying to keep calm herself. 'They will find her. Billy has got them all organized, and they are hunting every nook and cranny on the farm, from the top wall right down to the Cilgwyn road. They are walking down in a long line, all using big sticks to beat down the nettles and bracken and such like. They will find her, to be sure.'

The afternoon passed, and they did not find her. They insisted that I should stay at the Plas, which I found almost unbearable. Nobody ate or drank anything, such was the urgency of the search, in spite of the fact that it was a hot and sultry day. I received occasional reports from Billy, and the concern upon his face had increased in intensity every time he came back to the house. By six of the clock they had still not found her, and Billy drafted in as many of the neighbours and cottagers from Cilgwyn as he could. They started to search on the common and up on the mountain. Somebody went over the mountain to fetch Joseph in case he, as a 'knowing man', could see where she was. He came, and gave me some reassurance, but even he could not help. Grandpa, who was almost exhausted by the frantic searching, had come to talk to me earlier, and I had told him of my fears of an abduction. He appreciated my concern immediately, and went down to town at five of the clock to check on the whereabouts of Rice, Watkins, Lloyd and Beynon. He returned at six-thirty, having set all his spies to work, and said that if anything untoward had been going on we should certainly know about it by the time darkness fell.

Time passed. Joseph went off to join the search. I could hear the despairing shouts tumbling down from the mountain and echoing round the *cwm*: 'Daisy! Daisy! Where are you?' Those of us left in the house felt impotent and frightened, and I was constantly on the edge of panic. The only thing that stopped me from screaming hysterically was the presence of the other three children, who insisted on clinging to me and would not let go.

At nine of the clock Billy came in, utterly exhausted and dejected. 'Mistress Martha,' he moaned. 'I fear that we will have to call off the search for the day. Dusk is falling, and we cannot see what we are doing. The bracken on the mountain is so high between all the big stones and crevasses that she could be anywhere, and I fear that if we carry on stumbling about any longer somebody will break a leg. We will start again at first light tomorrow. I am sorry that we have not been successful.'

'No, Billy,' I protested. 'You have all worked heroically, and I thank you from the bottom of my heart. Call all of those good people back to the Plas, and let us give them something to eat and drink.' I slumped back on my chair in a state of total desolation, and I felt the tears streaming down my cheeks.

Suddenly I sat bolt upright, as if a shaft of lightning had passed straight through me. 'I know where she is!' I said to the other children, and to everybody else who was with us in the parlour. 'Don't worry! She is perfectly all right!' I leaped to my feet, scattering children in all directions, and ran to the kitchen. 'Billy, please will you get me a candle lantern with plenty of candles? I will go and get her. I don't want anybody with me. Darkness will be falling soon, but thank God it is a fine and warm evening. There is enough light for me to find my way for half an hour or so, but I will need the lantern for the return journey. I will see you all in an hour!'

And I went rushing off, carrying with me a lantern, some candles, a tinder box, and a blanket to wrap round my frightened child, leaving everybody in the house in a state of shock. As I walked up towards Ffynnon Brynach I passed several searchers coming down, and told them not to worry. So convinced was I of the inevitable outcome of my expedition that I believe I even managed to give them a smile and a cheery wave. I reached the spring, somewhat out of breath, for the climb was quite a steep one, and anointed myself with a few splashes of the water. It was cool and fresh on my brow, and helped to keep me calm. But in truth I was now not at all concerned about my little girl, and after resting for a few minutes I carried on upwards, climbing at a measured pace. I knew the way so well that I could have walked it with my eyes closed, or in pitch darkness. Every bluestone boulder, every little hollow, every flaming furze bush, every strip of springy turf was familiar to me. I passed patches of late summer bracken beaten down by the searchers only an hour earlier, and crevasses and rocky crags that had already been examined minutely by my dear friends, frantic and exhausted and miserable as they must have been. Up I went over the middle rocky bank, along the grassy terrace to the right, and up again onto the long scree slope. Up across the blue-grey slab with the long crack in the middle of it, then left to the place where the highest daffodils grow on the mountain in the early spring.

I stopped in order to catch my breath, and turned and looked back for the first time over the darkening *cwm*. The sun was already down, but I could yet pick out the mosaic of little woodlands, cottages and farms, stone walls and paddocks and fields. The air was still enough for me to hear the sweet sound of the waterfall near Trefelin and Cilgwyn Mill. The Plas was just visible, and I saw that there were crowds of people all round it, gazing upwards and following my progress. I waved at them, and they all waved back.

I turned and continued, to the left, up over the five big boulders covered in lichen and moss, down into the hollow with the little ash tree, past the crags where there are patches of white crystals glistening in the rock, and finally between the two rough stones leading into the grassy passageway with rocky outcrops above it, to left and right. I knew now that I would have been quite invisible from anywhere in the *cwm* even on the brightest and clearest of summer days. I also knew that no matter how intensively the searchers had picked their way across the mountain face, they would not have found this place; it had once belonged to old St Brynach, and now it was mine, and, Daisy's. I breathed deeply, and looked at the tumbled crag above and to the right. The old raven, and his mate, and four youngsters, now almost fully grown, were perched on their rock, watching me in silence. I gave them a wave, and went to fetch Daisy.

Ahead of me was the little rowan tree and the two pillars of blue rock which flanked the entrance to the cave. Long dry grasses and a few droopy fronds of fern covered it, but I brushed them aside and squeezed in through the entrance. It was pitch black inside, and I could see nothing at all. But I said quietly: 'Daisy, *cariad*, it's Mam. Time to come home.'

I heard a little stirring at the far end of the cave and knew that she had been asleep. I took out my tinder box and got a little flame going, and lit one of my candles. The light flooded the whole place, and there she was, the picture of innocence, not at all afraid, and rubbing her eyes. Somehow, I managed to control my emotions and to resist the urge to scold her or interrogate her. I simply walked across to her, folded her into my arms, and embraced her for a long time. 'Hello, Mam,' was all she said. I wrapped the blanket round her shoulders.

'Now then, *cariad*, it's late and past your bedtime,' said I. 'Shall we go down? It's pitch black outside. I will hold the lantern in one hand, and you hold on tight to my other hand, and we'll be quite all right.'

So the two of us made our slow and tortuous way down the mountain, stopping every now and then to listen to the owls in Gelli Wood. Below us we could see the lights of the Plas. As we walked we talked, and I discovered that my sweet, strange child had simply decided that she was bored picking runner beans all those hours ago, and that she would go for a walk on the mountain. She had climbed up and up, hidden by the tall bracken, and had been so absorbed by butterflies and little birds and pretty flowers that she had probably been quite oblivious to the shouts coming from the Plas and from the searchers during the afternoon. At last , she said, she felt a bit tired, and then a nice raven had flapped along in front of her, up and down and back and fore, a few yards at a time, and she followed it for a while. She didn't know exactly where she was, but she was not particularly troubled, since it was a warm day and the raven looked very friendly. And then the big black bird perched on the little rowan tree, so she went up to it and saw the slit in the rock between the two bluestone pillars. She said that she peeped inside, and found this lovely cool cave with a bed of moss at the far end. So she just went inside and cuddled down and went to sleep. What could I do but smile to myself at the charming innocence of her tale?

Then we came down to Ffynnon Brynach, and found Billy and Bessie waiting there. When they saw little Daisy holding my hand Bessie squealed with delight and Billy shouted, 'Miss Daisy! Miss Daisy! Are you all right, *bach*?' And they both insisted on giving Daisy and me great hugs, and there was such pandemonium that the four of us fell over in a pile. Billy sat straight down in the bubbling water of the spring pool and got his bottom soaking wet, which caused Daisy to have an uncontrollable fit of the giggles.

At last we calmed down and marched in a procession down the last bit of the path to the house. Billy carried Daisy on his shoulders and I carried the lantern. We had to go cautiously, since there was a confusion of shadows and stones and bracken patches to negotiate, but we descended safely. As we approached the house we saw upturned eager faces, illuminated by the lights from the windows. Every window in the place seemed to have a candle in it, and it looked like Heaven. Billy shouted: 'Miss Daisy is safe! Miss Daisy is safe and sound!' and in response a loud cheer went up and echoed about the *cwm*.

My recollections of our arrival in the yard are somewhat hazy, for that was the moment when emotions which had been kept in check were finally released; there were cheers, and tears, and laughter, and embraces, and dogs barking, and children hopping and dancing, and general chaos. I dare say a good deal of ale was consumed.

At last the children are tucked up in bed, fast asleep. The house is quiet and the candles have been extinguished. I am sitting at my desk trying to make sense of what has happened during the day. There will be no recriminations, and I will say nothing further about Daisy's adventure to the sweet child herself. I have already assured poor Sian that she was entirely blameless in the matter, and have told her that she has my complete confidence and respect. Suddenly I feel a surge of emotion in my breast and my hand is shaking. I think the intensity of the day has been too much for me, and I cannot write more.

17 August 1806

Last night, I am ashamed to say, I cried myself to sleep like a baby. I cannot find the right words for the emotion which overcame me, but I felt utterly desolate, vulnerable, isolated and alone in the world, even though I knew full well that I was surrounded by love.

In retrospect, now that twenty-four hours have passed, I believe that it was the vulnerability of my position that struck me with the greatest force and caused me to crumble like a dried eggshell beneath a rolling pin. My knowledge of the treasure-hunting aspirations of my enemies, my fears of an abduction of one of the children, and the heavy responsibilities which I now have to bear on my shoulders, have all created a longing within my breast for a good man at my side. Somebody to talk to late at night and early in the morning, when the rest of the world is asleep. Somebody with whom I can share the burden which life has given me. Somebody who will give me love and beauty and peace and security to replace the energy which seems constantly to be draining out of me. Can I go on, year after year, supporting others, caring for them, fighting battles for those who are in danger? I cannot. I cannot, for I do not have the strength.

But crushed and feeble, and emotionally drained as I am, I will not give in to despair. I will stick to the promise that I made to myself some months back, and I will not allow the storm waves to roll over me. I will make my own destiny.

It was in this frame of mind, before breakfast this morning, that I decided to go and visit Master Owain Laugharne at Llannerch. I had no idea what I was going to say to him, or what I hoped to achieve; maybe I was simply in need of some intelligent male company. The rest of the household made a very slow start, for all of them – family and servants – were exhausted after yesterday's frantic search for little Daisy. Mrs Owen and I ate breakfast together, while the rest of the house was fast asleep. 'Let them be,' I said to her. 'They deserve it. I happen to feel wide awake. Goodness knows why.'

'I dare say, Mistress, that your emotions have been too much tumbled about for proper sleep. But don't you worry – tiredness will probably overtake you later in the day, and tonight you will surely sleep the sleep of the angels.'

'You are probably right, Mrs Owen,' said I. 'By the way, I think everybody should take a break from the harvest today. The day will be very hot, and the glass is high, so let us assume that all will be well if we continue tomorrow.'

'That will be appreciated, Mistress. Poor Billy and Shemi and Will are so tired that if you put them in a barley field with scythes in their hands they will probably fall asleep on the job and cut each other's feet off.'

When the rest of the household emerged, with bleary eyes and sore heads, I told them the good news, and there was a deal of relief all round. There were many other jobs about the farm which needed doing, at a gentle pace and in the shade. The children, all four of them, came downstairs with Sian, looking as bright and shiny as new silver shillings. They were in a good humour, and Daisy of course loved being the centre of attention especially since this made her big sister Betsi jealous. She talked of being led on her adventurous walk by ravens and fairies, who took her to a magic cave full of gold and silver; and of course nobody believed her. I asked Sian to take the children for a picnic by the river at Cilgwyn Mill. They were all delighted with the idea, and immediately fell to cutting slices of bread and cheese and raiding the larder for assorted favourite things.

When Bessie was putting up my hair I told her that I was minded to pay a visit to Master Owain Laugharne.

'By yourself, Mistress?'

'Of course. Who else should I take with me?'

'Well, it is somewhat irregular for a lady to go visiting a bachelor gentleman unannounced, and without a chaperone.' And then she added, with a little smile on her face: 'There is no knowing what might happen.'

'It is still not ten of the clock, Bessie, and I don't even know if he will be there.'

'Of course you must go. If you meet him you can always say you are just out for a walk, and express great surprise at the encounter. He may well be at home, for the Llannerch harvest is finished, and his servants will be away today helping with the harvest at Plas Pontfaen. It is a Thursday, and on Thursdays he normally looks round the estate.'

'You are remarkably well informed about the movements of Master Laugharne, if I may say so.'

'Let us say, Mistress,' said Bessie with a smile, 'that I make it my business to be well informed on matters that might have an effect upon your well-being.'

So it was that at eleven of the clock, with the sun already high, I set off on a little walk in the direction of Plas Llannerch. Purely by chance, I had chosen to wear my prettiest red cotton dress and my white bonnet with silk ribbons. I walked along the lane towards Dolrannog and Penrhiw, entranced by heavy-seeded grasses and late summer flowers and busy butterflies and frantic bees. I waved to Mary Tucker as I went past, and she shouted: 'Good morning to you, Mistress Martha! So glad to have the wonderful news about Daisy *bach*!' Then I dropped down the rutted cart-track into the thick woodland of Cwm Gwaun, and soon I was in the shade of the ancient beech trees which overlooked the Llannerch walled garden. As I entered the yard at the side of the mansion I encountered Mistress Fanny Gwilym, the oldest of the Llannerch servants. She was cleaning the butter churns beside a water-spout. 'How nice to see you, Mistress Martha!' She smiled. 'A lovely day for a walk. Would you be looking for the young master?'

'Not particularly,' I lied. 'I just thought I should wander down and enjoy the summer flowers here in the valley. They are so much more beautiful than those which we have up on the mountain.'

'Well, in any case, he isn't here. Went over to the pandy on the other side of the valley, he did, about half an hour since. He will be sorry he missed you.'

'Not to worry,' said I. 'In any case, please give him my compliments when he returns. I will carry on with my walk. Good day to you!' And I carried on with my walk, which purely by chance took me across the Cwm Gwaun road and in the direction of Pandy.

I knew Pandy well, for it is the fulling place to which we all take our heavy woollen weaves so that they can be cleaned of oil and beaten into flannel. It was only about a quarter of a mile away, on a good cart track leading up a little side valley. It is not the pleasantest of places, for there is a big pond there, fed by the water of the Gwaun River where it comes cascading down from the high and soggy moorlands to the south. A crude leat carries the water away from the river into the pond. There is a rough stone building adjacent, with a waterwheel that drives a couple of heavy drop-hammers which splash into the water of the pond and beat and batter the woollen fabrics which are placed beneath them. Iolo Ifans the pandy-man has special recipes which he uses to assist in removing lanolin, binding the woollen fibres and colouring the flannel; I know not what most of his strange liquids are, but I do know that he pays a good price for animal and human urine, which many of the labourers who live in the *cwm* collect diligently throughout the year.

Luckily, today the waterwheel was resting and the drop-hammers were silent. There was only a trickle going through the pond, which was stinking and green and all but obliterated by clouds of mosquitoes and flies. I held my nose as I went by, following the track where it started to rise up on the valley side. There was no sign of Iolo or his wife or children, either in the cottage by the track or at the pandy itself, and I surmised that they must all be away at Gelli Fawr or Tregynon helping with the harvest.

I climbed up the track beside the cascading river, and when I was far enough from the smell of the pandy to stop and catch my breath I sat on a grassy bank in the cool dark shade of an oak tree. The woodland rang with birdsong and resonated with the humming of insect wings. I lay on my back and looked up at the canopy of leaves over my head, trying to count the number of greens and textures I could see within the leafy boughs. I think I nodded off for a minute or two, but then I was startled to hear a little snatch of music drifting through the trees. It faded away, and then it came again, carried on the breeze. It was unmistakably the sound of somebody singing. A man singing. It drew me like a magnet, and so I got to my feet and walked on up the track until I got to the start of a series of cascades in the adjacent river. In the winter, when there is a torrent roaring down off the mountain, this is a dangerous place indeed, and I know that poachers have been drowned in the deep rock pools where three-pound trout are reputed to lurk. There was not much water in the river today, to be sure, and the cascades and waterfalls were mere streams, but the lower pools were full of cool, clear water.

The sound was coming from one of the higher pools, louder and sweeter. The man was singing, in a fine tenor voice, in Welsh. I recognized the tune from my childhood; it was the one my father called 'The White Lilac Tree'. I walked on up the track for a little way, and then, to locate the source of the music, I had to make my way, as gingerly and quietly as possible, into a thicket of bushes and tall ferns. At last I was able to peep through the leaves of a little hazel bush, and then I saw him. Owain Laugharne, as naked as the day he was born, floating on his back in the biggest and deepest of the rock pools, with his eyes closed, singing at the top of his voice. His voice was beautiful, and he was beautiful.

The pool was only about fifteen feet across, but it was very deep. On the far side of it there was a wall of black shaly rock, smoothed by cascading water over thousands of years. Where there were little crevices, ferns and mosses and liverworts were thriving, no doubt fed and watered by spray when the river is in flood. To the left there was a jagged waterfall with just a trickle of water flowing down its face; to the right, where the water of the pool spilled out, there was a jumble of smooth black boulders and stones, ending abruptly at the edge of the next waterfall downstream. Tall trees towered over the pools and the river bed, and some of them had dropped branches or fallen over into the river; branches and roots and rotting tree trunks were jumbled together, all dripping with moisture and supporting clusters of greenery and summer flowers. The sunlight streamed through the tree canopy in shafts and slivers of light, dappling the river banks and the pool which Owain occupied. I thought that the Garden of Eden must have been very similar.

I could not take my eyes off him. His body was illuminated by sunlight and surrounded by shadow, and I could see every detail of it. Why had he been named Owain, when he should have been called Apollo?

His behaviour was so sweet, so natural, and so un-inhibited that I could hardly credit it. Was this the same young man who had been so stiff and uncertain of himself in my company? The same young man who, according to his sister Mary Jane, was almost obsessively concerned with learning the correct way of doing things? He must have been utterly convinced that nobody would pass along the pandy track today with the barley harvest in full swing, for country squires do not normally swim about in rock pools without any clothes on. So absorbed was I by the sound of his sweet voice and the sight of his lean body moving gently in the water that I became almost entranced; but I was jolted out of my reverie by the realization that his clothes were on a smooth rocky eminence between me and the rock pool. Indeed, they were no more than ten feet away from where I crouched behind my little hazel bush.

Suddenly he stopped singing, opened his eyes and swam towards me. I thought that he must have seen me in spite of the fact that I was well hidden, and very still. I hardly dared to breathe. He climbed out of the water and walked gingerly across the gravelly turf to the smooth rock where he had placed his clothes. Then he moved them to one side and stretched himself out on his back, having found a sunny spot where he could dry out gradually, and in comfort. He closed his eyes and looked as if he might go to sleep. I was mortified, but thanked the God of Mercy that I had not put any scent on before leaving the house; if I had done, he would certainly have smelt it. What was I to do? Fling aside my hazel boughs and fern fronds and say: 'Good day, Master Laugharne! How good it is to see you'? The poor fellow, I was sure, would never recover from the shock, and neither would I. There was nothing for it but to stay put, hardly breathing, not daring to move a muscle, and hoping that I could maintain my pose without getting cramp or suffering from exhaustion. So I continued to look at him, lying on his rock in the sun, so close that I could almost touch his skin and run my fingers through his hair.

He was listening to the birds, and to the whispering breeze, and to the gently murmuring and splashing stream. His chest rose and sank rhythmically as he breathed. I noticed that he was much slimmer than David, and I could make out his ribcage, but he was by no means undernourished, and had strong arms and legs. His stomach was flat and strong. He had very little body hair, and what he had was very blond. Below the waist his skin was as white as virgin snow, but his upper body was bronzed, and I thought that was the sign of a man prepared to work in the sun with his servants.

Water droplets trickled off his skin, and there was a funny little pool of water in his breast cavity. I noticed, more sharply than on my previous encounters with him, his fine nose and high cheekbones. His long golden hair settled about his head on the warm rock, and I noticed little rivulets of water streaming away down the natural slope and back towards the pool whence they had come. I am ashamed to say it, but I could not take my eyes off his private parts, which delicacy prevents me from describing in detail. Suffice to say that I have for too long been deprived of such things.

Then he turned over in order to dry his back, and I was able to examine the other side of him in considerable detail. His head was resting on the backs of his hands, and I could see in sharp focus the muscles on his back, his slim waist and his tight buttocks. I thought that in some way his back was even more beautiful than his front.

Suddenly he must have decided that it was time to go, for he sprang to his feet, rubbed the last droplets of water off his body with his shirt, and put on his breeches and stockings. Then he put on his shoes, shook out his shirt, and put that on too. He started whistling, strode past me so close that I could have touched him, and went back to the track. Then off he went down towards Pandy, and within thirty seconds he was gone. At last I was able to escape from my prison, and I was greatly relieved to be able to move my limbs again. For some minutes I jumped up and down and shook myself, and walked round in small circles on the rock where Owain had recently dried himself. I considered following him back towards Pandy, but thought better of it, for in truth I had had enough excitement for one day. So I sat on the rock, in the very patch of sunlight that Owain had recently graced with his naked body. I remained there for maybe

289

half an hour, thinking very beautiful thoughts; and when I judged that sufficient time had passed I retraced my steps back to the Cwm Gwaun road.

When I reached the road I decided not to return home through the Llannerch yard, but turned right and continued along the path that goes from Parc y Dyffryn towards Dolrannog and the Plas. Within thirty minutes I was home. Bessie was the only person in the kitchen. 'Why, Mistress Martha,' said she, 'you have a good colour on your cheeks and look as if you have had a fine walk in the sun. May I ask whether you saw Master Laugharne?'

'Oh yes, I saw him,' I replied. 'But the circumstances were not quite right for a conversation. Some other time.'

19 August 1806

Since I conducted my close examination of Owain's body a couple of days since, I must admit that I have thought of little else. I must try to pull myself together. Today, as we ate our breakfast, Grandpa said, with a twinkle in his eye: 'Martha, all day yesterday you went around in a daze, with a constant smile on your lips and a dreamy look in your eyes. Are you all right? Not going down with some summer ailment, I hope?'

And before I could answer, Bessie, cheeky as ever, said to everybody else: 'Very worried about her, I am, for this morning she looks just the same as yesterday. The children might just as well be on the moon, and there's no work we'll be getting out of her today. It's a good job the harvest more or less looks after itself.'

'Bessie!' said I, pretending to be upset, 'that's enough insolence from you, if you please. It so happens that I do feel quite mellow at the moment, as a result of thinking beautiful thoughts. I am trying to cultivate the habit.'

'There's nice for you,' said Mrs Owen, joining in the sport. 'Mellow is a good thing to be, and indeed I would like to be mellow myself. Would Mistress Martha like to share her beautiful thoughts with us?'

'No I would not! You can all go and find your own, and then we can all be mellow together.' And then the children joined in and made a competition of it, closing their eyes tightly and seeing who could think the most beautiful thoughts.

We were all out into the barley field by eight of the clock, since there was a good breeze and hardly any morning dew. Today it was Parc Gwyn, and we had twenty people at work, including Michael O'Connell, his wife and three children, and his brother Daniel, newly over from Wexford. I do not like to take on new labourers so late in the harvesting season, but Michael pleaded with me and said his brother was desperate for work. I interviewed him, and found him to be a pleasant and intelligent fellow; and indeed he has proved to be a hard worker who knows how to swing a scythe.

Work was proceeding well until, in the middle of the day, a terrible event occurred on the harvesting field. Michael's little boy Brendan, only five years old and a special friend of Daisy, was fooling about all by himself when the rest of us were sitting in the shade having our picnic. Suddenly he screamed such a scream as I never wish to hear again, and we all leaped to our feet to find that he had been playing with the scythes which the reapers had left, out of harm's way, hooked over a low branch. The little fellow had dislodged one of them and as it fell to the ground the blade, clean and sharp as the finest razor, had sliced into his leg right to the bone. There was blood everywhere, and pandemonium as his mother Molly became hysterical and Grandma Jane (who is reckoned to be expert at such things) desperately tried to staunch the flow of blood with shirts and kerchiefs and anything else that came to hand. Brendan's two little brothers and my own children were caught up in the panic and started screaming too, and I told Sian to take all of them back to the house. Some of the men became quite green at the sight of so much blood, and had to sit down.

I tried to help Grandma with her task, but the blood continued to flow, and soon we were using petticoats and tablecloths as well, and our own clothes became thoroughly bloodied. After thirty minutes of trying to help the screaming child I thought that we were fighting a losing battle, for his face was getting pale and his hands felt cold in spite of the heat of the day. Will went up to the barn to get a plank to carry the lad on, and Bessie ran to our medical chest to collect all the bandages we had. Then I had an inspiration. 'Shemi!' I said. 'Quickly! Take the chestnut pony, or whichever one you think is the fastest, and go over the mountain and fetch Joseph Harries! Tell him there is a boy bleeding to death here, and ask him to bring whatever medication may be appropriate.'

'Yes, Mistress Martha!' said the dear fellow, and ran down towards the paddock where the ponies were grazing. I knew that he would not even have to catch the one he needed, for they would all come to the gate as soon as they saw him. Within a minute or two he was away, riding bareback up onto the common and away towards Werndew.

We had to get the boy into the house, and so we bound up his leg with the remnants of my petticoat as tightly as we dared, laid him on the plank and held his leg high. Then his father Michael and uncle Daniel carried the plank and its precious burden back to the house. As we reached the kitchen the poor little fellow lost consciousness, and we all feared that he would die. We had still not managed to stop the flow of blood, and I could hardly credit that there could be so much blood inside one frail body. We laid him on some soft blankets on the kitchen table, on his back with a box under his injured leg to keep it high. Sian kept Dewi and his sisters out of the way, and since there was little that Billy, and the Jenkins boys, and the other reapers could do to help I told them they might as well continue with the harvesting. That would at least give them something positive to concentrate on.

Brendan was sinking fast, with his face as white as a new shroud and his pulse almost too weak to feel, when Joseph came rushing through the door. 'I was on my way when I met Shemi near Carn Edward,' he puffed. 'I knew something had happened and that it had something to do with blood. Now then, everybody, please stand aside.'

The first thing he did was to raise the boy's head and pour some brownish liquid down his throat. 'Sedative,' he said. Then he threw a little bagful of green plants of various sorts to Mrs Owen and said, 'One pint of boiling water on those, please, Mrs Owen, and chop and mix the whole lot up and keep it all simmering so as to make me a poultice.' She immediately got to work as directed, and Joseph proceeded to peel off the layers of blood-soaked cloths and bandages from the boy's leg. 'Well done, ladies,' he said. 'You have at least managed to slow the flow of blood. But this is a terrible injury, and I will have to work fast if the lad is not to lose the leg. Martha, do you have any boiled water that is cool? No? Then we will have to take a chance that the water from Ffynnon Brynach is clean. Please get me a big bowl of water straight from the pipe. Mistress Jane, clean cotton cloths if you please, freshly washed if possible.'

He then ran into the scullery and washed his hands and arms in soapy water that was as hot as he could bear. We women scurried about, following directions, with poor Michael O'Connell looking on, ashen-faced, and his wife Molly holding the unconscious boy's hand. Soon Joseph had the gaping wound cleaned, and he said: 'What did this? A freshly-sharpened scythe? Yes? That helps – it could have been a rusty old knife, and then we would really be in trouble. Now then, the Joseph Harries blood-stopping speciality. A good job the little fellow is asleep, or he would jump through the roof with the pain.' And he poured a clear liquid from a glass bottle all over the wound; as we watched, the blood started to congeal and the flow stopped.

'Good, good,' he said. He covered the lad with blankets so that only his head and the injured leg were showing. 'He is in a deep state of shock,' he said, 'and he must be kept warm.' Then he said to Grandpa, without taking his eyes off his patient for a second, 'Master Isaac, I have some stitching to do. Will you please fetch me your strongest magnifying glass? My eyesight is not what it was. Thank you. And Martha, please get me a roll of cotton thread and a small needle, put them in a saucepan of boiling water for three minutes, and then take them out and put them here on the table beside me on a clean cloth. Don't touch them with your bare hands, which may look clean but which are probably not.' He talked as he worked. 'I have discovered that in surgery carbolic acid is worse than useless. Cleanliness is everything.'

Next, he asked the men to move the heavy table to the window so that the injured leg was bathed in direct sunlight. Then he wrapped a clean cloth round his head, in order, so he said, to stop the sweat from his brow from dropping into the wound as he worked. And so Joseph set to, needle and thread in one hand, manipulating muscle and the other internal parts of the leg with the other. Sian held the magnifying glass exactly where he needed it. The operation went on for more than an hour, and Joseph concentrated so intensely that he hardly said another word. I had to monitor little Brendan's pulse. It almost stopped twice; on one occasion Joseph poured some medicine down the boy's throat to get it going again, and on the second he placed his hands, one on top of the other, on the boy's chest for several minutes, with the same result. As he worked, Mrs Owen and the other servants quietly gathered up all the bloody cloths and bandages and got them off to the washroom to be rinsed in cold water and then boiled in soap suds.

At last Joseph finished the final stitches on the skin of the boy's calf. He looked utterly exhausted, and his eyes were so tired that he kept on blinking in a manner that would have been comical in any other circumstances. 'Now then, Mrs Owen, the poultice should be soft and mushy by now. Soak a towel in cold spring water please, and pour on the poultice. Give it a minute to cool, and then hand it to me.' He straightened up, stretched his back, and groaned, for he had been working crouched over the boy for a very long time. 'Oh dear,' he said. 'Not as young as I ought to be.' Grandpa gave him a chair, and he sat down and looked round at the assembled company of about a dozen people. 'My goodness,' he said. 'I had no idea I had so many spectators. Now I have given away all my medical secrets, or at least some of them. No matter. The rest of the world will gain possession of all of them in due course, in any case.'

He turned to Brendan's parents, who were, very strangely for them, lost for words. He stood up and bowed. 'Delighted to make your acquaintance,' he said.

'Excuse me if I do not shake your hands just yet, but I am not quite finished. You are very lucky not to have lost your little boy today. I think he will be all right. He will not lose the leg, but it is very hard to repair everything inside it, and I fear that he may have a limp for the rest of his life. The chances are fifty-fifty. Let us hope for the best!'

'Here is the cloth with the poultice, Master Harries,' said Mrs Owen. 'Mind now, it's still a bit hot.'

'Ah, good, good,' said Joseph. He took it and wrapped it over the wound, and then wrapped more bandages around it to keep it in place. 'Right. Finished!' he said at last. 'Now I need a stiff brandy, my dear Martha, if you have such a thing.'

'Purely by chance, a few bottles came my way only last week,' I said, and poured him a tumbler full of the best duty-free liquid that money could quietly buy. Then I used the rest of the bottle up by pouring drinks for everybody else, for in truth we all needed something stronger than water.

Then Joseph did a very strange thing. He went to his bag and took out a piece of paper. He asked for a pen and ink. Then he turned his back on everybody and wrote something on the paper, and tucked it inside the bandage on the little patient's leg. Then he asked for the operating table, with the patient still on it, to be moved back to its accustomed place in the middle of the kitchen floor. He then walked five times clockwise round the table, and five times back again, muttering some very strange words which nobody understood. He was in a sort of trance. Then he stopped, closed his eyes, and breathed very deeply several times.

'Excellent!' he said with a smile on his face. 'I almost forgot the charming bit. Never quite sure about it myself, but it can't do any harm.'

After that we took the little boy and made a bed for him in the corner of the parlour, where it was cool and quiet. Joseph took his pulse and said it was steady and quite strong. Then he said that the lad would have to be watched constantly, and suggested that his mother or father should remain at his side for several days. He said that he would soon wake up and should be given plenty to drink, and that he should take some special iron medicine which he would make up in his cottage, if somebody would be so kind as to fetch it at seven of the clock. Will, who happened to look in with a view to reporting to the harvesters how the operation had gone, agreed to ride over the mountain as requested.

Joseph downed the rest of his tumbler of brandy, packed up his things, and embraced the little boy's parents. Not surprisingly, they were quite overwhelmed with gratitude. 'I will see you tomorrow in the middle of the morning,' he said, 'but if his condition worsens, send for me at once. Give him a little bit of warm broth later this evening. Not too much. I don't want him to be sick. Tomorrow he will have terrible pain, and his leg will swell up since there is very serious bruising. But the poultice will help, and in the afternoon I will give him something else to ease his distress. Goodbye!'

And he went into the yard, jumped onto his white pony, and trotted off towards the setting sun just as he had done many times before. Dear Joseph! All of us, including the Irish family, are lost in admiration. Wizard he may be, but he is also a born healer and a true man of science. Almost every time I meet him I discover some new talent.

Tonight all is quiet. Little Brendan woke up at about six of the clock and is very drowsy, but his mother is at his side. She and Sian will take it in turns to watch over him until daybreak. Today I have learned a great deal.

Michael O'Connell tells me that life is cheap in Ireland, but Joseph has reminded me – and the O'Connells – that life is to be cherished, and loved, and fought for, and considered more sacred than the highest altar or the grandest cathedral.

21 August 1806

Ten years ago, to the day, David and I were married by my brother Morys in a small and secret ceremony in his church near Carmarthen. I did not forget it. I woke up early, just as it was getting light, and before the children came rushing in I had thirty minutes to myself, remembering and celebrating the great love that we had for each other. I am pleased to report that I managed this with equanimity, having learned a good deal about controlling my emotions and directing my thoughts onto the beauty and the joy of his life and away from the ugliness and misery of his death. I am not a very godly person, but I managed to say a little prayer of thanks for our time together, and I asked the blessing of the Good Lord on his soul and on those whom David has left behind on the green and stony acres of Plas Ingli.

I have received a letter from Master John Fenton of Glynymel. In the middle of the morning a messenger arrived on a small grey pony, having ridden over from Fishguard. He delivered into my hand a perfumed envelope, and went off with Mrs Owen to get a drink of ale to cool himself off, while waiting to see if there might be a reply. Inside the envelope was the following letter, written by an erratic and extravagant hand:

From Master John Fenton

Glynymel, 20th day of August in the year of our Lord 1806

My dear Mistress Martha,

I do not recall that we have met, but I presume to address you in familiar terms since I feel that I know you perfectly well, having heard nothing but praise from all sides concerning your beauty and your intelligence. You may know that I am the oldest son of Squire Richard Fenton, and that in due course, God willing, I shall have the privilege of taking over both the substantial estate of my father, and the family fortune. I have recently returned from London, where I have been involved in certain business transactions and various matters of state. As you may know, I am privileged to be a friend and confidant of His Royal Highness the Prince of Wales, and to move in the most elegant and refined of circles to which the majority of local gentlemen can only aspire. Indeed, I count myself fortunate that my company is in such demand in the coffee houses and debating rooms of our fine capital city that I am able to spend relatively little time in West Wales.

I have been fully informed as to the sad circumstances surrounding the death of your esteemed husband, and pass on to you the sincerest of condolences. I can only sympathize with the considerable difficulties in which you now find yourself, with a young family to bring up and a great weight of responsibility upon your shoulders for the welfare of your estate, tenants and labourers.

You must, I declare, be greatly disadvantaged in your attempts to cope with such matters by the lack of a good man at your side who may give you guidance, physical comfort, and access to the delights of intelligent conversation and the gay social life of London. You may take it from me that this season's fashions are truly delightful, and indeed I have brought back with me from Madame Sylvia's excellent establishment in Bond Street the most beautiful of silk gowns which, I am assured, is exactly your size and just right for your colouring. I am also in possession of a most *exotic ruby necklace, the like of which has never before been seen west of Cardiff. May I make so bold as to pay you a visit on the morrow, and to make you a present of these items as tokens of my esteem?*

It is my sincere desire to meet you and, if the Good Lord should be willing, to lift you from the simple rural pleasures of this place to a life more genteel and – if I may suggest it – more fulfilling. Your beloved children deserve no less.

Be assured, my dear Martha, that I see it as my sole task in life to make you happy. If you truly seek happiness, I am the man who will provide it.

I await your reply with eager anticipation.

Your humble servant, Fenton

Postscript: You will be aware that the Beating of the Bounds of the Barony of Cemaes will take place at the end of next week. Is it your intention to ride out for the occasion? If so, it would be my pleasure to accompany you.

When I read this epistle, I could hardly credit it. I knew not whether to laugh or cry, whether to tear it up or mount it in a grotesque frame on the wall above my desk. In the event I read it again, and then collapsed in hysterical laughter. I was in my dressing room at the time, and Bessie came rushing in. Poor thing, she was greatly alarmed. She is now very good at reading, having taken lessons for some years, so I gave her the letter. Then she had a fit of hysterics too, and we had to hang on to each other in order to avoid falling over, and it was some little time before we could converse like civilized human beings.

'Oh, my goodness!' said she at last. 'That is quite the most wonderful letter I have ever read. You must be very honoured, Mistress.'

'I feel so privileged that I can hardly contain myself,' I said. 'Do you think it is a proposal of marriage?'

'Not a shadow of doubt about it. A confident fellow indeed, considering that he has never met you.'

'So what shall I do now?'

'I should have thought, Mistress, that a little note, short and to the point, will be appropriate.'

So I sat down for a few minutes and penned the following reply:

Plas Ingli, 21 August 1806

Sir,

I am in receipt of your letter dated 20 August, addressed to me in somewhat familiar terms.

I can assure you that I am perfectly happy and perfectly fulfilled, and that all is well at Plas Ingli. I am not sure that I need, or even aspire to, the sort of company that you appear to enjoy; and my wardrobe is already full of dresses which I have neither the time nor the inclination to wear. I am reliably informed that rubies do very little for me, and I am determined in future only to wear diamonds.

In the circumstances there would be very little point in meeting. I confirm that I will ride out for at least one of the days of Beating the Bounds, in the company of Master Isaac Morgan.

I thank you for your offer of physical comfort. I was sorry to hear, some time ago, of your affliction with an unfortunate ailment contracted as a result of giving physical comfort to others. I trust that you are now perfectly well again.

Yours etc., Martha Morgan, Mistress

I showed my letter to Bessie, and she read it and then had hysterics again. That started me off again too, and some minutes passed before I was in a fit state to put the letter into an envelope and address it to my dearly beloved Master Fenton. Bessie and I then staggered downstairs, past the parlour with its little patient and ever-attentive nurses, and thence to the kitchen. We both had red eyes and carried soggy kerchiefs. Grandma and Mrs Owen gave us some very disapproving looks, and indeed everybody within half a mile will have heard our uncontrollable laughter, including John Fenton's man.

Now he has gone off on his grey pony, and I suspect I have another enemy.

22 August 1806

Young Brendan is making good progress, and is eating well. He is still in the parlour with one or other of his parents at his side, but Joseph says that tomorrow he can get up and move about, and that in a couple of days he will be ready to go off with his family to their next harvesting location near Puncheston. The good wizard has called in faithfully twice a day since the accident, assessing the healing process, changing dressings and administering strange herbal remedies from the assortment of little glass bottles that he always carries around in his bag.

I have been talking at great length to the O'Connells – mother, father and two other little brothers besides Brendan. Poor things. The children are all under seven, and four other offspring have died. They are paupers in Ireland, never able to settle down, and driven from pillar to post by powerful squires who appear to control the whole country. They and various relatives were involved in the Irish Rebellion in 1798, in which they fought for the most basic of human rights – food in their bellies, a roof over their heads, employment, and warmth in the winter. When the rebellion was crushed, their hovel (about ten feet square) was burnt down by the authorities. Since then they have stayed with various relatives, but no parish vestry will admit to their being residents, so they have never been able to claim poor relief. They are too proud to beg and too poor to build a new cottage, even if they could find the land to build it on. They are very religious people, and they will not descend to crime. So they travel about, helping with the potato harvest in southern Ireland, making hay and reaping corn in Wales, picking apples in Hereford and hops in Kent. Except at the peak of the harvest, Michael is lucky to earn sixpence a day, Molly three-pence, and the three children a ha'penny each. Less than one shilling a day in total. Their life seems to consist of an endless cycle of earning a few shillings, spending them on food and clothes, and then earning a few more. They are quite overwhelmed by gratitude for what Joseph has done for them, and for the kindness which they have been shown by the rest of us; but in truth we could not have done less. Joseph has told them that there will be no bill for his services, and he gave them great pleasure when he said that their medical expenses would be paid – without their knowing anything about it – by the rich squires of Pembrokeshire who consult him on a regular basis.

I have been appalled at what I have heard of the brutality and corruption of the English rulers in Ireland, and am not at all surprised that insurrection appears permanently to be close to the surface on that sad and beautiful island.

24 August 1806

The O'Connells have gone to Puncheston, with tears in their eyes, and with such effusive gratitude that we all felt greatly embarrassed. As we waved them off down the lane, we were sorry to see them go, for they are kind and gentle people, always able to smile in spite of the adversity which life has heaped upon them. Daniel went off to Puncheston some days since, but walked back this morning, very early, so that he could carry little Brendan on his shoulders. Michael carried the bulk of their meagre possessions. Tomorrow they will all be working in the oats fields of Squire Bayles, who is a good fellow. It is too early to say whether Brendan will make a full recovery, but Joseph says he can move his foot about and wiggle his toes, so the signs are good. I wish we could have done more for them, but I paid them all at the agreed rate in spite of the fact that they did hardly any work, and I do believe that they are all a little plumper than when they arrived, as a result of Mrs Owen's cooking. We gave them some of our old clothes, and they all went off carrying substantial food parcels which Grandma Jane had made up for them with the help of Betsi, Daisy, Dewi and Sara.

Our own harvest is now almost finished, in spite of the disruptions of the last few days. We have fifteen people in Parc Mrs Owen today, and another twelve raking, pitching and carting in Parc y Blodau. The weather is beginning to turn, and there are some big black clouds over Mynydd Preseli, but Shemi says that we are safe until tomorrow, when we will celebrate harvest home.

Today, as we waved off the Irish from the kitchen door, Joseph stood with us, with a benign and beatific smile upon his face. When they had gone, I asked him whether we might sit in the garden for a few minutes since I had a number of matters which I wished to discuss. 'Of course, my dear Martha,' said he. 'I can always make a little time for the Mistress of Plas Ingli.' We sat on the new bench which Will has recently made for me using timber from a fallen oak tree. We exchanged news of

Rice, Beynon and Lloyd, and shared our pleasure that they appear too worried about curses, real or imagined, to do much mischief just now. Then I decided to share with Joseph the news that the conspirators were all driven by the desire to find a Plas Ingli treasure, real or imagined. I knew that Joseph was bound to pick up on this sooner or later, for his spy network is by no means inferior to mine. Much to my surprise, the lust for gold was news to him, so I had to pass on the intelligence received about a year ago from the likes of Gethin Griffiths and Patty Ellis.

'I have come to the conclusion,' said I, 'that Moses Lloyd, before he disappeared some years back, fed a story about gold and silver hidden in the ground to the old Squires Rice, Watkins and Howell, in the hope that they would help in his campaign to destroy the estate. We all know that he cursed us, and swore vengeance against us, and I believe he was driven by such hatred that he would have spread a multitude of lies and rumours about us, had he had the chance.'

'That is a reasonable supposition, Martha,' replied Joseph. 'He was no fool, that fellow Moses. He knew that jealousy and covetousness are the most insidious and powerful of vices, and that when sown and nurtured in the minds of others they can do untold harm.'

'In thinking over an explanation for this, I also suppose that the relative prosperity of our estate, by comparison to theirs, would have encouraged the fantasy that we were digging up a few gold coins, now and again, to keep us going.'

'Again, entirely reasonable. So how many people will be driven by this particular fantasy?'

'According to my information, there could be as many as five or six. Alban Watkins, for sure. I am certain that this is what has drawn him back to Newport. Then I think John Howell and Joseph Rice, both told the story of the Plas Ingli treasure by their fathers and both driven by the conviction that they have some right to it now that the old men are dead.'

Joseph nodded. 'And the walking wounded, Ifan Beynon and Matthew Lloyd? They must surely be a part of the conspiracy, having both been involved in the killing of dear David?'

'I think so. In the days when they used to drink and gamble and scheme with Rice and Howell, they may well have been kept on a leash by a promise of shares in the treasure. In any case, Beynon's personal lust for gold probably goes back a long way, to the time when he did all the dirty work required of him by the old squires. They had no spare money to pay him for his efforts, and I think he was kept going like an old donkey, with a carrot on a stick dangling a few inches in front of his nose.'

Joseph laughed at the image. 'All right. I cannot fault your logic on any of this. And we might have a further motive for David's murder, in addition to the matters which we discussed some time back.'

'And then Fenton, whose name keeps on cropping up in reports from town. I cannot really work out where he comes into the picture. Can you?'

'I too have a problem with Fenton,' said Joseph. 'He is a dangerous character, urbane and sophisticated, with polished manners and a multitude of contacts in high places, going all the way up to the Prince of Wales. He has – shall we say – a certain way with the ladies. He also has gambling debts, and at some stage those debts will be called in. Maybe he is owed money from the card tables by Rice and Howell, and maybe he too has been promised a pay day when the magical treasure is dug up?'

I thought this an entirely reasonable supposition, and told Joseph that it would probably do until some improved intelligence came our way. I told him about the extraordinary letter I recently received from Fenton, and he raised his eyebrows. I told him of my rejection of the fellow's impudent and arrogant approach, and he chortled with delight. 'Mistress Morgan, you are quite incorrigible!' said he. 'Not many ladies in this world have the courage to give Master Fenton such short shrift. You realize that you have now made an enemy of him?'

'I think I was that already.'

'Quite, quite. No matter. We can deal with him, as we can deal with the others. We have more friends than they do. Now, my dear Martha, we have to decide two things. First, with whom do we share this information about the lusting conspirators and the supposed Plas Ingli pot of gold? And second, what do we do about it?'

We both thought for a while, and then I said: 'Grandpa Isaac, my dear friend and adviser, must certainly be told. I will find an opportunity to do that later today. But for the moment, nobody else, since things would get out of control and there would soon be rumours flying all over the town. The sales of shovels and picks would go soaring upwards, so that there would be none to be had in the whole of north Pembrokeshire.'

Joseph laughed at this interesting speculation, and so did I, and then we got onto the second matter. I told him that I had the germ of an idea in my head, and that I should shortly wish to seek his advice about it. 'By all means, my dear friend,' he said. 'When you are ready. But I suspect that when you are ready, your plan will be so well considered that it will need little modification from me or anybody else.'

Then we turned to another thing which has been causing me much concern lately.

'Joseph,' I said, 'I am greatly worried about my ability to see things that others do not see. We have spoken of this before, but I am confused, and think I might be better off without this particular talent.'

'Excuse me, Martha,' said Joseph, 'but premonitions have the power to bless as well as curse. Were you not greatly blessed the other day, as were the rest of us, when you perceived that little Daisy was to be found in a particular place upon the mountain? And was not the O'Connell family equally blessed when I knew that somebody at Plas Ingli was harmed and needed help, a good thirty minutes before I met Shemi riding wildly across the common with your message? That little boy would surely have died if I had been delayed even by ten minutes. Such things have happened to me over and again during my life, and they will surely happen to you.'

'Yes, Joseph, I accept what you say. But this power frightens me.'

'That is as it should be, my dear Martha. Those who have power of any sort, and are not frightened by it, deserve nothing but contempt. We all know that power corrupts, but you and I have been given certain abilities and we must always be aware of the weighty responsibilities that go with them.'

'But I knew that David would die, and did nothing to stop it.'

'No, you did not know that. You knew that something terrible would happen to somebody dear to you, but you did not know it would be David. You could not have stopped it anyway. Fate is cruel, but also relentless, and cannot be diverted. She lurks invisibly behind every rotten tree, beneath every brittle layer of winter ice; she blows on every wayward spark that spits out of a fireplace, and drives every innocent wave that travels across the ocean. The fact that you and I catch glimpses of her now and then, and act to help those who might suffer from her predations, should be a source of at least a little satisfaction or pleasure.'

I saw that Joseph was right, and could not help smiling. 'Thank you, Joseph. I see that you have reached an accommodation with your strange powers, which are to be honest infinitely greater than mine. I have much to learn. But I will try; and in truth I have other rather more pressing matters of the heart and mind which will require my attention in the near future.'

'Oh, indeed? Would you like to elaborate?'

Just then I heard Betsi and Daisy laughing and shouting in the yard, and a moment later their pretty faces popped up over the garden wall. 'Mam, have you not finished talking to Master Harries yet?' asked Betsi.

'You said you would not be long,' complained Daisy. 'You promised us ages and ages ago that we could go and pick blackberries. We want blackberry tart for supper!'

'Yes, you are quite right, girls,' said I. 'Master Harries and I have had much to talk about. But a promise is a promise, and we had better get picking.'

I rose to my feet, as did Joseph, and I said to him: 'I shall elaborate next time we meet, by which time there may well be more to report.'

'I shall look forward to that,' said Joseph. He bowed, and took my hand and kissed it, and then did exactly the same to the girls, whom he called 'Mistress Betsi and Mistress Daisy', before taking his leave. They were of course thoroughly delighted, and remained in the best of humour during our blackberry-picking expedition.

Gentle Breezes

27 August 1806

Certain information has reached my ears concerning the unsavoury activities of my enemies. I have to admit to feeling some pleasure at their expense as I record the details on the pages of my little book.

At dinnertime yesterday Will asked if he might have a few words in private, and when the milking was finished he took me aside for a chat. He reported that Beynon and Lloyd have been blackmailing Joseph Rice for the past few months, and that he had just discovered that substantial sums of money were involved. 'Two sovereigns every month he has to find, Mistress Martha,' said Will, his eyes wide at the thought of it. 'That is a great deal of money, indeed, and the silence being bought must concern something enormous.'

'Do you have any idea what it is all about?'

'Not yet, Mistress, but my friend Benny is very interested. He will find out, just you wait and see.'

'And how does Master Rice pay the money over? Not in the open, and in the bright light of day, surely?'

'No,' replied Will, with a happy smile on his face. 'They sends messages, or rather Matthew Lloyd does.

310

And Master Rice has to drop the money somewhere so that Beynon can pick it up. Beynon keeps one sovereign himself, and passes the other over to Lloyd on the first day of every month. The lad who delivers Lloyd's messages for him just happened to get a peek at the contents of the last envelope, which said: *Grave of Daisy Wilkins, eleven of the clock, Friday evening*. He showed it to my friend Skiff, who can read, and who reckoned that would be the pick-up time. So he kept a watch on the churchyard, as one does, and sure enough, at ten of the clock who should come along but Master Rice, very furtive, and put something under a stone on Mistress Wilkins's grave. When a few minutes had passed, Skiff thought there would be no harm in having a look, and – would you believe it?– there happened to be two golden sovereigns there. He thought they were probably the proceeds of some wicked crime against the poor, and that it was his bounden duty to remove them. So now he is one sovereign better off, and so is Matthew Lloyd's messenger boy.'

'But Rice will swear that he left the money, and Lloyd will swear that he never got it, and the lad is bound to be suspected of stealing it.'

'Yes indeed, Mistress,' said Will. 'But he will swear that he did not tamper with the envelope, and that in any case he can't read. Lloyd will beat him, but he reckons that for one sovereign it's probably worth it.'

'And Lloyd will also surmise that Beynon is the one who may be doing the cheating?'

'Quite correct you are, Mistress. Me and my friends expect some interesting developments. We will keep you informed.' And Will gave me a big wink, and his face lit up with a broad grin, and he went back to mucking out the cowshed.

In the early afternoon the sea mist came rolling in from

311

Newport Bay, transforming the bright clarity of a late summer day into a murky pallor. So thick was it that we could not see across the farmyard from the kitchen door to the barn, and the mist wiped away the warmth of the sun to the extent that we all had to put on extra clothes. The children were very excited, as they always are on misty days when the air is still, and they went out into the orchard with Sian and Grandma Jane in order to play hide and seek.

I stayed in my room, pretending to work on the estate accounts but in reality pondering on the background to the blackmailing affair. What, I wondered, could it be that Rice was so desperate to hide? Not David's murder, for sure, because if that was made public, Rice would take Lloyd and Beynon down with him. And where was Rice getting the money from to pay off his blackmailers? Twenty-four sovereigns a year was enough to pay the rent of all the labourers' cottages in Cilgwyn, or to buy a prime Castlemartin black bull from Master Mirehouse of Angle every spring. Suddenly I thought of my friend Patty Ellis, and my heart missed a beat when I wondered whether she might have some role to play in the raising of the funds which Rice needed. He, after all, was blackmailing her, and he was in my estimation quite capable of squeezing her harder and increasing her suffering.

My mind was set at rest when I received a little note from Patty. It was delivered by Hettie, appearing like a ghost out of the mist on one of her periodic visits to fetch eggs and butter. This is what it said:

Parrog, 26th day of August 1806

My dear Mistress Martha,

I trust that you and your family are well, as I am. The greasy slug Rice, for whom I have to work so that he may pay his bills, or some of them, is still a worried man. He has not beaten me for some months, and that is something to be grateful for. I am glad to say I am beginning to make better use of the situation in which he and I find ourselves. A couple of months back, he tried to increase his share of my takings to 75 per cent, but I screamed and threw things at him, and got a knife and threatened to cut my own throat, and in the end he backed off and let things stay as they are.

He may be no higher in the scheme of things than a dung beetle, but he is not stupid, and he realizes that Patty Ellis dead or damaged is a great deal less valuable to him than Patty Ellis defiled. God only knows what he would do without the few shillings that I pass over to him each week.

But he is in trouble, Mistress Martha, as sure as spuds is spuds. There is a limit as to what I can do to raise the money he needs, but he is hunting for cash in a big way just now. I know not how much, or what for, but at the end of July he was in a frightful state, and at the moment his brow is dripping sweat and his countenance is black as thunder.

He has been dabbling in contraband, and has met up with Billy Truscott from Fishguard. This is not Truscott's patch, and he knows it, and nothing but trouble will come of it. Will you tell Gethin Dolrannog and your young man Will Owen? I dare say they will be interested.

Your loving friend, Patty

I thought that no reply was needed to this letter, so when Hettie left with her loaded basket I asked her simply to thank Patty for her message, next time she sees her, and to say that I will do as requested.

I then wandered down to the farmyard and found Will and Shemi repairing a *gambo* which had been damaged during the wheat carting. I knew that they were both still involved in the handling of duty-free goods, since they both disappear now and then around midnight, return in the early hours, and go round in a daze all the next day; so I thought there would be no harm in passing on

313

the news to both of them that Rice had recently met up with Truscott.

'Mistress Martha!' said Shemi. 'Well I never. How the devil did you find that out?'

'I never betray my sources,' said I, feeling as smug as a spy operating behind Master Bonaparte's front line.

'Good God!' said Will. 'That explains everything! You knew, Mistress, that Billy Truscott has been trying to move onto our patch? Before, he has done all his landings west of Fishguard. Rice has been dealing with Gethin up until now, he has, but he has probably negotiated a bigger cut with Truscott if he gets us off this coast and lets the Truscott family in. Nasty buggers they are, too. Brothers and other relatives working all along the South Wales coasts.'

Then Shemi chipped in. 'We always wondered who gave the tip-off to the Revenue last Easter,' he said, 'and almost got Will strung up on the gallows tree. There have been a couple of other close shaves since then as well, and we knew somebody was informing. Dickens Revenue Man pays well for information. Now we know whose deep pocket his silver shillings were being dropped into.'

Will looked concerned. He turned to me and said: 'We are sorry, Mistress Martha, to be telling you all this. It is not seemly for a lady like you to know the sordid details of what goes on in the creeks and coves between here and Fishguard.'

'Don't worry, Will. I am very discreet. And you may recall that Master Joseph Rice has not, in the past, shown any great affection for the Plas Ingli estate or us who live here.'

'Mistress Martha, may I take a few minutes to pop over to see Master Gethin?' asked Will. 'I think that he, and Master Abbs and Master Llewellin, will be very interested in this intelligence. A cargo is due in within the week. Steps may have to be taken.'

'Off you go,' said I, 'and send my regards to those good gentlemen.'

I hope that Patty's information might avert a disaster, and I await with interest news of further developments.

31 August 1806

Today has been a day like no other, when I have discovered something new and wonderful about the mysteries of the heart. It has been the fourth day of the Beating of the Bounds of the Barony of Cemaes, when a great procession travels from Newport out to Eglwyswrw, up onto Mynydd Preseli and Crymych, in a long loop along the south side of the mountain, and then back to Foeleryr and across Cwm Gwaun to Dinas before returning to Newport. The distance round the edges of the territory carved out by those old Norman barons must be at least forty miles, and every seventh year the Lord Marcher and a mighty multitude of common people ride and march round it. Goodness knows why, since for the most part one cannot see a boundary at all, but Grandpa Isaac, who always makes the whole journey even when it is afflicted by foul weather, says that in the old days the intention was to ensure that there was no encroachment onto Barony land or any unauthorized enclosures on the commons.

For the last three days Grandpa has been out from dawn to dusk on his rowan mare in the company of the faithful and loyal multitude. He has little respect himself for the Lord Marcher, who is an old fellow who cannot even be bothered to live in Newport. But he enjoys the social aspect of the whole business, and says that since virtually all of the freemen, burgesses and commoners are in the procession on horseback, a fine opportunity presents itself for the picking up of essential inform- ation. Besides, the Lord Marcher provides free food and ale at midday and at the end of the day's march, and Grandpa says that he might as well enjoy something at the Lord Marcher's expense in exchange for his loyalty. Last night he came back after dark, somewhat the worse for wear, and reported sadly that Squire George Bowen, old friend and leading magistrate in the area, is in financial trouble, having purchased several estates in recent years with borrowed money. His debts have spiralled upwards, and his creditors are getting nervous; thank goodness that none of our money is at risk, since I have made it a rule never to become involved financially with friends. But I am worried on behalf of my dear Ellie, since the knowledge of her father's financial mis- judgements will substantially affect her chances of a good marriage.

This morning I asked Grandpa Isaac if I might join him on the final day's ride, which was due to follow the boundaries of the parish of Newport. I thought it appropriate that I should attend, since I am, for better or for worse, the Mistress of this estate, and a public appearance would make a statement to the effect that I take my responsibilities seriously. Besides, I wanted to see who else might be in the procession. Grandpa was delighted at my suggestion, and so were the others round the breakfast table. It was a dry and misty day, so I promised the children that they could walk over the mountain with Sian and Bessie in the middle of the after- noon with a view to meeting the procession at Bedd Morris. They were thrilled at the prospect, even when I told them that they would be gently whipped by Grandpa at the site of the big standing stone to ensure that they would remember for the rest of their lives where the boundary of the parish is located. 'Oh, will it hurt, Great-grandpa Isaac?' squealed Betsi.

'Terrible, terrible it will be,' replied Grandpa, with a gleam in his eye. 'I will whip you so hard that you will remember the position of the boundary for at least two minutes!'

At ten minutes before nine of the clock Grandpa and I were at the starting point of the day's procession, by the lime kilns on the Parrog. I wore my summer riding habit and my blue bonnet, and Grandpa told me that he was greatly privileged to be riding in the company of such a pretty young lady. What a multitude we discovered already assembled! There must have been more than a thousand people milling about, and great excitement was in the air. Most of the local squires and their sons were there, on horseback like the wealthier burgesses and freeholders; and some of the local merchants and shopkeepers were also mounted, to the disgust of Huws Bayvil who thinks that they are acting in a fashion far above their natural station in life. Grandpa is delighted by the rising status of the commercial gentlemen of the town, and says that if wealth were a measure of status the merchants would all be riding with the Lord Marcher and most of the squires should be walking with the rabble at the back of the procession.

There were many greetings and introductions, and I realized that I was the only woman on horseback. The Beating of the Bounds was clearly intended to be a male activity. I had to be very civil to assorted young gentlemen who jostled for my attention. Mostly they were the same dreary fellows who had already paid me social visits at the Plas, enquiring as to my health, and the health of the children, and asking when I might be in a position to return their visits. Grandpa protected me from these well-meaning people with considerable aplomb, and I managed, I hope, to be civil and non-committal in all of my replies. Then I noticed Master Owain Laugharne, at the far side of the throng, mounted on a beautiful chestnut hunter. He was surrounded by a gaggle of mothers and daughters, and I suddenly realized that he was one of the most desirable young bachelors in the north of the county. I caught his eye, and since he was clearly trapped at that moment by social imperatives he shrugged his shoulders and rolled his eyes. I could not help laughing, and he smiled in return.

I was pondering on the charming and unaffected nature of his smile when I was reminded of the business of the day by a great cheer as the Lord Marcher, Thomas Lloyd, accompanied by his wife Mary and his son Tom, arrived from town in an open coach, having spent the night in the Prince of Wales Inn. Their natural residence should be the Castle, but it is habitable only by rats and jackdaws at the moment since the Lloyd family has not shown the slightest inclination to renovate it, let alone live in it. Clearly the social life of Carmarthen is more to their liking, and I am not alone in feeling aggrieved that they demand our allegiance when it suits them but otherwise do virtually nothing for Newport or its people. The Lord Marcher beamed benevolently upon the assembled masses, and patted a few tousled heads. He spotted me, and took the trouble to have a few words with me, but I was not impressed; he struck me as a man professing to be interested in others but in truth interested only in himself, and practised in the art of speaking while remaining quite ignorant of the finer art of listening. Then he was called away by the new Mayor, Daniel Thomas, who wanted the procession to get under way.

There was a little speech from Master Thomas,

announcing the business of the day and welcoming the
Lord Marcher and his family. He said that he and the
burgesses and other freemen were duty bound to inspect
the boundaries of the parish and to complete the full per-
ambulation of the Bounds of Cemaes commenced some
days ago. He said that encroachments onto the common,
or unauthorized enclosures, or unauthorized buildings,
would be inspected and dealt with, and called for the
appointment of a jury of good men and true who could
be depended upon to be honest servants of the Barony in
the event of disputes during the course of the day.
Twenty jurors were 'elected', although in truth like all
the best (and worst) elections everything had been
arranged in advance. Much to my surprise, the name
'Master Isaac Morgan' was called out, and Grandpa was
prevailed upon to join the jury at the head of the
procession. He was clearly not surprised at all, but when
he agreed to join the jury I was placed in something of a
dilemma since I could not possibly ride unaccompanied.
Grandpa winked, and then rode over to Master
Laugharne. He had a few words in his ear, and Owain
immediately excused himself from his colleagues and
rode round the edge of the crowd towards me.

Grandpa then rode off to the place where the jury
members – all twenty of them – were assembling, and
swearing oaths, and being presented with their badges
of office by the Lord Marcher.

Before Owain arrived at my side I was greatly
surprised when another rider, who must have been
hovering somewhere in the vicinity and watching
intently, rode straight up to me. He was a youngish
fellow, maybe in his thirties, dressed in a remarkably fine
cotton shirt with embroidered cuffs, a bright red silk
waistcoat, and yellow breeches. He was quite a small
man, and considerably heavier than he should have

been. He had a black beaver-skin hat upon his head. I remember thinking that he would have looked more in place at the card tables of St James's than he did on a small pony in rural West Wales. I noticed that his hands were soft and white – the hands of a man who has not done an honest day's work in his life. His face was podgy and pink, and it was obvious that he had been out in the sun of late, having previously hidden away from it with some determination. He addressed me in English, in a voice straight out of London. 'Mistress Morgan of Plas Ingli?' he asked. Then, without waiting for a reply, he continued: 'Pray forgive me, for I have made enquiries and have ascertained your name. We have not met, but we have corresponded, and I believe that you know my father. John Fenton, Glynymel. Delighted to make your acquaintance. I have ridden out with the procession round the Bounds of the Barony these last three days in the hope of meeting you, to no avail. Bothersome business indeed, mile after mile in the heat, and the flies on Foel Drygarn something terrible. Thank God for a decent hat. You may recall that I offered to accompany you on a section of the journey, and that you replied – perfectly reasonably, if I may say so – that Master Isaac Morgan would keep you company. Now, however, I see that he has been whisked away on jury service and has left you quite unprotected in the midst of all these rough people. May I offer you my protection on this difficult and dangerous journey?'

I was so fascinated by his incessant babble and by the affected and arrogant tone of his voice that I was quite unprepared for his question. However, I rapidly regained my wits. 'Master Fenton, it is a pleasure to meet you' I lied, also in English, 'since I have heard a great deal about you. I appreciate your offer. I recall our exchange of letters. However, we have not been formally introduced, and you will appreciate that it is a matter of paramount importance for a woman in my position to behave with decorum at all times. Master Isaac Morgan has indeed gone off to be sworn in as a member of today's jury, but I am happy to say that in anticipation of this duty he has made other arrangements for me to be escorted during today's ride.'

This was all going rather too far, for I was sure that Grandpa Isaac had made no such advance arrangements, but he had talked to Owain Laugharne, and that good gentleman was on his way. It now flashed through my mind that I was in a considerable predicament. The little episode was very public indeed, since Master Fenton and I, both perched upon our horses, were surrounded by many other mounted members of the local gentry and by townspeople who would be following the procession on foot. Everything we said was overheard, and diplomacy was needed. If I rode with Fenton the news would be all round the town as fast as a flash of lightning: 'Oh, did you see that Mistress Morgan rode out round the Bounds with Fenton Glynymel? There's interesting for you!' The very thought of it was appalling. The alternative was that exactly the same piece of news would circulate, but with the name of Owain Laugharne substituted. I hardly had time to contemplate the negative and positive aspects of the matter, and to weigh them in the balance, before Owain rode up alongside.

He doffed his hat and gave a deep bow, in so far as such a thing was possible when mounted upon a horse. 'Mistress Martha!' he said, with a smile upon his lips. 'How good it is to see you!'

'Master Laugharne, it is also a pleasure to see you again. You know Master Fenton of Glynymel?' The two gentlemen nodded to each other, and it was immediately

321

clear to me that they knew each other but that mutual affection was not a feature of their relationship.

I looked Owain straight in the eye and continued: 'In view of the fact that Master Isaac has unexpectedly been summoned to duty today Master Fenton has kindly offered to accompany me on the procession. However, I have just explained to him that prior arrangements have been made to cover just such an eventuality, and that you were invited long since, as a friend of the family, to offer your support to me during the day.'

Owain appreciated my dilemma in an instant, and rode to my aid like a knight in silver armour. 'Quite so, Mistress Martha,' he said smoothly. 'I indicated my willingness to ride with you to Master Isaac Morgan several weeks back, and I look forward to a day in your company.'

Without a further word John Fenton scowled, doffed his hat, turned his horse, and trotted away. I turned to Owain and whispered, 'Oh dear, I fear that Master Fenton is not amused. He is a man who is used to getting his own way. But thank you, Owain, for rescuing me from a terrible fate – I do not think I could have survived a day in that man's company.'

'My pleasure, Martha,' said Owain quietly. 'Your sanity is more important than his amusement. Let us now look forward to a pleasant day in the fresh air.'

And a pleasant day it was, blessed by warm sunshine and a gentle breeze and by company which could not have been bettered. With the jury all sworn in, off we went, in a set order as prescribed by tradition. At the head of the procession went a man carrying a big banner, which Owain said was the flag of the Barony. Then came a little band of musicians on horseback, one of them banging on a drum, another three tootling on bugles, and others playing on tin whistles and flutes. There followed a foot party carrying assorted other banners, most of them home-made, and inscribed with Welsh proverbs and mottoes. Next came the mounted members of the jury, and the freeholders, burgesses and aldermen of the town, and the Lord Marcher and his wife and son in their carriage, accompanied by the Mayor and his party. The procession was completed by a multitude of towns-people and labourers.

The atmosphere was jovial indeed, with a thousand conversations going on all at once, occasional bursts of laughter and applause from here and there, and happy faces all round. I received many smiling acknowledge-ments from the squires, burgesses and common people, some of whom were clearly amazed at the presence of a mounted female in the midst of such a congregation. More than one labourer made a point of coming up to me and saying, in Welsh, such things as: 'Well done, Mistress Morgan! Good to see that you are showing the gentlemen how times are changing!' It had not occurred to me that my presence was anything radical, for in truth I do not consider myself a very political person, but I admit that their comments did give me some amuse-ment and satisfaction.

The procession went along the estuary to the Afon Nyfer ford, then turned right, passing the church and ruinous castle before climbing Greystones Hill and pass-ing along the Cilgwyn road. This was not the precise route followed by the boundary of the Barony and parish, for that runs along the Afon Clydach, a tumbling stream with a stony bed and occasional cataracts that passes through dense woodlands in a narrow valley. No procession could possibly have followed the stream itself, and it gave me some pleasure to remember that the woods were full of unauthorized hovels built by poor labourers and vagrants who would certainly have been evicted if the jury had been able to get at them. There were also various deep bogs in the valley, far too dangerous to support the weight of mounted travellers. Soon our route took us past Plain Dealings and Brithdir, and I admit to a feeling of pride hereabouts that the road and the lands on either side of it belonged to Plas Ingli – my own sweet and lovely estate. People waved and cheered as we went past, and here I recognized everybody, and gave and received warm personal greetings. Then down and over the ford at Trefelin, past Cilgwyn Mill and on into Cwm Gwaun with its towering sides and magical oak woodlands. This all took time, since the procession moved along at a very gentle walking pace, and by the time we reached the narrowing of the valley at Llannerch we were all feeling very hungry and thirsty.

The great throng crowded into the yard of the old house, where various servants were waiting with tables piled high with loaves and cheeses and barrels of ale. Since this was Owain's residence he made a little speech, very nervously, welcoming everybody and acknowledging the generosity of the Lord Marcher in providing refreshments on a substantial scale. Everybody cheered and clapped, and there followed a somewhat chaotic picnic during which the gentry ate and drank with due decorum while the poor walkers made the most of the opportunity to get something substantial into their bellies. I, for one, did not begrudge it to them, for I am always mindful of the shocking conditions in which most of them live.

After a break of about an hour the party set off again. The going was very rough from this point on, passing along narrow tracks and soggy moorland up towards Carn Edward, along the mountain ridge towards Bedd Morris, and then dropping northwards towards Trecadifor and the coastal toll road. This was not carriage country, so the Lord Marcher took his leave with a promise to meet us later on near Dinas. Some riders and walkers also dropped out and returned home from Llannerch, but the hardy ones among us pressed on. Riding side-saddle across such terrain was not easy, but I had a wonderful time and found the ride thoroughly invigorating.

Owain was the very model of attentiveness and courtesy, helping me to dismount and mount whenever we stopped or had gates or steep banks to negotiate, holding branches aside for me when we were riding through woods and thickets, and finding the safest of routes across boggy and stony ground. As the day went on he relaxed more and more, and although our conversations were very public, with others involved or overhearing everything, we found ourselves joking and laughing in a manner so free and spontaneous that I could hardly believe it. I came to realize that I had discovered a man who laughs at the same things and who views the world in the same way as I. I also came to realize, from the light in his eyes, that he holds me in the highest regard, and by the end of the day there was such a fluttering of wings in my heart that I feared they would be heard by those around me.

At one stage in the afternoon Owain rode a little distance away from me in order to discuss some business with the Mayor, and as I watched him the image of his naked body stretched out on a rock at Pandy Pools came into my mind and would not go away. I saw before me not a black hat but a head of golden curls streaming with water; not a blue waistcoat but a slim and strong torso browned by the summer sun; not a pair of finely cut breeches but thighs and buttocks . . . 'Martha, you are a thousand miles away!' said a sudden voice in my ear, and I realized that Owain, the object of my impure thoughts, was back again at my side. 'Are you all right? Not suffering from fatigue, I hope?'

'Not at all,' I replied, trying desperately to sound calm and relaxed. 'I am perfectly all right, I assure you. I was just dreaming and enjoying the small pleasures of the day.'

And so we went on, with Owain proving to be a thoroughly entertaining companion while throwing me little puzzled glances now and then as he tried to work out the cause of my distraction. Distraction indeed, for while I should have been concentrating upon the communion of the spoken word, my mind was pre-occupied with his body and with communion of a different kind. Thank God that my imaginings were disrupted by our arrival at Bedd Morris, the great standing stone on the mountain road, where an excited crowd of parents and children was waiting for us. 'Mam! Mam! Here we are!' shouted Betsi, Dewi, Daisy and Sara, and in a trice they were crowding round my horse and begging me to dismount. Owain helped me down, and we all hugged as if I had just returned from some fearful expedition across the sands of the Sahara. Bessie and Sian were there too, full of smiles, and it transpired that they had all had a splendid picnic and had picked almost a bucketful of bilberries on the moor. Then Betsi and Daisy skipped off to greet all those whom they recognized. 'Hello, Great-grandpa Isaac! Hello, Master Owain!' they yelled, and it gave me great pleasure to observe the manner in which the little ones singled out Owain as the man best fitted to receive their news about bilberries and picnics and buzzards and curlews and so forth. To his eternal credit, he abandoned me for a while and listened with rapt attention to their babblings.

Then the Mayor made a little speech, and announced that all children present would be whipped so that they would never forget the position of the boundary of the Barony. There were lots of screams and giggles from the forty or so children who were in our company, and various parents and grandparents set to work on their gruesome task. Grandpa Isaac took out his horse whip and 'whipped' our four little ones with great theatricality, groaning under the weight of his exertions and shouting 'There now! Twenty lashes for you! Take that!' while he inflicted upon them no pain whatsoever. Great excitement all round.

Then it was time to go. The children, with Sian and Bessie, set off back along the mountain track towards the Plas, and the procession, led now by the Mayor, continued westwards to Mynydd Melyn and then down towards the coast road. With the sun settling towards the tip of Dinas Head, our route took us quite close to Werndew, the little cottage of my dear friend Joseph. How many times over the years, I wondered, have I passed this way, with joy or (more often) desolation in my heart? There he was, sitting on a big rock beside the procession route, and Owain and I exchanged a few cheerful words with him as we went by.

At the toll road we met up again with the Lord Marcher and his family in their carriage, and the whole procession turned towards Newport for the last triumphant lap of the journey, with the band playing their hearts out and the banners waving and chattering in the breeze. Just as dusk was falling we arrived back at the Parrog, to find another feast of cakes and ale awaiting us. The foreman of the jury announced to the Mayor that the Boundaries of the Barony and the Parish of Newport had been duly inspected, and that on this day, at least, no unauthorized activities had been discovered. Then the Mayor went over to old Thomas Lloyd and repeated the message. And that was that. A cheer went up from the weary riders and walkers of the procession, and from a host of onlookers, and the cakes and ale were consumed with great enthusiasm.

I took my leave of Owain and thanked him for his company and his kind attentiveness and courtesy, and I was sad that parting was a necessity. I rode home in the company of Grandpa Isaac as the last gleams of daylight were fading in the west. We have had our supper, the children are tucked up and asleep, and the house is quiet. As I look back on the day, I have to say that the story of my life has moved into a new chapter. It is now common knowledge within the communities of gentry and townspeople that Master Owain Laugharne and I have spent the day in each other's company. Many will have noted that we clearly enjoyed the experience. John Fenton, whom I observed with a darkening scowl upon his face as the day progressed, will be fully aware of what is going on, and will be confirmed as an enemy of both Owain and myself. And Grandpa, Bessie, Sian and the children will have seen, at close quarters, the flush upon my cheek and the sparkle in my eye when I am in Owain's company.

The genie is out of the bottle, and cannot be put back. I write these words with a little apprehension but more than a little pleasure. Tonight I will sleep well, and I trust that I will have sweet dreams.

1 September 1806

Justice moves swiftly and sometimes unexpectedly in these parts, without the involvement of the magistrates and beyond the reach of the long-armed criminal law. First thing this morning Billy, Shemi and Will asked if they might pop down into town in order to look at some new ploughs which Shoni Blacksmith has been manufacturing specially for heavy clay soils. I knew they must have another reason, but I said, 'Off you go then, but be sure to be back by midday, since I want the cattle and the horses moved onto fresh grazing before milking time.' They were quite happy to agree, and off they went, having borrowed some old sheets from Mrs Owen.

They returned at dinnertime, and sat at the kitchen table with the rest of us, grinning like sheepdog puppies. They tucked into their bread and butter and fresh mackerel, thoroughly enjoying my discomfort. They knew that I was longing to know what had been going on in town, but they would talk only of ploughs, and insisted on seeking my advice about the depth and width of furrow we should work towards, given that some of our soils are loamy and others heavy with clay. 'Something went on down in Long Street this morning,' was all they would say, 'but we were too busy with Shoni Blacksmith to pay much attention. Ask Master Isaac, since he was also in town this morning.'

As indeed he was. When he came back in midafternoon, very mellow after enjoying a few jars in the Royal Oak with his confederates, I asked him about the news.

'What news?' said he, all innocence, confirming my view that men are indeed the most irritating of creatures, with no appreciation of the need which is built into every woman on earth to know what is going on.

'Grandpa!' said I, with as much fierceness as I could muster. 'You know something happened in town this morning, and you probably know all the details. You might at least share this news with the rest of us.'

'Martha, my dear, my memory is not what it used to be, and in any case I have had too much to drink. It's a good job the chestnut pony knows the way home better than I do. I shall now have a little snooze, and perhaps by supper time my memory will have returned.' And off he went to his bed, leaving me feeling very angry indeed. The rest of my afternoon was quite spoiled, and I had to go for a walk on the mountain beneath a blazing sun in order to cool myself down.

At supper time, the first spoon had hardly touched the first bowl of *cawl* before I reminded Grandpa about my need to know the news from town. 'Ah yes!' said he. 'Now I remember. Down on Long Street. A great commotion. A visit from the *Ceffyl Pren* to Master Matthew Lloyd. And then, so I gather, the mighty beast paid a little visit to Master Joseph Rice down on the Parrog. And that was that, and I went back to my interesting conversation with Master Edwards Trefach and Master Prosser Frongoch.'

Still the other men refused to add details, and I now realize that great secrecy surrounds the *Ceffyl Pren* and the 'jury' that works with it. Nobody will ever admit to involvement with this primitive method of exacting retribution on those in the community who are held to be guilty of crimes against individuals or against society as a whole.

Grandpa continued to be in a silly mood throughout the meal, stringing us females along like so many puppies chasing after a bone. I had not realized that he could be so irritating, but the children greatly enjoyed the entertainment.

The story I was able to piece together goes something like this. Matthew Lloyd turned up, as he always does on a Friday morning, to enjoy a jar or two in the Black Lion with his crony Ifan Beynon. Apparently he was in a filthy mood, and I surmise that this is because of the disappearance of his latest payment from Joseph Rice into the grubby hands of two Newport lads. He and Beynon had a furious row and almost came to blows. Then Lloyd stormed outside, and was immediately confronted by the *Ceffyl Pren*, a massive and terrifying figure with a horse skull for a head, red marbles for eyes and tufts of straw for ears. No doubt it was closely related to the *Mari Lwyd* which paid us a friendly visit last Christmas. It was decorated with red ribbons and strips of cloth. Its body was covered in a white sheet, beneath which at least two men were prancing about. In attendance there were at least twenty other men, all dressed in white sheets with their faces blackened. Some of them wore women's bonnets; others wore old hats, with straw sticking out beneath them. They were the jury. I suspect that Billy, Shemi and Will were among them, for the white sheets returned to Mrs Owen at dinnertime were covered with great smudges of charcoal and tomato stains.

Lloyd was grabbed and tied to a chair, which was then raised aloft, placed on two long poles, and paraded through the streets of Newport. A great crowd of cheering and jeering townspeople followed close behind. This was strictly an illegal gathering, and should have been stopped by the constables or the magistrates, but none of them were to be seen; and indeed Grandpa, as a magistrate himself, appears to have done his best to avoid any contact at all with the crowds on the streets beneath his nose.

I was surprised to learn that Lloyd's crime was the seduction of a young girl, one Rosie Bebb, and the fathering of her bastard child. As a result the girl has been cast out of Ebenezer Chapel, publicly humiliated, and forced into pauperism, depending on the poor rate for even the simplest necessities of life. She has been abandoned by her Methodist parents, and lives on Long Street, in a hovel in the back garden of a kindly old gentleman called Billy Tomos. The child is now almost two years old, and her colouring, eyes and hair are so obviously those of Matthew Lloyd that his responsibility can no longer be denied. Lloyd, who has always refused to admit paternity and has even denounced the girl as a common whore, has fathered other bastard children in the town, and it seems that the town has finally decided not to tolerate his sowing of wild oats for a moment longer. The noisy procession made its way along East Street and down Long Street to stop outside Billy Tomos's front door. The *Ceffyl Pren* then presided over a mock trial at which Lloyd was asked by the foreman of the jury to admit that he was the father of Rosie's child. He refused, and was then buffeted about in his chair and anointed with rotten fruit before being asked again. He again refused, and the same thing happened, but for twice as long. Finally, the foreman asked again, and said that if he refused to admit paternity this time he would be taken to the ducking stool on the estuary and ducked twenty times 'regardless of whether he be alive or dead'.

At last, with the crowd baying for his blood, he broke down and admitted that the child was his. 'And what shall be the sentence?' asked the foreman.

'Five shillings per week to be paid to Rosie Bebb until the child shall be twelve years old,' came a booming voice from inside the horse skull, and there followed a roar of approval from the crowd.

'Master Lloyd, do you agree before all these witnesses?' Lloyd, his face covered with rotten tomatoes, potato peelings and bits of cabbage, protested that this was far too heavy a price to pay for an innocent mistake on his part, but he was again banged about in his chair and pelted with rubbish, and in the end had to agree to the penalty inflicted by the *Ceffyl Pren*. Somebody who could write then composed a notice that was attached to

Lloyd's chair. It read: *Lloyd Cwmgloyn, cost of wild oats 5/-per week*. He was then hoisted aloft again and paraded round the town so that everybody could see both him and the notice; and just to make sure that nobody went in ignorance of the sentence the crowd chanted and sang the words, with a drummer appearing from nowhere to give added emphasis.

Back outside the Black Lion, Lloyd was released, with a warning that if he should default on his payments to Rosie for even a single week, he would be revisited by the *Ceffyl Pren* and taken immediately down to the ducking stool, winter or summer, high water or low. Defeated and stinking of rotten vegetable remains, he was forced to fetch his horse from the back of the inn and was jeered out of town.

'Now then, my friends,' said the foreman of the jury. 'That was just the start. We have further business to transact. We will reconvene this court in thirty minutes down on the Parrog!' And the grotesque horse monster, its strangely attired attendants, and the local rabble, all headed down to the estuary and along the shore towards the little fishing port, cheering and chanting, skipping and dancing as if they were some primitive tribe in the jungles of Africa.

The time was now eleven of the clock, and the *Ceffyl Pren* knew that this was exactly the time at which Joseph Rice ate breakfast in his lodging house. Two of the jury knocked on the front door, and when it was opened by the good lady of the house, they politely invited themselves in and 'arrested' Rice as he sat at the breakfast table. He was dragged outside, to a wild cheer from the crowd, tied up and subjected to exactly the same treatment as Matthew Lloyd. This time the charge from the foreman of the jury was that 'Joseph Rice, late of Pentre Ifan, has passed on certain information to the men of the

Revenue Service which has been greatly prejudicial to the interests of the community and has brought harm to certain good people of this town.' He was asked whether he was guilty or not guilty as charged, and in response he furiously denied passing on any information relating to local duty-free transactions. He was pelted with rotten fruit and banged up and down in his chair, and then asked whether he had recently spoken with Dickens or Truscott. Everybody in the crowd knew that the one was the Milford Haven Revenue officer responsible for putting Will Owen into the lock-up, and that the other was the Fishguard smuggler who controlled the coast west of Fishguard. 'No, no, I deny everything!' whined Rice until the rotten fruit, and the banging up and down, and the promise of the ducking stool treatment, caused him to admit everything instead.

'Sentence him, sentence him!' shouted the crowd.

'Very well,' said the sepulchral voice from inside the horse skull. 'If Dickens or his men shall ever take a man from this coast and get him into jail, you shall go straight to the ducking stool for twenty duckings, alive or dead. And if Truscott or his men shall ever appear on this coast you shall have forty duckings, alive or dead. Do we all agree?'

'Agreed! Agreed!' shouted the crowd. And then the notice writer wrote out the words *Rice, Truscott and Dickens – send them all to Hell* on a big piece of paper, and pinned it to Rice's filthy shirt. He was then hoisted up, still tied to his chair, and paraded up the Parrog road into town, with the drum beating and the crowd chanting the words of the notice. He was dumped on the main crossroads in the centre of town and left to stagger home. And in just a few minutes the *Ceffyl Pren* and his attendants had disappeared, and the crowd had melted away.

And that was that. As we all sat round the supper table, mouths agape, Grandpa finished his remarkably detailed tale by saying: 'Of course, these sketchy details have been provided for me by various disreputable eye witnesses, and I have no idea whether they are true or not. I am really in ignorance of the whole affair, and I dare say that this whole episode has been greatly exaggerated. It is most likely that if Master Lloyd and Master Rice enter complaints, the magistrates will dismiss them as the rantings of deranged fellows who have old scores to settle. In any case, they will not find a single witness to support any accusations they may make.' And Billy, Will and Shemi nodded, and smiled in such an innocent and childlike fashion that I had to accept Grandfather Isaac's judgement on the matter.

Now that I am recording this late at night, in the quietness of my dressing room, I have to admit to a quiet pride in the compassion and good sense of the strange little community in which I live. And I am struck by a strange symmetry: Lloyd has to pay one sovereign a month to Rosie Bebb for the upkeep of his bastard child, which is exactly the amount which he obtains from Rice every month for keeping quiet about something or other, having passed over an equivalent amount to Ifan Beynon. Indeed, the proceeds of crime move about in the strangest of ways, with some of them, thanks to the *Ceffyl Pren*, being used to right an ancient wrong.

10 September 1806

For the last few days, I have tried not to think too much about the misfortunes of my enemies. While all the other residents of the house have been busy collecting apples from the orchard, blackberries from the hedgerows, and

335

bilberries from the common, I have been preoccupied with thoughts of my new friend Owain Laugharne. Images of his boyish good looks, his lean body clothed and unclothed, and his honest and open smile have flooded into my mind's eye so frequently that I must certainly have appeared very distracted. And at various times my half-hearted attempts to concentrate on other things have been disrupted by the obvious interest of others in the developing relationship between Owain and myself.

Bessie was the first to register her approval, in her usual roundabout way. On the morning after the Beating of the Bounds, while delivering hot water to my dressing room for my morning ablutions, she said: 'I noticed, Mistress, that you were well looked after during that long ride around the parish.'

'Indeed I was, Bessie. The intention was that Grandpa Isaac was to look after me, but he was unfortunately called away for jury service and alternative arrangements had to be made at short notice.'

'Whatever Master Isaac's intentions may have been, Mistress, or indeed your own, I am sure that everything worked out for the best.'

I smiled, and so did Bessie. 'I can assure you, Bessie,' said I with mock indignation, 'that there was no connivance on my part in any of Grandpa's wicked schemes. I am all innocence.'

'If you say so, Mistress.'

'You may not know that I was offered assistance by two gentlemen. I trust that, in your judgement, I made the right choice?'

'No doubt about it, Mistress,' said Bessie. 'From the rosy glow which surrounded you like a halo at Bedd Morris, I imagine that you have no doubts on the matter either. Master Laugharne is as fine a gentleman as you are ever likely to meet in these parts. The servants at Llannerch say that he is like a breath of fresh air about the place, strict and decisive when he has to be, but also very fair and concerned about his people. He is also a poet and a musician, so they say.'

'I was aware of that. I admit that I like him a good deal. Would you and the other servants give your blessing if I should see more of him?'

No doubt dear Bessie answered in the affirmative, but I confess to not hearing a word she said, since another image came flooding into my mind, and it occurred to me that I had already seen more of Owain than many delicate wives ever see of their prudish husbands in a lifetime of marital encounters in darkened bedrooms beneath heavy blankets.

Later on Grandma Jane thought, for the first time ever, that it might be a good idea to bring a bowl of fresh apples, pears and cherries up to my room. I knew what was coming. She pottered about for a while, trying to find the best place for the fruit bowl, and then she said: 'Isaac tells me that you had a pleasant day riding out with Master Laugharne from Llannerch.'

'I did indeed, Grandma. He was attentive and very gentlemanly, and I have to say that I enjoyed his company.'

'And might it be your intention, my dear, to meet him again?'

'And why not? I dare to think, Grandma, that he enjoys my company too.'

'That is all too plain for everybody to see. A number of our friends and neighbours were delighted to see you together, and I have heard many comments about how happy you looked.' Then she came and placed her hands upon my shoulders, and looked me straight in the eye. 'You deserve happiness, and you deserve love, my dear

Martha, after the traumas of the past. I pray that you will find both. It is obvious that Owain is very fond of you. If fate decrees that you should give your heart to a new man, let it be Owain, for I have never heard a bad word spoken about him.'

At this, I gave Grandma a warm embrace, for I had been uncertain thus far as to whether approval might be forthcoming from David's family. 'Does Grandpa approve? I need his blessing.'

'Indeed, I can assure you that you have it,' said Grandma. 'But you do not need it at all. Remember, Martha, that you are Mistress of this estate, and that you are in charge of your own destiny. No scheming fathers to interfere with your own instincts, no negotiations about marriage settlements, no subtle assessments of what might be a "good" marriage for the future of either of your two estates.'

Suddenly, with the mention of the word 'marriage', I began to feel afraid, for I had been so preoccupied with affairs of the heart that I had thought hardly at all about the practicalities of getting married to Master Owain Laugharne. I gasped, and whispered to Grandma as though I was afraid someone else might overhear me: 'Dear Grandma Jane, this talk of marriage makes me feel very frightened. I am not sure that I am ready for it. I am not sure that the children are ready for it. And after all the pain I have suffered, do I dare to let my emotions get carried away on a flood tide? What will happen if my love, or his, should fade and wither instead of blossoming?'

Grandma led me across the room, and we both sat on the edge of the bed. She put her arm round me. 'If things should go wrong, you or he, or both of you, will be terribly hurt,' she said quietly, in the voice of a sage. 'But it was always thus. Whenever a woman opens a door into her heart and lets love in, she takes a risk so great that it passes comprehension. But we keep on doing it. I have done it, and so have you. And we have both done it because the size of the risk is minuscule by comparison with the joys – emotional and physical – to be found in the Garden of Eden. Would you not agree?'

I smiled and nodded. 'Yes, yes – I know it. I have taken risks before, and I have to admit that in the matter of marriage you buy into pain as well as pleasure. Maybe it is just as well that one does not know in advance what might be the proportions of the one against the other. And thinking of life's little pleasures, here come four of them now.'

After a thunderous stampede upon the staircase, the door of my room burst open, and Betsi, Daisy, Dewi and little Sara stood there panting. 'Mam! Mam!' said Betsi, the self-appointed spokesman for the deputation. 'We have something very important to tell you!'

'Good gracious me!' said I. 'Is it very important indeed? Is it all right if Great-grandma Jane hears it too?'

'Oh, yes,' said Betsi. 'We have just had a meeting downstairs, and we have decided that Master Lougharne is a very nice gentleman. We think that you had better marry him.'

Harvest of Weeds

20 September 1806

Following the expressions of support for my friendship with Owain, I have decided to allow it to develop naturally and gently. It would not be seemly for him, or me, to make a great show of our affection, for it is still less than two years since David died. Besides, we still know very little about each other, and I have a natural fear that there may be some impediment – undiscovered thus far – that might come between us. I have spoken to all my friends, including Joseph, Ellie and Mary Jane, and they all advise me that Owain has an unblemished reputation. They all say that he is a gentleman thoroughly deserving of my affection, and Mary Jane (who is after all his sister) reports that he is behaving like a man besotted by love. She says that he is writing poetry and music when he should be planning cattle purchases and crop rotations, and I cannot help wondering whether any of the fruits of his labours will find their way into my hands. There is no doubt at all about the message carried in my heart, and while exercising caution I must do nothing which might cause Owain to become confused or despondent. I do believe that sensitivity and patience are two of his many virtues.

I have decided to take Master Laugharne into my confidence on certain matters. He invited me and the children to tea at Llannerch a couple of days since. Sian came too in order to make things respectable and to keep the children under control, for they adore Owain and were very excited. It was a showery day with the feel of autumn in the air. We walked the mile or so down through the woods to Llannerch, with tall white grasses brushing our faces and canopies of red and gold leaves over our heads. I believe that I was more excited than the children at the prospect of seeing Owain again, but I was more adept at keeping my excitement under control. He was on the front doorstep to greet us, and professed himself delighted that we were entering his house for the first time. He kissed my hand and took my coat and bonnet, and hugged all of the children. He was very welcoming and solicitous with Sian as well, which made her feel very flattered.

'Master Laugharne!' squealed Daisy. 'Will you sing us a song? Like the ones you sang for us before!'

'Now then, Daisy,' said I, greatly surprised. 'Master Laugharne is not a magical minstrel who can conjure songs out of a hat at a moment's notice.'

'Oh yes he is, Mam!' shouted Dewi, jumping up and down, and to prove the point Owain went into his parlour and came back carrying a big hat. With a flourish he took out of it a sheet of music paper, and after seating all of us in a row in front of him he launched into a rendition of a very silly song about a pink pig and a bucket of swill. The children were delighted, and so was I, for the sound of his fine tenor voice reminded me – if any reminding was necessary – of the occasion, only a month or so ago, when I had followed his music and discovered him naked at Pandy Pools.

I must have closed my eyes, and was pulled out of my

reverie by Betsi, who said: 'Wake up, Mam! Master Laugharne says it is time for tea!' And so it was. We enjoyed a most elegant tea, served by Owain's housekeeper in a sunny conservatory at the side of the house. Everything was quite perfect, and I was impressed that Owain entrusted the family's best bone china plates and cups to the tender mercies of the three girls and their brother. My heart was in my mouth more than once, for little Sara is but eighteen months old and is accident prone to boot, but nothing was smashed or spilt by the children, and in the event I was quite proud of their table manners. There was not a lot of poise or decorum involved, but we all had a very jolly time.

Then Sian and the children rushed off in the company of Owain's head man to inspect the animals, and he and I were left alone for a few precious minutes. 'Owain,' said I, 'I am intrigued by the business of the silly song. Would I be right in assuming that this is not the first silly song you have written and performed for the children?'

Owain laughed. 'Quite right you are, Martha,' he replied. 'This must be the fourth or the fifth. I am very fond of children, and especially, if I may say so, your children. Maybe I should have become a teacher instead of a squire. You might not have registered the fact, but following David's death I visited the Plas several times, and spent more time in the company of the children than I did in yours. You were either very melancholic, or pre-occupied with other things.'

'Oh, I am so sorry. I must have appeared very rude and very unappreciative indeed.'

'Not at all. I can hardly imagine the turmoil which must have afflicted you and your family at the time. I thought that in the circumstances it might be a nice idea to introduce a little humour into the children's lives, at least.'

'Thank you, Owain. I appreciate that kind gesture – as I am sure the children did, at the time.'

Then Owain showed me round the house, which was not as grand as I might have anticipated, with musty rooms, creaking floorboards and small windows. It was obviously a very old house, and Owain told me that certain parts of it went back to the days of Henry Tudor. Some of the furniture was new, but most of the carpets and curtains, tapestries and pictures were very old and worn, and Owain explained that they were a source of embarrassment to him. They were all left behind when Alban Watkins was arrested and flung into jail in London following his failed court case against our family in the autumn of 1797. When his wife and two daughters fled to Scotland, they took hardly anything with them. The Llannerch estate, and the house and all its contents, were sold to defray some of the Watkins debts, and most of the property was purchased by Squire Laugharne of Pontfaen, the father of Mary Jane and Owain. It was given to Owain, as the younger of two sons, with the challenge of repairing the damage done to land and buildings and stock over decades of mis-management. I knew, as did everybody else, that it was Owain's dream to turn the estate into a thriving enterprise of which he and the Laugharne family could be proud.

'I am afraid,' said Owain, 'that there are too many pieces of Watkins rubbish in this house for my liking. I would like to put them all onto a great bonfire and burn them up, but until the estate is paying its way properly my priority is to invest any spare cash in new stock, new implements and the repairing of barns and other build-ings. Then there are my excellent servants to look after.

The house can wait. Indeed, I cannot complain, for all of us under this roof have food in our bellies, and we manage to pay our bills.'

'You are too modest, Owain. I grant you that the house left by the Watkins family could do with some refurbishment, but the estate is in good heart, and I have heard many kind comments about your wise investments and careful husbandry.'

Since the talk had naturally turned to Alban Watkins, I thought that I might as well share with Owain my concerns about the wretched fellow's return from the penal colonies. I discovered that Owain knew a great deal about the history of the dispute between the Watkins family of Llannerch and the Morgan family of Plas Ingli. But he was just as bemused as I regarding the reasons for Watkins's return, and he was greatly entertained when I told him of my suspicion that Watkins' was driven by lust for some fantastical Plas Ingli treasure.

He roared with laughter, and said: 'Where on earth did he get that idea from? I thought it was common knowledge that the Plas Ingli money box melted away, or went up in smoke, during the terrible fire in the old house?'

'So it did, Owain,' said I, perfectly truthfully, and omitting to mention that the contents of the box were elsewhere at the time. 'But I suspect that the fantasy of the treasure goes back to the old days when Watkins was conspiring with Moses Lloyd, before his disappearance, to destroy the estate. You will have heard all about that from Mary Jane and others. I also suspect that the relative prosperity of Plas Ingli today has refuelled wild speculations of some secret hoard, and that Watkins has returned to find out where it is, and to claim it for himself.'

'A strange fellow indeed,' said Owain. 'And evil, too. Did you know that he has been prowling around Llannerch?'

'Oh? I am surprised that he dare show his face within ten miles of this place, for fear of being lynched by the servants, whom he treated so abominably before he was brought to justice.'

'I agree. Any one of a dozen people on this estate would be only too pleased to push a knife between his ribs. But he is very arrogant, and he has a way of intimidating people who are less well educated than himself.'

'So what has he been doing at Llannerch?'

'Generally trying to cause trouble. Wandering into the yard and the dairy, bossing the servants around, and grumbling about the theft of property which is rightly his. He upset Mary, my dairymaid, by instructing her to surrender all the butter churns and buckets into his possession, and then he angered my housekeeper by demanding the return of all the fabrics and furnishings in the house. He claims that all of the goods and chattels about the place were stolen from him during some great conspiracy, and threatens to take out a summons for their restoration.'

'I fear, Owain, that Master Watkins lives in a fantasy world. Just as he claimed that Plas Ingli belonged to him, he now appears to think that his mountainous debts, and the declaration of his insolvency, were wild fantasies dreamt up by his creditors in order to destroy him.'

'Anyway,' said Owain with a smile on his face, 'when my servants called me to their rescue, I sent him packing with a reminder that I have bills of sale and signed receipts for every single item on this estate, and I ordered him never to set foot upon Llannerch land again.'

'I wish I had been a fly upon the wall,' said I. 'That must have been an interesting little episode.'

After that, I informed Owain about my suspicions concerning Masters Rice, Lloyd, Beynon and Howell, and I was intrigued to discover that he did not seem at all shocked. Like everybody else in the community, he knew about the 'secret' duel between Rice and Lloyd, about their former friendship and their current bitter enmity. He knew about the punishment recently meted out to both of them by the *Ceffyl Pren*, and about the reasons for the animosity shown to them by the common people of the town. He also knew that Beynon and Lloyd are cronies, and that Howell and Fenton have been – and quite likely, still are – whoring, drinking and gambling partners of Rice. I explained that I had picked up various pieces of intelligence concerning their ill will towards Plas Ingli and me personally, and much to my surprise he said: 'I was aware of all that, Martha, and I too have been keeping an eye on things just in case you should ever need assistance.'

'Oh? Forgive me, Owain, but in my naivety I thought you were too preoccupied with artistic pursuits to take much notice of what is going on down in the town.'

At this he roared with laughter, and said: 'Thank you, Martha. I will take that as a compliment. But don't worry. I have more contacts in low places than you might imagine, and I have a pretty good idea what the criminal fraternity is up to.'

Then I laughed too, and was greatly intrigued by the discovery that there was more to this fellow than met the eye. I explained to him that I suspected that these two gangs of evil men were in desperate financial trouble, for a variety of reasons. He listened intently, and asked many questions. I also told him that the villains were most likely driven by the conviction that a part of the fabulous and imaginary Plas Ingli treasure was theirs by right, and that they might shortly make a move in order to discover where it was. I reminded him that Rice and Howell could well have heard about the mysterious treasure from their late fathers, who were both evil men in league with Alban Watkins and Moses Lloyd.

Owain absorbed all of this, and said that he had many more questions for me; but our conversation was terminated by the reappearance of Sian and the children, and we agreed that further discussions could wait for another day. Little Sara was very tired and grizzly, having missed her afternoon nap, so we all thanked Owain for his generous hospitality and took our leave. Once again, he kissed my hand and held it for just a little longer than would have been appropriate in polite circles. Sian noticed this, and could not resist a little smile. We set off back up the track towards Dolrannog and the Plas. I was sad to leave, but carried the warmth of our encounter with me all the way home.

Looking back, I am pleased that I have started to take Owain into my confidence on matters that might affect my own safety and the security of the estate. Although I do not think I am ready to share my thoughts about David's murder, I have discovered a good deal more about the Master of Llannerch today, and I like what I have seen. I am particularly gratified to find that from a modest distance he has been keeping a watchful eye on me and the estate. I think I have identified another guardian angel. But he is a great deal more to me than that, and while I sit here all alone at my desk, thinking that it is probably time for bed, I find myself fantasizing about the talents which he might one day demonstrate for me between the sheets.

21 September 1806

Autumn equinox. It has been a gentle, mellow day with a hazy sun and not a breath of wind. But there has been a whirlwind of news, and my feathers are still ruffled as a consequence.

It started during breakfast, when a messenger arrived at the kitchen door bearing a large bouquet of flowers. I recognized the messenger as one of Owain's servants, and indeed I recognized the flowers as having come from the Llannerch conservatory where we yesterday enjoyed afternoon tea. In the bunch there were chrysanthemums and dahlias, phlox and delphiniums, and late summer roses, red and russet and copper-coloured as befits the glories of an autumn day, with fern fronds and dry grasses around them. The whole bouquet was tied with a blue ribbon. The ribbon gave me almost as much pleasure as the flowers, for it indicated that he had worked out my favourite colour. There was an envelope as well, sealed with the Llannerch seal. With everybody looking on I had to open it, and was prevailed upon to read aloud the little poem it contained. It was short, and delicate, and was written in Owain's hand. It was about autumn, and made no direct reference to me, but when they heard it everybody smiled, and sighed, and both Grandma and Grandpa nodded and said, 'Amen, amen'.

'Martha,' said Grandpa. 'I think you have found yourself a true bard. Twelve lines and not a word wasted; the metres are excellent, the subtlety is a delight, and there is so much music in the words that no tune is required. The meaning is all in the sentiments which are unspoken.'

'Yes, Grandpa. I am sure you are right,' said I, without having the slightest idea what he was talking about.

'Would there be a reply, Mistress?' asked Owain's messenger.

'Yes, if you will give me a moment,' I replied, and I scribbled a note expressing my very great pleasure at the receipt of the flowers and the beautiful poem. I also asked him whether he might like to pay a visit on Saturday of next week at twelve noon, in the company of Mary Jane and her family, with a view to taking a picnic in the woods, weather permitting. I checked with the rest of the family and the servants as to whether this might be an acceptable idea, and they all expressed the most decided approval. So I sealed the message up, and off it went. Then I wrote an invitation to my dear friend Mary Jane and her family, and asked Shemi to deliver it to Trecwn. I am sure they will love to come if they can.

An hour later, with the children at their lessons and everybody else getting on with their tasks for the day, I was sitting in my room reading over Owain's poem and seeking to interpret its subtleties. I was also trying to come to terms with the fact that his affection for me is now about as public as it can be, clearly by intent. Flowers and poems do not often figure in the great scheme of things in this area, especially at breakfast time, and I thought them more appropriate to the warm olive groves of Tuscany than to the damp oak woods of Pembrokeshire. But this did nothing to diminish my pleasure, and in truth I was delighted that Owain had the support and approval of all the inhabitants of my house. A romantic gentleman indeed. I could hardly credit that he was the same fellow who was so hesitant, so shy and blushing, on the occasion of our first encounter . . .

Then there was a knock on the door. 'Mistress Martha,' announced Mrs Owen, 'Will have had a visit from one of the boys in town and he would like a word with you if it is convenient. Can I send him up? I will insist that he takes his boots off first.'

'Yes indeed.' I laughed. 'And I am very pleased to see that in spite of your mature years, Mrs Owen, your maternal instincts are still intact.'

She chuckled somewhere in the depths of her substantial bosom, and sent her son up the stairs.

'I have news, Mistress,' said Will, looking very delighted.

'How interesting. Please, Will, sit down here and tell me more.'

'It's about that bastard Joseph Rice, if you will forgive my language. Do you remember, Mistress, that we talked about the blackmailing business?'

'Of course.'

'Well, my friend Skiff have got the matter sorted out. He is a bright lad, that one. Always three steps ahead of the Revenue men and four steps ahead of the magistrates. He will go far, as sure as eggs is eggs.'

'Possibly all the way to Botany Bay?'

'Very probably, Mistress.' Will laughed. 'Anyway, Skiff started to think about all the local crimes in this area. He knows who did everything. Then he realized that there was one crime about four years ago, in November, that have always puzzled him and the other lads in town. Do you know Captain Luke Morris down on the Parrog?'

'Not personally, but I have heard about him. Not a very nice fellow by all accounts, and a crony of Joseph Rice?'

'Exactly, Mistress. Well, he came back from some voyage very well off, with wads of that new paper money in his purse. He had a wild party in his house, after which he found that two hundred pounds was missing. Big bother all over town, with the constables and the magistrates involved. Morris accused his servant girl Meg Billings of stealing the money, and beat her something terrible, but she pleaded innocence and nothing was ever proved. He sacked Meg, and then took on Patty Ellis instead. Meg went off and got a job with Squire Bowen at Llwyngwair, and she is still there. Very pretty girl, with wide hips and a big . . .'

'Spare me the details, Will. What happened next?'

'Ah yes. Skiff went down to see Meg and asked her about the robbery. She still swears that she had nothing to do with it, and she would not lie to Skiff. Then he asked her if she could remember all the people who were in the Captain's house drinking his gin on the night in question. She could recall about twenty names. One of them was Rice.'

'Now that is very interesting. But it doesn't prove anything.'

'Indeed not, Mistress Martha. But Skiff is no fool. He knows how the criminal mind works. Never shift your goods locally and fast; you either sit on them for a good while, if you can afford the time, or shift them somewhere else. What would Rice do if he had two hundred pounds of paper money in his pocket? Then Skiff realized that mid-November is the end of the social season in Tenby, when the *crachach* have their gay balls and musical evenings before going off to London. Not many from the local area join in with the Tenby season, but Rice was one of the ones who always did, until quite recently.'

I was getting quite intrigued by the ingenuity of this fellow Skiff, and thought that I should not like to get on the wrong side of him. Will continued with his narrative. 'So last week, Skiff took a little trip to Tenby, to have a swim in the sea and to meet some old friends. He got talking, and happened to meet a man who relieves the gentry of large sums of money by taking ridiculous

351

wagers. He had a clear recollection of one particular event, four years ago at the very start of the social season, which attracted some big bets.'

'More and more interesting, Will. Go on.'

'He put on a contest on South Beach. A donkey with a sixteen-stone man in the saddle, against a man carrying a sack of coal, over a one-mile course. All properly done, with judges and stewards and so forth.'

'Good gracious! Who won? The donkey, I presume?'

'No, no, the man with the coal,' chortled Will. 'The donkey was one of the ones used for giving children rides on the sands, and it did not even know how to run, even with something as light as a little boy on its back. The coalman walked, very slowly, for the whole mile and won by about a thousand yards.'

'I think I know where this is leading. And the bets?'

'The fellow in Tenby, who shall be nameless and would never say this to a magistrate, swears he has a clear memory of a shifty character named Rice from the north of the county who put down two hundred pounds in paper money, and lost the lot.'

'Case proved, Your Honour,' said I, quite lost in admiration. 'But how on earth did Lloyd find out about this?'

'That is still a mystery, Mistress. Maybe he found out the same way as Skiff. He used to go to Tenby a lot, in the days when he could afford it. Perhaps he picked up some local gossip about famous bets in years gone by, and put two and two together.'

'So Rice stole two hundred pounds from one of his own friends. Luke Morris is one of the hardest men in Newport. He will surely kill Rice if he finds out.'

'Quite right, Mistress. If I was in his shoes, I too would surely pay a couple of sovereigns a month in exchange for silence. On the other hand, I might just kill Lloyd and Beynon and save myself the expense.'

'Come come, Will. Wicked thoughts indeed. But Lloyd is smarter than that. You can be quite sure that if anything happens to him or Beynon, a sealed letter will be opened in some solicitor's office revealing the whole story of the crisp pound notes, the donkey and the coalman.'

'You are one step ahead of me, Mistress. If ever you want an exciting profession as a felon, just let me know, and I may be able to give you some contacts.'

'No thank you, Will,' I smiled. 'I have too many duties as it is, and too little time to succeed in any of them. Now then, you probably have work to do. And thank you for this information. Please pass on my thanks to your friend. Next time you go to town, please take him a dozen eggs and half a ham.'

When Will had gone, feeling very pleased with himself, I started to wonder about the native intelligence of some of the poor people of the town and country of Newport. What, I wondered, could poor people like Skiff, and Patty Ellis, and those who fish for herring, and those who stitch sailcloth in Havard's shipyard, do with a little education and a few opportunities for advancement in life? Many of them were certainly smarter, and a great deal more knowledgeable in matters of trade, than the buffoons who lord it over them and assume them all to be idiots. I thought it was high time that I renewed my acquaintance with Tom Paine's *Rights of Man*, and I was just reaching for it on my bookshelf when there was another knock on the door.

This time it was Bessie, with a letter from Patty. 'More gossip from town, Mistress Martha,' she said with a grin. 'You are having a busy day, indeed. At any rate, I hope the news will be to your liking. If there should be a reply, Hettie is here just now and will be departing back to the

Parrog after having a cup of tea and a slice of bread and jam.'

'Thank you Bessie,' said I. 'I will call if I am in need of a messenger.'

So I sat down by the window, looking out over the misty *cwm*, and read Patty's letter. This is what she said:

> *Parrog, the 21st day of September 1806*
>
> *My dear friend Mistress Martha,*
>
> *I trust that you and your loved ones are well. I am tired from overwork, but otherwise in health, and must be thankful for small mercies. Thank you for the eggs and the apples which you sent recently with Hettie – I am greatly enjoying them.*
>
> *I have news of Alban Watkins. Yesterday a ketch came in on the high tide from Bristol. On board was a fellow called Jake Nicholas, who used to live in Fishguard before being pressed into the Navy. He paid me a visit last evening, and after he had enjoyed more than his money's worth we got to talking. In the last five years he has been all over the world. When he was in Hobart he lost three fingers of his right hand in an accident, and was pensioned off. He found his way to Sydney, and worked on various ships taking convicts between New South Wales, Van Diemen's Land, and Norfolk Island.*
>
> *When he was in a coal mining place called Newcastle he got to hear of a convicted squire called Alban Watkins, and that rang a bit of a bell in his head. He made some enquiries in establishments of ill repute, and found that this particular fellow had just been given a free pardon by Governor Philip King and had been put aboard a ship for England, fare all paid, at high speed only a couple of weeks before. This, so they said, was to save his life, for if he had stayed a thousand convicts would have drawn lots for the privilege of beating out his brains with a shovel.*
>
> *And his crime? Jake said that the town was still buzzing like an angry beehive about it. Apparently a group of about twenty Irish convicts who were working the coal seams were so furious at the*

ill treatment and miserable rations they were getting from the mining manager that they decided to escape inland. They were driven, says Jake, by the wild dream that if they walked north away from Newcastle they would reach China, where they would find opium, and gold, and women, and food and drink in abundance. Watkins had been assigned to work as an assistant to the store manager, with about six months to go before he qualified for his precious ticket-of-leave.

The day before the escape, with everything planned, Watkins heard about it from a drunken Irishman. He was a convict himself, and knew all about the code of secrecy that they all subscribed to. But he ratted on the Irish, so that when the signal was given next day a contingent of fifty riflemen from the Newcastle barracks popped up from behind a hill and challenged the Irish to stop. The latter were carrying picks and shovels, but had no food or drink, and even if they had all escaped they would certainly have perished inside a few days.

Jake says that the Irish panicked, and a few of them attacked the soldiers. Three of the Irish were shot dead, and one of the soldiers was killed by a pickaxe. The rest of the convicts fled, and they were rounded up over the next couple of days and clapped in irons. According to Jake there were no proper trials. The three ringleaders were strung up on gibbets there and then. Twelve others were hauled before a court martial. Alban Watkins was the star witness for the prosecution, and attested to the involvement of all the Irish.

All were found guilty of rebellion and of the murder of the soldier, and a mass execution followed. Eight more gibbets were thrown up in a row on a hill overlooking the coal mine, and the eight convicted prisoners were put in iron cages and then hung by their necks, one after another. The other four, who were simple fellows who probably had little idea what was going on, were sentenced to three hundred lashes each – one hundred on the back, one hundred on the buttocks, and one hundred on the backs of their legs. Jake spoke to several convicts who witnessed the floggings, and even they, who were used to floggings and saw them almost every day, were made sick by the sight of such blood, and skin and flesh flying in all directions. The poor fellows took such a beating that their ribs and backbones were visible through the gore, and their buttocks looked like jelly, and their legs were so mangled that they could not walk. Three of them died within a few hours, and the last one, by some miracle, managed to survive.

Jake says that this all happened about three weeks before he arrived in Newcastle. He walked up behind the town, and saw there the crude graves of the three who died from their floggings. Not far away there were eleven gibbets with eleven rotting corpses dangling from them, each one in a sort of iron cage. The Governor had decreed that they should stay there until completely de-composed, as an example and a warning to others who might have rebellion in mind. Their eyes had gone and so had much of the flesh; the corpses were covered with maggots and flies, and crows were flapping about between one corpse and another. Stinking juices were dripping onto the ground beneath them. In the heat, says Jake, the stench was almost unbearable, and he was violently sick before he managed to get away from the place. He says that he still has nightmares about it.

After that, he was so appalled by New South Wales that he got out as fast as he could. He got onto the crew of a convict ship trading back home via Cochin on the Malabar Coast, and then found his way back here by way of Bristol.

Mistress Martha, I am sorry to have to describe all of this to you in such detail; indeed, I feel faint just from the writing of it. I hope it does not distress you. But I had to do it while it is fresh in my mind. I have no reason at all to disbelieve anything Jake has told me, and I judge him to be a kind and honest fellow.

So now we know the nature of the 'disaster' from which Master Alban Watkins saved New South Wales, and the treacherous 'bravery' for which he was rewarded with a free pardon and voyage home. If truth be told, he would not have survived a month if he had stayed anywhere in the colonies.

356

Now we know what kind of man we have as company in this sweet little town of ours, if we did not know it already.

Take care, and God bless you and your little ones.

Your friend Patty.

When I had finished reading this, I was shaking like a leaf, and hardly knew what to do or think. Then there was a knock on the door, and Bessie popped her head round it. 'Hettie is going soon, Mistress,' she said. 'Will there be any reply for Patty?' I shook my head, for I was incapable of words, and Bessie came rushing in when she saw the state I was in. She put her arm round me, pulled me to my feet, and led me over to the bed. Then she got me onto it, with my head on a soft pillow.

'My goodness, Mistress Martha,' she said, 'it is a very long time since I saw you in such a state. That was obviously not a very nice letter. Has Patty said something to upset you?'

'No,' I whispered. 'Patty is as kind and sweet as ever. It is just that the news I have received from her is not very pleasant. Will you please get me a small brandy?'

'I will get you a large one, since you obviously need it,' she replied. 'Just you stay put for a minute.' And off she went to get my drink and to tell Hettie that there would be no messages for the Parrog today.

It was still only about eleven of the clock in the morning, and I felt emotionally drained and ready for bed. But the brandy revived me, and at the dinner table the chattering of the children and the rest of the household did much to restore my spirits. But Grandma Jane noticed that I looked pale and strained, and with the assistance of the other women she devised a busy programme of activities for the children which would allow me to have the afternoon free. Off they all went, and I was left sitting alone at the table. Grandma came over to

357

me as I sat there, and took my hand in hers. 'You look as if you have had a morning of emotional highs and lows, my dear Martha,' she said. 'Flowers and poems at breakfast, followed by God only knows what. Why don't you seize the chance and walk in the fresh air while we and the children are busy with other things?'

So I climbed up alongside the water pipe to Ffynnon Brynach, anointed myself in its healing waters, and climbed up onto the jumble of bluestone boulders leading to the cave. The summit, I thought, could wait for another day. The old raven, alone this time, spotted me and watched me as I climbed. I followed the narrow path trodden, not so long ago, by Daisy *bach*, who was led along it, according to the latest version of her story, by fairies wearing red dresses and green bonnets.

Then I slipped between the bluestone pillars into the welcoming darkness. I sat there on my mossy cushion in perfect silence for maybe two hours, with my back against the wall and my knees drawn up to my chin. At first my mind was in a turmoil, for in the course of a single morning I had received a loving gesture from a romantic and handsome gentleman, a message (shot through, it has to be said, with humour) concerning the foolish thieving and gambling activities of a petty criminal, and finally news of such depravity and cruelty as I had never before encountered. Could mankind really be capable of such extremes of behaviour? How is it that some can show tenderness and compassion without measure, while others whose eyes see the same beautiful earth and whose nostrils breathe the same sweet air can use innocent souls in a manner fit only for the deepest recesses of Hell? Can it really be true that we are all members of the same human race?

I found no answers to my questions, but I wept for the Irish, and I wept for Owain, and Patty, and even for

Joseph Rice and Alban Watkins. I found a sort of peace, and in the cave of old St Brynach I breathed deeply and found – not for the first time – the strength to face once again the harsh light of day. I said to myself: 'These men will not defeat me and they will not harm the Plas or those who dwell beneath its blessed roof.' And having made my vow, I asked Brynach, and the old raven, and the angels of the mountain, for their assistance, and walked home through the scree slopes of blue boulders and the head-high swaths of red bracken.

24 September 1806

Two very strange fellows have arrived in the local area. One of them is tall and bald, and the other is short and hairy. They are dressed like medieval court jesters. The tall one, by all accounts, says he is a minstrel, and the short one claims to be an acrobat. They say that they are stopping off in Newport for a few days before travelling on to Ireland to entertain the simple people of that green and soggy isle. There is much talk about them in Newport, and I first got news of them yesterday when Gethin Griffiths called in on his way home from market. He says they are Cockneys, and that they have walked all the way from Portsmouth with very few possessions. As might be expected, they do not understand a word of Welsh, and this makes it somewhat difficult for them to communicate with most of the poor people in town.

When they arrived they stood out from the crowd like two spring lambs in the middle of a drove of black bullocks, and the Mayor wanted to throw them into the lock-up on the grounds that they were vagrants too far from their home parish. But they claimed that they were professional men, not vagrants or felons on the run, and nobody could show that they had been begging. Furthermore, said the tall one, they had money in their purses and had already taken a room in Mistress Matty Thomas's lodgings in Long Street. This turned out to be perfectly true, and the Mayor had to accept that they had every right to stay in the town so long as they did not bother anybody.

Last night Billy, Will and Shemi all went down to town to see if they could catch sight of these famous strangers, and sure enough they found them in the Royal Oak, sharing a few drinks with the locals. Billy has a good command of English, and he got talking to them, and interpreted for the others. He discovered that the tall one is called Tommy Ellis, and the short one Jeb Smith. They all urged the fellows to get out their instruments and strike up with a jolly tune or two, or to do a few somersaults and handstands in the middle of the bar-room floor; but they refused absolutely, saying that they were on holiday after an exhausting season in Portsmouth, and had to conserve their energies for their forthcoming appearances in Wexford town.

'Most peculiar fellows indeed,' said Shemi when he came in from the yard for breakfast this morning. 'We are not sure whether they are actually mad, or just pretending to be mad. We all had a bit of fun with them in the Royal Oak, and managed to get them to join in a few songs in the end, once they were well tanked up, but the one who says he is a minstrel has the worst singing voice this side of Cardiff.'

'And as for the one called Jeb Smith,' chortled Billy, 'he is so short-sighted that he can hardly focus on anything further away than the tip of his nose. If he tried to do a ten-minute session of acrobatics I would not fancy his chances of survival beyond the first ten seconds.'

We all listened intently, and soon there were gales of

laughter round the table as the three men told of the great entertainment which the Royal Oak regulars had enjoyed at the expense of the two Londoners. At last I said: 'Well, we are supposed to be famous in this town for the warmth of the welcome we extend to new arrivals, but it sounds to me as if all you fellows were very cruel with the strangers.'

'Oh, I shouldn't worry, Mistress Martha,' said Will. 'They took all the joking and teasing in good part, and they didn't need to pay for most of the ale they consumed. They were happy enough, I can assure you. And I dare say they are harmless.'

'I am not sure of that,' said Billy. 'Some of the boys in the inn think they are Revenue men in disguise, come to try to find out who is bringing in tax-free goods along this coast. Dickens from Milford is not having much success on that score, so maybe they are trying something new. Some of the other boys think they may have something to do with the press gang, sent to single out likely lads for their colleagues who might arrive at any time. There is word that five single men were pressed into the Navy at Haverfordwest only last week.'

'And then, of course,' added Grandpa, with a furrowed brow and a twinkling eye, 'they could be French spies, reporting direct to Master Bonaparte and sent in disguise into the Pembrokeshire countryside in order to report on troop movements and stir up rebellion.'

After this, further conversation was impossible as all of us became afflicted by chuckles, and then giggles, and finally hysterical laughter, and Grandma Jane almost choked on a slice of bread and cheese. In the end I had to remind all of them that there was work to be done, and sent them packing out of the kitchen. But as the day has gone on, almost all the conversation in the

361

household has turned upon Master Ellis and Master Smith, and I have to confess to being quite intrigued myself as to who they are and what they are doing here.

27 September 1806

There is more news of the Londoners, brought this time by Grandpa Isaac on his return from his afternoon drinking session in the Rose and Crown. He says that he witnessed a very interesting episode in which Master Ellis and Master Smith featured prominently.

Apparently he was sitting in his accustomed corner with Masters Gruffydd, Edwards and Prosser when who should come in but Alban Watkins. He looked like a worried man. He ordered a jar of ale, and sat by himself in a dark corner. He spoke to nobody. He probably did not notice Grandpa; and if he did he did not acknowledge him.

After about five minutes who should come in but the two Londoners. Grandpa says they were instantly recognizable as the two new arrivals in town, both from their voices and their attire. They looked, according to Grandpa, like two faded actors returning, in a bad mood, from an unsuccessful audition for small parts in *A Midsummer Night's Dream*. They went straight up to the innkeeper and Master Ellis said: 'We gather, sir, that amongst your customers in this excellent establishment you may have a certain Master Alban Watkins, late of Llannerch and New South Wales. If he is present, we should be delighted to make his acquaintance. Would you be so kind as to indicate his whereabouts?'

'No problem at all, sir,' replied the innkeeper, pointing into the corner. 'That would be the very gentleman, over there.'

And before Watkins could escape, the two fellows went over and confronted him. Grandpa says it was obvious that in spite of Watkins's heavy beard and the dim lighting, the two men recognized him. The recognition was mutual. 'Well well well,' said Master Smith, 'if it isn't Squire Watkins himself. What a pleasure it is to see you again after all this time!'

'And so good to see you looking so healthy and well fed,' added Master Ellis. 'Now then, we have a little business to complete. Shall we go outside?'

And without a further word from any of them, says Grandpa Isaac, they knocked aside Watkins's half-drunk mug of ale, grabbed hold of him under his armpits, and dragged him spluttering and protesting out through the door. Everybody else who was inside the inn followed, assuming that something very interesting was about to happen. They put him up against a wall and proceeded to give him a thorough beating. Grandpa says that Watkins, who is quite a large and powerful man, stood no chance at all, for the two Londoners knew more than a little about how to use their fists and their boots. The beating went on for about five minutes, and as it ran its course a substantial crowd gathered and watched in total silence. Nobody felt very inclined to assist Watkins, for he is not the most popular fellow in town. At last he slid to the ground, with his cheeks and lips split, his eyes swollen, and his face covered in blood. When he was on the ground they kicked him in the ribs a few more times, and then turned and walked off nonchalantly down towards the Parrog.

'In due course,' said Grandpa, 'Constable Wilson, who had been in the crowd and had seen the whole thing, went up to him and gave him some assistance. George the innkeeper, who had after all taken his pennies in exchange for a quart of ale, probably felt that he had better do his duty regarding his injured customer, and took him inside for repairs. He was groaning and moaning something awful, but the Londoners didn't use any weapons, and his injuries were not too bad. Nothing broken, apart from a couple of ribs maybe. But do you know what?'

'No, Grandpa. What?'

'Now there's a funny thing. Wilson Constable asked Watkins if he wanted to file a complaint against the Londoners for assault and battery, or attempted murder, or whatever, but he absolutely refused. Poor old John pleaded with him, for he was dying to arrest the Londoners and throw them into the lock-up, and earn a few shillings into the bargain, and he knew that with so many witnesses there would be no problem in obtaining a conviction at the Petty Sessions. But Watkins was quite insistent. He would not enter a complaint. So there we are. End of story. The whole town is talking about it, and there is no end of speculation as to what that little encounter was all about.'

Then he took a piece of paper, ignited it in the kitchen fire, and lit his pipe. He had the smug look on his face of a man who knows everything. He settled back into his favourite chair, took a few long puffs, and closed his eyes.

'All right, Grandpa, I know your little game,' said I. 'Come along, please. Tell us the whole story.'

After several more puffs, Grandpa said, 'Do the names Elias and Smyllie mean anything to you?'

I thought for a moment and said: 'Why yes. Were they not two of the corrupt legal fellows who helped Watkins with his claim upon our estate back in 1797?'

'Quite correct, Martha. As soon as the short fat one who calls himself Smith came into the Royal Oak I recognized him as Smyllie. Lewis Legal and I met him in London when we went up to fight the case in the

Chancery Court. He has lost weight and some of his hair has gone, but he is a very distinctive figure. An insignificant and corrupt clerk, he was, doing various bits of dirty work under the direction of an attorney called Thomas Elias. Actually he never was a proper attorney – no qualifications in the law or anything else, apart from some skills as a petty criminal. I never saw him in court, but I have no doubt at all that the tall bald one who calls himself Tom Ellis is Thomas Elias.'

'Oh, my God!' I exclaimed. 'And here they are in Newport, swaggering around town in the most ostentatious of costumes, and beating people up in broad daylight with never a thought of being brought to justice. I thought that all the conspirators were shipped off to the penal colonies?'

'Not so. You may recall that that was the fate of Watkins and Rice; but Elias and Smyllie, and another fellow called Elijah Willaby, were accessaries to the crime rather than the instigators, and they were let off by the judge relatively lightly. As I recall, they were all three sentenced to ten years of hard labour. Our new friends say they have been in Portsmouth. If they have been working on the chain gangs at the dockyard there, and have behaved well, they might well have been released early.'

'I am not sure that I would describe them as "friends", Grandpa. From what they did to Alban Watkins they do not seem to be very friendly people at all.'

'Anybody who beats Alban Watkins is a friend of mine,' said Grandpa. 'But we now have to work out why they are in Newport. Watkins probably never paid them for their work on his Chancery Court case, and he also landed them with six years or so of hard labour. So they have a grudge against him. But how did they know that he was back in Newport rather than in New South

Wales? And would their grudge have been powerful enough to bring them all the way from Portsmouth just to beat him?'

'I doubt that, Grandpa,' said I. 'There must be much more to it than that. This deserves some careful thought. Shall we consult with Joseph tomorrow? He may have other information, and it would be of benefit to get his assessment of the threat which these fellows may pose. I must say that I find it impossible, without meeting them, to decide whether they be fools, friends or fiends.'

And that is how we left it. I am sure that further interesting discoveries will follow.

28 September 1806

This morning, first thing, I wrote out a message to Joseph asking if he might like to call in for afternoon tea. Shemi rode over the mountain with my envelope, and was back home in time for breakfast. 'Master Harries says thank you very much,' he reported at the kitchen table. 'He has business in Newport, and after that he will come over to the Plas. Around three of the clock.'

The children, who were tucking in to their porridge at the time, heard this and were delighted. 'Mam! Mam!' said Daisy. 'If Master Harries is coming, do you think he will do some magic tricks for us? Jane from Penrhiw says he is a wizard and that he can turn sticks into snakes and stones into dragons and . . .'

'Hold on, Daisy,' said I. 'He is certainly a wizard, but not that sort of wizard. He has more important things to do, like helping poor people get well when they are sick. He is coming over to talk to Grandpa and me, and may not have very much time. But if you are good, maybe he will tell you a magical story.'

As the day went on, the weather deteriorated, and by the afternoon it was pouring with rain and very windy into the bargain. When Joseph arrived on his white pony, he was not feeling in a very magical mood, for he was soaked to the skin. Mrs Owen took care of him, settled him in front of the big fire in the kitchen, and found him some dry clothes. We gave him a big mug of hot tea, and this restored his spirits somewhat. The children demanded his attention, and to his credit he gave it to them. With the four of them sitting at his feet, their eager faces illuminated by the flickering firelight, he told them a long story about a mermaid who saved a fisherman from St Dogmael's when he was caught out at sea in a fearsome storm. In the pregnant pauses, of which there were many, he managed to gulp down his tea.

Then Sian took the children off to the nursery while Joseph, Grandpa and I settled into the parlour for our Council of War. 'Dear Joseph,' I said, 'thank you for calling in at such short notice on such a terrible day. I hope you don't end up with a chill on the chest after your soaking. But there are new people in town, and we need to talk.'

'Yes. I have heard all about them – and about yesterday's punishment session outside the Rose and Crown.'

'They are using false names, of course,' said Grandpa. 'I met one of them in London some years ago. Name of Julius Smyllie, part-time clerk and full-time petty criminal.'

'I had concluded as much myself,' said Joseph with a grin. 'He would be the one who now calls himself Jeb Smith. The one who calls himself Tommy Ellis would presumably be Thomas Elias?'

Grandpa looked amazed. 'Good God, Joseph!' he said, struggling with a mouthful of buttered scone. 'How did you know that?'

'You must remember, Isaac my friend, that once something goes into my head it stays there. I recall the accounts given by you and David about the court case in London. You told us that Watkins had been involved with three crooked legal people, and I assumed that these two fellows in Newport must be two of them.'

'Correct, Joseph. The other one was called Willaby.'

'Yes, I know. Yesterday evening I went down to town and found Master Smith and Master Ellis in the Barley Mow. I got chatting to them, and asked which part of London they were from. Limehouse, they said. Ah! What a coincidence, said I, and told them that I had once known a splendid fellow called Elijah Willaby from around those parts. Would they by any chance have known him? They looked extremely startled, and spluttered and huffed and puffed for a while. Then Master Ellis said they had indeed known him, but that he was now dead. Very sad to hear it, said I, and asked about the cause of death. Oh, it was nothing serious, said Master Ellis, and I said I found that very reassuring. And where did he die? On holiday in Portsmouth, said Master Smith.'

'That ties in with our information, Joseph,' said Grandpa. 'We know they have been in Portsmouth too. Probably all three of them were in the chain gangs there. By no means all prisoners survive the experience.'

I then told Joseph of our discussion concerning the motive for yesterday's beating, and I confessed that I found it difficult to understand why the Londoners should have walked all the way from Portsmouth just to beat Alban Watkins. 'If their grudge was so strong,' I said, 'why did they not come into town one dark night and simply slit his throat?'

'Because they need him alive, Martha,' said Joseph. 'The beating was just a gesture. Maybe it was simply to work off their frustrations, maybe it was payment for the blisters on their feet, or maybe it was payment for the death of their friend Elijah Willaby. Probably they blame Master Watkins for all their misfortunes. My theory is that they were in Portsmouth three months ago, having just been released from the labour camp. They heard – maybe in some alehouse near the docks – about a fellow called Watkins who had just come in on a ship from New South Wales, with a free pardon and lots of gold sovereigns in his pocket. A free pardon is a rare enough event to be the main talking point of the place for weeks if not months. Before they could catch up with him Watkins was gone, on another ship to Bristol, and heading for home.'

'So they followed him,' said Grandpa. 'But surely not just to beat him. There must be a great deal more to it than that.'

Then it all began to fall into place in my mind, and I asked: 'The fabulous buried treasure of Plas Ingli?'

'Of course,' said Joseph. 'For seven or eight years these fellows have thought of little else, as they slaved away in chains, fed on rations meagre enough to starve a cat, and living in conditions that the average pig would find unacceptable. I assume that during the court case in London they worked for Master Watkins in exchange for the promise of a share in the treasure. God knows what he told them about it; it probably grew larger every time he mentioned it, as did the certainty of obtaining it. Watkins had little else to pay them with, since he was destitute at the time of the case.'

'So they have come here to find the treasure, and to claim their share of it?'

'I am convinced of it. Watkins may well have told them, when they did their deal in London, that he knows

369

precisely where it is and that it is just a matter of going to the place and digging it up.'

'And we might further conclude,' said Grandpa, 'that they assumed that Watkins, now a free man again, was heading for Newport at high speed with but one thought in his head – namely to get hold of a shovel and pick at the earliest possible opportunity.'

'Precisely. They will now feel a little better, having given Watkins a good beating. They will be relieved that he has not already dug up the mythical treasure and disappeared with his pockets full of gold. But they will surely meet him again, and demand the right to work alongside him in the treasure pit.'

At this, I burst out laughing, and so did Joseph and Grandpa, for we all three had an image in our minds of two court jesters and a bearded and battered squire digging away in the middle of a muddy field in search of a treasure which did not exist. 'Poor Master Watkins!' said I. 'I almost feel sorry for him. He is damned if he tells them he does know where the treasure is, for he will then have to try to lead them to it. And he is damned if he tells them he doesn't know where it is, for they will not believe him. Such are the wages of sin.'

'So what do we do next?' asked Grandpa.

'Just keep an eye on things,' said Joseph. 'Masters Elias and Smyllie have Watkins under their control. They can do more or less what they want to him, for if he ever complains to the constable or the magistrates the whole story will come tumbling out. They are breathing down his neck, and he will be very worried. He is using up the golden sovereigns which he had in his pocket, for he has to live. And we can be quite certain that the Londoners will never get as far as Wexford. They will not leave this place, for fear that if they do Watkins will rush off and dig up the treasure, and abscond with the funds.'

'Oh dear, what a tangled business,' I said with a degree of resignation in my voice. 'The plot thickens by the minute. We now have two more treasure hunters in our midst, to add to Masters Rice, Fenton, Lloyd and Beynon, not to mention Master Watkins. Lloyd and Beynon are blackmailing Rice, Watkins is talking to Rice and Fenton and is being watched with eagle eyes by the two Londoners, and any one of these villains would probably have just cause for sticking a knife into the ribs of any one of the others.'

'Correct, Martha,' said Joseph. 'And let us not forget that they are in dire financial straits, all of them. They all survive on the proceeds of petty crime, and not one of them ever appears to have thought of the idea of doing a day's honest work in exchange for reasonable reward. And then we come to Captain John Howell, late of the Light Dragoons . . .'

'What do you mean, "late" of the Light Dragoons?' I asked, greatly surprised. 'Is Howell not in France, fighting against the French?'

'Not at all, Martha. At this moment he is in Fishguard, staying with his sister Mary and her husband, a merchant. His old mother lives in the same house. He arrived there yesterday, and all three of them want him out of the place as quickly as possible. The gossip is that he has been dishonourably discharged from the army. No details yet, but they will surely emerge. You may be quite certain that within a few days he will reappear in Newport and renew his acquaintance with his old friends Joseph Rice and John Fenton.'

This gave me a feeling of deep despair, for I realized that all four of David's murderers would now be gathered together again in one place. They were split two and two, it is true, but the prospect was none the less appalling, especially since it was more apparent than ever that all of them were desperately short of money and all driven by the lust for Plas Ingli gold. Joseph saw the shadow on my face, and came across the room. He put his arm round my shoulder, and said: 'There now, Martha, you need not get too worried. Remember that they are all so busy watching each other that they have little time for watching you and the Plas. Watkins is the one we must observe most carefully, and I have that in hand.'

'Thank you, Joseph. I too will make sure that my spies keep an eye on him. But things are coming to a head. Do you recall that I mentioned the germ of a plan which was growing in my mind?'

'Indeed I do.'

'Well, it has grown even more. We must not talk about it now, for it is time to think about supper for the children. But would you like to call in again, same time, same day, next week? I would value your advice and your participation.'

'That sounds intriguing, to be sure,' said Joseph, with a broad grin. 'How could a gentleman resist such an invitation?'

And he kissed my fingers, shook Grandpa's hand, gave a deep bow, and set off homewards through the rain.

I suspect that quite soon, for the first time in my life, I may be able to devise and execute a cunning plan which might save this house of angels from the depredations of evil men. My spies are already at work. Now I will choose my allies, lay my traps, and consider my offensive and defensive strategies. If success is to be the outcome of my enterprise, I will need the goodwill and active participation of a great many friends, and to a degree I will require foolish behaviour on the part of my enemies. But I have to press on, and if victory should follow it will be the most liberating and empowering experience of my short life. In truth I need such an experience. The miseries which have afflicted me since David's death will be entirely forgotten, to be replaced by euphoria. Red blood will course through my veins as never before, and even now as I anticipate the coming confrontation I feel a quickening of the pulse. I feel like a mighty general on the eve of a decisive battle. Queen Boudicca, you have a sister!

Highs and Lows

3 October 1806

We have had our picnic in the woods, and the occasion has restored my faith in human nature. Owain of course accepted my invitation with enthusiasm, as I hoped he would; and Mary Jane, husband Dafydd and little son William also found the time to join us.

Yesterday the children and I made most of the preparations ourselves, which put Mrs Owen's nose out of joint; but I explained to her that I wanted to do this for Owain and our other guests, and that I wanted the children involved rather than taking it for granted that wonderful food and drink would always appear as a result of somebody else's labours. She understood what I intended, and in the end went off with reasonably good grace to visit one of her daughters down in Nevern. 'Now if you please, Mistress Martha,' said she as a parting shot, 'no mess in my kitchen when I come back, and everything in its correct place.'

We had a thoroughly delightful time, with just a little assistance from Grandma Jane. First of all we made some dough out of wheat flour, and Daisy and Betsi baked three loaves of white bread. When they came out of the bread oven, crisp and crusty and smelling of Heaven, there were squeals of delight all round. Then we baked some scones and made a pile of Welsh cakes on the griddle, hoping that they would keep nice and fresh until the morrow. Will then turned up with a splendid five-pound sewin, and would not tell us where it had come from; I did not press him too hard for the information, and we baked it in the oven with herbs, let it cool down, and Grandma and Daisy stripped off all the flesh and got rid of the bones. Then they added gelatine and set it in a mould. While this was going on Betsi picked some late peas in the garden, shelled them and cooked them on the fire. Dewi, little Sara and I dug up a good pile of potatoes and all got in a frightful mess. We washed and peeled them together and boiled them to perfection, firm enough to cut cold into slices. Betsi collected a dozen brown eggs from the chicken shed and hardboiled them. Then I sent all four children out with some bowls to collect blackberries from the hedgerows, and while they were away I pulled down a nice lean ham and cut a supply of thin slices. When the children returned with half-filled bowls and purple fingers and lips, we sorted out the good clean fruit and added lots of sugar, and used it to make a beautiful blackberry pie. Daisy was in charge of that particular project, and she was very proud of the result when it emerged, steaming and fragrant, from the oven.

We had promised Mrs Owen that we would be finished with her kitchen by five of the clock, so that she could take over again in time to prepare supper. And ready we were, with everything covered over with muslin in the cold scullery, all pots and pans washed and dried, and sugar, salt, herbs, oils and spices all back in their appointed places. She was very impressed, and that made me feel very smug. The children were of course covered with flour, mud, juice and butter stains and various other picnic ingredients, and they all had to have a bath before supper. Their clothes – and mine – went straight into the wash. And so to bed.

This morning when I opened my shutters I saw that it would be a perfect autumn day, exactly right for the beginning of October. It was quite calm, with a rose-pink tint in the lightening eastern sky and wisps of mist down in the *cwm*. The children came rushing into my room at six of the clock and bounced about on the bed. They were too excited to sleep any more, so I cuddled them down under the blankets with me and told them a fairy story. Bessie came in with my morning cup of tea before I had finished, and was greatly taken by the sight of five tousled heads all in a happy row on my long pillow.

The morning was taken up with sorting out wicker baskets, cloths and napkins, china plates and mugs, silver cutlery and so forth. We got out all the food from the scullery and packed it down in a big hamper, and added a bowl of fresh salty butter, several small cheeses, pots of chutney and rhubarb jam, a pot of clotted cream, some bottles of Portuguese red wine, and a big bottle of sweet plum cordial for the children. By noon we were all ready. I did not dress the children up in their Sunday finery, for I knew they would get into a terrible mess. For myself, I chose my favourite red crinoline dress – the one with the flattering waistline and the deeply-cut top – and thanked the Good Lord in his Heaven that the day was warm enough to dispense with jackets and cloaks. Bessie put my hair up, and I used just a little rouge; but in truth I hardly needed it, since I have a healthy natural colour and have been out in the fresh air a good deal lately. I told Bessie that I would wear no jewellery apart from my wedding ring. When I was ready I stood in front of my full-length mirror to check that I looked presentable, and Bessie pleased me greatly when she said: 'Mistress

Martha, you look absolutely beautiful today – as radiant as a princess going to a royal ball. I do not think I have ever seen you looking so pretty. If Master Owain does not throw himself at your feet as soon as he sees you he must surely have a heart of stone.'

I laughed and said: 'You may be sure he will not do that, Bessie. He may be very romantic, but he will not fling himself upon the ground since that is not in the book of good manners. And he certainly does not have a heart of stone. Far from it. You may take it that I have already discovered what it is made of.' Bessie raised her eyebrows, and then we heard yells from the yard. I went out onto the landing and looked out of the window, and saw Owain striding towards the house, with the children rushing to greet him. He had no hat on his head. He wore a white shirt, open to the chest, blue breeches and black boots, and he carried a chestnut walking stick with a horn handle. I suddenly realized that my heart was pounding, and I felt like a fifteen-year-old who has just encountered love for the first time. Bessie knew exactly what was in my heart, and she pushed me towards the stairs.

'Off you go, Mistress,' she said. 'You are as ready as you ever will be. And I hope that you have the most wonderful day. You deserve it.' And as she gave me a little kiss on the cheek, I noticed that she had a tear in her eye.

No sooner had I welcomed Owain than the carriage from Trecwn came round the corner and into the yard, with dogs barking and more excitement from the children. There were embraces all round, and Uncle Owain swept up his little nephew William and swung him round until he got giddy, and then he had to do the same for Dewi and Sara as well. Luckily Betsi and Daisy did not insist on the same treatment, for they are both

377

reaching an age at which decorum matters. Mary Jane and Dafydd freshened themselves up in my dressing room, and without further ado we were off. I did not want any of the servants to accompany us, so Owain and Dafydd carried the big hamper between them, Mary Jane and I carried the smaller wicker baskets, and the children carried blankets and cloths and napkins in little baskets of their own. I had decided in advance that we should visit the waterfall near Cilgwyn Mill, just half a mile from the Plas. In no time at all we were there, spreading our blankets out on the mossy banks of the river, dappled with sunlight and shade. The sound of the waterfall dominated everything, although in truth it is only about ten feet high and in other circles might be dismissed as a very insignificant cataract. But it is beautiful none the less, with white water and bluestone boulders, and deep pools above and below it, and mosses, ferns and liverworts bobbing about in the spray.

Now that it is late, and I am sitting at my desk with book before me and pen in hand, I realize that I have no wish to record in detail the little happenings of the afternoon. My memories are hazy, and mellow, and very happy indeed. We all ate and drank far too much, and my guests were afterwards full of praise for the most wonderful picnic they had ever enjoyed. The five children had a wild and energetic time, playing silly games on the river bank, throwing flat pebbles and trying to make them bounce on the water, exploring in nooks and crannies, collecting berries, and trying to catch fish. They gathered different sorts of leaves, red and yellow and gold now that the autumnal colourings are spreading across the woodland canopy. Owain devoted more time to them than he did to me, and sang songs for them and told them nonsense rhymes. I did not mind one little bit, and loved every minute of watching them together. Once, I caught Mary Jane's eye as she watched me watching them, and she gave me the sweetest and gentlest of smiles.

When we had the chance we four adults lay on our backs listening to the sounds of falling water, busy insects and woodland birds. Owain and I talked endlessly, with the children and with each other, and I was greatly touched when Mary Jane and Dafydd took all of the little ones for a few minutes and went off hunting for squirrels and otters with them. With all that noise going on there was not the slightest chance of finding anything with four legs, but the joy was in the searching rather than the finding. While they were away Owain held my hand and sent a wave of emotion through me from head to toe; he wanted to say something, but before he could find the right words Dewi, my sweet angel, came rushing up with the intention of showing us a big orange slug, and the moment passed. Such is life in the real world, we thought, as we exchanged smiles.

After three perfect hours in our wooded dell, the children started to get tired. William and Sara were so exhausted that they fell asleep on our big blanket. Quietly we packed everything up, and we left the big hamper at the side of the waterfall so that Owain and Dafydd could carry the little ones home. I said that I would ask Will and Shemi to fetch the hamper later on, and indeed they did, with the reward of finishing off the remains of the picnic feast. So we made our weary way home, with Owain carrying Sara and Dafydd carrying his little boy, and we women dragging the other tired children along behind. As I watched Owain striding ahead with my sweet baby in his arms, I realized that what I have in my heart is more than respect, more than admiration, more than affection.

Although I hardly dare to write these words in the

pages of my diary, and I feel a flutter of apprehension in my breast, I think that I have found love again.

5 October 1806

For the last two days I have not been able, nor have I tried, to keep Owain out of my mind. It is probably perfectly obvious to everybody in the house that I am in love, but they are undoubtedly happy with the fact, and so am I. The picnic taught me – as I thought it might – many new things about this fine and gentle man, and not least his easy and loving relationship with his sister and her family, and with my own beloved children. They adore him and love every minute in his company, and I am inclined to trust their judgement.

Yesterday morning I received another pretty bouquet of flowers from Owain, and another little poem. I did not read this one out loud for the rest of the family, and that was just as well, for it is specifically a poem about me, and I am not inclined to share it with anybody. I will slip it between the pages of my diary and keep it there, and look at it often. With the poem there was a little note, thanking me for the pleasantest afternoon of his whole life, and expressing the joy he felt in my company and in the sweet innocence of my children.

My dearest Martha, he wrote, *every time I meet you, every time I tread the same sweet earth as you and breathe the same fragrant air, I lose a little more of my heart and find it replaced by yours. I rejoice in the fact that your beauty fills my heart and my mind, so that everything else by comparison appears grey and dismal. I have things to tell you, and soon. May I call in on Friday next, in the middle of the morning? Please agree to it, or I fear that you will break my heart.*

Your loving friend Owain.

What was I to make of that? Of course I agreed to it, and responded as warmly as might be appropriate. Now I am like an excited child, and can hardly wait for Friday to come. I am warmed by the glow of my own love, and warmed further by the passion of as good and beautiful a man as I am ever likely to meet. I am as sure as I ever have been about anything that on Friday Owain will declare his love for me. I have spoken again to Grandma and Grandpa, for they must have mixed emotions about the imminent arrival of a new man to take the place of our beloved David; but they are as generous as they are wise, and I have their blessing.

My sense of euphoria is disturbed, to some small degree, by news which came today from Fishguard. There was a message from Lewis Legal, the faithful attorney who has looked after our family affairs for many years. He reported that there was a burglary in his office last night, executed with considerable skill. No money was taken from his safe, and indeed no attempt was made to break into it; but many of his piles of dusty documents were rifled through, and some papers were taken. He is still trying to discover what is missing, but he is certain that the thieves have taken an old map of the Plas Ingli estate, and also the estate accounts for the last ten years. He says that he has not reported the loss to the Fishguard constable, who is an idiot, but that he has asked Joseph Harries to investigate. He is sure, as am I, that Joseph will get to the bottom of this affair and will bring the guilty person or persons to justice. Master Lewis says that he would like to keep the burglary quiet, but he fears that news of it will soon be all over town. Two of his junior clerks discovered the ransacked office when they came in to work early in the morning, and a carpenter and a glazier will be needed to repair the damage done. He says, with some resignation, that he cannot depend upon their discretion.

I shared this information with Grandpa, and he appeared neither surprised nor worried. 'Huh!' said he. 'This could be the work of any one of the fellows who are obsessed with the Plas Ingli pot of gold – or maybe several of them working together. God knows what they think they will learn from what they have stolen. Do they think they will find a cross on the map with the words "Here be Treasure" alongside it? And our financial affairs are pretty well common knowledge anyway, down to the rents we receive and the tithes we pay. If I were you, my dear, I shouldn't bother too much about this. You have other far more important things to concentrate upon.'

8 October 1806

Today it is a Black Thursday, and I have been dragged from the breezy heights of elation and expectation and cast, not for the first time, into a dark and desolate pit. Is it my fate in life to see happiness before me, just beyond my fingertips, and to reach for it with the eagerness of a child, and to see it then cruelly snatched away? My day of misery started in the middle of the morning, when Owain's man brought an envelope for me. I was a little surprised, since Owain was due to call and see me – as I thought, in order to declare his love – on the morrow. But I took the envelope up to my room, opened it with eager fingers, and read the note inside. It was short and to the point. This is what it said:

> *Llannerch, Thursday the 8th day of October 1806*
> *My dearest Martha,*
> *Please forgive me, but our meeting arranged with much eager*

anticipation on my part for tomorrow had better be called off. Something has happened which, when you find out about it, will undoubtedly cause you great distress, and I am eternally sorry about it. I have been naive, and I am appalled that people should think so ill of me, and that you and your reputation should have been harmed as a consequence.

In the circumstances both you and I need time to reflect. Please be assured that concern for your happiness is uppermost in my mind, and that every moment away from you is a moment of suffering.

Your loving friend Owain

When I had read it I felt as if my heart had been turned to stone and that the blood in my veins had been transformed into ice. I sat staring out of the window for I know not how long, and then read the letter again and again. I could not understand its language, or the cause of its writing. What was happening to me? What was happening to Owain? How was it that a man so sensitive and so kind only a few short days ago could write such a letter today?

The house was quiet, and I thanked God that the children were away with the little ones from Penrhiw collecting mushrooms in Parc Newydd. After a while there was a gentle knock on the door, and Bessie appeared. I had my back to her as I sat by the window. 'Mistress Martha,' she said, 'the man from Llannerch is still here, and he wonders if there might be a reply.' I shook my head. Bessie could not see my face, but she knew at once that there was something wrong. 'I will return straight away, Mistress,' she said, and ran downstairs to send Owain's man on his way. Then she came upstairs again with a glass of water, and insisted that I take a few sips.

She sat next to me, and put her arm round my

shoulder, and at that point my self-control dissolved, and I wept. She let me weep until there were no tears left in my heart. And then she said gently: 'The letter from Owain?' I nodded, and wiped my eyes and tried to compose myself. 'Would you like me to read it too?' I nodded again.

Bessie read it, and read it a second time. Then she said: 'I think I know, Mistress, what this is all about. A very difficult situation has arisen. But it is obvious from the letter that he loves you.'

'You think so? That is not the way it looks to me. From where I sit, this looks like a letter which terminates our relationship and dashes all my hopes of happiness.'

'No, Mistress. Look at it again. His heart is broken and I suspect that his suffering is even greater than yours. But damage can always be repaired, and you must never give up hope!'

I smiled slightly and was just a little reassured by her optimism. 'Now then,' she continued, 'your eyes have been full of stars these last few days since the picnic, and you may not have paid attention to what has been going on in town. There has been a certain amount of malicious gossip. I hoped it would go away, but it obviously has not, and now it has reached the ears of Master Owain out at Llannerch. He is even more isolated from the affairs of the world than you are.'

'Malicious gossip? About me and Owain?' I asked. 'Surely there must be a mistake, since both he and I have taken great care to act with the utmost discretion at all times.'

'True, Mistress, and he is such a gentleman that I dare say he thinks very deeply about touching your hand, let alone any other part of you. But this is not about the extent of your relationship. I fear that it is more serious.'

384

Again I felt the blood draining out of my face, and I was grateful that I was not standing up. 'Dear Bessie,' I whispered. 'You had better tell me.'

'If you will forgive me, Mistress, I would prefer that you should be told by Master Isaac and Mistress Jane, for they were in town yesterday and will be more aware of what is a somewhat technical matter.'

'All right, Bessie. If they are in the house now, would you please go and fetch them?'

So Bessie departed, and ten minutes later Grandma and Grandpa came up to my room. They looked quite distressed, and it was clear to me that Bessie had told them about Owain's letter and my reaction to it. I showed them the fateful piece of paper. They read it, and then I asked them to explain to me what was going on.

We sat, all three of us, on the edge of the bed. 'Let us start at the beginning,' said Grandpa. 'Some of this goes back to the time of the Beating of the Bounds, when you and Owain clearly took some pleasure in each other's company, which was there for all the wide and inquisitive world to see . . .'

'I had nothing to hide!' I blurted out. 'If I enjoy another's company, man or woman, I am not afraid to show it, and I will not conduct my social life in dark corners and behind closed doors!'

'Calm down, Martha *bach*,' said Grandma, and placed her hand upon mine. 'Just hear Isaac out.'

'I am sorry,' said I. 'I did not mean to be rude.'

'Don't worry, Martha. I appreciate that things are difficult for you. At any rate, on the day after the peregrination round the parish boundaries, certain whisperings began in town to the effect that Owain was setting his sights upon you as a very desirable widow with an estate much larger and more profitable than his own.'

385

Now all the blood that had previously drained out of my face returned with a rush, and I said: 'But that is preposterous! I have never met anybody in my life who is less cynical and calculating than Master Owain!'

'That may well be. But tongues were wagging in any case. Remember that Owain is a second son with no great prospects. His estate was impoverished when he took it over, and is only worth six hundred pounds a year. Plas Ingli is worth at least three times as much, and people have seen how it has risen like a phoenix after the fire of 1794 to the point where it now has five tenanted farms, and hardly any debts.'

'Quite so!' said I, with my eyes blazing. 'Through hard work and dedication on the part of you two good people, and your son William, and your grandson David, and now all of us beneath this roof! And have we not already paid a sufficient price for our success?'

Grandma saw that I was close to tears again, and she put her arm round me. Grandpa stopped for a few moments while I took another sip of water. Then he continued. 'You, and all of us in this house, know that he is an honourable man, and we are sure that he loves you. But that may not be as it appears to certain small-minded people in town. Remember that as the law stands, if Owain marries you he will become the Master of a very large estate. Plas Ingli and Llannerch will be joined. He will be transformed from being a slightly eccentric small squire – with more interest in poetry than in pigs – into a very powerful gentleman indeed. Certain people may not feel comfortable with that, and others will actually be threatened by it.'

Now my passion was spent, and I gave way again to despair. I buried my head in my hands and sighed, deep and long, for the loss of innocence and the loss of love. 'There now, Martha,' said Grandma Jane, in a voice full of consolation. But in truth she did not know what else to say.

'So for better or for worse,' continued Grandpa, 'there are those in town who are intent upon painting Owain as a rogue and a calculating opportunist, and portraying you as an innocent and gullible widow with a young family, and desperate for male company. Such talk was probably inevitable, and I curse myself for not warning you of it. You were so happy in your growing love, Martha my dear, that I could not bear to say anything that might disturb your innocent pleasure. God knows you have had little enough of innocence, and little enough of pleasure. I am so, so sorry that this has happened.'

I moaned again, and there was a long silence. At last I said: 'Grandpa, where are these rumours coming from?'

'We are not sure, my dear. Your friends, quite unknown to you, have been looking into it. But I feel certain that the people behind this whispering campaign are Rice, Watkins, Lloyd, and Beynon. John Fenton is not a happy man either, especially since you have snubbed him on at least two occasions. He may have something to do with it.'

'I am sure you are right. Oh dear, is there no end to their wickedness? Can they not just leave me alone, so that I may try to find some happiness?'

'I fear, Martha, that there may be worse to come,' said Grandpa, with his jaw set firm. 'They are not finished with us yet. But neither are we finished with them. We have the weight of the law behind us, and the support of the people of the town. We will defeat them, you take it from me. But we will need great resolve and just a little cunning.'

There was another long silence. Then I said: 'Is that it, Grandpa? I think it is probably enough for today.'

'I am afraid, Martha *bach*, that it is not. There is another element to the gossip, and you had better hear it from me rather than from somebody else. Are you strong enough?'

'I think so. I am rather experienced at listening to bad news.'

'It is something that I also expected, but failed to warn you about. You heard about the burglary at Lewis Legal's office in Fishguard?'

'Yes, of course. No great damage done, and nothing much lost, by all accounts. Have you and I not already concluded that one of our enemies was behind it?'

'Indeed we have. And I still believe that to be true. But the talk in town is that Owain was behind it.'

'Owain? But that is preposterous! Owain involved in petty crime? I have never met a man who is less inclined to criminal activities in all my life.'

'Quite so. You know that, and so do all those who know him. But for those who do not know him, or who wish to harm him, the burglary is very convenient indeed. For the wagging tongues of Newport, the idea of Owain stealing Plas Ingli maps and checking up on the estate accounts is a godsend; according to them, the wicked and grasping fellow was simply doing a little additional research, and was checking up on your assets before seriously setting about the task of acquiring them.'

Grandma Jane then stood up in front of me. She managed a little smile. 'And that, Martha, is the extent of our bad news,' she said. 'You may now appreciate, I think, the reason for Owain's letter. The poor fellow had to do something. What he did may have been hasty and ill-judged, and maybe his words might have been more diplomatic, but he has acted for the best. He is quite right in thinking that any contact between you in the near future will be misconstrued, and may well lead to further malicious chatter. You and he will both be harmed. Do you see that?'

'I suppose so,' I said bleakly. 'Do you think he still loves me?'

'Of course he does,' replied Grandma. 'It is perfectly obvious from his letter.'

'Can you just be patient for a few days, my dear?' asked Grandpa. 'We may well get further news from town, and you may be assured that many people are working on your behalf in order to get to the bottom of this business.'

'Should I write to Owain?'

'Maybe you should. But my advice would be to wait for a day or two until you have calmed down and had more time to disentangle this complicated business inside your head. And maybe your heart needs a day or two to recover, too.'

And so we decided to leave things for a little while. The rest of the day has passed in a black haze, and I have little recollection of anything else that happened at mealtimes, or round about the house, or with respect to the children. Sian has taken good care of them and protected them from too much contact with my desolate mood; and dear Bessie and Grandma Jane have taken care of me. I cannot write more. I trust that I will find some consolation in sleep, and that the haze will clear away with the dawning of a new day.

11 October 1806

Three days have passed since I received Owain's letter, and they have been three days of misery and confusion. I have tried to maintain some sort of normality in my life, and have tried to be a loving mother to the children and a fair Mistress to my servants. But I have read the letter a hundred times more, and I still cannot understand why Owain should have acted so precipitately, and why he wrote in terms which were bound to cause me distress. Why did he not have the courage to come and see me instead of writing? He seems to think that by cutting off contact he is acting to protect me – but could it be that his main interest is to protect himself and his reputation? And is he really a free agent? He is very loyal to his father, and it may be that he is under pressure from the old Squire to protect not just his own reputation but also the good name of the Laugharne family. I feel as if I am trapped in a maze; every time I explore a new avenue I come to a dead end, and I still cannot find the way out.

And I am lonely. I long to talk to Owain, and I long for his company, for the touch of his hand, for the warmth of his smile. I dare not think ill of him. I have already given him so much of my heart that if I betray him, or hurt him, I fear that he will walk away and take it with him. And what then? An empty landscape, devoid of warmth and security and passion, stretching away to the far horizon. That is not the world I wish to inhabit.

This morning, dismayed by my own inability to affect the course of events, I recalled the promise that I made to myself more than a year ago – namely that I would seek to make my own destiny. The advice I have been given by everyone in this house is that I should not act without due consideration, that I should be patient, that I should await developments. In other words, that I should do nothing. But for days, or weeks, or months? I decided that I could not for a moment longer live with this uncertainty and inactivity. I was certain that Owain would be working hard to undo the harm that has been done to us by wicked tongues. I wanted to find out what his strategy was, and considered setting off, there and then, for Llannerch. But then it occurred to me that such a move might cause difficulty for him, or his servants, and might be seen by others as the action of a huntress in pursuit of her quarry; so I thought better of it. I went to see Joseph instead.

I walked over the mountain, surrounded by swirling cloud and anointed occasionally by flurries of rain, and felt better for it. As luck would have it, the Werndew front door was wide open. Joseph was in his kitchen, crushing up some dried herbs with a mortar and pestle. As soon as he saw me in the doorway he dropped what he was doing, and rushed over to me. 'My dear Martha!' he said. 'How good it is to see you. I have been expecting you for three days.'

'How can that be?'

'You are in deep trouble just now, and you always come to see me when you are in trouble.'

'You are quite right, Joseph. I am very miserable indeed. I just do not know what I should do next . . .'
And I am afraid that at that point I dissolved into tears, and flung my arms round his neck, and hung on to him for dear life, and soaked his collar. He said nothing, but stroked my head as a father would with a small child, until I stopped my sobbing. Then he sat me down at his fireside, and made a pot of tea.

'You know about the wicked rumours which have been flying around about Owain and me?'

'Of course, my dear friend. I have been aware of them for a month or maybe more.'

'Then why did you not tell me about them when we met a couple of weeks ago? That would have been a kindness.'

'In retrospect, you are right. But we had other matters to discuss. And like Master Isaac, I hoped that they would simply fade away, as most silly rumours do. I was surprised when Owain came to consult me on the matter just a few days ago. He reported that, on the contrary, they had increased in intensity, and the burglary at Lewis Legal's office in Fishguard has added another dimension.'

'But Joseph, when rumours spread across the land-scape like smoke, upwind there has to be a fire, and somebody has to feed the fire.'

'Yes, and we have all been trying to find out who that person or persons may be. Between us, Owain and I have been making enquiries. He has been working like a man possessed, trying to protect you from the accusation that you are a man-hunting widow . . .'

'Just as my instinct, Joseph, is to try to protect him from the slander that he is a cynical and opportunistic squire seeking a good marriage.'

And then Joseph suddenly burst out laughing, and slapped his thighs in that disconcerting way of his. 'What a funny business this is!' he exclaimed. 'Two dear friends of mine, forced apart but longing to be together, each one trying to protect the other from the slanders of some petty fellows with wagging tongues. Cheer up, Martha. This is a very small drama indeed. Nobody is actually getting hurt . . .'

'Excuse me, but I am terribly hurt, and so, I suspect, is Owain.'

'Of course. You are quite right. I am sorry to appear so flippant. It is a bad habit of mine. Do you love him?'

I was greatly taken aback by this question out of the blue. But I swallowed hard and nodded.

'Good, good. He is a splendid fellow, and you could not do better than to give him your affection. You know, I suppose, that he loves you?'

'I have dared to hope that,' said I. 'But I have not been

certain of it, and a letter which he recently wrote to me caused me such distress that my uncertainty has turned into doubt.'

'Do not doubt it for a moment, Martha. I suspect that Owain has hardly slept for the last three days, and he and his friends in town have been moving mountains in order to track down the source of the rumours. Certain fellows whom Owain trusts have spoken quietly to many of the locals, and have bought a great many jars of ale for them. They have tracked back from one source to another, very diplomatically, with a hundred trails reducing to fifty, and fifty to twenty-five, and so forth. All of the trails lead eventually to Alban Watkins and Joseph Rice.'

I sighed from sheer relief. 'I thought as much. And there is no room for doubt?'

'Not a shadow of doubt. Owain's sources are impeccable.'

'Something must be done about it, Joseph!' said I, suddenly fired up with enthusiasm. 'This very day, before setting out over the mountain, I decided that I should not allow the waves of cruel fate to wash over me, but that I should take decisive action and make my own destiny. The trouble is, I do not know what decisive action to take.'

Joseph burst out laughing again. 'Dear Martha,' he chuckled. 'You are quite wonderful! Owain, if he wins your hand, will never have to endure a dull moment once you and he are beneath the same roof! I understand your impatience, but I urge you not to take any action that might conflict with what Owain is doing. I am not a party to all his plans. But I can tell you that at his behest, and with instructions from Lewis Legal, I am looking into the burglary. I have examined the office in Fishguard, and am following a number of very interesting lines of evidence. I expect to have identified the culprit, and the name of the person who hired him, within a few days. You and Owain will be the first to know. Owain can then expose these malicious rumours for what they are, and we will have solid grounds for several indictments. Convictions will certainly follow.'

'Thank you, Joseph. I do hope you are right. I will keep a low profile for the moment. But I can admit to you, as my oldest and dearest friend, that I am longing to see Owain again and to talk over all these matters with him. Is there some way in which we can meet in secret? Can you arrange it?'

Joseph took several sips from his cup of tea, and ate a slice of fruit cake. Then, after several minutes, he said: 'I have a better idea. Why not meet in public, and expose the activities of Watkins and Rice before the very people whose support you need – the ladies and gentlemen of the north Pembrokeshire gentry? In two weeks one of the biggest events of the social calendar will be taking place at Glynymel – Squire Richard Fenton's Autumn Ball. The Squire has the highest regard for you. I am already invited, and old Master Fenton owes me a few favours. With a little encouragement from me he will invite both you and Owain. I will find an opportune moment during the proceedings to denounce the perpetrators of the Fishguard burglary, and I will also present evidence that Rice and Watkins are responsible for the foul rumours which have afflicted you. They are both social outcasts anyway, and people will accept my evidence. Then it is up to you and Owain to demonstrate, in whichever manner you choose, that your relationship is based upon affection rather than convenience.'

'Dear Joseph! Thank you! I will do it! Several crows to

394

be killed with one stone. Do you think that Owain will co-operate?'

'Of course he will. The proposal which I have devised will appeal to his romantic nature. Besides, does he not love you?'

And with my spirits lifted, I thanked Joseph yet again for the provision of a shoulder to weep on, for his keen listening ear, for his wise counsel, and for his tea and fruit cake. I walked home over the common through the drizzle, and was not at all bothered about getting wet.

20 October 1806

In the last week or so there have been a number of developments, most of which are quite pleasing to me.

On the domestic front, the children are thriving, and in the last few days I have been able to give them more of my attention and more of my love since my own temperament has been more settled. Daisy is still a difficult child, liable to sulks and tantrums; but Betsi, who is three years older, is very loving and attentive with her, and is a very responsible big sister. They are both, in their own ways, as pretty and dainty as little fairies. Dewi, three years old and still full of the wonders of creation, is a little fellow who will, in years to come, have young ladies swooning at his feet; with his rosy cheeks, tousled blond hair and wide brown eyes he charms everybody he meets. He is certainly the most handsome little boy in the world; but I have to admit, in my calmer moments, that I may be prejudiced. And Sara *bach*, the apple of my eye, my gift in compensation for the death of David, is as calm and lovely as ever; she is now nineteen months old, and her vocabulary is increasing by the day. Sian is a wonderful nursemaid, growing in her skills as her little charges grow around her. Without her, God only knows how I would have carried my dear family through the last two years of tribulation.

The anger which I feel in my breast whenever I think of my enemies is lessened to some degree by news of the misfortunes which afflict them. Will, Gethin, Patty and other friends who keep an eye on things in Newport have reported on all of them, and I feel a degree of quiet satisfaction about the manner in which their lives are falling apart.

Lloyd and Beynon have made alternative arrangements for the collection of their tribute from Joseph Rice; Skiff has not yet worked out the new system, but he is confident that more golden sovereigns will come his way before long. Beynon is still at Berry Hill, living at the expense of those members of his large family who know how to do an honest day's work. The arm which he broke during the struggle prior to the killing of my dear husband is deformed, and still gives him pain. He is a haunted man, and he is more convinced with every passing day that curses placed by a wizard and a witch are the cause of all his misfortunes.

There is very bad blood between Rice and Lloyd, and their mutual animosity has been increased by the public humiliations which they have both received at the hands of the *Ceffyl Pren*. Rice does not know which way to turn in his attempts to find a dishonest sovereign or two, for he has Truscott and the Revenue men pressing him eastwards and the *Ceffyl Pren* pressing him west. Patty is aware of his weakening position, and she has felt secure enough (with a little encouragement from me) to reduce the proportion of her takings that she hands over to him. He cannot harm her, for without her he would starve. He still behaves like a man on the run, and still hires the two local bullies called Sion and Huw ap Ifan to look after him. How he pays them, or what hold he has over them, is a mystery at present.

The episode with the *Ceffyl Pren* was the last straw for Matthew Lloyd's young wife; she has left him and returned to her parents in Brynberian, and she has taken their small child with her. For some weeks he has lived on his own in his dark hovel on the Cwmgloyn estate, still estranged from his brother Meredith, and still suffering from the injury received in the duel with Rice. I know how he finds the money that he has to pay over for the upkeep of his bastard child; but I cannot imagine how he finds the money he needs for food, and ale, and clothing.

I am told that this very morning our friends from London have moved out of their lodging house (or rather, they were thrown out for not paying their rent) and have moved in with Lloyd. His accommodation presumably comes somewhat cheaper. It was inevitable, in my mind, that Masters Elias and Smyllie would eventually form an alliance with Lloyd and Beynon; they have no great affection for Alban Watkins, and their only interest is in keeping a watchful eye on him. And they have nothing in common with Rice or Howell, who belong to the social group loosely referred to as 'fallen gentry'.

And talking of the fallen gentry, I have received no recent news of Master John Fenton. He may have moved down to Tenby, as he often does in the autumn; or he may be lurking unseen in the bushes. I have my doubts about the latter possibility, since he is not built for lurking, and he would not wish to get his breeches dirty.

Three days since, Joseph sent me a note with further information on the ending of Captain John Howell's military career. Apparently he has not been in France at all, but has been based in various places along the east coast of England, originally waiting for Master Bonaparte to invade, and more recently celebrating the fact that the French army has gone off to do something else instead. Some army officers have obviously had too little fighting to do, and too much time on their hands, for Howell was eventually hauled up before his superiors for something that happened in a house of ill repute in Rye. It was not serious enough to justify a court martial, but he was stripped of his colours and sent packing in disgrace. So here he is again. His brother-in-law has thrown him out of his house in Fishguard, and he has moved in with Rice down on the Parrog. I hear that he has money in his pocket, presumably the last of his army pay, but he will have no pension and he has been stripped of his uniform, his status and his pride. He is surly and arrogant, but he is a more sophisticated bully than Ifan Beynon. He also infuriates almost everybody he meets by demanding respect without earning it; this sort of behaviour does not go down well in Newport. According to the innkeepers of the town he is not a happy fellow, and he has already been involved in three nasty fistfights with the locals.

As for Watkins, he is living with an old cousin in town, and is being carefully watched by Smyllie and Elias, and various others as well. He is still sporting a black eye and various other facial injuries acquired during his beating by the Londoners; and he holds his stomach as he walks, as if he is in pain. The assumption that he would form an alliance with Rice and Howell was well founded; they have been seen together on many occasions, and Will reports to me that the Plas Ingli treasure is consistently one of their topics of conversation. Last week, one of my spies spotted him at a cock-fight in Pengelli Woods, where he put down six golden sovereigns on a white rooster and lost it all.

He had been drinking heavily and attacked the man who had taken his money off him, upon which he was dragged away and slung into a muddy pool in order to cool off. He stormed off, covered in mud and slime, and swearing vengeance on all and sundry, as is his wont.

On the matter of the rumours relating to Owain and myself, more evidence has emerged to confirm the finding that Rice and Watkins are the instigators. Will and Patty have both told me that they have no doubts on the matter, and indeed Rice has boasted and laughed about the difficulties which he has caused us on a number of occasions. I have also been pleased to discover that Owain and his confederates have started a campaign of counter-rumours to the effect that Rice and Watkins are acting maliciously out of a desire for revenge against our two families, having both lost their estates – and indeed their families – because of their own evil conspiracies in the past. This is no rumour but the truth. The townspeople know most of the details already, and I am optimistic that any further lies spread by these evil fellows will fall upon stony ground and transform themselves into weeds that will choke them.

My latest message from Joseph about the burglary in Fishguard is that his enquiries are close to a conclusion, and that he is confident of tying up all loose ends within the next few days. I am as certain as can be that at the ball on Friday all will be revealed.

In writing all of this, I am struck by the fact that the enemies lined up against me are miserable fellows, malcontents and misfits to a man. Do they have any happiness, any colour, any music, any serenity in their lives? I doubt it. They creep about in the shadows, afraid of everything that moves. They are all surrounded by mistrust, and intrigue, and hate. My intuition tells me that each one of them expects to die a violent death, and that this will indeed come to pass. Any one would betray his cronies in exchange for a silver shilling, driven by a lust for power and for wealth, living in a fantasy world, dreaming about things that are unattainable, unaware that while they squander time life is slipping by. Maybe they are only sustained by dreams, since the reality they know is too painful to bear. In writing thus about them I am almost sorry for them, and wish that I could help them; but then I am forcefully reminded that these men are evil. They have no respect for the sanctity of life, no experience or understanding of beauty, no conception of what it is to love. Four of them, now gathered together in Newport, are the four men who murdered my husband, and I have sworn that they will pay a just price. I vowed long ago that I would have no dealings with them and would not exchange a single word with them until each and every one of them is sentenced to hang. I hold firm to that vow. As for the others, like Watkins and Fenton, Smyllie and Elias, they are evil, but perhaps to a lesser degree; and for them, I am happy to let justice take its course.

Enough of these dark and dismal matters. I have also to record that yesterday I received a most beautiful invitation, as did Grandpa Isaac and Grandma Jane, to the Glynymel Autumn Ball. On the back of my card, old Squire Fenton had written:

My dear Mistress Martha, I do hope that you will grace our little celebration with your beauty. You may also be interested to know that an invitation has gone to Master Laugharne of Llannerch. Your friend Richard Fenton.

This little note brought me just as much pleasure as the invitation itself, for it signalled the fact that Squire Fenton, his wife and probably many of his confederates were already treating the foul rumours about Owain and me with the contempt they deserve. The old man wishes us well, and that means a great deal to me.

And to cap it all, this morning I received another bunch of flowers from Owain, with a little note attached. It said:

My dearest Martha, I have received a kind invitation to Squire Fenton's Autumn Ball. I understand that you have also been invited. I cannot wait to meet you there, and am counting down the hours. I have spoken to Joseph, and am aware of developments. I pray to God that at the ball, among our friends, we will be able to clear away mistrust and establish that your affections, and mine, are spontaneously and naturally given and received. Your loving friend and admirer, Owain.

What more is there to add? We are six days away from the ball. I will try not to appear too preoccupied with the business of counting between now and then, but in one hundred and forty hours from now I hope, God willing, to touch Owain's hand, and look into his eyes, and show the world that I have given him my heart.

27 October 1806

I am ashamed, and distraught, and overwhelmed by revulsion at the recollection of my own disgraceful behaviour. I hardly dare write about it, but I must; in writing these words I may do my penance and learn my lesson. Maybe I will read them again in the years to come, and feel shame welling up inside me, and that will be as it should be.

The Glynymel ball was a time of joy for almost everybody else, and a time of infamy for me. My departure

401

from virtue and my descent into intemperance began before I left the Plas. I spent almost the whole day getting ready, and gave attention to the minutest details of my dress, my hair, my cleavage, my jewellery, my eyes, my lips, and my complexion. I was so excited that I could not eat, and that was the start of my downfall. How Bessie put up with my irritable and ungrateful comments throughout the day, I shall never know. She is truly an angel. I have never been a bride preparing for a wedding, since my own marriage to David was a secret and furtive affair; but I suppose I felt the same turbulent emotions, perspiring palms, obsession with detail, and physical expectation, as a virgin bride on the way to the altar. It was all quite absurd, and in retrospect no way for the respectable Mistress of Plas Ingli, widow and mother of four, to behave. But I could not help myself, and I suppose that the emotional highs and lows of my relationship with Owain must have had something to do with it.

We were due to leave at seven of the clock, and while Billy prepared the carriage and Grandma and Grandpa were getting dressed in their room I was already treading water and listening to the ticking of the clock. I asked Bessie for a stiff drink of brandy to calm my nerves. 'I would not advise it, Mistress,' she said. 'You have eaten nothing all day, and it will surely go to your head.' But I behaved like a petulant child, and insisted on it. Then, half an hour later, I had another stiff brandy, while Bessie's face registered dismay and apprehension in equal measure.

Then off we went, on a fine dry evening. The old folks and the servants were very tolerant of the fact that I was slightly tipsy as I climbed into the carriage with Billy's help. They all knew that my excitement was related to the fact that I would meet Owain again after a difficult three weeks filled with misunderstandings and rumours. What they did not know was that there would also be a theatrical performance from Joseph during which the villainy of Rice and Watkins, and possibly others, would be revealed.

We arrived in a crunching of wheels and a clattering of hooves at the front door of Glynymel. The house is big, and very beautiful, and there were candle lanterns everywhere, in all of the windows, around the yard, among the trees and in the garden. There was a silver moon in the sky, and although it was too cool for nocturnal promenades under the stars I thought it a perfect evening for romance. Squire Fenton and his wife Anne were on the front doorstep, and they greeted us with warmth and courtesy. There seemed to be servants everywhere, and the place was already filling with guests. Grandma and I were shown to the Ladies' Room, where we duly made ourselves presentable. She looked slim and very elegant, and I was once again reminded forcefully that she is only a little over sixty, with a bloom upon her cheek and a spring in her step. No wonder, I thought, that Grandpa Isaac is still very much in love with her after all their years together.

Then we went and mingled. Many of my friends were there, including Ellie and Mary Jane, and we chatted, and laughed, and sampled the good things laid out in the music room. The food looked excellent – delicate and imaginative – and the drinks were like nectar. There was a quartet playing in the parlour, where in due course there would be dancing. There were a few army officers present, doing their best to look dashing, but most of the guests were members of the local gentry and wealthy merchants and their wives from Fishguard and Newport. Among the younger people were some of those who had set their sights on me in past months, and

I did my best to behave with due courtesy when they now greeted me and asked after my health.

But in truth my memories of the first part of the evening are somewhat hazy, for I was paying hardly any attention to what went on around me. I was waiting for Owain. Every time a coach drew up at the front of the house I found my way to one of the French windows to see whether it was he who descended and came into the house. An hour or more passed, and still he did not come. Mary Jane saw my concern, and indeed she was a little worried herself about the non-appearance of her dear brother; but she had to give most of her attention to her husband Dafydd, who wanted to eat first and dance second. Grandpa and Grandma also saw the concern writ large upon my face, and they too became apprehensive. But they could not devote all their time to looking after me, for many other guests were intent upon talking to them and sharing the latest gossip concerning local families. So I passed from one group of friends and acquaintances to another, and for most of the time I had a glass in my hand. I should have been hungry, but when the large cold table was attacked by a multitude of guests armed with Wedgwood plates, silver cutlery and linen napkins, I was not among them.

Then Joseph arrived, very late. He found his way over to me, and there was concern on his face. I was not sure at first whether his concern was caused by my flushed cheeks and erratic movements, or whether there was something more serious behind it. He took me to one side where nobody else would overhear us. 'Martha, my dear,' he whispered. 'You have been drinking too much. I urge you to be cautious. I am late because I have had a strong premonition that something has happened to Owain. Something else has occurred, too, which means that I will not be able to speak as we planned this evening. Do you understand?'

I was struck dumb by this revelation, and all I could do was nod. 'I must now go and talk to Squire Fenton in the privacy of his study,' he said. 'I will be back in a few minutes. Are you all right here?' I nodded again, and off he went.

I know not why, but I was overtaken by despair. I was terrified, and lonely, and like an idiot I convinced myself in an instant that I had been abandoned. Owain, the man to whom I had given my heart, was no man at all. At the first sign of controversy, on first discovering the whisperings about his motives in seeking my affection, he had turned and run. Poet, artist, dreamer, sender of sweet messages and posies of flowers. A fellow with no spine, and feet of clay. How dared he deceive me and lead me along, right up to the last message of just a few days ago? How dared he leave me in this throng of people, abandoned to their ridicule and scorn? I was incandescent with fury, and at the same time utterly distraught. I could not bear, in the circumstances, to remain for a moment longer in the company of jolly people who were talking, and laughing, and eating and drinking, and dancing. The gentlemen of the orchestra, fiddling away furiously, mocked me as their music invited guests to step out with smiles upon their faces and flirt discreetly with one another on the dance floor. I felt physically sick. I knew that I must either become hysterical and destroy my reputation for ever, or run and find a sanctuary somewhere.

With tears welling up in my eyes, I slipped away from the parlour, nodded to the servants in the entrance hallway, and fled up the main staircase. I think I was looking for the drawing room, but in truth I had not the faintest idea where it was. I found myself on a long landing with doors on either side. I panicked, and I think I may have collapsed. Then I realized that somebody was holding me in a tight embrace, and saying, 'There there, Mistress Martha, everything will be all right.' And I broke down and wept, for I know not how long. I did not know it at the time, but the man holding me and caressing me was Master John Fenton.

My memories are hazy, but I recall that very gently, while I was still weeping as if for the sins of the world, and still hanging on to him as if my life depended upon it, he opened a door, moved me quietly into one of the rooms off the passage, and closed the door silently behind us. He was no fool, and he knew the ways of women, for he let me weep until there was no more weeping to be done.

Then, before I had the wit to prevent it, his lips were upon mine, and his hands were upon my back. I can hardly bear to write about it, but such was my state of inebriation and despair that I did not resist as I should have done, and it was only when he pressed me down on the bed and lifted himself over me that I roused myself to scream in horror and revulsion, and tried to fend him off. However, my strength was no match for his, and a moment more would have been catastrophic.

'God damn you, sir!' said a voice of thunder, coming from a figure standing in the bright light of the doorway. 'How dare you, sir? How dare you betray me within the walls of my own house! Infamy, sir! Get out of this house this minute, and never return! You will never again call me father, and I will never again call you son. Not another penny for you, sir, whether I be alive or dead!'

I was suddenly sober, and aware of my compromising position. I could hear loud music and stamping feet and clapping hands downstairs. But my fear was as nothing compared with the panic displayed by John Fenton. He was off me and off the bed in an instant, dragging up his breeches and trying to cover himself while Squire Richard Fenton, a man renowned for his gentle manners and equable temperament, attacked him with a horsewhip. There was no more shouting, and John Fenton said not a word, but his father whispered with venom beneath his breath as he struck out with his whip: 'Damn you, sir! May you rot in Hell! How many times have I saved you in the past? Never again. Never again. If you are not out of this house in two minutes, I will kill you with my own hands!' And the wretched fellow fled out into the passage without looking back, and disappeared.

I did my best to cover up my dignity. The old squire was in a frightful state, and I could see that he was shaking like a leaf, but even under conditions of extreme provocation he is wiser than a copse full of tawny owls. He closed the door quietly and came over to the bed. 'It is probably best in the circumstances, my dear Martha, that we do not involve any others at this stage,' said he. 'I think it best that this little episode remains a secret between you and me.'

'Thank you, Master Fenton. I am very grateful indeed,' was all that I could say.

'Did he hurt you?'

'No, I think I am all right.'

'Did he . . . ?'

'No, but if you had been a minute later I fear you would have been too late.'

'Well, thank God for it. Or thank Joseph. Downstairs, as soon as he realized that you were missing, he asked me where you might be. I knew immediately, and was already on my way to this room when I heard you scream. If it is any consolation to you, you are not the first young lady to have been transported to this particular bed.'

That was no consolation to me at all. Then the full realization of what had almost happened to me hit me like a wall of cold water. I started to shiver, and my teeth started to chatter, and I felt the blood draining out of my face. The Squire got me beneath the blankets, with a soft pillow under my head. He fetched me a drink of cold water, and then another, and gradually my equilibrium returned. I had a splitting headache, and my mouth felt as if it was full of sand. My emotions were so confused, and my remorse so great, that I hardly knew what to say to the Squire who had saved me. 'Thank you, sir, for your intervention,' I whispered miserably. 'Owain never came. Owain never came . . .'

He came over to the bed and held my hand. 'I know,' he said in the gentlest of voices. 'Something has happened to him, and we shall soon find out what it is. But tonight you must stay here. You are in no fit state to go home. Tomorrow you will feel much better . . . or, more likely, just a little better. You know you have drunk too much?'

'I know it only too well.'

'Now then. Tonight's events will remain a secret between you and me. I swear that I will never tell another soul – not even my dear wife. Luckily there was so much noise from the dance floor at our moments of highest drama that nobody else will have heard your scream, or my shouting. And all the servants were downstairs.'

'What shall we tell people?'

'Simply that you felt unwell, possibly as a result of something you ate, and became sick, and had to be packed off to bed. Perfectly plausible, and no one can disprove it!'

I managed a weak smile at last, and said: 'Dear Master Fenton, you are so kind. How will I ever repay you?'

'By being happy, my dear Martha. And by inviting me to your wedding.'

Then there was a knock on the door, and Mistress Anne was standing there, with Grandpa and Grandma, Joseph, Mary Jane, and assorted servants all standing behind her. The Squire called them in, and between us we fed them our cock and bull story. I cannot say whether they believed us, but in my estimation we did a good job of storytelling. They fed the news back to the other guests, who were of course speculating as to the reasons for my disappearance. And so the Squire returned to his duties as genial host, and the ball went on, far into the night. By all accounts, a very good time was had by everybody except me. Grandpa and Grandma took their leave at an hour appropriate to their age, and Billy delivered them safely home. A sweet housemaid called Mair was detailed to look after me, and she found a nightdress for me. Then she tucked me up and got me off to sleep, and stayed in my room with me all night.

This morning, when I woke up in a strange bed and a strange house, I felt terrible. But I was treated with the greatest of courtesy, and prevailed upon to eat a good breakfast. There was no sign of Master John Fenton. Then I was desperate to get home to my children and to the security of my own room and my own bed. Quietly I asked if I might now take my leave, and the Squire laid on his coach for me. I asked the old fellow whether he had any news of Owain, and he had not. We said our farewells, and I thanked the members of his household for their great kindness to me. Perhaps I should not have done it, but I could not resist throwing my arms round the Squire's neck, and giving him a little kiss on the cheek. He smiled, and so did his dear wife Anne.

I was delivered like a queen back to the Plas, to the

great delight of the children, who had never seen such a big coach in the yard before. Bless them, they were full of concern for me, and hugged me and kissed me as if I had been away for a month. I said that I was not feeling very well, and that I needed more sleep. So I slept.

By mid-afternoon I felt a great deal better. I got up and decided to start writing. It is now five of the clock, and in writing my appalling narrative I have experienced a degree of cleansing. More serious and prolonged cleansing will be needed, of that I have no doubt. I need time to collect my thoughts, and time to come to terms with what almost happened to me. I have tried, in the past, to work out how to handle grief, and I must now learn how to handle guilt.

Now there is a commotion in the yard, so I must stop.

28 October 1806

It is late at night. Rain is beating against the windows, and a westerly gale is screaming its way past the Plas and roaring through the blue rocks of the mountain. I am exhausted after another day of turbulent emotions. Owain is in my bed, fast asleep and breathing easily. I will get little sleep myself, unless I nod off in my bedside chair. I will spend most of the night watching over him, and Grandma Jane will help too since she is a skilled nurse.

The latest assault upon my heart and mind started yesterday, in the late afternoon. A chaise came bouncing into the yard, to an accompaniment of clattering hooves and a great deal of shouting. 'Get him inside quickly!' shouted somebody. 'And be careful with him, or you may do more harm than good!' I was wearing only a nightdress and dressing gown at the time, so I flung on

410

some clothes and rushed downstairs. As I entered the kitchen, Will and his friend Skiff were carrying a limp body in from the yard. They placed him gently on the kitchen table. His blond hair was caked in blood. I knew immediately that it was Owain. Before I had time to react, Joseph came striding in, followed by Patty Ellis from the Parrog, and shortly afterwards by all our own servants who had been working outside and had been attracted by the noise.

Joseph caught my eye at once, and said: 'Good day, Martha. He is very badly injured. We will talk later. But for now I have work to do. Mrs Owen and Mistress Jane, I will appreciate your help. Get all of his clothes off, as I need to examine him properly. Cut them off with scissors so that you don't have to move him too much. Bessie, I will need boiling water and as many bandages and cloths as you can find. Everybody else, out of the kitchen please, including you, Martha. You are too involved here, and will do more harm than good. Go and take care of the children.'

We all obeyed meekly, and trooped into the parlour. I was so shocked by this turn of events that I felt quite faint, and Patty put her arm round me and led me to a chair. Luckily the children were not in the house at all; Sian had taken them for a walk in the woods so that I could get some peace and quiet. Peace and quiet indeed! Patty gave me a glass of water, and after some minutes I began to feel better. 'I'll wager you are not used to being spoken to like that!' said she. 'But Master Harries is probably quite right in the circumstances.'

Joseph's tone of voice was the least of my worries, and I said so. There were sounds of hectic activity in the kitchen, and muffled voices. I accepted that there was nothing I could do. So I said: 'Well, Patty, you had better tell me what this is all about.'

'Skiff knows more about it than I do,' she replied. 'I just found him this morning when I was out for a walk along the estuary.'

'What on earth do you mean?'

'Just what I say. I was walking along the path towards the ferry, through the reed beds, when I heard a moaning noise coming from somewhere on my left. Good God, I thought, there is somebody there! So I went and investigated. Then I found this fellow all covered in blood, and battered and bruised. Very nice clothes. I did not recognize him. He was only just conscious. The tide was coming in, and I knew that if I left him there he would be drowned. Luckily two of the shipyard workers came by, on their way to work, and I yelled to them to come and help, and we dragged him up onto the path.'

'Then, Mistress Martha, I came past, walking my dog,' said Skiff. 'I know everybody's face, and I recognized straight away that it was Master Laugharne. Anyway, I had heard last night that this same gentleman had been involved in a spot of bother in the Black Lion in the middle of the afternoon, and so I was already looking for him.'

'You mean Owain had been involved in a fight? That would not be like him at all.'

'Not a fight, exactly, Mistress. From what my friends tell me, Alban Watkins, John Howell and Joseph Rice were in the corner, plotting something or other. Two of my mates were trying to listen in, but those bastards the Ifan brothers were also there, keeping an eye on Rice, so they could not get too close. Then who should come in but Master Owain Laugharne, and confronted the three crooks in the corner. He said that he had been hunting everywhere for them, and that he was glad to have caught up with them at last. He accused them of spreading false rumours and of damaging the good name of himself and Mistress Morgan of Plas Ingli. He said that he would, that very afternoon, be making out an indictment against the three of them for slander, insulting behaviour and sowing discord, and said that he had many witnesses who would attest to the truth of his complaint. He also said that he would, that very evening, denounce all three of them at a social event to be held in Fishguard.'

'Oh, no!' I moaned. 'What a stupid fellow! How could he be so naive?'

'Stupid indeed, Mistress,' said Skiff. 'And perhaps not very used to dealing with the low life of the Newport taverns. But very brave, I have to say. I would not have done that.'

'So what happened next?'

'My mates tell me that there was a short conversation between Rice, Howell and Watkins. Then Rice said, "Deal with him", and Sion ap Ifan and his brother got up, grabbed Master Owain and dragged him outside. He is not a very big fellow, and those two brothers are built like prize bulls, so he had no chance against them. My mates ran outside after them, but they were gone. Then they came to fetch me, which was stupid of them, for when we all got back to the inn Rice and his confederates had gone too.'

'I appreciate your concern for Owain's welfare, Skiff.'

'Not so much that, Mistress, I have to confess. Our job is to protect you, and we knew that there was some romantic attachment between you and Master Owain, so we thought that if anything nasty happened to him, you would quite likely be very upset.'

'You are quite correct in that,' said I, swallowing hard. 'I have to confess, Skiff, that I was unaware of the extent of your involvement in looking after me and my estate.'

'It is something we choose to do, Mistress. At any rate,

we got fellows out all over town in no time at all, but we found not a trace of Owain or any of the others. Then it got dark, and we kept a watch on all the Newport and Parrog inns. Then Will came down to the Rose and Crown for his Friday night drink, and I was able to put him in the picture.'

Will took up the story. 'We got even more fellows on the case, Mistress, but to no avail. What was I to do? I knew that you were out at the ball at Glynmel, and so was Master Isaac. The constables, all three of them, would be more of a hindrance than a help. I knew that all the magistrates were at the ball too, so there would be no point in trying to get hold of any of them. I knew that Master Owain was supposed to go to the ball too, and that you would be very upset if he did not turn up.'

'Sadly, you are quite correct,' I sighed.

'So then I thought of Master Joseph Harries. I thought that wizards do not normally go to Pembrokeshire balls, and that he would certainly be at home. I thought that maybe he could summon up some spirits to tell him where Master Owain was. So I borrowed a pony off a friend and rode over to Werndew at the gallop. He was not at home. Hell and damnation! All I could do was to leave a note on his table. I am not very good at writing, Mistress, as you know, but I went in, lit a candle from the fire, found some paper and a pen and ink, and scribbled something to say that Master Owain was taken away by villains in town and that I was fearful for his safety.'

'Well done, Will. You could not have done more.'

'You may not know it, Mistress, since you were not here yourself, but I was out all night with my friends, searching. No trace of anything anywhere. At first light I was hunting up on the rough ground behind the church-yard when who should appear but Master Harries on his white pony. "Thank you for your note, Will," says he. "I have not been in bed myself, and have been searching along the Nevern road with my candle lantern. Thank goodness for some daylight at last." We searched together, and then one of my mates came running up and said that Master Owain had been found down near the ferry. And you know the rest.'

'What a business! So I suppose you all went down to the estuary, and Joseph took charge of the situation, and you commandeered a chaise from somebody, and decided that it would be best to bring Owain straight back here for treatment?'

'Indeed, Mistress Martha,' said Patty. 'Master Joseph thought he might die if we took him all the way back to Llannerch. He said time was of the essence. So me and Skiff held him fast in the chaise, with Caleb Jones driving, and Joseph and Will came galloping on their ponies.'

'You are truly angels, all of you,' I said. 'I thank you from the bottom of my heart.' But I could not wait out in the parlour for a moment longer, and so I went back into the kitchen and closed the door behind me. Owain was still stretched out on the kitchen table, naked as the day he was born, but he was conscious. His chest was covered in bandages, and he had other bandages on his arms and legs. His teeth were chattering, but his eyes were open, and when he saw me he even managed a little smile. A wave of relief swept over me, and I ran across to him and kissed him on his forehead and held his hand. Joseph was washing his hands in hot soapy water, and he smiled as he looked up.

'Now then, Mistress Morgan, this will not do,' he said with great severity and a twinkle in his eye. 'Disobeying instructions, as usual. I thought I told you to stay away from here? It is not seemly for a fine lady to look upon

415

the body of a young bachelor squire, or even an old married one for that matter.'

'Don't you worry, Joseph. I will probably survive the experience.'

'Anyway, we are ready. Mrs Owen, cover him with sheets, if you please. He has been out all night in the cold, and it is a wonder he has survived. Thank goodness and mercy it was not raining. Can you find a nightshirt for him? Get him upstairs, and tucked into bed if you please.'

'Put one of David's nightshirts on him,' said I, 'and put him in my bed.' Mrs Owen raised her eyebrows, and I said: 'Please. I insist on it.'

Owain was drifting in and out of consciousness, but with the help of Will and Shemi and Skiff he was carried upstairs. 'Be careful,' said Joseph. 'He has not broken anything, so far as I can make out. But he has received a severe beating, and he has cuts and lacerations all over his body, and very serious bruising. I have stitched him up and dressed his wounds as best I can, and I do not want any of them opening up again.'

Soon he was in my bed, fast asleep. Bessie offered to sit by his bedside for the first couple of hours, since I wanted to talk to Joseph. Downstairs, I thought that we had better offer our unexpected guests something to eat and drink; but Grandma Jane had already anticipated that, and having cleared and washed the kitchen table she was sitting people down round it. Soon a veritable feast of bread, salty butter, cheeses, cold potatoes, ham and other cold meats had appeared from the scullery, and all were supplied with mugs of steaming sweet tea. Spirits revived as soon as it was apparent that Owain would pull through, and before long there were full bellies, and laughter as well as talk around the table. Joseph said that Owain was suffering most of all from severe chilling, and that he would take some hours to warm up again. He said that he would have to be watched continuously for at least three days, and encouraged to drink warm liquids every few hours if possible. He said that he might develop a serious fever, and that if he did, I was to call him over at once. He said there was no damage to the head, so far as he could make out, and that that was a great blessing in the circumstances.

'Now, my dear Martha,' he said at last, 'I am utterly exhausted, and I must go home and get some sleep.' He had a pallor on his cheeks, and his eyes were bloodshot and sunken in their sockets. His grey hair was stiff and matted with sweat. I realized that the dear man had not slept for thirty-six hours, and that the same could be said for Will and Skiff, who had been up all night searching for Owain. 'Thank you, Joseph,' I said. 'I see that you, and others of my dear friends, look as if you could sleep for a week. But you are in no fit state to ride that pony of yours. You will certainly fall off.' Then Caleb Jones Siop Fach offered to take Joseph home in his chaise, and the good doctor gladly accepted the offer.

Soon, having given all of them the warmest of embraces, I was waving them off, with Caleb driving and Joseph, Patty and Skiff crammed into the back. Darkness was just creeping up from the *cwm* towards the slopes of the mountain. 'Thank you all,' I shouted after them. 'You have all been the best of friends to me today.' And they were gone. Will staggered off to bed, with instructions to sleep for as long as he wished, day or night. Joseph said that he would return on the morrow, to collect his pony and to talk further.

Then the house was quiet. Grandpa, Grandma and Mrs Owen cleared up the mess in the kitchen and refused absolutely to allow me to help. They sent me packing, and I was left with my thoughts. Not for very long, because Sian and the children arrived back, demanding their supper. They were all very surprised indeed to find Master Owain in my bed, and I spent quite a while trying to explain to them, without getting too involved in the sordid details, the circumstances that lay behind it.

29 October 1806

Owain is still in my bed and I am outside it. I am tempted to creep in between the sheets, but that would probably not be good for his health. He is fast asleep, and is recovering at a remarkable rate. Joseph is pleased with his patient, and I am, to say the least, delighted. It is my turn to keep watch, and I would happily do it for weeks or months if it should be needed. But my ecstasy is all but wiped out by the knowledge of what has happened to this man to whom I have given my heart, and whose courage is almost beyond belief. I have to record the following.

This morning I received a kindly letter from Squire Fenton, enquiring after my health, and I sent him a reply affirming that I was very much better, and thanking him for the multitude of kindnesses shown towards me. He will know what I mean.

More details have emerged about recent events, and for these I have to thank my remarkable friend Joseph, who came over to fetch his pony. Grandpa joined us, and we three sat in the parlour, drinking a nice cup of tea since I am sworn off alcohol. 'Now then, dear friends,' said Joseph. 'We have much to catch up on. Where shall I start?'

'Perhaps the matter of the ball?' said Grandpa,

sending a shiver down my spine, but I did not want to betray any concerns about what might emerge, so I nodded.

'Yes, right then. The ball. Master Isaac, you might not know that Martha and I had made certain plans to expose the wickedness of our enemies. Owain was in the picture, and he was fully in agreement.'

Grandpa was surprised by this, since I had not warned him in advance about Joseph's plans for a public denunciation. Now I explained everything to him, and he nodded his approval. 'Excellent idea,' he said. 'But Owain's non-appearance caused that plan to fall by the wayside?'

'To a degree, yes,' said Joseph. 'But there was another matter too, relating to the burglary in Lewis Legal's office. I did not resolve that particular issue until the afternoon of the ball, so there was no time to communicate my findings to Owain and Martha. I could not have publicly denounced the man behind it at the ball.'

'Why on earth not, Joseph?'

'Because the man behind it was John Fenton, Squire Fenton's errant son. I could not possibly have accused him of a serious crime in such company, beneath the Squire's own roof. The shock might well have killed him.'

He had a considerable shock as it was, thought I, and he came out of it looking remarkably well.

'At any rate,' said Joseph, 'with Owain absent without leave, and some uncertainty as to the reasons for his absence, I decided not to create any unnecessary ripples on the surface of the pond.' And then he turned to me. 'Did you know, Martha, that John Fenton has been around recently?'

'Oh yes,' I replied, 'I know it.' And I thought it best, in the circumstances, not to elaborate further. So I changed

419

the subject. 'How did you discover about his involvement in the burglary?'

'It was very straightforward. Lewis Legal asked me to investigate, and paid me for the privilege, which I thought was very kind. There was a broken window at the back of the office, where the burglar got in. The frame was smudged, as if it had been wiped clean, and when I examined it through my magnifying glass I found traces of dried blood. There were more traces of blood on the red carpet in the office, although it was so filthy, as befits an attorney's office, that nobody else had noticed them. The burglar had cut himself very seriously. The fellow involved was from Fishguard, I was sure, since he had entered by the most vulnerable route and had chosen the only window not visible from any other property. There are five known burglars in Fishguard. With the help of assorted low friends I set about finding the one with a recently cut hand, and at last I found him. I went to see him, but he would not admit anything. I went to see him again, and he was very scared. Somebody had been putting pressure on him, and he was in fear of his life if he spoke.

'Time was running out, so in the end I had to resort to the unfashionable tactic of pinning a note on his door though in the past I've always found it produces results. It said:

'Billy Filbert, I know what you have done. Tonight I will consult my book and will take steps to ensure that you are punished in a manner that will surely shock all the people of this town. This magic will only be removed if you write down the name of the man who hired you on a piece of paper, and pin it to the door of Dinas church at precisely four of the clock, this very afternoon. Harries Werndew.*

'Very unpleasant business, and I do not enjoy playing on the superstitions of simple people. But it had to be done. At any rate, I watched the church, and he turned up as the clock struck four, and looked round furtively. He pinned a piece of paper to the door, and ran off. It said *John Fenton Glynymel*.'

I had to laugh, and so did Grandpa. 'Up to your old tricks again, Joseph!' he chuckled, and took a sip of tea.

'So that's that one out of the way,' said I. 'Now we come to the matter of Owain's escapade in town. What do we know about it?'

'I have certainly not been able to gather much,' said Grandpa. 'Now that he is recovering, he admits that he was foolish in confronting Rice and his cronies in the way that he did, but he says that he had to do something, and thought it would be fair to give them advance warning of the legal action he was about to take. Brave and honourable, but stupid at the same time, if you ask me. He obviously did not reckon that the Ifan brothers would be in there, protecting Master Rice.'

'I have spoken to him too,' I said. 'I have pressed him over and again to say what happened after he was dragged out of the Black Lion. He claims that he cannot remember anything, and I cannot work out whether he is telling the truth.'

'He may well be, Martha,' said Joseph, with a dark shadow on his face. 'People sometimes shut out horrific things from their minds. You realize that he was tortured with a knife?'

I was dumbstruck, and I must have become so pale that Grandpa came and put his arm round me and encouraged me to take a sip of tea.

'You have to know it. I told you that there were cuts on his body, and you may have seen some of them yourself. There was a pattern to them. They were not the random slashes of a knife attack. I have treated plenty of those in my time, and I know the signs. Neither were they slashes through his clothes; his shirt and breeches were covered with blood, but they were otherwise quite unharmed. The cuts were inflicted, slowly and deliberately, on his bare skin.'

'Oh, my God. Oh, my God,' was all I could say. Grandpa was similarly appalled, and could find no words to express his disgust.

'We are dealing with very unpleasant fellows here,' continued Joseph. 'The Ifan brothers would not have done this – they are simply a pair of bullies, and if things had been left to them they would probably have cracked Owain's skull and dumped his body in the river.'

'So what is your conclusion as to what happened?' asked Grandpa.

'I have given this some thought, and reckon that the Ifan boys gave Owain a beating with their fists in some dark alley, that Rice, Watkins and Howell then joined them, and that the five of them took Owain off to some secret place for interrogation . . .'

'But surely that cannot have been their intention from the beginning?' I asked, having recovered my power of speech. 'After all, Owain's appearance in the Black Lion was not anything which they had invited or orchestrated.'

'True. We are talking here about a piece of opportunism. Rice and his cronies probably realized it would not be a good idea to kill Owain, since there were too many witnesses to his abduction. So they probably thought that a beating followed by an accidental death would be better. If the tide had been rising when they dumped him, he would have been drowned. But it was falling in the middle of the night, and that saved him, for the tide had not returned to full flow when Patty came upon him in the reeds.'

'But what can have been the motive for the unimaginable terror to which they subjected him?'

'Some people enjoy inflicting pain, my dear Martha. I imagine that Masters Rice, Watkins and Howell are among them. But I suppose they thought Owain might know where the Plas Ingli treasure is to be found, and I suppose they thought that he would tell them rather than be cut to pieces. Probably, in the end, he passed out, and at that point they decided to take him back down to the estuary and dump him.'

'And we know the rest,' said Grandpa.

There followed a long silence, as all three of us sought to come to terms with the full horror of the situation, and with yet more evidence of the utter depravity of these men sent from Hell. Then Joseph stood up abruptly. 'My friends,' he said, 'we have looked into the face of evil quite enough for today. I will now go home. I urge you not to give in to despair, in spite of what has happened to Master Owain. This morning, as I walked here over the common, I had a powerful premonition, and I know two things: first, that a great conflict is about to break over us; and second, that we will triumph. Do not doubt it for a moment.'

'Oh, Joseph, I do hope that you are right!'

'Do not doubt it, Martha. You have mentioned several times that you have a germ of a plan in your mind. Has the germ yet grown into something bigger?'

'Yes, it has. I see more and more clearly what has to be done.'

'Good, good. Let us therefore meet in a few days' time, by which time Master Owain will be fit enough to join us in our discussions. In the meantime, Martha, will you speak to him? I suggest that you take him entirely into your confidence, if that is what your heart tells you. You might also try to elicit further details of what happened to him at the hands of the enemy, if he can bear to talk about it.'

I nodded. 'I will try, Joseph. I will work on my plans, if I can empty horror out of my head to the extent that rational thought becomes possible. Will you join us at two in the afternoon on Wednesday?'

Joseph agreed, and hugged both of us, and said, 'Goodbye, dear friends. Keep steady – we will triumph!' And off he went back to Werndew, leaving Grandpa and me to return to normal domestic duties.

1 November 1806

Now I am as angry as Queen Boudicca. Never in my life have I felt such fury in my breast, and I will not tolerate the activities of those devils for a moment longer. I will suffer at their hands no more, nor will I allow them to inflict further suffering on other innocent souls. I swear before God, and before St Brynach and the angels of Carningli, that I will bring them all to justice within a week. Matters have come inexorably to a conclusion, and I welcome it.

I have had no time to wring my hands and dress in sackcloth and ashes over what happened at Glynymel; that can come later. There has been far too much to do.

On the day after my meeting with Grandpa and Joseph, Owain was much better. He was in great pain, but he is strong, and young, and his wounds are healing well, and he was much more ready to divulge his secrets. I spent the whole afternoon at his bedside, and we talked about everything, or almost everything. The only things which I did not tell him related to the events in John Fenton's bedroom, the location of the real Plas Ingli treasure, and my spying upon him in the Pandy Pools. But we talked about David's death and my utter conviction that he was murdered by Rice, Howell, Lloyd and Beynon. We talked about the children, and about David's will, and about our efforts to bring the villains to justice. I was as honest as I could be about my tendency towards melancholia and about my wild swings of temperament, and I was entertained to discover that he had already worked all that out for himself. He told me about his somewhat sheltered upbringing at Pontfaen, his shyness, and his preference for artistic rather than practical pursuits. And he admitted to being too trusting of others and too naive in the ways of the world. We talked about estate affairs, both at Llannerch and Plas Ingli. We talked about our recent misunderstanding arising out of the false rumours spread by our enemies, and I apologized to him, with tears in my eyes, for doubting him, and misjudging his motives. He was equally effusive with me, and admitted that he had made grave errors of judgement in responding to the rumours, and begged my forgiveness for the distress he had caused to me and others. He told me more about his investigations into the activities of Watkins and the other villains, and admitted that his visit to the Black Lion the other afternoon was just about the most foolhardy thing he had done in his life.

'It was very stupid, Owain,' said I, 'for it almost resulted in your being taken away from me and placed in a coffin.'

He looked at me, and smiled through his scratches and bruises. Then he said: 'Martha, can I tell you something which I should, if fate had not intervened, have told you some little while ago?'

He took my hand, drew it to his lips, and kissed it. I whispered, 'Please do,' and swallowed hard.

'I have loved you since the moment I first saw you,' he said. 'Even when you were married to David. With you and he so clearly happy, and with your beautiful children growing up, there was nothing I could do but love you from a distance, and resign myself to a life in purgatory. But then . . . but then . . .'

At this point his voice cracked. I realized that tears were streaming down my cheeks, but I said: 'Dearest Owain, that is the sweetest and strongest thing I have ever heard. And I was fool enough to think you a coward. Will you ever forgive me? But you must know that my heart is so full of love for you that I can hardly contain it. And my love grows with every day that passes.'

Then I could not stop myself, and I bent over him and gave him a long kiss on his bruised lips. He lay flat on his back, covered only by a light blanket, and I could not help noticing a rising bump halfway down the bed. I patted it, and said: 'I am very glad to observe, my dear Owain, that those villains were only able to inflict limited damage when they got hold of you the other day!' He spluttered, and blushed, and then roared with laughter, and so did I, and I had to calm him down when I realized that his laughter was causing him some pain round his battered ribs.

The barriers between us having thus been broken down, we continued to talk, and at last he opened up on the matter of the torture to which he had been subjected by his captors. It was painful for him in the extreme, but he described how they had taken him to a shack in the woods near Allt Clydach. Much to his surprise, John Fenton was already in the hut when they arrived. They had then interrogated him about the wealth of Plas Ingli

426

and Llannerch, and particularly about the Plas Ingli treasure which they supposed to be buried somewhere in our stony soil. He told them that the treasure was a fantasy and that there was no location to give them; but they would not believe him, and so they started to cut him, repeating the question over and again, obtaining the same answer, and cutting him again until he passed out. I held his hand tightly as he talked of this, and I could hardly bring myself to listen. But he finished his narrative, and then said that he supposed that they had carried him unconscious to the estuary later on, and left him to die.

I felt that there was now a more powerful bond between us than I had ever thought possible, and I believe that Owain felt the same, for we had both suffered in our different ways at the hands of these monsters. We held hands, and together we swore that we would obtain justice.

2 November 1806

We have had our meeting, this afternoon around Owain's bed, and everything is in place for the final confrontation. We talked for more than two hours. I have developed my battle plans, and shared them with the others. Tactics have been modified to some degree as a consequence of wise comments from my three beloved men, but I am now satisfied that we have considerable entertainment in store.

News came from Patty that John Fenton, whose crimes can now be added to those of the others, is homeless and has moved in with Joseph Rice. There are now three of them crammed into Mistress Billings's little room down on the Parrog, and I am certain that that is an unsustainable situation. Lloyd has defaulted on his latest payment for his bastard child, and is convinced that the *Ceffyl Pren* will be paying him a visit any day now. Will tells us that Beynon, miserable and surly fellow that he is, has fallen out with his relatives and that they want him out of Berry Hill. Smyllie and Elias, still dressed in their idiotic jesters' outfits, spend most of their time spying on Alban Watkins. They no longer buy drinks in the inns of Newport, and this leads Skiff and his friends to the view that their money has run out. Watkins is known to have been borrowing money of late at very high rates of interest, and Grandpa Isaac says that he is destitute. The whole miserable bunch of them are down at heel, and are in Owain's view increasingly likely to do something very dangerous or very stupid. I just hope that we can implement our plan of action before we ourselves get harmed.

Owain will soon be well enough to go back to Llannerch, but Plas Ingli will be where the drama will unfold, and I hope he will be here when it happens.

I do not want the little ones to be around us over the next week, for I fear for their safety, and would never forgive myself if anything were to go wrong with our plans. So I have today sent them off with Sian to stay with my brother Morys and his wife and children in Haverfordwest. I asked them a few days since, and received a kind message back to say that they would be only too delighted to help. I was tearful when they left, and could hardly bring myself to let them go. But they were more interested in their adventure than they were in me, and simply said 'Bye bye Mam' in a perfectly matter of fact way. Then they hopped into the carriage, and begged Billy to gallop as fast as he could over the mountain, since they were longing to see their little cousins. Such are the ways of children.

We have briefed all our friends in Newport as to what is going to happen, and they all know the roles they have to play. They are all sworn to secrecy, and not a word of our conspiracy will reach the ears of any of our enemies.

The next few days will be exciting ones, and I pray that nothing will go wrong. I have passion in my breast and fire in my belly, but my head is cool and calm, and I am convinced that I have thought of everything.

Autumn Gale

3 November 1806

We have set things in motion. The weather is perfect for our purpose, cool and dry, and Shemi has consulted his weather-wise animals and advises us that the dry spell will last at least until next weekend.

I have been rushing about a great deal today, being as ostentatious as possible. I took the trap, with Will driving, and went first to Newport. I chatted on the street with a good many people, and went to see the Rector. I drank his tea and ate one or two of his Welsh cakes, but conducted no business with him whatsoever. A visit to the Rector is always a good way to get tongues wagging. I called in at various shops including Price Very Nice and Jones Siop Fach. I looked at the most expensive things I could find, and tried a daring and exquisite silk dress which Master Price has recently brought in from London. I bought nothing at all, but that was not the purpose of the exercise; the whole point was that I should be seen during the course of my shopping expedition. I called in to see three of the Newport merchants, including Elijah Collins, Shoni James and Shoni Richard, enquired as to their recent and likely future purchases, and drank more tea and ate more

Welsh cakes. Then I went down to the Parrog, waving cheerfully to everybody we passed on the way, and called in at all the warehouses on the quay to enquire about vessels expected and what their cargoes might be. I asked to be notified as soon as the next trading vessel came in. The warehouses are all visible from the lodging house inhabited by Rice, Howell and Fenton, and I was certain that my visits would be observed. I then walked over to the lime kilns and asked the lime burners their current prices and the quantities of lime that might be available for carting next week. And to cap it all, I took a short walk over to Master Havard's shipyard on the estuary and told him I was interested in a 60 per cent share in his next vessel, which I wanted to be a sloop with the name *Golden Sovereign*.

After that I returned to town and called on Will Final Testament. With him, I did talk about real business, and talked frankly about my plans. He was greatly amused, if a little apprehensive, about what might happen in the coming days, but he agreed to do two things. First, he would advise those brought before the magistrates without charging any fees; and second, he would gently let slip in one or two places round town that Mistress Morgan was looking into some major purchases of property in the town and on the Parrog. The date on which purchases might well be negotiated was to be the 6th day of November.

Then, having said my noisy farewells on Will's front doorstep, I went to see the Steward of the Barony to ask whether any properties owned by the Lord Marcher might be available for purchase over the coming weeks. The Steward, one Morris Hughes, is a miserable fellow who drinks too much and works too little, but he has a loose tongue and drinks in the same places as Lloyd and Beynon. They will soon know that Master Hughes and I have been talking.

431

During my conversations in town I discovered that many people had heard about the terrible treatment meted out to Owain by Rice and his cronies. There was universal admiration for the manner in which Owain had confronted the villains in the Black Lion. It was common knowledge that the Ifan brothers had been involved, and there was a seething anger directed towards the whole gang because of the attempted murder of a well-liked young man. Everybody knew of the mutual attraction between Owain and myself, and everybody knew that he was now at the Plas recovering from his injuries; and I was greatly heartened by the expressions of concern for his welfare and the hopes of many people that we would both find happiness in each other's company. I was more than a little relieved to discover that the stupid rumours about Owain's cynicism and my gullibility have not been given much credence by the more sensible people of the town. Most people now seem to know that the rumours emanated from Rice and his cronies, and this has increased their resentment towards them.

After our visits to Newport and Parrog, Will and I rattled in the trap all the way to Fishguard, and called on Lewis Legal. I had real business with him, but once again I knew that my visit would be noticed by some of the locals and discussed in low places. Master Lewis has shared many adventures with the Morgan family of Plas Ingli, and he is a dear friend. We chatted of this and that. Then we talked about the burglary in his office. He had already been informed by Joseph that John Fenton was the man behind it. With no direct evidence of that, Master Lewis had been thinking of making out an indictment against the ignorant fellow who was paid to do the stealing; but I convinced him to let that rest for a while, since the poor man is scared out of his wits anyway, by the fear of a curse from Joseph and by Fenton's bullying. I said that the burglar would not squeal in court and that he would be sent down while Fenton would walk free. Much better, said I, to do things the other way round: catch Fenton first for some other crime and then hit him with the evidence about the burglary during the legal process. He agreed at last with this strategy, although I had to use some of the most potent weapons in my female armoury in order to obtain his acquiescence. It is well known that he likes nothing better than a pretty lady. He knew all about the activities of Rice, Howell, Watkins and Fenton, and is just as appalled by them as I am; but when I described my plans to him he chuckled with glee, and agreed to advise the villains in prison for nothing, and to defend them in court.

Then I returned to the Plas, feeling very pleased with myself. On the way home Will and I talked about my visits and the progression of my campaign, and he said that he would pass on the word to his friends, who would in turn ensure that a good deal of talk goes on round Newport and on the Parrog about my 'business activities' during the day. The word would be about already that something significant would be happening at the Plas on the 5th day of November. By tomorrow, I thought, there would be nothing much else talked about in the inns and shops of the town.

Owain was in my bedroom, up and about, still bandaged and looking battered, but able to walk without assistance. I greeted him with a moderately energetic embrace, since anything more severe might have hurt him, and a kiss on the lips. He was very frustrated by his enforced inactivity, but we sat together for a long while and I told him everything about my day's activities. He was delighted with the progress already made, and was greatly touched by the messages which I passed to him

433

from many good folks in town wishing him a speedy and complete recovery from his injuries.

While I was going about my business, and Owain was feeling frustrated, Grandpa Isaac was also very busy. He dressed in his best breeches and jacket, put some shiny boots upon his feet and a feathered hat upon his bald head, and rode off on our finest hunter to visit the local gentry. Most of his visits were unannounced, which is somewhat improper, but Grandpa knows nearly all the local squires thoroughly well, and I am sure they will not have been offended by his galloping arrivals at their front doors. He visited more than a dozen squires during the day, and spent time with each of them in private conversation. He discovered a great resentment almost everywhere towards the brutal and corrupt activities of Watkins, Rice, Matthew Lloyd and the rest of them, with a number of squires saying, 'Something should be done about them.' Grandpa assured them that something was indeed being done. Those whom he could trust, like Bowen Llwyngwair, Edwards Llwyngoras and Prosser Frongoch, were brought into his confidence and told the truth about our plans. Owain's father John Laugharne of Pontfaen was fully informed and gave his wholehearted approval; this was of course necessary because of the close involvement of his son. Mary Jane and Dafydd Stokes were also visited at Trecwn and told everything. They thought our scheme was very risky, but could think of nothing better.

Those were the easy visits. The more difficult ones were the visits to the frosty old squires who have no great love for the Plas Ingli estate or the Morgan family, and Grandpa said that these were very hard work. Nevertheless, he went through with trips to the likes of Rees Laugharne Pengelli Fawr, Price Llanychaer, and Owen Gelli Fawr in the hope of improving relations and in order to inform them – very gently – of our interest in acquiring more property. 'How much property?' asked the squires, one by one. 'Oh, a thousand acres or so,' said Grandpa in reply to each of them. When asked, as he inevitably was, about the source of the funding for these prospective purchases, Grandpa says he was suitably and mysteriously evasive.

By this evening, messages will have been flying all over north Pembrokeshire, from the mansions of our friends as well as our enemies, to the effect that the Morgan family is in the property market and that considerable sums of money will shortly be at our disposal. Grandpa returned home a short while ago, well pleased with his efforts. He stripped off his stiff and formal clothes, got back into his comfortable working outfit, and settled down happily by the fire with his pipe in one hand and his glass of brandy in the other.

In addition, Bessie, Mrs Owen, Billy, Shemi and Will have all been to town at various times, mentioning to friends and acquaintances, quite confidentially of course, that they will all shortly be receiving substantial wage increases, with a special bonus to be paid very soon, on the sixth day of the month. They have been making discreet enquiries as to the prices of new boots, new clothes, new tools and so forth. Shemi has been having the most fun of all, and has been round to all the local horse merchants, putting it about that he will soon be purchasing a stallion of his own, and showing himself not at all surprised at some of the prices he has been quoted.

This afternoon, after my long talk with Owain, I packed him off to bed again, for he still needs a great deal of rest, and went down to town on my own pony. I visited all the local blacksmiths and ironmongers, and made a great show of examining picks and shovels. Then

I purchased a pick and a shovel from each of them, paid cash on the nail, and asked for delivery first thing in the morning. Tomorrow, before breakfast, five delivery boys will be on their way to the Plas, and the whole town will be speculating as to the reasons for this sudden interest on our part in excavating equipment. Among those doing the speculating will be Watkins, Rice and their cronies, and Lloyd and Beynon and their cronies. The money spent on all this hardware is not wasted, since we need new shovels and picks anyway.

After that I rode off to see Squire Jethro Gittins of Tredrissi and Squire Mark Higgon of Tredafydd. They are both magistrates, and I wanted to ascertain whether they might both be available for a Petty Sessions in three days' time. They confirmed that they were indeed available, and inquired as to my interest. All I would say was that I would be asking for several arrest warrants very shortly, and that there might well be indictments requiring their wise attention in the pursuit of justice. I said that in my view they were the fairest and most knowledgeable of all the local magistrates, and that I had heard on many occasions that they were quite incorruptible. I was sure, said I, that they could be relied upon utterly to see that justice was done in the most impartial fashion. They were both very flattered, and I am as confident as any lady can be that there will now be a satisfactory degree of partiality in their coming deliberations. As for Squire Gittins, he still hopes that his son Mostyn will marry me, so I dare say that his goodwill can be taken for granted.

And the final piece of subterfuge concerned the map. For the last couple of days Owain, who is too incapacitated to do too much else, has been trying out his skills as a forger. We found a scruffy old map of the estate as it was fifteen years ago, and Owain has been inscribing onto it, in matching ink and with matching pen strokes, various lines and measurements, with a cross marked in the middle of one of our top fields which goes by the name of Parc Haidd. This afternoon, by prior arrangement, Billy rode down into town and called in to see Will Final Testament. Before entering the door he happened to drop an envelope onto the ground. On it were inscribed the words *Master Will Probert, from Morgan Plas Ingli in strictest confidence.* Inside the envelope was Owain's map and a note from me which said:

> *Plas Ingli, on the 2nd November 1806*
>
> *My dear Master Probert,*
>
> *Here is the map of which we spoke. Please be assured that matters will be concluded on the 5th day of this month, and that on the following day I shall wish you to act on my behalf in the matters which we have previously discussed.*
>
> *Yours very sincerely, Martha Morgan (Mistress)*

Purely by chance this envelope was picked up by one of Skiff's friends and carried directly to Rice's lodging house on the Parrog. The resident villains were all at home. The urchin concerned made a great scene on the front doorstep, in discussion with John Howell. He refused to go inside. Finally he managed to sell the envelope in exchange for a golden sovereign, handed it over and disappeared behind the lime kilns.

Another urchin observed all of this, and went over to where Smyllie and Elias were sitting on a wall, where they always sat when they were spying on Alban Watkins. The poor fellows didn't have a sovereign in their pockets, but they did have three silver shillings between them, and in exchange for that the urchin revealed that the document just handed over at the lodging house was an envelope from Mistress Morgan Plas Ingli to Master Probert the lawyer, stolen after being accidentally dropped on the ground. When asked what it contained, the child said that he thought it was a scruffy old map with a cross on it. Smyllie and Elias almost fell off their wall. The child ran off at high speed before they had a chance to recover their money from him. According to Patty, who was looking out of her window at the time, they had a rapid consultation, and set off at the trot along the estuary track. She knew that this was the shortest and most direct route towards Berry Hill and Cwmgloyn, and she was in no doubt that they were heading off to report directly to Beynon or Lloyd.

We have now done all that we can do for today. We have had an extremely jovial supper, and I have thought better of my decision to give up alcohol. Owain is fast asleep in my bed, and I am sitting at my desk, jotting down my recollections and feeling well satisfied. As usual, I will sleep on the spare mattress on the floor, even though I might wish it otherwise. Things are moving very rapidly, and it is too late to turn back now. The excitement in the air is palpable, and I hope I can relax enough to sleep.

4 November 1806

One day to go. We have had a quieter day today, allowing gossip to spread and allowing the villains to work themselves up into a feeding frenzy. We have gone about our business as usual at the Plas, but news has come from Patty that Smyllie and Elias tried to break in to Rice's lodging house during the night, no doubt in an attempt to steal the mysterious map. They were repelled by the defenders, but much blood was spilt, and the whole lot of them will now have sore heads. Mistress Billings was not amused.

Early in the morning we were reminded that not everybody is involved in the business of plotting and planning when we had a short visit from Daniel O'Connell, the uncle of the little boy injured by a scythe during the barley harvest. He knocked at the kitchen door and insisted on seeing me personally. When I came down he smiled, and so did I, for he is a pleasant fellow, but in truth I was surprised to see him, for I thought he had long since left the neighbourhood. He said that he had been working here and there, because he liked it in these parts, and added that he would shortly be returning to Ireland. As to the purpose of his visit, he said he simply wanted to report that little Brendan has made a remarkable recovery, and is walking with just the slightest limp. 'What wonderful news!' said I.

Just now, said Daniel, the rest of the O'Connell clan are in the north of England, helping with the potato harvest. He said that he had had a message from his brother Michael, asking him to report on the little boy's progress and to pass on their gratitude to all of us, and to Master Harries in particular, for saving his young life. 'You are all good people here,' said Daniel, 'and we thank you from the bottom of our hearts. We will never forget you.' I think he had a tear in his eye. And with that he turned on his heel, and walked off down the track towards the Cilgwyn road.

During the day we have placed a very obvious watch upon Parc Haidd, which is a high and exposed field blessed with good stone walls all round it and deep sandy soil in the middle. Shemi, Will, Billy, Gethin, Skiff and assorted labourers from the estate have all taken it in turns to stand guard, three at a time. They were not very happy about it, poor fellows, since there was a cold November wind blowing, but they were sustained by bowls of hot soup and plenty of bread and cheese carried up from the Plas by Bessie and Mrs Owen.

To our great satisfaction, as the day progressed, the signs of spying activity increased on all sides. Owain and I remained in the house for most of the day, with a perfect view from the back windows of the mountain and the top fields. Parc Haidd was particularly easy to see since there are no trees or bushes in the way. With the aid of Grandpa's excellent spyglass we first of all spotted heads popping over the summit of the mountain, and we knew that assorted villains had climbed up on the Newport side so as to get a good view of proceedings. We spotted other signs of activity round on the flank of the mountain towards Carn Edward, and yet more signs near the high wall that marks the estate's eastern boundary near New England. We looked out through all the other windows of the house too, and were delighted to spot spying activity in two or three other places. Somebody was even watching us from Carnedd Meibion Owen, far away on the other side of the *cwm*; we knew it because whenever the sun broke through the cloud we saw reflected sunbeams glinting on somebody's spyglass.

Joseph turned up at midday, ready to stay the night. We had an amiable lunch, and afterwards the three men and I met in the parlour and reviewed the state of our preparations, and the plans for tomorrow. We were now certain that the people on top of the mountain were Watkins, Rice, Howell and Fenton, possibly accompanied by the Ifan brothers. Billy, who has eyes like a hawk, says he spotted two very big fellows on the skyline, and a shorter man with a heavy grey beard. The people on the eastern boundary of the estate, closest to

Nevern, were probably the members of the Lloyd gang, and this is supported by the fact that Mair Williams Gelli, on her way back from town this morning, spotted four heavily cloaked figures crossing the Cilgwyn road halfway up Greystones Hill. That looked to us as if there are six members in the one gang and four in the other. The two gangs may well have spotted each other, since they probably have spyglasses; but we decided that that should not bother us too much, and indeed will have the effect of increasing the tension between the two gangs and raising the chances of a violent confrontation between them. They may well be so preoccupied with watching each other, we thought, that they would fail to notice the other things going on around them.

We speculated about the effect that the increasing tempo of arrivals and departures at the Plas during the day might have upon the villains; but again we decided that this would most likely confirm them in their conviction that something was about to happen, and would simply increase their mad lust for some, if not all, of the miraculous treasure that was shortly to appear before them.

In our discussions Owain proved to be very perceptive and clear in his thinking, and this gave me great pleasure. He pointed out one issue which we had not addressed previously, and that was the matter of firearms. We thought it possible, after due consideration, that some and possibly all of the villains are in possession of muskets and pistols, and maybe even explosives. Owain said that we must not allow even the slightest possibility that these weapons, if they exist, could be used against Billy, or Shemi, or Will, or any other of our dear friends. He suggested certain modifications to our plans, and we agreed with these, and Billy and the others have now been briefed.

With a degree of certainty that all of the villains were temporarily out of the way, I went down to town in the late afternoon and visited all three of the constables. I told them that I had reason to believe that certain dastardly deeds would be done at Plas Ingli tomorrow evening, and requested their attendance. I said it was inevitable that at least ten wicked and violent fellows would have to be apprehended, and when they heard this each of them cringed and thought they might have other urgent business to attend to. I was having none of that, and said I would report them to the Lord Lieutenant for dereliction of duty if they did not turn up with ropes and irons at the ready; and I promised them ample assistance in making arrests. Then I went down to see Patty and knocked on her front door, having decided that I was no longer worried about wagging tongues on that score. She was not otherwise engaged, thank goodness, and I said that I would need her assistance for an hour or so. We did a little tour of the back streets of Newport, and called in at most of the disreputable inns, and in no time at all we had obtained a veritable army of knights in shining armour who all promised to assemble at the Plas, without their armour or their steeds, one hour after dusk tomorrow. I asked all of them to walk up from town without lights, since secrecy was of the essence. I promised that they were needed for a noble enterprise and that they would be well rewarded; but in truth they probably knew that this was all something to do with Rice and Lloyd and their cronies, who were no friends of theirs, and they needed little encouragement.

Then I asked dear Patty if she would like to come back with me to the Plas in order to enjoy the fun which was to come. I need my female troops around me, and she leaped at the chance. It was dark when we arrived home, and none of the villains on the mountain will have spotted her arrival.

Now the Plas is quiet, and everybody but me is in bed trying to sleep. The house is crammed full; but with the children away Joseph and Skiff have taken over the nursery, and Patty is sleeping in Sian's bed. We all retired early in anticipation of the events to come. I will collapse onto my mattress in just a few minutes. As I write I can hear rain on the roof, and indeed Shemi forecast that there would be some showers in the night, followed by good weather tomorrow. The watchmen in the field have oilskins to keep them dry, and a roaring fire to keep them warm.

The sound of the rain brings me some innocent pleasure, since we know from their flickering candle lanterns that the villains are all out there still, ill-equipped for bad weather, and probably by now thoroughly wet and miserable. They will not dare to light fires for fear of being spotted. Some of them, like Lloyd, Beynon and Watkins, will be suffering from ancient injuries; others will be nursing more recent ones. They are all destitute, hungry, thirsty and dirty. Some of them are homeless. Poor fellows – I almost feel sorry for them.

5 November 1806

We have won a stunning victory, and a wave of euphoria has swept over the Plas. We have had a party this evening like no other in living memory, with feasting, and drinking, and laughing and dancing. Suddenly, fear and tension have been swept away. I think that I have never been so happy; other happinesses in my life have been anticipated and gradually attained, but

this one is special, since it has sprung out of the deviousness and brutality and greed of our enemies. True, our
triumph has been planned for, and hoped for, but right
up until the last minute I hardly dared to believe in it, for
so many things could have gone wrong. Hardly anything did go wrong, and since seven of the clock this
evening I have been dancing on clouds and hugging
angels. I must have embraced a thousand times during
the course of the evening, and five hundred of those
embraces were reserved for Owain. I fear that I have
done further damage to the poor dear man's ribs, and set
his recovery back by a week; but I could not help myself.

I must start at the beginning. At dawn three more of
our labourers went up to Parc Haidd and relieved the
night watchmen. We were all up early, and over breakfast we went through our plans for one last time, making
sure that everybody knew exactly what they were
supposed to do. There were some low clouds wafting
about, but the rain had stopped, and the weather was
perfect for our purposes. We did some spying out of our
windows, and saw that the villains were still in their
chosen positions. Billy and Will did the milking as usual,
Shemi fed all the other animals, watered the heavy
horses and checked the sheep, and Mrs Owen and Bessie
completed the usual tasks in the dairy. Grandma went to
the garden and dug up some potatoes and pulled up a
few leeks. I fed the chickens, ducks and geese, collected
the eggs, and took the dogs for a run around a couple of
the bottom fields. Grandpa went for his usual walk
along the boundaries of the farm, taking care not to
notice anything untoward. Joseph went for a pleasant
stroll up to Ffynnon Brynach and back. Patty kept out of
sight. Hettie arrived from the Parrog to collect her eggs
and butter, and did not go away again, since we anticipated that we would need her. To all appearances, life

went on as normal at the Plas, and this must have been very frustrating for the soggy villains.

Then in mid-morning Billy, Shemi, Will and Skiff emerged from the barn, each one carrying a brand-new shovel and pick, and marched up to Parc Haidd making a good deal of noise. Demonstrating great skill in the matter of theatricals, they consulted a map, one way up and then the other, and discussed at length which field was which. Having finally decided that they were in the right one, they started measuring. First, Billy paced from one side of the field to the other. Then they decided that his paces were too long, and Will did the pacing instead. They decided to use a big stone to mark the place where the treasure was buried. They laboriously dragged it from one of the stone walls and plonked it in an agreed position. Then they re-measured, and moved it a few yards. Then they repeated the whole process several times over. Then Mrs Owen rang the bell at the front door, and Billy shouted 'Dinnertime!', and they threw their tools to the ground and trooped down to the house.

They could hardly contain themselves as they walked, and collapsed in hysterics as soon as they came through the kitchen door. We hoped that the villains did not hear the gales of laughter. We congratulated the men on their acting ability, and we all enjoyed a good dinner. We tried to imagine what was going on in the spying positions established by the villains.

Since the field was now unguarded, we assumed that the dastardly fellows would creep closer to Parc Haidd. And so they did. Occasionally, as we looked out of the upstairs nursery window, we caught glimpses of Rice and his confederates moving among the boulders and crags on the flank of the mountain, and we hoped that none of them would break a leg. Then we saw the tall bracken moving near St Brynach's holy spring. They were sliding on their stomachs down the stony slope, trying to remain invisible. At last all six were installed behind the northern stone wall at the edge of Parc Haidd. Simultaneously Lloyd and his confederates were scrambling over one stone wall after another, also trying to remain invisible, and approaching from the east. We saw them perfectly clearly; indeed, we could hardly miss them, since Elias and Smyllie still had their jesters' hats on. Idiots to the last, I thought. Soon all four of them were huddled up behind the eastern stone wall of Parc Haidd. The field that they were in had twenty young bullocks in it, and the animals took a great interest in their newly arrived friends. Those of us who were look-ing on from the safety of the house could hardly contain ourselves as we thought of the paroxysms of fear that must have been afflicting the two Londoners, who had probably never been within a hundred yards of one frisky bullock before, let alone twenty.

In the middle of the afternoon, having allowed sufficient time for the villains to get stiff and cold and irritable, Billy and the other diggers emerged from the Plas and ambled back up to the field. They did more measuring and more debating, and finally decided on exactly the spot where the treasure was buried. Then they sat down and had a little picnic. Finally, they started digging. Gradually the hole got deeper and the piles of sandy soil around it became higher. Dusk began to fall, and they were still going down. They went and fetched some candle lanterns, and continued in the darkness. By the time they were down to about six feet it was seven of the clock, and pitch dark. Then Mrs Owen rang the Plas Ingli bell again, and Billy said, 'Suppertime, boys!' Then the four of them had a big argument. Billy said that there was less than one foot to go, and thought they should continue before going off for supper, but the others argued in very loud voices that they could finish the job off in five minutes after supper. Billy was out-voted, and so they threw down their shovels and picks, took their lanterns, and trudged off down towards the Plas.

At last they reached the Plas, went into the kitchen and closed the door behind them. This was the signal for the opening of the Gates of Hell up in Parc Haidd. Candle lanterns appeared on both the northern and eastern sides of the field, shadowy figures scrambled over stone walls, and there was a mad rush towards the big hole in the ground. It was difficult from the windows of the Plas to see what was going on, but we all heard the sounds of a mighty battle – thuds, thumps, shouts and curses, and the clash of metal against metal. We even heard the wild tinkling of the bells on the jesters' hats. Thankfully, there were no gunshots, and we concluded that the villains had not brought with them either pistols or muskets. We let the pandemonium go on for as long as we dared, and then Mrs Owen rang the Plas Ingli bell with groups of five strokes, four times. Immediately more than twenty candle lanterns were lit behind assorted stone walls, in the lane and in the Plas Ingli yard, and the defenders of law and order sprang into action. They sprinted up to the field. Some of them rushed through the gate and others vaulted over the walls, and then they moved in to arrest the enemy.

It was difficult to see from the house what was going on, but later we pieced it together from various descriptions. Apparently the two gangs hardly noticed that their enterprise was at an end, or that they were con-fronted by superior forces, for they were all too preoccupied with trying to kill each other. Rice and Lloyd were the most vicious, and they were discovered in the bottom of the pit, assaulting each other with

447

shovels. The sides of the pit collapsed, and they were lucky not to be buried alive. Some of the boys from town had to dig them out, still snarling at each other even though they were half dead. Beynon and Howell were going at it with their fists serving as hammer and tongs, grappling and rolling about in the spoil by the side of the pit. The Ifan brothers, living up to their reputation as fellows with big bodies and small brains, were chasing Elias and Smyllie round the field in the pitch darkness, wielding pickaxes and threatening (in Welsh) to tear them limb from limb. All four of them had to be over-powered by superior numbers. Billy said he thought it best to intervene; two of them spoke no English and the other two spoke no Welsh, so there was little chance of a negotiated truce.

After twenty minutes of chaos, the conspirators were finally overwhelmed and subdued. There was blood everywhere, and one of the Ifan brothers had a very serious injury in his side which he claimed had been inflicted by a Cockney pickaxe. Beynon was suffering from agonizing pain in the arm which he broke in the struggle prior to David's death. Otherwise the injuries were relatively minor – black eyes, lacerated faces, battered shins and skulls, and bruised bodies. Their clothes were filthy, and in shreds. They were all still conscious, but not all able to walk, so some of them had to be carried down to the Plas. Even after being captured, they continued to kick and yell, and the language was not at all suitable for the ears of a lady. Rice and Lloyd, in particular, were fighting mad in their attempts to get at each other, and could be kept apart only with the greatest difficulty. They were marched and dragged down from the field in a ragged procession illuminated by candle lanterns, to the accompaniment of much cheering and jeering.

When they entered the yard every person except myself went out to inspect the captured rogues. I would not have any of them in the house, so they were paraded over to the barn and hauled inside. I watched them from the landing window, but it was so dark, and they were so filthy and dejected, that I could not distinguish one from another. Indeed, even if they had all been dressed in their Sunday finery, and if the midday sun had been shining upon them, I would not have recognized them; for I had vowed many months ago that I would not meet or speak to any of my husband's murderers until the day that they were finally crushed by the full weight of the law. The others recognized them all right, and people like Patty and Owain, who had suffered terribly at their hands, must have felt powerful emotions as they were dragged past them into the barn. Once inside, they were all stretched out on the threshing floor and trussed up with chains and ropes. Grandpa said afterwards that even in an untrussed state they would not have had the energy to stand, let alone effect an escape.

After a little while Billy came out of the barn and crossed the yard to the house. I could see his face in the light of his candle lantern, and it bore a worried expression.

'Mistress Martha,' he said. 'There's only eight of them. Watkins and Fenton are missing.'

My heart missed a beat. Like an idiot I said: 'Are you quite sure?'

'Quite sure. No doubt about it.'

'Can you find out from the others when and where they were last seen? Perhaps you could try a little gentle interrogation on them.'

'It will be a pleasure, Mistress,' said Billy, and returned to the barn. I could see from my window that Billy and Grandpa Isaac dragged each of Watkins's confederates

449

to their feet, one by one, and took them out into the yard for questioning out of the earshot of the others. No violence was required, and the whole matter was dealt with quite quickly. Then Billy, Grandpa and Owain returned to the house. The four of us sat round the kitchen table.

'Now then,' said Grandpa. 'There are at least thirty good fellows guarding the prisoners, and Joseph and the women are setting about the unpleasant task of cleaning and dressing their wounds. Strange fellow, Joseph. He would spend an hour stitching up a condemned man's split head just so that he could go to the gallows two minutes later looking tidy.'

'On the matter of the whereabouts of Master Watkins and Master Fenton,' said Billy, 'the other four all say that they left them on the summit of the mountain. Fenton refused to descend through all those nasty crags and crevices for fear that he might do himself a damage, and Watkins declared that he was too old and stiff for such escapades.'

'So they trusted those other evil fellows, Rice, Howell and the Ifan brothers, to dig up the treasure and simply hand it over to them later?'

'No no,' said Grandpa. 'They all say that a deal was struck. In compensation for being spared the crawling and the digging, Watkins and Fenton swore on oath that they would each forfeit twenty golden sovereigns when the share-out was done. They agreed to meet up at midnight back at Rice's lodging house on the Parrog.'

'Very good,' I said. 'We have to believe that they are all four telling the truth. Come to think of it, there is no reason for them to lie, since they have no great incentive to let Watkins and Fenton go free while they themselves head for the rope and the drop.'

'I agree, Martha,' said Owain. 'Back to business, and

we must be quick. From the summit Watkins and Fenton will have observed the failure of their enterprise and heard all the chaos in Parc Haidd. They probably assume that all four of their friends are captured. So where will they go now?'

'Certainly not back to the Parrog,' said Grandpa. 'They will assume that warrants are out for their arrest, and that a search party will soon be after them. But first they have to get off the mountain. The north flank is not as steep and boulder-strewn as the south side, but neither of them will know the sheep tracks, and they will be stumbling about in the pitch blackness. They will both be in a mad panic. I should not be surprised if one or both of them was to fall and get injured.'

Owain turned to Billy. 'Now then, Billy,' he said. 'Can you get twenty of your fellows up onto the mountain with lanterns, to search the summit and the north side?'

'Certainly, Master Owain,' said Billy. 'We can take three groups. Will can take a few of the boys from town, Skiff can take a few more, and I will go with the labourers from the estate. Shemi can stay behind with five or six to keep an eye on the prisoners.' And so he rushed off, and within a few minutes three search parties were heading, with new candles in their lanterns, up onto the bracken-covered bluestone slopes.

I was concerned that there were still two villains on the loose, but Owain put his arm around my shoulder and said: 'Don't you worry, Martha. Our friends will find them. Even if they don't, and even if Watkins and Fenton have managed to get off the mountain, they are abject cowards and they will run as far as their fat little legs will carry them away from Carningli and the Plas. Once daylight comes, there will be search warrants and a price on their heads, and I am sure they will be caught. If one thing is certain it is this – they will

451

never again trouble you, or me, or your beloved estate.'

I had to accept the common sense of what Owain was saying, and in any case there was no time for further contemplation. Somewhat belatedly, the three constables from Newport turned up, and I formally made a complaint that the eight men whom we had apprehended had trespassed on our land and had caused an affray. That was enough for the members of the two gangs to be arrested and charged. Once they were in the custody of the constables they had to be got to the Newport lock-up, so Shemi got two of the ponies out of the paddock, harnessed them to a cart and a *gambo*, and placed them at the disposal of the law officers. The prisoners, still trussed up so tight that they could hardly move, were dragged to their feet and out of the barn. Rice, Howell and the Ifan brothers were dumped onto the cart, and Lloyd, Beynon, Elias and Smyllie onto the *gambo*. Then off they went, with the constables and half a dozen of Shemi's friends in attendance. The town boys said that they would stand outside the lock-up and watch the prisoners like owls all night, although in truth the criminals were all so exhausted that escape could not possibly have been an option.

And then they were gone. There was no waving, no jeering. We all stood in silence, and watched them as they disappeared into the darkness down the track towards the Cilgwyn road. The four men who had murdered my dear husband, and four more of their accomplices, were on their way to prison at last. In half an hour they would all be behind bars. There was a sort of anticlimax as the Plas became quiet, and I felt an emptiness and a heaviness of heart – no sense of relief, let alone triumph.

Then there was nothing for it but to celebrate, for that was what everybody else wanted to do. Grandpa fetched a barrel of ale and some big jars of duty-free brandy from the cellar. Mrs Owen organized the other women, including Patty and Hettie, in the scullery and the kitchen, and soon the makings of a mighty feast began to appear – loaves of bread, bowls of salty butter, piles of buns, plates of cold meats, a jugged hare, two whole baked sewin, vegetables and fruits, sauces and chutneys, fresh cream in abundance, fruit preserves and delicate sugary sweetmeats. In no time at all kettles and saucepans were whistling and bubbling on the fire, and almost all of our supplies of plates and cutlery were taken out and placed on the kitchen table.

'Good gracious me!' I said to Mrs Owen. 'Where have all these provisions come from?'

'From our larder, Mistress,' replied the miracle-worker, 'with a little bit of planning. You have been a bit preoccupied these last few days, if I may say so, and might not have noticed the kitchen activity. I assumed that we might have a multitude in this evening, and they will no doubt start arriving at any moment.'

And indeed they did. First our tenant families – the Griffiths family of Dolrannog Isaf, the Williamses of Gelli, the Tuckers of Penrhiw, and the Pritchards of the other Dolrannog – arrived, all bearing gifts. Then the folks from Brithdir. They could not have escaped the commotion up in Parc Haidd, and indeed many of them will have seen the lights and heard the yelling warriors from their windows. Most of their men had indeed been volunteers in the Plas Ingli Defence Force. Now the women and children appeared, carrying jugs of milk, eggs, potatoes and whatever else they could afford, as contributions to the feast. Then the labourers and their families appeared from Penrhiw Fach and Plain Dealings, Brynaeron and Trefelin, Brithdir Bach and Waun Isaf. They too carried gifts of food and drink, bless them, although they could ill afford the gesture. Then some of our other neighbours appeared, including Edwards Trefach, Prosser Frongoch, and Rhys Cilshafe, carrying with them their congratulations at our victory and expressing their delight at the manner in which we had brought the villains to their knees. Some of our friends from town turned up, having anticipated something from all the gossip that has been flying around in the shops and inns, and having seen the prisoners paraded through the town on the way to the lock-up on Long Street. Shemi and the constables had told them all about the battle, and they were thoroughly amused.

We could not possibly seat all those who arrived, so the eating and drinking had to be done standing up, and we could hardly move for the crowd in the kitchen and parlour. The crush became even more intense when the search parties started to arrive back from the mountain. Will, and then Billy, and then Skiff came back with their fellows, all exhausted and frustrated at their failure to apprehend the missing villains. There was no trace of them anywhere, although Billy said he had been to the summit himself and had seen all the signs of their occupation of the grassy hollow near the topmost crags. 'Don't worry, Mistress,' he said. 'We will get them. All the boys are prepared to resume the search tomorrow at first light, and when the clerk is awake we can get an arrest warrant organized. Once there is a price on their heads – and maybe even without it – anybody who sees them will grab them in a flash, for they are not the sorts of fellows who will be very clever at resisting arrest.'

'Very true, Billy,' I said. 'Thank you for your wonderful efforts and for your reassurance. Let us hope that within the next day or so there will be two new arrivals in the Newport lock-up, which is, I dare say, already

454

somewhat overcrowded. Now then, you and your friends need some refreshments.'

The hungry and thirsty fellows joined the feast, and soon, as the ale and the brandy soothed sore joints and loosened dry tongues, there was so much noise that one could hardly hear oneself think. Everybody had a personal story from the Battle of Parc Haidd to relate; each of the participants, and each of the observers, had experienced or seen something different. Because much of the action had taken place in the dark, I dare say there was a great deal of imagination involved in some of the stories that were told.

Somebody started singing, and before long sweet traditional airs were echoing round the *cwm*, although not very sweetly sung. The Jenkins boys and various others had brought their fiddles and their flutes, and Bessie and Will asked whether they might use the threshing floor in the barn as a dance floor. 'Of course,' said I. 'Off you go. Just be careful with your candle lanterns, with all that unthreshed barley piled high.' So off they went, and the feast was transformed into a *twmpath*, and everybody had a wonderful time.

As the evening went on I managed to relax more and more, and Owain stayed close by my side. Both he and I drank far too much, and ate too much, and talked too much, and did too much embracing with each other and with those who wished us well. At last, well after midnight, those of our neighbours with small children took their leave, and those of us who had been emotionally involved in the planning of the campaign to bring the villains to their knees realized that we were far more exhausted than those who had been directly involved in the battle. Grandpa and Grandma slipped away to their room, next Joseph excused himself and said good night, and then I realized that Owain was finding it difficult to keep awake. He was, after all, still recovering from his injuries, and was still in pain. So I packed him off to my bed, and he is already asleep.

I am sitting at my table, tired and just a little tipsy but with my brain too active for sleep. The kitchen downstairs is still echoing with laughter and buzzing with conversation; the sounds of music and dancing feet and clapping hands are drifting across to the house from the open doors of the barn. I dare say that many of our guests will get no sleep at all tonight, and that we will have a considerable crowd for breakfast.

6 November 1806

Life is gradually returning to normal, although we have had another unusual day. I have hardly been able to keep track of the myriad comings and goings.

At first light, true to their word, the three search parties ate a quick breakfast and were off again up onto the mountain. Where they found the energy from I will never know, for most of them had been carousing in the barn all night. They were out for most of the morning, and returned empty-handed around noon. More searches are under way in town and in the countryside round about, but there is a consensus that Watkins and Fenton may well have escaped from the area already, and may be in hiding in Tenby or Cardigan. They never returned to Rice's lodgings on the Parrog, and we got a report this afternoon that at least one very filthy fellow got onto the Cardigan coach first thing this morning some distance to the east of the town. If they are still in the area, they will be found, for every hovel, cave and hut is known to somebody and will be searched. Indictments have been entered against both of them for burglary, trespass, sowing discord, nuisance, and assorted other offences; and Owain has asked for a charge of attempted murder to be brought against them. Arrest warrants have been issued. It turns out that they both owe considerable sums of money in town, and some of the local traders have offered a reward of twenty sovereigns for their capture alive. They are, I presume, no good to them dead.

The wheels of justice have started to grind over the imprisoned villains, and I have no inclination to feel sorry for them. Four of them – Smyllie, Elias, Sion ap Ifan and his brother Huw – are silly fellows and bullies who deserve to be brought to justice, but I hope that the law does not deal too harshly with them. The other four are the men who killed my beloved David in cold blood and dragged me to the very edge of insanity; and while I seek not to be vengeful or vindictive, I am not inclined to forgive them. Let justice take its course. I am particularly pleased that we have managed to get them behind bars without committing any offence ourselves. We have certainly been devious and have led them by their noses into a situation from which they could not escape; but they have only their own greed and gullibility to blame. We have not damaged any of their property, or abused them or assaulted them, and when they face our complaints against them in court they cannot have any grounds for counter-claims against us. Their defence, in my estimation, will be virtually non-existent.

This morning, when Bessie and Patty and I had a few quiet moments together in my room, we shared a glowing satisfaction at the peculiarly feminine nature of our campaign against the villains; and we enjoyed a good deal of laughter when we thought that we had brought the two gangs to the dark and fateful pit in the middle of

Parc Haidd without the use of any force whatsoever, by a process more akin to seduction than rape. In fairness, our beloved menfolk had gone along with the plan enthusiastically, and it could not have been implemented without their participation and their skill in matters of detail, but we thought we deserved more than a little credit.

It wasn't long before people started arriving. First were Lewis Legal and Will Final Testament, who had to be briefed as to the events of yesterday evening. They both chortled with delight, and agreed that they would act for us when the two gangs were brought to the Great Sessions. However, they also agreed the line they would take with the criminals today, and went down to the lock-up to talk to them. They offered their services to the two gangs for nothing, and none of the offenders was in a position to refuse their advice since there are no other attorneys in town.

The clerk to the justices and local scrivener, one William Daniels, arrived at my invitation in mid-morning, and we started entering indictments. We did not need our legal friends for this, since both Grandpa Isaac and Owain are magistrates, and they know the right words to use. By the time poor Master Daniels went back to his office in town, he had a pile of documents almost too heavy to carry, and I was running short of writing paper. Each and every one of the prisoners had to have his own indictments, and they covered affray, trespass, stabbing, extortion, resisting arrest, sowing discord, unlawful entry, swearing, assault, attempted murder and a host of other things. Many of the complaints came from me, but others were entered by Patty, Grandpa Isaac, Owain and Joseph. After much thought, I decided that I would now take out an indictment against Rice, Howell, Beynon and Lloyd for the murder of Master David Morgan of Plas Ingli on the 12th day of February in the year of our Lord 1805. This would ensure a trial at the Great Sessions in Haverfordwest before a judge and jury. The Clerk to the Justices was very surprised at this, but Joseph advised that his evidence was strong enough to stand up under cross-examination, and that it would certainly obtain the prosecutions we desired since the associated cases against the villains would already have amply demonstrated their brutality, their deviousness, and their disregard for the law.

Down in town, we gather that there were so many volunteers for guard duty outside the lock-up that the constables had to organize a rota system. Shemi was there for most of the day, and reported that just as for the battle and the searches of the mountain, nobody wanted paying or rewarding in any way. He says that the instinct of almost everybody in town is to ensure a safe and happy future for me and my family, to bring the villains to justice, and to ensure that nothing is left to chance until they are all safely incarcerated in Haverfordwest gaol. I was immensely touched by this, and was close to tears as I realized – having often in the past forgotten it – that this warm and lovely community is indeed populated by angels. As the story of the battle and its outcome goes round town, many of the angels are laughing, and Shemi says there is great admiration for the manner in which we led the whole community into a mire of wild speculations in the days before the final confrontation. Everybody sees why it was needed, and nobody is offended.

The news from the lock-up is that the two gangs are in separate cells, still snarling and throwing insults at each other. Each of them is in leg irons, and although they have been fed and allowed to wash they are so dirty and ragged that Shemi says he has never seen a bunch of vagrants and beggars to compare with them. Will Final Testament has spoken to Rice and his cronies, and Lewis Legal to Lloyd and his gang. They have all been advised to admit to trespass and affray, since there is no likelihood of successful defence on those matters, but they have not been told what else of a legal nature might hit them. And they have all been advised, in private meetings with the attorneys, to seek to mitigate their own culpability by making complaints against their colleagues for leading them astray and against their enemies for assault and attempted murder. So poor Master Daniels and one or two other scriveners have been writing all day. Sion ap Ifan is entering an indictment against Elias for attempting to murder him with a pickaxe, and against Smyllie for grievous bodily harm, and against Joseph Rice for extortion, breach of contract, and encouraging him to undertake criminal activities. Rice is accusing Matthew Lloyd of attempted murder, and vice versa. Howell is accusing Beynon of attempted murder and Rice of obtaining money by false pretences. Smyllie is accusing Elias of extortion, and Huw ap Ifan of attempted murder. And so it goes on. What the poor magistrates will make of it all, goodness knows.

The Clerk to the Justices, acting on my recommendation, took a break from his writing and went to see Squire Gittins and Squire Higgon, and they have both agreed to convene a Petty Sessions tomorrow at two of the clock in the afternoon in the Sessions House on East Street. Then Master Daniels returned to the writing out of indictments. He was probably not particularly sorry, for he gets a small fee for every one he writes out, and by this evening he will be a wealthy man.

Back at the Plas, we have received a stream of social visitors, all coming to give their congratulations and felicitations. Even the Rector turned up to express the gratitude of the community for the manner in which we had brought eight evil men to book. If the members of the community had really suffered so much at their hands, and had really felt so strongly about them, I felt more than a little disappointed that everybody else had left it to us; but I did not say that to the Reverend Mr Devonald. Mary Jane and Ellie called in, and I was delighted to discover that they were both fully aware of the female tactics which we had employed, and gratified at their successful outcome. Those who could not come sent messages, and there were errand boys, some on horseback and others on foot, coming and going all day. I could never have imagined what interest there has been in our conflict with these two gangs, or the satisfaction which their incarceration has brought to so many.

Now it is evening, and things are quieter. Skiff and all his friends have returned home to their hovels and cottages in town. Hettie has returned to the Parrog. Our tenants and labourers are all getting back to their humdrum lives on the land. Joseph and Patty are still here, and indeed they are very welcome to stay, but they too have other things to do, and they will go home tomorrow after the Petty Sessions. Their beds are needed, and on the day after tomorrow I will go to Haverfordwest and fetch Sian and the children. I miss the little ones dreadfully, and I miss the music of their laughter about the place, and we will all be relieved to have them back among us.

And Owain will have to go back to Llannerch, for his servants need him and indeed he feels that it is his duty. He will take my heart with him, for in these last days of tension and high adventure he has been a solid rock at my side, calm in the midst of chaos, rational and clear-thinking while others have been impulsive and urging action while others (including myself) have preferred to talk. He is still in a good deal of pain from the deep lacerations on his skin, but he has not complained once or sought to draw attention to himself. His courage is beyond question. And he has been prepared to risk loose talk by remaining at the Plas, in my bedroom and indeed in my bed, during his recuperation.

Before all these departures occur, we have the small matter of the Petty Sessions tomorrow afternoon. That will, I have no doubt, be an occasion which will pass into local folklore.

7 November 1806

The Petty Sessions have been held, and they were a severe disappointment to all of us. We achieved our objectives, of course, and by now all eight of our enemies are behind bars in Haverfordwest castle; but in the court hearing there was so little in dispute, and the evidence against the villains was so overwhelming, that the entertainment value of the afternoon was strictly limited.

We all turned up at court in good time, and had to be let in since we were the principal plaintiffs. Owain came with us, on his first outing in public since his appalling experiences at the hands of Rice and his cronies. There were hundreds of people outside, including various squires and their wives, merchants and common people, and they greeted us with cheers as we went in. Many of them wanted to get in, and indeed over forty of them had offered to appear as witnesses for the prosecution; but there was no room, and only about a dozen people gained entrance. Then the two magistrates appeared, settled down behind their table, and asked the Clerk to the Justices about the nature of the day's business.

'Thirty-six indictments, your honours, all relating to the activities of eight defendants, whose names you have before you.'

'Thirty-six?' gasped Squire Higgon. 'It is hard enough dealing with one or two at a Petty Sessions. Are they complicated, and do they relate to serious charges?'

'Indeed they do, your honours. They include murder, attempted murder, burglary, affray, assault, extortion . . .'

'Enough, enough,' said Squire Gittins. 'Can you not reduce the number of indictments to more manageable proportions?'

'Afraid not, Squire. I only managed to write out thirty-six in the time I have had. I have been asked to do at least another twenty.'

'Oh dear. Then we had better cope as best we can. Do you have indictments against all of the defendants?'

'Yes, your honour. The one with the least number of complaints against him is Master Ellis, whose real name is Master Elias, and he has just the four.'

'Do you mean that the names down on this piece of paper are not the real names of the defendants?'

'Who can tell, your honour? They tell me who they are, and I have to believe them.'

'Oh dear,' groaned Squire Gittins, who was probably wishing already that he was somewhere else. 'This looks like being a complicated afternoon. Right. Let's move on. Who is representing the plaintiffs?'

'I am, sir,' said Joseph, rising to his feet.

'Are you a trained attorney, Doctor Harries?'

'No sir, but I don't think that will make too much difference.'

'Very well. And now, Master Daniels, who is representing the defendants?'

'Nobody, sir. Master Lewis and Master Probert have advised them as to their best course of action, but sadly today they are otherwise engaged. No other attorney in the locality is prepared to appear for them, either paid or unpaid.'

'Not surprising, I suppose,' said Squire Higgon. 'Well, let's get on with it. Now then, fetch the defendants from the lock-up, Master Wilson, if you please.'

So the constable walked the forty yards down to the Long Street lock-up, and brought them up, in single file, under an armed guard made up of twenty local lads holding bludgeons and axes. As they walked up the street there was abuse and jeering from the locals, and some of them came in with their already filthy clothes decorated with bits of rotten eggs and tomatoes. After a good deal of commotion all eight of them were installed in a makeshift dock, still with irons on their legs and guarded by the three constables. Now, for the first time, I was face to face with them. None of them would look me in the eye.

After the oaths had been sworn, and after Smyllie and Elias had admitted, under pressure from Joseph, that their names were not Smith and Ellis, the proceedings could begin. 'Doctor Harries, what are the charges?'

'So many, your honours, that I do not know where to start. Some of them may fall under the jurisdiction of this court, but others will certainly require referral to the Great Sessions. Shall we content ourselves for the moment with trespass and affray? All of the defendants are charged, on fifteen indictments, with trespassing on land belonging to Mistress Morgan of Plas Ingli, with stealing various pickaxes and shovels, and with causing an affray which prevented Master Billy Ifans and others from going about their lawful business.'

'And what was their lawful business?'

'A perfectly routine matter, your honours. They were digging a hole in order to bury a dead sheep.'

464

At this, pandemonium broke out in the court. All of us who were there as plaintiffs could not keep our faces straight, and there was a danger that we might all explode with laughter; but luckily the magistrates did not notice our scarcely concealed mirth because all of the defendants were shouting and snarling and rattling their chains. The noise went on for several minutes, with cries of 'Lies! Lies!' and 'What about the treasure?' echoing round the courtroom.

At last the magistrates managed to restore some sort of order, and Squire Higgon said: 'Doctor, they seem to be shouting something about a treasure. Do you wish to say something about that?'

'Pure fantasy, your honours,' replied Joseph in his best legal voice. 'I can assure you that there is no treasure in that hole or anywhere else. But it is a very good field for burying dead sheep because the soil is soft and deep and sandy. What the defendants think about the hole in the ground is a matter for them. With respect, may we return to the charges?'

'Hm. Yes, indeed. Defendants, do you understand the charges?'

And then there was pandemonium in the court again, with all eight of them yelling and gesticulating, and shouting insults at each other. The constables had to get between the two gangs in order to prevent grievous bodily harm being done. Somewhere above all the hullabaloo I heard Squire Higgon shouting 'Guilty or not guilty?' over and again. He and Squire Gittins finally lost patience. They both hammered on their table with their little wooden hammers, and something approaching silence was restored.

'Outrageous behaviour, sirs! Quite outrageous!' stormed Squire Higgon.

'Contempt of court of a most dastardly kind!

Contempt of court!' shouted Squire Gittins. 'We find all eight defendants guilty, without further ado, of contempt of court. We also find that the charges of affray and so forth are proved since the defendants refuse to plead.'

'All the indictments presented are in our view reasonable,' said Squire Higgon, calming down a little. 'Record that, Master Daniels, if you will. Also record the fact that the eight defendants are found guilty of a most serious contempt of court.' Then he turned to them and said: 'You, sirs, are remanded in custody in Haverfordwest gaol until you shall be brought to trial at the next Great Sessions. There, the matter of contempt of court will be dealt with, along with all of the other matters referred to in the indictments submitted by Doctor Harries and other representatives on behalf of their clients. No bail will be considered in view of the behaviour of the defendants.'

'Master Daniels, make sure that all of the paperwork is submitted to the court in good time,' added Squire Gittins. 'Now then, you may swear in fifteen special constables to help you to transport these fellows to Haverfordwest, and we authorize you to hire three wagons for the purpose. Court dismissed!'

The defendants were dragged back to the lock-up and kept out of harm's way for an hour or so while the special constables and transport were organized, and then the procession set off along the Cilgwyn road with jeering crowds running alongside the wagons. Then they were over the ford at Trefelin, up and over the mountain, and away, on a route and to a destination that I knew only too well from my own cruel incarceration of some years ago. I took some satisfaction from the fact that the men responsible for that evil act in 1797 were Benjamin Rice and George Howell, now both dead. Their sons

Joseph Rice and John Howell were now making the same journey, partly at least because of my own determination to see justice done to evil men.

The two magistrates retired downstairs to the bar, intent upon liquid refreshment in sufficient quantity to restore their equilibrium. Grandpa Isaac and Joseph joined them. Owain and I, and the rest of the Plas Ingli contingent, emerged into the daylight to cheers and yells of delight from the crowds outside. We had to describe the proceedings to them in detail, and they became even more gleeful. Then we said our farewells. Patty went back to her cottage, a free woman at last, and able to think about her future. Owain came back with us to the Plas to gather up his things.

Then, having embraced all the members of my household as warmly as he dared, and having thanked all of them for their loving care and devotion during his recuperation, he took his leave. I found parting very difficult, for I had enjoyed having him in my bed even if I had been outside it. Before he went downstairs we kissed long and hard, and again declared our growing love for each other. I must not be too sad, for his house is less than a mile away, and we will contrive to meet on most days over the weeks to come.

Now the house is quiet, and we all have to adjust to new circumstances, free of threats and almost free of challenges. I hope I shall be able to cope. Tomorrow I shall fetch the children, and they will do their best to keep me out of mischief.

Calm after Storm

10 November 1806

The calm after the storm is always a strange time, and mind and body both take time to adjust to changed circumstances. Three days is not enough to come to terms with what has happened to me and my enemies, and I have had three nights with very little sleep. True, I have been back in my own bed, and the children are back in theirs after having a wonderful time in Haverfordwest, but I miss Owain terribly. In addition, dark and distressing moods have been afflicting me as I recall my misadventure at the Glynymel ball. On several occasions I have come out in a cold sweat with the realization that John Fenton came within an inch of taking my virtue from me, and that it was partly my own fault. I think I am discovering what guilt means, and how it can affect the most resolute of souls.

I do not know what to do with myself, and my strange and irritable mood has not been eased by the weather. The first of the winter storms has hit us with a vengeance, with a wild wind screaming in from the west and carrying with it a veritable deluge of cold rain. The wind and the rain have stripped the autumn-coloured leaves from the trees, and now their branches are standing stark and bare against the sky. Yesterday the children and I could not get out at all, and even when wearing their oilskins the men got soaked as they went about their tasks of milking and caring for the animals. Billy went up to the top fields to inspect the sheep, and reported that the pit in the middle of Parc Haidd, freshly dug and six feet deep, has been so affected by the deluge that its sides have caved in. Now, he says, there is nothing much there but a muddy hollow filled with water. For some reason, that news made me unutterably sad, and I could not help reflecting on the disappearance of the focal point of our recent triumph against our enemies, and the ephemeral nature of things in general.

After the excitement of their stay with their little cousins in Haverfordwest, the children have been argumentative and bored, and I have not been very clever at entertaining them. Their mood was not improved yesterday by the foul weather, and by the fact that they have all got running noses and sore throats. But Sian has been a bubbling and cheerful angel as usual, and has done her best to keep them entertained with puzzles, and drawing sessions, and stories, and mysterious enterprises involving bits of wood and glue and string.

Grandpa and Grandma have been exhausted, and have done little but sleep for the last two days; and even the servants have been wandering about in a daze, going about their tasks with a degree of resignation which is unusual. I must try to understand them and try to understand myself, but at the moment the Plas is a strange and moody place.

This blessed place has once again shown its capacity for refreshment and renewal. I must say that the sun helps. This morning Bessie Sunbeam, not for the first or last time, came to my rescue and to the rescue of all who live beneath this roof.

After breakfast the cloud banks were suddenly swept away to the east, and the sun came out, and rays of sunshine streamed through our east-facing windows. Bessie was making my bed while I tried to decide which dress to wear for the day. 'Thank God for the sunshine, Mistress Martha,' she said. 'I trust that it will make you feel a little better.'

'Whatever do you mean, Bessie?' I snapped.

'Well, Mistress, we have all noticed your strange mood since the day of the Petty Sessions. We are not entirely surprised. I dare say that episode used up more of your reserves of energy than you might be prepared to admit.'

'You are probably right, Bessie. I am sorry for my short temper, but I do feel a strange emptiness in my heart.'

'Missing Master Owain, I dare say?'

'Yes, of course. I am very fond of him indeed, and I am not sure how I would have coped with that business of the treasure hunt if he had not been here by my side.'

'Well, Mistress, he is hardly very far away. No doubt he will be popping in very soon to pay his respects and remind you of his affection.'

She puffed up the pillows and tucked down the blankets. Then she added: 'Do you know what I think?'

'Tell me, Bessie.'

'I think you have had too much of people lately, and that you need to get up onto your mountain again.'

Suddenly I realized that she was right. Golden sunshine entered my soul. I sprang to my feet, and went over to hug my dear servant and friend. 'Bessie *bach*, how I love you!' I cried. 'You know me better than I know myself. You are perfectly right. Of late I have had no time to myself, no room to move, no air to breathe. But now the rain has stopped and the sun is shining. Will you put out my warm woollen dress and cloak? And my stout boots?'

And in fifteen minutes I was striding up the lane towards the common, with the west wind on my cheeks and the warm sun on my back. When I passed Parc Haidd I looked at the soggy hollow that had once been the pit of temptation for our enemies, and found it not a sad place but a symbol of the stupidity and greed of men. This cheered me up very much.

I sat on the big stone adjacent to Ffynnon Brynach, and looked out over my little world. The *cwm* was still streaming with water after all the rain of recent days, but the sunlight had turned muddy bogs into silver pools, and angry rills and rivulets into delicate threads of gold. With most of the leaves now blasted off the trees, I realized that the woodlands and the hedgerows had acquired patterns and traceries that had been missing since the days of plumping buds and unfurling leaves back in the spring. The air was clear and cool, and I could see with wonderful clarity the subtle colourings of Foeldrigarn and Frenni Fawr in the distance. The scents of damp earth and golden winter-flowering furze and brittle bracken reminded me that I was not very far from Heaven after all, and that this place, even in a season of storms and shortening days, had a strange power to bond me to itself.

I had no wish to escape, and walked on through the familiar wilderness of bluestone boulders and crags, up over one terrace and scree slope after another, winding my way upwards until I was at last on the summit. My lovely panorama was unchanged: the grey waters and scudding waves of Cardigan Bay to the north, the far crags of Pencaer and Dewisland to the west, the purple interlocking horizons of Mynydd Preseli to the south, and the crags and copses and fields of the *cwm* to the east. Below my feet, feeling so close that I might almost reach them with a decent throw of a pebble, were the gleaming and steaming roofs of the cottages of Newport – inhabited by the very people who had recently given me such encouragement and support during the battle with my enemies.

On the topmost crag, as ever, the west wind was strong and constant, and if there were any cobwebs in my hair they were soon removed. I suddenly felt like a child, and I stood on the highest tip of rock, fighting against the wind to keep my balance, and spread my arms wide, and closed my eyes. I felt that I was flying through the air, with the wind pressing on my face and breast and stomach, my dress streaming out behind me, and my cloak flapping and fighting to break free. My long hair, so often tamed and contained, now became a plaything of the wind. I thought that this must be what it is like to be an angel.

Then the wind dropped for a second, and I lost my balance, and the magic disappeared. I tumbled down onto the grassy hollow beside the crag, thinking that this is what it must be like to be a fallen angel, and I laughed at my own childishness and at the sheer elation and free-dom of the moment. On my back on the wet grass, I gazed for a while at the wide sky and the racing clouds, and the old raven, quiet guardian of the mountain, sailed on wide black wings across my field of vision. I remem-bered that this was precisely the place where Watkins and Rice and their confederates had huddled, just a week or so ago, while they spied upon the Plas and lusted after their imaginary treasure. To my surprise, I was not at all disquieted by this, and indeed I felt a calm satisfaction that they were now sitting in a stinking dungeon while I had repossessed my sacred mountain.

I realized that I was getting wet and dirty, and that Bessie would be disgusted with my appearance when I returned. So I climbed to my feet. Now I had had enough of the wild summit, and needed time in my sanctuary. So I climbed down, round the flank of the mountain, onto my hidden path across the scree slope, treading carefully because the rocks were very wet and slimy. Soon I was squeezing into my cave, which I had not visited since the appalling episode with little Daisy. I recalled the horror of that day, and the cold fear that I had experienced about the imagined abduction of one of my little ones, and the surging relief of discovering that my fear was unfounded and that all was well.

I sat on my bed of moss at the back of the cave for a long time, finding nurture and nourishment in the blessed silence. I wrapped myself in my cloak, and felt warm and comfortable. No birdsong, no sounds of bleating sheep, no barking dogs, no lowing cattle. Just a gentle whispering of the wind, and an occasional rustle from the fern fronds at the cave entrance. I must have fallen asleep, because when I was next aware of my surroundings it was almost dark inside the cave. I peeped out, and realized that it must be four of the clock, for the light was fading fast. So I said farewell to St Brynach and scrambled down among the rocks, and just as it was getting dark I stepped into the warm glow of the kitchen.

Daisy came running up to me and flung her arms around my neck. 'Do you know what, Mam?' she said breathlessly. 'This morning, when you were out for your walk, we looked up at the mountain and there, right up on the top summit, there was an angel. A real angel, with big wide wings and a long white dress and streaming hair. There was a sort of golden light shining on her. She was there for ages, and then she just flew away. Did you see her, Mam?'

'No,' I replied. 'I suppose I must have been looking the other way at the time.'

20 November 1806

A body has been found this morning on the estuary, in exactly the place where Owain was dumped and left for dead some weeks back. It was found by one of the ship-yard fellows who was walking along the path from the ferry to the place where he works. Apparently he walks that way every day, back and fore, and first noticed a bit of a stench a few days ago. This morning, with the wind in the north, it was overpowering, so he went to investigate, in among the tall reeds round about high water mark. He was shocked almost out of his wits by what he found.

From what I hear, the body was badly decomposed. It was a man dressed in bits and pieces of ragged clothes. He had matted hair and the remnants of a heavy beard. His eyes had been taken by the crows; and where his stomach had been there was a pit, excavated by rats. Parts of the corpse were heaving with maggots, and round it there were clouds of flies. The skin was shrivelled and soggy, but there was quite a lot of it left, maybe preserved by the salt water of the estuary.

Within half an hour of the discovery there was a crowd on the path near the reed-bed, and somebody had fetched Havard Medical. He came along, took one look at the disintegrating and stinking corpse, and declared it to be that of a vagrant. 'Happens all the time,' he said. 'Usually they die by the lime kilns because of the fumes. This one was probably drunk, and fell asleep in the reeds, and died from the cold.' The body could not be left where it was, so some of the shipyard workers wrapped cloths round their faces as protection against the vapours of rotting flesh, and moved it onto a makeshift bier, and took it to the mortuary. Doctor Havard went off to do the necessary paperwork. As luck would have it, Joseph was in town at the time, and he heard the news about the grotesque discovery. He thought that there might be more to this business than met the eye, and so he got the key from Davy Death three doors away. He let himself in, and as soon as he saw the human remains on the cold slab he knew that he was looking at all that was left of Alban Watkins.

He immediately sent a message to Havard Medical, and the poor fellow had to return to the grisly and putrid corpse and work with Joseph on the matter of identification. The task could not have been a pleasant one and could only be completed with the aid of large quantities of carbolic acid. But there was no doubt about it. The beard and hair colours were right, and there was just enough skin left on the face to recognize the scar across the nose that was one of Watkins's most distinctive features. The wizard and the medical man together measured body height and build, and they matched what both of them recalled of the evil fellow. Then Joseph made a terrifying discovery. He looked closely at the shreds of flesh and muscle on the throat, using his magnifying glass, and said to Doctor Havard: 'William, my dear fellow, this man has had his throat cut. He was murdered.' The doctor was amazed, but when he was shown the evidence, he had to agree. Then Joseph made another grotesque discovery. The shreds of shirt across

Watkins's chest were black, and initially he thought that this was black mud from the estuary; but then he looked more closely, and realized that it was old and congealed blood. He took some cleaning substance and loosened and peeled off the fabric. When he looked at the skin beneath he saw that it had been cut with a sharp knife, with several deep and long cuts, parallel and a couple of inches apart.

'Look at this, William,' said Joseph. 'What do you think?'

Havard examined the cuts, and looked quite horrified. 'Oh my God,' he said. 'I have never before seen such a thing. Torture?'

'Quite so. I have seen it once before, but it would betray a confidence if I were to give you the details. You will find out in due course.'

The two experts attempted to work out the date on which Watkins had died, using their knowledge of rates of putrefaction and so forth. They estimated that he could have been dead about two weeks. There was nothing more to discover, and nothing more to do. Joseph left Doctor Havard to complete his paperwork and to arrange an inquest. It will have to be tomorrow; the corpse cannot be left to rot any more, for fear of its becoming a hazard to public health.

Joseph came straight from the Parrog to give me the news. I was so appalled when I heard it that I hardly knew what to say. Even now, some hours after his departure back to Werndew, I cannot come to terms with it. I fear that I will be too afraid to close my eyes tonight, for if I do I am certain that my dream world will be inhabited by maggoty cadavers and demons from Hell.

I have sent a message to Owain and asked him to call in to discuss an urgent matter tomorrow at three in the afternoon. He will certainly come. Joseph will come too, and of course I will involve Grandpa Isaac as well. I hope that between us we will be able to work out the implications of this nightmarish discovery, and that I can obtain some reassurance that our contacts with evil men, alive or dead, are finally over.

21 November 1806

The inquest was held this morning. Joseph was present. The jury viewed the corpse, although some of them could hardly cope with the stench. The Coroner took statements from witnesses, formally recorded the facts discovered by Joseph and Havard Medical, and then concluded that 'Master Alban Watkins, lately resident on the Parrog in Newport, was murdered on or about 6 November 1806 by a person or persons unknown.' Since Watkins's only relative, his old cousin, was not willing to get involved at all, his body was then dumped into a pauper's grave outside consecrated ground, sprinkled with lime, and covered up.

At three of the clock we held a meeting of our War Council, as planned. I hope to God it will be the last. Owain had heard about the grotesque discovery on the estuary, but not the details. When he heard about the precise location at which the corpse had been dumped, and about the cutting of Watkins's chest, he was appalled, and I saw a tensing of his body. He knew far too much about the terror, and the pain, which Watkins must have endured before he was finally despatched with a slice across the throat. Joseph had to stop for a while, and I held Owain's hand as the four of us sat in silence for several minutes. Then Owain nodded, and Joseph completed his narrative.

'What devil could have done this?' I asked.

'Well,' replied Joseph. 'I have given the matter some thought. I have dismissed robbery as a motive; no self-respecting footpad would wish to rob, let alone kill, somebody who must have looked like a vagrant or a beggar. The most obvious suspect has to be John Fenton, for the two of them came down off the mountain together on the night of the Battle of Parc Haidd.'

'But why would Fenton have done such a thing?' asked Grandpa Isaac. 'He is a soft fellow, and I am not sure about his capacity for brutality and cold-blooded murder. Could they have fallen out, and had a furious row, and blamed each other for the fiasco which had overtaken their confederates?'

'I doubt that,' said Joseph. 'This does not have the hall-mark of a fight between old friends ending in hot-blooded murder. Remember that the killer knew exactly where Owain had been left to die, and went to the trouble of dumping the corpse in the same spot. Fenton would have had no reason to do it, and he would not have had the energy anyway to drag a heavy man from wherever he had been killed. But there is certainly a bizarre symbolism in the choice of the final resting place.'

'I agree with that,' said Grandpa. 'The murderer must have known where and how Owain was found. How many people knew about that?'

'The whole town,' I replied. 'Patty, and Skiff, and most of the shipyard workers, and quite a lot of others besides were actually there, and news spreads fast. You can con-firm that, Joseph, since you were there as well?'

Joseph nodded. 'Quite correct, Martha. We do not get very far with that line of enquiry. But then, on the matter of symbolism, think of the cuts on Watkins's chest.'

'Could they not have been done after his death?' asked Grandpa.

'I doubt it, Isaac. There was so much blood that I think the cuts were made when he was alive – exactly as happened with Owain. If the cuts had been made even a minute or two after death there would have been hardly any blood at all.'

'This may sound like a weird suggestion,' said Owain, 'but could this have been some sort of ritual sacrifice, with torture followed by murder? Something to do with secret societies, or witchcraft or wizardry, Joseph? You know about such things.'

'No. In all my years of study I have never come across such a case. There are certainly foolish people around who profess to use black magic to do the work of the devil, but I know all of the likely candidates within fifty miles of this place, and none of them could have done this. There would be no point at all in starting a witch-hunt.'

'So where does this get us?' I asked. 'If you do not think it was Fenton, where else do we go with our suppositions?'

'Well,' said Grandpa, 'Watkins was not short of enemies, that's for sure. He has bullied and victimized all sorts of people in town since he arrived back from the penal colonies, and even before he was sent out there he was a monster. I personally know at least half a dozen poor people in and around town who would happily have slit his throat if given half a chance.'

'I can vouch for that,' said Owain. 'Remember that I now employ most of his former servants and have to look after most of the labourers on the Llannerch estate who endured years of misery during his time as squire. He sent three people to the gallows for trifling offences, and I know of at least five others who died as a direct consequence of his cruelty and vindictiveness. The murderer may well be one of my own people.'

'There would be a nice symmetry to that,' said Joseph, 'in spite of the appalling nature of what has happened. Watkins was one of those who tortured you and left you for dead. Not many people know you were tortured – those beneath this roof, and those beneath yours.'

'Oh my God!' said I. 'Should we suspect one of our own servants or friends? I cannot believe that Shemi, or Will, or Billy could have done this even to our worst enemy.'

'And I cannot believe it of my servants either,' said Owain. 'Even in retribution for the injuries inflicted on me by my tormentors, I cannot think that they could have carried out an execution in such a cold-blooded and calculating fashion.'

'I have to accept what you say,' said Joseph. 'You know your servants far better than I do. I am still mystified as to who did this. Revenge was surely the motive, but maybe that is as far as we can go. Perhaps, my friends, we had better not investigate this murder too closely. We wanted Watkins strung up from the gallows anyway, and this execution has simply brought forward his demise and saved us all from the bother of an additional court case.'

And so, on that somewhat callous note, we had to leave it. Now, at the end of the day, I have to record that we are really no further forward in working out what happened to Watkins before his body was dumped, and who was responsible. Neither Doctor Havard, nor Joseph, nor the town constables, nor the local magistrates appear keen to take the matter any further. One senses that there will not be much mourning in town for the loss of Master Alban Watkins, nor many prayers said for his departed soul.

Having concluded the business of the meeting this afternoon the four of us took a cup of tea together, and enjoyed some of Grandma Jane's special fruit cake, and talked of more cheerful things. In particular, we took great pleasure in hearing from Hettie that Patty and her sailor friend Jake Nicholas are to be married. That is, if they can find anybody to do the marrying, since ladies of easy virtue expect no favours from Rector Devonald and his church. At any rate, Patty has given up her dubious profession, and Jake has promised to make an honest woman of her. He is wildly and passionately in love with her, says Hettie, and everybody on the Parrog knows it. Maybe that is because she gave him more than his money's worth on the occasion of their first meeting; but I am sure there is more to it than that, since she is very pretty, and also far too intelligent to be confined to a grubby boudoir for the rest of her working life. Jake has bought a share in a small fishing boat, and he is a skilled seaman and a hard worker, so I am sure he will do well. I am quite delighted by the news, since I am very fond of Patty. We have shared many secrets, and I feel that there is a strong bond of friendship between us.

Tomorrow Owain and I will go down to town in the trap. We will have a beautiful time together, whatever the weather does. We will do some shopping. We have decided that we are no longer afraid of wagging tongues, and we will both take delight in showing off our mutual affection for the rest of the world to see. Then we will go and visit Patty and Jake, which gesture will cause a few raised eyebrows but will be of inestimable value to the happy couple.

3 December 1806

November has gone, and I am grateful for its passing, for it was a month too full of turbulent emotions. Enough of mistrust, and brutality, and rage, and fear and deception. I want December to be a month of love, culminating in a quiet and joyful Christmas season. I trust that it will be the month in which Owain and I can settle on our future together. I have seen him every day, and every day brings a deepening of my love. Every moment in his presence is sheer joy. And I know that the feeling is reciprocated; he tells me so, and he is not a man who lies. I also want December to be the month in which stability and joy are wrapped like a warm blanket round my lovely children, and the month in which decisions affecting the Plas can be shared. I have tried taking responsibility, and in truth I have enjoyed it, but it is a tiring business when there are four little ones demanding attention and deserving love; and I am minded to rediscover the joys of sharing my office and my bed with a good man.

Yesterday I thought that the matter of Alban Watkins had been put to rest, and that the world had more or less forgotten about him; but today I have been reminded that unhappy ghosts do not disappear as quickly as one might like. This morning a trap rolled into the yard. I saw it coming, and did not recognize the trap, the driver or the passenger. She stepped out onto the cobbles, looking around her uncertainly. She was quite an attractive lady, perhaps just a little younger than I, modestly dressed in a black dress and bonnet and a grey cape. I met her at the kitchen door, with Dewi hanging on to one hand and little Sara on the other.

'Mistress Martha Morgan?' she asked.

'Yes indeed,' I replied. 'And these are two of my little ones, Dewi and Sara. I do not believe we have met.'

'I think we have, a long time ago. My name is Rose Watkins. I am the daughter of Squire Alban Watkins.'

I almost collapsed with the shock, and Rose smiled.

Her smile was open and honest, and that was almost as much of a shock for me. 'I am sorry to arrive unannounced,' she said, 'and I appreciate that you may wish to have nothing to do with the Watkins family ever again. But I was in Pembrokeshire and I had to come because I have something for you that might be of interest.'

I recovered my composure, and encouraged Dewi and Sara to go off and play with their two big sisters. 'I must apologize for my reaction just now,' I said, managing a smile myself. 'Please come in and let Bessie take your cape. Before we go any further, may I ask whether you know about . . .'

'Yes, I know it all. My uncle Benjamin, who is Father's cousin, wrote to my mother in Dundee the day after they found his body. We got the news on the day before we were planning to come to Pembrokeshire for a family wedding. We decided that we should still come, in case there were any matters to be tied up. We have had a very long and difficult journey, but here we are.'

Her pretty face had the shadows of tragedy upon it, and I admired her courage in coming to visit the very place that had been the focus for so much of her father's hatred. She had tears in her eyes, and I thought she might break down, so I took her hand and led her into the parlour. I asked Bessie to make us a cup of tea and to prepare some buttered scones.

It was difficult for me to know where to start, but she took the initiative. 'I have told you about one letter,' she said. 'Now I must tell you about another. It was written on the third day of November, just one month ago, and sent off with the Cardigan mail coach on the same day. It was written to me, and not to my mother, and it contains important information. It is no good to me, and I want you to have it.'

'Are you sure?' I asked, not knowing what to think. 'I have no wish to be party to the contents of a private letter written by a father to a beloved daughter.'

'I insist. Take it, please, and read it.'

With some trepidation I took the folded sheet of paper and opened it. This is what it said:

Parrog, 3rd day of November 1806

My darling Rose,

You have received no communication from me for many years, and that is but one of many things in my life for which I am truly sorry. It is probably too late to make amends or to seek forgiveness from you and your dear mother for the miseries which I have heaped upon you. But there are things I need to say, for I fear that the end is near. You will probably never see me again, but I pray by the goodness of God that these few words may remind you that I have always endeavoured to give you happiness.

At this point I was so amazed that I looked up from my reading. Poor Rose was sitting with her back straight as a new poker, doing her best to look impassive. I thought it best to say nothing, and continued reading.

I have to make a confession. First, I confess that in the days before my conviction and transportation to the penal colonies I used fraud and deception and a deal of wickedness in plotting with Benjamin Rice, George Howell and Moses Lloyd to destroy the Plas Ingli estate. First, I was jealous of it, and then my jealousy was transformed to hate by the encouragement of the others, and my hate was turned into an obsession with obtaining possession of it. I promise you, my darling, that I never wished Mistress Morgan or the other people in the house any physical harm, and that I did all in my power to keep a rein on the wild plans of the others. Moses Lloyd especially was like a madman, driven by a desire for destruction; I wanted to do things with a degree of

484

finesse, through the courts. But that is all history now, and I was punished for my misdeeds.

When I returned to Newport in July, and joined up with Joseph Rice, John Howell, Matthew Lloyd and Ifan Beynon, I was horrified to discover that they had killed David Morgan of Plas Ingli during last year's cnapan game on Berry Sands. I swear by Almighty God that these four men committed the murder, and that they told me of it with their own lips. They swore me to secrecy on pain of death. I know that I will die soon, and if some justice can come through the writing of these words, so be it.

I have done many other wicked things in my life, but I will not write of them for fear of distressing you. But be assured, dearest daughter, that all of my actions against Plas Ingli in recent months, and my involvement in the terrible things done to Master Owain Laugharne, were driven by the desire to possess the Plas Ingli treasure. Not for its own sake, I have to say, but out of a simple desire to become wealthy again, as our dear family was in generations past, and to recover Llannerch, and to bring your mother, and you and your dear sister Daisy, back from Scotland to the place where you all belong.

Years ago Moses Lloyd told me on oath that there was a treasure at Plas Ingli, and that he knew where it was. He swore to each of us that if we helped him to obtain it we would share it out and would never want for anything again. Then he disappeared. I do not believe he took the treasure with him; if he had, we would surely have heard of it. Throughout my years of imprisonment, pain and deprivation I have been sustained by the belief that the treasure is still there. It was this belief that brought me home.

Dearest Rose, I will never know the truth of this matter. Go to Mistress Morgan if you can, and ask her: what is the truth of it? Then, if God wills it, you at least shall know that I have been driven by truth rather than fantasy, and will think of me a little more kindly.

God bless you, and may you be happy.

Your loving father, Alban Watkins

And then, beneath the signature, Rose had written this.

I swear by Almighty God that I am Rose Watkins, the daughter and rightful recipient of this letter. I confirm and swear that this letter is written in the hand of my father Alban Watkins, and that it is his signature that follows it. My purpose in writing this is to seek justice for the Morgan family and to bring to book the four named men who killed Master David Morgan.

Rose Watkins, Dundee, Scotland, 15th day of November 1806

When I had read this I was so shocked that I buried my head in my hands for several minutes, trying to collect my thoughts. Was it all hypocrisy? Was Watkins quite mad? Was it the product of his conviction that he was about to die? I could not work out the answers. But the letter had a sort of grandeur about it, and a degree of pathos. And I had to admire Rose's nobility in writing a postscript on the letter, and in handing it over to me. She, at least, thought that enough evil had been done, and that it was time for justice. It was heartening to know that there was some good blood flowing in the veins of the Watkins clan. But now she wanted an answer to the question posed in the letter, and I had to choose my words very carefully indeed.

At this point Bessie brought in some tea and scones, and served them for us, and took her leave. We made some small talk.

'My dear Miss Watkins,' I said at last. 'This letter is very moving, and I admire your courage in coming here and giving it to me. Thank you from the bottom of my heart. I will seek to use it discreetly, in a manner that does not bring further trouble to your family, in order to obtain justice for the killing of my beloved husband. Now, to the question asked by your father. I can assure you that his treasure-hunting obsession was very misguided, and that the notion of a wonderful treasure buried in the ground in the field called Parc Haidd was nothing but imagination. There never was a treasure there, and indeed I have it on good authority that when the old house burned down in 1794 the Plas Ingli money chest, and its contents, were consumed by the flames. All that was left afterwards were a charred lock and the melted straps of the box; I was not there, but I have been assured of the truth of this by many who raked through the ashes.'

'So Moses Lloyd and my father and the other squires were driven by a wild fantasy?'

'I cannot say what was in Moses Lloyd's mind,' I replied, 'and I cannot presume to know what he might have said to others. He has not been seen by anybody of my acquaintance since the time when I was so cruelly incarcerated and punished by your father's friends. But yes, I believe they were all driven to a hole in the ground by a fantasy.'

Rose looked as if a great weight had been lifted from her mind. She smiled, and relaxed, and we were both keen to let the conversation turn to other matters. So we talked of children, and farming, and politics, and Scotland, and at last it was time for her to go. I liked her very much. I will probably never see her again, but to echo the words of her father, I hope that God will bless her, and that she will find happiness.

Now she has gone. I have escaped from a tight situation without actually telling any lies. I will have to show the letter to Owain, Grandpa and Joseph, and I am sure that they will wish to pass it on to Lewis Legal for use in the forthcoming court case at the Great Sessions. I am not sure of its status in law, but I feel that it will help to convince judge and jury that murder was done in that fateful *cnapan* game last year, and that there is no doubt as to the identity of the murderers.

4 December 1806

It is now only ten days until the Great Sessions in Haverfordwest, and we have had appalling news from the gaol in the old castle where the prisoners are kept. Joseph and Lewis Legal have been back and forth several times to consult with the Clerk of the Court. The poor fellow is so concerned with the number of prisoners apprehended during the Battle of Parc Haidd, and the sheer weight of indictments arising from it, that he fears that the business of the Sessions will simply grind to a halt. So he has been trying to make some agreement with our legal representatives which might simplify matters.

Well, matters are simpler today than they were yesterday, since there is now one fewer prisoner to deal with. Joseph Rice, whom I have always thought of as the brains behind much of what has happened here, is dead. He was strangled in his cell by John Howell following a furious argument, and apparently the Ifan brothers who were in the cell with them chose not to intervene. Whether that makes them accomplices to the murder I am not sure.

Joseph brought the news this morning, on his way back from Haverfordwest. He has only the slimmest of details, but he understands that the four members of Rice's gang were in the same cell, shackled up with leg irons, and having to endure the most filthy and primitive of conditions. I know what that is like, for I have endured them myself. Presumably the members of Matthew Lloyd's gang were in another cell; indeed, if they had all been put together the two gangs would have been at each other's throats like fighting tom-cats, and not one of them would have survived. Joseph says that according to the gaoler, Rice and Howell had been surly and argumentative ever since their arrival at the castle, and had come to blows on several previous occasions. Some days ago, he says, Huw ap Ifan got a black eye himself when he tried to separate them, and clearly decided after that that there was no point any longer in trying to keep the peace. Apparently, yesterday evening the fight that finally led to the death of Joseph Rice was over a bowl of gruel. Rice said that Howell had been given more gruel in his bowl than the gaoler had put into his own. He complained about preferential treatment, and asked Howell to give him a few spoonfuls so as to restore equality. Howell refused, and Rice threw his own gruel all over Howell, and one thing led to another. At the end of it Rice lay on the floor of the cell, covered in gruel, and dead.

When I think about this I feel a sort of emptiness. I do not feel sad, for I wanted this man strung up on the gallows anyway. Neither do I feel triumphant, for one cannot be elated over the death of another human being, no matter how evil he might have been. And Joseph Rice certainly was evil. I have to admit to seeing the episode and the death in the prison cell not exactly as a laughing matter, but certainly as one containing an element of black humour. Maybe the Grim Reaper had a smile upon his face when he wrapped his cloak round Joseph Rice; for here was a murderer and extortionist, a man driven for years by the insane lust for gold, finally brought low by a fight over porridge in a filthy prison cell. In a gruesome way, I think Rice's demise had both poetry and justice in it.

Joseph will call in and tell Patty about the death of the

last of the Rice family; Patty will not be as restrained as I, and I know that she will have a considerable celebration at the demise of her tormentor.

Only three of David's murderers are now left to stand trial at the Great Sessions. The judge wants to concentrate on that case, for it is the most serious one. Lewis Legal will represent us, and Joseph will be the star witness. There will be other witnesses too, and I was amazed to learn from Joseph today that since David's death he has been building up a file with sworn affidavits and all sorts of other information in it. He says that it is now more than twelve inches thick. Over the months, quite unknown to me, he has been quietly working on the case, and has identified five new witnesses who have agreed to appear in court. Where he finds the time I do not know, in between all the healing work and solving of mysteries that goes on at Werndew; but he is truly a man driven by a passionate desire for justice. And justice will be done.

Talking of my dear friend, at our meeting today I passed over Alban Watkins's letter. Joseph read it with interest, and expressed a quiet satisfaction on the basis that this confirmed a number of views which he had already formed about the fellow. He was not sure whether the judge would allow it as evidence in the murder trial, and assumed that the defence attorney would question its authenticity. But he added, with a twinkle in his eye, that its introduction could not do any harm, and that the handwriting could be authenticated by comparing it with certain other documents written by Alban Watkins which were already in Lewis Legal's possession. I was intrigued by this, and asked Joseph whether such documents might be quite old. 'Yes indeed,' he replied. 'I have seen them myself. They date from the time when Watkins laid claim to the estate

490

almost ten years ago. We must be thankful, my dear Martha, that attorneys belonging to the old school never throw anything away, and that Master Lewis belongs to the old school.'

One further matter relating to the forthcoming court cases. Hettie came up from the Parrog last evening with a big grin on her face. In her hands she carried a bundle of papers wrapped up with a blue ribbon. They proved to be the Plas Ingli map and estate accounts which had been stolen from Lewis Legal's office in Fishguard a couple of months back. So much has been going on here that I had forgotten all about them, and I suppose that even Joseph had written them off. But Hettie says that Mistress Billings, the owner of the lodging house used by Rice and his cronies on the Parrog, has had a big clearing out session. Without knowing of Rice's death she has finally given up hope of ever getting any of the rent money that she is owed, although she has an indictment for her arrears sitting somewhere in the middle of the pile of documents on the Clerk of the Court's table in Haverfordwest. She has of course re-let the room used by the conspirators, but until now she has been storing all their possessions in a cupboard in the hope of selling them. Nobody wanted to buy them, and in truth there were only a few clothes, some bags, a few pairs of old boots, and various bits and pieces of personal possessions. In the end Mistress Billings went through everything, gave all the useful items to poor people in the town, and kept a few things for herself including a sturdy army bag belonging to John Howell. She checked to see that she had emptied everything out of it, and then felt something in a hidden inside pocket. It proved to be the bundle of Plas Ingli papers. She immediately gave them to Hettie, and asked her to return them to me at the Plas.

So another piece of the puzzle falls into place, and our court case is strengthened even further. If necessary, I am sure that Mistress Billings will give evidence for us; the involvement of the Rice gang in the Fishguard burglary is now proved beyond any doubt, and Master John Howell, late of the Light Hussars, has 'receipt of stolen goods' added to the long list of crimes for which he will be held to account.

12 December 1806

The matter of Alban Watkins's death has still not been put to rest alongside his decomposing corpse. His ghost has come to haunt me yet again. It happened like this.

This afternoon I was exhausted and a little on edge, because we have had three days of bothersome meetings with our attorneys and with Joseph Harries, working out the details of our case (or cases, for there are many of them) at the Great Sessions in two days' time. That has made me apprehensive enough, for I will have to take the witness stand over and again; but matters have been made even more wearing by the constant stream of people who have been turning up for briefings and to make statements. They are all friends, and many of them will come with us to the Sessions and will appear as witnesses, but I have had to be sociable with all of them, and now I want the whole wretched business to be over and done with.

So I was not in the best of moods when a horseman galloped up the driveway just a few minutes after the last of our guests had departed. I was lying on my bed and hoping to enjoy the sound of silence. Bessie came in and said: 'Excuse me, Mistress Martha. I know you are trying to relax, but there is a fellow here on a horse. He has a letter for you, and he will not give it to anybody else.' I groaned, and followed Bessie down to the yard.

The horseman did not dismount. 'Mistress Martha Morgan?' he asked. I nodded, and he said: 'This is for you.' I thought I could trace a touch of Irish in his voice, but he said no more, and handed me a sealed envelope. Then he wheeled his horse round and was gone.

'Not a very sociable fellow,' said Bessie, 'but quite nice-looking.'

'Agreed and agreed again,' said I. 'But I don't feel very sociable just now either. I shall take this envelope and return to my bed to read its contents at my leisure.'

And that is what I did. It was just as well that I was lying down, for the letter read as follows:

Ireland, 6th December 1806

My dear Mistress Morgan,
This letter will come to you by the hand of a friend of mine who is shortly to travel across from Wexford to Cardigan. I had to write to you, for I knew that you would be troubled by the death of Alban Watkins, and that you would be wondering how and why it happened. I respect you as a good and kind and beautiful lady. If I am to confess to anybody I will confess to you. No priest hiding in a confessional will ever hear of this, nor even a priest beside my deathbed. In truth I do not expect to die in bed.

I am the man who killed Alban Watkins. You know me as Daniel O'Connell, and think me to be the brother of Michael; but I am no brother of his, and O'Connell is not my real name. You may recall that I visited you some little while back to report on the progress of the little fellow Brendan. That report was real, and the thanks of all of us was real, and the affection of all of us towards you and your gentle and warm family was as real as ever could be.

First, you will need to know why. I come from a poor family, and we live in a part of Ireland ruled by brutal squires. When I

493

was six my older brother was strung up on the gallows for poach-
ing a rabbit. When I was eight two of my sisters died from
starvation. They called it something else, but it was starvation all
right. Some years back three of my brothers and one cousin got
caught up in a rebellion in Wexford. They did nothing much, but
were caught blockading a road and that was enough to get them
the death sentence. That was commuted to transportation; they
were sent to Portsmouth, festered in chains there for more than a
year, and were then shipped to New South Wales for fourteen
years. I do not know everything, for only one of my brothers could
write. He wrote only three times in five years, and his letters were
censored. But I got news of what was going on in other ways.

The four of them were troublesome, from what I can gather, and
were sent to a place called Newcastle where they were digging
coal. The manager there was like the devil incarnate. There was no
rule of law, and he buggered some men, and had others lashed, and
had others strung up on his portable gallows on a whim. He killed
thirty-three Irish and maimed God knows how many others through
lashings with the cat. In the end the prisoners got him, and there
was not much left of him when they had finished. They chopped
him up with their shovels and fed him to the crows. There was
only one man who was worse, and his name was Alban Watkins.
He came to work in the store, and was soon the manager's
favourite fellow. I will not distress you by describing what went
on between them, but I have it on record. There were suspicions
that he was ratting on his fellow prisoners, but nothing solid.
Then a gang of Irish prisoners decided to escape and walk to
China. My three brothers and my cousin were among them. It
turned out to be a fiasco. Charlie Boswell got drunk, and blabbed,
and Watkins was listening. The military knew all about what was
planned, and the soldiers were waiting. Some fellows were killed,
and those that did escape were soon rounded up. There was a sort
of trial, and Watkins was the big man whose evidence sent nearly
all of them to the gallows. My brothers and my cousin were
among them. I will not distress you by giving you the details,

494

but they were left hanging there until nothing was left of them.

I heard of all this from various sailors and from fellows who belong to the same organization as myself. I have no reason to doubt it. Normally monsters like Watkins are dealt with – in due course – by other fellows in New South Wales who have long memories. I thought that that would be the way of justice in his case. But then I got a message saying that Watkins had been given a free pardon, and that the Governor had got him out of Newcastle and onto a ship for home as fast as a streak of lightning. He was already home by the time I found out all of this, for news travels round the world very slowly. We knew he was from Pembrokeshire. I was given the job of finding him and dealing with him; but in truth I needed little encouragement or instruction from anybody else, for he had killed four of my own family, and had to be executed.

When I had read this far, I had to put down the letter, and close my eyes, and seek to ease the palpitations of my heart. For several minutes I just lay on my bed, trying to come to terms with the horror of it all. Could there really be so much wickedness in the world? Could men really behave with such inhumanity towards other men? I could hardly believe that this horror story, recounted some months back by Patty in her letter, was now returning to haunt me. Watkins had been a monster all right; and the details of the tale, no doubt told and re-told across the oceans by sailors and then told again a thousand times in Ireland, exactly matched those given to Patty by Jake. At last I had the strength to continue my reading, with trepidation in my heart since I knew what was coming.

At last I found out where Watkins had come from, and where he now was. I latched onto Michael O'Connell and his family, and trained the little ones to call me 'uncle'. I knew how to swing a scythe and do most other farming things, and in truth I enjoyed my time with them. At last I found my quarry. I got to know where he was living, who he drank with, and how he moved about the place. I needed to get him when he was alone, but that was not easy, for he almost always had company, and indeed I think he made a point of never going out by himself, even in broad daylight. I had to watch and wait. The more I watched and waited, the more I discovered about the evil that was being done, and being planned, by this man and his cronies. I made good contacts with Skiff and the other low fellows in town, and I can tell you, Mistress Morgan, that when it comes to the activities of Watkins you do not know the half of it.

Then one day, in the Black Lion in Newport, I had a stroke of luck. I got talking to a fellow called Jake. You might know him. He has been a sailor, and has been to New South Wales, and has even been to Newcastle. When he was there he saw the bodies of my brothers and cousin rotting on their gallows, and confirmed all the details of the story that I had picked up from other sources. Like me, he was horrified by what Watkins had done, and he said he was still suffering from nightmares as a result of what he saw all those months ago. He said he would help me, but that he would not do any killing. And so we agreed to work together. I came and went, for I had to earn a few shillings to live on, and Jake said he would contact me if he saw an opportunity coming. One day I got a message from him that said, 'Come now. Things are moving fast.' So I came.

We met at Patty's cottage. Probably the locals thought that there was some group frolicking going on, but indeed there was not, for we had serious things to plan. Patty told us about what had happened to Master Laugharne. She seemed to know everything, including details of what had happened in the inn, how they had beaten him, how they had tortured him with a knife, and how they had dumped him near the river and left him to die. She even showed us the exact place where she had found him moaning among the reeds.

496

I started to form an idea in my mind as to how the execution of Alban Watkins might work out. We watched the cottage where he was holed up with Rice and the others. Then one day, I think it was on 5 November, the four of them left and walked up through town. They met up with the Ifan boys, and the six of them went up past the castle, heading for the mountain. Jake and I had watched you and your family laying your elaborate trail of deception, and we were very amused. We knew that a big treasure hunt and probably a huge set-to was coming, but we did not want to get mixed up in it. We decided to go up onto Carnedd Meibion Owen, across the cwm, and to watch what was going on from there. Jake has one prize possession from his days as a sailor in His Majesty's Navy, and that is a remarkable spyglass. Although the rocks are a long way from Carningli, we could see perfectly all that went on, and we watched through the night.

The next day we were amazed to see that Watkins and Fenton stayed on top of the mountain while most of the villains crept closer to the field where the hole was. They were no fools, we thought, for they are intent upon avoiding the action and simply sharing the spoils afterwards. We gave chase when they disappeared.

Jake has been on the mountain a lot, and he knew which path they were on. We intercepted them at a place called Carn Llwyd, up on the common and a good way from the nearest house. We had a bit of a struggle with them, but they were exhausted and frightened, and we dragged them to the ground. Maybe we were a bit complacent, but Fenton suddenly wriggled like an eel and sprinted off in the pitch darkness. Maybe it was a mistake, but I said to Jake, 'Oh, let him go. He won't get far without his lantern. Let the Plas Ingli folks pick him up tomorrow.' I gathered the next day that he had got down to the Cardigan road and hidden somewhere in a hedge, and had managed to get on a coach going east next morning.

Not that we were very worried about Fenton. Watkins was our man, and now we had him. He was scared almost out of his wits.

We gagged him to keep him quiet, trussed him up and carried him round the edge of the town and down to the ferry. We are sure that nobody saw us, since it was now late at night. We looked back and saw the lights of the search parties on the mountain, and felt some innocent pleasure on account of the fact that we had beaten them to it.

We went to the precise spot where Master Laugharne had been left to die, on the edge of the estuary, in among the high reeds. There Jake left me. Then I informed Alban Watkins that he was sentenced to death, and told him why. I told him that four of the men betrayed and sent to the gallows by him in Newcastle were my relatives, and that he would now pay the price. I also told him that I knew what he had done to Master Owain Laugharne. I told him that he would suffer first, that he would then be executed, and that then he would be left for the birds and the maggots to consume, just as he had left eleven Irishmen hanging up as food for birds and maggots under the New South Wales sun. I could see from his eyes that that was almost enough suffering. But not quite enough. So I got out my knife, stripped back his shirt, and marked him on his chest just as he had marked Master Laugharne. At first he was conscious, but then he passed out. There was a great deal of blood. Then I executed him by slitting his throat. I took away the ropes that we had used to bind him, and left him there. I do not know how long it might have taken for people to find his body, but I hope that the birds and the maggots had their fill first.

Next day I said farewell to Jake and walked to Fishguard. As I went, I heard from some people about what they called 'the Battle of Parc Haidd'; and you will be pleased to know that they were very delighted with its outcome. I got onto a ketch heading for the Irish coast, and landed not far from Wexford. Now I am at home. You will never see me again.

I know that I can trust you, Mistress Morgan, never to show this letter to anybody or to follow it up. It would in any case serve no purpose, for justice has been done, and I have taken it upon myself to avenge wrongs done to you and Master Laugharne, and *to my own family, by a man who came to earth straight from Hell. Now he is back where he came from. I have named names, but I know you will never pass them on, for those who have helped me have suffered enough already. They are good people, who deserve to be left alone and to have the chance of making a new life together.*

I trust that this letter has not shocked you too much. I have killed before, and I may kill again, if I have just cause. Injustice turns men into victims and martyrs, fighters and executioners. And my beloved land is a land destroyed by injustice. Pray God that it never happens to your pleasant country of Wales, for it is a place of fond memories for me.

If life had been different for you and for me, I might have loved you and I might have deserved your love. When I came to see you a little while back it was partly to tell you about little Brendan; but in truth I came to see you for the last time, for I knew what was ordained and I knew that I would never see you again. You truly have a passion in your heart, and a lust for life, and a beauty that makes men mad; and I pray to God, if He is prepared to listen to one such as I, that men's madness and lust for you will never bring you harm.

Farewell, from an Irish friend

When I had finished this letter, I am afraid that I was shaking like a leaf. I flung the letter to the floor, and wept for a long time. I have a sense that in the middle of my torrent of tears, Bessie came to the door, and looked in, and went out again. She knew that I needed to cry until there were no more tears. What she did not know was that once again I was weeping not for myself, but for the world.

At last I stopped, and found an uneasy peace within my breast. I thought that there must be, on the evidence of this letter, a sort of madness within all men, and that women such as I are not always to blame for it. Could they not, I thought, use subtlety a little more, and the vengeance of the cold knife a little less? And would not the world then be a kinder and safer place?

I picked up the letter from the floor and put it back into its envelope. I will never show it to anybody, and I will never breathe a word about its contents. Not even Owain will know. I have been given a confession, brutal and callous as it may be, and I will keep the secrets of the confessional. As far as Jake and Patty are concerned, I will never give them the slightest hint, through speech or eye, that I know what I know.

I hope to God that the ghost of Alban Watkins is now behind me, and that I will never meet it again. Whatever happens, I hope that never again will I need to write of him in the pages of this book.

14 December 1806

The trials have been held in Haverfordwest before judge and jury, and justice has been done. Justice – that strange and noble thing for which I have striven over the better part of two years. For all this time it has been beyond my grasp. Now I have reached it, and it has turned and embraced me, and yet I take no great joy in writing about it. I feel as if all the blood has been drained out of me, as if all emotion has been sucked out of my heart, as if my brain has been cudgelled to the point where it is incapable of sensible thought.

But I will try to record the happenings of the last two days, in spite of being very tired.

We all knew that the court cases would be heard over two days, because of the way the system works. I said my fond farewells to the children; little Sara was weepy, but I knew that Sian and Bessie would look after all four of them with more than their usual loving devotion. We set off before six in the morning, on a dark day with low cloud and flurries of cold rain. There must have been nigh on a hundred people from Newport making the journey over the mountain, and we assembled at New England on the Cilgwyn road in our carriages and coaches, traps and chaises. A good many were on horseback. We all had our candle lanterns, and those who were exposed to the elements were covered up as well as could be managed in cloaks and capes and oilskins. Some of the poorer people had nothing better than smocks and hessian sacks to keep them dry, and during the journey they got very wet, but they insisted on coming, and I was very moved by their determination to appear as witnesses. All this for me and Owain and the Plas Ingli estate! I had of course anticipated it, but I could hardly believe it when it happened, and the sight of our long lantern-lit procession winding slowly down into the *cwm* and then into the cloud and rain over the bare mountain made me feel very humble.

We were in town by nine of the clock. It was still hardly light enough to see what was what, but we made our way up to the Guildhall at the top end of town and crowded inside. It was a small and scruffy building, not at all as grand as I had imagined, and there was not room for all of us to sit. Owain and I sat together, with Grandpa and Grandma alongside us. There was a good deal of bowing and scraping and ceremonial, no doubt designed to engender respect for the law. The judge was robed in scarlet and bewigged in white, and we were all encouraged by the usher to stand whenever he came or went, which was frequently. Lewis Legal, Will Final Testament and Joseph sat at the front, as did some defending lawyers from Haverfordwest who had reluctantly agreed to do something to help the seven villains to protect themselves against the welter of evidence that would shortly be thrown at them.

After a good deal of legal business which I found extremely dull, the seven defendants were brought in and sat in a row in a dock which had been specially extended for the occasion. They looked emaciated and very dejected, but at least they had reasonable clothes on their backs, and I thought that the good deacons of Bethesda must have been at work again, ministering to the miserable fellows in the cells, bringing them food and clothing and comfort, and never once inquiring as to their innocence or guilt. I was lost in admiration for those kind people, for I knew that I could never have found such goodness in my own soul, assaulted as I have been over and again by evil.

There was a swearing of oaths, and then most of the day was taken up by the judge and his jury of magistrates dealing with a mighty pile of indictments which had been written out by Master Daniels of Newport and other scriveners. Most of them were the same ones that had been produced at the Petty Sessions, but there were a good many more, including seven (one against each defendant) alleging contempt of court and entered by the Newport magistrates. Each indictment was heard in the same way by the judge and jury: it was read out, and the judge asked the defendant whether he was guilty or not guilty as charged, and the defendant said, 'Not guilty', and then Lewis Legal would present a summary of the evidence and maybe call one witness, and next the defence lawyer would make a feeble point or two, and finally the jury foreman would say, 'True Bill!' and that was that. Several of the indictments were entered by the defendants against their erstwhile colleagues, alleging attempted murder, assault and battery, extortion, breaking and entering and so forth, and there was so much bickering and arguing among them that the judge had to get very fierce with them on occasion. I felt sorry for the defending lawyers, for they knew not whether they were coming or going, and I suspect that they had had precious little co-operation from Howell, or Lloyd, or any of the others. It went on all day, with just one break for dinner, and by the end of it we were all very stiff and very bored. Then the judge summoned us all to appear in court again next day. He stood up, and we all had to stand up, and he went off somewhere with his jurors and minions, no doubt to get a stiff drink. We trooped out into the dark and streaming streets of the town, not knowing quite what to do with ourselves.

Owain saw that I was very tired, and insisted that we should go straight to the Bethesda manse, where Morys and Nansi were waiting for us. We stayed there together with Grandma Jane and Grandpa Isaac. The house was very crowded with five of them and four of us, but we managed. We had a pleasant meal and a quiet evening, and got off to bed early. We saw nothing at all of Joseph, Master Lewis and Master Probert; no doubt they were closeted away somewhere in town, working out their strategies for the presentation of evidence and the questioning of witnesses and defendants. As for the rest of the Newport contingent, the visit to Haverfordwest was a rare opportunity for them to sample the delights that the place had to offer, and the inns did exceptionally good business. It is not often that the county town gets an invasion of a hundred Welsh people down from the hills, but luckily there were no incidents, and Welsh and non-Welsh speakers appear to have enjoyed each other's company. At any rate, there were a few sore heads at the second day of the trial.

Now I must sleep. I will continue my narrative

tomorrow, by which time I trust that I will have
recovered my strength.

15 December 1806

I have slept well, and I have had a day with the children
which has restored my spirits. Not that my improved
mood has done anything to lighten the blackness of my
narrative. To continue.

We were all on duty again at nine of the clock. There
were many legal submissions, and this time there was a
petty jury to be sworn in, so it was mid-morning by the
time the judge was ready to start. The defendants were
brought in, and he said he had decided to deal with the
cases in two groups. In the morning he would deal with
Lloyd, Beynon and Howell, who were all charged
with murder and a host of other crimes. He assumed
that this would take until mid-afternoon. Then he would
deal with Huw and Sion ap Ifan, Elias and Smyllie, who
were charged with lesser crimes, the most serious of
which were contempt of court and attempted murder.
This had all been agreed with the lawyers in advance. So
then he sent the Ifan boys and the Londoners back to the
cells, leaving Lloyd, Beynon and Howell in the dock.

They were all charged with murder, and all pleaded
not guilty. Lewis Legal was in charge of things for the
prosecution, and I was very impressed. He is like a wise
old owl, seeing everything, missing nothing, fluent in
both Welsh and English, and always several steps ahead
of the game. Joseph was the star witness. He presented
all the evidence relating to David's murder in the *cnapan*
game with cool authority, and was very concise. He used
no notes, and maintained eye contact with the judge and
with members of the jury throughout. None of it was

504

hearsay, and where he needed other witnesses Master Lewis produced them from the back of the court to swear on oath that they had seen Howell in an agitated state after the game, that Lloyd had been soaked to the skin after struggling in the water, and so forth. The case mounted up and ever upward, and Joseph proved to be a great deal more expert in the business of cross-examination than the poor fellows who tried to cross-examine him. The judge was the only one who asked pertinent questions, and Joseph dealt with these with due courtesy and total confidence. There was clearly a strong mutual respect between them, and I suddenly recognized, through the fog of court procedure, that these two had met before and had an established working relationship. Billy gave evidence on the injuries which he had seen on David's body, which were more extensive than I had realized; and then I remembered that he had prepared my dear husband's body for burial and must have seen everything. I found Billy's evidence most difficult to listen to, and I fear that I almost became faint, but Owain was at my side and was very attentive. He held my hand hard, and I was able to remain in my seat. Doctor Havard appeared as a witness and confirmed everything which Joseph and Billy had said, and when asked by the judge why he had not recommended 'murder' as the cause of death at the Coroner's inquest, he got in a frightful tangle which helped our case very considerably.

Then Lewis Legal presented the letter given to me by Rose Watkins, and read out the relevant section to the jury before the defending lawyers had a chance to stop him. They immediately objected that the letter could be a forgery, and went on about hearsay and so forth; and Master Lewis produced other documents written by the hand of Alban Watkins; and a good deal of argument ensued, all of which, in the minds of the jury, must have served to emphasize the guilt of the accused.

At last the three defendants were cross-examined by Master Lewis. They huffed and puffed and blustered, and accused Joseph and the other witnesses of telling lies, but when they protested their innocence the wise old fellow concentrated on little inconsistencies in their stories like a barn owl which has heard a mouse in the long grass at a distance of twenty yards. They took refuge in the fact that this had all happened a long time ago, and that their memories were imperfect, but Lewis would not let them escape that easily, and kept pecking at them, until they refused to answer any more of his questions. They would not admit culpability, but the judge warned them that their silence might be interpreted as an admission of guilt, and several members of the jury nodded when he said it.

When it came to summing up, Lewis developed his thoughts on the motives that might have driven the three defendants, bringing into mind the discussions between Joseph and Grandpa and myself all those months ago. Clearly it had all been in Joseph's file, and clearly the file had been passed in its entirety to the lawyers. Again, he was very concise. Then he summarized the main lines of evidence, and ended by saying to the jury: 'Gentlemen of the jury, I submit to you that these three men, together with one Joseph Rice, now deceased, conspired to murder Master David Morgan at the *cnapan* game on the twelfth day of February last year. They had motive enough. Having conspired with each other, they waited for an opportunity to carry out their plan. That opportunity was provided by the fortuitous arrival of a fog bank, and they took their chance. They rode Master Morgan out of the game to the water's edge, and there they cruelly and callously beat him with fists, boots and cudgels, and held him under the water until he was dead. The evidence is incontrovertible. I ask you for a guilty verdict. I ask that all three prisoners should pay the ultimate penalty, and that each one should be hanged by the neck until he is dead.'

At this point the whole thing became too much for me, and I think I must have fainted. At any rate, I have no further recollection of the proceedings, and came to my senses later on in some small annexe to the courtroom. Owain and Grandma were with me. I had a drink of water, and then I had to go outside and walk about in the fresh air for a while with Owain supporting me. He was as kind and strong and gentle as may be imagined. 'Well done, *cariad*,' he said to me with a reassuring smile. 'You were remarkably brave and controlled in there, considering the nature of the evidence to which you have been forced to listen. I was very proud of you.' I smiled back, not just because of his reassurance but also because it was the first time he had ever called me '*cariad*' or 'darling'. It was strange, I thought, that it should be in the context of an occasion dominated by memories of my beloved David, cut down in his prime by four evil men. Truly, I thought, out of suffering comes love.

I know about the rest of the morning proceedings only from what Grandpa and Joseph told me afterwards. Apparently the final submission by the lawyer for the defendants was a miserable business indeed. He burbled on at great length, and Grandpa thinks that in the middle of the legal rigmarole the point he was trying to make was that because there were no independent witnesses to the murder, it did not happen. He says that neither the judge nor the jury appeared very impressed.

The judge then looked at his pocket watch, and as he did so Lewis Legal sprang to his feet and asked to make a procedural point. The judge nodded, and Master Lewis said: 'Forgive me, your honour, but I will appreciate your guidance. The three prisoners before you in the dock are charged between them with a further twenty-seven offences, following the withdrawal of various others which we do not wish to pursue. John Howell is charged with the murder of Joseph Rice in Haverfordwest gaol before two witnesses, Sion ap Ifan and Huw ap Ifan. He is also charged with contempt of court, and with the attempted murder and wounding of Master Owain Laugharne, receiving stolen goods and various other offences. Matthew Lloyd is charged with the attempted murder of Joseph Rice, now sadly deceased, and with contempt of court, extortion, affray, trespass, and other crimes. Ifan Beynon is charged with the attempted murder of Huw ap Ifan, and with extortion, handling stolen goods, affray, fraud (not for the first time), trespass, theft and other matters. These are all serious crimes, and many of them, if proved, carry the death penalty. There is a practical limit to the number of times that a man can be hanged by the neck until he is dead. We believe that the charges are so well founded that, with respect, we will obtain convictions on all of them. Is it your wish, your honour, that we should press ahead with each and every one of these cases, or will you wish to consider them as relevant matter in your summing up, and then in your sentencing should the defendants be found guilty?'

Joseph told me afterwards that this was all rather naughty, since the lawyer for the defence is supposed to have the last word prior to the judge's summing up. But the judge did not bat an eyelid, and said: 'Thank you, Master Lewis. I will consider this during the break. Court is now adjourned for one hour!' And he rose, and so did the jury and members of the public, and he went off for his dinner, and so did the rest of them.

Some of the Newport people took dinner in various inns, but I was so worked up and apprehensive that I could not eat, and accordingly Owain and I walked about the town in the fresh air. It did me good. Owain encouraged me to believe that all would be well, and that I might not even be required to give evidence. I prayed in my heart that I would not need to stand in the witness box and face my enemies, and judge and jury, and the packed courtroom full of supporters. Not because I was afraid of the truth, or indeed of the process of the law, but because I was tired, so tired, of the whole miserable business. I just wanted it over and done with.

The judge helped to speed me, and the rest of the courtroom population, towards a sensible conclusion immediately after the resumption of the hearing. He said, before the defendants and the jury and everybody else, that he had digested things during his dinner break. He would now give his summary, and would then ask the jury for a verdict. After that, he would decide what to do about the other charges against the three defendants. His summing up took about half an hour, and I thought it very fair. He highlighted doubts where they existed, but there were in truth very few, and the weight of evidence against my three enemies appeared to grow greater with every minute of his discourse. Then he asked the gentlemen of the jury to leave and consider their verdicts. We settled down for a long wait, and started chatting with one another. I started to relax myself, for I knew now that there was nothing more that Master Lewis, or Joseph, or anybody else, could do for our cause. Then, within three minutes, the members of the jury were trooping back in again. The judge was quite taken by surprise, and so were the rest of us. Suddenly I felt my palms sweating, and there was a knot in my stomach.

509

'Members of the jury, have you chosen a foreman?'

'We have, your honour.'

'Foreman, have you reached your verdicts?'

'We have, your honour.'

'Well then, let us proceed. Do you find John Howell guilty or not guilty as charged?'

'Guilty.'

'Do you find Matthew Lloyd guilty or not guilty as charged?'

'Guilty.'

'Do you find Ifan Beynon guilty or not guilty as charged?'

'Guilty.'

In such perfunctory fashion was justice done by the will of the people and with regard to the law of the land. I looked at the faces of the three men in the dock. Howell was impassive; Lloyd and Beynon were shaking, with white faces and staring eyes, and white knuckles gripping the rail round the dock. I could take it no more, and finally broke down in Owain's arms. But luckily I was not the only one displaying emotion, for the Guildhall was suddenly resounding with shouts and cheers from the Newport contingent and indeed from others in the public gallery who had come in, I suppose, for the entertainment. I realized that I was by no means the only one who had been suffering from the tension of the occasion, for there were others in the room – not least Owain and Patty, and some from Parrog – who had had to endure the defendants' villainy in the past.

At last I recovered, and the judge managed to restore some sort of order. He thanked the jury for their verdicts, and said that he would deliver sentences at the end of the day. That was a formality, since all three had to be sentenced to death. He said that he would dispense with the other cases brought against Howell, Lloyd and

Beynon, on the basis that he had familiarized himself with the details and would bear them in mind when giving his sentences. The prisoners were then taken back to the cells to await the pronouncement of their fate.

There was no time for relaxation, for the judge was obviously intent on getting things over and done with. He asked the jury to stay put, and had the Ifan brothers and the Londoners marched into the dock. Now there was a very different atmosphere, for it was clear from the start that Smyllie and Elias are quite mad and that the Ifan boys are no better and no worse than a pair of backstreet bullies. But the charges against them were serious, and there was another pile of indictments to be dealt with. Will Probert now took over on our behalf, with Lewis Legal and Joseph whispering in his ear and passing him notes, and a very effective attorney he was too. The judge decided that he would accept evidence on assorted charges but would ask the jury for verdicts only on the most serious charges against each individual prisoner. Will Final Testament chose to press the charge on the Ifan brothers of the wounding and attempted murder of Master Owain Laugharne. Against Smyllie he pressed the charge of affray and contempt of court, to which the Ifan brothers' lawyer added a charge of attempted murder. And against Elias he pressed the charges of assault, causing grievous bodily harm, and breaking and entering with intent to commit a felony. All of the charges, if proved, carried the death penalty.

The cases droned on and on all afternoon. Thankfully I was not required to enter the witness box at all, but poor Owain was, and he had to show the courtroom the scars across his chest. The people in the gallery gasped in horror when they saw them, and when Joseph gave his medical opinion as to how they had been caused. The wounds were certainly enough to obtain the death penalty against the Ifan brothers (and indeed against John Howell) even if there had been no other evidence before the court and no other witnesses to attest to their wickedness. One after another the Newport people took the witness stand, swore the oath, and gave their evidence. Master Probert questioned them expertly and quickly. In most cases the defending lawyer chose not to cross-examine them.

Then the prosecuting and defending legal gentlemen made their final statements, and the judge made his summary. He said in conclusion that he wanted the jurors to bear in mind the piles of indictments which still stood on the table before them, unopened and unconsidered. 'Some of these ancillary matters may be irrelevant,' he said, 'but I can assure you, gentlemen, that I have examined them and that I find them all to be well founded. They would not have reached this table if the grand jury had not, in yesterday's deliberations, found them to be true bills. You might wish to bear in mind that no less than fifteen of them charge the defendants with offences that carry the death penalty, and you might wish to consider that they constitute evidence of a certain mode of behaviour on the part of the defendants that can at best be referred to as antisocial, violent and lawless. You might also examine whether the defendants have a predisposition towards criminality, and whether the community in which we live might be better off without them.'

When he had finished speaking, the judge sent the gentlemen of the jury out to consider their verdict, and they trooped off to some secret room, looking more dead than alive. In no time at all, they were back again, delivering their unanimous guilty verdicts. After the judge's summing up, I realized that that outcome was pretty well inevitable.

There was then a short delay while the judge went to his room for a few minutes and the court officials fetched Lloyd, Beynon and Howell back from the cells. Then, with the seven of them standing there in a row looking like soldiers before a firing squad, the judge returned, placed his black cap upon his head, and gave his verdicts: 'John Howell, Matthew Lloyd, Ifan Beynon, Huw ap Ifan, Sion ap Ifan, Thomas Elias and Julius Smyllie, I sentence you each to be hanged by the neck until you are dead. May God have mercy upon your souls, each and every one of you. I now recommend to His Majesty the King that Howell, Beynon and Lloyd be not considered suitable for the Royal Mercy, such is the severity of the crimes for which they are now convicted. As for the others, I consider that theirs are lesser crimes which have, so far as I can see, resulted in no fatalities. I ask His Majesty the King to consider, in his wisdom, the Royal Mercy and to commute their sentences to transportation for a period of fourteen years. Court dismissed!'

The prisoners were taken away, and I felt a strange mixture of emotions as I watched them go. I know I will not see any of them again.

At the end of it all Owain and myself and the two old folk were so exhausted that we did not have the strength or the inclination for wild celebrations. We had been too close to everything that had gone on in court. That is not to say that Billy, and Patty, and Will and Skiff and the others did not have a thoroughly good time. I dare say that they did, from the looks in their eyes next morning, but I prefer not to know too much about it. Outside the Guildhall there was a great deal of embracing, and indeed many tears of joy, as we met my dear parents from Brawdy, and Owain's parents from Pontfaen, who had all been in the public gallery.

513

We returned to the Bethesda manse, and later on Lewis Legal, Will Final Testament and Joseph all joined us there for supper. It was a quiet and somewhat sombre occasion, with elation and satisfaction beneath the surface, and congratulations and thanks given and received, but on the faces of all of us round the supper table there was a deep sadness. We had, after all, been in a confrontation with evil, and we had observed the workings of the law at close quarters. We were all too aware that because of actions initiated by us, albeit in defence of ourselves and our loved ones, three men would hang within the month and four others would be shipped to New South Wales, or Van Diemen's Land, or some such hellhole. The chances were that they would not see out their fourteen years of hard labour beneath a merciless sun, with the lash of the cat upon their backs and irons on their ankles. Indeed, may God have mercy upon them all.

Dark Night and Rising Sun

16 December 1806

Now the Newport contingent is back in town, and the whole of the community is talking of nothing but the court case. Never before in this place, I suspect, have so many individuals been prepared to stand up and be counted, often at great personal risk, in order to rid the community of a perceived evil. The wicked conspiracy perpetrated by Rice, Lloyd and the rest of them was driven by a lust for gold, but it manifested itself in many forms, just like the maggots and flies and other creeping creatures that consumed the body of Alban Watkins. Extortion, torture, burglary, lies, intimidation and even murder were things that the conspirators lived with day by day, and appear to have been comfortable with. For many months the community put up with their antics with a degree of stoicism that I find hard to credit; but then the people of the town and country of Newport decided that enough was enough, and got rid of them. And what I find greatly moving is that this process of cleansing has not been done through riot and rebellion but through respect for the due process of the law.

Joseph told me on the way home yesterday that he spoke after the trials to the judge and some of the jurors

515

from the Great Sessions. He appears to know them well, and he says that they were greatly moved by the number of witnesses who gave up two days of earnings to make the journey across the mountain in support of those who had entered indictments. That, apparently, is very unusual, for in their experience most witnesses to crimes are reluctant to appear in court because of intimidation and revenge. The winning of our guilty verdicts, one after another, must have been due in no small part to the fact that there were nigh on a hundred common people inside and outside the court who were prepared to give evidence in an alien environment. What is more, they were willing to subject themselves to hostile cross-examinations in English, a language which is for many a foreign tongue spoken by clever and arrogant people.

Thus has my faith in humanity been restored, after a good many months during which it has wavered. Now I hope that I can get back to the business of running this estate, giving time to my children, laughing with my servants, and planning my future life with Owain. He has not yet asked me to marry him, but he surely will, and when he does I have no doubts at all about my answer.

Today we have had one of those extraordinary days which we occasionally get in December. After the miserable weather that afflicted us during our expedition to Haverfordwest, the cloud wafted away during the night and gave us a morning with frost on the ground and rime on the trees. Then the sun came up, and the work of Jack Frost was removed within an hour, and we have had a day such as we normally expect in June. And what is more, miracle of miracles for a place such as this, there was not a breath of wind between dawn and dusk. Above us, the old blue mountain shimmered in the heat.

I have been very tired, and the servants know it and

tell me that they are not surprised. So at their insistence I installed myself in the sunlit garden and stayed there for the whole day, with the children playing around me. The house had a constant stream of visitors, most of them coming to talk about the court cases and to give their congratulations, but Grandpa and Grandma dealt with them all. Bless them, they refused to let any of the callers see me, and refused to allow me to worry about any of them. So in the security of the walled garden I told the children stories, and we played little games, and we hunted for creepy crawly things in among the weeds where the vegetables normally grow. There are still some late flowers cheering up my herbaceous borders, and we picked posies for the house. The sun, low in the sky, was so bright that I had to use my sunshade in the middle of the day. After we had eaten a picnic on the lawn, little Sara, light of my life, got tired of playing with the others and sat on my lap, and then went to sleep in my arms. I do believe that I nodded off too. So the day passed in a warm and golden haze, and I was able to be a real mother again, giving my love to my children and receiving it back multiplied a thousandfold.

18 December 1806

Complacency always was one of my failings, and now it has carried me to Hell and back. Yesterday, only a day after my serene and wonderful time in the garden with the children, some of the terrors visited upon others have finally been visited upon me, and I am still shaking with the recollection of them.

It started early in the morning, when Shemi asked if he could have a word after breakfast. He looked pale, and I thought that he might have had a few too many celebratory pints in the Royal Oak the previous evening. He came into my bedchamber and closed the door after him.

'Mistress Martha,' he said, with a break in his voice, 'I have something serious to tell you. I wondered whether or not I should say anything, what with so much happening lately, but then I thought . . .'

'Please, Shemi. I have coped with a fair bit, and can probably cope with your news. Go ahead.'

'Well, Mistress, I did promise you a long time ago not to keep secrets from you on such matters. I have seen another battle in the sky.'

Immediately I felt the colour draining from my face. 'Oh no. Oh no,' I said, and I had to sit on my bed. Shemi stood rooted to the spot. He did not know what to do, poor fellow, for comforting his Mistress was not one of the things assumed to be included in his working week. I buried my face in my hands, and spent a long time in silence. Then I stared out of the window across the misty *cwm*. Did I really want to hear about this? The last time Shemi had seen a battle in the sky was one month before David's death. On that occasion I had seen it too, and it was followed by unimaginable horrors. What horrors were now in store for me and my family? I hardly dared to think about it, and tried to shut it out of my mind. But it kept on coming back again, and I had no option but to enquire further.

'Where, Shemi?'

'Last night, right over Carningli.'

'That sounds a bit too close to home for comfort.'

'That's what I thought, Mistress. But it wasn't so bad really.'

'What do you mean?' said I, raising my eyes to meet his. 'A battle is a battle, and as far as premonitions go that means death and destruction.'

518

'Yes indeed, Mistress. But it was different from the other one. Not so big, for a start. And not going on for so long. One hell of a struggle, there was, and I must say I was pretty scared, but one army was dark-coloured and the other was sort of white and glowing.'

'Good gracious. Do you mean devils against angels, that sort of thing?'

'I can't say, Mistress. There was no horns and wings at any rate, as far as I could see.'

'And how did it end?'

'Very interesting, it was. The dark army, after losing many warriors on the field of battle, turned and fled. Then there was a great noise from trumpets, as if there was thousands of them, and the white army went straight up into the sky and disappeared.'

'And then? Was there a light?'

'Yes, Mistress. The whole landscape was bathed in it. It was after midnight when I was walking home from town, and it was just as if it was daytime for several minutes.'

'And the colour of the light?' I asked, with a cold fear in my heart, knowing that the battle in the sky before David's death had been followed by a red light.

'White, Mistress.'

'Oh, thank the Good Lord for that, ' I said, feeling some colour returning to my cheeks. 'That, Shemi, means there will be peace after the terror. I am not sure that that brings me any consolation, but at least I will probably have a few weeks to prepare myself for whatever is to come. But I saw nothing at all, and that is strange. I hope beyond hope, my dear Shemi, that it will not be you who has to suffer this time. Just you take care, and keep your eyes open for untoward occurrences. Thank you, at any rate, for the information; you have been very kind to tell me.'

'And you take care yourself, Mistress,' said Shemi, heading for the door. 'Mind you now, if you needs any help, just you be sure to shout, and me and Will and Billy will be right with you.'

I smiled, and nodded, and off he went to muck out the cowshed. I was left with my thoughts. I sat down on the bed and pondered on what might happen to me or to Shemi in the days to come, and how I might respond to one crisis or another.

19 December 1806

Twenty-four hours have passed, and it is now a little easier for me to give a narrative of what happened on the best and worst day of my life. Complacency, as I said, always was one of my failings, and round about dinner-time, as I thought about various occurrences which might deserve to be called disasters, one of them unfolded before my very eyes with a speed and ferocity that I had totally failed to predict. And, worst of all nightmares, the disaster involved one of the children.

I was in the kitchen, helping Mrs Owen to make a good meaty *cawl* for dinner, when I heard galloping hooves and the splashing of wheels through puddles. My heart missed one beat, and then several more. I knew immediately that it was our one-horse trap returning from town. Straight after breakfast Grandpa Isaac and Grandma Jane had taken the children on a jolly trip to do some Christmas shopping and to try on some new coats and boots at Jones Siop Fach. Now they were returning at a speed which must have endangered all those on board. Mrs Owen and I rushed for the door simultaneously. We reached the yard just as Grandpa pulled up the horse and leaped down from the driving seat. I saw at once that there were only three children in the back with Grandma Jane.

'Martha!' shouted Grandpa, his face white. 'Sara is missing!'

In an instant I recalled the anguish which I had felt back in the summer when Daisy had gone missing and had been found in my cave. I knew straight away what had happened. Abduction – the worst nightmare of any parent, and this time involving Sara, my golden child who had brought me consolation after David's death and had done more than any other to bring light into my life. And I knew without conscious thought that the man responsible was John Fenton, the man whom I had all but forgotten, the one enemy who was still roaming free. This was the nightmare presaged by the recent battle in the sky.

There was no time for histrionics or for fainting attacks. The three children jumped down off the trap and ran up to me, their faces as white as Grandpa Isaac's. They knew there was something desperately wrong, and I had to hold all three of them tight. 'Tell me, Grandpa, where and when.'

'In town, when we were at Siop Fach. We were inside, and Annie Jones was fitting some boots for Daisy. The two little ones were bored, and they went outside to watch the horses on the street. We told them to stand on the front doorstep of the shop, since it was Dewi's turn next to try on some boots. A few minutes later we called him in, and in he came, without Sara. "Where is your little sister?" Jane asked. "Gone with a nice man," said Dewi. We rushed out onto the street straight away, the whole lot of us. There was no trace of Sara, and in truth hardly anybody else on the street apart from one or two tradesmen going off on horseback in the distance. Trying not to upset the little fellow, we asked him what the nice man looked like, and what he had said to Sara, and where he had taken her. Dewi said he was not very tall, with nice clothes and a silver walking stick, and that he spoke to Sara very softly and nicely. He said Sara should come with him to see a secret round the corner, and then took her hand, and off she went with him. Along East Street, towards the Nevern road.'

'John Fenton. The bastard!' I said.

'We don't know that, Martha,' said Grandpa. 'It could have been anybody.'

'You might not know it, but I do. What did you do next?'

'There was only one thing to do. We left the other three with Annie Jones and rushed along East Street and looked up and down the side streets as well. The three of us, Jane, Caleb Jones and I, split up and ran down different streets. No sign of Sara anywhere. We tried the inns and knocked on doors up and down the street. Nobody had seen anything. There were very few folks around, since most are at work at this time of day. Then we thought we had better get back here with Betsi, Daisy and Dewi at high speed, since we did not want them tangled up in some frantic manhunt. Caleb has got all the local boys out of the inns, and has roused the three constables, and there is now a huge hunt going on all over town, house to house. As the news gets around, more and more people will join it. Even before we left, emotions were running high. God help him if they find him.'

'It's not he who needs God's help, but Sara.' We had not a second to lose. I looked into the children's frightened eyes, and said: 'Now then, you three. No tears, if you please. We must all be very brave. We will find Sara, you can be sure of that. Now, I want you to stay in the house with Sian and Bessie for the time being. Can you do that? Betsi, can you please look after the little ones for me?' Betsi nodded, and the other two nodded, and they went meekly into the house under Sian's wing, with Bessie in attendance. Then, while Grandpa led the pony and trap over towards the stable, I asked Mrs Owen to ring the bell with groups of five strokes at a time – the same signal that we had used to call all the labourers and the boys from town into action in Parc Haidd on 5 November. It echoed round the *cwm*, and within minutes the first people started to arrive. Shemi, Billy and Will came in from the fields. Men came from all the cottages and farms on the estate, and from further afield. Grandpa immediately organized them into search parties, and they went off in groups towards town. We knew that Fenton would not take Sara up onto the open ground on the mountain, so there was no point in searching there. But he might have taken her to some old building in town, or into the woods of the Nevern valley or somewhere among the reeds or copses along the estuary. I felt sure that he would not take her away on one of the roads on horseback or in a trap or other vehicle, since that would certainly attract attention.

I knew that I needed Billy, Shemi and Will close at hand, and I asked them not to join the searches. But there were two people whose help I desperately needed. I sent Will on one pony to fetch Owain from Llannerch, and Shemi on another over the mountain to bring Joseph from Werndew. Grandpa saddled up his hunter and rode back down to town to help with organizing the search there.

There was now nothing I could do until Owain and Joseph arrived. I tried to stay calm, and sat with the children since I knew that that would force me to practise self-control. Thirty minutes passed. I tried to eat some *cawl*, but could not.

Then I heard galloping hooves again, and a horseman clattered to a halt in the yard. I knew what was coming. 'Letter for Mistress Morgan,' said he. It was not in an envelope, but was simply a piece of paper rolled up and tied with twine. I took it from him with shaking hands, unrolled it and started to read it to myself. This is what it said:

I have your daughter. Now I want you as well. If you do not come within one hour, I will kill her. The time is now one of the clock.

Meet me at the bottom of Greystones Hill. Walk, if you please. Bring this letter with you and show or read it to nobody else. No weapons, nobody following you – if you disobey any of this, I will kill her.

I have nothing to lose, but you do. That is why I know you will come.

You know who I am.

The man on the horse said: 'A smart fellow gave it to me on Greystones Hill. Gave me a shilling too. Will there be a reply, Mistress?' I shook my head and ran into the house to look at the kitchen clock. It was half past one. It takes half an hour to walk to the bottom of Greystones Hill from the Plas. I stuffed the letter into the pocket of my dress, grabbed a cloak, flung it over my shoulders, and put on my strong boots. Then I strode out of the kitchen and headed for the driveway. I was walking so fast that Bessie had to run alongside me to keep up. 'Mistress Martha!' she pleaded. 'What are you doing? Where are you going?'

'To fetch Sara,' I replied.

'But where?'

'I cannot tell you, for fear of endangering her. On no

account must anybody follow me, whatever your instincts may be. I insist on it. When Owain and Joseph arrive, tell them that Fenton has Sara, and that I have gone to get her. They will know what to do for the best.' And then I strode away like a mad thing, leaving Bessie in my wake. All I could think about was the time, and Sara's safety. Like a fool, I thought not for a moment about myself, or of what was to come.

I passed a couple of people on the road, going the other way, but my mind was so set on reaching my destination that I know not whether I acknowledged them. I walked down Greystones Hill, and as I reached the stile at the bottom I saw that he was standing in the field on the other side. He motioned me to climb over the stile. He was holding a long knife in one hand and a pistol in the other. 'Well done, Mistress Morgan,' he said, very softly. 'I knew you would come. I dare say the maternal instinct is very strong. God knows why. I never did like small children myself.'

'How do I know that you have her?'

'I knew you would ask that. Will these convince you?' And he held up Sara's little shoes for me to inspect. There was no doubt that they were hers.

'Now then. We cannot stand here chatting like a couple of neighbours in a street market. This way, if you please; you first, and me after, so that I can see what you are doing.' His voice was so soft that it was almost a whisper. I thought it surreal, as if we were two children hiding in a cupboard and trying to ensure that nobody could hear us.

He motioned me to start walking along the path that ran along the edge of the field. As we walked, he asked me for the letter. I took it out of my pocket and handed it to him. 'Good, good,' he said, after examining it. 'I would not want this getting into unauthorized hands. If this business were ever to come to court, I dare say it would do my case no good at all.' Then he tore it into small pieces, dropped the fragments into the mud, and trampled them in until they had disappeared. We kept on walking. I became intrigued by his obsession with detail, and thought that this fellow might prove very difficult to deal with. He did not look mad to me, and therefore his actions, in contrast to those of Moses Lloyd some years since, might be too well considered for comfort. This realization increased the sense of unease within my breast, but I managed to control myself and did not panic.

We reached another stile at the far end of the field. We climbed over it and then stopped. He motioned me to stand by the stile, and stood behind me where he could get a clear view back across the field to the first stile and the roadway on Greystones Hill. 'Now then, Mistress Martha Morgan,' he said. 'We shall see if you have betrayed me. If anybody comes after you within the next half-hour, I will shoot you and then kill the child.'

We stood there for thirty minutes, watching the road. Thank God that nobody came. For the first few minutes there was silence between us, and then the tension became unbearable, with me looking at the road, and him behind me with a pistol in my back. 'This makes me nervous,' I said. 'Can I please turn round and face you?'

There was a long silence, and then he said: 'All right. Why not?' I turned and looked at him. 'Keep your hands out, with your palms towards me. There is no knowing what sort of arsenal you have got hidden beneath that cloak of yours.'

I did as he instructed. For the first time, I noticed what he was wearing – grey breeches and socks, a white shirt, a florid embroidered waistcoat, and a brown jacket that was too big for him. He wore no hat, and he had well polished black shoes on his feet. He had lost a lot of weight since our last meeting, and there was more colour in his cheeks, but his eyes were cold and there was a hunger in them.

'Well now,' he said, with his eyes flicking back and forth between me and the road. 'This is very pleasant, is it not? A brisk walk in the winter countryside is always good for the constitution.'

'I think I would prefer to be at home with my children about me.'

'Come come. Do you not enjoy my company? I recall that once upon a time you did not object to it.' I flushed, and he noticed it and laughed. 'I see that the recollection causes you some embarrassment, Martha. May I call you Martha? I always think that all these formalities that we have to put up with, Mistress this and Master that, create such barriers between people.'

'Call me what you like, sir. What about my child? For all I know, you might have killed her already.'

'No,' he whispered. 'I am a man of honour. She is quite all right, I can assure you.'

'Then where is she?'

'You will find out, all in good time. Fast asleep, looking like a little angel.'

I suddenly felt panic in my breast. 'What do you mean, asleep? How could a child who has just been abducted sleep, when her instincts would be to scream for her mother?'

'Don't you worry on that score. Before I took her out of town, I gave her a little magic drink and told her that it would help her to see secret things that other people could not see. Kicking and screaming children are very difficult to carry about. Very trusting she was, and drank it down without a murmur. I am very good with magic

527

potions, and have frequently put them into the drinks of beautiful young ladies in the past. They act very quickly, and have the desired effect. I also know a lot about doses. Your little baby will sleep for a good hour yet.'

Then I paled, and my eyes widened with horror. I choked, and asked: 'Have you . . . ?'

'No, Martha,' he said. 'How could you think me capable of such a thing? I am a man with perfectly normal appetites, as you know full well. I do not even like little girls, until they reach the age of sixteen or thereabouts. Your Sara is unharmed. That having been said, I will happily slit her throat if I cannot get what I want.'

Then he looked at his watch. 'Good. Half an hour has passed without stupid servants in hot pursuit. Start walking again, if you please.'

And I had to continue along the path, with him a few paces behind me. We turned right and left, crossed one field after another, went through gates, and over various stiles, and then into the woods. I had never been in this area before, and I was soon quite lost. Among the trees, and in the flat light of a cloudy winter day, I could not even work out where the points of the compass were. We must have walked for about half a mile. Then we came to a clearing with a small hovel only twenty yards in front of us, and a green open area beyond. 'Home sweet home,' said Fenton. 'Please go inside. I never lock the door. People in these parts are entirely trustworthy, as I am sure you have discovered yourself.'

I pushed the door open and went inside. It was very dark, for there was only one small window. I had to wait for a minute or two while my eyes adjusted to my new environment. It was a typical labourer's hovel, maybe fifteen feet by ten, with a rough thatched roof and an earth floor. Inside there was one wooden bed, a couple of low chairs and a table, all crudely made. On the table there were a few pieces of earthenware crockery, some cutlery and some scraps of food. There was a simple fireplace at the far end, with ashes and half-burnt logs in it, but there was no chimney. In one corner there was a bag and a jumble of clothes. In another corner there was a pile of dry straw, and lying on it was my beloved Sara, with her blond ringlets framing her face. I could not resist rushing across to her, and before Fenton could stop me I grabbed her and hugged her to my breast. Thank God. She was warm, and I could feel her gentle breath against my cheek.

'Did you not believe me, Martha?' asked Fenton, coming inside and closing the door. 'I am a gentleman, and gentlemen do not lie. She is perfectly all right, I assure you. So far. Now, put her down. Put her down, I say!'

Suddenly he was speaking normally, for he clearly felt that there was no longer any need to whisper. And there was real menace in his voice. He was not at all afraid of being overheard, and that meant that the cottage was very isolated. This realization filled me with dread. He was standing by the door, still with the knife in one hand and the pistol in the other. I put Sara down gently onto her bed of straw.

'Now then, Martha,' he said. 'May I call you that? Yes, of course I can. You and I have certain matters of business to conduct.' His voice was shaking, and he appeared breathless. I realized that he was more nervous than I. I looked into his eyes, and saw that he was not just apprehensive but in a state of high tension, like a drawn bow. I needed to breathe deeply, and to keep my self-control, if something appalling were not to happen.

'What do you want?' I asked.

'Two things. First of all, I want the exact location of the Plas Ingli treasure. You and I know that the business in

Parc Haidd was a charade, and that my colleagues and I were all fools to be taken in by it. You and I know that it is really somewhere else. I want it and I need it, since times are hard. If necessary, you will lead me to it through a crowd of servants. I will have Sara, and I will have a knife to her throat, so you will co-operate. And second, I want you.'

At this, I closed my eyes, hardly able to bear what I was hearing. Fenton laughed. 'Now then, Martha, don't be coy,' he said. 'Do you not recall that we have unfinished business? Some little time ago, if my memory does not deceive me, we enjoyed a little comfort in my favourite bed in my father's house. Surely you have not forgotten?'

'I have not forgotten, sir. I have regretted it ever since. I had had far too much to drink.'

'That may be. Drink is very good for loosening a woman's inhibitions and opening her legs. Now then, Martha, which first and which second? I am very generous in the matter of choices, as in many other things.' Then he walked across the cottage to where Sara was sleeping, and put his knife within an inch of her throat. I circled round, keeping as far away from him as possible. 'Remember that I can despatch this little one in a second. Pistol shot or knife? Maybe the latter, for guns are nasty noisy things. This knife is very suitable for the task. It cuts well, as I have already discovered from certain operations conducted upon the chest of one Master Owen Laugharne.'

Then the full horror of the situation hit me, and I felt that the breath had been beaten out of my lungs. I thought that I might pass out, and felt myself swaying. I grabbed hold of one of the chairs to stop myself from falling over. Now I understood that this man was indeed mad. I should have realized it before, but had taken him to be a soft fellow, incapable of violence. Foolish, irresponsible, dangerous complacency. If he had marked Owain with the very knife that was now in his hand, he would certainly have no compunction in slitting Sara's throat and taking his pleasure with me. I struggled to regain my composure, but found it almost impossible.

'My dear Martha, you look pale,' he said. 'Are you not well? Come over here and lie on the bed. That will surely make you feel better.'

'I think I prefer to stand, thank you,' I whispered, for in truth I could not manage anything louder. 'Was it really you who cut Owain with the knife?'

'Yes, it was my pleasure. The others were too squeamish. In fact, I thought I might have two pleasurable experiences on the same night – first the marking of the wretched poet to whom the Mistress of Plas Ingli has apparently given her heart, and second the possession of the Mistress herself. I left here at nine, knowing that with a good horse at a canter I could get to Glynymel in an hour, even in the dark. I assumed, my dear Martha, that you might be more than a little upset at Owain's non-appearance. A perfect assessment indeed! I slipped into the house by the back entrance, had a warm bath, changed into something civilized, and went on to the upstairs corridor just as you came up the stairs. The rest, as they say, is history.'

I could hardly credit the extent of this man's cold cynicism. Now I needed time to work out what to do next, so I said: 'Whatever else may befall me and my child in this cottage today, sir, may I ask how you come to be here, and how you have planned for this confrontation? You have clearly given matters some thought.'

'Indeed I have. I have thought of nothing else, since the day of the charade in that field on your farm. I was

531

lucky to get out of the grips of those two fellows who jumped on Watkins and me in the darkness near Carn Llwyd. They appeared to be more interested in him than me. God knows why, but there it is. They just let me go. I got down to the Nevern road and hid in the hedge till morning. It was so cold I thought I might freeze to death. Then I waved down the Cardigan coach, when it came along, and hopped on board. It stopped at Eglwyswrw, and the driver asked me for my fare. I had not a single penny in my pocket, so he threw me off. A pity that, but I was at least out of Newport and away from the hue and cry. I walked to Haverfordwest, mostly at night. I talked to a couple of vagrants on the way; they thought I was one of them, since I was just as ragged and dirty as they were. They told me the latest funny story from Newport, about some idiots who had got caught fighting over an empty hole in a field and had all got slapped into the lock-up. Very hilarious, they thought. I got to Haverfordwest and convinced one of my old friends to put me up. He was reluctant, since I owed him rather a lot of money, but what are friends for? He gave me some of his old clothes – those I am standing in today. Then I stole a nice walking stick and a hat from one of the inns in town, and after that I looked quite respectable. When I was in town I heard of a convoy with eight prisoners coming in from Newport for incarceration in the gaol. Then I knew that all of our plans had come to nothing. Stupid idiots that they were.'

'Did you know that Rice was killed by Howell while they were in the county gaol?'

'Of course. News travels quickly in the county town. A pity that. Rice was the only one with any brains, and he might have got them all a bit more organized in court.'

'Did you find out about the Quarter Sessions?'

'I could hardly have missed the news if I had been on the moon. The town was talking of nothing else. I kept out of the way, since all the inns and boarding houses seemed to be full of Newport people, and I thought I might be recognized. When they had all gone home I picked up on all the details. A bad business, Martha.' Now there was menace in his voice again. 'You have a lot to answer for, and you will have to be punished. How does it feel to be responsible for seven death sentences and two already dead?'

'Excuse me, sir, but you know that they were not exactly innocent fellows, any of them.'

'Damn you, Martha Morgan! They were my friends!' His face reddened, and he put down his pistol, and hammered the wall with his fist. He was fighting to keep his self-control. 'Now, enough of this.' And he left his position by Sara's straw bed and came over to me, with the knife in his right hand. He thrust it under my chin, and I could see that he was getting agitated. With the tip of the knife only an inch from my throat, I played for even more time. God knows why, since there was no prospect of anybody finding me or Sara in this isolated place. But I suppose that the instinct for survival takes a hand in deciding the actions of desperate people.

'Before we reach the end of this business, sir, will you tell me how you came to be in Newport and how you came to take little Sara? If I am to die, I have to know it.'

'Very well. A simple matter. I came back to Newport about a week ago. I had to, since my friend in Haverfordwest threw me out. I got a lift with a fellow fetching some lime. I moved into this cottage – very safe and secure, since the locals think it is haunted. Nobody will come near it. We used it occasionally when we were staying on the Parrog. As I told you, we brought your friend Master Laugharne here when we needed to interrogate him and spill some of his blood. Messy business. I assumed when I got back here that I would find Watkins in residence. No sign of him. Then I went down to town one night and overheard some fellows talking about the body found on the estuary a month back. I assumed that it must have been Watkins, and that he had been done in by those two fellows who jumped on us. I was not really surprised – his days were numbered, with so many people out to get him.

'As for the child, I just waited. I knew that all of them would come to town sooner or later, for their Christmas shopping. I watched Greystones Hill, knowing that they would come down it eventually. It could have been any one of them, but I thought it might be easiest with the smallest. And then along they came, bright and breezy, this very morning, with only the old folks looking after them. A wonderful stroke of luck, as I'm sure you will agree. I just followed them into town, discovered which shop they were in, and the rest you can work out for yourself. Now then, what is all this about dying? Who said you were to die, Martha?'

'That, I am afraid, is the logic of it. You cannot let me live with the knowledge that I have about you and your activities. And in any case, you have revenge in your heart. Your instinct is that if all your friends are to die, my death might be some small compensation.'

'You are right in that. But I do not always follow my instincts. If I let you live, I might obtain some innocent pleasure from extracting occasional payments from you. You have some dark secrets, Martha, one of which is the little episode in the Glynymel bedroom. I am sure that you would not wish Master Owain Laugharne to know about that, for a start. Oh, I know you survived with your virtue intact, but what if I were to set it about that

534

it was only my father's intervention that held you back from a willing – a very willing – surrender?'

'You would not dare!'

'Oh yes I would. You have set your heart on Master Laugharne, as he has on you. Very well. Bless you both, and I wish you many happy years together. But my silence will have a price. How shall I be paid? Money is so sordid, I always think. This treasure business has put me right off it. No, I think your body will do very well, every now and then, when I fancy it.'

Again, I felt my blood running cold. I felt that my capacity for clear thought was departing me, and as if I was in an ocean of despair, sinking with a weight round my legs and no prospect of struggling back to the surface. I started to say things without being too concerned about whether I might later regret them. 'All right. I will do a deal with you. Will you swear on oath to spare little Sara and let her go unharmed?'

'That depends on the price you are prepared to pay,' he replied, still holding the knife an inch from my throat.

'Do what you will with me, as long as you do not harm her.'

'And the treasure? Do not forget the treasure, Martha. You must remember, surely, that it was the treasure which brought us to this romantic spot in the first place?'

'All right. If you will spare my life as well as hers, I will tell you where it is, or else recover it and hand it over to you in a way to be arranged.'

'The latter appears more appealing. After all, if you are dead, there will not be a lot of pleasure to be had from you in years to come. I will have to trust you not to take half the treasure and keep it for yourself. But I am sure you are a trustworthy person who would never think of betraying a business partner. We have a deal?'

I nodded. There was in truth nothing else I could do, with a knife at my throat. 'We have a deal.'

'Good, good.' Then he backed off, still holding the knife, and returned to where Sara was sleeping in the corner. He knelt beside her and held the knife over her. 'Now then, to business. The light will be fading soon, and this child will soon wake up. Go over to the bed.' I knew what was coming, but had to do as instructed. 'Right. Now take your clothes off.'

I was shaking like a leaf, and when I tried to speak the words would hardly come. 'Is that necessary?' I whispered. 'It is cold without any fire in this place.'

'Don't you worry about that. I will soon warm you up. You might have all sorts of weaponry hidden among those skirts of yours, and I do not fancy a knife in my back. That would certainly have the effect of reducing my pleasure. Take your clothes off. Now.'

With a resignation the like of which I have never felt before, and wish never to feel again, I started to undress. First my cloak. Next, my bonnet. Then my boots and stockings. Then my bodice. Then I had to unbutton the front of my dress to loosen it. I let it fall to the ground around my feet. I had played this game many times before with David, but then the act of undressing was a part of the act of love, and was always something very sensual for me. I hoped to God that it might be so again in the future, with Owain. But now the whole thing was cold, with not an ounce of excitement in it. I went through the motions, and I saw through the gloom that Fenton was still holding the knife an inch from Sara's throat. Oh, my God, I thought, will he never lose his self-control? Is there never to be a moment of respite?

Then two things happened simultaneously. Fenton stood up, and cleared his throat. He was still holding the knife, and he was still on his guard, but I could see from the front of his breeches that he was very aroused. At the same time I heard the alarm call of a blackbird outside in the wood, and I knew that there was somebody there. Fenton was an urban creature, and would probably not have noticed it if a flock of a thousand starlings had flown in through the cottage window and out through the door. In any case, his mind was on other things, and he did not react to the sound at all. With a glimmer of hope in my breast, I thought I had better try some play-acting. So I caught his eyes with mine and held them, not because I felt like a seductress but because I wanted his full attention lest there should be further sounds from outside. I shook my hair free, so that it fell around my bare shoulders. I loosened my outer petticoat and let that drop. Then I loosened my stays, which involved some contortions, but at last I got them free and dropped them to the ground, exposing my breasts. Then I undid the ties of my second petticoat, the soft one against my skin, and let that drop. At last I stood quite naked in front of him. It was cold, and I started shivering, and not just because of the temperature. But I held his eyes, and would not let them go.

'That's better. A little co-operation at last.'

He stood and looked at me. Then he moved across the room and stood a few feet in front of me. He took off his jacket and waistcoat. 'Well now,' he said. 'What a rare privilege, to have the most beautiful woman in Wales standing before me in all her glory. Did you know that that is what they say about you? No? Well, you are very well protected from wagging tongues and lusty squires by your own precious virtue and by those old folks and your devoted servants at the Plas. You hardly ever go out, and nobody can get within a mile of you, which is a cause of great distress to gentlemen such as I.'

'Sir, I am a widow, and the mother of four children,' I said, with my teeth chattering from the cold.

'Yes yes, I know all of that. But I think I like what I see. Black-haired and passionate, just like Princess Nest. You are a good deal more desirable, Martha, and a good deal more accessible, than the Plas Ingli estate. I placed a wager with John Howell that I would possess you before Christmas; and I think the time has come to win my wager.'

'You will recall that John Howell is in no position to pay up . . .'

'To hell with John Howell! Now, lie on the bed and open your legs,' he said, and I had to obey. It was a short box bed, and its crumpled woollen blanket was rough on my back. He came and stood over me. Still I looked straight into his eyes, but I could see at the edge of my field of vision that he was still holding the knife. The same knife with which he had cut the stripes onto Owain's chest. What would he do with it now? Had I the courage, or indeed the strength, to fight him? But I knew that I could not fight, for all of the resources of nervous and physical energy which had sustained me thus far suddenly seemed to have drained out of me. I was also quite trapped by the high wooden sides of the bed.

'What will it be?' he said, unbuttoning the flap on his breeches with one hand while still holding the knife in the other. 'With violence or without? Rape is a sordid business, and I prefer to have nothing to do with it if at all possible. Too much energy is dissipated. Seduction is much sweeter, and easier all round. With violence or without, my dear Martha?'

'Without,' I whispered, having now resigned myself to my fate and totally lost the capacity to resist. He knew that my will was broken. He put down the knife on the floor at the side of the bed, and finished unbuttoning his breeches. Then he shook them down and knelt over me. The vile creature let himself down upon me, tried to kiss me on my mouth, and started to fondle my breasts. I wanted to scream, but could not. I pressed my hands against his chest, but I had no strength in my arms, and he was too heavy and too strong for me. Revulsion, terror and resignation swept through me like an ice-cold flood, and I realized that my assumption of some rescuer outside the hut had been a foolish mistake. There was nobody there. Everything was lost. I turned away, and closed my eyes. He moved one hand down to my private parts, and touched me, and I knew then that he was about to enter me. I think I almost fainted.

'God damn you, sir! How dare you, sir?'

Suddenly I was restored to my senses, but at the same time utterly confused. Were those not the words shouted by Squire Fenton on the occasion of the Glynymel ball? Was I dreaming, or wide awake? I was awake indeed, as soon as the full weight of John Fenton was yanked off me. I saw in the dim light that the newcomer was Owain, in a rage such as I had never thought possible. I sat up and saw that he had thrown Fenton to the floor. There was a furious struggle in progress, in the midst of which I saw that Fenton was scrabbling about trying to get hold of his knife. His right hand was almost touching it. I jumped out of the bed and grabbed it, and he realized what had happened and uttered a string of obscenities. I then ran across the room and picked up the gun. Now I had the gun in one hand and the knife in the other, but not being very good with weapons I did not know what to do with either. Even if I had been a fearsome warrior I could not have done much, for the two men were locked in conflict and crashing about the place, colliding with chairs and table and bed, seeking to land blows upon each other. They used fists and booted feet to inflict damage, sometimes on the floor, and sometimes standing up. If I had tried to shoot or plunge the knife into Fenton I would probably have killed Owain instead, so I had no option but to let the battle take its course.

Eventually I realized that Owain was the stronger of the two, and I saw that Fenton's movements were somewhat restricted because of the fact that his breeches were around his knees. But then he found some energy from somewhere, and hurled Owain against the edge of the bed. Owain slumped to the floor, winded and gasping for breath. Fenton was about to leap on him, but I shouted: 'Leave him, sir, or I will blow your brains out!'

I dropped the knife and levelled the pistol straight at his head. I was less than ten feet from him, and now I walked towards him. I would have pulled the trigger, too, but then he shouted, 'Damn you both! May you rot in hell together!' He pulled up his breeches, turned and rushed out through the door. He ran without thinking towards the green open area between the cottage and the trees, and realized too late that he was running straight into a bog. I came to the door with the gun, and saw what was happening. The shaking surface held his weight until he was about twenty yards into it, and then the matted mosses and rushes gave way, and his legs sank in to the knees. He struggled to pull his feet clear of the sucking and stinking morass of water and rotten vegetation, but the more he struggled, the deeper he sank. At last he lost his balance, and fell over. He tried to get up onto all fours, but his hands sank in as well, up to the elbows and then inexorably deeper. I was horrified as I watched, and then Owain regained his breath and came and stood at my side outside the cottage door.

'Can we get him out?' I asked.

'Impossible,' he said. 'He is too far in, and there are no

planks or ladders or ropes here. If we try to get to him we will sink too.'

And so, rooted to the spot with the sheer terror of it all, we watched him die, as unfortunate cattle and sheep had died at this place through centuries past. He knew he was going, and screamed like a man being dragged down to Hell. Never again do I wish to hear such screams. Soon his chest was in the water, and then his back, so that only his shoulders and head were clear. He was still screaming when he went under, and then his mouth filled with water, and it became quiet. The top of his head disappeared, and there was a slight movement on the surface of the bog, and then everything was still. The soft green mosses and rushes and patches of brown streaky saturated peat looked as cool and serene as they might have done on a midsummer day.

At last the high emotions of the afternoon caught up with me, and I collapsed into Owain's arms. I wept a flood of tears and hung on to him as a drowning woman might hang on to a log. I do not know for how long my desperate embrace lasted, but it must have been for many minutes, and the blessed man held me as I needed to be held.

'Hello, Mam. Why have you not got any clothes on? Hello, Master Owain.'

So said a little voice from the door. And there stood Sara. That started me off all over again, and I ran to her and swept her up in my arms, and hugged her, and swung her round, and laughed and cried at the same time. She laughed too, and thought this was a splendid game. At last I regained some of my composure, and I saw that Owain was leaning on the door with a quizzical look on his face. In spite of the horrors we had just been through, he managed a smile. I managed to smile back at him. I put Sara down, and held both his hands in mine.

It was almost dark, and we could hardly see each other. Suddenly I realized how absurd the situation was. Here was I, the respectable Mistress of Plas Ingli, standing in the middle of a wood on a freezing cold winter evening, stark naked, holding hands with a fully dressed young gentleman, with a small daughter looking on.

'Martha,' said Owain, laughing. 'God knows what the deacons of Caersalem would think if they saw us now. I have seen a great deal more of you today than decorum permits. But I very much like what I see. *Cariad*, will you marry me?'

'I thought you would never ask,' said I. Then I turned to Sara and asked: 'Now then, Sara *bach*, do you think I should marry Master Owain?'

'Oh, yes please!' said she, skipping up and down and clapping her chubby hands.

'There is your answer, dearest Owain,' I said. And we kissed long and hard, with Sara holding my hand.

'Now then, Mistress Martha,' said Owain when we had to stop for breath. 'There is a serious risk of your getting a chill and my getting over-excited. I think we had better get you dressed. And then I think we had all better go home to the Plas.'

20 December 1806

There is not very much more to relate. I got dressed as quickly as I could, and checked that Owain was not too badly injured from his ferocious struggle. He had many bruises on his face and body, but miraculously there was no blood. Then I took Fenton's pistol and his knife – the one which had left permanent scars upon Owain's chest – and flung them out into the middle of the bog. They sank instantly without trace. Then we took the wretched fellow's meagre belongings, stuffed them into his bag, weighted it down with stones, and flung that too into the bog. There was then no trace at all of Fenton's occupation of the cabin, either inside or out.

Then Owain hoisted Sara up onto his shoulders, and we walked home through the semi-darkness. He knew exactly where he was going, and we did not take a single wrong turning. I remarked upon this, and he said: 'Don't forget, Martha, that I have been here before, quite recently on an occasion I would prefer to forget, and also on other occasions when I was a boy. We called it the "spirit hut" and we thought it was haunted because moans and screams were often heard in the vicinity. I have known the reason since I was a lad; now you know it too. Fenton was not the first. Somebody may well have heard him from a distance, and today's events will perpetrate the ghostly myth.'

As we walked along the narrow path, with Owain striding ahead with little Sara on his shoulders, how I loved him! This humble and shy man had saved my virtue, and probably my life, and I could hardly imagine what might have been the culmination of the episode in the hut if he had not intervened. I also pondered on the strange symmetries which have come into my life. David's death had been presaged by a battle in the sky; and so too had the fateful and yet wonderful events of this long day of days. Owain, fully clothed, had watched me naked, and now knew a good deal about the contours and details of my body, just as I had watched him naked in Pandy Pools back in the balmy days of August. One day, I thought, I will tell him about that.

When we got back to the Plas there was pandemonium and more tears and hugs and laughter. They were all there, including Joseph. We had to assure everybody that Sara was perfectly unharmed, and so was I. We would not tell them what had happened, and indeed on the way back to the house Owain and I had agreed that we would take the secret with us to our graves. All we would say was that I had found Sara, and that Owain had found me and her, and that we had managed to escape from a difficult situation. He had got some bruises on his face from walking into a tree in the dark. Nobody pressed us. They all probably realized that there was more to this escape than might meet the eye, but they also appreciated that some things are best left unknown.

Now, as a priority, Billy, Will and Shemi took the trap and rode down to town in the darkness to call off the search parties and stop the house to house searches being conducted by the constables. They are telling everybody that Owain and I found Sara, quite unharmed, in an empty cottage, and that the abductor must have fled because of all the noise and searching going on. Let us hope that the good people of Newport, who have come to our aid once again, will believe what they are told.

When we had a moment, I took little Sara upstairs and asked Joseph to follow. She was still very drowsy, and I told him that I had found her asleep, presumably from some sedative that Fenton had given to her. He smelt her breath and looked carefully into her eyes, and said, 'Quite safe, Martha my dear. Probably valerian. Give her some fruit cordial to drink, well diluted with plenty of water. She will sleep well tonight, and tomorrow she will be fine. She may not remember a great deal about what has happened to her, but perhaps that is just as well.'

'Indeed it is, dear Joseph,' said I, as I kissed him on the cheek. 'That may be one of the few kind things that Fenton ever did in his life.'

One final matter which I find intriguing. I asked

Owain today, when he and I had tea together in the parlour, how he had known where I had been taken and how he had managed to get there so quickly. 'That was not so difficult,' he said. 'I arrived here at the same time as Joseph, shortly after you left to walk to Greystones Hill. The others warned me not to follow you, but I knew you were in grave danger, and would not be deterred. I assumed that Fenton had taken Sara, and would take you, to the same cottage in the woods that he and his cronies had used to torture me. It was, after all, perfectly safe, protected as it was by an aura of ghostliness. But I was not absolutely certain, and I dared not go to the wrong place for fear that you might both be killed. Joseph noticed my uncertainty and said: "Owain my friend. Are you uncertain as to where they are?" I replied that I was almost sure. "Ask me a question then," he said, pulling out of his pocket a little crystal on a string. "The answer has to be yes or no." So I asked, "Are they at the spirit hut? Yes or no?" Joseph held the crystal on its string for a minute or two, and then it started moving in a circle. "Yes," said Joseph. "You will find them there."'

Then, said Owain, he rushed off as fast as his legs could carry him. He did not go the direct way, since he assumed that Fenton would be watching the path from the Greystones Hill stile. Quite correct, said I, and told him that if he had gone that way the story of the afternoon would certainly have been very different. Instead, he said, he ran down past Brithdir into the valley, and worked his way through the woods by various other tracks. He thought that his arrival at the hut had been ruined by the frightened blackbird, but after waiting for some minutes for a reaction which never came, he crept up to the window very slowly, peeped inside and saw what was going on. His reactions from that point on

545

were, he admitted, instinctive and impulsive, and when he rushed into the hut he had no thought of weapons or anything else but saving me. And that was that, he said.

'My dear Owain,' I said. 'You came at exactly the right time. I trust that your timing, in the future, will be just as impeccable.'

He looked just a little shocked, and then burst out laughing, and almost choked on his slice of apple pie.

21 December 1806

Little Sara appears to be quite unaffected by her abduction, and thinks it was all a happy game. Owain is recovering well from his battle, as I am from my naked ordeal. I have hardly had time to think of the horrid manner in which Fenton met his death, but I dare say that in weeks to come I will hear his screams again and will wake in the middle of the night covered in a cold sweat. But, if all goes according to plan, I will have a good man at my side who will know precisely why I am distressed, and will be able to give me consolation. Thinking back on it, there was a cruel symbolism in that evil man's demise, sucked down to Hell in the manner of Don Juan.

Now that life is restored to some sort of normality, I have work to do in my own heart. The price of justice is a high one, and I will have to pay it. Three villains are already dead, and three others will hang. The Londoners and the Ifan brothers will go to the penal colonies and will probably not survive. Ten deaths to come to terms with. And all my fault? Surely not, but I do feel guilt. I have been so obsessed with the pursuit of justice that I fear I may have lost sight of the distinction between justice and vengeance. Can I find it in my heart to forgive these men? In all truth, not yet; but as I forgive the little ones for their tantrums and their bullying, and for the grief they bring me from time to time, so must I find greater forgiveness for Watkins and Howell and the rest of them. Nothing will have been achieved if I do not seek to become a kinder and a gentler person. I will work on it in the silence of my cave, and I know that Owain will help me, for he is a man who holds no malice in his heart, and appears to have an instinctive understanding of what forgiveness really means. I pray for the acquisition of just a little of his strength and his compassion.

At Christmas I will close this diary, for I have a wedding to plan. Then, early in the New Year, Owain, the dear man who lives already in my heart, will take over my bed as well. We will not live at Llannerch, for it is a dark place, and full of shadows. We will live at the Plas, a place of morning sunshine on the flank of Angel Mountain.

From now on, writing in my diary might prove to be difficult, and as I think about the nature of the evenings that lie ahead I think that I may well be busy with other things. I can hardly wait for that time to come, when my body is pressed against his, my breath mingles with his, and we are finally joined in passion. It has been too long in coming. For almost two years I have lived the life of a nun, and I fear that it does not suit me. I have two years' worth of love to give to Owain, but I must try not to overwhelm him with it. However, I think I might obtain some pleasure, and indeed give some to him, by teaching him something new. As I write this I feel my heart beating faster, and I am greatly aroused. My hand shakes as I write, and my handwriting wavers, and I suppose this proves, if proof is needed, that I am in love. I must

547

try to be patient, but patience is a virtue for which I have never had much respect.

Now I have calmed down a little. Something else occurs to me, and amuses me, namely that my technique of writing in Dimetian Welsh will, as from the day of my marriage, no longer guarantee security. There are hardly any people left in this world who understand, write and read the Dimetian dialect, but Owain is one of them. There are many secret things in this diary which I do not want him to read. At least, not yet.

I think I might play a little game with Owain, or my children, or anybody else who might fancy it in years to come. The little picture of the Plas, which I gave to David some years since and which now hangs in the parlour, has a part to play. I will lay a trail leading from the picture to a riddle and thence to Pontfaen, where Owain grew up. He loves the old library there, and its dusty tomes. He has a special affection for the plays of Master Shakespeare, and I am minded to allow my secret diary to cuddle up in between a Jewish gentleman from Venice and two others from Verona. The plays concerned are two of his favourites. I am sure the gentlemen will not mind, and that they will keep my modest literary efforts warm. At *Hen Galan*, in three weeks or so, Owain's parents will invite us over to Plas Pontfaen as usual, and I will find my way into the library, and execute my plan.

22 December 1806

Three weeks ago, after the completion of the court case in Haverfordwest, I wrote a long and newsy letter to my dear sister Elen in Bath. I said that all was well, and told her about Owain, but thought it best not to enter into any details of the events of recent months. If I had done, my letter might have turned into a book! I know that Elen is alone, and obsessed with her music teaching, and in my letter I wondered whether she might like to join us for Christmas at the Plas.

Today I received a sweet reply from her, full of news, and enquiring after my health and that of the children. She wrote that she is eager to meet Owain, but thought that she might defer a visit till next summer. And she ended her letter with the following words, which I found very entertaining:

> The Christmas season is a very jolly one in Bath, although I shall miss my dear friend Jane who moved to Southampton last year following the death of her old reverend father. I am already invited to gay balls and other festivities. Although it is wet and grimy and crowded here, with much building going on, I like this place and am nicely settled in. I think I am a town girl at heart. Please forgive me for saying so, my dear sister, but unlike you I need a good deal of stimulation for my mind and my spirit, and nothing ever happens in Wales.
> Your loving sister, Elen

23 December 1806

I am sitting at my desk early in the morning, with a weak winter sun doing its best to remove the traces of a hard night frost. Billy is outside in the yard, stamping his feet and clapping his mittened hands as he tries to keep warm. As he exhales his breath condenses and swirls about his head, and catches the sunlight, and forms a halo.

It is almost two years since the death of David, the bravest and kindest of husbands and the gentlest and most loving of fathers. Since the day he went to his grave

I have experienced the extremes of emotion and have been swept back and forth on tides of despair and hope, serenity and turmoil. I have been on a long journey of self-discovery, and I am tired. I have learned how to live with grief and selfish misery, and after according them due respect I have finally sent those old impostors packing. I have seen brutality and depravity on a scale which, only a year ago, I could never have imagined. I have learned some of the arts of survival, and I have discovered how to exert some influence over my own fate. The downfall of my enemies was, for me, a time of empowerment and liberation rather than celebration. In the last year I have experienced both high farce and abject terror, and have discovered that while motherhood is life's greatest blessing it carries with it fear and apprehension on a scale which I could not have imagined.

I have rediscovered love, and on Christmas Day Owain and I will announce to our two families that we are to be married. There will be tears, but they will be tears of joy. Then, a few days after Christmas, we will celebrate Owain's 26th birthday. Together.

I thank God that somehow, in spite of the appalling events that have overtaken us, my beloved children and the rest of my family and loyal servants have survived. Our bodies and minds are scarred, but I trust that the wounds will heal. The Plas, this old bluestone house on the flank of Brynach's stony mountain, is truly a house inhabited by angels. Those who live beneath its roof have behaved with honour and courage in the face of the most severe provocation from our enemies, and we have even managed to fight some of our battles with smiles on our faces. Somehow we have brought wicked men to justice, with the aid of a prostitute, a smuggler, a wizard, assorted urchins and petty thieves, and a political assassin. There are those in this area who would class all of my friends as common criminals, beyond redemption and fit only to be clapped in irons and transported to the colonies. As far as I am concerned, they are all angels who have delivered a multitude of blessings to me and my loved ones, young and old.

And in spite of everything, the Plas Ingli treasure, known only to me, is still in the ground.

I write this in the House of Angels, on the 23rd day of December 1806.

Martha Morgan

GLOSSARY OF WELSH TERMS

Bach: 'little one' (a term of endearment)

Calennig: New Year's gift

Cantre'r Gwaelod: the Lowland Hundred, submerged in Cardigan Bay

Cariad: darling

Cawl: traditional Welsh broth, made with mutton and chopped vegetables

Ceffyl Pren: the wooden horse (creature used in folk traditions)

Cnapan: old ball game, thought to be a forerunner of rugby football

Crachach: gentry or 'establishment' (derogatory)

Cromlech: prehistoric structure with pillars and a capstone

Cwm: valley or hollow in the hillside

Duw: God

Ffynnon: spring or water source

Gambo: a flat two-wheeled cart with no sides

Gwlad y Tylwyth Teg: fairy land, under the sea in Cardigan Bay

Gwylnos: wake night or vigil, before the funeral

Heddwch: peace (shouted during *cnapan* games in order to stop play)

Hen Galan: the Old New Year, 12 January

Hirwen-gwd: an old tradition involving the lifting of a shrouded corpse up inside the chimney of the deceased person's house

Mari Lwyd: literally 'grey Mary'; old tradition involving a horse skull – part pagan custom, part debased miracle play

Parc Haidd: barley field

Parrog: flat land along a shore or estuary (Newport's seaside community)

Perllan: literally 'orchard', but used for a marked board in connection with the wassail ceremony

Plas: big house or palace

Plygain: candlelit service ending at dawn

Simnai fawr: big chimney, large open fireplace

Sul y Blodau: Flower or Blossom Sunday, the Sunday before Easter

Toili: phantom funeral, interpreted as an omen of a death to come

Tolaeth: a death omen, usually heard as the sound of coffin making

Twmpath: jolly evening of song and dance (literally tump)

Wrach: witch or hag

Y tair ysbrydnos: the three spirit nights, May Eve, the Eve of St John, and Hallowe'en

ON ANGEL MOUNTAIN
By Brian John

In 1796, impetuous Martha Morgan becomes the mistress
of the struggling Plas Ingli estate, at only eighteen years
old. Though she loves her husband David dearly,
she is desperately lonely in a strange house, and her
quick wit and cutting humour make her as many
enemies as friends.

There are mysteries surrounding the great fire that
devastated the estate but Martha's questions about it
remain unanswered. Nobody else seems to realise that their
haughty servant Moses Lloyd, the disinherited son of the
local squire, is not as trustworthy as Martha's husband hopes.
The local gentry think that she is far too clever for her
own good and indeed it seems inevitable that Martha
will fall into a trap set to lead her to the gallows.
How can she possibly escape?

On Angel Mountain is a gripping tale in the tradition
of Winston Graham's *Poldark*

0 552 15327 3

CORGI BOOKS